LAW, POLICY AND REPRODUCTIVE AUTONOMY

Reproductive choices are at once the most private and intimate decisions we make in our lives, and in some instances also among the most public. Reproductive decision making takes place in a web of overlapping concerns – political and ideological, socio-economic, health and healthcare – all of which engage the public and involve strongly-held opinions and attitudes about appropriate conduct on the part of individuals and the State.

Law, Policy and Reproductive Autonomy examines the idea of reproductive autonomy, noting that in attempting to look closely at the contours of the concept, we begin to see some uncertainty about its meaning and legal implications – about how to understand reproductive autonomy and how to value it. Both mainstream and feminist literature about autonomy contribute valuable insights into the meaning and implications of reproductive autonomy. The developing feminist literature on relational autonomy provides a useful starting point for a contextualised conception of reproductive autonomy that creates the opportunity for meaningful exercise of reproductive choice. With a contextualised approach to reproductive autonomy as a backdrop, the book traces aspects of the regulation of reproduction in Canadian, English, US and Australian law and policy, arguing that not all reproductive decisions necessarily demand the same level of deference in law and policy, and making recommendations for reform.

Law, Policy and Reproductive Autonomy

Erin Nelson

·HART·
PUBLISHING
OXFORD AND PORTLAND, OREGON
2013

Published in the United Kingdom by Hart Publishing Ltd
16C Worcester Place, Oxford, OX1 2JW
Telephone: +44 (0)1865 517530
Fax: +44 (0)1865 510710
E-mail: mail@hartpub.co.uk
Website: http://www.hartpub.co.uk

Published in North America (US and Canada) by
Hart Publishing
c/o International Specialized Book Services
920 NE 58th Avenue, Suite 300
Portland, OR 97213-3786
USA
Tel: +1 503 287 3093 or toll-free: (1) 800 944 6190
Fax: +1 503 280 8832
E-mail: orders@isbs.com
Website: http://www.isbs.com

British Library Cataloguing in Publication Data
Data Available

ISBN: 978-1-84113-867-1

Typeset by Hope Services, Abingdon
Printed and bound in Great Britain by
TJ International Ltd, Padstow

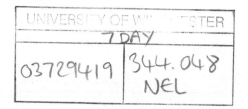

For Jim, Emily, Sam and Talia,
and in memory of my grandmother, Rose

Preface

The issues discussed in this book have occupied my professional life, in one way or another, for the better part of a decade. As I am sure is the case for all book authors, I have mixed feelings about the project coming to a close. There is of course the relief that comes with having finished a large project, but also some sadness that my deep engagement with the issues I have written about here is going to end, or at least change.

As I note in the Introduction, my aim in this book is to nudge the discussion around reproductive autonomy in a slightly different direction. Instead of continuing to explore new technologies and new reproductive choices from the standpoint of whether we should be free to make them without interference, I urge consideration of the *meaning* of reproductive autonomy before turning to its implications for regulation of reproductive decision making. The common law often refers to the notion of reproductive or procreative autonomy without ever engaging with the essential question of the contours of the idea.

The first part of the book thus draws on ideas from philosophy and bioethics in an attempt to answer some questions about what we really mean by reproductive autonomy, and the remaining parts seek to apply that meaning to various regulatory questions. One of the primary motivations for this project was to attempt to find a way to understand reproductive autonomy that has some resonance with feminist thinkers who dispute the focus on autonomy in reproductive decision making. I am well aware that there will be many who disagree with my approach, and I am under no illusions that I have managed to answer all of the questions. But I hope that I have at least shown the potential value of an analysis that demands a deep engagement with these questions.

My other main aim in this project has been to make law and policy on these topics in these jurisdictions a bit easier to locate. The pace of change in this area is remarkable, and at times I have felt as though I am chasing a fast-moving train in attempting to keep up. The law and policy as stated here are current to 1 August 2012, although in some areas it has been possible to include later developments.

I am hardly the first to observe that writing a book involves the assistance and support of many others, but that it can also be lonely work. Many of my colleagues, past and present, have listened to me carry on about some of these issues, and I thank them for indulging me and for helping me sharpen my arguments: Barbara Billingsley, Russell Brown, Ubaka Ogbogu, Zubin Master and James Stribopoulos have been cheerful participants in conversations about aspects of this work (Ubaka and Zubin even took the time to read a chapter and provide helpful and encouraging comments). Colleagues from other institutions have also provided helpful feedback and support: Alta Charo, Roxanne Mykitiuk, Carolyn McLeod and Jeff Nisker. This book evolved out of my doctoral dissertation, and I also want to thank my dissertation examination committee at Columbia University (Carol Sanger, William Sage, Patricia Williams and Ariela Dubler) for their insightful comments and their encouragement. My former and current Deans, David Percy and Philip Bryden, have been very supportive of this project, and I thank them for that. Three colleagues in particular stand out for their incredible patience and their repeated assurance that I could write this book. Annalise Acorn, Bruce Ziff and Tim Caulfield were always ready to give a pep talk and provide encouragement, as well as comments and advice on the mechanics of getting a book written, and I want them to know that there is literally no way that this book would have happened without their help.

I am very grateful to the organisations that have provided support for this project. I benefitted from a grant from the Social Sciences and Humanities Research Council of Canada in the very early days of my exploration of these topics, and more recently the University of Alberta has provided critical and much appreciated support. I also want to thank my student research and editorial assistants, Daryk Gorrie and Leanne Monsma, for their excellent, and much appreciated, work.

I also wish to thank Richard Hart and his assistant, Rachel Turner, for their patience and support.

Lastly, I want to thank my family. Emily, Sam and Talia, you have shown a remarkable degree of understanding and patience during the writing process, and I want you all to know how much I appreciate it! And Jim, you have been amazing. There is truly no way that I would have been able to do this without you. Thank you.

Erin Nelson
Edmonton, Alberta
October 2012

Acknowledgements

Parts of this book contain material that has been previously published and revised. In Chapters 2–8, much of the material referring to Canadian law and policy first appeared in my chapter 'Regulating Reproduction' in Jocelyn Downie, Timothy Caulfield and Colleen M Flood (eds), *Canadian Health Law and Policy*, 4th edn (Markham, LexisNexis Canada, 2011) 295–340. That information is reprinted here with permission of the publisher LexisNexis Canada Inc. Parts of Chapter 6 first appeared in 'Reconceiving Pregnancy: Expressive Choice and Legal Reasoning' (2004) 49(3) *McGill Law Journal* 593–634. Part of Chapter 7, section V. first appeared in my chapter 'Informed Consent: Reasonableness, Risk, and Disclosure' in Jocelyn Downie and Elaine Gibson (eds), *Health Law at the Supreme Court of Canada* (Toronto, Irwin Law, 2007) and is included here with permission from Irwin Law. Parts of Chapter 8 first appeared in my article 'Comparative Perspectives on the Regulation of Assisted Reproductive Technologies in the United Kingdom and Canada' (2006) 43 *Alberta Law Review* 1023–1048; these sections are reprinted here with the permission of the Alberta Law Review. Parts of Chapter 9, sections III., IV. and V. (relating to surrogacy, parentage and reproductive tourism) first appeared in my article 'Global Trade and Assisted Reproductive Technologies: Regulatory Challenges in International Surrogacy' (2013) 41(1) *Journal of Law, Medicine and Ethics* 240–253.

Summary Contents

Contents

Table of Cases

Australia

Canada

European Court of Human Rights

France

India

Ireland

Israel

Netherlands

United Kingdom

United States of America

Table of Legislation

Australia

Statutory Instruments

United States of America

Table of Conventions, Treaties, etc

1

Introduction

No society, no religion, no culture, and no system of national law has been neutral about issues of human reproduction.[1]

R EPRODUCTIVE CHOICES ARE at once the most private and intimate decisions we make in our lives, and yet they undeniably also have public dimensions. Reproductive decision making takes place in a web of overlapping concerns – political and ideological, socio-economic, health and healthcare – all of which engage the public and which involve strongly-held opinions and attitudes. Decisions about reproducing, about whether and how to use one's reproductive capacity, whether to 'bear and beget' children, are deeply meaningful to us as individuals, and of profound consequence to society. These decisions play a key role in 'determin[ing] the shape and meaning of one's life.'[2] And it is now possible actively to make decisions about childbearing in ways that would not have been open in the past. We now have choices about aspects of the reproductive process that, in the past, were matters of chance; we routinely see evidence of the social concerns that these issues raise in the popular press[3] and popular culture.[4] The shift from reproduction as a matter of chance to an opportunity for deliberate choice has yielded a need for greater State involvement in reproductive activity. The introduction of medical products and procedures to prevent conception, to terminate pregnancy and to initiate pregnancies in vitro, has created a need for regulation aimed at consumer protection and quality control, much as is the case with other medications, medical devices and procedures. But the complexities introduced by increased choice in reproduction go beyond issues of safety and quality, in that they also introduce new ethical concerns. Reproductive choices, controversial as they sometimes are, demand a carefully-balanced response from

---

[1] Rebecca J Cook, Bernard M Dickens and Mahmoud F Fathalla, *Reproductive Health and Human Rights: Integrating Medicine, Ethics, and Law* (Oxford, Oxford University Press, 2003) 3.

[2] John A Robertson, *Children of Choice: Freedom and the New Reproductive Technologies* (Princeton, NJ, Princeton University Press, 1994) 24.

[3] See, eg, Mark Henderson, 'First "Designer Baby" Could Save His Brother', *The Times Online* (London, 9 November 2004), <www.timesonline.co.uk/article/0,,8122-1380616,00.html>; Rob Stein, 'A Boy for You, a Girl for Me: Technology Allows Choice: Embryo Screening Stirs Ethics Debate', *Washington Post* (14 December 2004) A01; Karen Chen, 'Fertility Experts Debate the Risks of IVF Twins', *Ottawa Citizen* (10 September 2012), <www.ottawacitizen.com/health/Fertility+experts+debate+risks+twins/7215343/story.html>; Michael Hanlon, 'Three-parent IVF is a Chance to Create a Generation Free From Mitochondrial Diseases', *Telegraph* (Chatham, 17 September 2012), <www.telegraph.co.uk/science/9548387/Three-parent-IVF-is-a-chance-to-create-a-generation-free-from-mitochondrial-diseases.html>; Reuters, 'First Mother to Daughter Uterus Transplant Carried Out in Sweden', *Vancouver Sun* (19 September 2012), <www.vancouversun.com/health/women/First+mother+daughter+uterus+transplant+carried+Sweden/7265488/story.html>.

[4] There are several movies dealing with a number of the issues raised by assisted reproductive technologies: *Godsend* (2004); *Baby Mama* (2008); *Inconceivable* (2008); *My Sister's Keeper* (2009).

law and policy. Intervention by the State in the context of reproductive decision making is necessary but also dangerous – necessary in order to protect the rights and interests of individuals, and dangerous because if it goes too far, regulation can have destructive effects on individuals and on society as a whole.

I. REPRODUCTIVE AUTONOMY IN LAW

Reproductive autonomy – the ability to be self-determining and to act on one's own values in making decisions about reproduction[5] – is an important concept in law and policy. Legal support for reproductive autonomy is found in the Canadian[6] and American[7] Constitutions, international instruments (such as the International Convention on Civil and Political Rights,[8] the Convention on the Elimination of Discrimination Against Women,[9] the International Conference on Population and Development[10] and the European Convention on Human Rights[11]) and the common law. There does not seem to be much, if any, disagreement around the idea that freedom of choice in reproductive matters is a significant aspect of the freedom to map the course of one's own life. Yet in attempting to look closely at the contours of the concept, we begin to see some uncertainty about its meaning and legal implications, about how to understand reproductive autonomy and how to value it.

The development of the legal conception of reproductive autonomy relates to women's claims to access to contraception and abortion services; it stems from assertions that women should be free from coercion in reproduction.[12] North American jurisprudence around reproductive autonomy thus has its origins in relation to bodily integrity and decisional privacy. Whether or not the law has explicitly recognised it as such,[13] the struggle for the right to safe, timely abortion is where we locate the origins of reproductive autonomy.

Early judicial commentary on the notion of reproductive autonomy is found in the American contraception and abortion cases. In *Eisenstadt v Baird*, for example, Justice Brennan stated that

---

[5] See, eg, Emily Jackson, *Regulating Reproduction: Law, Technology and Autonomy* (Oxford, Hart Publishing, 2001) 2–9; Carolyn McLeod, *Self-Trust and Reproductive Autonomy* (Cambridge, MA, MIT Press, 2002) 2. For a discussion of autonomy generally, see Catriona Mackenzie and Natalie Stoljar, 'Introduction: Autonomy Refigured' in Catriona Mackenzie and Natalie Stoljar (eds), *Relational Autonomy: Feminist Perspectives on Autonomy, Agency, and the Social Self* (Oxford, Oxford University Press, 2000) 3.

[6] *R v Morgentaler* [1988] 1 SCR 30, 63 OR (2d) 281.

[7] See, eg, Robertson (n 2) (arguing that US constitutional jurisprudence supports a broad reading of reproductive autonomy or, as he labels it, procreative liberty).

[8] International Covenant on Civil and Political Rights (adopted 19 December 1966, entered into force 23 March 1976) 999 UNTS 171, Arts 17, 23.

[9] Convention on the Elimination of All Forms of Discrimination Against Women (adopted 18 December 1979, entered into force 3 September 1981) 1249 UNTS 13, Art 16(1)(e).

[10] 'Programme of Action of the International Conference on Population and Development', UN International Conference on Population and Development (Cairo 5–13 September 1994) UN Doc A/CONF.171/13/Rev.1, Ch VII.

[11] European Convention on Human Rights and Fundamental Freedoms (adopted 4 November 1950, entered into force 3 December 1953) UNTS 213.

[12] Onora O'Neill, *Autonomy and Trust in Bioethics* (Cambridge, Cambridge University Press, 2002) 50.

[13] As is discussed in ch 5, the law around abortion in the UK and Australia has not developed in such a way as to recognise women's autonomy explicitly.

[i]f the right of privacy means anything, it is the right of the individual, married or single, to be free from unwarranted governmental intrusion into matters so fundamentally affecting a person as the decision whether to bear or beget a child.[14]

In *Roe v Wade*, the US Supreme Court expanded on this analysis in articulating the contours of a constitutional right to abortion, holding that 'The detriment that the State would impose upon the pregnant woman by denying this choice altogether is apparent.'[15] In striking down Canada's therapeutic abortion law, Chief Justice Dickson noted the profound implications of a woman's inability to choose freely to terminate a pregnancy:

> At the most basic, physical and emotional level, every pregnant woman is told . . . that she cannot submit to a generally safe medical procedure that might be of clear benefit to her unless she meets criteria entirely unrelated to her own priorities and aspirations. . . . Forcing a woman, by threat of criminal sanction, to carry a foetus to term unless she meets certain criteria unrelated to her own priorities and aspirations, is a profound interference with a woman's body and thus a violation of security of the person.[16]

Madam Justice Wilson took an even more expansive view, recognising that a woman's decision to terminate a pregnancy has 'profound psychological, economic and social consequences,' but also that it is a decision that 'deeply reflects the way the woman thinks about herself and her relationship to others and to society . . . Her response to it will be the response of the whole person.'[17]

The cases on contraception and abortion tend to refer with approval to the idea that procreative decisions are of an acutely intimate and personal nature. The cases also recognise the importance of the freedom to make such decisions and acknowledge the universality of the relevant principles.[18] As Mr Justice Munby put it:

> Decisions on such intensely private and personal matters as whether or not to use contraceptives, or particular types of contraceptives, are surely matters which ought to be left to the free choice of the individual. And, whilst acknowledging that I have had no argument on the point, I cannot help thinking that personal choice in matters of contraception is part of that 'respect for private and family life' protected by Article 8 of the [European Convention on Human Rights]. The reasoning of the Supreme Court of the United States of America in *Griswold*, *Eisenstadt* and *Carey* no doubt reflects a different constitutional background, but are not the underlying principles the same?[19]

In addition to articulating an intense and very personal interest in being able to choose not to reproduce, courts have also noted the importance of the 'right to reproduce' in considering issues such as non-consensual sterilisation of persons with intellectual

---

[14] *Eisenstadt v Baird*, 405 US 438 (1972) 453.

[15] *Roe v Wade*, 410 US 113 (1973) 153. Justice Blackmun went on to refer to the potential medical and psychological harm, as well as the distress, that could be caused by forcing a woman to bear an unwanted child.

[16] *Morgentaler* (n 6) 56–57 (cited to SCR). In *Morgentaler*, the Supreme Court of Canada found the Criminal Code (RSC 1970, c C-34) provisions dealing with abortion to be unconstitutional and therefore invalid, on the basis that they violated s 7 of the Canadian Charter of Rights and Freedoms, Pt I of the Constitution Act, 1982, being Schedule B to the Canada Act 1982 (UK), 1982, c 11.

[17] *Morgentaler* (n 6) 171 (cited to SCR).

[18] In *Smeaton v Secretary of State for Health* [2002] EWHC 610 (Admin), [2002] 2 FCR 193, the English High Court was called upon to address 'the legality of the prescription, supply and use of the morning-after pill' in England (para 3). The petitioner asserted that the pill (also known as the 'emergency contraceptive pill') is an abortifacient.

[19] *Ibid* para 398.

disabilities.[20] In *Skinner v Oklahoma*, the United States Supreme Court expressed what is taken to be the 'strongest precedent'[21] in favour of a broad right to autonomy in the reproductive context, referring to procreation as a 'basic civil [right]' and holding that

> [t]he power to sterilize . . . may have . . . farreaching and devastating effects. . . . There is no redemption for the individual whom the law touches. Any experiment which the State conducts is to his irreparable injury. He is forever deprived of a basic liberty.[22]

And in *E (Mrs) v Eve*, in which the mother of an extremely aphasic woman sought to have her daughter sterilised, Mr Justice La Forest noted the 'growing legal recognition of the fundamental character of the right to procreate'.[23]

In spite of these unequivocal and eloquent statements about the deep interest we have in making our own decisions about whether or not to 'bear or beget' children, courts have on occasion faltered in attempting to articulate the contours of reproductive autonomy. In the United States, for example, the Supreme Court has made clear that its view of reproductive autonomy is limited, holding that although a woman has a constitutional right to choose abortion, this right does not

> [carry] with it a constitutional entitlement to the financial resources to avail herself of the full range of protected choices. The reason why was explained in *Maher*: although government may not place obstacles in the path of a woman's exercise of her freedom of choice, it need not remove those not of its own creation. Indigency falls in the latter category.[24]

And in *Re B*, after noting that in an earlier decision of the Family Court[25] 'the judge rightly referred to . . . a basic human right, namely the right of a woman to reproduce,' Lord Hailsham proceeded savagely to criticise the decision of the Supreme Court of Canada in *Eve*.[26] He ultimately permitted the sterilisation of an intellectually disabled woman, stating that

---

[20] In *Skinner v Oklahoma*, 316 US 535 (1942), the US Supreme Court invalidated an Oklahoma statute that granted the state the power to sterilise persons who had been convicted three times of particular criminal offences.

[21] Robertson (n 2) 36.

[22] *Skinner* (n 20) 541.

[23] *E (Mrs) v Eve* [1986] 2 SCR 388, [1986] SCJ No 60, 419–20 (cited to SCR). This case concerned an application by the mother of an intellectually disabled woman to have the woman sterilised. Mr Justice La Forest referred to the 'grave intrusion on a person's rights and the certain physical damage that ensues from non-therapeutic sterilization without consent' and concluded that 'it can never safely be determined that such a procedure is for the benefit of that person' (*ibid* 431). Similar comments have been made by judges in other jurisdictions. In *Re Jane* (1988) 85 ALR 409, 418–20, for example, Nicholson CJ suggested that there is a right to procreate, or to choose not to do so. In *Marion's Case*, which was decided a few years after *Re Jane*, the Australian High Court recognised the 'fundamental right to personal inviolability' but left open the question of whether 'there exists in the common law a fundamental right to reproduce which is independent of the right to personal inviolability' (*Secretary, Department of Health and Community Services v JWB and SMB (Marion's Case)* (1992) 175 CLR 218, 253).

[24] *Harris v McRae*, 448 US 297 (1980) 316. The Court went on to say: 'The financial constraints that restrict an indigent woman's ability to enjoy the full range of constitutionally protected freedom of choice are the product not of governmental restrictions on access to abortions, but rather of her indigency. Although Congress has opted to subsidize medically necessary services generally, but not certain medically necessary abortions, the fact remains that the Hyde Amendment leaves an indigent woman with at least the same range of choice in deciding whether to obtain a medically necessary abortion as she would have had if Congress had chosen to subsidize no health care costs at all. We are thus not persuaded that the Hyde Amendment impinges on the constitutionally protected freedom of choice recognized in *Wade*' (316–17). See also *Maher v Roe*, 432 US 464 (1977).

[25] *Re D (A Minor) (Wardship: Sterilisation)* [1976] Fam 185.

[26] *Re B (A Minor) (Wardship: Sterilisation)* [1988] AC 199.

[t]o talk of the 'basic right' to reproduce of an individual who is not capable of knowing the causal connection between intercourse and childbirth, the nature of pregnancy, what is involved in delivery, unable to form maternal instincts or to care for a child appears to me wholly to part company with reality.[27]

The cases provide only a partial picture, as they consider only certain aspects of reproductive regulation and reproductive autonomy, rather than making broad statements about its implications. While it is fair to say that there is strong legal support for the notion of reproductive autonomy, at least in relation to abortion, contraception and sterilisation, questions remain as to whether these statements add up to more than the sum of their parts. Can we extrapolate from statements in favour of reproductive autonomy in the abortion and contraception context to support for the use of pre-natal diagnostic testing in an effort to avoid bearing a child with a genetic abnormality? Does the right not to be involuntarily sterilised entail a right to access technological means of procreation where one is unable to conceive a child without such assistance? Does the apparent endorsement of a strong, negative rights approach to the question of avoiding reproduction translate into a similar privileging of positive rights to access reproductive technology?

As assisted reproductive technologies (ARTs) have developed and become normalised, it has become increasingly clear that reproductive autonomy can be understood to encompass more than simply freedom from coercion in reproduction. It is commonplace to see claims that such things as the freedom to use pre-natal tests, the freedom to use technological means to facilitate procreation and the freedom to select for or against specific traits in our offspring, potentially involve the exercise of reproductive autonomy.[28] Arguably, the statements in cases that have considered aspects of reproductive autonomy lend themselves to this broader understanding of the freedom to make choices in an area of our lives that is central to our self-definition.[29] Yet, at the same time, new technologies evoke issues and concerns that are distinct from the more basic questions raised in the early cases. Courts have had to consider the implications of reproductive autonomy in the context of surrogacy agreements,[30] disputes over the disposition of surplus embryos created as a result of infertility treatment[31] and cases where a woman has sought to attempt conception using her male partner's sperm after his death.[32] These cases require courts to consider conflicting rights or interests in reproductive autonomy where, for example, former partners cannot agree on the disposition of embryos created for purposes of in vitro fertilisation. Not surprisingly, these types of

[27] *Ibid* 204. It has been pointed out that the view taken of B's capacity by the Law Lords is particularly pessimistic: see, eg, Jonathan Montgomery, 'Rhetoric and "Welfare"' (1989) 9 *OJLS* 395, 398–99. See also Jackson (n 5) 63, noting that the English courts have tended to 'ignore the fluidity of incompetence'.

[28] See, eg, Jackson (n 5); Robertson (n 2); Dorothy Roberts, *Killing the Black Body: Race, Reproduction, and the Meaning of Liberty* (New York, Vintage, 1997); Allen Buchanan *et al*, *From Chance to Choice: Genetics and Justice* (Cambridge, Cambridge University Press, 2002).

[29] See, eg, Roberts (n 28); Robertson (n 2).

[30] *In the Matter of Baby M*, 109 NJ 396 (1988); *Johnson v Calvert*, 851 P 2d 776 (Cal 1993); *Jaycee B v John B*, 42 Cal App 4th 718 (1996).

[31] *Davis v Davis*, 842 SW 2d 588 (Tenn 1992); *Kass v Kass*, 696 NE 2d 174 (NY 1998); *AZ v BZ*, 725 NE 2d 1051 (Mass 2000); *JB v MB*, 783 A 2d 707 (NJ 2001); *Re the Marriage of Litowitz v Litowitz*, 48 P 3d 261 (Wash 2002); *Evans v Amicus Health Care Limited & Others* [2004] EWCA Civ 727, [2005] Fam 1.

[32] Although these cases generally do not frame the issues with reference to reproductive autonomy, see, eg, *AB v AG (Vic)* (Supreme Court of Victoria, Gillard J, 21 July 1998); *R (Blood) v Human Fertilisation and Embryology Authority* [1997] EWCA Civ 3092; *Hecht v Superior Court*, 20 Cal Rptr 2d 274 (Cal App 1993); *Hall v Fertility Institute of New Orleans*, 647 So 2d 1348 (La App, 4th c 1994).

cases create some uncertainty about the implications of reproductive autonomy for law and policy making.

It seems obvious that abortion and contraception rights are necessary in order for women to enjoy autonomy and to participate fully in civic life. A more difficult argument to make is that access to ARTs equally fits within our conception of what is needed to respect reproductive autonomy. The cases frame reproductive autonomy as a vast concept and articulate sweeping ideas about its importance; these judicial statements have been relied upon to ground broader arguments about reproductive autonomy, both in terms of what it means and what it demands of the State. As reproductive technologies have developed and changed, we have seen the issues that confront judges and policy makers become more complex, but because the cases do not give sufficient depth or clarity to the concept, it is not always clear what reproductive autonomy demands. My project here is to consider ideas and arguments from philosophy and bioethics around autonomy and reproductive autonomy, both in terms of what it means and what it demands, and to apply those ideas in considering what shape legal regulation of reproductive decision making should take.

II. THE STRUCTURE OF THE BOOK

This is a study of reproductive regulation, the meaning of reproductive autonomy and the implications of its meaning for the regulatory enterprise. The aim is twofold: first, to make some arguments about the meaning of reproductive autonomy and its implications for law and policy; and, secondly, to create a resource for those interested in law, policy and reproductive decision making in Canada, the United States, the United Kingdom and Australia. Given the pace of change that has marked the law in some of the areas of reproductive regulation, it is useful and important to have a point-in-time resource explaining the legal and policy landscape. It is also useful to introduce and highlight Canadian and Australian law and policy in particular, as law and policy in these jurisdictions are less well known to many readers than UK and US law and policy.

The book is divided into four parts. In chapter two, I consider the nature of reproductive autonomy by examining literature from philosophy and bioethics. I explore the developing feminist literature on relational autonomy, and though I think that it provides a useful starting point for considering autonomy from a more inclusive perspective, I ultimately conclude that a relational analysis is not an approach I am comfortable adopting. Instead, I suggest that we work with an array of philosophical ideas about autonomy to arrive at a deeply contextualised account of reproductive autonomy, one that is concerned with creating the opportunity for meaningful exercise of reproductive choice. This broad approach is particularly appropriate where, as here, we are concerned with issues at the intersection of law and reproductive medicine, and with their particular impact on women.

Judicial and academic commentary around reproductive autonomy in a variety of contexts suggests the adoption of an inclusive understanding of the concept. Given the importance of the freedom to make one's own reproductive choices, particularly in relation to women's lives,[33] reproductive autonomy surely must mean more than simply the

---

[33] Indeed, Robertson suggests that reproductive autonomy is of 'central importance to individual meaning, dignity, and identity' (Robertson (n 2) 16).

legal ability of a woman to obtain an abortion or access to reproductive technologies. Our understanding of this concept should 'encompass the full range of procreative activities, including the ability to bear a child, and it must acknowledge that we make reproductive decisions within a social context, including inequalities of wealth and power'.[34] I also suggest that a strong link between reproductive autonomy and reproductive health would help to ground policy development around reproductive choice.

In chapter three, I turn from thinking about how to understand reproductive autonomy to considering how to respect it. In other words, based on this contextual understanding of reproductive autonomy, how should the State approach regulating reproduction? In this context, I argue for a model that takes as its starting point the notion that there is a 'core' of reproductive autonomy in which I locate decisions that engage women's bodily integrity. Reproductive autonomy need not be viewed as monolithic, but instead should be understood as including a vast number and array of decisions that may not all demand the same level of respect from the State. I suggest we can create a model that places these core issues at its heart, entitling them to maximal respect from the State (which includes the provision of resources). While other reproductive decisions are also entitled to respect, they do not demand as much from the State as do decisions that engage women's bodily integrity. I also argue here that a contextualised approach to reproductive autonomy requires a coherent and thoughtful approach to regulating reproductive decision making. The development of a comprehensive framework to guide law and policy on all aspects of reproductive regulation is not a realistic aim. But one step in the right direction would be the creation of a national reproductive health strategy, which would permit the bringing together of experts in healthcare, law and policy, and would help to highlight the relationship of reproductive health and reproductive autonomy. Though a national reproductive health strategy would not answer all of the questions raised by a reproductive autonomy analysis, it could provide a starting point for consideration of policy directions.

The remaining three parts of the book take a detailed look at law and policy related to various aspects of reproductive decision making, drawing on examples from Canada, Australia, the United States and the United Kingdom. When I began this project, I thought that considering law and policy in several jurisdictions would be useful in terms of thinking about the lessons Canada might learn from these other jurisdictions, as well as providing a focal point for critique. As I have progressed through this work over the years, what I have found instead is that most of these jurisdictions can be criticised for their positions on several of these issues, but most of all, they can be criticised for failing to adopt any coherent policy framework for legal and policy decision making in this area. The analysis of several different jurisdictions with different histories but which share a liberal democratic tradition, adds depth and richness to the discussion. Such an approach does allow for us to draw lessons from one jurisdiction that can be applied in others but, more than anything else, shows how important it is to address these issues from a policy orientation (as opposed to *no* policy orientation), and in particular a policy orientation that acknowledges the importance of reproductive autonomy for women.

All four jurisdictions have taken *ad hoc* approaches to regulating reproduction, as a result of which this study of law and policy around reproductive decision making in these jurisdictions reveals some interesting contradictions. For example, in the UK and in some Australian states, abortion remains a criminal offence, yet it is generally available and is

[34] Roberts (n 28) 6.

(at least partially) publicly funded. In Canada, there is no criminal law against abortion, yet in some geographic locations there are no abortion providers. The procedure is therefore available only to those who are not prevented by other responsibilities, or by financial straits, from traveling to other jurisdictions. In the US, abortion and contraception are constitutional entitlements, but abortion services can be very difficult to access due to restrictive legislation (both in terms of funding for abortion services and in terms of other restrictions, including mandatory waiting periods and parental consent rules for minors). Moreover, prescription hormonal contraception is often not covered by health insurers, and emergency contraception in particular can be extremely difficult to access.

Numerous areas of law and policy are covered here, from birth control and abortion to surrogacy arrangements and parentage laws, and several more besides.[35] None of these areas is covered exhaustively; my purpose is to give a sense of the legal and policy landscape in the various jurisdictions. I have included this wide array of issues because, in order fully to appreciate the important role reproductive decision making plays in women's lives, it is essential to look at reproductive decision making through a wide lens. The juxtaposition of all of these areas helps to highlight the importance of context in reproductive regulation, as it illustrates the ways in which women's lives are affected by regulation of reproduction and the impact on women of our continued failure to regulate with a view to fostering reproductive autonomy. Another reason for including all of these areas is that much contemporary scholarship on reproductive autonomy has shifted its focus to regulating 'new' technologies', and I wanted to concentrate some attention on contraception and abortion, to show how much work is yet to be done to establish meaningful opportunities for the exercise of reproductive autonomy even in those less contemporary, arguably more settled areas of law.

In spite of the emphasis I place on the importance of reproductive autonomy in regulating reproduction, I also acknowledge the limits of a reproductive autonomy analysis. This analysis cannot resolve all of the issues that fall to be considered in thinking about how particular areas of reproductive decision making should be regulated. That said, given the significance of reproductive autonomy – in particular, its significance to women – the task for law and policy is to create conditions under which reproductive autonomy can be exercised meaningfully.

The pace of change in reproductive science and technology is astonishing. Even as we attempt to create law and policy, the ground is shifting underfoot. We cannot hope to fashion a set of fixed, explicit rules to guide law and policy makers. But we can – and must – take steps to work toward the development of a coherent approach to legal and policy decision making in the reproductive context.

---

[35] And there are many others which could be considered but which I do not include.

Part One

Reproductive Autonomy in Theory and Practice

2

Reproductive Autonomy in Theory

WHAT IS REPRODUCTIVE autonomy? Though much discussed in legal
and bioethics literature, many questions remain unanswered about what is
meant by reproductive autonomy. There is little disagreement that freedom
of choice in reproductive matters is critically important, but as a concept, reproductive
autonomy remains somewhat inchoate. In part, the ambiguity is a result of the incomplete theorisation of the concept; in turn, this is tied to the contested nature of autonomy
itself.

My aim in this chapter is to bring the discussion and debate around autonomy in ethical theory more fully into our thinking about autonomy, and particularly reproductive
autonomy, within bioethics and law. I recognise that there are many questions and
issues I cannot resolve here; my objective is to take a first step toward a more concretely
theorised idea of reproductive autonomy, which in turn can help to inform and shape
law and policy around reproductive decision making. My argument is that we need a
more robust foundation for reproductive autonomy, and I begin by addressing that
foundation. Most philosophers and bioethics scholars would agree that reproductive
autonomy is not a distinct concept within ethical theory, but it is clear that in order to
define reproductive autonomy, we must first understand something about autonomy
more generally. While I cannot pretend to do justice to philosophical theories of autonomy here, I cannot make coherent arguments about what reproductive autonomy
entails without working through philosophical and bioethical arguments about autonomy. This chapter therefore undertakes that exploration in some detail.

I begin with a discussion of autonomy in philosophy, in which I attempt to tie together
various conceptual details. These details include: the nature of the autonomous person;
the prevailing views of the conditions precedent for autonomy; the relationship between
autonomy and liberal theory; and current conceptions of autonomy in bioethics. I then
turn to a discussion of the feminist critique of autonomy, and from there to feminist
articulations of autonomy, with a focus on relational autonomy. Those who are not
interested in the entire preliminary discussion might wish to skip ahead to the second
part of the chapter, which focuses on reproductive autonomy. Here I discuss the feminist
critique of reproductive autonomy and my arguments for a way forward. I argue that
the critique of reproductive autonomy raised by feminist theorists is not a reason to
reject the concept. Instead, we must reconceptualise reproductive autonomy based on a
rich and nuanced conception of autonomy itself.

I. WHAT IS AUTONOMY?

To say that autonomy is an important concept in philosophy, bioethics and law is to state the obvious. Yet aside from this broad claim about its significance in these theoretical and practical realms, there is little agreement about the nature of autonomy and its meaning in moral or political philosophy, applied ethics or law. Indeed, it seems that after decades of debate and discussion, we have more questions than answers about autonomy's meaning and implications.

In very general terms, autonomy is the prerogative of the individual to live her own life, in accordance with her own values and desires: to live by her own lights. The ideas of self-governance and internally directed decision and action are core characteristics common to all accounts of autonomy, in spite of the profound differences among theorists around the specific conceptual details. And these differences are indeed profound. Autonomy has been used to describe a wide range of ideas,

> sometimes as an equivalent of liberty (positive or negative in Berlin's terminology), sometimes as equivalent to self-rule or sovereignty, sometimes as identical with freedom of the will. It is equated with dignity, integrity, individuality, independence, responsibility, and self-knowledge. It is identified with qualities of self-assertion, with critical reflection, with freedom from obligation, with absence of external causation, with knowledge of one's own interests. . . . It is related to actions, to beliefs, to reasons for acting, to rules, to the will of other persons, to thoughts, and to principles. About the only features held constant from one author to another are that autonomy is a feature of persons and that it is a desirable quality to have.[1]

Depending on the lens through which it is viewed, autonomy can be seen as 'rational self-maximization',[2] as freedom, as achievement, as a series of competencies requiring certain skills or attributes,[3] as a procedural ability to subject one's motivations and actions to critical reflection, and as 'the self-imposition of the universal moral law'.[4] But as some philosophers have pointed out, a number of the ideas that have come to be associated with autonomy are actually separate notions that have been grafted onto autonomy through popular representations; this is particularly true of conceptions of autonomy that connect it with ideas of independence and (financial) self-sufficiency.[5]

---

[1] Gerald Dworkin, *The Theory and Practice of Autonomy* (Cambridge, Cambridge University Press, 1988) 6. By this Dworkin means that 'autonomy' refers to an abstract concept which is filled out with different content by different authors (*ibid* 10). In other words, 'when it comes to specifying more concretely what principles justify interference with autonomy, what is the nature of the "self" which does the choosing, what the connections between autonomy and dependence on others are, then there will be different and conflicting views on these matters' (*ibid* 9–10).

[2] Diana Tietjens Meyers, 'Feminism and Women's Autonomy: The Challenge of Female Genital Cutting' (2000) 31 *Metaphilosophy* 469, 477. As Meyers notes, rational choice views of autonomy 'identify autonomy with devising plans that maximize satisfaction'.

[3] Diana Tietjens Meyers, *Self, Society, and Personal Choice* (New York, Columbia University Press, 1989).

[4] John Christman, 'Autonomy in Moral and Political Philosophy' in Edward N Zalta (ed), *The Stanford Encyclopedia of Philosophy*, Spring edn (2011), at <plato.stanford.edu/archives/spr2011/entries/autonomy-moral/>. As Christman explains, for Kant, this forms the ground of our moral obligations and of the respect others owe to us.

[5] See, eg, Marilyn Friedman, *Autonomy, Gender, Politics* (Oxford, Oxford University Press, 2003) 47–50.

A. The autonomous person

Autonomy – as a concept relevant to persons – has its roots in the Enlightenment. As religion and religious ideas around morality and moral behaviour began to give way to arguments grounded in science and rationality, views of human agency also faced challenges. The rejection of religious moral principles as the point of reference for evaluating the morality of actions led to the need for an alternative secular foundation. Although most contemporary accounts of autonomy depart significantly from his conception, Immanuel Kant's moral philosophy is an important starting point in any discussion of autonomy. Kant, an Enlightenment philosopher, saw autonomy being grounded in practical reason ('our ability to use reasons to choose our own actions'[6]) and guided by self-imposition of universal moral law. As Jeremy Waldron explains, for Kant, 'A person is autonomous in the moral sense when he is not guided just by his own conception of happiness, but by a universalized concern for the ends of all rational persons'.[7] In Kantian moral philosophy, autonomy grounds an obligation to treat persons with respect, 'as ends in themselves'.[8]

Contemporary accounts of autonomy in general adopt a far more individualistic view of autonomy than did Kant. Indeed, there is little argument among modern theorists on this point. Instead, the debate and discussion centre on the nature of autonomy as an individualistic concept, and discussion of what it means to be an autonomous person. Modern theories of autonomy build on Kant's views, but generally part ways with Kant in that they ground autonomy in the individual capacity to adopt a set of values and reflectively to endorse those values, such that one's decisions or choices are based on values and reasons that are truly one's own.

B. Conditions for autonomy

In the most general terms, in order to exercise autonomy, one must have the liberty or freedom to make decisions and act on them. But according to most theories of autonomy, there are additional conditions that must exist in order for a person to be autonomous. Most theorists subscribe to two prerequisites for autonomy; these are referred to as authenticity conditions and competency conditions.[9] Authenticity conditions are those that describe the ability to reflect on and endorse or identify with one's 'first-order' desires, so that one is able to act on values that in some concrete sense are one's own.[10] Competency conditions refer to the agent's capacity to be autonomous. Different accounts of autonomy require different competency conditions, but typically these conditions include the capacity for 'self-control . . . rational thought, and freedom from

---

[6] Christman (n 4).

[7] Jeremy Waldron, 'Moral Autonomy and Personal Autonomy' in John Christman and Joel Anderson (eds), *Autonomy and the Challenges to Liberalism: New Essays* (Cambridge, Cambridge University Press, 2005) 307.

[8] This notion of the obligation to treat others with respect is echoed in the bioethics literature on autonomy, particularly in the context of the obligation to respect patient autonomy (typically understood as patients' choices).

[9] Christman (n 4); Carolyn McLeod, *Self-Trust and Reproductive Autonomy* (Cambridge, MA, MIT Press, 2002) 106–10.

[10] Christman (n 4); McLeod (n 9) 109–10.

debilitating pathologies, systematic self-deception and so on' – attributes that permit the individual to lead her life in a manner that is consistent with the values she has adopted.[11]

Marilyn Friedman describes the requisite competencies as including the capacity to have and understand values and commitments, the ability to take on 'valenced attitudes' toward one's values and commitments,[12] the capacity to act in ways that reflect one's commitments and values, and the ability to persist in acting in harmony with one's values and commitments in the presence of some degree of interference.[13] Friedman notes that the ability to act in harmony with one's own values in the face of obstacles is not often emphasised in the literature around autonomy, but seems significant nonetheless, given that 'the more [someone] can succeed in pursuing her concerns despite resistance,' the more autonomous she is.[14]

Different theories of autonomy take different positions as to whether autonomy is purely a procedural notion that is content-neutral (meaning that there are no requirements as to values or commitments that an autonomous agent can or must have), or whether it also has substantive requirements.[15] Content-neutral or procedural accounts of autonomy do not constrain the kinds of value commitments that an agent must have if he or she is to be considered autonomous. For the conditions of a procedural account of autonomy to be satisfied, the agent need only engage in the requisite type of critical reflection on her values (or at least be capable of doing so).[16] Such accounts are content-neutral because they do not insist on specific content in an individual's values, beliefs, desires or attitudes – or perhaps more accurately, do not place certain kinds of values or beliefs 'off-limits'.

Substantive accounts of autonomy – to a greater or lesser degree – do place limits on the value commitments that autonomous persons can have.[17] Substantive accounts of autonomy reject content neutrality in favour of some constraints on the values and pref-

---

[11] Christman (n 4). Meyers describes autonomy as a 'competency' that requires supportive conditions in order to flourish (Meyers (n 3)). It is not an 'all or nothing' construct but a matter of degree. Full autonomy is rare; persons can be minimally, moderately or maximally autonomous, depending upon their facility in exercising autonomy competency skills (*ibid* 205). More specifically, autonomy competency is described as requiring skills of self-discovery, self-definition and self-direction. Meyers defines autonomy competency as 'the repertory of coordinated skills that makes self-discovery, self-definition, and self-direction possible' and as the ability to act in ways that resonate with values one has previously considered and affirmed as one's own (*ibid* 76).

[12] Friedman (n 5) 13.

[13] *Ibid*. She further explains that choices and actions are autonomous only if they 'mirror wants or values that an acting person has reflectively reaffirmed and that are important to her' (*ibid* 14). More specifically, autonomous choices are self-reflective, they stem from what a person cares deeply about, and they are 'relatively unimpeded' by conditions that interfere with self-reflection, including coercion, manipulation and deception (*ibid* 14). Friedman further specifies that choices must be self-reflective in two senses. First, autonomous choices must be partly caused by the individual's 'reflective consideration of her own wants and values' and, secondly, they must reflect wants and values that the individual has 'reflectively endorsed' (*ibid* 14). Lastly, she notes that wants and values that are 'relatively important' to an individual are those that are both deep and pervasive (*ibid* 6). Depth refers to the fact that the particular value 'tend[s] to be chosen over other competing wants and values' and pervasiveness indicates that the particular want or value is 'frequently salient' in a person's life (ie it is relevant to many of the situations she faces) (*ibid* 6).

[14] *Ibid* 13.

[15] See, eg, Christman (n 4).

[16] Catriona Mackenzie and Natalie Stoljar, 'Introduction: Autonomy Refigured' in Catriona Mackenzie and Natalie Stoljar (eds), *Relational Autonomy: Feminist Perspectives on Autonomy, Agency, and the Social Self* (Oxford, Oxford University Press, 2000) 3, 13–14.

[17] See, eg, *ibid* 13–17; Catriona Mackenzie, 'Relational Autonomy, Normative Authority and Perfectionism' (2008) 39 *Journal of Social Philosophy* 512.

erences of agents,[18] and 'on what people can autonomously choose'.[19] On a substantive account of autonomy, certain choices or lifestyles are impermissible because they do not sit comfortably with our intuitions about what it is that autonomous people want.[20] Substantive theories of autonomy can be either 'weak' or 'strong'. Strong substantive theories require certain values or commitments on the part of autonomous persons, in essence stipulating that if persons do not endorse these values, they are not autonomous.[21] Weak substantive theories do not specify particular values or desires that persons must hold, but do place 'further necessary conditions on autonomy that operate as constraints on the contents of the desires or preferences capable of being held by autonomous agents'.[22] As Paul Benson explains, strong substantive accounts in some way preclude persons from preferring or valuing certain things 'without sacrificing some autonomy'.[23]

This is an important tension: on the one hand, procedural accounts of autonomy might be too ready to recognise as autonomous a person who reflectively endorses values that suggest that he or she is not autonomous; but on the other hand, substantive accounts might be too demanding and thereby too readily find that individuals lack autonomy.

In defending a content-neutral conception of autonomy, Marilyn Friedman suggests that substantive conceptions hold that in order for a person's choices to be respected as being autonomous, her choices must demonstrate her recognition of the value of autonomy.[24] In her view (and the view of many others[25]), this demand is too stringent because it fails to acknowledge as autonomous many decisions that meet a significant qualitative threshold in satisfying the requirements of content-neutral accounts.[26] Friedman offers a further reason, in addition to her conceptual arguments, for a content-neutral approach to autonomy;[27] namely, that it is more inclusive in terms of who may be considered autonomous (and, by extension, whose choices are worthy of respect).[28] This, in turn, fosters a broader sense of the equal worth of individuals.

C. Autonomy and liberalism

Autonomy as a contemporary idea is very closely linked with liberal political theory, where a primary focus is the relationship between the individual and the State.[29] Liberal

---

[18] Mackenzie and Stoljar (n 16) 19. See also Paul Benson, 'Feminist Intuitions and the Normative Substance of Autonomy' in James Stacey Taylor (ed), *Personal Autonomy: New Essays on Personal Autonomy and Its Role in Contemporary Moral Philosophy* (Cambridge, Cambridge University Press, 2005) 124, 133.

[19] Meyers (n 2) 477.

[20] See, eg, Marina AL Oshana, 'Personal Autonomy and Society' (1998) 29 *Journal of Social Philosophy* 81. See also Mackenzie (n 17) 512; John Christman, 'Relational Autonomy, Liberal Individualism, and the Social Constitution of Selves' (2004) 117 *Philosophical Studies* 143.

[21] Mackenzie and Stoljar (n 16) 19.

[22] *Ibid.*

[23] Benson (n 18) 133.

[24] Friedman (n 5) 20. Benson disagrees with this assessment of substantive accounts of autonomy, noting that not all strong substantive theories demand that a person's choices accord with the value of autonomy. He also faults Friedman for overlooking the potential of weak substantive theories to contribute to feminist conceptions of autonomy (Benson (n 18) 139).

[25] See, eg, Friedman (n 5); Christman (n 20); Meyers (n 2).

[26] Friedman (n 5) 20–21.

[27] *Ibid.* Friedman posits that the conceptual arguments demonstrate that substantive and content-neutral accounts of autonomy are more or less equally convincing for conceptual and intuitive reasons.

[28] *Ibid* 23. See also Christman (n 20) 152.

[29] John Christman and Joel Anderson, 'Introduction' in John Christman and Joel Anderson (eds) (n 7) 1.

theory is concerned with the legitimate role of the State in limiting individual freedom,[30] and the liberal tradition treats individuals as the 'unit of analysis' for purposes of political philosophy. The individual is who we must have in mind when building State institutions. The rights and interests of the individual are what count in terms of creating boundaries between individual and State, and in determining what constitutes a legitimate exercise of State power.

In this context, autonomy is critical as a means of protecting the individual from the State, or protecting a space for individual decision making and self-governance. Autonomy is necessary in order to preserve the interests of the individual from the collective. Thus, many accounts of autonomy that draw on the liberal tradition focus on the separateness, individuality and self-sufficiency of the autonomous person. The emphasis is on separating or insulating the self from the group or community.

The emphasis in liberal theory on individual free will and the vital importance of the boundary between the individual and the collective has led to the tendency to identify, even conflate, the liberal idea of autonomy with the separate, isolated, self-sufficient individual. The resulting image of the autonomous self has been called a 'caricature' of autonomy, 'exemplified by the self-sufficient, rugged male individualist, rational maximizing chooser of libertarian theory'.[31] Feminist and communitarian critiques of autonomy are often critiques of this caricature, as will be explained in more detail in section II. below.

D. Autonomy in bioethics

Discussion of autonomy is ubiquitous in the bioethics literature, but interesting questions arise when considering the meaning of autonomy in bioethics, as to whether philosophers and bioethicists are even talking about the same concept. Largely, the disconnect exists because autonomy in bioethics has not been fully theorised – there is in the bioethics literature 'no theory of autonomy that spells out its nature, its moral implications, its limits, how respect for autonomy differs from respect for persons (if it does), and the like'.[32]

In the healthcare ethics context, the notion of autonomy is usually used in reference to the need to respect patient autonomy; in other words, respect by healthcare providers for the autonomy (and autonomous choices) of their patients. The concept of autonomy in bioethics, as it has been traditionally understood, draws on liberal ideas about the self and about the role of the individual in making healthcare decisions.

Although Kant's name is often invoked in the philosophical and bioethics literature, many contemporary accounts of autonomy and of what is demanded by the obligation to respect it are more closely aligned with John Stuart Mill's views of liberty.[33] Mill's

---

[30] *Ibid* 4.

[31] Mackenzie and Stoljar (n 16) 5.

[32] Tom L Beauchamp, 'Does Ethical Theory Have a Future in Bioethics?' (2004) 32 *Journal of Law, Medicine & Ethics* 209, 214. Beauchamp points to Dworkin's theory of autonomy as being the 'most detailed' theory of autonomy in bioethics, but argues that it falls short in many respects. He also bemoans the lack of work building on some of the ideas found in Dworkin's theory (such as the idea of content-neutrality in relation to autonomy) and the lack of work tying autonomy theory to practice, but fails entirely to mention any of the feminist literature on autonomy that has embarked on those projects.

[33] Onora O'Neill, *Autonomy and Trust in Bioethics* (Cambridge, Cambridge University Press, 2002) 30.

contention – that individual liberty can be constrained only by the liberty of others and by the obligation not to harm others – resonates with the bioethics literature in its demand for respect for patient autonomy and in its disavowal of paternalism. As Mill explains, in *On Liberty*:

> [T]he sole end for which mankind are warranted, individually or collectively, in interfering with the liberty of action of any of their number, is self-protection. That the only purpose for which power can be rightfully exercised over any member of a civilised community, against his will, is to prevent harm to others. His own good, either physical or moral, is not a sufficient warrant. He cannot rightfully be compelled to do or forbear because it will be better for him to do so, because it will make him happier, because, in the opinions of others, to do so would be wise, or even right. These are good reasons for remonstrating with him, or reasoning with him, or persuading him, or entreating him, but not for compelling him, or visiting him with any evil in case he do otherwise.[34]

Both Kantian and Millian views of autonomy have been subject to criticism – Kant for being hyper-rational and leaving no room for affect, emotion or relationships, and Mill for being overly individualistic and consumer-orientated.[35] The focus on reason within Kantian autonomy arguably does miss the mark in terms of decision making, particularly in relation to healthcare, given the centrality of emotion and relation in this realm. And Mill's arguments about liberty can certainly be taken to lead to the conclusion that what is best for human flourishing is an ever-increasing list of options – and again, this seems to neglect the nuances of choice making, especially in the context of healthcare and reproduction.

There is a vast literature on the idea of autonomy in bioethics.[36] In spite of the volume, however, there is one conception of autonomy in healthcare ethics that dominates the field; that developed by Tom Beauchamp and James Childress in their groundbreaking work *Principles of Biomedical Ethics*.[37] In order to create a practically useful approach to ethics for healthcare decision making, Beauchamp and Childress draw on many high-level ethical theories, while recognising that none of these theories – including Kantianism and utilitarianism – is suited for wide use in the bioethics context. Ultimately, they distill four principles of bioethics: autonomy, beneficence, non-maleficence and justice. While Beauchamp and Childress do not make the claim that autonomy is the foremost of the four principles, the focal point within the bioethics literature has been on autonomy.[38]

---

[34] John Stuart Mill, *On Liberty*, 2nd edn (Cambridge, MA, Ticknor and Fields, 1863) 23.

[35] See, eg, O'Neill (n 33) 45–48 (referring to the way in which Mill's ideas have been used to support a 'consumerist' view of autonomy); Annette Baier, *Moral Prejudices: Essays on Ethics* (Cambridge, MA, Harvard University Press, 1994) 18–32; Tom L Beauchamp and James F Childress, *Principles of Biomedical Ethics*, 6th edn (New York, Oxford University Press, 2009) 348–49 (referring to Kantian theory).

[36] Tom Beauchamp has referred to 'thousands of publications' on the topic (Beauchamp (n 32) 216).

[37] The first edition of the book was published in 1979; the most recent edition in 2009 (Beauchamp and Childress (n 35)). Numerous authors refer to the dominance of the Beauchamp and Childress account – see, eg, O'Neill (n 33); Carl Schneider, *The Practice of Autonomy: Patients, Doctors, and Medical Decisions* (New York, Oxford University Press, 1998); Rebecca Kukla, 'Conscientious Autonomy: Displacing Decisions in Health Care' (2005) 35(2) *Hastings Center Report* 34, 35 (noting that Beauchamp and Childress version remains dominant in spite of multiple attacks); Rebecca L Walker, 'Medical Ethics Needs a New View of Autonomy' (2009) 33 *Journal of Medicine and Philosophy* 594, 595.

[38] Paul Root Wolpe, 'The Triumph of Autonomy in American Bioethics: A Sociological Perspective' in Raymond De Vries and Janardan Subedi (eds), *Bioethics and Society: Constructing the Ethical Enterprise* (New York, Prentice Hall, 1998) 38; Raanan Gillon, 'Ethics Needs Principles – Four Can Encompass the Rest – And Respect For Autonomy Should be "First Among Equals"' (2003) 29 *Journal of Medical Ethics* 307.

The principlist account of autonomy (or, more specifically, of respect for autonomy) explained by Beauchamp and Childress takes as its focus the autonomous nature of a particular choice, action or decision, rather than the autonomous nature of the person making the decision.[39] Autonomous actions, on this view, are those that are intentional, voluntary[40] and based on substantial understanding of relevant facts. A deliberate choice made by a person who has 'acquired pertinent information and [has] relevant beliefs about the nature and consequences of their actions'[41] and who is choosing voluntarily, is autonomous and requires respect.

Beauchamp and Childress claim – quite rightly – that autonomous persons and autonomous decisions are distinct concepts with distinct implications. They justify their focus on autonomous choices rather than autonomous persons by appealing to practical considerations and by suggesting that the conceptions of autonomy articulated by moral philosophers demand too much. They argue that accounts of the autonomous person rule out the potential for exercise of autonomous choice by all but the very few who meet the conditions that these ethical theories stipulate.[42] They also claim that, in practical terms, it does not follow from the fact that a person is generally autonomous that all of his or her decisions are autonomous. Autonomous persons can make non-autonomous decisions if, for example, they lack information or are coerced into acting.[43] Likewise, autonomous decision making by a person who would not ordinarily be considered 'autonomous' cannot be ruled out.[44] Beauchamp and Childress claim that autonomy in decision making is a matter of degree, and that bioethics must attend to the character of a particular decision rather than the character of the individual making the decision. They also assert that our approach to decision making and to action does not accord, at least not in everyday life, with the idea that first-order desires are all subjected to careful reflection to determine whether they can be identified with our second-order desires.[45]

Arguably, it makes sense for bioethicists to be primarily interested in the autonomous nature of particular choices rather than in the autonomous person.[46] It is at least theoretically possible to know whether a person has made a decision without sufficient information, or that a decision or action has been coerced. And when this occurs, remedial action can be taken.[47] By contrast, it is not possible to know when a decision that appears to be autonomous has been reached because a person has actually failed to act autonomously according to the procedural or substantive accounts of autonomy in philosophical theory. In other words, we cannot know whether a decision has been made in spite of one's reflectively endorsed values.

---

[39] Beauchamp and Childress (n 35) 100. Faden and Beauchamp also frame autonomy in this way: Ruth R Faden and Tom L Beauchamp, *A History and Theory of Informed Consent* (Oxford, Oxford University Press, 1986) 237.

[40] Or substantially free from coercive forces.

[41] Beauchamp and Childress (n 35) 127.

[42] As they put it, 'Few choosers and few choices would be autonomous if held to the standards of higher order reflection' (*ibid* 101).

[43] *Ibid* 100; Faden and Beauchamp (n 39) 8, 235–37.

[44] Faden and Beauchamp (n 39). Faden and Beauchamp refer to the non-autonomous person '[mustering]' the resources to make an autonomous choice (*ibid* 8).

[45] *Ibid.*

[46] Walker (n 37).

[47] *Ibid* 604–05. Walker notes that when a healthcare provider determines that a patient has made a decision on the basis of insufficient or incorrect information, the situation can be remedied by providing that information and allowing the patient to decide.

To a large extent, respect for autonomy has been subsumed within the (bioethical and legal) doctrine of informed consent;[48] in practice, the Beauchamp and Childress formulation of respect for autonomy can be understood as a requirement to respect patient informed consent to specific diagnostic or treatment interventions.[49] As Rebecca Kukla explains:

> [W]hile bioethicists know that the concept of informed consent does not exhaust the rich concept of autonomy, many still take it as a governing assumption that in the practical domain of health care, concerns about autonomy can be translated into concerns about self-determination, which can in turn be translated into concerns about informed consent.[50]

In other words, in healthcare settings, securing informed consent does the work of respecting autonomy.

This prevailing conception of autonomy has come under criticism for its failure to extend the debate about autonomy's meaning beyond the patient–provider interaction in the context of informed consent.[51] As noted earlier, Beauchamp has acknowledged the under-theorisation of autonomy in bioethics; he has described the connection between ethical theory and bioethics as 'contingent and fragile'.[52] Beauchamp locates blame for this phenomenon in the inability of moral philosophers to bridge the divide between theory and practice, and urges continued attention to the development of practically useful ethical theories. But perhaps part of the problem here is the sharp divide that the principlist account seeks to draw between autonomous persons and autonomous choices. Even if Beauchamp and Childress are right to distinguish between autonomous choices and autonomous persons, it does not follow that bioethics should focus on one to the exclusion of the other.

Rebecca Walker argues that the principle of autonomy as currently understood in bioethics cannot do the work we need it to. Walker acknowledges the dilemma faced by bioethicists, in that

> [t]he practically useful account of autonomy that is currently appealed to in medical ethics is conceptually inadequate. On the other hand, conceptually adequate accounts of autonomy are less practically useful and seem to provide suspect grounds for interference with patient decisions.[53]

Walker's point is this: the prevailing account of autonomy in bioethics is not able to identify instances of actual failures of autonomy in decision making. Even where a person is sufficiently informed, is choosing deliberately and is not coerced into a particular decision, it is possible for his decision to be non-autonomous because it is clearly at odds with the

---

[48] Susan Dodds, 'Choice and Control in Feminist Bioethics' in Mackenzie and Stoljar (eds) (n 16) 213.

[49] Although autonomy has traditionally been viewed as the moral foundation that justifies the need for informed consent, this view has been challenged, see, eg, James Stacey Taylor, 'Autonomy and Informed Consent: A Much Misunderstood Relationship' (2004) 38 *The Journal of Value Inquiry* 383.

[50] Kukla (n 37) 35.

[51] Dodds (n 48). Feminist theorists have been engaged with this question for some time; this is discussed in more detail in section III.B. below.

[52] Beauchamp (n 32) 209.

[53] Walker (n 37) 605. What Walker means by 'suspect grounds for interference' is that we do not have any realistic way of knowing when a person is making a decision based on 'weakness of the will' or is being irrational (and is therefore making a decision that does not align with his or her reflectively endorsed values). If a provider seeks to claim that a decision that is voluntary, deliberate and informed is nevertheless non-autonomous because of weakness of the will on the part of the patient, they will have a hard time justifying that claim.

individual's deeply-held values.[54] However, she acknowledges that ethical theories of autonomy that describe the autonomous person by reference to his or her ability to subject first-order desires to a process of reflection (and endorsement) do not give us a practical means of assessing the autonomous nature of a particular decision and might lead to interference with patient decision making for improper reasons. Walker's suggested solution is to 're-cast "respect for autonomy" in medical ethics as support for the conditions that are conducive to autonomous decision making on the one hand and abidance by the decisions of autonomous persons made under those conditions on the other hand'.[55]

Walker's arguments point to a conception of autonomy in bioethics that seeks to connect philosophical accounts of the autonomous person with current thinking about respect for autonomy as a way to a richer and more nuanced account of autonomy in bioethics. This is in keeping with a move in bioethics to consider a broader array of questions[56] and in keeping with my own thinking about how we ought to understand reproductive autonomy, as is elaborated on in section IV. below.

In addition to respecting autonomous decisions, respect for autonomy in bioethics also means giving individuals the freedom to choose among healthcare options. Medical care has evolved (particularly in the United States[57]) to become a business much like any other, and in the wake of the rise of managed care and the resulting influence of investors and others in the physician–patient relationship,[58] the idea of consumer choice has become prevalent.[59] In this context, respecting autonomy has come to mean giving a wide scope for individuals to choose how to approach caring for their own health.

In spite of the contested nature of 'autonomy' as a concept, it continues to dominate the health law and healthcare ethics literature. And a number of contemporary social trends – including the growth of bioethics as a discipline,[60] the increasing focus on

---

[54] *Ibid* 597–600.

[55] *Ibid* 605–06.

[56] Howard Brody, *The Future of Bioethics* (Oxford, Oxford University Press, 2009); Susan Sherwin, 'Looking Backwards, Looking Forward: Hopes for *Bioethics*' Next Twenty-Five Years' (2011) 25 *Bioethics* 75, 77–78.

[57] See, eg, Council on Ethical and Judicial Affairs, American Medical Association, 'Ethical Issues in Managed Care' (1995) 273 *Journal of the American Medical Association* 330; Ezekiel J Emanuel and Nancy N Dubler, 'Preserving the Physician-Patient Relationship in the Era of Managed Care' (1995) 273 *Journal of the American Medical Association* 323; Steffie Woodhandler and David U Himmelstein, 'Extreme Risk: The New Corporate Proposition for Physicians' (1995) 333 *New England Journal of Medicine* 1706; Frank A Chervenak *et al*, 'Responding to the Ethical Challenges Posed by the Business Tools of Managed Care in the Practice of Obstetrics and Gynecology' (1996) 175 *American Journal of Obstetrics and Gynecology* 523.

[58] Mark A Rothstein, 'The Growth of Health Law and Bioethics' (2004) 14 *Health Matrix* 213. Rothstein notes (*ibid* 214): '[H]ealth care is now big business. In the United States, health care spending in 2001 was $1.4 trillion, representing approximately 14.1 percent of GDP. The practice of medicine is increasingly concentrated in large conglomerates, including for-profit health care delivery companies and managed care organizations. . . . Finally, the health insurance industry, by pre-approving or rejecting medical interventions, has in many instances blurred the distinctions between those who provide health care and those who provide reimbursement for health care.' See also Alan R Nelson, 'Medicine: Business or Profession, Art or Science?' (1998) 178 *American Journal of Obstetrics & Gynecology* 755.

[59] It has been noted that the bioethics movement gained strength in the 1960s and 1970s due to a number of parallel social trends, including the civil rights and consumer movements – see, eg, Madison Powers, 'Some Reflections on Disability and Bioethics' (2001) 1(3) *American Journal of Bioethics* 51; David J Rothman, 'The Origins and Consequences of Patient Autonomy: A 25-Year Retrospective' (2001) 9 *Health Care Analysis* 255; Sydney A Halpern, 'Medical Authority and the Culture of Rights' (2004) 29 *Journal of Health Politics, Policy and Law* 835.

[60] See, eg, Rothstein (n 58); Glenn McGee, 'Bioethics for the President and Bioethics for the People' (2002) 2(2) *American Journal of Bioethics* 1.

consumer choice and consumer participation,[61] radical changes in healthcare delivery marked by a shift from the medical model to the business model,[62] rapid developments in healthcare technology[63] and a pronounced focus on an ethic of individual responsibility for health[64] – mean that the predominance of autonomy as a key moral value in healthcare is likely to continue for some time to come.

II. FEMINIST CRITIQUE OF AUTONOMY

Feminism, according to Marilyn Friedman, has a 'love–hate' relationship with autonomy.[65] Like feminism itself, the feminist critique of autonomy is varied, ranging from the claim that autonomy is not possible because there are no 'selves'[66] to the argument that autonomy is possible but not desirable because of its association with traditional liberal ideas around abstract individualism, rationality, self-sufficiency and separation.[67] In relation to bioethics more specifically, the feminist critique draws on strands of the arguments made around autonomy generally. In particular, these arguments tend to focus on the fact that mainstream conceptions of autonomy ignore the social nature of individuals,[68] that reproductive choices cannot be viewed as truly autonomous given pervasive pronatalist social pressures,[69] and the claim that the focus on autonomy in bioethics tends to marginalise other important values.[70]

---

[61] James C Robinson, 'The End of Managed Care' (2001) 285 *Journal of the American Medical Association* 2622; Daniel Callahan, 'Bioethics' in Stephen G Post (ed), *Encyclopedia of Bioethics*, vol 1, 3rd edn (New York, Macmillan Reference USA, 2004) 278; Alexander Morgan Capron, 'Law and Bioethics' in Stephen G Post (ed), *Encyclopedia of Bioethics*, vol 1, 3rd edn (New York, Macmillan Reference USA, 2004) 1369.

[62] Rothstein (n 58). See also, Paul Starr, *The Social Transformation of American Medicine* (New York, Basic Books, 1982); Mary R Anderlik, *The Ethics of Managed Care: A Pragmatic Approach* (Indianapolis, Indiana University Press, 2001) 179.

[63] Rothstein (n 58).

[64] See, eg, Meredith Minkler, 'Personal Responsibility For Health? A Review of the Arguments and the Evidence at Century's End' (1999) 26 *Health Education and Behavior* 121; Tammy Horne and Susan Abells, *Public Remedies, Not Private Payments: Quality Health Care in Alberta* (Edmonton, AB, Parkland Institute, 2004).

[65] See, eg, Marilyn Friedman, 'Autonomy and Social Relationships: Rethinking the Feminist Critique' in Diana Tietjens Meyers (ed), *Feminists Rethink the Self* (Boulder, CO, Westview Press, 1997) 40.

[66] Judith Butler, *Gender Trouble: Feminism and the Subversion of Identity* (New York, Routledge, 1990).

[67] See, eg, Friedman (n 5) 47–50; Mackenzie and Stoljar (n 16) 8–9. Other 'anti-autonomy' arguments advanced by feminists include the claim that mainstream ideas of autonomy mistakenly assume the transparency of selves, while psychoanalytic theory tells us that some aspects of the self can remain hidden to 'conscious self-reflection' and the argument that such conceptions of autonomy elevate reason over emotion (Friedman (n 65) 41–42).

[68] See, eg, Mackenzie and Stoljar (n 16); Jennifer Nedelsky, 'Reconceiving Autonomy: Sources, Thoughts and Possibilities' (1989) 1 *Yale Journal of Law and Feminism* 7; Susan Sherwin, 'A Relational Approach to Autonomy in Health Care' in Susan Sherwin *et al* (eds), *The Politics of Women's Health: Exploring Agency and Autonomy* (Philadelphia, Pa, Temple University Press, 1998) 19; Anne Donchin, 'Understanding Autonomy Relationally: Toward a Reconfiguration of Bioethical Principles' (2001) 26 *Journal of Medicine and Philosophy* 365, 367. See also Anne Donchin, 'Reworking Autonomy: Toward a Feminist Perspective' (1995) 4 *Cambridge Quarterly Healthcare Ethics* 44.

[69] Robyn Rowland, *Living Laboratories: Women and Reproductive Technologies* (Bloomington, Indiana University Press, 1992) 248.

[70] See, eg, Joan C Callahan and Dorothy E Roberts, 'A Feminist Social Justice Approach to Reproduction-Assisting Technologies: A Case Study on the Limits of Liberal Theory' (1995–96) 84 *Kentucky Law Journal* 1197; April Cherry, 'Choosing Substantive Justice: A Discussion of "Choice", "Rights" and the New Reproductive Technologies' (1997) 11 *Wisconsin Women's Law Journal* 431.

Often, the feminist critique of autonomy is actually a critique of liberal political phil-osophy, or of the cultural ideal that has grown out of traditional liberal theory. As Joan Callahan and Dorothy Roberts explain:

> The atomistic ontology of persons underpinning Locke's theory continues to anchor liberalism in its several contemporary varieties, including liberal feminism . . . Filled out, the fundamental social notion at work in liberal ontology is that persons are radically individualized agents, that the uniqueness of human beings is characterized by the capacity for rationality and auto-nomy, and that the protection of individual autonomy is the keystone of a morally well-ordered society.[71]

The critique outlined by Callahan and Roberts relates to general communitarian[72] and feminist critiques of the liberal conception of autonomy, based as it is on the liberal individualistic ideal. In essence, the argument is that the liberal notion of autonomy is inadequate because of its failure to take into account our interdependent natures.[73] The communitarian critique, in common with one aspect of the feminist critique, is particu-larly concerned with the social (as opposed to isolated) nature of the self, and the import-ance of social relationships to self-identity and self-consciousness.[74] But the concerns of feminists diverge rather sharply from those of communitarians in that the latter do not engage with issues that have particular significance for women, but rather '[condone] or [tolerate] traditional communal norms of gender subordination'.[75]

Many feminists have expressed concern specifically about the individualistic nature of autonomy, as traditionally conceived.[76] The mainstream interpretation of the auto-nomous man arguably envisions one who is

> self-sufficient, independent, and self-reliant, a self-realizing individual who directs his efforts toward maximizing his personal gains. His independence is under constant threat from other (equally self-serving) individuals: hence he devises rules to protect himself from intrusion. Talk of rights, rational self-interest, expediency, and efficiency permeates his moral, social and political discourse.[77]

From a feminist perspective, autonomy thus represented is not only objectionable, but also harmful to the interests of oppressed groups. It is also antithetical to the important

---

[71] Callahan and Roberts (n 70) 1201–02.

[72] See, eg, Alasdair MacIntyre, *After Virtue: A Study in Moral Theory*, 2nd edn (Notre Dame, Ind, Notre Dame University Press, 1984); Michael Sandel, *Liberalism and the Limits of Justice* (Cambridge, Cambridge University Press, 1982).

[73] See, eg, Donchin, 'Reworking Autonomy' (n 68); Donchin, 'Understanding Autonomy Relationally' (n 68); Nedelsky (n 68); Sherwin (n 68); Jocelyn Downie and Susan Sherwin, 'A Feminist Exploration of Issues Around Assisted Death' (1996) 15 *St Louis University Public Law Review* 303.

[74] See, eg, Sandel (n 72). See also Marilyn Friedman, 'Feminism and Modern Friendship: Dislocating the Community' in Cass R Sunstein (ed), *Feminism and Political Theory* (Chicago, University of Chicago Press, 1990) 143, 145–54.

[75] Friedman (n 74) 145.

[76] See, eg, Lorraine Code, 'Second Persons' in Lorraine Code, *What Can She Know: Feminist Theory and the Construction of Knowledge* (Ithaca, NY, Cornell University Press, 1991). Code's critique has been termed 'symbolic' in that it is directed not at any specific theory of autonomy but at the popular interpretation of autonomy into a particular character ideal (Mackenzie and Stoljar (n 16) 6). See also Callahan and Roberts (n 70); Friedman (n 5) 85–86. It bears noting here as well that even the feminist analysis of liberal philosophy as exemplified by Callahan and Roberts tends to portray liberalism in quite narrow terms that do not accord with the views espoused by a number of modern liberal thinkers such as Joseph Raz and Martha Nussbaum (Joseph Raz, *The Morality of Freedom* (Oxford, Oxford University Press, 1986); Martha C Nussbaum, *Sex and Social Justice* (Oxford, Oxford University Press, 1999)).

[77] Code (n 76) 77–78.

feminist goal of substantive equality.[78] It is legitimate, then, for feminists to question whether autonomy is a value worth defending.

But is this autonomy – this state of self-sufficiency, independence and (arguably) self-ishness that is occupied by hyper-rational individuals bereft of any relationship ties? Arguably, the claim that autonomy has been distorted into a harmful concept rests on a fundamental error, or on a caricature of autonomy. While in popular understanding, autonomy has become linked with independence and self-sufficiency, these ideas are distinct from philosophical understandings of autonomy.[79] As Friedman notes, 'financial independence is no constitutive part of autonomy. If the clichés of autonomy ("think for yourself") suggest any sort of independence at all, it is independence of mind or behavior.'[80]

A. From feminist critique to feminist articulation: relational autonomy

In spite of the pronounced feminist ambivalence toward autonomy, feminists are increasingly recognising the crucial importance – to women – of a robust conception of autonomy. This has led to an evolution in feminist thinking. Instead of simply criticising traditional liberal views of autonomy, many feminist philosophers and bioethicists are working to redefine autonomy.[81] In exploring how traditional ideas of autonomy might be reconfigured to make the concept more friendly to their aims, feminist philosophers have acknowledged that autonomy is too vital to feminism to be abandoned.[82] A number of feminist theorists have advanced ideas about how autonomy might be reconceived to acknowledge properly the social nature of individual selves; this evolving conception of autonomy is referred to as 'relational autonomy'.[83] The term 'relational autonomy' applies to a wide variety of perspectives, which

[78] Martha Albertson Fineman, *The Autonomy Myth: A Theory of Dependency* (New York, The New Press, 2004). Fineman refers here to a much more substantive notion of equality than the formal equality which dominates American law.

[79] Friedman (n 5) 48–50. Martha Fineman explores the mythic dimensions of autonomy, independence and self-sufficiency in the American public policy discourse around the family. The definition of autonomy on which she bases her critique is taken from an English language dictionary, which makes the very error Friedman describes in depicting autonomy as though it were independence. In turn, independence is defined in the same dictionary with reference to freedom from any need for support or aid (Fineman (n 78) 7–8).

[80] Friedman (n 5) 48.

[81] See, eg, Mackenzie and Stoljar (n 16); McLeod (n 9) (a feminist consideration of the relation between self-trust and autonomy in the reproductive decision-making context).

[82] See, eg, Donchin, 'Understanding Autonomy Relationally' (n 68); Friedman (n 65); Friedman (n 5); Mackenzie and Stoljar (n 16); Nedelsky (n 68).

[83] Nedelsky is widely considered to be the first theorist to propose a relational conception of autonomy (Nedelsky (n 68)). As others have noted, however, feminist conceptions of relational autonomy are not alone in their recognition of the centrality of relationships to the constitution of the self. Emily Jackson points out that many 'mainstream' liberal thinkers acknowledge the centrality of our connections with others to our sense of who we are (Emily Jackson, *Regulating Reproduction: Law, Technology and Autonomy* (Oxford, Hart Publishing, 2001) 4). Nussbaum observes that prominent liberal philosophers (including John Stuart Mill, David Hume and John Rawls) build an 'other-inclusive psychology . . . [and] affiliation with and need for others into the very foundations of their accounts of human motivation' (Nussbaum (n 76) 60). As Mackenzie and Stoljar note, the conception of autonomy that is the target of much of the feminist critique is a 'caricature of individual autonomy' (Mackenzie and Stoljar (n 16) 5). See also Friedman (n 65) 47–51 (describing the 'convergence' of feminist and mainstream conceptions of autonomy). Friedman refers to her conception of autonomy as a 'social conception' of autonomy, as opposed to a relational conception, but she draws on some aspects of feminist theories of relational autonomy in her work, which is why I include her here.

are premised on a shared conviction . . . that persons are socially embedded and that agents' identities are formed within the context of social relationships and shaped by a complex of intersecting social determinants, such as race, class, gender, and ethnicity.[84]

The feminist conception of autonomy as relational arises out of the claim that the value of autonomy is central to feminist aspirations, but that the liberal model is not suited to a perspective that acknowledges the constitutive nature of social relations to one's sense of self and one's ability to exercise self-determination.[85] Although liberal conceptions of autonomy have been emphatically criticised by feminist theorists, feminism is not prepared to renounce freedom or the idea of 'a human capacity for making one's own life and self'.[86] Feminism must therefore address the tension between the individual and the collective, and the reality that democratic outcomes can threaten autonomy.[87] In other words, the task is to construct a theory that sufficiently accounts for both the social and individual natures of human beings. As Jennifer Nedelsky explains:

> [F]eminists are centrally concerned with freeing women to shape our own lives, to define who we (each) are, rather than accepting the definition given to us by others (men and male-dominated society, in particular). Feminists therefore need a language of freedom with which to express the value underlying this concern. But that language must also be true to the equally important feminist precept that any good theorizing will start with people in their social contexts.[88]

Relational conceptions of autonomy originate in relational (or 'different voice') feminism,[89] which draws on Carol Gilligan's work on women's unique approach to moral reasoning.[90] Gilligan claims that women reason with a 'different voice' than do men, and that women's moral reasoning is based on an 'ethic of care' as opposed to the masculine 'ethic of justice'.[91] Different voice feminism sees value in the different modes of knowing and reasoning employed by women, and claims that reasoning based on an ethic of care 'might serve as a better model of social organization and law than existing "male" characteristics and values'.[92] In part, this is based on the greater interdependence of women compared to men, and on the notion that women 'value relationships more than individual rights'.[93] Women are different from men, and different in ways that count for moral theory, social organisation, law and legal institutions. Different voice feminists have called for reform to both substantive law and to legal process, charging that women's unique way of reasoning has the potential to point us in the direction of better laws and institutions.

---

[84] Mackenzie and Stoljar (n 16) 4.

[85] *Ibid* 7.

[86] *Ibid* 8.

[87] *Ibid* 21, 33. See also Jennifer Nedelsky, 'Law, Boundaries, and the Bounded Self' (1990) 30 *Representations* 162, 169.

[88] Nedelsky (n 68) 8–9. See also Nedelsky's book, collecting her thoughts and arguments around relational autonomy, Jennifer Nedelsky, *Law's Relations: A Relational Theory of Self, Autonomy, and Law* (New York, Oxford University Press, 2011) 121.

[89] Relational feminism is also referred to as 'cultural' feminism – see, eg, Katherine T Bartlett, 'Gender Law' (1994) 1 *Duke Journal of Gender Law & Policy* 1; Martha Chamallas, *Introduction to Feminist Legal Theory*, 2nd edn (New York, Aspen Publishers, 2003) 62–68.

[90] Carol Gilligan, *In a Different Voice: Psychological Theory and Women's Development* (Cambridge, MA, Harvard University Press, 1982).

[91] *Ibid.*

[92] Bartlett (n 89) 11.

[93] *Ibid.*

While the source of relational accounts of autonomy is relational feminism, relational autonomy has extended beyond these origins, and many feminists who adopt a relational approach to autonomy do not necessarily describe themselves as relational feminists.[94] Indeed, many feminists find the tenets of the different voice approach troubling, given the danger of regress toward traditional ideals of femininity and domesticity that arise from a focus on women's differences from men.[95] And, as Catharine MacKinnon has argued, women's different voice originates in male dominance – it is not about women's individuality and self-identification as carers, but about the value men have placed on being cared for by women.[96] Some relational theorists deliberately distance themselves from relational feminism more broadly. As Susan Sherwin explains:

> I explicitly distinguish my use of the term *relational* from that of some other feminist authors, such as Carol Gilligan . . . who reserve it to refer only to the narrower set of interpersonal relations. I apply the term to the full range of influential human relations, personal and public. Oppression permeates both personal and public relationships; hence, I prefer to politicize the understanding of the term *relational* as a way of emphasizing the political dimensions of the multiple relationships that structure an individual's selfhood, rather than to reserve the term to protect a sphere of purely private relationships that may appear to be free of political influence.[97]

From a liberal perspective, autonomy is essential to protect the individual from the 'intrusion of the collective'.[98] Feminism, too, recognises the need for a space in which individuals may make their own choices based on their own values, and not those imposed by community. But at the same time, feminist thinkers acknowledge that the ability to make one's own choices is not possible or meaningful in isolation from relationships. Rather than a 'static human characteristic',[99] autonomy is a capacity, the development of which depends on 'constructive relationship'.[100] Since relationships can both nurture and obstruct one's capacity for autonomy, the key is ensuring that relationships (personal and institutional) are structured in such a way as to encourage the development of autonomy.[101]

Feminist philosophers are alive to the fact that socialisation can have profound effects on one's ability to develop the skills needed in order to exercise autonomy.[102] At the same time, however, they insist that such socialisation does not preclude autonomy.[103] Those who have been oppressively socialised may be only minimally autonomous, and their autonomy skills may not be well-developed or well-coordinated, but they may

---

[94] Sherwin (n 68) 19–20.

[95] See, eg, Catharine MacKinnon, *Feminism Unmodified: Discourses on Life and Law* (Cambridge, MA, Harvard University Press, 1987); Joan C Williams, 'Deconstructing Gender' (1989) 87 *Michigan Law Review* 797.

[96] MacKinnon (n 95) 38–39.

[97] Sherwin (n 68) 19–20.

[98] Nedelsky (n 87) 167.

[99] *Ibid* 168.

[100] *Ibid.*

[101] *Ibid* 169. See also Nedelsky (n 68) 12 (where Nedelsky notes that intimate and 'public' relationships alike can 'either foster or undermine autonomy').

[102] Friedman argues that the distinctions between mainstream and feminist accounts of autonomy (in terms of their focus on the social self) are not as marked as many have claimed (Friedman (n 5) 81–97).

[103] Indeed, as Meyers notes, although large numbers of individuals are systematically subordinated, 'some of these individuals are exemplars of autonomy, and few of them altogether lack autonomy' (Diana Tietjens Meyers, 'Intersectional Identity and the Authentic Self? Opposites Attract!' in Mackenzie and Stoljar (eds) (n 16) 151, 152).

nevertheless be capable of eventually achieving a greater degree of autonomy, given supportive social conditions.[104]

B. Tensions in relational autonomy

i. Relational autonomy and the self

There is an important and unresolved tension within feminist theories of the self, between the significance of the social and of the individual. This tension comes into sharp relief in terms of the details of relational autonomy. Clearly, autonomy requires a social context, without which it would be 'pointless and meaningless'.[105] And emphasising the social nature of autonomy has utility in helping to subvert the potential for conceptions of autonomy to subscribe to an excessively individualistic ideal.[106] But some feminist accounts of autonomy also recognise an important role for individualism. The significance of individuality within feminist theories of autonomy stems, in part, from the reality that individuals are physically separate, embodied selves with their own identities, life histories and experiences. It also stems, in part, from the recognition that the 'social' (social relationships, social conditions) can frustrate as well as foster one's ability to act autonomously.[107] If social conditions prevent one from acting in concert with one's 'deep values or commitments' then one is prevented from acting autonomously.[108] Similarly, the social context in which one finds oneself might hinder one's ability to develop and exercise autonomy competency.[109]

Some accounts of relational autonomy suggest that there is 'a social component built into the meaning of autonomy',[110] which suggests that the very conditions that define autonomy include 'requirements concerning the interpersonal or social environment of the agent'.[111] Friedman points out that this inchoate notion that social relationships are 'constitutive' of autonomy[112] remains unresolved in feminist philosophy, and that an important question therefore persists in respect of feminist accounts of autonomy that tend to this view – what does it mean to say that autonomy is inherently or constitutively relational?[113] Does it mean that autonomy can only be expressed in and through relationships (either in a general sense, or with reference to particular sorts of relationships)? Or that autonomy is a characteristic of relationships rather than a characteristic of individuals? Or that a person can be autonomous only if the right sorts of relationships are in place in her life?

---

[104] Meyers argues that boys typically demonstrate a higher degree of autonomy than girls because boys are socialised in ways that give them greater scope for practicing skills of self-assertion in action, whereas girls are 'reared to assume one, narrow, privatized, subordinate role' (Meyers (n 3) 166).

[105] Friedman (n 5) 17.

[106] *Ibid* 15–16.

[107] *Ibid* 16–18.

[108] *Ibid* 18.

[109] *Ibid*.

[110] Nedelsky (n 68) 33–34.

[111] Christman (n 20) 147. Christman argues that in order for a conception of autonomy to be '*uniquely* "relational" or "social"' there must be some social conditions that are 'conceptually necessary requirements of autonomy rather than, say, contributory factors' (*ibid* 147–48).

[112] Friedman (n 5) 96.

[113] *Ibid* 96–97.

John Christman maintains that it is important to distinguish between related but distinct aspects of relational views of autonomy.[114] As he explains:

> It is one thing to claim that social conditions that enable us to develop and maintain the powers of authentic choice and which protect the ongoing interpersonal and social relationships that define ourselves are all part of the background requirements for the development of autonomy. ... It is another thing, however – and a more dangerous and ultimately problematic move ... to claim that being autonomous *means* standing in proper social relations to surrounding others and within social practices and institutions.[115]

My own view is that autonomy, while deeply social, is not itself constituted by social relations. Frankly, I am at something of a loss as to what it means to say that autonomy is 'constitutively' social. Christman and Friedman are right to be concerned about views of autonomy that appear to posit it as a property of relationships, as opposed to a characteristic of individuals (who are inextricably embedded within relationships), given the oppressive potential of some relationships, particularly for women. Autonomy, then, is a 'social project ... but ... ultimately resides in individuals'.[116]

ii. Relational autonomy and perfectionism

Another important tension in accounts of relational autonomy is the fact that many – if not all – of these accounts adopt a substantive or 'perfectionist view'[117] because what makes a theory of autonomy *'uniquely* "relational" or "social" is that among its defining conditions are requirements concerning the interpersonal or social environment of the agent'.[118] The defining feature of a relational account of autonomy is the insistence on particular social conditions as 'conceptually necessary'[119] for autonomy – as distinct from conditions that contribute to the development of autonomy. While the full implications of adopting a relational understanding of autonomy are not spelled out in these accounts, at a minimum, what this entails is that only persons who are in certain kinds of relationships or social conditions are autonomous. Christman focuses on Marina Oshana's relational view of autonomy as an example of such an account. I would argue that Anne Donchin's account fits here as well. Donchin asserts that the relational view that she favours 'recognizes a social component that is built into the very meaning of autonomy'.[120] She argues that autonomy is reciprocal and collaborative: reciprocal in that it involves a 'dynamic balance among interdependent people',[121] and because 'the self-determining self exists *fundamentally* in relation to others'.[122] The collaborative aspect relates to supporting those for whom we are responsible in the development of their autonomy:

---

[114] Christman (n 20) 158.
[115] *Ibid*.
[116] Sherwin (n 68) 39.
[117] Christman (n 20) 146.
[118] *Ibid* 147.
[119] *Ibid*.
[120] Anne Donchin, 'Autonomy, Interdependence, and Assisted Suicide: Respecting Boundaries/Crossing Lines' (2000) 14 *Bioethics* 187, 188.
[121] *Ibid* 191.
[122] *Ibid*.

Any tenable conception of personal autonomy is bound to be subject-centered; but a *social* conception that is relational in this stronger sense will take into account the need for a network of personal relationships to develop and sustain competencies necessary to act as self-determining, responsible agents.[123]

As others have noted, the result of a 'thoroughly relational view'[124] of autonomy such as that adopted by Oshana is to equate the protection of individual autonomy with the protection of the relationships identified by relational theorists as the ones that count. Most relational accounts of autonomy are not *thoroughly* relational – they are interested in the social and relational conditions that permit or foster the development of autonomy capacity, and they quite rightly assert that these conditions have been largely ignored in liberal accounts of autonomy. The difficulty with the label of relational autonomy becomes evident here, in that there is nothing *inherently* relational about this approach to autonomy. Like Christman and Friedman, I am optimistic that a liberal approach to autonomy can indeed find the space to emphasise (more than has been the case to date) the importance of 'securing the social conditions that are required for the enjoyment of autonomy, conditions relating to education, social structures and opportunities, access to basic resources, housing, and so on'.[125]

Relational theorists can be credited with this important contribution. But we need not rename autonomy to take account of this insight, and we ought to be very cautious about doing so, as the label 'relational autonomy' might lead in a direction that would be a mistake to pursue. It could, as Christman argues, lead to the exclusion from autonomy of those who do not stand in 'proper social relations' to other individuals and to the institutions of social life.[126] Surely the aim of relational theorists is not to limit the reach of autonomy and thereby limit its utility in the fight against oppression. Indeed, it is hard to imagine that proponents of a relational account seek to rein in rather than expand autonomy's reach in respect of whom we count as autonomous.

Arguably, not all relational accounts of autonomy are perfectionist (or substantive) accounts. There is a potential conflict between taking oppression seriously and recognising the way in which it can work to impair autonomy, on the one hand, and recognising the need to expand the category of bearers of autonomy on the other. Meyers and Friedman both offer what can be described as content-neutral theories of autonomy,[127] in that their accounts of autonomy do not define substantive or normative conditions against which decisions can be measured to determine whether they are in fact autonomous. On these accounts, in very general terms, as long as decisions individuals make, or desires individuals have, arise from their reflections about their authentic selves, they can be considered autonomous. Meyers distinguishes her 'skills-based processual account' of autonomy from both 'value-neutral' and 'restrictive, value-saturated'

---

[123]   *Ibid* 192.
[124]   Christman (n 20) 156.
[125]   *Ibid*.
[126]   *Ibid* 158.
[127]   Mackenzie and Stoljar locate Meyers' theory within the general category of procedural theories, which they equate to content-neutral theories (Mackenzie and Stoljar (n 16) 17), as do McLeod and Sherwin (Carolyn McLeod and Susan Sherwin, 'Relational Autonomy, Self-Trust, and Health Care for Patients who are Oppressed' in Mackenzie and Stoljar (eds) (n 16) 259, 263). Friedman herself refers to her theory as content-neutral (Friedman (n 5) 19–25).

accounts.[128] In her view, value-neutral theories pay too little attention to oppressive socialisation, while value-saturated accounts tend to exaggerate its impact.[129] The peril inherent in substantive accounts of autonomy is that they mistake the *possibility* that cultural norms (as opposed to autonomous reflection) have led to a particular decision being made for the *certainty* that this is the case.

iii. Some reservations about relational autonomy; and a middle ground?

Early in my thinking about reproductive autonomy, I was attracted by the idea of relational autonomy and sought to develop an account of reproductive autonomy using the ideas developed by theorists who endorse that approach. Along the way, I reconsidered. The more I attempted to understand (and explain) the differences between relational autonomy and autonomy, the more elusive the ideas seemed to become.

Perhaps this should not be surprising. Relational autonomy is a project under construction; its contents have not been fully articulated, nor has its architecture been fully sketched out.[130] It may be the case that some of my criticisms are premature, or that my questions and concerns will at some point be answered. But for now they are sufficiently pronounced that I am not prepared to adopt an account of autonomy based in relational theory.

My most significant reservations are these: first, and most obviously, relational autonomy and autonomy are not irreconcilable.[131] There is no reason why autonomy (as it has generally been conceived) cannot take context – including relationships – into account.[132] It is perhaps the case that traditional accounts of autonomy seem not to do so, or do not do so very well, but that does not mean that they cannot do so. Secondly, and more importantly, I think that the 'relational autonomy' label is actually unhelpful in furthering our understanding of autonomy. Because it tends toward the notion that autonomy inheres in relationships rather than persons, it can be understood to mean that if you are not in the right kinds of relationships – or if you are in the 'wrong' kinds – you cannot be autonomous. Indeed, as discussed above,[133] this is precisely what some relational theorists appear to suggest. Lastly, I think that there is a risk that relational theories of autonomy could be used to justify paternalistic ideas and arguments about which decisions can legitimately count as autonomous. The concerns about oppressive socialisation made by many relational theorists are at the root of this worry. As I have acknowledged, the influence of social pressures is vital in theories of autonomy. This concern can be handled in a variety of ways – generally by the imposition of competency conditions (such as self-trust, self-worth, self-discipline, the ability for rational thought) and

---

[128] Meyers (n 2) 487. Benson explains that Meyers' theory is not strictly content-neutral, because the set of autonomy competency skills she describes 'seem to import specific values into the account' (Benson (n 18) 135). In particular, Benson is referring to the skills of 'self-nurturing' and the connection between these skills and self-worth.

[129] Meyers (n 2) 479.

[130] Jennifer J Llewellyn and Jocelyn Downie, 'Introduction' in Jocelyn Downie and Jennifer J Llewellyn (eds), *Being Relational: Reflections on Relational Theory and Health Law* (Vancouver, UBC Press, 2012) 1 (noting the 'patchwork nature' of the literature on relational theory).

[131] Sheila AM McLean, *Autonomy, Consent and the Law* (London, Routledge-Cavendish, 2010) 27–30; Jackson (n 83).

[132] Christman (n 20).

[133] Above, section II.B.i.

sometimes by the imposition of substantive conditions as to which kinds of decisions can count as autonomous. Ultimately, there is no theoretical solution to the problem of oppressive socialisation, and this highlights a potential problem with relational approaches to autonomy. We are faced with the reality that socialisation can impair autonomy or one's ability to exercise autonomy. But we cannot test whether a person's decision is actually autonomous by 'undoing' socialisation and then assessing whether the person makes the same decision.

What some relational theorists seem to seek to do instead is to claim that decisions that are influenced by oppressive socialisation cannot be autonomous and therefore need not be respected. In writing about Caesarean section rates and autonomy, Sylvia Burrow discusses Caesarean section on maternal request.[134] She claims that although it may appear that adding the option of surgical delivery on request increases women's autonomy, this understanding is based on a 'limited view' of autonomy. As she explains, 'Social pressures can influence the decision to have a cesarean in a way that undermines rather than fosters autonomy'.[135] But on this understanding, it seems that the only time women's reproductive choices can be autonomous is when they conform to the intuitions of some feminists as to the kinds of decisions that can be conceived of as autonomous.

For all of these reasons, I am unprepared to adopt a relational approach to autonomy. But while I reject the 'relational autonomy' label, I agree wholeheartedly with the argument in favour of a more nuanced and contextualised understanding of autonomy, and I argue that we need to develop such an approach specifically in relation to reproductive autonomy. Relational accounts of autonomy have much to offer, and can help to inform a richer understanding of autonomy. As Sherwin explains:

> A relational approach to autonomy allows us to maintain a central place for autonomy within bioethics, but it requires an interpretation that is both deeper and more complicated than the traditional conception acknowledges – one that sets standards that involve political as well as personal criteria of adequacy.[136]

In my view, a better alternative to the relational view of autonomy is to adopt what Friedman identifies as a 'social' conception of autonomy. Friedman's account of autonomy is an example of a feminist approach that is rooted in liberalism, and which therefore recognises the importance of individualism.[137] But Friedman also endorses feminist attempts to reconceive some of liberalism's most important concepts, including autonomy and rights, into forms that are compatible with feminist recognition of the reality of oppression. As she notes:

> Liberalism is generous with autonomy in theory, seeing its value at the foundations of justification for political order. In practice, as we know all too well, actual societies claiming liberal principles and pedigrees have disregarded the viewpoints of many groups among the governed, thereby suppressing the personal autonomy of the members of those groups. This shameful history might prompt us to jettison liberal principles altogether. This is not, however, the only

---

[134] Sylvia Burrow, 'On the Cutting Edge: Ethical Responsiveness to Cesarean Rates' (2012) 12(7) *American Journal of Bioethics* 44.

[135] *Ibid* 46.

[136] Sherwin (n 68) 44. Donchin has, like Sherwin, articulated the need for integrating a relational conception of autonomy in bioethics in order to retain a central place for autonomy, 'if only autonomy can be severed from the individualistic assumptions about social relations imbedded in modern moral theories' (Donchin, 'Understanding Autonomy Relationally' (n 68) 367). See also Donchin, 'Reworking Autonomy' (n 68).

[137] Friedman (n 5) 66–73.

response open to us. We can instead revise liberal principles specifically to counteract whole-sale historical exclusion of certain groups from the liberal legitimation project.[138]

Friedman envisions autonomy as an essential element in the fight against oppression. She maintains that while it is certainly not the only, nor even the most important moral value, autonomy

> is nevertheless vital and momentous for a great multitude of human lives across many cultural boundaries and other human differences. This ideal . . . can be . . . particularly inspirational . . . for those who, in the course of living their lives, must cope with the all-too-familiar human wrongs of abuse, exploitation, domination, and oppression.[139]

While the precise nature of relational autonomy remains somewhat ambiguous, it ultimately, and most significantly, responds to the need to contextualise autonomy, to recognise that autonomy is a competency developed and exercised in the context of individual and institutional relationships, and to acknowledge that the constitution of these relationships may foster or impede an agent's ability to exercise autonomy. From a feminist standpoint, one of the most important contextual factors is oppression – particularly women's oppression. The argument for reconceptualising autonomy as relational seeks to acknowledge the disadvantages faced by women (and by other marginalised groups) within our conception of autonomy. The response to oppression demanded by a contextualised understanding of autonomy is concerned with both autonomous choices and autonomous persons. Such an approach to autonomy demands that we consider the context of the individual in providing opportunities for the exercise of autonomy (including opportunities to make 'choices that are not influenced by the wishes of those who dominate them'[140]). This view of autonomy also tells us that it is inappropriate to respond to oppression by usurping the decision-making capacity of those who lack autonomy capacity or autonomy-related skills. Rather, we must endeavour to ameliorate the conditions that lead to oppressive socialisation in the first place, by educating and counselling individuals making healthcare decisions, as well as by supporting them in their deliberative processes.[141]

As Carolyn McLeod and Susan Sherwin note, relational autonomy 'seeks politically aware solutions that endeavour to change social conditions and not just expand the options offered to agents'.[142] Just as healthcare policy has come to recognise the social determinants of health, I understand relational autonomy to be concerned with the determinants of autonomy. And I see a social conception of autonomy as capable of incorporating these concerns in a meaningful way.

III. FROM AUTONOMY TO REPRODUCTIVE AUTONOMY

Reproductive autonomy, like autonomy itself, is an elusive concept and a contested idea with seemingly inestimable implications. Many see the origins of reproductive autonomy as a concept arising out of the struggles over birth control and abortion that began

---

[138] *Ibid* 76.
[139] *Ibid* 4.
[140] Sherwin (n 68) 37.
[141] *Ibid* 38.
[142] McLeod and Sherwin (n 127) 260.

in the mid-nineteenth century.[143] Avoidance of coerced reproduction was the point – the battle for reproductive autonomy was a battle for women's right to control their own reproductive capacities by preventing or terminating unwanted pregnancies. This phrase (and its many synonyms, including procreative liberty, procreative autonomy and reproductive freedom) has come in the twenty-first century apparently to mean something more.[144] As O'Neill observes:

> [Reproductive] technologies opened the way to possibilities of self-determination and self-expression in reproduction that went far beyond the avoidance of unwanted children . . . Appeals to autonomy were invoked to support use of (and even guaranteed and subsidised access to) a wide variety of assisted reproductive technologies, ranging from hormone treatment to IVF, to the use of eggs, sperm and gestation provided by others, from post-menopausal pregnancy and *post mortem* paternity, to cloning and the production of so-called 'designer babies'.[145]

The early articulations of reproductive autonomy in both law and bioethics are very much a product of liberal ideas around individual choice and individual rights. Possibly the most well-known and influential comprehensive approach to reproductive autonomy (or, as he refers to it, procreative liberty) is that articulated by John Robertson.[146] According to Robertson, 'Full procreative freedom would include both the freedom *not* to reproduce and the freedom *to* reproduce when, with whom, and by what means one chooses'.[147] In a later version of the definition, he states that procreative liberty is 'the freedom to decide whether or not to have offspring and to control the use of one's reproductive capacity'.[148] Given the central importance of reproduction 'to personal identity, to dignity, and to the meaning of one's life',[149] Robertson asserts that taking procreative liberty seriously requires a 'strong presumption' in favour of the freedom to make reproductive decisions for oneself, unless 'tangible harm to the interests of others can be shown'.[150]

Robertson also argues that procreative liberty applies equally to traditional and technological modes of reproducing. Accordingly, he notes that most of the concerns about

---

[143] See, eg, John A Robertson, 'Procreative Liberty and the Control of Conception, Pregnancy and Childbirth' (1983) 69 *Virginia Law Review* 405; Reva Siegel, 'Reasoning from the Body: An Historical Perspective on Abortion Regulation and Questions of Equal Protection' (1992) 44 *Stanford Law Review* 261; Reva Siegel, 'Abortion as a Sex Equality Right: Its Basis in Feminist Theory' in Martha Albertson Fineman and Isabel Karpin (eds), *Mothers in Law: Feminist Theory and the Legal Regulation of Motherhood* (New York, Columbia University Press, 1995) 43.

[144] See, eg, Robertson (n 143); Ronald Dworkin, *Life's Dominion: An Argument About Abortion, Euthanasia, and Individual Freedom* (New York, Alfred A Knopf, 1993); John A Robertson, *Children of Choice: Freedom and the New Reproductive Technologies* (Princeton, NJ, Princeton University Press, 1994); John Harris, 'Rights and Reproductive Choice' in John Harris and Søren Holm (eds), *The Future of Human Reproduction: Ethics, Choice and Regulation* (Oxford, Clarendon Press, 1998) 5; Elizabeth Reilly, 'The "Jurisprudence of Doubt": How the Premises of the Supreme Court's Abortion Jurisprudence Undermine Procreative Liberty' (1998) 14 *Journal of Law and Politics* 757; Judith F Daar, 'Assisted Reproductive Technologies and the Pregnancy Process: Developing an Equality Model to Protect Reproductive Liberties' (1999) 25 *American Journal of Law & Medicine* 455.

[145] O'Neill (n 33) 57–58.

[146] Robertson is certainly not alone – others have made similar arguments – but of these, Robertson's account is the most fully developed.

[147] Robertson (n 143) 406.

[148] Robertson, *Children of Choice* (n 144) 16.

[149] *Ibid* 24.

[150] *Ibid* 41–42. Robertson does not claim that procreative liberty is absolute, but would place the burden of demonstrating such harm on those who would claim that procreative liberty should be limited.

potential harms raised in relation to the use of reproductive technologies are based on speculation or are grounded in moral objections and thus do not meet the 'high standard necessary to limit procreative choice'.[151]

Though his definition of procreative liberty appears comprehensive, Robertson adds an important caveat:

> [N]ot everything that occurs in and around procreation falls within liberty interests that are distinctly procreative. Thus whether the father may be present during childbirth, whether midwives may assist birth, or whether childbirth may occur at home rather than in a hospital may be important for the parties involved, but they do not implicate the freedom to reproduce . . .[152]

Robertson is indeed correct in his basic assertion – it is impossible to argue cogently that decisions about abortion and contraception implicate reproductive autonomy, and that decisions about whether to use 'high tech' methods to reproduce (such as in vitro fertilisation (IVF), intracytoplasmic sperm injection (ICSI), or preimplantation genetic diagnosis (PGD) do not. Decision making about technological means of reproduction implicates reproductive autonomy, regardless of the fact that it involves the use of technology and is therefore not natural, or that it falls outside the relational context of procreative activity and might threaten traditional understandings of the family.[153]

But while Robertson's approach to procreative liberty is expansive, it leaves much to be desired. He views procreative liberty as bifurcated into two distinct liberty interests – the freedom not to reproduce and the freedom to reproduce. This position is what permits his conclusion that questions about women's preferences during pregnancy and childbirth are not necessarily distinctly procreative.[154] As to what they might be if not procreative, Robertson does not elaborate. His approach fails to include in reproductive autonomy a good number of procreative activities and events that take place after the decision to reproduce has been made. His exclusion of such aspects of reproduction from procreative liberty seems largely to discount the experience of reproduction from the reproducing woman's point of view.

Robertson also inserts the notion of 'reproductive responsibility' into his discussion of procreative liberty. He notes that the question of whether a particular act of reproduction (or a particular reproductive decision) is responsible or irresponsible can be answered by taking into account a number of factors: the reproductive interests at stake, 'the ease or burdens of avoiding reproduction', and the impact of a reproductive decision on offspring and on society.[155] When, on balance, individual reproductive decisions are irresponsible, the State may permissibly intervene.[156] In general, Robertson would limit State intervention to non-coercive measures, owing to the presumptive primacy of procreative liberty, although he is prepared to allow that coercive means may be justified in limited circumstances.

The idea of irresponsible reproduction surfaces primarily in Robertson's discussion of the acceptability of involuntary contraception and sterilisation,[157] as well as in the context

---

[151] *Ibid* 35.
[152] *Ibid* 23.
[153] *Ibid* 32–34.
[154] *Ibid* 23.
[155] *Ibid* 72–78.
[156] *Ibid* 78–80.
[157] *Ibid* 69–93.

of pre-natally caused harm to offspring.[158] In both instances he supports non-coercive methods of obtaining women's compliance (and he is principally, though not exclusively, concerned with women's irresponsibility), either with the use of long-acting contraception such as Norplant or with medical advice during pregnancy. In the case of contraception, such methods can include informing women of the option, subsidising its availability and providing financial incentives (provided the incentives are not too large, in which case they might more plausibly be viewed as coercive). In the context of pre-natal behaviour, Robertson favours education, counselling and the provision of better pre-natal care over criminal sanctions and forced medical treatment, but concedes a role for the latter in particularly egregious cases.[159]

In addition, in Robertson's formulation (which can generally be referred to as the traditional liberal formulation) procreative liberty is a negative liberty; in essence, it requires no more of the State (or others) than a hands-off, permissive approach.[160] While this perspective is preferable to one permitting significant restrictions on reproductive choice, it is ultimately unsatisfactory, as it will undoubtedly result in the denial of meaningful reproductive choice for those who are economically and socially disadvantaged.[161]

There have been many critiques of the traditional liberal position, on a variety of fronts, but this account of procreative liberty has nevertheless proved very influential, particularly in the United States. In part, this is due to the 'bitterly divisive abortion debate'[162] in the US, and its influence on the debate around reproductive choice more generally. Alta Charo points out that pro-choice groups have been 'led . . . into extreme libertarian positions lest the principle of reproductive choice be undermined'.[163] She suggests that the 'abortion wars' have led to a search by opponents of abortion 'for proxy wars . . . as opportunities to rehearse arguments on the value of biologic but nonsentient human existence'.[164] If the debate around the right to die is influenced by abortion politics, it should be no surprise that notions of reproductive autonomy are similarly affected.

Liberal arguments in favour of procreative liberty are not without their critics. As one of Robertson's notable critics, Dorothy Roberts,[165] explains, the liberal conception of reproductive autonomy fails to recognise the issues of social justice that require consideration in this context. According to Roberts:

> Liberals' defense of reproductive liberty as a 'moral right' central to 'personal identity, meaning, and dignity' is a compelling reason to ensure the equal distribution of procreative resources

---

[158] *Ibid* 173–94.

[159] *Ibid* 181–90.

[160] Robertson, *Children of Choice* (n 144).

[161] See, eg, discussion in ch 4 (section II.B.); ch 5 (section IV.A.), and ch 8 (section V.B.).

[162] R Alta Charo, 'Realbioethik' (2005) 35(4) *Hastings Center Report* 13, 13. Charo's argument in this piece is that outcomes of bioethics debates are heavily influenced by political arguments, often more so than they are affected by the merits of the bioethics arguments themselves. Charo also points out that economic factors can play a key role as well – in nations with public health systems, physicians are a part of the decision-making structure around which services ought to be funded and which not. By contrast, in the US, the system of private payment leads to physicians becoming 'allies with their patients in a consumerist demand for more patient autonomy in purchasing services'. And, as she notes, this reality has 'obvious implications for fields of medicine that straddle the "disease" and "lifestyle" distinction, such as infertility treatment'.

[163] *Ibid* 13.

[164] R Alta Charo, 'The Celestial Fire of Conscience – Refusing to Deliver Medical Care' (2005) 352 *New England Journal of Medicine* 2471, 2472.

[165] Dorothy Roberts, *Killing the Black Body: Race, Reproduction, and the Meaning of Liberty* (New York, Vintage, 1997).

in society. Liberals give no good reason why our understanding of procreative liberty must adopt a baseline of existing inequalities or why the deepening of those inequalities should not weigh heavily in our deliberations about policies affecting reproduction.[166]

In other words, to approach reproductive autonomy as requiring only that the State not restrict our ability to make reproductive decisions for ourselves in accordance with our own priorities, is to fail to recognise the steps that might be necessary to create conditions in which reproductive autonomy can meaningfully be exercised. Roberts' project is to expose the racism of reproductive law and policy in American history, noting that *'regulating Black women's reproductive decisions has been a central aspect of racial oppression in America'*.[167] To this end, she supports an approach that focuses 'on the connection between reproductive rights and racial equality',[168] and that explicitly takes social justice into account. For Roberts, an approach to reproductive liberty based on privacy rights alone privileges the reproductive choices of those with wealth and power, and discounts both '"private" obstacles' to reproductive choice[169] and government interference (short of coercion)[170] that constrains reproductive decision making.[171]

Emily Jackson has also made the argument for reproductive autonomy, albeit from a perspective different from that of John Robertson.[172] Like him, she advocates in favour of a wide scope for reproductive freedom, but for Jackson that concept has a meaning distinct from that subscribed to by Robertson. Jackson draws on a number of feminist commentators in characterising autonomy more broadly than do traditional liberal accounts.[173] She notes that the version of liberal autonomy that is often critiqued by cultural or relational feminists as being excessively individualistic is a 'particularly narrow and impoverished conception of autonomy',[174] as it focuses myopically on an insular, atomistic self. Ultimately, she argues that it is possible to conceive of autonomy in a much richer, more meaningful way.

Jackson takes seriously the claims that individuals are social beings and that the capacity for autonomy develops in a social context. She maintains that 'without socialisation within a strong network of relationships, an individual's right to self-determination would be both meaningless and irrelevant'.[175] But the fact that individuals' preferences are shaped (and constrained) by their social realities does not mean that we are justified in dismissing them as inauthentic.[176] Rather, being free to act on our preferences, inevitably socially constituted as they may be, is crucial to our sense of self.[177] Moreover, Jackson argues that meaningful respect for reproductive autonomy demands more than a negative liberty approach. It not only requires recognition of the capacity of a particular individual to act on 'preferences that are *already* fully formed and clearly articulated',[178] but also

---

[166] *Ibid* 296.
[167] *Ibid* 6.
[168] *Ibid* 294.
[169] Racism, systemic social prejudice and the unequal distribution of wealth (*ibid* 297).
[170] Such as the use of incentives to deter poor, Black women from reproducing (*ibid*).
[171] *Ibid*.
[172] Jackson (n 83).
[173] In particular, Jackson refers to the work of Nedelsky, Friedman, Meyers and Nussbaum (*ibid* 3–8).
[174] *Ibid* 2.
[175] *Ibid* 5.
[176] *Ibid* 7.
[177] *Ibid* 6.
[178] *Ibid* 7.

must acknowledge that 'positive provision of resources and services may be necessary in order to assist people both to work out their own priorities and to realise them'.[179]

Robertson uses the language of procreative liberty rather than autonomy, but his justifications for the presumptive primacy of procreative liberty are autonomy-related, in that they speak to the importance of being able to make one's own reproductive choices in harmony with one's own values. Indeed, he refers to the centrality of decisions around reproduction to one's identity, dignity and the meaning of one's life. As he puts it:

> [D]eprivation of the ability to avoid reproduction determines one's self-definition in a direct and substantial way. It . . . centrally affects one's psychological and social identity . . . [similarly] being deprived of the ability to reproduce prevents one from an experience that is central to individual identity and meaning in life.[180]

These reasons do not justify merely a negative liberty approach to reproductive autonomy,[181] but demand that we also consider issues of equality and social justice, and recognise the connections between reproductive health and reproductive autonomy, and between socio-economic status and reproductive autonomy. They also demand that we attend to the concerns that arise because of oppressive socialisation and its effects on reproductive autonomy.

My use of the phrase reproductive autonomy, in contrast to reproductive 'freedom' or 'liberty', is deliberate, as it implies a deeper understanding of what it means to be self-determining in making reproductive decisions. Although autonomy and liberty are often used as though they are synonyms, as should be clear from the discussion on autonomy earlier in this chapter, they are not.[182] Typical modes of interference with liberty (the use of force, coercion) also interfere with autonomy (understood as self-determination), and liberty is a 'necessary [condition] for individuals to develop their own aims and interests and to make their values effective in the living of their lives'.[183] But, as the preceding discussion shows, 'Autonomy is a richer notion than liberty, which is conceived either as mere absence of interference or as the presence of alternatives'.[184]

Reproductive autonomy has two facets: personal and political.[185] Reproductive autonomy can refer to the actual making of autonomous decisions about reproduction, guided by one's own values and commitments. It also speaks to the question of whether and to what extent constraints can be erected by the State around one's freedom to make reproductive decisions, based on the interests of the collective (or of others, external to the decision itself).

---

[179] *Ibid* 7–8.
[180] Robertson, *Children of Choice* (n 144) 24.
[181] See, eg, Roberts (n 165).
[182] Dworkin (n 1) 14.
[183] *Ibid* 18.
[184] *Ibid* 107.
[185] These facets correspond to the personal and political senses in which autonomy itself can be understood. In describing autonomy as a political ideal, Dworkin states that here autonomy is 'used as a basis to argue against the design and functioning of political institutions that attempt to impose a set of ends, values, and attitudes upon the citizens of a society' (*ibid* 10). Meyers describes this as 'legal autonomy' (she frames political autonomy as being attributed to Nation States, and explains it as the obligation of States to respect one another's political autonomy) (Meyers (n 3) 10). Legal autonomy refers to the idea of a 'private sphere in which individuals are free to pursue their own projects in their own ways'.

The tendency of commentators whose understanding of reproductive autonomy is drawn from liberal thought (including Robertson, John Harris[186] and Julian Savulescu[187]) has been to focus quite narrowly in terms of what is demanded by way of respect for individual autonomy in the clinical interaction, as well as with respect to the extent to which the State may permissibly constrain the scope of reproductive freedom. In terms of personal autonomy, as is the case in bioethics more generally, the key question in assessing the autonomous nature of a particular reproductive decision is whether informed consent was obtained. From the standpoint of the political sense of autonomy, the main concern is that the State not unduly restrict the scope of freedom to make reproductive decisions.

As feminist critics have noted, taken together, these focal points lead to the tendency to reduce reproductive autonomy to a right to demand an ever-expanding array of technologies for purchase by consumers.[188] Even assuming that this is a legitimate aim for reproductive autonomy arguments, the narrow focus means that a number of important issues are overlooked.

A. Feminist critique of reproductive autonomy

The feminist critique of reproductive autonomy (and of Robertson's arguments in particular),[189] has largely focused on objecting to his valorisation of individual freedom, and has not attempted to take him on on his own terms, so to speak. There are not many well-developed feminist accounts of reproductive autonomy.[190] Instead, because Robertson has been an influential and prolific contributor to the legal and ethical literature around procreative liberty, a great deal of energy has been expended in responding to his arguments. In general, feminists focus on why autonomy is not the only value we should be concerned about in relation to reproductive decision making, and on what harms might ensue from allegiance to an ethic that is overly deferential to procreative liberty.

Arguably, the feminist 'opposition' to reproductive autonomy is not opposition to reproductive autonomy itself but to the liberal, individualistic, negative liberty conception of reproductive autonomy. Most feminists, even those who object to ARTs, favour reproductive autonomy in relation to, for example, contraceptive use and abortion. And virtually all feminist social justice supporters would permit access to ARTs.[191] Feminist

---

[186] Harris (n 144); John Harris, 'Sex Selection and Regulated Hatred' (2005) 31 *Journal of Medical Ethics* 291.

[187] Julian Savulescu, 'Sex Selection: The Case For' (1999) 171 *Medical Journal of Australia* 373; Julian Savulescu, 'Procreative Beneficence: Why We Should Select the Best Children' (2001) 15 *Bioethics* 413; Julian Savulescu, 'Deaf Lesbians, "Designer Disability" and the Future of Medicine' (2002) 325 *British Medical Journal* 771.

[188] See, eg, Susan Sherwin, *No Longer Patient: Feminist Ethics and Health Care* (Philadelphia, PA, Temple University Press, 1992) 134.

[189] Which also apply to arguments raised by others, including Harris and Savulescu.

[190] Although Dorothy Roberts both critiques Robertson and argues in favour of a social justice-orientated approach to reproductive autonomy (Roberts (n 165)). It is encouraging to see that feminist scholarship continues to contemplate an important role for reproductive autonomy – see, eg, Pamela Laufer-Ukeles, 'Reproductive Choices and Informed Consent: Fetal Interests, Women's Identity, and Relational Autonomy' (2011) 37 *American Journal of Law & Medicine* 567; Jody Lyneé Madeira, 'Woman Scorned?: Resurrecting Infertile Women's Decision-Making Autonomy' (2012) 71 *Maryland Law Review* 339.

[191] Callahan and Roberts (n 70) 1210.

concern tends to revolve around the way in which reproductive autonomy is interpreted and valued, rather than being antagonistic to the very idea of reproductive autonomy. In short, the position taken by many feminists in respect of Robertson's views on reproductive autonomy is to say 'if that is reproductive autonomy, we don't want it'.

In part, the feminist critique around the liberal vision of procreative liberty is concerned with the focus on State neutrality in the context of reproductive decision making and the contention that reproductive autonomy demands only that the State not interfere with individuals' reproductive decisions.[192] As many feminists have argued, the notion of reproductive autonomy as simply a negative liberty is, for many women, woefully inadequate.[193] It is of little use to tell a woman that she is free to terminate her pregnancy if she cannot afford to pay for the abortion procedure,[194] or if she is required to travel not once but twice[195] to a distant clinic in order to have the procedure, and her job, or her child or elder-care responsibilities make that travel impossible. State neutrality might permit her to make the decision but at the same time deprive her of the means to carry it out. The same goes for reproductive technologies on the other end of the spectrum – ARTs. Women and couples are free to seek IVF or other assisted conception services, but the enormous financial cost of such services puts them out of the reach of most women.[196] Poor women are free to bear children should they wish to, but when welfare benefits are tied to women refraining from having further children,[197] freedom is elusive.[198]

There are, of course, deeper, more fundamental feminist criticisms of the very idea of procreative liberty and the meaning accorded to it by 'reproductive liberals'.[199] These critiques are closely tied to critiques of assisted reproduction, and object to the notion

---

[192] *Ibid* 1231–33.

[193] See, eg, *ibid*; Jackson (n 83); MacKinnon (n 95). Although Jackson's account is not explicitly feminist, it has been described as 'woman-centred' (Susan Millns, 'Exploring the Boundaries of Reproductive Autonomy' (2003) 9 *Res Publica* 87).

[194] See, eg, MacKinnon (n 95) referring to *Maher v Roe*, 432 US 464 (1977) and *Harris v McRae*, 448 US 297 (1980), cases in which the US Supreme Court held that a constitutional right to abortion does not entail State funding of abortion services.

[195] More than half of American states have passed legislation requiring that women wait a specified amount of time (usually 24 hours) between mandatory abortion counselling and the abortion procedure (Guttmacher Institute, 'State Policies in Brief: Counseling and Waiting Periods for Abortion' (2 August 2012), at <www.guttmacher.org/statecenter/spibs/spib_MWPA.pdf>). Given that many US counties lack abortion providers, this mandatory waiting period can mean that women have to travel twice in order to obtain abortion services (Guttmacher Institute, 'In Brief: Facts on Induced Abortion in the United States' (August 2011), at <www.guttmacher.org/pubs/fb_induced_abortion.pdf>). In 2008, 87% of all US counties lacked an abortion provider; and while 95% of all abortion facilities provide services at eight weeks' gestation, only 64% offer abortion services at 13 weeks or later. The numbers drop sharply after that point, with only 11% of providers offering abortion services at 24 weeks.

[196] The average cost of an IVF cycle varies considerably among jurisdictions. According to a 2009 study, the average costs for a standard IVF cycle in 2006 were as follows: United States $12,513; Canada $8,500; Australia $5,645; and the United Kingdom $6,534 (Georgina M Chambers *et al*, 'The Economic Impact of Assisted Reproductive Technology: A Review of Selected Developed Countries' (2009) 91 *Fertility and Sterility* 2281). In 2011, the median cost of an IVF treatment cycle in the US was $24,373 for IVF, and $38,015 for IVF using donor eggs (Patricia Katz *et al*, 'Costs of Infertility Treatment: Results from an 18-month Prospective Cohort Study' (2011) 95 *Fertility and Sterility* 915).

[197] Or tied to the woman's 'consent' to the use of long-acting contraception (Roberts (n 165) 109–10, 209–10).

[198] *Ibid*; Sherwin (n 188).

[199] Janice G Raymond, *Women as Wombs: Reproductive Technology and the Battle Over Women's Freedom* (San Francisco, Cal, Harper Collins, 1993). Raymond describes reproductive liberalism as enshrining several dominant principles, including 'procreative liberty, gender neutrality, privacy, individual rights, and unlimited choice' (*ibid* 76–77).

that regulation of ARTs must, in most cases, facilitate individual preferences. There are also strong objections to the claim that reproductive autonomy entails a right to reproduce. Several distinct arguments have been made in relation to assisted reproduction and reproductive autonomy, including those expressing concern that the very availability of ARTs reinforce the notion of maternity as 'woman's destiny'.[200] Critics also worry about the strain of infertility treatment on women,[201] and argue that the medicalisation of reproduction fostered by ARTs leads to a diminution of women's power over reproduction (and a corresponding increase in men's power).[202] Some also assert that consent to treatment in the infertility context is a myth.[203]

These critiques of procreative liberty seem fundamentally to be critiques of the liberal articulation. These feminist critics do not seem to envision that procreative liberty could be understood in any other way. They are deeply suspicious of the liberal account of procreative liberty and worry that its unstated purpose is to create not just a right to use reproductive technologies, but *'the right to use . . . reproductive [persons]'*.[204] The rhetoric becomes quite heated, with claims that 'procreative liberty institutionalizes the commodification of women as means of procreation' and 'is rooted in the quest for children who are technologically and contractually vetted'.[205] Some have even called for a ban on reproductive technologies such as IVF, egg donation and surrogacy, arguing that the technologies violate women's bodily integrity.[206] They assert that reproductive technologies encourage 'women . . . to negate their own bodies, treating their bodies as instruments for their own or someone else's reproductive goals and splitting their bodies from their selves'.[207]

Some feminists who contest the claim that wide latitude should be afforded to reproductive choice in the context of a right to reproduce nevertheless strongly support women's rights to access contraception and abortion services.[208] But in spite of what appears to be a commitment to the importance – for women – of reproductive choice, they caution against interpreting reproductive choice broadly enough to include support for a 'right to reproduce'. Christine Overall argues, for example, that although there is a solid foundation for the recognition of a 'strong' right not to reproduce, it does not follow ethically, politically or logically, that a similarly robust right to reproduce also

[200] See, eg, Callahan and Roberts (n 70) 1211; Cherry (n 70) 439; Sherwin (n 188).
[201] See, eg, Gena Corea, *The Mother Machine: Reproductive Technologies from Assisted Insemination to Artificial Wombs* (New York, Harper & Row, 1985); Sarah Franklin, *Embodied Progress: A Cultural Account of Assisted Conception* (London, Routledge, 1997).
[202] See, eg, Corea (n 201); Raymond (n 199); Christine Overall, *Ethics and Human Reproduction: A Feminist Analysis* (Boston, MA, Allen & Unwin, 1987) 124, 167–70.
[203] See, eg, Callahan and Roberts (n 70) 1227; Sherwin (n 188) 128–29.
[204] Raymond (n 199) 78–79.
[205] *Ibid* 79.
[206] *Ibid* 208. Raymond asserts that women must be permitted to terminate unwanted pregnancies, as the alternative would be to coerce women into pregnancy and childbearing, but she does not specify why abortion does not also violate women's bodily integrity (Janice G Raymond, 'RU486: Progress or Peril?' in Joan C Callahan (ed), *Reproduction, Ethics, and the Law: Feminist Perspectives* (Bloomington, Indiana University Press, 1995) 284). Though many of these concerns about ARTs were initially raised a decade or two ago, they still have currency with the critics (Renate Klein, 'From Test-Tube Women to Bodies Without Women' (2008) 31 *Women's Studies International Forum* 157).
[207] Raymond (n 199) 205. Rowland echoes many of Raymond's concerns, and agrees that the use of reproductive technologies should cease (Rowland (n 69) 300–301). Both Raymond and Rowland take the view that regulating the technologies implies their acceptance and is thus the wrong approach (Raymond (n 199) 205–08; Rowland (n 69)).
[208] Overall (n 202) 167–68.

exists.[209] Her primary concern is that 'In endorsing an uncritical freedom of reproductive choice, we may also be implicitly endorsing all conceivable alternatives that an individual might adopt; we thereby abandon the responsibility for evaluating substantive actions in favour of advocating merely formal freedom of choice'.[210] In particular, she worries that acknowledgement of a right to reproduce in a 'strong sense' would 'require the acceptance of certain implications about which feminists should have serious reservations'.[211] Among these worrying implications, Overall includes the concerns

> that fertile men married to infertile women are entitled to the services of surrogate mothers, and that surrogate mothers should be legally compelled to surrender their children after birth . . . [and] that if a man offers his sperm to fertile women and they all reject him, then his right to reproduce has been violated. . . . It could be used as a basis for requiring fertile people to donate gametes and embryos to assist the infertile.[212]

Overall asserts that feminists who favour a right to reproduce are really only concerned with discrimination in the provision of infertility treatment services to single and lesbian women. This difficulty can, in her view, be remedied by an insistence upon the provision of these services without discrimination, and need not lead to recognition of a right to reproduce.

The feminist critique of liberal reproductive autonomy is, in part at least, well aimed. The concern with Robertson's treatment of surrogacy (for example) is justified, given his apparent willingness to privilege the needs and interests of infertile couples who wish to use surrogacy in order to procreate over the needs and interests of the women who will provide surrogacy services. In favouring presumptive enforcement of collaborative reproduction agreements, Robertson's focus is quite clearly on the infertile couple, who should have the right to reproduce collaboratively, and who require some certainty about the legal implications of their collaborative enterprise.[213] He argues that prohibiting payment for surrogacy services, if it significantly reduces the likelihood that an infertile couple would be able to secure an agreement for the provision of such services, would inappropriately interfere with the procreative liberty interests of such couples.[214] The procreative liberty of the surrogate is minimised in his account.

As with feminist views around autonomy in philosophy, there are tensions within feminism in relation to reproductive autonomy. There is a reluctance, at least among some feminists, to agree that reproductive autonomy deserves the attention that it has

---

[209] *Ibid.*

[210] *Ibid* 125.

[211] *Ibid* 170.

[212] *Ibid.*

[213] Robertson, *Children of Choice* (n 144) 125–26. Robertson does advert to the fact that, in his view, gamete donors and surrogates also benefit from the certainty that exists when the parties are aware that their contractual arrangements will be respected and enforced, but it is quite clear that his chief concern is the procreative liberty of the infertile couple seeking to use collaborative means to reproduce.

[214] *Ibid* 141. There are, of course, many arguments that may be raised in opposition to prohibiting payment to surrogates, including that the exploitative potential of the practice of surrogacy is not limited to its commercial form, or that it will simply drive the practice underground where surrogates run even higher risk of exploitation. Robertson does consider the potential for exploitation of women as a result of the practice of surrogacy, but ultimately does not dwell on the procreative liberty of those who provide surrogacy services. What is particularly interesting about Robertson's arguments on preconception agreements in relation to his general position on procreative liberty – specifically the negative liberty aspect of procreative liberty – is his failure to acknowledge that his position in fact grants State support to the rights and interests of the commissioning couple in a surrogacy agreement by backing them with the power of the courts. Nedelsky makes a similar point about property rights in 'Reconceiving Autonomy' (n 68) 18–19. So much for State neutrality.

had within the bioethics literature. For these scholars, the reaction to the 'triumph of autonomy' has been to suggest that autonomy is not the only value and in some cases might not be the most important value. Sometimes this is framed as a claim, like that made by Burrow,[215] that social pressures faced by women in making reproductive decisions mean that what might appear to be autonomous choices are in fact not autonomous. I have also heard a related claim made by my some of my feminist colleagues in conversations and at academic meetings, wherein the argument is that particular reproductive decisions do not require respect (presumably even if they are autonomous), because autonomy in such cases is outweighed by other values, such as women's equality.[216] In this latter iteration, certain choices by individual women are impermissible because they conflict with the (more important) aim of recognising women's equality.

The claims about the threats posed by ARTs are clearly also claims about reproductive autonomy. If choosing infertility treatment amounts to yielding to the socially-created 'need' to be a mother, or surrendering (to medicine) control over one's reproductive processes, even where such actions conflict with one's deeply-held values and commitments, then by definition these choices cannot be autonomous. The same holds for the assertion that consent to the use of ARTs is nothing more than fantasy, given social pressures, societal norms around women's roles and pressure from a male partner. But these critiques reveal a deep disconnect between women's experiences of infertility, their choices about infertility treatment and the characterisation of these choices by feminist critics. As Margarete Sandelowski has explained, no one is 'more introspective and self-conscious' in making reproductive decisions than infertile couples 'compelled to find the way to parenthood'.[217] It is difficult to imagine a clearer example of the exercise of autonomous choice in the reproductive context.

While I share many of the concerns raised by feminist theorists in relation to prevailing interpretations of reproductive autonomy, I do want to pause here and point out my unease with this tendency. I am not suggesting that we need not concern ourselves with women's equality. Perhaps it is a more important aim than the realisation of individual autonomy. But I do not see how failing to respect the autonomy of some persons can help us reach the ideal of equality. Equality and autonomy are bound up in important and intractable ways, and though I share the concern at the heart of the feminist objection to autonomy, I worry about the implications of placing certain kinds of decisions out of bounds in terms of what we can consider autonomous. As I said in explaining my reservations about relational autonomy, there is a risk that the intuitions of feminist and relational theorists will be prioritised over the needs of individual women. In the reproductive choice context, this has the potential to rule out some reproductive choices because they do not fit with feminist intuitions about what autonomous women can legitimately choose. Relational theorists might disagree with my interpretation, but this is a potentially paternalistic tendency in that it suggests that these theorists know what women really want and that they must therefore protect women – individually and collectively – from their own misguided choices.

---

[215] Above (n 134 and accompanying text).

[216] Although she does not explicitly make this argument, Elisabeth Boetzkes discusses this concern in general terms (Elisabeth Boetzkes, 'Equality, Autonomy, and Feminist Bioethics' in Anne Donchin and Laura Purdy (eds), *Embodying Bioethics: Recent Feminist Advances* (Lanham, MD, Rowman and Littlefield, 1999) 121).

[217] Margarete Sandelowski, 'Fault Lines: Infertility and Imperiled Sisterhood' (1990) 16 *Feminist Studies* 33, 43.

Feminist claims and critiques in the arena of reproductive autonomy – like feminist approaches generally – are diverse. Jackson suggests that the diversity in the feminist response to ARTs (and generally also reproductive autonomy[218]) can be attributed to feminist 'ambivalence about whether motherhood should be considered empowering or oppressive or both'.[219] While Jackson is absolutely right in her assertion that feminists are deeply ambivalent about the significance of motherhood, this alone does not explain the divergent nature of the feminist critique of ARTs and of reproductive autonomy.

Given the sizable diversity among feminist approaches, any attempt to distil a single reason for feminist positions on questions such as motherhood and reproduction is unwise. I suggest that feminist ambivalence in relation to reproductive autonomy is rooted in concerns around the history of reproductive regulation. There is a long history of abortion regulation from which we can draw lessons about what types of abortion regulation benefit, and what types harm, women. Assisted reproductive technologies are, by contrast, new, and we therefore have no historical record that demonstrates precisely how women are affected by various regulatory approaches.[220] As a result, the concerns raised by feminists critical of reproductive autonomy (most of which centre on the use of the concept to justify entitlements to access to an ever-expanding list of ARTs) are, to varying degrees, speculative. But feminist suspicion of mainstream medical approaches to women (much of which is arguably justified[221]), especially in relation to reproductive health and reproductive decision making, means that these speculative concerns come to carry a great deal of force in feminist thought.

History may not have taught us much (yet) about the effects on women of access to various ARTs, but it has taught us a great deal about social and medical attempts at controlling women's reproductive lives. Added to this reality is the very practical reluctance on the part of feminists to leave the substantive questions around reproductive decision making to the non-feminist (and, in some cases, antifeminist) majority. As Overall points out, a strong stance in favour of the inclusion of a right to reproduce within the scope of reproductive autonomy 'shifts the burden of proof onto those who have moral doubts about the morality of technologies such as IVF and practices such as surrogate motherhood'.[222] Many feminists have deep reservations about ceding ground to the proponents of a broad scope for reproductive autonomy for all of these reasons.

Is there a way to recognise the importance of reproductive autonomy in all reproductive decisions women might make without adopting an uncomfortably liberal stance in relation to reproductive choice? Reproductive decision making can involve a multitude of discrete decisions that may take place at various points in a woman's life, many of which have

---

[218] For the most part, the feminist critique around reproductive freedom has been in relation to ARTs, as opposed to, eg, abortion and contraception. There is generally widespread agreement that women must have access to abortion in order to be able to determine the shape of their own lives – see, eg, Raymond (n 206); Rowland (n 69) 276–77; Catharine A MacKinnon, 'Reflections on Sex Equality Under Law' (1991) 100 *Yale Law Journal* 1281, 1317–18.

[219] Jackson (n 83) 175.

[220] The newness of some technologies could be disputed, particularly donor insemination. They are, at least, new on the political agenda, relative to abortion.

[221] It was, after all, physicians who demanded regulation of abortion in their campaign to wrest professional dominance over reproductive healthcare from midwives – see, eg, Siegel, 'Reasoning from the Body' (n 143) 281–87.

[222] Overall (n 202) 170.

distinct implications for the lives of individual women, women as a collective and society generally. Adopting an attitude that favours respect for reproductive autonomy can mean different things, depending on the nature of the decisions themselves and the context in which decisions are made. Understandably, many feminists are reluctant to adopt an unlimited commitment to respect for reproductive autonomy because they fear the effects of such a position on women and women's interests. I suggest that there is a solution to this problem that does not entail rejecting an inclusive conception of reproductive autonomy, and that is to develop a more nuanced, contextual conception of reproductive autonomy.

B. Relational autonomy and reproductive decision making

Feminist articulations of relational autonomy have begun to be incorporated into feminist work in bioethics. Susan Sherwin draws on work by feminist philosophers who have adopted a relational view of autonomy, and applies their ideas and arguments to the bioethics context, where respect for patient autonomy has become profoundly important.[223] Like most bioethicists, Sherwin considers autonomy to be an essential value in the healthcare context, given that failure to respect autonomy can lead to exploitation of patients. In her view, however, the prevailing conception of autonomy fails to capture the socially constituted nature of individual selves, and has failed to direct attention toward the significant differences among individuals. For Sherwin, a relational view of autonomy emphasises the important differences among individuals (including the varying effects of privilege and oppression) and the effects that these differences have on one's ability to exercise autonomy.[224]

Relational autonomy, according to Sherwin, helps us to understand why simply offering all persons the same range of options does not necessarily mean that all will be equally autonomous with respect to a particular decision. But, at the same time, recognising the effects of oppression on one's ability to develop and exercise autonomy skills does not imply that those who are oppressed are non-autonomous. Indeed, as Sherwin points out, it is sometimes the case that those who are 'multiply oppressed' may have the least to lose by insisting on change in the status quo, and therefore may be more likely to resist structures and institutions that perpetuate oppression.[225]

As Susan Dodds has argued, the traditional liberal model of autonomy that pervades bioethics is 'undertheorized' and misses a great deal that is especially important to women in healthcare decision making.[226] This is particularly the case in relation to reproductive decision making. Because the traditional preoccupation of bioethics has been the behaviour of healthcare providers, considerations of autonomy tend to focus on the potential for providers' interference in patient decision making. In essence, Dodds argues (and, as is clear from the earlier discussion on autonomy in bioethics, she is not alone in this view), autonomy is identified with informed consent, and this 'narrow focus on consent as the sole locus for autonomy considerations in medicine has worked to constrain debate about

[223] Sherwin (n 68) 19.
[224] *Ibid* 35.
[225] *Ibid* 38.
[226] Dodds (n 48) 213–18.

autonomy in health care'.[227] Taking informed consent as representative of autonomy 'makes it easy to overlook other limitations on autonomy in health care'.[228]

Dodds' point is that the traditional approach to autonomy in healthcare has led to the failure of bioethics to recognise the constraints on decision making that are peculiar to the healthcare context. Simply ensuring that an individual has been provided with the information needed to make a decision, and that she has made a decision that appears to be 'her own', does not necessarily mean that the decision is autonomous.[229]

While Dodds agrees with the relational autonomy approach outlined by Susan Sherwin, she is not uncritical of Sherwin's claims. In particular, she would apply Sherwin's ideas not only to those who experience oppression, but also to those in grave medical need. The features of the healthcare context that can constrain autonomy, she notes, apply equally to anyone facing critical healthcare decisions.[230] Dodds also faults Sherwin for her continued emphasis on choice as being representative of autonomy. She concedes that Sherwin calls for a re-examination of the processes of medical decision making, but asserts that, ultimately, Sherwin fails to inquire into the process by which individuals develop the capacity to exercise autonomy.[231] Dodds argues that

> an adequate understanding of autonomy in health care must not be restricted to an examina-
> tion of the exercise of autonomy through choice but must also encompass an understanding of
> the ways in which autonomy is developed or . . . the ways in which the array of "autonomy
> competencies" are fostered, shaped, and potentially thwarted.[232]

According to Dodds, Diana Meyers' autonomy competencies[233] approach requires systems and structures that foster the development of autonomous selves.[234] The implications of this approach for healthcare ethics and policy are significant. Dodds claims that Meyers' theory requires the provision of a basic level of universal access to healthcare, recognition of the role that socialisation plays in healthcare settings[235] and the provision of support for those who face threats to their autonomy due to healthcare emergencies.[236] In other words, more is required of the State than simply relying on the rules

---

[227] *Ibid* 213.

[228] *Ibid* 213–14.

[229] *Ibid* 217. As she points out in relation to individuals who do not appear to be fully autonomous (her example is a person in the early stages of dementia), it is possible that respecting a decision as autonomous because it has been made after the provision of the requisite information and because it appears to correspond with the individual's 'stable preferences' might be the wrong thing to do. For example, the person might have failed to understand (or to recall) some of the key aspects of the information provided, and so the decision might not be autonomous even though it appears that way outwardly.

[230] *Ibid* 224–25.

[231] I disagree with Dodds here, as I think it is quite clear that Sherwin is concerned with much more than choice and its relation to autonomy. She puts forward a position that focuses, as does Dodds' argument, on the oppressive conditions which frustrate the development and exercise of autonomy skills for women (and other oppressed groups).

[232] Dodds (n 48) 226.

[233] Meyers, as noted earlier (n 11), has developed a theory of autonomy competency, noting that autonomy involves the capacity to exercise skills such as self-discovery, self-direction and self-definition to achieve what Mackenzie and Stoljar refer to as 'an integrated but dynamic self' (Mackenzie and Stoljar (n 16) 17). See also Meyers (n 3); Diana T Meyers, 'Personal Autonomy and the Paradox of Feminine Socialization' (1987) 84 *Journal of Philosophy* 619.

[234] Dodds (n 48). See also Mackenzie (n 17).

[235] Here, Dodds primarily refers to persons who require and receive long-term healthcare (such as children who are born with chronic illness or serious disability), or residential care in a healthcare facility (Dodds (n 48) 229). See also Donchin, 'Understanding Autonomy Relationally' (n 68).

[236] See, eg, Dodds (n 48) 228–31.

intended to ensure that providers obtain informed consent before treating their patients. In relation to reproductive autonomy more specifically, it is clear that theories such as that espoused by John Robertson are not adequate to the project outlined by Dodds, given their emphasis on State action that threatens to limit or restrict the scope of pro-creative choice. Such a focus obscures the extent to which an individual's choices may be profoundly constrained for reasons unrelated to outright interference by the State.

But Dodds' claims also help us recognise additional concerns with John Robertson's procreative liberty arguments, including, for example, his comments about procreative liberty and provider autonomy in the ART service provision context. In canvassing the ethical issues around the welfare of offspring conceived using ARTs, Robertson notes the numerous sources of potential risks to offspring: namely, risks resulting from the use of the technologies themselves, from poor parenting and from non-traditional family structures.[237] He explores the ethical paradox of the problem of offspring welfare from the perspective that ARTs

> may lead to situations in which the child has a less favorable physical, psychological, or social situation than healthy children born after coital conception in a married nuclear family setting. But the only way to prevent those effects would be to eschew use of the ART that makes the birth of the child possible. This is the famous philosophical problem that Derek Parfit and others call 'the non-identity problem' – the person protected never benefits because they are never born.[238]

Robertson concedes that, even where children are not actually 'harmed' by being born through the use of ARTs, it is necessary to consider their welfare in making professional and policy decisions around ART use. He concludes that although adequate respect for procreative liberty means that it will rarely (if ever) be appropriate to prohibit the use of particular ARTs in particular situations, 'wide room [should be left] for physician discretion over whether to offer ART services in many of those situations'.[239]

In reference to the question of access to ARTs for gays, lesbians and persons with disabilities, Robertson suggests that physicians who provide assisted reproduction services must ensure that they do not discriminate against gays and lesbians, or against persons with disabilities, even where they 'have moral reservations about facilitating such births'.[240] He does, however, envisage a role for provider autonomy in making decisions about appropriate recipients of ART services. A provider would be justified, for example, in refusing to provide services to a single man 'with no partner or child-rearing skills [seeking] to inseminate a surrogate mother whom he has hired to produce a child whom he will then rear on his own'.[241]

This example illustrates that Robertson's own conception of procreative liberty, comprehensive as it is, fails to capture the contextual backdrop to reproductive decision making. It thus neglects to account for the influence of socialisation and relationships, and the possibilities for a robust account of reproductive autonomy. First, in claiming discretion on behalf of physicians to determine whether a particular individual will be

---

[237] John A Robertson, 'Procreative Liberty and Harm to Offspring in Assisted Reproduction' (2004) 30 *American Journal of Law & Medicine* 7, 24–30.
[238] *Ibid* 8.
[239] *Ibid*.
[240] *Ibid* 39.
[241] *Ibid* 38. Presumably, the same reasoning could be applied in the case of a single woman with no partner or rearing skills who requests artificial insemination.

permitted to reproduce (or to make his or her own reproductive decisions), he fails to interrogate a key underlying assumption – that physicians (or other ART providers) have some expertise or training in assessing the competence of others to rear children.[242] Secondly, the very example Robertson has chosen – that of single parenthood – has not been empirically proven to correlate with (much less cause) poor outcomes for children.[243] Thirdly, Robertson seems to be unaware of, or to disregard, the potentially oppressive nature of the physician-patient relationship. He equally overlooks the reality that physicians enjoy the power they have only because of the status accorded to them as a result of the organisation of social institutions, and because of a culture that grants them that power.[244] Lastly, a richer account of reproductive autonomy would advocate in favour of putting social supports in place in order to permit the meaningful exercise of reproductive autonomy by the man in the example, rather than dismissing his desire to parent because, from the perspective of his physician, he is not suited to that role.

A richer understanding of reproductive autonomy, by contrast, emphasises the context within which reproductive decision making takes place, and insists that we attend to both the political and the personal autonomy implications of reproductive autonomy. Part of the context that we need to be concerned with is the question of whether we are at liberty to make the choice in question. In other words, in order to make an autonomous decision about terminating a pregnancy, that option (ideally) needs to be available. In a society where abortion is prohibited by way of criminal penalties and strict enforcement, a woman can come to an autonomous decision to end a pregnancy, but not have the freedom to act on her decision.[245] There is another aspect to this context, however, and that is the social and relational context of the woman who is pregnant and trying to decide what to do. Does she want to proceed with the pregnancy, and raise the child, but feel unable to because of her financial circumstances? If she chooses to terminate her pregnancy because the financial reality of her life makes child-rearing inconceivable, her decision may not be autonomous on this contextualised view. If the decision to terminate the pregnancy conflicts with her own values, it is arguably not autonomous, and we need to acknowledge the constraints she faces as being autonomy-limiting. Similarly, a woman who lives in a jurisdiction where abortion services are unavailable and who has child-care or elder-care responsibilities that she cannot neglect, may 'choose' not to travel in order to obtain an abortion, but a context-driven view of autonomy would not count that choice as autonomous. The fact that she is free to seek an abortion does not signify that her decision not to abort is an autonomous one. In order to create conditions in which reproductive autonomy can be meaningfully exercised, the State's obligations go beyond simply allowing women to continue or terminate pregnancies, to demanding the provision of support that makes both choices realistically available.

---

[242] As Jackson notes: 'Infertility clinicians do not receive training in assessing future parenting ability, and nor will they have access to the sort of detailed information that ought to inform such a complicated assessment.' (Emily Jackson, 'Conception and the Irrelevance of the Welfare Principle' (2002) 65 *MLR* 176, 194)

[243] *Ibid*. Jackson notes that although the fact of single parenthood is often associated with negative effects on children's welfare, the reality is much more complex; factors such as poverty and family breakdown tend to be more significant than the mere absence of a second parent.

[244] Chris MacDonald, 'Relational Professional Autonomy' (2002) 11 *Cambridge Quarterly of Healthcare Ethics* 282, 285.

[245] Although we know that, in such circumstances, women often resort to unsafe, illicit means to terminate their unwanted pregnancies. For a contemporary example, see Jack Hitt, 'Pro-Life Nation', *The New York Times Magazine*, 9 April 2006, 40.

IV. REPRODUCTIVE AUTONOMY: A WAY FORWARD

So where does all of this leave us in terms of developing a theoretical foundation for reproductive autonomy? Even Robertson has pointed out that we still lack a fully theorised account of procreative liberty, that our thinking remains 'inchoate'.[246] Based on a robust and contextualised view of autonomy, we can begin to work our way toward a more complete conception of reproductive autonomy.

Although some liberal thinkers have interpreted autonomy broadly,[247] liberal political philosophy has traditionally not been particularly successful at taking into account the ways in which social context and oppression can affect one's ability to become an autonomous person and to make autonomous choices. Most notably, liberal philosophy has failed to attend to the manner in which oppression and social context impede the development of autonomy-related skills, and shape individuals' beliefs, desires, attitudes and values.[248] Liberalism's failure on this front is, in part at least, a result of the way in which liberalism understands autonomy. A political system based on a conception of autonomy that is primarily concerned to ensure that people have choices, but that is reluctant to spell out too many conditions as to evaluating the genuineness of those choices, will generally be satisfied as long as choices are present. From a traditional liberal point of view, as long as neither men nor women are coerced into reproducing, or sterilised without their consent, or prohibited from choosing technological means of reproducing, all is well. But, as a richer conception of autonomy helps to highlight, all is not well when we fail to acknowledge the uneven effects of reproductive decision making (and reproduction itself) on men and women, and particularly on women who are multiply disadvantaged.

As noted in the earlier discussion on autonomy (see section I.C. above), our conception of the nature of the autonomous citizen has implications for political philosophy and for the derivation of political principles.[249] As Christman and Anderson explain,

> debates over the . . . social conditions necessary for [the] exercise [of autonomy] ultimately turn on issues of the scope of privacy, the nature of rights, the scope of our obligation to others, claims to welfare, and so on – the very issues that are at the heart of discussions of liberalism regarding the legitimate political, social, and legal order.[250]

In other words, our conceptions of autonomy and of the autonomous self have important implications for how we structure the State. More specifically, our conception of reproductive autonomy has important implications for how we regulate reproductive decision making. This, then, is why we have to start with a more finely-grained, contextual view of autonomy – so that we end with a rich and nuanced appreciation of what it takes to respect reproductive autonomy. Traditional liberal accounts of autonomy (and, by implication, of what is necessary in order to respect autonomy) miss too many things, especially things that are important to women's ability to exercise meaningful reproductive choice.

---

[246] John A Robertson, 'Assisting Reproduction, Choosing Genes, and the Scope of Reproductive Freedom' (2008) 76 *The George Washington Law Review* 1490, 1491.

[247] Raz, for example, speaks to the importance of having a meaningful array of options in order to be able to make autonomous choices (Raz (n 76) 373–77). See also Jackson (n 83) 1–9; Nussbaum (n 76) 55–59.

[248] Mackenzie and Stoljar (n 16) 22.

[249] Christman and Anderson (n 29).

[250] *Ibid* 1.

Relational theorists might argue that the answer to this problem is to look to a relational account of autonomy. Indeed, they would suggest that this is precisely what they mean when advocating a relational approach to autonomy. I have already outlined my concerns with the label 'relational autonomy' – in particular, the suggestion inherent in the word 'relational' that what we need to worry about in this context is relationships. Clearly, relationships play a key role in reproductive decision making. But ultimately what I am concerned about is respect for individuals' reproductive decisions. It is critically important that we firmly ground reproductive autonomy on respect for the autonomy of individuals, particularly individual women.[251]

Arguably, liberalism must (and does) respect and promote individual freedom of choice and is committed to the ideal of the equal worth of persons as choosers.[252] But we need to go further in considering the context in which decisions are made. It is not enough to assume that a decision or an action is autonomous (and therefore deserving of respect) based primarily, if not solely, on the question of whether it was based on the consent or choice of the decision maker. Even where liberal thinkers, like Martha Nussbaum, demand a background of basic equality and respect individuals' decisions within that context, they do not go far enough to ensure that we are creating conditions which permit meaningful choice. To be sure, Nussbaum goes a considerable distance to remedy some flaws in traditional accounts of liberalism, particularly the failure of most liberals to note that the private family sphere can be a site of oppression for women.[253] But, I would argue, her conception of autonomy does not sufficiently account for social context.

Again, it is essential to ensure that we concern ourselves with both autonomous persons and the choices they make. A significant challenge in turning our attention to the question of whether a person has acted autonomously is the impossibility of actually knowing whether a decision or action is premised on or consistent with a person's deeply-held values.[254] I do not have a ready answer to this concern, neither can I suggest a way in which we may determine in practice whether a particular choice is autonomous from this perspective. But even if we cannot actually tell whether a person is autonomous or has acted autonomously, we can focus some attention on ensuring that the conditions in which a person is asked to make choices are conducive to the development of autonomy and the potential for autonomous choice.

In accusing traditional liberalism of failing to take context adequately into account, I mean both that liberal conceptions of autonomy often (though not always) envision separate, self-interested man as their subject, *and* that such conceptions of autonomy isolate the autonomous chooser (even when this individual is seen as socially embedded) from the social context in which she is making choices. In other words, such conceptions of autonomy tend to isolate people from one another and call autonomy the thing that these isolated selves do, and they isolate people from the rest of their lives in respect of the particular decision being made. Even where liberals acknowledge that individuals are inherently social – that is, where they acknowledge that individuals develop as

---

[251] Nussbaum (n 76).

[252] *Ibid* 57. It should be noted, however, that Nussbaum has been criticised for being illiberal in the extent to which she focuses on these issues within her understanding of autonomy: see, eg, Anne Phillips, 'Feminism and Liberalism Revisited: Has Martha Nussbaum Got It Right?' (2001) 8 *Constellations: An International Journal of Critical and Democratic Theory* 249.

[253] Phillips (n 252) 251–52.

[254] This is discussed in section I.D. above. See also Walker (n 37).

autonomous beings because of, and only in connection with, relationships with others – they nevertheless attempt to isolate individual decisions and view them out of the context of the decision maker's life, as though this context has no (or only minimal) importance with respect to the decision in question.

To my mind at least, the separation of individuals as a part of autonomy is less worrying than the separation of individuals from the context in which they live. Some degree of individuation of persons is important, even if only valuable to specific individuals in certain aspects of their lives. It may be the case that many individuals make autonomous decisions on the basis of the value they place on their relationships with others and their concern for what others care about. But there must still be a space in which we are each free to decide what matters most to us as individuals and to determine how we wish to behave, even (maybe especially) when these values and desires disrupt our relationships. The recognition that some level of individuation might be a good thing is, in and of itself, not harmful – even for those who subscribe to the idea that women care mostly about relationships, and that they often base their decisions on preserving relationships and on the needs and interests of others. It only becomes problematic when individuation itself is the goal that must be met in order for a person to count as autonomous.

In isolating the chooser from her context, a liberal version of reproductive autonomy misses a lot of important things, particularly things that are important to women. This traditional view is too ready to agree that granting everyone the same options is sufficient to create conditions for the meaningful exercise of reproductive choice. It is less concerned with the overlapping influences that shape reproductive choice. A contextualised view of autonomy, by contrast, requires us to think about these influences, including the fact that, almost 35 years after the birth of the first IVF baby and in a context where over five million children have been conceived using ARTs,[255] we have only in the past few years seen any attempt at comprehensive, long-term research into the safety of IVF and related technologies.[256] The existence of ARTs speaks to the importance placed by our society on genetic relatedness, and is evidence of our tendency to medicalise social problems. The fact that comprehensive research into the safety of ARTs was not conducted prior to their introduction into clinical practice (and indeed, has still not been conducted) illustrates that concerns over health outcomes for women and children take second place to the march of progress in ART practice.

An example of the contrast between the concerns of a traditional liberal as opposed to a contextualised conception of autonomy might be useful. An infertile couple sees a fertility specialist for some information about treatment options and possibilities. The male partner is infertile; he has a very low sperm count. The specialist discusses

---

[255] European Society of Human Reproduction and Embryology, 'Press Release: The World's Number of IVF and ICSI Babies Has Now Reached a Calculated Total of 5 Million' (2 July 2012), at <www.eshre.eu/ESHRE/English/Press-Room/Press-Releases/Press-releases-2012/ESHRE-2012/5-million-babies/page.aspx/1606>.

[256] As William Buckett and Seang Lin Tan note: 'The first studies comparing rates of congenital abnormalities in children conceived as a result of assisted reproductive techniques . . . with those in children conceived spontaneously were published . . . some 10–15 years after the advent of IVF.' (William M Buckett and Seang Lin Tan, 'Congenital Abnormalities in Children Born After Assisted Reproductive Techniques: How Much is Associated with the Presence of Infertility and How Much With Its Treatment?' (2005) 84 *Fertility and Sterility* 1318, 1318) See also Martine De Rycke, Inge Liebaers and André Van Steirteghem, 'Epigenetic Risks Related to Assisted Reproductive Technologies: Risk Analysis and Epigenetic Inheritance' (2002) 17 *Human Reproduction* 2487, 2488: 'The widespread, almost immediate clinical application of IVF and ICSI in assisted reproduction, without any adequate experimental phase, as well as the invasive nature of some of the techniques, have led to a debate concerning the safety of these techniques.'

infertility treatment for individuals in their circumstances, and gives them a basic list of their options. He mentions donor insemination, but glosses over it and does not encourage questions about it, emphasising IVF with ICSI instead (which will, if successful, allow the couple to have a child that is genetically related to both of them). The couple, having spoken with friends and family, are generally aware of their options for treatment, and their discussion with the specialist does not reveal anything surprising. They spend a few weeks discussing whether to pursue infertility treatment, then return to see the specialist, having decided to go ahead with IVF and ICSI.

From a liberal point of view, this decision appears to be autonomous – the couple were provided with information about their options, they considered the options and arrived at a decision. A context-focused perspective, however, would have to consider more factors before concluding that the decision is autonomous, at least on the part of the female partner. Given societal expectations of women with respect to childbearing, and women's known willingness to defer to their partner's feelings about infertility treatment,[257] respect for the woman's autonomy requires more of the physician in terms of time for careful explanation of the risks, costs and success rates of donor insemination compared to IVF with ICSI. Taking a broader view of what makes a decision autonomous can illuminate these otherwise hidden contextual factors. In the end, the decision might be the same, but the contextualised view asks us to widen the lens through which we contemplate the autonomous nature of the decision, and to think beyond informed consent in terms of how we understand autonomy.

Access to abortion provides another example of the contrast between a more traditional and contextualised conceptions of reproductive autonomy. Granting women equal freedom to access abortion services would satisfy most who hold a liberal view. But freedom to obtain an abortion means something very different to a woman who lives in a large city where abortion services are quite readily available than it does to a woman who lives in a rural area with no service provider. It also means something very different to a woman who has the means (or insurance coverage) to pay for the abortion than it does to a woman with no insurance and no ability to pay. A context-driven view of autonomy explicitly takes these contextual factors into account. It is not satisfied by the bare assertion that abortion is legally available to all of these women, and that therefore all are equally able to make an autonomous decision about whether or not to carry a pregnancy to term.

A contextualised conception of autonomy demands that we consider the range of decisions that must be permitted to be made autonomously. But unlike most accounts of reproductive autonomy, it also focuses our attention on the question of whether conditions exist that actually permit (or foster) the meaningful exercise of reproductive choice.

In addition to directing our focus more broadly, a deeper, contextualised understanding of reproductive autonomy directs us explicitly to consider the social, institutional and policy contexts that play a role in shaping reproductive decisions. Emily Jackson notes that the objection has been raised that healthcare dollars allocated to the provision of infertility treatment would be better spent in attempts to reduce the incidence of infer-

---

[257] See, eg, Gay Becker, *The Elusive Embryo: How Women and Men Approach New Reproductive Technologies* (Berkeley, University of California Press, 2000) 136: 'Women often stated they would prefer the use of a [sperm] donor to adoption because they could experience pregnancy and childbirth. When men favored adoption over donor insemination, however, women usually deferred to their husband's feelings . . .'

tility, by focusing on its causes, including pelvic inflammatory disease.[258] As she quite correctly points out, funding research into the causes and prevention of infertility does not add to the meaningful reproductive options of those who are infertile.[259] Such research is, however, necessary in order to alleviate the problem of infertility in the future, which will improve the reproductive options of those who would, without prevention, become infertile. Jackson supports the call for research related to prevention of infertility, but does not connect the need for this research with improved possibilities for reproductive choice. A contextual understanding of autonomy would go farther and include the lack of research and treatment funding for infertility prevention within the scope of providing meaningful reproductive options. Such a conception of autonomy would recognise that the direction of the research agenda and the development of particular technologies and treatments (to the exclusion of others) form a part of the context in which reproductive decisions are made. Thus, policy makers considering which aspects of reproductive medicine to fund, or into which to encourage research, might, on this type of approach to autonomy, decide that healthcare dollars would be better spent on strategies for prevention, rather than on funding IVF, or at least that some spending should be directed toward prevention.

A. Reproductive autonomy and reproductive health

One aspect of reproductive decision making that is notably absent from most arguments around reproductive autonomy is reproductive health. From a legal perspective, the notion of autonomy is often expressed in the language of rights. This is evident from the case law, which refers variously to the 'right to reproduce', the 'right to privacy' (which encompasses the right to make private reproductive decisions) and the 'right not to reproduce'. As I have argued, Robertson's binary characterisation of procreative liberty into the 'right to reproduce' and the 'right not to reproduce' leaves much to be desired in terms of a deeper understanding of reproductive autonomy. And feminist criticisms of rights language in this context demonstrate both the poverty of this view for women's reproductive autonomy and the potential over-breadth of rights language when framed from the point of view of a right to reproduce.[260] Arguably, along with reconceiving autonomy from a contextualised standpoint, we also need to reconceive rights.[261] I suggest that a way forward is to move away from the right to reproduce/right not to reproduce dichotomy, toward a notion of reproductive autonomy (and reproductive rights)

---

[258] Jackson (n 83) 199.

[259] Whether IVF itself is a meaningful option depends heavily on a number of factors. Success rates for IVF treatment vary considerably depending upon clinic statistics, including age limits, number of embryos transferred in any given cycle and other factors. In 2009 in the US, the overall live birth rate following IVF using non-donor eggs was 30% (with donor eggs, the birth rate was 55%). The woman's age at time of treatment has a significant effect on success: the live birth rate for women under 35 years of age was 41%, for women between 35 and 37 years, it was 32% and for women between 38 and 40 years, 22% (Centers for Disease Control and Prevention, American Society for Reproductive Medicine, Society for Assisted Reproductive Technology, *2009 Assisted Reproductive Technology Success Rates: National Summary and Fertility Clinic Reports* (Atlanta, US Department of Health and Human Services, 2011) 33). In the UK, 2008 data show an overall success rate of 24%, and for women under 35 years, a success rate of 33% (Human Fertilisation and Embryology Authority, *Fertility Facts and Figures 2008* (London, HFEA, 2010) 4–5).

[260] See, eg, Overall (n 202).

[261] Jennifer Nedelsky, 'Reconceiving Rights as Relationship' (1993) 1 *Review of Constitutional Studies* 1.

that centres on reproductive health. Such an approach incorporates ideas of equality into the notion of self-determination in reproductive matters, and may also exert a significant influence on the State.[262]

As nations that subscribe to the goals of the International Conference on Population and Development,[263] Canada, the US, the UK and Australia have committed to developing a comprehensive national policy approach to population and development issues, which includes reproductive health.[264] A clear understanding of reproductive autonomy is essential to the development of such a policy, and reproductive health itself is essential to the ability to exercise reproductive autonomy. It seems logical, therefore, explicitly to recognise this connection, and to parallel our understanding of reproductive autonomy on that of reproductive health. The definition of reproductive health adopted by the ICPD is broadly based and looks beyond medical factors:

> Reproductive health is a state of complete physical, mental and social well-being and not merely the absence of disease or infirmity, in all matters relating to the reproductive system and to its functions and processes. Reproductive health therefore implies that people are able to have a satisfying sex life and that they have the capability to reproduce and the freedom to decide if, when and how often to do so. Implicit in this last condition are the right of men and women to be informed and have access to safe, effective, affordable and acceptable methods of family planning of their choice, as well as other methods of their choice for regulation of fertility which are not against the law, and the right of access to appropriate health-care services that will enable women to go safely through pregnancy and childbirth and provide couples with the best chance of having a healthy infant.[265]

This definition refers to a number of issues that are key to consideration of autonomy in reproductive decision making, including the importance of freedom to make one's own decisions and the need for information to support autonomous decision making. In addition, there are echoes here of factors that are essential to a social or contextualised conception of autonomy, including the need for access to methods of family planning and to healthcare services that will permit the meaningful exercise of reproductive choice.

[262] Marie Fox, 'A Woman's Right to Choose? A Feminist Critique' in Harris and Holm (eds) (n 144) 77, 99–100.

[263] 'Programme of Action of the International Conference on Population and Development', UN International Conference on Population and Development (ICPD) (Cairo, 5–13 September 1994) UN Doc A/CONF.171/13/Rev.1, Ch VII.

[264] *Ibid* Art 13.5: 'Governments, with the active involvement of parliamentarians, locally elected bodies, communities, the private sector, non-governmental organizations and women's groups, should work to increase awareness of population and development issues *and formulate, implement and evaluate national strategies, policies, plans, programmes and projects that address population and development issues*, including migration, as integral parts of their sectoral, intersectoral and overall development planning and implementation process.' (emphasis added)

[265] *Ibid* Art 7.2. Admittedly, it is problematic to rely on a definition that conditions the freedom to make reproductive decisions on the legality of the means chosen, in order to support an understanding of reproductive autonomy that should guide the law. The purpose of the qualifier 'which are not against the law' is to permit the existence of legal limitations on reproductive health services in nations that take the view that restrictions on reproductive freedom are morally acceptable: see, eg, Rebecca J Cook, Bernard M Dickens and Mahmoud F Fathalla, *Reproductive Health and Human Rights: Integrating Medicine, Ethics, and Law* (Oxford, Oxford University Press, 2003) 79. The approach used by the ICPD is nevertheless instructive in that it demonstrates the broad vision given to reproductive health by the various States that have committed to the goals of the ICPD. The scope of reproductive autonomy should be similarly broad and recognise that being autonomous in reproduction means being able to act in accordance with one's authentic values in respect of the full range of reproductive choice. Reproductive health and well-being are essential ingredients of that ability.

In my view, one essential piece of the regulatory puzzle in the reproductive health context is a policy framework with clearly articulated objectives. There seems, however, to be little explicit recognition in the literature around reproductive autonomy of the importance, for both reproductive autonomy and reproductive health, of explicit policy on these matters. As will be seen from the discussion of various legal and policy issues related to reproduction in the chapters that follow, Canada, the US, the UK and Australia have all taken an *ad hoc* approach to the regulation of reproductive decision making. None of these jurisdictions has anything resembling a coherent national policy approach to regulatory control of reproduction. Worldwide response to reproductive health itself has been described as 'fragmentary', which has led to slow progress in improving reproductive health in general.[266] Many have contended that the legal regulation of reproduction should be guided by an ethic of strong respect for reproductive autonomy. But the conceptions of reproductive autonomy relied upon by these commentators do not seem to require the deeper engagement with issues of reproductive health that is demanded by a contextualised understanding, neither do they regard as essential the development of national, comprehensive policy strategies around reproductive health and reproductive autonomy.[267] Reproductive autonomy cannot be properly respected in the absence of explicit policy that attends to both its own importance and the importance of reproductive health. To take just one example of the intimate connection between reproductive health and reproductive autonomy, it is well known that pelvic infection is a significant cause of infertility; indeed, it is responsible for approximately one-third of all instances of infertility internationally.[268] Thus, it seems clear that the only way forward in terms of reducing infertility and, in turn, mitigating its consequences, requires a concerted effort directed at the prevention and cure of cases of pelvic infection.[269]

A context-focused understanding of reproductive autonomy will also highlight the ways in which social, economic, political and legal factors can have significant influences on women's (and men's) reproductive health. Clearly, the 'underlying socio-legal causes [that] affect and injure women's status and autonomy, [also affect] their reproductive health'.[270] Rebecca Cook, Bernard Dickens and Mohammed Fathalla refer to four

---

[266] Cook *et al* (n 265) 47.

[267] This is to be expected from an account of reproductive liberty that challenges the validity of most State regulation of reproduction, like that of Robertson. Although Harris and Savulescu both argue strongly against restrictive State intervention, both seem prepared to concede a role for the State: see, eg, Harris (n 144) 30–31; Savulescu, 'Deaf Lesbians' (n 187). Emily Jackson takes the position that '*Unregulated* reproduction would unquestionably not be the best way to enhance reproductive freedom,' but does not argue for a comprehensive, explicit policy, beyond stating that the development of the law should be guided by respect for reproductive autonomy (Jackson (n 83) 318).

[268] Cook *et al* (n 265) 47. The authors also note that infertility that is secondary to pelvic infection is the most resistant to treatment. The rate of infertility thought to be caused by pelvic infection varies among jurisdictions; it is much lower, for example, in the US than in African countries (Harold C Wiesenfeld *et al*, 'Subclinical Pelvic Inflammatory Disease and Infertility' (2012) 120 *Obstetrics & Gynecology* 37). The rate of pelvic inflammatory disease is also much higher among some groups even in the same jurisdiction (Maurizio Macaluso *et al*, 'A Public Health Focus on Infertility Prevention, Detection, and Management (2010) 93 *Fertility and Sterility* 16e1, 16e2 (noting that the rate of Chlamydia infection in African American women is eight times the rate in white women)).

[269] Cook *et al* (n 265) 47. The authors note, more specifically, that 'The magnitude of the problem of infertility will not be ameliorated except by a reduction of sexually transmitted diseases (STDs), by safer births that avoid post-partum infection, and by decreasing the need for the resort to unsafe abortion practices'. See also Rebecca J Cook and Mohammed F Fathalla, 'Advancing Reproductive Rights Beyond Cairo and Beijing' (1996) 22 *International Family Planning Perspectives* 115, 119–20.

[270] Cook *et al* (n 265) 19.

factors that act as determinants of reproductive health: 'providence, people, politicians, and providers of health services'.[271] These four factors also determine, to a large extent, one's capacity to exercise reproductive autonomy.

From a political perspective, law and policy have obvious implications for reproductive autonomy, and so can healthcare systems, institutions and providers. A contextualised understanding of reproductive autonomy lends itself to recognising this important connection between reproductive health and reproductive autonomy, and to seeking solutions that will improve both. In the chapter that follows, I explore in more detail the context in which reproductive decision making takes place, and I sketch out a framework that focuses on women's reproductive needs and interests.

---

[271] *Ibid* 18.

3

Theory to Practice: Respecting Reproductive Autonomy

I N THE FOREGOING chapter, I outlined a theoretical foundation for the idea of reproductive autonomy. I argued that reproductive autonomy must be a focal point in regulating reproduction, given the critical impact that reproductive decisions can have on one's life, including one's ability to live an autonomous life. While the discussion in that chapter illustrates that the nature of precisely what it means to be an autonomous person and to live an autonomous life is far from settled, it is clear that one must have the capacity, together with some accompanying social conditions, to be the author of one's own life story.

I have also argued in favour of an inclusive approach to reproductive autonomy to guide policy development and legal decision making in the context of reproductive regulation. I now turn to considering what that means in terms of translating our understanding of reproductive autonomy into a regulatory approach that demonstrates respect for reproductive autonomy. Ideally, respect for reproductive autonomy requires the adoption of an explicit, comprehensive policy framework aimed at creating conditions in which reproductive choice can be exercised meaningfully. This ideal is not achievable – the scope of law and policy around reproductive decision making is vast, encompassing too many areas and involving too many actors for this to be a manageable goal. That said, I think it is critical that we develop a thoughtful and attentive approach to reproductive law and policy that seeks to ensure that reproductive autonomy is respected. As I note in chapter one, an important step in this endeavour is the creation of a national reproductive health strategy to create space for consideration of the issues by those with expertise in healthcare, ethics, law and policy.

I have argued that reproductive autonomy should be understood in a deeply contextualised way, and the first section of this chapter addresses the context of reproductive decision making. After highlighting the contextual backdrop to reproductive decision making, particularly in terms of the context of women's reproductive lives, I argue that a framework to guide law and policy that respects reproductive autonomy should take a specific shape. This framework, though not demanded by, is certainly supportable on the basis of a contextualised understanding of reproductive autonomy, and places reproductive decisions engaging women's bodily integrity at its core. I conclude with some brief comments on the nature of the interest in reproductive autonomy and the question of whether there is (or should be) a right to reproductive autonomy.

I. REGULATION AND RESPECT FOR REPRODUCTIVE AUTONOMY

A. The context of reproductive autonomy: women's reproductive lives

Currently, reproductive activities and decisions are regulated in a fragmentary and incoherent way. Regulation may be described as *ad hoc*, in that decisions are made as issues arise for consideration. An *ad hoc* approach to reproductive regulation fails adequately to protect reproductive autonomy because it adopts no particular direction for the development of law or policy, let alone one based on an ethic of respect for individual choice in reproductive matters. Indeed, it appears actively to avoid the adoption of a coordinated, thoughtful approach to policy making. With no policy aim, agenda or direction, we have nothing against which to measure progress, and no ability or metric to figure out how we might work toward achieving policy goals. Clearly, it is neither possible nor desirable to specify a uniform approach to all of the myriad questions that arise in relation to reproductive autonomy. My aim here is to start to formulate a framework for policy making – in other words, a method or approach to sorting out how to answer these questions.

The socially grounded, context-dependent idea of autonomy I outlined in the previous chapter asks us to take women's needs and interests into account in valuing or respecting reproductive autonomy. Context is particularly important in reproductive decision making, and helps to highlight the ways in which women's reproductive autonomy is distinctly affected by social realities and constraints. When law and policy fail to respect reproductive autonomy, although it is problematic for women and men alike, it is particularly troubling for women. Reproduction can have dramatically different effects on the lives of men and women. Reproduction takes place in a context within which women's bodies, needs and interests have a central role. Reproductive activity is literally located within women's bodies. As a result, women's lives intersect with medicine and law in the reproductive context more frequently and more variably than do men's lives. This means that a fragmentary and unreflective approach to reproductive regulation has uneven effects on women and men. Women's capacity for reproductive autonomy is also tied much more intimately to reproductive health than is the case for men. Women's ability to be autonomous in reproductive decision making depends on their level of reproductive health, as well as the accessibility of reproductive health services and the structure of the healthcare system.

An integrated and coherent policy approach to the regulation of reproduction is demanded by women's reproductive needs and interests. Separating abortion policy from reproductive health policy, contraceptive policy or ART policy engenders a situation in which it is easy to lose sight of how various laws and policies can interact to the detriment of women's interests. Abortion law and policy in the US is an interesting example of this very problem. The US Constitution grants women a fundamental right to privacy, within the scope of which they are entitled to make decisions about whether to terminate a pregnancy,[1] yet federal and some state policies prevent public funding for abortion services. In fact, current legal policy in many American jurisdictions is apparently aimed at getting as close as possible to, but not overstepping, the line between placing obstacles in

---

[1] US Const amend XIV.

the way of women seeking abortion services and creating an 'undue burden' on women's exercise of their privacy rights.[2]

As a result of their biological role in reproduction, women in their reproductive years bear a disproportionate share of the global burden of sexual and reproductive health conditions.[3] This burden includes medical as well as non-medical costs to women that result from reproductive and sexual health conditions, as well as from lack of control over reproduction. The medical costs of unwanted pregnancy are weighty, and include complications of pregnancy and childbirth;[4] risk of infection, infertility and death due to unsafe abortion; and infant death or ill health.[5] And the personal, economic and social costs can be equally profound. Women who are unable to control their fertility and who therefore have mistimed or unwanted pregnancies face more limited life options, because they have fewer opportunities for education and training, and for paid work.[6] Put concisely, women pay in all sorts of ways when they are unable to exercise reproductive autonomy, including, sometimes, with their lives. Research demonstrates that when women can control the timing of their pregnancies and the spacing of their children, they are more likely to enter or remain in educational programs, and therefore are more likely to have better employment prospects and to be able to participate more fully in social and political life in their communities.[7] The connection between meaningful reproductive choice and improved life prospects is bidirectional. The more life opportunities women have, the more likely they are to become further empowered to take charge of their own reproductive lives.[8]

Women also suffer a disproportionate impact from the ongoing politicisation of women's reproductive health.[9] In addition to the added vulnerability to reproductive

---

[2] *Planned Parenthood of Pennsylvannia v Casey*, 505 US 833 (1992). And in others, it is aimed at realising a reversal of the United States Supreme Court decision in *Roe v Wade*, 410 US 113 (1973). A number of states have passed legislation that would prohibit abortion in all but the most limited circumstances, in anticipation of the potential reversal of *Roe v Wade* by the US Supreme Court (Louisiana (Title 40, Public Health and Safety, RS 40:1299.30); South Dakota (SD Codified Laws § 22-17-5.1(2011))). Mississippi and North Dakota have similar laws on the books as well (Guttmacher Institute, 'State Policies in Brief: Abortion Policy in the Absence of Roe' (1 August 2012), at <www.guttmacher.org/statecenter/spibs/spib_APAR.pdf>). Policy activity around abortion in the US has been intense in 2011 and 2012; this is discussed in more detail in ch 5.

[3] See, eg, United Nations Millennium Project, Task Force on Child Health and Maternal Health, *Who's Got the Power? Transforming Health Systems for Women and Children* (London, Earthscan, 2005). The Task Force refers to the global burden of sexual and reproductive health conditions as representing 17.8% of all Disability Adjusted Life Years (DALYs) lost, and notes that for women in their reproductive years (ages 15–44), the burden of these types of conditions is 31.8% of all DALYs lost (*ibid* 72).

[4] See, eg, Rebecca J Cook, Bernard M Dickens and Mahmoud F Fathalla, *Reproductive Health and Human Rights: Integrating Medicine, Ethics, and Law* (Oxford, Oxford University Press, 2003) 22–33.

[5] UN Millennium Project (n 3) 72.

[6] Susan A Cohen, 'The Broad Benefits of Investing in Sexual and Reproductive Health' (2004) 7(1) *Guttmacher Report on Public Policy* 5; Heather Boonstra, 'The Impact of Government Programs on Reproductive Health Disparities: Three Case Studies' (2008) 11(3) *Guttmacher Policy Review* 6; Susan A Cohen, 'Family Planning and Safe Motherhood: Dollars and Sense' (2010) 13(2) *Guttmacher Policy Review* 12. This lack of opportunity, in turn, can also have impacts on society more generally, related to economic and social development (Susheela Singh *et al*, *Adding it Up: The Costs and Benefits of Investing in Family Planning and Maternal and Newborn Health* (New York, Guttmacher Institute and the United Nations Population and Development Fund, 2009)).

[7] Cohen, 'Family Planning and Safe Motherhood' (n 6).

[8] Rebecca J Cook, 'International Human Rights and Women's Reproductive Health' (1993) 24(2) *Studies in Family Planning* 73, 83.

[9] This is particularly the case in the US, where politics and ideology play a significant role in shaping public health policy. The Food and Drugs Administration's (FDA's) 2004 decision not to make emergency contraception available without a physician's prescription in direct contradiction of the recommendations of their scientific experts is just one example. Another is the Bush administration's 'abstinence only' policy in relation to

health and non-medical problems alike that comes from being female, women face restrictions on access to needed reproductive health services due to ideological forces that shape the political landscape.[10] Nowhere is this more striking than in the US, where, although women have a constitutional right to abortion, restrictions on access continue to multiply (including laws that require parental consent for minors who seek abortion services, restrictions on insurance coverage of abortion, mandatory waiting periods, mandatory counseling).[11] The Affordable Care Act,[12] a policy initiative of the Obama Administration, will radically alter the American healthcare system. One of the focal points for political debate respecting this legislation is the inclusion of funding for many preventative health services that are critical to women's health – including contraception.[13] The reach of the political heat around reproductive decision making also extends far beyond America's national boundaries. For four decades, US policy has placed obstacles before women in developing countries who depend on foreign financial aid for the availability of reproductive health services. The Helms Amendment bars the use of US foreign assistance funding in the provision of abortion services.[14] For many years the US also restricted access to services and information through the 'global gag rule'[15] which precluded foreign organisations in receipt of USAID funding to deliver family planning services from providing information about the availability of legal abortion.[16]

Canadian initiatives in foreign assistance have also come under fire. In 2010, prior to hosting a G8 summit meeting, the Canadian Government announced its maternal and child health program.[17] The Canadian initiative targets improving maternal and child health and reducing maternal, newborn and child mortality. It calls for action by the G8 nations on interventions that comprehend the continuum of care. The scope of such interventions has been acknowledged to include 'antenatal care; post-partum care; family planning, which includes contraception; reproductive health; treatment and prevention of diseases; prevention of mother-to-child transmission of HIV; immunizations;

HIV prevention: see, eg, Adrienne Germain, 'Playing Politics with Women's Lives' (2004) 305 *Science* 17; Cynthia Rothschild, 'Abstinence Goes Global: The US, the Right Wing, and Human Rights' in Gilbert Herdt and Cymene Howe (eds), *21st Century Sexualities: Contemporary Issues in Health, Education, and Rights* (New York, Routledge, 2007) 178.

[10] See, eg, Shereen El Feki, 'The Birth of Reproductive Health: A Difficult Delivery' (2004) 1(1) *Public Library of Science Medicine* 010.

[11] Current law and policy on abortion are discussed in more detail in ch 5. In the contraception context, the FDA's intransigence on non-prescription access to emergency contraception provides a particularly frightening example of the extent to which ideology can drive science policy (Miriam Schuchman, 'Stalled US Plan for Plan B' (2005) 173 *Canadian Medical Association Journal* 1437; Alastair JJ Wood, Jeffrey M Drazen and Michael F Greene, 'A Sad Day for Science at the FDA' (2005) 353 *New England Journal of Medicine* 1197).

[12] Patient Protection and Affordable Care Act of 2010, Pub L No 111–148, 124 Stat 119, as amended by the Health Care and Education Reconciliation Act of 2010, Pub L No 111–152, 124 Stat 1029 (codified as amended throughout 42 USC).

[13] *Ibid* § 2953 (codified at 42 USC § 713 (2011)). The exemption from participation for religious employers has been a significant political issue (R Alta Charo, 'Warning: Contraceptive Drugs May Cause Political Headaches' (2012) 366 *New England Journal of Medicine* 1361; John Halsey, 'The Shortcomings of Contemporary Political Rhetoric' (2012) 8(2) *Pitt Political Review* 9, 11).

[14] Susan A Cohen, 'US Overseas Family Planning Program, Perennial Victim of Abortion Politics, Is Once Again Under Siege' (2011) 14(4) *Guttmacher Policy Review* 7.

[15] See, eg, El Feki (n 10) 012; Germain (n 9).

[16] Germain (n 9). The 'gag rule' has since been rescinded by President Barack Obama (Rob Stein and Michael Shear, 'Funding Restored to Groups That Perform Abortions, Other Care', *Washington Post*, 24 January 2009, at <www.washingtonpost.com/wp-dyn/content/article/2009/01/23/AR2009012302814.html>).

[17] Paul Christopher Webster, 'Nutrition and Integrated Health Care to Highlight Canadian Plan to Fight Child and Maternal Mortality, Minister Says' (2010) 182 *Canadian Medical Association Journal* E397.

and nutrition,'[18] as well as initiatives focused on water sanitation and equality for women. There is no disagreement as to the urgency of the need for or the potential benefits of taking comprehensive action to improve maternal and child health, and Canada has been recognised as a leader for its commitment to these issues. Yet almost as quickly as the initiative was announced by the Harper Government, questions were raised as to whether the Government's notion of 'family planning' included access to abortion.[19] The initiative drew harsh criticism for excluding abortion from its definition of family planning, as maternal health cannot be achieved without reproductive health, and that, in turn, entails access to legal and safe abortion.[20] Editors at *The Lancet* went so far as to call the move 'hypocritical and unjust',[21] noting that the Canadian Government provides Canadian women with access to safe abortion services and yet refused – for solely political reasons – to include such services in its international intiative.

In addition to drawing our attention to the tightly-woven connection between reproductive autonomy and reproductive health, a contextualised approach to reproductive autonomy insists that we consider the extent to which reproductive decision making implicates women's relationships, both personal and public. Women make reproductive decisions within a network of relationships – their intimate relationships with a partner and with other family members (including children), their relationships with healthcare providers (physicians, nurses, midwives and others) and their relationships with the healthcare system. All of these relationships have the potential to influence women's decisions about reproductive matters. In situations where a woman's male partner is opposed to having children, her sexual, contraceptive and possibly abortion-related behaviours will be, at least in part, determined by his lack of interest in reproducing. Where a woman feels that her existing children would suffer by the addition of more children to her family, her reproductive decisions will undoubtedly be shaped by this concern.[22] Her physician's attitude may also have a profound impact on a woman's reproductive choices. A 2003 report of the Canadian Abortion Rights Action League (CARAL) relates the story of a woman in New Brunswick who was told by her family physician that not only would he not refer her to another provider for an abortion, but that if he found out that she obtained an abortion, he would remove her and her family from his patient roster.[23] And lastly, the structure of the healthcare system can play an important role in shaping women's reproductive decisions. The accessibility of contraception (including emergency contraception), abortion and infertility treatment services

---

[18] 'G8 Development Ministers Meeting: Chair's Summary' (Canadian International Development Agency (CIDA), 28 April 2010), at <www.acdi-cida.gc.ca/INET/IMAGES.NSF/vLUImages/G8/$file/G8-DEV-MINISTERIAL-CHAIR_S-SUMMARY-28-APRIL-2010-EN.pdf>.

[19] 'No Abortion in Canada's G8 Maternal Health Plan', *CBC News*, 26 April 2010, at <www.cbc.ca/politics/story/2010/04/26/abortion-maternal-health.html>.

[20] Cohen, 'Family Planning and Safe Motherhood' (n 6) 15; 'Editorial: Canada's G8 Health Leadership' (2010) 375 *The Lancet* 1580; 'G8 Maternal Health Initiative Draws Flak', *CBC News*, 23 June 2010, at <www.cbc.ca/news/world/story/2010/06/23/g8-maternal-health-initiative.html>.

[21] 'Editorial: Canada's G8 Health Leadership' (n 20) 1580.

[22] The research on women's reasons for seeking abortion bear this out (Lawrence B Finer *et al*, 'Reasons U.S. Women Have Abortions: Quantitative and Qualitative Perspectives' (2005) 37 *Perspectives on Sexual and Reproductive Health* 110, 116; Maggie Kirkman *et al*, 'Reasons Women Give for Abortion: A Review of the Literature' (2009) 12 *Archives of Women's Mental Health* 365).

[23] Canadian Abortion Rights Action League, *Protecting Abortion Rights in Canada: A Special Report to Celebrate the 15th Anniversary of the Decriminalization of Abortion* (Ottawa, Canadian Abortion Rights Action League, 2003) 24.

can determine what steps a woman must go through in order to access reproductive health services, and indeed whether she is able to access the services at all.

As is clear from the foregoing, women's reproductive decision making and reproductive health are interdependent, and both, in turn, are heavily influenced by social context. Reproductive healthcare, according to the International Conference on Population and Development (ICPD) Programme of Action, includes

> family-planning counselling, information, education, communication and services; education and services for prenatal care, safe delivery and post-natal care, especially breast-feeding and infant and women's health care; prevention and appropriate treatment of infertility; abortion . . . including prevention of abortion and the management of the consequences of abortion; treatment of reproductive tract infections; sexually transmitted diseases and other reproductive health conditions; and information, education and counselling, as appropriate, on human sexuality, reproductive health and responsible parenthood.[24]

This list of interventions aimed at improving reproductive health illustrates the many points in a woman's life at which her reproductive health needs are identical to her basic health needs. The conclusion that we must take reproductive health into account in considering reproductive autonomy is inescapable. I do not mean to suggest that all reproductive needs are medical needs – far from it. But it is essential to recognise the close connection between women's social and political circumstances (as individuals and collectively), and their ability to access reproductive health services and exert some measure of control over their own reproductive lives.

For women in their childbearing years, reproductive health is inextricably connected to overall health.[25] The importance of accessible, good quality reproductive healthcare to women's health cannot be over-emphasised. Access to reproductive health services can lead to improved access to other types of healthcare and related services.[26] Maternal mortality remains an enormous challenge in the developing world: estimates indicate that between 342,900 and 550,000 women died as a result of pregnancy or pregnancy management in 2008.[27] Approximately 60,000 to 70,000 maternal deaths each year are caused by unsafe abortion.[28] In addition, each year, millions of women suffer from pregnancy-related illness or disability.[29] Maternal health is also critical to child health and development, in that where a mother dies or becomes ill, her children's health and development suffer.[30]

---

[24] 'Programme of Action of the International Conference on Population and Development', UN International Conference on Population and Development (ICPD) (Cairo, 5–13 September 1994) UN Doc A/CONF.171/13/Rev.1, Ch VII, Art 7.6.

[25] As noted by Anand Grover (UN Special Rapporteur), 'The right to sexual and reproductive health is an integral component of the right to health' ('Interim Report of the Special Rapporteur on the Right of Everyone to the Enjoyment of the Highest Attainable Standard of Physical and Mental Health' (3 August 2011) UN Doc A/66/254, 4).

[26] Cohen, 'Family Planning and Safe Motherhood' (n 6) 14.

[27] These estimates come from two studies based on different methodologies, and there remains significant uncertainty about the accuracy of the figures, but the authors of the study that arrived at the lower estimate (342,900) are confident that their methods have led to a more accurate figure (Margaret C Hogan *et al*, 'Maternal Mortality for 181 Countries, 1980–2008: A Systematic Analysis of Progress Toward Millennium Development Goal 5' (2010) 375 *The Lancet* 1609). The larger estimate is drawn from World Health Organization data (Singh *et al* (n 6) 6).

[28] Hogan *et al* (n 27); Anthony D Falconer *et al*, 'Scaling Up Human Resources for Women's Health' (2009) 116 (Supp 1) *BJOG: An International Journal of Obstetrics and Gynaecology* 11.

[29] World Health Organization, *The World Health Report 2005 – Make Every Mother and Child Count* (Geneva, 2005); Véronique Filippi *et al*, 'Maternal Health in Poor Countries: The Broader Context and a Call for Action' (2006) 368 *The Lancet* 1535, 1536.

[30] Filippi *et al* (n 29).

As important as it is to note the close tie between reproductive health and women's (reproductive) autonomy, it is also essential to acknowledge the dangers in asserting this close connection, given the potential for the further medicalisation or 'healthicization'[31] of women's lives. The relationship between women's health and reproduction is complex and multi-faceted, and the boundaries between the social and medical aspects of procreation are neither sharp nor clear.

The phenomenon of medicalisation in relation to women's health is wide-ranging. Many issues in women's social lives have become medicalised, including domestic abuse, lesbianism, eating disorders and reproductive issues, including 'childbirth, birth control, infertility, abortion, menopause and PMS'.[32] As Susan Sherwin notes, medicalisation of women's lives has created 'double-binds' for women, in that it has led to the '[characterization] as pathological various bodily and mental states that are typical of women'.[33] But as feminist writers have also acknowledged, medicalisation is sometimes the result of women's health advocacy – this advocacy does not uniformly resist medicalisation but seeks to make medicalisation work for women. In some instances this means resisting medicalisation; in others, it means working to demand or change medicalisation.[34]

The ICPD Programme of Action defines reproductive health comprehensively to include 'physical, mental and social well-being'.[35] There are risks in defining reproductive health so broadly that it purports to include 'social health'. Indeed, some have argued that, in order to prevent the extension of medical authority into the more value-laden contexts of mental and social health, definitions of health and illness should be limited to physical matters, where value judgements are more clearly grounded in physiologic norms.[36] And while feminists generally share these concerns about expanding the sphere of medical influence and authority, the feminist position on defining health broadly is (unsurprisingly) not uniform.

---

[31] Peter Conrad refers to the process of 'healthicization' as the characterisation of social or behavioural activities as 'medical risks for well-established biomedical conditions' (Peter Conrad, 'Medicalization and Social Control' (1992) 18 *Annual Review of Sociology* 209, 223). He contrasts 'healthicization' and 'medicalization' as follows: 'With medicalization, medical definitions and treatments are offered for previous social problems or natural events; with healthicization, behavioral and social definitions are advanced for previously biomedically defined events . . . Medicalization proposes biomedical causes and interventions; healthicization proposes lifestyle and behavioral causes and interventions. One turns the moral into the medical, the other turns health into the moral.' See also Faith T Fitzgerald, 'The Tyranny of Health' (1994) 331 *New England Journal of Medicine* 196.

[32] Conrad (n 31) 222. See also Susan Sherwin, *No Longer Patient: Feminist Ethics and Health Care* (Philadelphia, PA, Temple University Press, 1992) 179.

[33] Sherwin (n 32) 180. Sherwin cites the examples of the presence or absence of menstruation, 'being too fat or too thin, eating too much or too little' and exercising insufficiently or excessively as areas into which medical authority has insinuated itself by claiming that all of these states evidence ill-health (*ibid* 179). Further, Sherwin notes that behavioural norms of femininity are characterised by mental health providers as 'unhealthy' for adults.

[34] See, eg, Wendy Mitchinson, 'Agency, Diversity, and Constraints: Women and Their Physicians, Canada, 1850–1950' in Susan Sherwin *et al* (eds), *The Politics of Women's Health: Exploring Agency and Autonomy* (Philadelphia, PA, Temple University Press, 1998) 122, 132–33 (describing the adoption of twilight sleep during labour and childbirth; as Mitchinson notes, women demanded twilight sleep, but the result of their successful demand 'was in some respects a diminishment of their involvement in childbirth'); Kathryn Pauly Morgan, 'Contested Bodies, Contested Knowledges: Women, Health, and the Politics of Medicalization' in Susan Sherwin *et al* (eds) (*ibid*) 83, 110–11.

[35] 'Programme of Action' (n 24) Art 7.2.

[36] See, eg, Daniel Callahan, 'The WHO Definition of Health' (1973) 1(3) *Hastings Center Report* 77; Christopher Boorse, 'On the Distinction Between Disease and Illness' (1975) 5 *Philosophy & Public Affairs* 49.

Although sympathetic to concerns about 'the worldview that imagines personal lives can be neatly fragmented into physical, mental and social components',[37] Laura Purdy maintains that the notion of social health should be excised from definitions of health to avoid its potentially dangerous applications,[38] and argues that the 'useful work' that can be done by a concept of social health can also be achieved in its absence. Purdy claims that even absent a notion of 'individual "social health" ', we can make the necessary connections between physical or mental disease and 'social arrangements'.[39] Further, she prefers the use of moral or political language to achieve the same end, without medicalising social issues such as domestic abuse; she asserts that we can avert the extension of medical authority into areas where its practitioners have no claim to specialised knowledge or expertise.[40]

Though she recognises the risk in subscribing to a definition of health that might further expand and entrench medical authority in women's lives, Susan Sherwin sees the need for a broad definition of health in more pragmatic terms. As she explains, the ideal solution for feminists would involve 'development of means to respond to the many different kinds of human need, without having to force every sort of problem into the medical model'.[41] But until such social change is effected, Sherwin argues in favour of maintaining a broad definition of health. In part, this is based on the concrete reality that health tends to be the only foundation on which the State can be motivated to support those in need.[42] Sherwin's reasoning is particularly persuasive in the reproductive health context.[43] In the short term, at least, there may be much to be gained by working from the position that women's reproductive health demands respect for women's reproductive autonomy. We must, however, do so thoughtfully, given the complicated and potentially negative interactions between medical authority and women's lives.

B. The foundation: women's bodily integrity

In addition to advocating a comprehensive approach to reproductive autonomy in law and policy, I want to propose a focal point for, or core of, the idea of reproductive autonomy. That core is located, to my mind, in women's bodily integrity. For the sake of clarity, by bodily integrity, I mean one's ability to decide what will be done with and to one's body.[44] This definition acknowledges the relation between bodily integrity and

---

[37] Sherwin (n 32) 193.
[38] Laura Purdy, 'A Feminist View of Health' in Susan M Wolf (ed), *Feminism & Bioethics: Beyond Reproduction* (New York, Oxford University Press, 1996) 163, 166–67. Purdy cites, in particular, the example of Samuel A Cartwright (Samuel A Cartwright, 'Report on the Diseases and Physical Peculiarities of the Negro Race' in Arthur L Caplan, James J McCartney and Dominic A Sisti (eds), *Health Disease and Illness: Concepts in Medicine* (Washington, DC, Georgetown University Press, 2004) 28).
[39] Purdy (n 38) 166.
[40] *Ibid.*
[41] Sherwin (n 32) 194.
[42] *Ibid.*
[43] *Ibid* 179–200.
[44] There are, of course, other possible understandings of bodily integrity that extend the concept to include notions of the inalienability of certain bodily parts or substances: see, eg, Cynthia B Cohen, 'Selling Bits and Pieces of Humans to Make Babies: *The Gift of the Magi* Revisited' (1999) 24 *Journal of Medicine and Philosophy* 288; Suzanne Holland, 'Contested Commodities at Both Ends of Life: Buying and Selling Gametes, Embryos, and Body Tissues' (2001) 11 *Kennedy Institute of Ethics Journal* 263. For a critique, see Carolyn McLeod and Françoise Baylis, 'Feminists on the Inalienability of Human Embryos' (2006) 21(2) *Hypatia* 1. For an ongoing interest in one's personal health information, see, eg, *McInerney v MacDonald* [1992] 2 SCR 138,

autonomy, in that it adopts a perspective that includes the individual's interest in being secure from violations of the body by others, and in being able to control, or determine the actions of, her own body.[45]

The articulations of the legal underpinnings of reproductive autonomy reside in cases involving questions closely related to women's bodily integrity.[46] The cases on abortion, sterilisation and contraception all focus to some extent on the implications of the reproductive law or policy at issue for bodily integrity. They also recognise the significance of bodily integrity from an emotional or psychological (as opposed to simply physical) perspective.[47] As then Chief Justice Dickson put it in *R v Morgentaler*:

> At the most basic, physical and emotional level, every pregnant woman is told by the section that she cannot submit to a generally safe medical procedure that might be of clear benefit to her unless she meets criteria entirely unrelated to her own priorities and aspirations. Not only does the removal of decision-making power threaten women in a physical sense; the indecision of knowing whether an abortion will be granted inflicts emotional stress. Section 251 [of the Criminal Code] clearly interferes with a woman's bodily integrity in both a physical and emotional sense. Forcing a woman, by threat of criminal sanction, to carry a foetus to term unless she meets certain criteria unrelated to her own priorities and aspirations, is a profound interference with a woman's body and thus a violation of security of the person.[48]

126 NBR (2d) 271, 148 (cited to SCR) (La Forest J), where medical records are referred to as 'information that goes to the personal integrity and autonomy of the patient'. See also Timothy Caulfield and Nola M Ries, 'Consent, Privacy and Confidentiality in Longitudinal, Population Health Research: The Canadian Legal Context' (2004) Special Supp *Health Law Journal* 1, 24–26. In addition, from a psychoanalytic standpoint, it has been argued that the right to bodily integrity has not only physical, but also social and symbolic aspects, that demand attention. Drucilla Cornell has argued that individuation demands that a subject be permitted both to 'project . . . bodily integrity' and to have it be recognised by others (Drucilla Cornell, 'Bodily Integrity and the Right to Abortion' in Austin Sarat and Thomas R Kearns (eds), *Identities, Politics, and Rights* (Ann Arbor, University of Michigan Press, 1995) 21, 27). She explains that, for example, 'The denial of the right to abortion should be understood as a serious symbolic assault on a woman's sense of self precisely because it thwarts her projection of bodily integration and places the woman's body in the hands and imaginings of others who would deny her coherence by separating her womb from her self'. Lastly, for argument and critique relating to the law's approach to the notion of bodily integrity and its dependence on the 'normative physical body that occupies a bounded space', see Kristin Savell, 'Sex and the Sacred: Sterilization and Bodily Integrity in English and Canadian Law' (2004) 49 *McGill Law Journal* 1093.

[45] See, eg, *Ciarliariello v Schachter* [1993] 2 SCR 119, 100 DLR (4th) 609, 135 (cited to SCR): 'It should not be forgotten that every patient has a right to bodily integrity. This encompasses the right to determine what medical procedures will be accepted and the extent to which they will be accepted. Everyone has the right to decide what is to be done to one's own body. This includes the right to be free from medical treatment to which the individual does not consent. This concept of individual autonomy is fundamental to the common law and is the basis for the requirement that disclosure be made to a patient. If, during the course of a medical procedure a patient withdraws the consent to that procedure, then the doctors must halt the process. This duty to stop does no more than recognize every individual's basic right to make decisions concerning his or her own body.' Wim Dekkers, Cor Hoffer and Jean-Pierre Wils refer to this approach to bodily integrity as a 'person-oriented' (as opposed to 'body-oriented'), and note that it has wide acceptance in law and medical ethics (Wim Dekkers, Cor Hoffer and Jean-Pierre Wils, 'Bodily Integrity and Male and Female Circumcision' (2005) 8 *Medicine, Health Care and Philosophy* 179, 183).

[46] See ch 1, section I.

[47] Cornell argues for an even broader, psychoanalytically-based understanding of bodily integrity, one that subsumes the concept of 'the process of integration' (Cornell (n 44) 22). Based on Lacan's account of individuation, Cornell envisions the conditions of individuation as 'social and symbolic' and asserts that the right to bodily integrity must encompass the right of each individual to 'project herself as whole over time'. Cornell claims that, given the significance of women's reproductive capacities to their bodily integrity, the abortion right is necessary for the 'minimum conditions of individuation necessary for any meaningful concept of self-hood'. See also Drucilla Cornell, *The Imaginary Domain: Abortion, Pornography and Sexual Harassment* (New York, Routledge, 1995) 94.

[48] *R v Morgentaler* [1988] 1 SCR 30, 63 OR (2d) 281, 56–57 (cited to SCR).

Even in cases considering the imposition of a tort law duty of care toward the fetus, some courts refer to the 'extensive and unacceptable intrusions into . . . bodily integrity' that would be occasioned by such a change in the law.[49] The extension of the notion of bodily integrity in this context is interesting, in that it acknowledges that reproductive decisions have implications for the quotidian as well as extraordinary aspects of women's lives. Imposing tort liability on women does not itself require any interference with the woman's person. All it demands is that she live up to a standard of careful behaviour in her conduct while she is pregnant. But, as the courts have recognised,

> this argument fails to take into account . . . [t]he unique relationship between a pregnant woman and her foetus . . . Everything the pregnant woman does or fails to do may have a potentially detrimental impact on her foetus. Everything the pregnant woman eats or drinks, and every physical action she takes, may affect the foetus. Indeed, the foetus is entirely dependent upon its mother-to-be . . . a pregnant woman's every waking and sleeping moment, in essence, her entire existence, is connected to the foetus she may potentially harm. If a mother were to be held liable for prenatal negligence, this could render the most mundane decision taken in the course of her daily life as a pregnant woman subject to the scrutiny of the courts.[50]

The notion that women's bodies and health are uniquely affected by reproductive technologies is explicitly recognised in Canadian ART legislation,[51] lending support to the argument that a policy approach to reproductive autonomy ought to take women's interests into account in a peculiarly meaningful way. Any harms caused by the techniques involved in assisted reproduction will be visited on women, not men. Women experience the discomforts and risks of fertility treatment, including the side-effects of the hormones used to suppress and stimulate ovulation,[52] the surgical procedures involved in extracting oocytes[53] and the hazards of multiple pregnancy as a result of assisted reproduction procedures.[54]

---

[49] *Dobson (Litigation Guardian of) v Dobson* [1999] 2 SCR 753, 214 NBR (2d) 201, para 23 (cited to SCR). See also *Stallman v Youngquist*, 125 Ill 2d 267 (1988). In *Stallman v Youngquist*, the Supreme Court of Illinois refused to recognise a claim in negligence by a fetus, subsequently born alive, against his or her mother for the unintentional infliction of pre-natal injuries caused by her negligent driving, holding that to impose such a duty would violate pregnant woman's rights to privacy and bodily integrity.

[50] *Dobson v Dobson* (n 49) para 27 (cited to SCR).

[51] Assisted Human Reproduction Act, SC 2004, c 2, s 2(c): 'The Parliament of Canada recognizes and declares that . . . (c) while all persons are affected by these technologies, women more than men are directly and significantly affected by their application and the health and well-being of women must be protected in the application of these technologies . . .'

[52] Ovarian hyperstimulation, a step in the IVF process, involves the administration of hormones to stimulate the ovaries to produce as many eggs as possible. Women who undergo ovarian stimulation often experience a form of ovarian hyperstimulation syndrome (OHSS), which can be mild (the ovaries become swollen and painful), moderate (accumulation of fluid in the abdomen or chest, which can lead to nausea, bloating and other gastrointestinal symptoms) or severe ('excessive weight gain, fluid accumulation in the abdomen and chest, electrolyte abnormalities, over-concentration of the blood, and rarely the development of blood clots or kidney failure') (*Assisted Reproductive Technologies: A Guide for Patients* (Birmingham, AL, American Society for Reproductive Medicine, 2011) 16). There is ongoing research into the related question of whether the use of fertility drugs can lead to increased risk of ovarian cancer.

[53] *Ibid.* These risks include bleeding, infection and the very rare possibility of damage to blood vessels or organs (including the uterus, bowel and bladder).

[54] PG Crosignani *et al*, 'Multiple Gestation Pregnancy' (2000) 15 *Human Reproduction* 1856. Concerns about multiple pregnancy have led to policy initiatives aimed at reducing the number of multiple gestation pregnancies caused by infertility treatment: see, eg, Peter Braude and the Expert Group on Multiple Births After IVF, *One Child at a Time: Reducing Multiple Births After IVF* (London, Human Fertilisation and Embryology Authority, 2006); Jason K Min, Paul Claman and Ed Hughes, 'Joint SOGC–CFAS Guideline No 182: Guidelines for the Number of Embryos to Transfer Following In Vitro Fertilization' (2006) 28 *Journal of Obstetrics and Gynaecology Canada* 799; Yakoub Khalaf *et al*, 'Selective Single Blastocyst Transfer Reduces the Multiple Pregnancy Rate and

The recognition of the singular role played by women in the reproductive process also accords with the Programme of Action adopted by the ICPD,[55] and with human rights approaches to reproductive health more generally.[56] The ICPD '[places] women at the centre of an integrated approach to reproduction',[57] population and development, and acknowledges the complex, interdependent nature of women's social status and roles, and their ability to exert control over their own reproductive capacities. Clearly, reproductive health and reproductive rights require a range of other rights beyond those concerned specifically with health:

> A woman's right to decide the number and spacing of her children depends upon her status, her ability to safeguard her own health and that of her family, and her right to act as an independent adult. It also depends on her ability to participate as a citizen in her community, to earn a living, to own and control property and to be free from discrimination on the basis of gender, race, class, and religion. Ultimately, reproductive choice is meaningful only when it is part of this full constellation of rights.[58]

The ICPD Programme of Action appears to recognise the ways in which culture and law are shaped by patriarchal assumptions about women and their capacity for roles other than motherhood. These underlying assumptions must be subverted in order for society to accept the need for reproductive rights for women. At the same time, the acceptance of such rights will further undermine the oppressive ideology that has led to the refusal to recognise reproductive autonomy and reproductive rights.[59] Indeed, it has been suggested that women's 'rights to liberty [and] security of the person . . . are unattainable without comprehensive, accessible, and affordable reproductive and sexual health services and the freedom to make decisions about their fertility and sexuality'.[60] The ICPD Programme of Action explicitly acknowledges the need to eliminate discrimination against women, and to empower women by promoting their full and equal participation in political, economic and social life.[61]

Increases Pregnancy Rates: A Pre- and Postintervention Study' (2008) 115 *BJOG: An International Journal of Obstetrics and Gynaecology* 385; American Society for Reproductive Medicine and Society for Assisted Reproductive Technology, 'Guidelines on Number of Embryos Transferred' (2009) 92 *Fertility and Sterility* 1518; Fertility Society of Australia Reproductive Technology Accreditation Committee, *Code of Practice for Assisted Reproductive Technology Units* (Melbourne, Fertility Society of Australia, 2010); 'One at a Time: Better Outcomes From Fertility Treatment' (*One at a Time*, 2012), at <www.oneatatime.org.uk/index.htm>.

[55] 'Programme of Action' (n 24) Art 7.2.

[56] See, eg, Cook (n 8); 'Economic, Social and Cultural Rights: The Right of Everyone to the Enjoyment of the Highest Attainable Standard of Physical and Mental Health – Report of the Special Rapporteur, Paul Hunt' (16 February 2004) UN Doc E/CN.4/2004/49.

[57] 'Economic, Social and Cultural Rights' (n 56) 5.

[58] Bharati Sadasivam, 'The Rights Framework in Reproductive Health Advocacy – A Reappraisal' (1997) 8 *Hastings Women's Law Journal* 313, 325.

[59] See, eg, Paula Abrams, 'Reservations about Women: Population Policy and Reproductive Rights' (1996) 29 *Cornell International Law Journal* 1, 2. As Abrams explains: 'Women have been valued historically for their capacity to bear children. Reproduction, along with other aspects of women's lives, has generally been controlled by men. One element of this control is the devaluation of women's judgment. The legal and cultural devaluation of women's reasoning ability creates substantial social ambivalence towards ceding reproductive autonomy to women. Further, the role assigned to women by patriarchal society – essentially of service to family, husband, and children – is antithetical to an image of woman as an individual entitled to self-determination.'

[60] Women's Coalition for the International Conference on Population and Development, 'Reproductive Health and Rights are Human Rights' (International Women's Health Coalition, 2001), at < http://www.iwhc. org/index.php?option=com_content&task=view&id=2483&Itemid=824>.

[61] 'Programme of Action' (n 24) Art 4.1. The article goes on to note: 'The power relations that impede women's attainment of healthy and fulfilling lives operate at many levels of society, from the most personal to the highly public.'

Not only is it the case that women experience reproduction and reproductive decision making differently than do men, women's reproductive capacity has long been a site of, and rationale for, women's oppression. [62] Women have historically been denied power because of their reproductive roles[63] and, what is more, 'Many of the social disadvantages to which women have been subjected have been predicated on their capacity for and role in childbearing'.[64] The history of reproductive regulation is a history of attempts to enforce a traditional view of women and their proper social roles. Nineteenth-century laws 'criminalizing contraception and abortion were explicitly premised on the view that women are "child-rearers"'[65] whose place is in the home, while men belong in the 'marketplace and the world of ideas'.[66]

Beyond the biological and social facts of reproduction are the social facts of child-rearing. While reproduction can have profound effects on the lives of men and women alike, its more profound and potentially negative consequences are largely lived by women. Women are responsible for the 'vast majority of the labor necessary to make infants into adults'[67] and women's status as mothers 'defines [their] identity, relations, and life prospects in diverse social arenas'.[68] Social scientists have long recognised that even when women work outside the home, they remain primarily responsible for the organisation and maintenance of the home.[69] They have also pointed to evidence of the impact motherhood (and motherwork[70]) can have on women's career prospects. Statistics illustrate this in graphic terms: 'it has been estimated that a woman with children in Britain loses as much as 57 percent of lifetime earnings after 25 compared to her childless counterpart.'[71] In the US, career interruptions as brief as one to two years exact significant penalties – 'women lose an average of 18% of their earning power when they take an off-ramp . . . Across sectors, women lose a staggering 37% of their earning power when they spend three or more years out of the workforce.'[72]

Given the clear and dramatic impact of reproduction on women's lives, and the asymmetrical effects it has on women and men, it is clear that respect for reproductive autonomy means different things to women than to men. A mistimed or unwanted preg-

---

[62] Cook (n 8) 83.

[63] In addition to being punished when they 'transgress . . . stereotype-driven norms' ('Interim Report of the Special Rapporteur' (n 25) 6).

[64] Catharine A MacKinnon, 'Reflections on Sex Equality Under Law' (1991) 100 *Yale Law Journal* 1281, 1308.

[65] Reva Siegel, 'Reasoning from the Body: A Historical Perspective on Abortion Regulation and Questions of Equal Protection' (1992) 44 *Stanford Law Review* 261, 356.

[66] Ibid, quoting *Mississippi University for Women v Hogan*, 458 US 718 (1982).

[67] Siegel (n 65) 375.

[68] Ibid 373. As MacKinnon puts it ((n 64) 1311–12): 'A narrow view of women's "biological destiny" has confined many women to childbearing and childrearing and defined all women in terms of it, limiting their participation in other pursuits, especially remunerative positions with social stature.'

[69] Most notable is Arlie Hochschild, *The Second Shift* (New York, London Books, 1989). A 2001 study confirms that things have not changed dramatically since Hochschild first identified the problem – '40% of highly qualified women with spouses felt that their husbands create more work around the house than they perform' (Sylvia Ann Hewlett and Carolyn Buck Luce, 'Off-Ramps and On-Ramps: Keeping Talented Women on the Road to Success' (2005) 83(3) *Harvard Business Review* 43, 44).

[70] I borrow this term from Lorna Turnbull, *Double Jeopardy: Motherwork and the Law* (Toronto, Sumach Press, 2001).

[71] Sandra Fredman, *Women and the Law* (Oxford, Clarendon Press, 1997) 180, referring to H Joshi and H Davies, *Childcare and Mothers' Lifetime Earnings: Some European Contrasts* (London, Centre for Economic Policy Research, 1992) 19. As Fredman notes ((n 71) 180): 'While women without children continue to make inroads into male-dominated occupations and professions, their counterparts with children are . . . severely restricted in the type of jobs and the level of pay available to them.'

[72] Hewlett and Luce (n 69) 46.

nancy is a very different matter for a woman than for a man, however sensitive and involved he may be.[73] The threat of forced medical intervention in pregnancy may anger and frustrate the male partner of a pregnant woman, but it will not violate *his* person or implicate *his* values in the same way that it will hers. Lack of timely access to emergency contraception may force a woman, not a man, to choose to terminate or proceed with an unwanted pregnancy. For all of these reasons, many feminists have advocated an approach to reproductive choice based on equality rather than privacy. The approach to reproductive autonomy I suggest here, based on a model that places women's bodily integrity at its centre, builds ideals of equality into the very idea of reproductive autonomy.[74]

The aim of grounding reproductive autonomy in women's bodily integrity is not to ignore or belittle the contribution men make to the procreative process; it is simply to recognise that the bodily integrity of men is generally not implicated in the process of reproduction (with the important exception of conception, when that is a result of sexual intercourse).

Placing decisions engaging women's bodily integrity at the core of reproductive autonomy creates, quite literally, a woman-centred model. The significance of this model is both practical and symbolic. In the practical sense, reproductive activity largely centres on women's bodies. When reproduction occurs as a result of sexual intercourse, fertilisation, implantation, pregnancy and childbirth take place in the woman's body. When reproduction involves the use of technologies such as IVF, artificial insemination, pre-natal diagnosis or pre-implantation genetic diagnosis, certain aspects of the process occur outside the woman's body. But even where she is not the infertile partner, infertility treatment revolves around her body.[75] Symbolically, placing the woman at the centre of discussions about reproductive autonomy will go some distance, if not all the way, to alleviating feminist concerns[76] around the use of reproductive technologies, and will

---

[73] As Siegel points out, the notional availability of giving up a child for adoption is not an option that many women choose, 'for the simple reason that few women are able to abandon a child born of their body' (Siegel (n 65) 371–72). She notes that women form emotional bonds with their future children through the course of pregnancy, and often feel substantial pressure to raise a child they have borne. For more in-depth discussion on women's experiences of adoption, see Anne B Brodzinsky, 'Surrendering an Infant for Adoption: The Birthmother Experience' in David M Brodzinsky and Marshall D Schechter (eds), *The Psychology of Adoption* (New York, Oxford University Press, 1993); Merry Bloch Jones, *Birthmothers: Women who have Relinquished Babies for Adoption Tell Their Stories* (Chicago, IL, Chicago Review Press, 1993); Ann Fessler, *The Girls Who Went Away: The Hidden History of Women Who Surrendered Children for Adoption in the Decades Before Roe v Wade* (New York, Penguin Press, 2006).

[74] For arguments relating to abortion as an equality right, see, eg, MacKinnon (n 64); Siegel (n 65); Catharine A MacKinnon, *Toward a Feminist Theory of the State* (Cambridge, MA, Harvard University Press, 1989) 246. For arguments related to the possibility of retaining privacy rights to abortion, with a focus on gender equality, see, eg, Anita L Allen, 'The Proposed Equal Protection Fix for Abortion Law: Reflections on Citizenship, Gender, and the Constitution' (1995) 18 *Harvard Journal of Law & Public Policy* 419, 421; Anita L Allen, 'Coercing Privacy' (1999) 40 *William and Mary Law Review* 723; Linda C McClain, 'Reconstructive Tasks For a Liberal Feminist Conception of Privacy' (1999) 40 *William and Mary Law Review* 759; Jack M Balkin (ed), *What* Roe v Wade *Should Have Said: The Nation's Top Legal Experts Rewrite America's Most Controversial Decision* (New York, NYU Press, 2005).

[75] See, eg, Gay Becker, *The Elusive Embryo: How Women and Men Approach New Reproductive Technologies* (Berkeley, University of California Press, 2000); Jane Haynes and Juliet Miller (eds), *Inconceivable Conceptions: Psychological Aspects of Infertility and Reproductive Technology* (Hove, Brunner-Routledge, 2003).

[76] These concerns exist on several levels, including the more general feminist concerns around liberal notions of choice: see, eg, MacKinnon (n 64); Robin L West, 'The Difference in Women's Hedonic Lives: A Phenomenological Critique of Feminist Legal Theory' (1987) 3 *Wisconsin Women's Law Journal* 81; Robin West, 'Jurisprudence and Gender' (1988) 55 *University of Chicago Law Review* 1; Joan Williams, 'Gender Wars: Selfless Women in the Republic of Choice' (1991) 66 *New York University Law Review* 1559; Catriona Mackenzie and Natalie Stoljar, 'Introduction: Autonomy Refigured' in Catriona Mackenzie and Natalie Stoljar (eds), *Relational Autonomy:*

highlight the need for a conception of reproductive autonomy that incorporates equality and social justice concerns. It will serve to remind us that, ultimately, women bear the corporeal burdens of both fertility and infertility. It will also acknowledge the centrality of the woman's physical body in respecting her choosing mind.

Grounding respect for reproductive autonomy on women's bodily integrity can also be justified on the basis of the instrumental value of women's reproductive autonomy. Marilyn Friedman explains that autonomy has both 'intrinsic' and 'instrumental value'.[77] That is, autonomy is valuable not only in and of itself, but also because it can foster other values; in particular, acknowledging one another's autonomy can help us to recognise that we are all morally equal.[78] As Friedman points out, practices and patterns of male dominance frustrate the realisation of women's autonomy and their moral equality.[79] In conditions of male dominance, men are more able to exercise their autonomy, and women are 'denied . . . respect for their moral competence'.[80] Ultimately, when those who are dominated or oppressed are able to act in accordance with their own values, their own moral competence is recognised and this, in turn, can promote the realisation of moral equality for all. Friedman argues that the autonomy of women living under conditions of male dominance is more valuable than that of men, given its potential to advance this important social goal.[81] We therefore 'all have good reason to advance women's autonomy whenever possible'.[82]

Traditionally, law and policy have not only privileged men's reproductive interests over those of women,[83] but have privileged the reproductive interests of wealthy men over poor men[84] and the interests of white men over those of men of colour.[85] If Friedman's claim is correct – that the autonomy of those who are oppressed is more valuable than of those who are dominant – then the explicit recognition of women's reproductive interests in respecting reproductive autonomy will arguably go some distance toward promoting social recognition of the reproductive equality of all persons.

Feminist Perspectives on Autonomy, Agency, and the Social Self (Oxford, Oxford University Press, 2000) 3. Feminist concerns have also been raised in relation to specific questions related to the regulation of reproduction, including the medicalisation of women's bodies, questions about women's social roles and the need for support for caregivers, to name just a few: see, eg, Morgan (n 34); Sherwin (n 32); Erin Nelson, 'Reconceiving Pregnancy: Expressive Choice and Legal Reasoning' (2004) 49 *McGill Law Journal* 593, 614.

[77] Marilyn Friedman, 'Autonomy and Male Dominance' in John Christman and Joel Anderson (eds), *Autonomy and the Challenges to Liberalism: New Essays* (Cambridge, Cambridge University Press, 2005) 150, 167.

[78] *Ibid.*

[79] *Ibid* 168. Friedman describes male dominance as a pervasive, universal phenomenon involving 'men's greater control . . . of resources and power and men's control of women's sexuality and reproduction' (*ibid* 151).

[80] *Ibid* 168.

[81] *Ibid* 169.

[82] *Ibid.*

[83] See, eg, Margaret Brazier, 'Reproductive Rights: Feminism or Patriarchy?' in John Harris and Søren Holm (eds), *The Future of Human Reproduction: Ethics, Choice, and Regulation* (Oxford, Clarendon Press, 1998) 66.

[84] The forced sterilisation of over a million people in India, many of whom were poor men, during the Emergency Period in the 1970s is one example: see, eg, Mohan Rao, *From Population Control to Reproductive Health: Malthusian Arithmetic* (New Dehli, SAGE, 2004) 45–49; Rajani Bhatia, 'Ten Years After Cairo: The Resurgence of Coercive Population Control in India' (Spring 2005) 31 *Different Takes* 1. A combination of factors led to the implementation of forced sterilisation practices in spite of the lack of official government sanction. States faced cuts in the financial aid received from the central government if they failed to reach sterilisation targets. To this end, the states put in place various incentives to promote sterilisation – government permits were withheld until a 'sterilisation certificate' was produced, school admission was denied to children whose parents had more than three children, and those who were displaced by 'slum clearance' were offered housing only if they agreed to be sterilised.

[85] Dorothy Roberts, *Killing the Black Body: Race, Reproduction and the Meaning of Liberty* (New York, Vintage, 1997) 66, 90.

Some might hesitate to agree with a broad approach to understanding reproductive autonomy;[86] the reason for this hesitation probably relates to the potential implications that including a particular kind of decision within reproductive autonomy might have for the State. We might be loath to include decisions about using high-tech treatments for infertility within the scope of reproductive autonomy, because that might preclude the State from regulating access to the use of the technology, or it might go even further and require the State to provide genuine access by covering some or all of the costs associated with the treatment. But this confuses the distinction between understanding and valuing reproductive autonomy. We can at once understand it broadly and yet not be committed to respecting every decision that engages reproductive autonomy in precisely the same way. In embracing an ethic of respect for reproductive autonomy, we are not necessarily opening the doors to all choices a person might wish to make. A commitment to respect reproductive autonomy means different things in different contexts. In other words, including a woman's right to use pre-implantation genetic diagnosis to choose embryos that will produce blue-eyed children within our understanding of reproductive autonomy does not necessarily commit us to granting that decision the same level of respect that we give to her right to terminate an unwanted pregnancy.

Instead of understanding reproductive autonomy as a monolithic concept,[87] it is helpful to adopt a more nuanced approach that comprehends reproductive autonomy as protecting a sphere of decision making that includes a wide variety of decisions. Within this broad sphere of protected decisions exist differential levels or zones of respect into which particular exercises of reproductive autonomy can be fit. Diagrammatically, we might conceptualise this as a series of concentric circles depicting these different zones of respect. All decisions that involve an exercise of reproductive autonomy will fit somewhere within this model, but that does not necessarily imply that all reproductive autonomy-related decisions are entitled to the same degree of respect.[88]

---

[86] Onora O'Neill argues that reproductive autonomy does not include 'rights to access' reproductive technologies, and she claims that reproductive autonomy (or autonomy, period) is not a solid foundation on which to base an entitlement to the use of reproductive technologies (Onora O'Neill, *Autonomy and Trust in Bioethics* (Cambridge, Cambridge University Press, 2002) 65). Others who would disagree with a broad approach are the feminist critics of reproductive autonomy referred to in ch 2.

[87] John A Robertson, *Children of Choice: Freedom and the New Reproductive Technologies* (Princeton, NJ, Princeton University Press, 1994) 17. Robertson notes that 'the reproductive interests claimed under the canopy of procreative liberty are not monolithic or unitary, but consist of a congeries of interests in procreating, avoiding procreation, having or not having a genetic connection, using one's reproductive apparatus, selecting or controlling offspring traits, and the like'.

[88] There is another reason, a practical reason, for taking a nuanced approach to valuing reproductive autonomy, and that is that there are different levels of comfort with a position of strong support for reproductive autonomy. The evolution of reproductive technologies has created increasingly complex questions and considerations surrounding the exercise of reproductive autonomy. This, in turn, might lead to a tempering of judicial willingness unequivocally to endorse an expansive view of reproductive autonomy. An example of this phenomenon is evident in the United States Supreme Court abortion jurisprudence: see, eg, *Maher v Roe*, 432 US 464 (1977). See also R Alta Charo, 'Children by Choice: Reproductive Technologies and the Boundaries of Personal Autonomy' (2002) 4 *Nature Cell Biology* S23. This potential for softening of support for an inclusive understanding of reproductive autonomy tells us that we need to find a new way to understand reproductive autonomy so that we can accord it the deference it demands. The risk in failing to come up with a new approach to reproductive autonomy is this: if popular and legal support for reproductive autonomy weakens in relation to decisions at the margins, then support for all of reproductive autonomy might become attenuated. If strong support for reproductive autonomy comes to be perceived as necessarily endorsing the use and availability of technologies that are not widely defended, the foundations of reproductive autonomy might weaken: see, eg, Ted G Jelen and Clyde Wilcox, 'Causes and Consequences of Public Attitudes Toward Abortion: A Review and Research Agenda' (2003) 56 *Political Research Quarterly* 489. Jelen and Wilcox suggest that attitudes toward abortion, which have remained remarkably stable over time, may begin to change as 'questions of biotechnology

From another angle, this means that decisions which form the core of reproductive autonomy are entitled to a maximal amount of respect and that concerns related to the entitlements or interests of others have very little bearing on decision making.[89] As we move toward the outer zones, an individual's decisions, while still entitled to respect, become slightly less compelling, and the concerns, rights, needs and interests of others may have more significance.

My aim in crafting this model is not only to help us to resolve some of the dilemmas relevant to exercises of reproductive autonomy, but primarily to point our inquiry in the right direction, particularly in the case of newer technologies or practices. In an area as complex, ethically charged and potentially broad as that of reproductive decision making, it is not possible to find a 'one size fits all' solution. Distinct considerations will animate the various areas of reproductive decision making where law, policy and healthcare become entangled, and distinct approaches may be required depending on the interests at stake. But it is nevertheless useful to approach these various questions and issues from a starting point that demands a focus on the needs and interests of women in the reproductive decision making context, while keeping in mind that finding a clear, principled solution to every possible reproductive autonomy dilemma is an elusive goal at best.

The contentious aspect of this model will of course be attempting to specify where each type of reproductive decision should fit, and determining how properly to value decisions at each level within the model. This will necessitate a thoughtful and balanced approach. Essentially, reproductive autonomy is an interest that is based on women's bodily integrity, and decisions implicating this aspect of reproductive autonomy are entitled to the utmost respect from the State. Such decisions require the State to provide conditions which optimally permit the exercise of this aspect of reproductive autonomy, meaning that State funding may legitimately be demanded to best respect autonomous decision making. As we move away from the woman's body, the interest diminishes in intensity; less deference will be required, and there will be more room to balance other interests against those of the individual seeking to assert her reproductive autonomy.

II. A RIGHT TO REPRODUCTIVE AUTONOMY?

As is borne out by both the theoretical discussion in the preceding chapter and by the more detailed examination of various topics in the chapters that follow, the nature of the interest in reproductive autonomy is unclear.[90] Is it a moral claim,[91] a legal right, a constitutional right, a right based on principles of international law or all of the above? Abortion is framed as a right, or at least having some 'rights' dimensions in Canada and

(including variations on human cloning) become increasingly prominent in public discourse. As different value choices come into play . . . and as different vested interests are created, it is difficult to imagine that abortion politics will not be transformed in some very basic ways.' (*ibid* 498)

[89] Unless, of course, the individual making the decision wishes to take the entitlements or interests of others into account.

[90] This question is further complicated as a result of the fact that it may be answered distinctly in each of the four jurisdictions being considered, as the legal and constitutional issues are somewhat distinct. Detailed consideration of the legal and constitutional underpinnings of the State will not be undertaken here; my purpose is simply to raise this issue for consideration.

[91] See, eg, Mary Warnock, *Making Babies: Is There a Right to Have Children?* (Oxford, Oxford University Press, 2002).

the US, in contrast to Australia and the UK. In the US jurisprudence around sterilisation of persons with intellectual disabilities, the courts have sometimes alluded to a fundamental right to procreate, but then proceeded to disregard the right for the purposes of the application before them.[92] In the course of deciding not to impose liability on a pregnant woman toward her fetus, the Supreme Court of Canada repeatedly referred to the fundamental privacy and autonomy rights of women without ever explicitly stating the foundation of those rights.[93] And in the ART regulation context, important interests are adverted to but are not necessarily referred to as 'rights'.[94]

While it is beyond the scope of this project to contemplate questions around the nature and dimensions of rights more broadly, and of whether the interest in reproductive autonomy can, for example, legitimately be characterised as a constitutional right, it is helpful to highlight some relevant considerations.

There is clear support for the assertion that reproductive autonomy is constitutionally protected,[95] and in some jurisdictions, aspects of reproductive autonomy have been found to have constitutional dimensions.[96] The wisdom of arguing that reproductive autonomy is constitutionally protected is obvious, particularly given historical examples of State action taken to abrogate reproductive autonomy, such as eugenics-based laws.[97] Case law in the United States certainly suggests the existence of a constitutional right to reproduce[98] and to avoid reproducing.[99] Even in cases considering the non-consensual sterilisation of intellectually disabled women, courts have opined that a person who is not capable of deciding whether to be sterilised has a constitutional right to the option. In *Re Valerie N*, the Supreme Court of California concluded that a statutory provision that prohibited the sterilisation of 'wards or conservatees' violated the privacy and liberty rights of these individuals.[100]

Canadian jurisprudence does not provide a definitive statement as to the nature of the interest in reproductive autonomy, but there are suggestions that at least some aspects of

---

[92] Roberta Cepko, 'Involuntary Sterilization of Mentally Disabled Women' (1993) 8 *Berkley's Women's Law Journal* 122, 133–35. See also discussion of *Secretary, Department of Health and Community Services v JWB and SMB (Marion's Case)* (1992) 175 CLR 218, in ch 1 and ch 4.

[93] *Dobson v Dobson* (n 49).

[94] And, indeed, in a number of cases, parties have had to litigate a matter to have their rights recognised: see, eg, the discussion on ART regulation in Australia (see ch 8, section III.B.). It should be noted that rights are referred to in s 2 of the Assisted Human Reproduction Act (n 51).

[95] In particular this is the case with respect to contraception and abortion (see ch 4 and ch 5 for more detailed discussion).

[96] Canada and the US both have 'bills of rights' within their Constitutions (Canadian Charter of Rights and Freedoms, Part I of the Constitution Act, 1982, being Schedule B to the Canada Act 1982 (UK), 1982, c 11; US Const amend I, II, III, IV, V, VI, VII, VIII, IX, X). In the UK, the Human Rights Act 1998 (UK) (together with the European Convention on Human Rights (ECHR) (European Convention on Human Rights and Fundamental Freedoms (adopted 4 November 1950, entered into force 3 December 1953) UNTS 213)) confers protection similar to that provided by a constitutional bill of rights. Australia is somewhat unique, in having neither a constitutional bill of rights, nor a general human rights law that protects similar rights. There have been attempts made in Australia to enact a statutory bill of rights, but to date this has not been successful other than in the State of Victoria (James Allan, 'You Don't Always Get What You Pay For: No Bill of Rights for Australia' (2010) 24 *New Zealand Universities Law Review* 179).

[97] Alberta has a particularly appalling history in this regard, see, eg, Timothy Caulfield and Gerald Robertson, 'Eugenic Policies in Alberta: From the Systematic to the Systemic?' (1996) 35 *Alberta Law Review* 59. For discussion of the eugenic past of the United States, see, eg, Roberts (n 85) 65–70; Robertson (n 87) 89–91.

[98] *Skinner v Oklahoma*, 316 US 535 (1942).

[99] See, eg, *Roe v Wade* (n 2); *Griswold v Connecticut*, 381 US 479 (1965); *Eisenstadt v Baird*, 405 US 438 (1972).

[100] *Re Valerie N*, 707 P 2d 760 (Cal 1985) 771.

reproductive autonomy (in particular, the right to abortion) are constitutionally protected. There is no case that specifically addresses the nature of the interest in reproductive autonomy, but aspects of the issue have been considered. For example, the Supreme Court of Canada's decision in *R v Morgentaler* considers the abortion issue.[101] *R v Morgentaler* does not recognise a right to abortion within section 7 of the Canadian Charter of Rights and Freedoms,[102] but a more limited right to access to abortion without arbitrary and unfair administrative obstacles. In *E (Mrs) v Eve*, Justice La Forest (for the Court) refused to permit non-consensual sterilisation of an apparently intellectually disabled woman, noting the 'growing legal recognition of the fundamental character of the right to procreate'.[103] Further, the courts have recognised a psychological dimension to the right to 'security of the person' enshrined in section 7, and have applied this aspect of section 7 in cases involving parental rights.[104]

Reproductive rights and, by implication, reproductive autonomy also have human rights dimensions.[105] The ICPD in Cairo in 1994 marked a turning point in the understanding of reproductive health as 'fundamental to individuals, couples and families, as well as to the social and economic development of communities and nations'.[106] In 2003, the United Nations Commission on Human Rights confirmed that 'sexual and reproductive rights are integral elements of the right of everyone to the enjoyment of the highest attainable standard of physical and mental health'.[107] Sources of rights related to reproductive health include Article 17 of the International Covenant on Civil and Political Rights (ICCPR) (freedom from arbitrary or unlawful interference with privacy or family),[108] Article 8 ECHR[109] (the right to respect for family life), Article 23 ICCPR and Article 12 ECHR (right to found a family), Article 16(1)(e) of the Convention on the Eradication of all forms of Discrimination Against Women (CEDAW)[110] (the right to determine the number and spacing of children) and Articles 12 and 24 of the International

---

[101] *R v Morgentaler* (n 48).

[102] Canadian Charter of Rights and Freedoms (n 96). It is possible that in the near future, the courts will have to address the question of a right to autonomy more directly; this is a central issue in *Carter v Canada (Attorney General)*, 2012 BCSC 886, [2012] BCJ No 1196 (the plaintiffs are arguing that the criminalisation of assisted suicide is unconstitutional).

[103] *E (Mrs) v Eve* [1986] 2 SCR 388, [1986] SCJ No 60, 419–20 (cited to SCR).

[104] See, eg, *New Brunswick (Minister of Health and Community Services) v G (J)* [1999] 3 SCR 46, 216 NBR (2d) 25. It is certainly arguable whether decisions relating to exercises of reproductive autonomy are akin to parenting decisions; my only aim in using the parenting cases is to provide an example involving considerations similar to those in a hypothetical case concerning an issue of reproductive autonomy. The psychological dimension of the right to security of the person was also significant to Dickson J's decision in *R v Morgentaler* (n 48).

[105] Cook (n 8). There have been feminist criticisms of the use of rights-based strategies in the reproductive health/rights context, based on concerns around the 'gender-blind nature of international law', the implementation of the CEDAW, and the location of reproductive rights 'within the family and conjugal union' which is for all intents and purposes a heterosexual partnership constituted along traditional patriarchal lines (Sadasivam (n 58) 325–28). See also Rebecca J Cook, 'Reservations to the Convention on the Elimination of All Forms of Discrimination Against Women' (1990) 30 *Virginia Journal of International Law* 643.

[106] 'Economic, Social and Cultural Rights' (n 56) para 7.

[107] 'Commission on Human Rights Resolution 2003/28: The Right of Everyone to the Enjoyment of the Highest Attainable Standard of Physical and Mental Health' (22 April 2003) UN Doc E/CN.4/RES/2003/28, Preamble, para 6.

[108] International Covenant on Civil and Political Rights (adopted 19 December 1966, entered into force 23 March 1976) 999 UNTS 171, Arts 17, 23.

[109] ECHR (n 96).

[110] Convention on the Elimination of All Forms of Discrimination Against Women (adopted 18 December 1979, entered into force 3 September 1981) 1249 UNTS 13, Art 16(1)(e).

Covenant on Economic, Social and Cultural Rights[111] (the right to health). There is also support for reproductive rights in the proceedings of the ICPD[112] and the Fourth World Conference on Women.[113] The statements of rights found in the various human rights conventions are broadly formulated, but have been interpreted in such a way as to recognise the propriety of some State-imposed limitations.[114]

Characterising the interest in reproductive autonomy as a legal or a constitutional right has significant implications, particularly in the context of legal claims, in the larger context of law and policy around matters of reproductive health and reproductive decision making. But the existence of a legal right as such is not essential to a conclusion that reproductive autonomy demands respect in law and policy.[115] The existence (or not) of a constitutional right is indisputably relevant, but even if there is no such right (or even if there is, but it only partially protects reproductive autonomy), good public policy should be based on respect for the individual interest in reproductive autonomy.

Although there is abundant support for the argument that persons have the right to make their own reproductive decisions, it is not necessary fully to articulate the contours of the right in order to delineate the State's responsibilities in terms of respecting reproductive autonomy. The State should respect and seek to foster reproductive autonomy, not simply because it can be characterised as a right or because the State could face legal challenge for its failure to do so, but because ultimately, autonomy (in general *and* in matters of reproduction) has instrumental value to the State. Only through respect for reproductive autonomy can women become full participants in social and civic life, and the ability of all persons to participate as full citizens is ultimately of benefit not just to individuals but to the State itself.

Even if there is a constitutional right to reproductive autonomy, the scope of the right itself might not be sufficiently comprehensive to create conditions for its meaningful exercise. American abortion jurisprudence is a clear example of this very problem. And while the Canadian Constitution protects a basic level of rights that may not be abrogated by the State,[116] little support can be found in existing jurisprudence for claims that would require positive State intervention.[117] Further, the existence of a

---

[111] International Covenant on Economic, Social and Cultural Rights (adopted 16 December 1966, entered into force 3 January 1976) UNGA Res 2200 (XXI).

[112] 'Programme of Action' (n 24).

[113] 'Fourth World Conference on Women: Beijing Declaration and Platform for Action' (17 October 1995) UN Doc A/CONF.177/20.

[114] Governments may create incentives or disincentives to influence reproductive choice, but 'cannot apply compulsion or coercive means' (Cook *et al* (n 4) 176).

[115] This, it seems, is along the lines of what Emily Jackson argues in saying '[t]he right to reproductive self-determination that I defend in this book is not an absolute right to, for example, have a baby or an abortion, rather it is a right to have one's reproductive choices treated with respect' (Emily Jackson, *Regulating Reproduction: Law, Technology and Autonomy* (Oxford, Hart Publishing, 2001) 9).

[116] As Justice Iacobucci has noted: '[T]he *Charter* is not an exhaustive catalogue of rights. Instead, it represents a bare minimum below which the law must not fall. A necessary corollary of this statement is that the law, whether by statute or common law, can offer protections beyond those guaranteed by the *Charter*.' (*R v Oickle*, 2000 SCC 38, [2000] 2 SCR 3, para 31)

[117] See, eg, Helen Hershkoff, 'Positive Rights and State Constitutions: The Limits of Federal Rationality Review' (1999) 112 *Harvard Law Review* 1131; Diana Majury, 'The *Charter*, Equality Rights, and Women: Equivocation and Celebration' (2002) 40 *Osgoode Hall Law Journal* 297, 330–31. There are exceptions: see, eg, *Eldridge v British Columbia (AG)* [1997] 3 SCR 624, (1997) 151 DLR (4th) 577 (where it was held that s 15 of the Charter was violated by British Columbia's failure to pay for sign language interpreters in the context of access to healthcare by deaf persons). See also *New Brunswick (Minister of Health and Community Services* (n 104), where it was held that s 7 of the Charter required the Government to provide state-funded counsel to a woman whose children the state sought to remove from the family home. Many scholars have argued in favour

legal right[118] may not fully answer questions about how the law should resolve conflicts between individuals where both have a right to reproductive autonomy and where the rights of both parties cannot be fully respected. In the context of disputes around the disposition of cryopreserved embryos, for example, the fact that each progenitor has a right to reproductive autonomy that must be respected does not itself provide any guidance as to how conflicts between the rights of the parties are to be resolved.[119]

To be sure, the question of rights is central to the State's task in regulating reproduction. Being able to assert a legal or constitutional right is of critical value in situations where State action threatens to restrict reproductive choice. But, as will be seen in the chapters that follow, many of the issues that arise in the context of reproductive autonomy while related to rights, do not necessarily directly implicate rights. And even where rights are in issue, particularly constitutional rights, the ultimate decision depends on a weighing of values or policy aims – meaning that clear and well-developed policy arguments (of the type I seek to make here) are essential to the outcomes of rights claims adjudication. To that end, the following chapters examine several areas of reproductive regulation, with a view to situating them within the above-outlined model of reproductive autonomy, and sketching the contours of a policy approach that appropriately respects a contextualised conception of reproductive autonomy.

of finding positive rights in the Charter; they include Martha Jackman, 'Poor Rights: Using the *Charter* to Support Social Welfare Claims' (1993–94) 19 *Queen's Law Journal* 65; Martha Jackman, 'The Right to Participate in Health Care and Health Resource Allocation Decisions Under Section 7 of the Canadian Charter' (1995–96) 4(2) *Health Law Review* 3; Margot Young, 'Case Comment: Rights, the Homeless, and Social Change: Reflections on Victoria (City) v Adams (BCSC)' (Winter 2009/10) 164 *BC Studies* 103.

[118] Legal and constitutional rights can be distinguished generally on the basis that States create legal rights and can therefore abrogate them, while they cannot similarly interfere with constitutional rights. Moreover, we tend to think of legal rights as being exercisable against other private individuals, while constitutional rights operate to protect us from State (or public) power.

[119] See, eg, the embryo disposition cases mentioned in ch 9, section II.B. See especially *Evans v Amicus Health Care Limited & Others* [2004] EWCA Civ 727, [2005] Fam 1, para 110: 'The fact is that each person has a right to be protected against interference with their private life. That is an aspect of the principle of self-determination or personal autonomy. It cannot be said that the interference with Mr Johnston's right is justified on the ground that interference is necessary to protect Ms Evans' right, because her right is likewise qualified in the same way by his right. They must have equivalent rights, even though the exact extent of their rights under Article 8 has not been identified.' Ms Evans unsuccessfully argued her case before the European Court of Human Rights, claiming that the consent provisions in Sch 3 to the Human Fertilisation and Embryology Act 1990 (UK), violated her rights under Arts 8 and 14 ECHR (n 96) (*Evans v The United Kingdom* (2007) 46 EHRR 34).

Part Two

Avoiding Reproduction

4

Law, Policy and Contraception

I. INTRODUCTION

WOMEN HAVE ATTEMPTED, with varying degrees of success, to use birth control since ancient times.[1] The intensity of the desire to limit fertility and the ingenuity (and sometimes desperation) with which that objective has been pursued throughout history speaks to the profound impact that unwanted and mistimed pregnancies have on women's lives, and to the pressing need for access to effective and safe contraception.

Women have used a variety of methods to prevent conception or induce abortion.[2] The effectiveness of early methods of birth control is uncertain – while some herbal methods employed by women thousands of years ago do appear to have properties that might make them effective as contraceptives, many methods employed to limit fertility are clearly not effective.[3] Many of today's contraceptives are simply contemporary versions of very old 'technologies'.[4] The major modern breakthrough in contraceptive options was the development of the oral contraceptive pill. Since the introduction of the pill in the 1960s, research into new contraceptive methods seems to have slowed markedly. As of 2002, only a small number of pharmaceutical companies were actively pursuing research into new methods; most were choosing instead to adapt existing products and methods.[5] This is not to suggest that nothing new has happened on the research and development front – examples of new or adapted contraceptive techniques include long-acting contraceptive injections and emergency contraceptive pills, as well as long-term implantable devices and intra-uterine contraceptive devices. But there has been nothing new on the scale of the pill.

Although newer, very effective methods of birth control are readily available, the most commonly-used methods of birth control in Canada, the US, the UK and Australia are oral contraceptive pills and condoms.[6] Both of these methods are reversible and have

---

[1] Indeed, Plato and Aristotle wrote about and debated the need to limit family size (Angus McLaren, *A History of Contraception: From Antiquity to the Present Day* (Oxford, Basil Blackwell Inc, 1990)). See also Robert Jütte, *Contraception: A History* (Cambridge, Polity Press, 2008).

[2] See, eg, John M Riddle, *Eve's Herbs: A History of Contraception and Abortion in the West* (Cambridge, MA, Harvard University Press, 1997).

[3] *Ibid.* See also McLaren (n 1).

[4] Heather Boonstra *et al*, 'The "Boom and Bust Phenomenon": The Hopes, Dreams, and Broken Promises of the Contraceptive Revolution' (2000) 61 *Contraception* 9, 23.

[5] See, eg, *ibid*; Constance Holden, 'News: Research on Contraception Still in the Doldrums' (2002) 296 *Science* 2172.

[6] See, eg, Farhat Yusuf and Stefania Siedlecky, 'Patterns of Contraceptive Use in Australia: Analysis of the 2001 National Health Survey' (2007) 39 *Journal of Biosocial Science* 735; Amanda Black *et al*, 'Contraceptive Use Among Canadian Women of Reproductive Age: Results of a National Survey' (2009) 31 *Journal of Obstetrics and Gynaecology Canada* 627; Deborah Lader and the Office for National Statistics, *Opinions*

reasonably good efficacy when used perfectly. Typical use, however, results in significant failure rates (around 9 per cent for the pill, and 17 per cent for condoms).[7] The fact that these are the options most women choose does not indicate that they reflect women's actual preferences, or that women would not welcome innovative methods. Decisions about contraceptive use reflect a wide variety of considerations that include age and reproductive stage of life, fertility status and intentions, and social factors.[8]

In spite of the existence of safe, effective and acceptable methods of contraception, unintended pregnancy accounts for an estimated 86 million pregnancies annually. This translates into approximately 33 million unintended births, 41 million induced abortions and approximately 11 million miscarriages.[9] The proportion of unintended pregnancies relative to total pregnancies is approximately 41 per cent;[10] in the US and the UK, estimates suggest that closer to half of all pregnancies are unintended.[11] The numbers are staggering, but actually reflect a global decline in the pregnancy rate over the past decade; this decline is in part explained by increasing contraceptive use. Yet the persistently high numbers of unintended pregnancy illustrate a significant unmet need for access to birth control.[12] The need and demand for contraception varies in scope and in specifics – women and couples in developing nations need education about contraception and affordable access to modern methods of birth control, while teens and young women in developed countries often lack access to birth control due to legal and policy-based restrictions.

Unintended pregnancy is not caused solely by lack of access to contraceptive products and services. Many factors play a part in the continuing high rates of unplanned preg-

Survey Report No 41: Contraception and Sexual Health, 2008/09 (Newport, Office for National Statistics, 2009) 19; William D Mosher and Jo Jones, 'Use of Contraception in the United States: 1982–2008' (2010) Series 23, No 29 *Vital and Health Statistics* 1.

[7] Guttmacher Institute, 'In Brief: Facts on Publicly Funded Contraceptive Services in the United States' (May 2012), at <www.guttmacher.org/pubs/fb_contraceptive_serv.pdf>.

[8] Edith Gray and Peter McDonald, 'Using a Reproductive Life Course Approach to Understand Contraceptive Method Use in Australia' (2010) 42 *Journal of Biosocial Science* 43, 44.

[9] Susheela Singh, Gilda Sedgh and Rubina Hussain, 'Unintended Pregnancy: Worldwide Levels, Trends, and Outcomes' (2010) 41 *Studies in Family Planning* 241, 243.

[10] *Ibid* 241.

[11] Louise Bury and Thoai D Ngo, *'The Condom Broke!' Why do Women in the UK Have Unintended Pregnancies?* (London, Marie Stopes International, 2009) 5; Lawrence B Finer and Mia R Zolna, 'Unintended Pregnancy in the United States: Incidence and Disparities, 2006' (2011) 84 *Contraception* 478. As Finer and Zolna note, there are significant disparities in unintended pregnancy rates, with women aged 18–24 and poor women having significantly higher rates of unplanned pregnancy. Data around Canada's rate of unintended pregnancy are more difficult to find, but a recent study carried out by the Public Health Agency of Canada suggests that (based on self-reporting by women) at least 27% would have liked to be pregnant at some later time, or not at all (*What Mothers Say: The Canadian Maternity Experiences Survey* (Ottawa, Public Health Agency of Canada, 2009) 31). Australian data on unintended pregnancy rates are also difficult to find, but authors suggest that the relatively high abortion rate in Australia (19.7 abortions per 1,000 women) indicates a significant level of unintended pregnancy (Melissa K Hobbs *et al*, 'Pharmacy Access to the Emergency Contraceptive Pill: A National Survey of a Random Sample of Australian Women' (2011) 83 *Contraception* 151).

[12] Unmet need for birth control exists when women of childbearing years (defined by these authors as ages 15–49) who are sexually active and want to avoid pregnancy are not using any method of contraception, or are using a 'traditional method' of birth control (Jacqueline E Darroch, Gilda Sedgh and Haley Ball, *Contraceptive Technologies: Responding to Women's Needs* (New York, Guttmacher Institute, 2011) 9). Traditional methods of birth control include withdrawal and periodic abstinence; modern methods are hormonal contraceptives and barrier methods, see, eg, Sharyl J Nass and Jerome F Strauss (eds), *New Frontiers in Contraceptive Research: A Blueprint for Action* (Washington, DC, The National Academies Press, 2004) 21.

nancy, including women's perceptions about their risk of pregnancy.[13] But at a minimum, it appears that much more can be done, in terms of both innovation and development of new, acceptable and effective methods of birth control, and in educating women and men about the available alternatives. Indeed, the need for innovation in contraceptive options has been noted, and concerns have been raised about the lack of activity in research and development into new contraceptive methods.[14]

In addition to the urgent need for new and better methods of birth control, it remains the case that barriers to access to available methods of birth control continue to exist, and respect for reproductive autonomy demands that these barriers be addressed. Among the concerns that must be addressed by law and policymakers are lack of access due to financial constraints and concerns around accessibility of birth control in light of conscientious objection.

Contraception fits within the nucleus of the bodily integrity model of reproductive autonomy.[15] While contraception is theoretically an issue with which both men and women are concerned, almost all currently available contraceptive methods are ultimately the responsibility of women. Women's inability to gain timely access to appropriate contraceptive methods potentially threatens their bodily integrity by requiring them either to bear an unwanted child or seek an abortion. Based on a contextual approach to reproductive autonomy that places women's interests at its core, the State must facilitate timely and appropriate access to contraceptives for those who wish to use them. This includes ensuring the availability of a range of safe and effective contraceptive options, and providing meaningful access to these choices. While contraceptives are generally available in most Western nations, barriers to access continue to exist; respect for reproductive autonomy demands that these barriers be dismantled.

On the opposite end of the spectrum from the question of improving access to contraception is the spectre of coerced or non-consensual imposition of contraception. One important issue that needs consideration from the standpoint of respect for reproductive autonomy is the worry that some of the more effective methods of contraception – which tend to be those that do not require a great deal of 'user input' – can be used coercively.

In this chapter, I consider legal and policy issues related to access to contraception. The first half of the chapter considers a number of barriers to access to contraception; these include regulatory barriers, financial barriers and provider conscientious objection. Emergency contraception is considered separately (see section II.D.), as a sort of case study in how these barriers to access work in practice. The second half of the chapter explores the issue of non-consensual birth control, primarily the non-consensual sterilisation of persons with intellectual or developmental disabilities.

---

[13] See, eg, Hobbs *et al* (n 11); Gunilla Aneblom *et al*, 'Knowledge, Use and Attitudes Towards Emergency Contraceptive Pills Among Swedish Women Presenting for Induced Abortion' (2002) 109 *BJOG: An International Journal of Obstetrics and Gynaecology* 155; Caroline Free, Raymond M Lee and Jane Ogden, 'Young Women's Accounts of Factors Influencing Their Use and Non-use of Emergency Contraception: In-depth Interview Study' (2002) 325 *British Medical Journal* 1393; Anna Glasier *et al*, 'Advanced Provision of Emergency Contraception Does Not Reduce Abortion Rates' (2004) 69 *Contraception* 361.

[14] Boonstra *et al* (n 4) 10.

[15] A related issue – that of provider responsibility for negligence in performing birth control procedures or giving birth control advice – is considered in ch 7.

II. POLICY AND ACCESS TO CONTRACEPTION

Birth control has not always been an issue for legal regulation, although religious and social concerns have played an important role in perceptions around the use of contraception and in attempts at regulating or restricting access.[16] Some historians have claimed that knowledge of contraceptives was widespread among women prior to and during the Middle Ages, and that the knowledge was lost when midwives (or wise women) were persecuted as witches.[17] With this loss of knowledge among women themselves came the possibility of medical or professional control over contraception and abortion, together with the possibility of State restriction and control. Whether or not this is an accurate history, it is certainly the case that as science and medicine progressed and new, more effective methods of birth control were developed, professionalisation and medicalisation of birth control occurred, and with it, the potential for State control.

In both Canada and the US, the use of contraception was unlawful from the late nineteenth century until the 1960s. The Canadian Criminal Code[18] of 1892 criminalised the provision of contraceptives; the criminal prohibition was finally removed from the Code in 1969.[19] In 1873, the US Comstock Laws[20] made it an offence to disseminate information about birth control. The federal prohibition was declared unconstitutional in 1938, but state laws remained in place until 1965, when such laws gradually began to fall. First, in *Griswold v Connecticut*,[21] married couples were permitted access to contraception (and information about contraception); then, in 1972,[22] the United States Supreme Court held that the right to privacy recognised in *Griswold* applied equally to non-married couples. Finally, in *Carey v Population Services International*,[23] the Court held that the State of New York had demonstrated no compelling interest that would justify a ban on provision of contraceptives to minors under 16 years of age.

Australia and the UK have never had criminal prohibitions on the use of contraceptives, although in both countries, medical and religious opinion has historically acted to restrict the availability of contraceptive products and devices.[24]

Although the histories differ, access to contraception has presented challenges in all four jurisdictions, and all continue to struggle with strategies to address unplanned pregnancy and its personal and social costs.[25] That reducing the rates of unplanned pregnancy is an

---

[16] See, eg, Jütte, (n 1) 75–89; Riddle (n 2) 206–15; Angus McLaren and Arlene Tigar McLaren, *The Bedroom and the State: The Changing Practices and Politics of Contraception and Abortion in Canada, 1880–1997*, 2nd edn (Toronto, Oxford University Press, 1997) 15–22.

[17] Riddle (n 2) 10.

[18] Criminal Code, SC 1892, c 29.

[19] Criminal Law Amendment Act, SC 1968–69, c 38.

[20] Comstock Act, 17 Stat 599, c 258 § 2 (1873).

[21] *Griswold v Connecticut*, 381 US 479 (1965).

[22] *Eisenstadt v Baird*, 405 US 438 (1972).

[23] *Carey v Population Services International*, 431 US 678 (1977).

[24] See, eg, JC Caldwell and H Ware, 'The Evolution of Family Planning in Australia' (1973) 27 *Population Studies* 7 (noting the prohibition on the sale of contraceptives by anyone other than pharmacists); Hera Cook, 'Unseemly and Unwomanly Behaviour: Comparing Women's Control of Their Fertility in Australia and England from 1890–1970' (2000) 17 *Journal of Population Research* 125.

[25] See, eg, Bury and Ngo (n 11); Kerryn O'Rourke, *Background Paper: Time for a National Sexual and Reproductive Health Strategy for Australia* (Public Health Association of Australia, Sexual Health and Family Planning Association of Australia and Australian Reproductive Health Alliance, 2008); Jayne Lucke *et al*, 'Unintended Pregnancies: Reducing Rates by Improving Access to Contraception' (2011) 40 *Australian Family Physician* 849.

extremely important social goal is borne out by the observation that it is 'one of the most important reproductive health goals identified by the US Department of Health and Human Services'.[26]

Criminal prohibitions on contraceptive use, as once existed in the US and in Canada, clearly violate reproductive autonomy. But the absence of legal prohibition does not necessarily result in access to effective, affordable birth control. In other words, liberalising access to contraceptives from a legal standpoint does not entail the removal of practical barriers to access. Currently, contraceptives are widely available in Canada, the US, the UK and Australia,[27] yet as is clear from the data on unintended pregnancy rates, access remains less than ideal. There are multiple reasons for lack of contraceptive use, some of which relate to women's perceptions around risk of pregnancy,[28] but financial, structural and political reasons also play a role; these latter reasons are the focus of this section.

A. Regulatory barriers to access

Canada can claim a barrier to access to contraceptives that is unique among the jurisdictions under study here, and that is the Canadian regulatory environment itself. In 2001, Health Canada proposed guidelines for industry respecting the development of hormonal contraceptives for women.[29] According to the authors of a 2004 study on the availability of contraceptive methods in Canada, the proposed Guidance included 'recommendations for clinical trials . . . in excess of the current requirements in Europe and the United States'.[30] The original proposal 'had the potential to discourage contraceptive research in Canada and to block registration of new products'.[31] The Guidance was modified after being challenged by the Society of Obstetricians and Gynaecologists of Canada. The authors of the study note that, irrespective of whether Health Canada was operating under the restrictive requirements found in the draft proposal, as of 2004, no oral contraceptives had been approved for sale in Canada since December 1997.[32]

Through conducting a comparative analysis of the availability of contraceptive products in Canada and other countries, the study's authors found that Canadian women have

---

[26] Finer and Zolna (n 11) 478.

[27] In some instances, the availability of birth control methods has translated into attempts at coercive birth control. In the US, shortly after Norplant (an implantable, long-acting hormonal contraceptive) became available, many women were encouraged to use it (as a condition of receiving welfare, for example), and one California woman was required to 'consent' to using Norplant as a condition of probation (*People v Johnson*, 5 Cal App 4th 552 (1992), in Dorothy Roberts, *Killing the Black Body: Race, Reproduction, and the Meaning of Liberty* (New York, Vintage, 1997) 151–52). See also Michelle Oberman, 'Commentary: The Control of Pregnancy and the Criminalization of Femaleness' (1992) 7 *Berkeley Women's Law Journal* 1; John A Robertson, *Children of Choice: Freedom and the New Reproductive Technologies* (Princeton, NJ, Princeton University Press, 1994) 71–72; Rebecca Dresser, 'Long-Term Contraceptives in the Criminal Justice System' in Ellen Moskowitz and Bruce Jennings (eds), *Coerced Contraception? Moral and Policy Challenges of Long-Acting Birth Control* (Washington, DC, Georgetown University Press, 1996) 134.

[28] See, eg, Aneblom *et al* (n 13); Free *et al* (n 13); Glasier *et al* (n 13); Hobbs *et al* (n 11).

[29] The final version of the Guidance is available from Health Canada's website ('Health Products and Food Branch, Guidance for Industry: Clinical Development of Steroidal Contraceptives Used by Women' (*Health Canada*, 2002), at <www.hc-sc.gc.ca/dhp-mps/alt_formats/hpfb-dgpsa/pdf/prodpharma/contracep-eng.pdf>).

[30] Dianne Azzarello and John Collins, 'Canadian Access to Hormonal Contraceptive Drug Choices' (2004) 26 *Journal of Obstetrics and Gynaecology Canada* 489, 490.

[31] *Ibid* 489.

[32] *Ibid*.

access to a significantly smaller range of hormonal contraceptive products available world-wide than women in the US, France, Sweden, Denmark and the UK. At the time the study was conducted, Canadian women had access to 35 per cent of contraceptive products available worldwide, and 37 per cent of the available hormonal contraceptives.[33] In contrast, women in the US had access to 58 per cent of all contraceptives and 59 per cent of hormonal contraceptives; figures for the UK were 52 per cent and 54 per cent, respectively.[34] In the case of newer contraceptive products, Canadian women had access to the fewest options, as only 22 per cent of these products were available in Canada.[35]

The study also points out that while Canada tends to be approximately six months behind the United States in terms of the time required for regulatory approval of new drug products, as of 1 January 2004, Canada was 29.6 months behind for six contraceptive products seeking regulatory approval.[36] The authors concluded that

> Canada appears to be lagging behind other countries with respect to the availability of hormonal contraceptive options. A wider choice of contraceptive options, including a variety of dosage forms, routes of administration, and chemical entities, can improve access to effective contraception . . . [and] reduce the number of unplanned and unwanted pregnancies . . .[37]

While it is not clear that having fewer contraceptive options necessarily compromises reproductive autonomy, limited access can have significant effects on women's ability to choose effective and acceptable methods. As the study authors note, 'Different dose regimens and routes of hormonal contraceptive administration offer a range of efficacy, side-effect profiles, and advantages and disadvantages that allow each woman to make an optimal choice'.[38] In addition, wider choice may improve compliance with drug regimens, leading to more effective use of hormonal contraceptives.[39] In turn, more effective use of contraception means fewer unplanned pregnancies, with their attendant personal and social costs.

The existence of this regulatory barrier to access helps to illustrate the importance of adopting a contextualised account of reproductive autonomy. It is essential to look at a wide array of contextual factors in assessing whether law and policy demonstrate respect for reproductive autonomy. From this standpoint, it is instructive to note the divergence between Canada and other countries in terms of contraceptive availability, and to recognise that questions need to be asked about why Canadian women face limited options. It is also very significant to note the much greater delay for approval of contraceptive medications compared to other medications, and to consider the implications of this regulatory stance for women's reproductive autonomy. It is difficult to know the extent to which the concerns outlined here continue to affect Canadian women in terms of their ability to access a wide range of contraceptive methods, including newer contraceptives. But it is clear that an ethic of respect for reproductive autonomy means that women

[33] *Ibid.*

[34] Figures for other countries studied are as follows: France 44% and 54%; Sweden 44% and 50% (*ibid* 495–97).

[35] Women in Denmark have the greatest number of options (67% of available products) (*ibid* 496).

[36] *Ibid* 495. The authors note that hormonal contraceptive products and hormone replacement therapy products all required longer review times than Viagra, a drug used in erectile dysfunction. The shortest approval time for an HRT product was 111 days longer than the approval time required for Viagra. It is unclear why this is the case, because information is not readily available (*ibid* 495, 498).

[37] *Ibid* 499.

[38] *Ibid* 496–97.

[39] *Ibid* 497.

should not face more limited options than they otherwise might as a result of the vagaries of the regulatory scheme.

B. Financial barriers to access

Funding for contraceptive products and services is a key policy issue, and financial barriers to access pose complex problems. It is essential to note that the differing approaches taken in the different jurisdictions under consideration here reflect, in part, the significant distinctions in overall health care system structure. While the UK, Australia and Canada all have universal public healthcare insurance systems, the systems are structured very differently. Together with the varied nature of the products and services involved in the provision of contraception, these structural or systems-based differences lead to a great deal of variation in how care related to birth control can be accessed.

The UK's National Health Service (NHS) provides all forms of contraception at no cost through General Practitioners and family planning clinics.[40] Elective sterilisation is funded within the NHS for both men and women, but it is also available privately, without the wait attendant upon services in the public system.[41] Australia's healthcare system also provides some coverage for contraception and sterilisation, either through its public or subsidised private system.[42] Intrauterine devices and sterilisation are covered, and some sexual health and family planning clinics also offer contraceptives for free or at a very low cost.[43] In spite of subsidies for contraceptives in Australia, barriers to access do exist. This is particularly the case in rural Australia, where it is often necessary to travel long distances in order to obtain products and services, and where women face difficulty in obtaining timely physician appointments.[44]

In the US, issues of funding and access to contraceptives are complex, to say the least. Most healthcare coverage in the US is accomplished through private insurance plans, usually obtained through one's employer.[45] There is also health insurance coverage in the public sector through Medicare, Medicaid and other related programs.[46] The current US healthcare insurance system (which is set for comprehensive reform in the coming years) leaves approximately 50 million Americans uninsured and millions more underinsured.[47] According to a 2009 estimate, 40 per cent of poor women of reproductive age lack

---

[40] Emily Jackson, *Regulating Reproduction: Law, Technology and Autonomy* (Oxford, Hart Publishing, 2001) 16.

[41] *Ibid.*

[42] Australia's national healthcare system includes partial coverage of prescription drugs (National Health Act 1953 (Cth), Pt VII). Currently, the maximum cost of a prescription is $34.20, but 'concession card holders' (low income earners, armed services veterans and some others (*ibid* s 84(1)) pay a maximum of $5.60 per prescription.

[43] *Ibid.*

[44] Lucke *et al* (n 25).

[45] Carmen DeNavas-Walt, Bernadette D Proctor and Jessica C Smith, *US Census Bureau, Current Population Reports, P60-239, Income, Poverty, and Health Insurance Coverage in the United States: 2010* (Washington, DC, US Government Printing Office, 2011).

[46] Barbara S Klees, Christian J Wolfe and Catherine A Curtis, *Brief Summaries of Medicare & Medicaid: Title XVIII and XIX of the Social Security Act* (Washington, DC, Centers for Medicare and Medicaid Services, Department of Health and Human Services, 2010).

[47] DeNavas-Walt *et al* (n 45). A 2012 study found that in 2011, 26% of Americans experienced a gap in health insurance coverage (Sarah R Collins *et al*, 'Gaps in Health Insurance: Why So Many Americans Experience Breaks in Coverage and How the Affordable Care Act Will Help' (The Commonwealth Fund, April 2012), at <www.commonwealthfund.org/Publications/Issue-Briefs/2012/Apr/Gaps-in-Health-Insurance.aspx>).

healthcare insurance,[48] meaning that they are left to 'rely on a patchwork quilt of under-funded family planning programs for their reproductive health care'.[49] Contraceptive coverage under Medicaid is inconsistent, due to 'stagnation' of federal funding: although the population segment that relies on publicly-funded family planning services continues to increase (largely due to increasing poverty), funding for family planning services has remained the same (or has been reduced) in over half of the states.[50] Even where services are available to women through these public programs, access to effective and desirable methods of contraception can be frustrated because although federally-funded clinics are required to offer a range of contraceptive methods, they are not required to provide all Food and Drugs Administration-approved (FDA-approved) methods.[51]

Most Americans are covered by private healthcare insurance programs; in general these programs are available to individuals and their families through employers.[52] While most such plans cover the costs of prescription drugs, many do not cover the full range of FDA-approved contraceptive drugs and devices.[53] Several states (currently 28) have passed 'contraceptive equity laws' which require health insurers that cover pre-scription drugs to cover contraceptive methods and services.[54] In 20 of the 28 states with contraceptive equity laws, however, exemptions permit religious employers or insurers to refuse to cover contraceptive services where provision of such coverage would violate their religious beliefs.[55] In addition to these formal exemptions (some of which are suf-ficiently broad to exempt secular organisations that object on moral grounds to the pro-vision of contraceptive coverage[56]), some employers self-insure, rather than purchasing insurance coverage from a commercial insurer, and are therefore not caught by contra-ceptive equity laws.[57] Lastly, even where a woman has private insurance that does cover contraceptive services, these policies include co-payment or deductible provisions that mean that women must still pay some of the costs of obtaining contraceptives.[58]

---

[48] Rachel Benson Gold *et al*, *Next Steps for America's Family Planning Program: Leveraging the Potential of Medicaid and Title X in an Evolving Health Care System* (New York, Guttmacher Institute, 2009) 10.

[49] Eve Espey, Ellen Cosgrove and Tony Ogburn, 'Family Planning American Style: Why It's So Hard to Control Birth in the US' (2007) 34 *Obstetrics & Gynecology Clinics of North America* 1, 8. Publicly-funded family planning services are delivered in the US through a combination of Title X of the Public Services Act of 1970, Pub L No 91-572 and through Medicaid. See also Gold *et al* (n 48).

[50] Espey *et al* (n 49) 9.

[51] Reproductive Health Technologies Project and the Alan Guttmacher Institute, *The Unfinished Revolution in Contraception: Convenience, Consumer Access and Choice* (Washington, DC, Alan Guttmacher Institute, 2004) 7.

[52] Collins *et al* (n 47).

[53] 'In Brief: Facts on Publicly Funded Contraceptive Services in the United States' (n 7); Center for Reproductive Rights, 'Contraceptive Equity Laws in the States' (4 January 2006), at <http://reproductiverights.org/en/project/contraceptive-equity-laws-in-the-states>; Guttmacher Institute, 'State Policies in Brief: Insurance Coverage of Contraceptives' (2 August 2012), at <www.guttmacher.org/statecenter/spibs/spib_ICC.pdf>.

[54] 'State Policies in Brief: Insurance Coverage of Contraceptives' (n 53).

[55] *Ibid*.

[56] *Ibid*.

[57] Espey *et al* (n 49) 9. Another important barrier to access in the US is the phenomenon of hospital mergers, wherein non-religious institutions merge with religious hospitals. In the past 25 years, over 100 such mergers have taken place, and roughly half of these mergers have led to the reduction or elimination of reproductive health services. According to one study: 'There are now 91 counties in the US where a Catholic hospital is the sole provider of health care, and in 95% of those counties Catholics are minorities.' (Nikki Zite and Sonya Borrero, 'Female Sterilisation in the United States' (2011) 16 *European Journal of Contraception & Reproductive Health Care* 336, 339)

[58] Espey *et al* (n 49) 10–11. The authors explain that the Medical Expenditure Panel Survey conducted in 2004 found that insured women paid, on average, $14 per package of pills. A related concern is that 'insurance regulations often limit the number obtained at the pharmacy to a single pack', likely making ongoing compli-ance more challenging (*ibid* 11).

In an attempt to alleviate some of these (and many other) financial barriers to access to healthcare in the US, plans and legislation are in place to effect sweeping reform of the healthcare system. As noted in an earlier chapter, women bear the burdens of the politicisation issues related to reproductive health;[59] in the debate around healthcare reform, the politicised nature of policy making around women's health has once again been revealed. The Patient Protection and Affordable Care Act[60] holds enormous promise for improvements in access to reproductive health services generally, including access to contraceptive services.[61] One of the most fiercely-contested aspects of the legislation has been the Department of Health and Human Services mandate respecting contraceptive services.[62] The mandate requires all healthcare insurance plans to provide coverage at no cost (meaning that insurers cannot require deductibles or co-payments) for all FDA-approved contraceptive methods. The decision, which is based on recommendations by the Institute of Medicine,[63] has been challenged by several states as well as by religiously-affiliated employers. These groups – although exempted from the requirement to offer policies that cover contraceptive services – argue that compelling insurance companies to provide this coverage to their employees violates their right to freedom of conscience and religion.[64]

The evidence establishes that mandating coverage for contraceptive services increases the likelihood of consistent contraceptive use,[65] translating into fewer unplanned pregnancies and fewer abortions. Yet abortion opponents are among the most vocal in this debate.[66] As one group of authors notes, 'The high rate of unintended pregnancies in the United States graphically demonstrates that this confusion . . . damages both human health and financial soundness'.[67] It is too soon to tell whether the enormous potential benefits of the contraceptive mandate (and the Affordable Care Act more generally) will be realised, but they are certainly not on the immediate horizon, as full implementation of the legislation is years away and, in the meantime, the law faces numerous challenges.

In marked contrast to that of the US, Canada's healthcare system provides universal coverage of physician and hospital services.[68] Canada's system has evolved since initially conceived, but it remains true to its roots in its organisation around physician and hospital services. The focus on coverage of physician services and in-hospital care has

---

[59] This is discussed in ch 3, section I.A.

[60] Patient Protection and Affordable Care Act of 2010, Pub L No 111–148, 124 Stat 119 (codified as amended throughout 42 USC).

[61] See, eg, Adam Sonfield, 'Contraception: An Integral Component of Preventive Health Care for Women' (2010) 13(2) *Guttmacher Policy Review* 2; Adam Sonfield and Rachel Benson Gold, 'Editorial: Holding on to Health Care Reform and What We Have Gained for Reproductive Health' (2011) 83 *Contraception* 285.

[62] Patient Protection and Affordable Care Act of 2010 (n 60) § 2953 (codified at 42 USC § 713 (2011)). The exemption from participation for religious employers has been a significant political issue (R Alta Charo, 'Warning: Contraceptive Drugs May Cause Political Headaches' (2012) 366 *New England Journal of Medicine* 1361; John Halsey, 'The Shortcomings of Political Rhetoric' (2012) 8(2) *Pitt Political Review* 9, 11).

[63] Institute of Medicine, *Clinical Preventive Services for Women: Closing the Gaps* (Washington, DC, National Academies Press, 2011).

[64] See, eg, Charo (n 62) 1362; Ellen R Shaffer, Mona Sarfaty and Arlene S Ash, 'Contraceptive Insurance Mandates' (2012) 50 *Medical Care* 559, 560.

[65] Brianna M Magnusson *et al*, 'Contraceptive Insurance Mandates and Consistent Contraceptive Use Among Privately Insured Women' (2012) 50 *Medical Care* 562.

[66] See, eg, Charo (n 62); Shaffer *et al* (n 64) 560.

[67] Shaffer *et al* (n 64) 560.

[68] For a detailed discussion of the structure of the Canadian healthcare system, see William Lahey, 'Medicare and the Law: Contours of an Evolving Relationship' in Jocelyn Downie, Timothy Caulfield and Colleen M Flood (eds), *Canadian Health Law and Policy*, 4th edn (Markham, LexisNexis Canada, 2011) 1.

important implications for coverage of contraceptive products and services. Coverage of prescription medications is provided by all provinces when those drugs are used by hospital inpatients, but outpatient use is not comprehensively covered by most provincial healthcare insurance plans.[69] Provincial plans also do not provide non-prescription contraceptives such as condoms, spermicides and contraceptive sponges.[70] The cost of an intra-uterine device (IUD) is also not covered by most provincial healthcare plans, although the office visits for the prescription of the device and its insertion and removal are covered as they are insured physician services. Sterilisation procedures (tubal ligation and vasectomy) are covered by most provincial healthcare insurance plans.[71] Hormonal contraceptives and contraceptive devices such as the IUD may be covered under supplementary private insurance plans. Contraceptives can be obtained free of charge (or at a subsidised rate) in some sexual health clinics and some university health service clinics.[72]

The UK approach – the provision of all (or at least a very broad range of) available contraceptive methods without charge – is unquestionably the best way to demonstrate meaningful respect for reproductive autonomy. In Canada, the US and Australia, women and couples continue to face significant financial barriers to accessing contraception. In Canada and Australia, access to contraceptive methods can depend on which province or state is one's home, or on one's status (as a student, for example), or even whether contraceptive services are sought from a family doctor or a sexual health clinic. But overall, availability is variable and unpredictable, depending on the specific contraceptive an individual seeks to use, and where they live. From the perspective of respect for reproductive autonomy, this state of affairs is unsatisfactory, to say the least. Women should not face financial barriers in attempting to use contraception, and they should not be pushed into choosing a potentially less desirable or more risky option because that option is available without charge while more acceptable options are financially prohibitive.

Ironically, in the Canadian system, because of the organisation and structure of the healthcare system around physician and hospital services, the most affordable contraceptive option may also be the most permanent – surgical sterilisation. While the provision of tubal ligation or vasectomy without charge is not coercive, it may nonetheless be

---

[69] *Ibid* 26. Some provinces have 'pharmacare' programs that provide some prescription drug coverage: see, eg, British Columbia Ministry of Health Services, 'Welcome to Pharmacare' (*Province of British Columbia*), at <www.health.gov.bc.ca/pharmacare/index.html#>; Manitoba Health, 'Manitoba Pharmacare Program: About the Manitoba Pharmacare Program' (*Province of Manitoba*), at <www.gov.mb.ca/health/pharmacare/index.html>.

[70] Some contraceptive methods are available without charge to certain individuals (eg, those who attend sexual health or university health clinics) or in certain jurisdictions (where prescription drugs are covered), but availability is variable and unpredictable, depending on the specific contraceptive an individual seeks to use, and where in Canada the individual lives.

[71] Generally speaking, provincial healthcare insurance plans cover medically necessary services provided by physicians; this includes surgical services, and in most provinces surgical sterilisation procedures are covered. Insertion of IUDs is covered by provincial healthcare insurance plans, as this, too, is a medically necessary service provided by a physician, but the cost of the device itself (which can range from approximately $90.00–$400.00) must be paid by the patient (G Menard, M Pineau and S Laplante, 'Abstract: A Cost-minimization Analysis Comparing Mirena® with Oral Contraceptives' (2001) 4 *Value in Health* 165; Sheila Wijayasinghe, 'Ask a Health Expert: Should I Use an IUD for Birth Control?' *The Globe and Mail* (Toronto, 8 March 2011), at <www.theglobeandmail.com/life/health-and-fitness/ask-a-health-expert/should-i-use-an-iud-for-birth-control/article569781/>).

[72] Amanda Black *et al*, 'SOGC Clinical Practice Guideline No 143: Canadian Contraception Consensus, Part 1 of 3' (2004) 26 *Journal of Obstetrics and Gynaecology Canada* 143, 152.

cause for concern when viewed within the broader context of contraceptive choices. If women are led to choose sterilisation even where it is not an optimal method of contraception in their particular circumstances (that is, where they wish to have more children in the future), because it is more affordable than non-permanent options, then the autonomous quality of the choice arguably becomes questionable. Poor women who wish to avoid pregnancy in the short term may be led to the most permanent contraceptive option (or to no option at all), due to the costs of other methods.

A broad, contextualised view of reproductive autonomy makes clear that in Canada, the US and Australia, policy makers are failing to respect reproductive autonomy in their approach to access to contraception. As in the case of abortion,[73] the US is the only jurisdiction in which citizens have a constitutional right to use contraceptives, and yet it is the jurisdiction in which gaining access to contraceptives, for some women at least, can be most difficult. A potential answer to this concern seems clear: the healthcare system should provide funding for a wide range of contraceptive options, as is done in the UK. This has been shown to be a cost-effective approach.[74] And not only would this approach lead to a better range of options for women, it would also help to reduce the incidence (and associated costs) of abortion, as well as the social costs created by unwanted and mistimed pregnancies.

C. Providers as barriers to access: conscientious objection

Another appreciable roadblock to access in the contraceptive context is conscientious objection by healthcare professionals. Provider objection to the provision of contraceptive services can make access difficult, particularly for low-income women and those who live in rural areas.[75] The frequency with which conscientious objection poses a problem for contraceptive access is unclear, but anecdotal accounts illustrate that it does occur.[76] A growing number of pharmacists assert a right conscientiously to object to the provision of services (and to the provision of referrals to other providers who will furnish the requested service) that they find morally or religiously offensive.[77]

An important consideration in the context of provider objection is the scope of permissible objection. This turns largely on what it means to participate in the provision of

---

[73] Abortion regulation is discussed in ch 5.

[74] See, eg, Alistair McGuire and David Hughes, *The Economics of Family Planning Services: A Report Prepared for the Contraceptive Alliance* (London, Contraceptive Alliance, 1995); Department of Health, *Choosing Health: Making Healthy Choices Easier*, Cm 6374 (London, The Stationery Office, 2004); Department of Health, *Findings of the Baseline Review of Contraceptive Services* (London, The Stationery Office, 2007) 7; Kelly Cleland *et al*, 'Family Planning as a Cost-Saving Preventive Health Service' (2011) 364 *New England Journal of Medicine* e37.

[75] See, eg, Lucke *et al* (n 25), Tania Khan and Megan Arvad McCoy, 'Access to Contraception' (2005) 6 *Georgetown Journal of Gender and the Law* 785; Holly Teliska, 'Obstacles to Access: How Pharmacist Refusal Clauses Undermine the Basic Health Care Needs of Rural and Low-Income Women' (2005) 20 *Berkeley Journal of Gender, Law and Justice* 229. Conscientious objection is discussed in relation to abortion services in ch 5, section IV.C.

[76] See, eg, Mike Mastromatteo, 'Alberta Pharmacist Wins Concessions in Right-to-refuse Case', *The Interim* (Toronto, December 2003), at <www.theinterim.com/2003/dec/02alberta.html>; Barbara Sibbald, 'Nonprescription Status for Emergency Contraception' (2005) 172 *Canadian Medical Association Journal* 861; 'Lloyds Pharmacy Probe Over Pill Refusal in Sheffield', *BBC News* (10 March 2010), at <http://news.bbc.co.uk/2/hi/uk_news/england/south_yorkshire/8557816.stm>.

[77] See, eg, Mastromatteo (n 76); Allison Grady, 'Legal Protection for Conscientious Objection by Health Professionals' (2006) 8 *Virtual Mentor* 327.

contraceptive products or services. Some providers assert that their religious or moral values require not only that they decline to perform or prescribe an objectionable procedure or treatment, but that they must also refrain from referring their patient to a non-objecting provider.[78] Karen Brauer, head of an organisation called Pharmacists for Life International, puts the matter of referral very plainly:

> That's like saying, 'I don't kill people myself but let me tell you about the guy down the street who does'. What's that saying? 'I will not off your husband, but I know a buddy who will?' It's the same thing.[79]

Though Canada has no law directly addressing conscientious objection, there are signals that lead to the fairly safe conclusion that Canadian law requires physicians (and other providers) who object to participating in certain procedures for reasons of conscience to refer their patients to a provider who does not similarly object.[80] In *Zimmer v Ringrose*, the Alberta Court of Appeal held that a physician's failure to refer his patient to a local physician who would facilitate an abortion amounted to negligence (for failure to provide appropriate follow-up care).[81] While this case does not deal with a refusal to refer because of conscientious objection (indeed, the physician's reason for referring his patient to a US practitioner rather than a local physician was to ensure the abortion took place as soon as possible), it does indicate that the courts are likely to see a failure to provide an appropriate referral as negligence tantamount to abandonment. As Rebecca Cook and Bernard Dickens note, *McInerney v MacDonald*,[82] which holds that physicians owe fiduciary duties to their patients, must surely require that physicians place their patients' well-being ahead of their own personal convictions.[83]

The UK does not have specific legislation on point with respect to contraception, but section 4 of the Abortion Act 1967 provides that

> no person shall be under any duty, whether by contract or by any statutory or other legal requirement, to participate in any treatment authorised by this Act to which he has a conscientious objection . . .[84]

The Act itself does not define 'participate' but the courts have read the section narrowly, limiting the right to object to those who are involved in the procedure or treatment.[85]

In the US, although the vast majority of states have legislation that protects objecting providers from being required to participate in abortion services, only 14 states have

---

[78] Ryan E Lawrence and Farr A Curlin, 'Physicians' Beliefs about Conscience in Medicine: A National Survey' (2009) 84 *Academic Medicine* 1276.

[79] As quoted by Rob Stein, ''Pharmacists' Rights at Front of New Debate', *Washington Post*, 28 March 2005, at <www.washingtonpost.com/wp-dyn/articles/A5490-2005Mar27.html>.

[80] See, eg, *Zimmer v Ringrose*, 28 AR 69, [1981] 4 WWR 75; Rebecca J Cook and Bernard M Dickens, 'Access to Emergency Contraception' (2003) 25 *Journal of Obstetrics and Gynaecology Canada* 914.

[81] *Zimmer v Ringrose* (n 80).

[82] *McInerney v MacDonald* [1992] 2 SCR 138, 126 NBR (2d) 271.

[83] Cook and Dickens (n 80) 914–16.

[84] Abortion Act 1967 (UK). Australian abortion legislation also contains conscience clauses: see, eg, Criminal Law Consolidation Act 1935 (SA), s 82A(5) (no duty to participate in abortion if provider conscientiously objects, but not exempted from participating if procedure is needed to save life or prevent grave damage to health); Abortion Law Reform Act 2008 (Vic), s 8 (provider must inform woman of his/her conscientious objection and refer the woman to another provider whom he/she knows does not conscientiously object); Criminal Code Act 1924 (Tas), s 164(7); Medical Practitioners (Maternal Health) Amendment Act 2002 (ACT), s 55E (no duty to carry out or assist in carrying out an abortion); Medical Services Act 1982 (NT), s 11(6) (no duty to terminate or assist in terminating a pregnancy if provider conscientiously objects to doing so).

[85] See, eg, *Janaway v Salford Area Health Authority* [1989] AC 537; *Barr v Matthews* (2000) 52 BMLR 217.

similar laws in place relating to contraceptive products and services.[86] Even where conscientious objection is permitted, however, most state legislation provides that the objecting provider must refer or help the patient to make alternative arrangements for access to the medication.[87] Some states, by contrast, have legislation either requiring the provision of emergency contraception in some circumstances[88] or, more broadly, precluding pharmacies from declining to fill prescriptions on the basis of moral or religious objections.[89]

There is a dearth of case law relating to provider obligations and the role of conscience, and although some jurisdictions have legislation on point,[90] the question is largely left for policy makers to address. Some healthcare professional governing bodies do allow providers to refuse to participate in treatment where doing so would violate the provider's personal values or beliefs, while others make it clear that the ability conscientiously to object is contingent on the timely provision of care to the patient.[91] The Pharmaceutical Society of Australia's Code of Ethics, for example, states that a pharmacist has 'a right to decline provision of care based on a conscientious objection,' but that the exercise of this right should not prevent patient access to healthcare. The pharmacist who wishes to decline to provide care because of conscientious objection 'should inform the consumer of the objection and appropriately facilitate continuity of care for the consumer'.[92]

Julian Savulescu has argued that conscientious objection has no place in medicine; in his view, 'A doctor's conscience has little place in the delivery of modern medical care'.[93]

---

[86] Guttmacher Institute, 'State Policies in Brief: Refusing to Provide Health Services' (1 August 2012), at <www.guttmacher.org/statecenter/spibs/spib_RPHS.pdf>. Of the 14, six states have laws that explicitly permit individual pharmacists to refuse to dispense contraceptives.

[87] A Wisconsin pharmacist was disciplined by the professional pharmacy regulator in the state when he refused to fill *and* refused to transfer to another pharmacy a prescription for oral contraceptives (*Noesen v Wisconsin Department of Regulation and Licensing, Pharmacy Examining Board*, 751 NW 2d 385 (Wis App 2008)).

[88] Guttmacher Institute, 'State Policies in Brief: Emergency Contraception' (1 August 2012), at <www.guttmacher.org/statecenter/spibs/spib_EC.pdf>.

[89] Thaddeus Mason Pope, 'Legal Briefing: Conscience Clauses and Conscientious Refusal' (2010) 21 *Journal of Clinical Ethics* 163.

[90] See above (n 84).

[91] See, eg, Daniel W Brock, 'Conscientious Refusal by Physicians and Pharmacists: Who is Obligated to Do What, and Why?' (2008) 29 *Theoretical Medicine and Bioethics* 187; Lisa H Harris *et al*, 'Obstetrician-Gynecologists' Objections to and Willingness to Help Patients Obtain an Abortion' (2011) 118 *Obstetrics & Gynecology* 905; Zuzana Deans, 'Conscientious Objections in Pharmacy Practice in Great Britain' (2013) 27 *Bioethics* 48.

[92] 'Code of Ethics for Pharmacists' (*Pharmaceutical Society of Australia*, September 2011) 6, at <www.psa. org.au/download/codes/code-of-ethics-2011.pdf>. The UK's General Pharmaceutical Council requires objecting providers to inform the relevant authorities or individuals and 'refer patients and the public to other providers' (General Pharmaceutical Council, 'Standards of Conduct, Ethics and Performance' (July 2012) 10, at <www.pharmacyregulation.org/sites/default/files/Standards%20of%20conduct%20ethics%20and%20 performance %20July%202012.pdf>). Likewise, the Ontario College of Pharmacists permits providers to decline to provide care where doing so would conflict with their 'view of morality or religious beliefs and if the pharmacist believes that his or her conscience will be harmed by providing the product or service,' but also states that the objecting provider must ensure that the patient is able to access the required service or product from an alternative source, with minimal inconvenience or suffering (Ontario College of Pharmacists, 'Position Statement on "Refusal to Fill for Moral or Religious Reasons"', at <www.ocpinfo.com/client/ocp/OCPHome. nsf/web/Position+Statement+on+Refusal+to+Fill+for+Moral+or+Religious+Reasons>).

[93] Julian Savulescu, 'Conscientious Objection in Medicine' (2006) 332 *British Medical Journal* 294, 294. But see Frank A Chervenak and Laurence B McCullough, 'Conscientious Objection in Medicine: Author Did Not Meet Standards of Argument Based Ethics' (2006) 332 *British Medical Journal* 425; Vaughan P Smith 'Letter: Conscientious Objection in Medicine: Doctors' Freedom of Conscience' (2006) 332 *British Medical Journal* 425.

Yet the trend appears to be to recognise the validity and legitimacy of conscientious objection, as long as it does not compromise patient care. Indeed, as Alta Charo has noted, legislation proposed in Wisconsin a number of years ago would have permitted objecting physicians to refrain from advising patients about emergency contraception, IVF and even therapies developed with the use of fetal tissue (which include the varicella vaccine, as it was developed using tissue from aborted fetuses).[94]

While I would not go as far as Savulescu and suggest that providers' conscientious objections are irrelevant, respect for reproductive autonomy necessarily limits a provider's freedom to decline to provide services on the basis of conscientious objection. In short, objection can be permitted only in circumstances where it does not have the effect of nullifying women's reproductive autonomy. Ideally, healthcare professionals should not be required to participate in procedures or services they find morally objectionable. There must, however, be limits to the protection of provider conscience where such protection threatens women's health and well-being because it threatens their ability to access healthcare services. The balance that needs to be struck is that between professional autonomy and professional obligations, and women's needs and interests must not be allowed to be enslaved by provider's moral views.[95]

D. Emergency contraception and barriers to access

As noted earlier, in spite of the persistent barriers to accessing contraception, most women in the US, the UK, Australia and Canada who wish to use contraception are able to do so. This suggests that for the most part, there is not a great deal to be concerned about in relation to access to contraception. The legal and political response to emergency contraception belies that theory. In this section, I shall consider access to emergency contraception, as a kind of 'case study' of how barriers to access operate in practice.

Emergency contraception (EC)[96] is the most recent contraceptive option to provoke controversy in all four of these jurisdictions. Emergency hormonal contraception is a form of hormonal contraception that is effective in preventing pregnancy if taken within 72 hours[97]

---

[94] R Alta Charo, 'The Celestial Fire of Conscience – Refusing to Deliver Medical Care' (2005) 352 *New England Journal of Medicine* 2471.

[95] For an interesting discussion of the place of conscientious objection in the Canadian reproductive health context, see, eg, Cook and Dickens (n 80); Howard Bright, 'Access to Emergency Contraception' (2004) 26 *Journal of Obstetrics and Gynaecology Canada* 111; Rebecca J Cook and Bernard M Dickens, 'In Response' (2004) 26 *Journal of Obstetrics and Gynaecology Canada* 112; Sean Murphy, 'Access to Emergency Contrac·ption' (2004) 26 *Journal of Obstetrics and Gynaecology Canada* 705; Rebecca J Cook and Bernard M Dickens, 'Reply' (2004) 26 *Journal of Obstetrics and Gynaecology Canada* 706.

[96] There are two methods of emergency, or post-coital, contraception. One is hormonal, and the other is the insertion of an IUD within five days of unprotected sex, or up to five days 'from the earliest calculated day of ovulation' (Simone Reuter, 'The Emergency Intrauterine Device: An Endangered Species' (2003) 29(2) *Journal of Family Planning and Reproductive Health Care* 5). The emergency IUD will not be discussed here.

[97] There is a newer EC option available in Europe (ellaOne) and the US (ella). The drug used in this regime is ulipristal acetate, which has been shown to be effective for up to five days (or 120 hours) after unprotected intercourse. Older EC methods (including the Yuzpe regimen and levonorgestrel) have been shown in some studies to be somewhat effective even if taken between 72 and 120 hours after unprotected intercourse: see, eg, Isabel Rodrigues, Fabienne Grou and Jacques Joly, 'Effectiveness of Emergency Contraception Pills Between 72 and 120 Hours After Unprotected Sexual Intercourse' (2001) 184 *American Journal of Obstetrics & Gynecology* 531; Helena von Hertzen *et al*, 'Low Dose Mifepristone and Two Regimens of Levonorgestrel for Emergency Contraception: A WHO Multicentre Randomised Trial' (2002) 360 *The Lancet* 1803; Charlotte Ellertson *et al*, 'Extending the Time Limit for Starting the Yuzpe Regimen of Emergency Contraception to 120 Hours' (2003)

of unprotected intercourse.[98] Emergency contraception is most effective if used within 24 hours of unprotected sex (when it prevents 95 per cent of expected pregnancies) and least effective if used more than 49 hours post-intercourse (when it prevents only 58 per cent of expected pregnancies).

The potential for emergency hormonal contraception was discovered when researchers observed that the use of estrogen and progesterone could interfere with the menstrual cycle, even if ingested post-coitally. The first scientifically validated EC regime used a method designed by Canadian physician Albert Yuzpe and his colleagues in the mid-1970s. At the time, the Yuzpe group noted that these hormones produced changes to the lining of the uterus that made implantation unlikely.[99] In general, however, the mechanism of action of emergency hormonal contraception was not well understood until quite recently, and this has proved significant in terms of opposition to wider access to EC. Newer research has shown that EC is effective primarily because it inhibits or delays ovulation and may also inhibit fertilisation.[100] Post-fertilisation effects cannot be ruled out – it is possible that EC interferes with implantation, just as is true of other hormonal contraceptives (and even of breastfeeding).[101] But EC has no effect on an established pregnancy and is not an abortifacient.[102] This knowledge has not diminished opposition to EC in some quarters, and this has meant that women seeking access to EC continue to face roadblocks based on conscientious objection from both physicians and pharmacists.

After the discovery of the Yuzpe regimen, a number of manufacturers began to introduce dedicated EC products.[103] Emergency contraception was first available to women who already had a prescription for oral contraceptives (the original Yuzpe regimen was based on taking a certain number and type of pills after unprotected intercourse), or with a physician's prescription. It is clear from the efficacy data that time is of the essence

---

101 *Obstetrics & Gynecology* 1168; Suk Wai Ngai et al, 'A Randomized Trial to Compare 24h Versus 12h Double Dose Regimen of Levonorgestrel for Emergency Contraception' (2005) 20 *Human Reproduction* 307; Olukayode A Dada et al, 'A Randomized, Double-Blind, Noninferiority Study to Compare Two Regimens of Levonorgestrel for Emergency Contraception in Nigeria' (2010) 82 *Contraception* 373.

98 EC prevents 89% of expected pregnancies if used within 72 hours of unprotected intercourse. There are two primary methods of EC. One uses a high dose of combination oral contraceptive pills containing both estrogen and progesterone/levonorgestrel (the Yuzpe method); the other is levonorgestrel alone, which is marketed under the brand name 'Plan B' (Rebecca J Cook, Bernard M Dickens and Mahmoud F Fathalla, *Reproductive Health and Human Rights: Integrating Medicine, Ethics, and Law* (Oxford, Oxford University Press, 2003) 289). The efficacy rates given here are for levonorgestrel (Task Force on Postovulatory Methods of Fertility Regulation, 'Randomised Controlled Trial of Levonorgestrel Versus the Yuzpe Regimen of Combined Oral Contraceptives for Emergency Contraception' (1998) 352 *The Lancet* 428).

99 See, eg, Albert A Yuzpe et al, 'Post Coital Contraception – A Pilot Study' (1973) 13 *Journal of Reproductive Medicine* 53; Albert A Yuzpe and WJ Lancee, 'Ethinylestradiol and dl-Norgestrel as a Postcoital Contraceptive' (1977) 28 *Fertility and Sterility* 932; Charlotte Ellertson, 'History and Efficacy of Emergency Contraception: Beyond Coca-Cola' (1996) 28 *Family Planning Perspectives* 44.

100 James Trussell and Beth Jordan, 'Editorial: Mechanism of Action of Emergency Contraceptive Pills' (2006) 74 *Contraception* 87; Kristina Gemzell-Danielsson, 'Mechanism of Action of Emergency Contraception' (2010) 82 *Contraception* 404.

101 Trussell and Jordan (n 100).

102 See, eg, *ibid*; James Trussell and Elizabeth G Raymond, 'Emergency Contraception: A Last Chance to Prevent Unintended Pregnancy' (*Emergency Contraception*, June 2011), at <ec.princeton.edu/questions/ec-review.pdf>.

103 Lisa L Wynn and Angel M Foster, 'The Birth of a Global Reproductive Health Technology: An Introduction to the Journey of Emergency Contraception' in Angel M Foster and Lisa L Wynn (eds), *Emergency Contraception: The Story of a Global Reproductive Health Technology* (New York, Palgrave Macmillan, 2012) 3, 6–8.

for women who need access to EC. Given the need for prompt access and the potential delay entailed by the need for a physician's prescription, access to EC without a prescription is thought by many experts to be the best way of ensuring that EC is used to maximum effect.[104]

In the UK and Australia,[105] and now Canada, one form of EC (levonorgestrel) is available without a physician's prescription, and may be obtained directly from a pharmacy.[106] In the US, levonorgestrel may be obtained by men and women aged 17 or older without a prescription,[107] and ella (ulipristal acetate) is available only by prescription. Women aged 16 and under cannot access any EC in the US without a prescription.[108] Although the same general approach is being taken to improve access to EC in Canada, the US, the UK and Australia, both the extent of the changes made and the process by which the changes have been implemented have been markedly different among these jurisdictions.

In the US, the manufacturer of the EC pill known as 'Plan B' requested over-the-counter status for the drug in 2001. An expert advisory committee of the FDA was convened to consider the request. The committee 'overwhelmingly' voted in favour of non-prescription status for Plan B.[109] The advisory committee's conclusions and recommendations were later endorsed by FDA staff, but in 2004, FDA management rejected the manufacturer's application for non-prescription status on the basis of concerns about the potential effect of over-the-counter availability on the sexual behaviour of young adolescents.[110] The FDA informed the manufacturer that the medication could not be made available over-the-

---

[104] A number of organisations support non-prescription access to EC, including the American College of Family Physicians, the International Planned Parenthood Federation, the American Public Health Association, the American College of Obstetricians and Gynecologists, the Royal College of Obstetricians and Gynaecologists, and the Society of Obstetricians and Gynaecologists of Canada (International Consortium for Emergency Contraception, 'Support for EC', at <www.cecinfo.org/what/supportForEC.htm>). See also Anna Glasier and David Baird, 'The Effects of Self-Administering Emergency Contraception' (1998) 339 *New England Journal of Medicine* 1; David A Grimes, 'Switching Emergency Contraception to Over-the-Counter Status' (2002) 347 *New England Journal of Medicine* 846; International Consortium for Emergency Contraception, 'Policy Statement: Improving Access to Emergency Contraception' (July 2003), at <www.cecinfo.org/publications/PDFs/policy/ImprovingAccess_EC_English.pdf>.

[105] In both of these countries, EC may be obtained after a request and brief consultation with a pharmacist. This means of access has been available in Australia since January 2004 (Hobbs *et al* (n 11)) and in the UK since 2001 (University of Aberdeen, Faculty of Family Planning and Reproductive Health Care Clinical Effectiveness Unit, 'FFPRHC Guidance: Emergency Contraception' (2003) 29(2) *Journal of Family Planning and Reproductive Health Care* 9, 13). The newer EC ulipristal acetate is available in the UK and the US with a prescription.

[106] In Canada, Plan B (levonorgestrel) is no longer under Federal Government control. This means that it is up to provincial and territorial regulatory bodies to determine how the drug may be sold. Provincial and territorial regulators act on the basis of recommendations made by the National Drug Scheduling Advisory Committee (Joanna N Erdman and Rebecca J Cook, 'Protecting Fairness in Women's Health: The Case of Emergency Contraception' in Colleen M Flood (ed), *Just Medicare: What's In, What's Out, How We Decide* (Toronto, University of Toronto Press, 2006) 137, 138–39).

[107] Megan L Kavanaugh, Sanithia L Williams and E Bimla Schwarz, 'Emergency Contraception Use and Counseling After Changes in United States Prescription Status' (2011) 95 *Fertility and Sterility* 2578. The FDA initially allowed over-the-counter access only for women aged 18 and older (Trussell and Raymond (n 102)). In 2009, the FDA was ordered by the US District Court for the Eastern Circuit to take action to make Plan B available to 17-year-olds as well.

[108] See Rebekah E Gee *et al*, 'Behind-the-counter Status and Availability of Emergency Contraception' (2008) 199 *American Journal of Obstetrics & Gynecology* 478.e1. For a discussion of the FDA's decision, see Alastair JJ Wood, Jeffrey M Drazen and Michael F Greene, 'A Sad Day for Science at the FDA' (2005) 353 *New England Journal of Medicine* 1197.

[109] Wood *et al* (n 108) 1197. The committee was made up of experts in obstetrics and gynaecology and in non-prescription drug availability, and voted 23:4 in favour of non-prescription status for Plan B.

[110] *Ibid.*

counter either until it demonstrated that adolescent women (16 or younger) would be able to use the drug safely. Alternatively, it could create a new label for the drug and a distribution system that made it available over-the-counter only to those over 16 years of age, but only with a prescription for those aged 16 or younger.[111] The FDA's decision has been criticised for its clearly political nature, given the overwhelming evidence in support of non-prescription status,[112] but, as noted above, Plan B is currently available over-the-counter only to those aged 17 or older.[113]

Some US states have sought to improve access to EC via various methods. These include permitting access to EC without a prescription in certain circumstances, limiting pharmacists' ability to decline to provide EC and mandating that EC must be provided by hospital emergency rooms to women who have been sexually assaulted.[114] Other states have taken steps to limit the accessibility of EC, such as excluding EC from family planning services covered by Medicaid, and excluding EC from their mandatory contraceptive insurance coverage.[115]

In the UK, as in the US, EC was first introduced as a prescription-only medication. It quickly became apparent that given the narrow window of opportunity for effective use of EC, the need for a physician appointment and prescription would pose a significant barrier to use of EC to prevent pregnancy.[116] When a status change from prescription-only medicine to pharmacy medicine was initially proposed, the manufacturer of the then available EC pill resisted the change, apparently due to concerns about potential liability for adverse events.[117] Ultimately, the change in status was effected after action by the Secretary of State for Health, and EC became available from pharmacists without the need for a physician's prescription.[118] Emergency contraception has been available to women in the UK in this fashion since 2001, and more recently it has become available to women under age 25 at no cost.[119]

Ann Furedi argues that, at least in the case of Britain, the manufacturer of the first dedicated EC product (Schering Health Care Limited) did not approach the launch of its new product with any enthusiasm, and that the company's apparent reluctance has had an important and continuing impact on usage rates.[120] This, together with mixed messages about sex and morality in British society, and the continued efforts of anti-abortion advocacy groups, has meant continued challenges to those who would like to see the method more widely accepted and used. As Furedi puts it,

---

[111] This ruling is contrary to the advice of the FDA's own medical expert advisory committee, as well as that of the American College of Obstetricians and Gynecologists and several other healthcare provider organisations (Megan L Ranney, Erin M Gee and Roland C Merchant, 'Nonprescription Availability of Emergency Contraception in the United States: Current Status, Controversies, and Impact on Emergency Medicine Practice' (2006) 47 *Annals of Emergency Medicine* 461, 463).

[112] See, eg, Wood *et al* (n 108).

[113] Above (n 107).

[114] 'State Policies in Brief: Emergency Contraception' (n 88).

[115] *Ibid.*

[116] Ann Furedi, 'Britain: Contradictory Messages about Sexual Responsibility' in Foster and Wynn (n 103) 123.

[117] *Ibid* 127–28. At the time (the early to mid-1990s), the only dedicated EC product available was a combination product, meaning that it contained estrogen as well as progesterone.

[118] The Prescription Only Medicines (Human Use) Amendment (No 3) Order 2000 (SI 2000/3231) (UK).

[119] Furedi (n 116) 125.

[120] *Ibid.*

The tragedy of the provision of EC in the United Kingdom is that the extension of access into pharmacies did not become a means to normalize its use. It did not lead to a situation where it was marketed effectively by a maker keen to maximize its use. Instead it has remained shrouded in stigma, a product that women really 'shouldn't' need.[121]

Although early efforts to provide a dedicated EC product to Australian women were initially hindered by abortion politics, once it became available, EC progressed from prescription to non-prescription status very swiftly.[122] Levonorgestrel was approved as a prescription-only drug in 2002, and the application for change to non-prescription status was instigated virtually upon its approval by the relevant authorities.[123] By January 2004, EC had become available upon request from pharmacists.[124] There was some resistance to the status change, both by medical professional bodies and by religious organisations.[125] The concerns expressed by the medical profession related to the potential for adequate counselling by pharmacists, in part because of the difficulty of ensuring private consultations in the pharmacy setting.[126] Physicians also expressed reservations about the inability of pharmacists to follow patients who request EC to ensure that they are offered testing for sexually-transmitted infections.[127] In spite of these concerns, the transition from prescription-only status took place within an unusually short time frame, with the regulatory body waiving the typical time requirements.[128]

In spite of ready access to EC in both Australia and the UK, concerns have been raised about its unrealised potential, given relatively low rates of use.[129] One of the primary reasons for the low usage is the perception on the part of women that they are at low risk for pregnancy.[130] In Australia, another potentially significant barrier to increased use of EC is the prohibition on direct-to-consumer advertising, meaning that women may lack knowledge about use of EC and where to obtain it.[131]

In Canada, the deregulation of EC happened in two stages. In 2005, EC was changed to non-prescription status across Canada, meaning that it could be kept 'behind the counter' in pharmacies and obtained by women upon direct request to the pharmacist.[132] While this meant that the impediment to access created by the need for a physician's prescription was cleared away, other obstacles emerged. Concerns were raised around cost – pharmacies were charging a counselling fee in addition to the cost of the drug –

[121] *Ibid* 136.

[122] Helen Calabretto, 'Australia: Organized Physician Opposition to Nonprescription Status' in Foster and Wynn (eds) (n 103) 207, 211–13. Calabretto notes that in the mid-1990s, anti-abortion groups in Australia attempted to link EC with mifepristone, asserting that EC was an abortifacient. The campaign was evidently very successful, as this erroneous idea persists today, with many women in Australia 'still confusing the ECP with mifepristone' (Hobbs *et al* (n 11) 156).

[123] Calabretto (n 122) 213.

[124] Hobbs *et al* (n 11).

[125] Calabretto (n 122).

[126] *Ibid* 214–16.

[127] *Ibid.*

[128] *Ibid* 214. Calabretto notes that the regulatory body (the National Drugs and Poisons Schedule Committee of the Therapeutic Goods Administration (TGA)) ordinarily requires two years of clinical use within Australia before it will consider a schedule change.

[129] See, eg, Furedi (n 116); Hobbs *et al* (n 11).

[130] Hobbs *et al* (n 11). This is a finding that has been reported in many studies of EC usage: see, eg, Aneblom *et al* (n 13); Free *et al* (n 13); Glasier *et al* (n 13).

[131] Calabretto (n 122) 207–08. Hobbs *et al* (n 11) 156 note that they 'found that poor knowledge of the ECP is significantly associated with its nonuse'.

[132] Government of Canada, 'Regulations Amending the Food and Drug Regulations (1272 – Levonorgestrel)' (2004) 138 *Canada Gazette* 1633.

and around privacy, based on the information collection practices of many pharmacists who dispense EC.[133]

The privacy concerns centred on a form recommended for use by the Canadian Pharmacists Association (CPhA). The form asked for 'personal data, including the woman's name, address, the date of her last menstrual period, when she had unprotected sex, and her customary method of birth control . . . [and] . . . the reason for dispensing the medication'.[134] Objections were raised to the practice of collecting this information, as it could deter women from seeking access to EC because of their fears around the collection and storage of sensitive information. Privacy commissioners in a number of Canadian jurisdictions articulated concerns about the CPhA form, noting that pharmacists do not normally collect personal information when they dispense Schedule II drugs.[135]

The proposed solution to these remaining barriers to access was to make EC available without the need for pharmacist intervention. In May 2008, the second stage of deregulation occurred, and Plan B became a Schedule III product, meaning that it can now be sold off-the-shelf with no need for consultation with a pharmacist.[136] The decision to approve Plan B as a Schedule III product was based on the recommendation of the National Association of Pharmacy Regulatory Authorities (NAPRA). In theory, this means that women throughout Canada should be able to purchase EC without pharmacist involvement, just as they would purchase any number of other items at the pharmacy. However, the scheduling change recommended by NAPRA is not binding on provincial and territorial regulators, and at least two provinces have declined to make the change.[137]

As explained above, the uncertainty about the mechanism by which EC prevents pregnancy has played a role in creating barriers to access for women wishing to use it. The resistance to wider availability of contraception (especially for minors[138]), and EC in particular, is largely founded on conservative politics. Emergency contraception is often claimed by pro-life organisations to be a form of early abortion because it might prevent implantation of a fertilised egg.[139] In the UK, the decision by the Secretary of State for Health to permit pharmacists to dispense EC without a prescription was challenged by an organisation called the Society for the Protection of Unborn Children (SPUC). SPUC argued that the decision facilitates the commission of criminal offences by allowing abortion in circumstances where abortion would not be permitted under UK abortion legislation.[140] In rejecting the challenge, the court held that 'miscarriage' in the Offences

---

[133] Erdman and Cook (n 106) 146–49; Laura Eggertson and Barbara Sibbald, 'Privacy Issues Raised Over Plan B: Women Asked for Names, Addresses, Sexual History' (2005) 173 *Canadian Medical Association Journal* 1435.

[134] Eggertson and Sibbald (n 133) 1435.

[135] Laura Eggertson, 'Ontario Pharmacists Drop Plan B Screening Form' (2006) 174 *Canadian Medical Association Journal* 149.

[136] Laura Eggertson, 'Plan B Comes Out From Behind the Counter' (2008) 178 *Canadian Medical Association Journal* 1645. Another EC product, NorLevo, has since also been approved as a Schedule III product (Donald B Langille, Michael Allen and Anne Marie Whelan, 'Emergency Contraception: Knowledge and Attitudes of Nova Scotian Family Physicians' (2012) 58 *Canadian Family Physician* 548).

[137] In Saskatchewan, EC is kept behind the counter; and in Québec, EC may be obtained by prescription from a pharmacist (*Pharmacy Act*, RSQ c P-10, s 17(6)). See Plan B website at <www.planb.ca/where.php>.

[138] See, eg, Roxanne Mykitiuk and Stephanie Turnham, 'Legal Dimensions of Adolescent Sexuality' (2004) 26 *Journal of Obstetrics and Gynaecology Canada* 991.

[139] Jackson (n 40) 87; Center for Reproductive Rights, 'Governments Worldwide Put Emergency Contraception into Women's Hands: A Global Review of Laws and Policies' (September 2004), at <www.reproductiverights.org/pdf/pub_bp_govtswwec.pdf>.

[140] *Smeaton v Secretary of State for Health* [2002] EWHC 610 (Admin), [2002] 2 FCR 193.

Against the Person Act[141] means 'the termination of an established pregnancy, and there is no established pregnancy prior to implantation'.[142] The court noted that the EC pill (or 'morning-after pill', as it was referred to in the judgment) works prior to implantation and that it cannot interfere with an established pregnancy.

Uniquely in the US, safety has been a major issue with respect to non-prescription access to EC, particularly safety for women aged 16 and younger. That this concern is specious is quite obvious when placed in context with the FDA's approach to other medications. As one group of authors explains:

> [O]ther over-the-counter drugs, such as acetaminophen and aspirin, can cause death when taken inappropriately. At a meeting of a similar FDA advisory committee, data were presented indicating that acetaminophen ingestion results in 56,680 emergency department visits, 26,256 hospitalizations and 458 deaths in the United States every year; a large number of these events affect persons younger than 17 years of age. The FDA has shown no inclination to restrict the availability of these drugs to young people by requiring them to have a prescription. Why not?[143]

E. Access to contraception and reproductive autonomy

The history of the development of and access to EC clearly illustrates the interplay of multiple barriers to access that work to interfere with reproductive autonomy. Over time, regulatory barriers, cost and provider conscientious objection have all played a role in restricting women's ability to access EC. In addition to these important barriers to access, manufacturer's interests (or lack thereof) in creating and marketing effective methods of EC, and politics around abortion and sexual morality, have also been implicated in preventing or hindering access to EC.[144]

I have argued that respect for reproductive autonomy requires that women's access to effective and desirable methods of contraception must be facilitated. This may involve interrogating and removing regulatory and financial barriers to access, and requires that women's needs and interests prevail over the moral or religious objections of some healthcare providers.

Contraception is an interesting case study from the standpoint of my arguments about the nature of reproductive autonomy and what it, in turn, demands from the State. While opposition to contraception continues in some circles, it is limited in scope and pervasiveness. There is no legitimate reason why, in a country like Canada or the US, the UK or Australia, any woman who wishes to use contraception should have any difficulty accessing it. Respect for reproductive autonomy clearly requires coordinated efforts on the part of regional and national governments and health professional regulators to remove regulatory and financial barriers to access, and to make it clear that women's autonomy will not successfully be obstructed by the consciences of healthcare providers. It is not possible to continue to deal with these issues in an *ad hoc* fashion if meaningful change and progress are to be realised.

[141] Offences Against the Person Act 1861 (UK).
[142] *Smeaton v Secretary of State for Health* (n 140) para 17.
[143] Wood *et al* (n 108) 1198.
[144] Calabretto (n 122) 211–12; Furedi (n 116); Wynn and Foster (n 103) 8–11; Lisa L Wynn, 'United States: Activism, Sexual Archetypes, and the Politicization of Science' in Foster and Wynn (eds) (n 103) 39.

Indeed, from the standpoint of respect for reproductive autonomy, it is difficult to imagine a plausible justification for the persistence of barriers to accessing effective contraception. There is no dispute as to the importance of a woman's ability to plan the timing of her childbearing, neither is there any disagreement as to the societal ramifications of access to effective birth control. And yet, in developed nations in the twenty-first century, we continue to see extremely high rates of unintended pregnancy. Contraception will never be perfect and there will always be unintended pregnancies. But surely we can expect better.

III. NON-CONSENSUAL BIRTH CONTROL

Sterilisation is the most commonly used form of contraception worldwide,[145] and in so far as those who are sterilised have made an autonomous choice in that respect, its use is (in Western democracies, at least) uncontroversial. That said, its use in some contexts – such as the 'emergency' period in India in the 1970s, where 8.1 million people were sterilised in 1976[146] – provides cause for significant concern.[147] Closer to home is the legacy of the Eugenics Movement in Canada and the United States. The movement saw some Canadian provinces and several American states pass legislation permitting the non-therapeutic (in other words, non medically-necessary) sterilisation of persons with mental illness, developmental or intellectual disabilities and other traits deemed socially undesirable.[148] Although most such laws have now been repealed,[149] concerns remain about coercive practices; most commonly when intellectually disabled or mentally-ill women (or men) are sterilised without their consent.[150]

---

[145] United Nations, Department of Economic and Social Affairs, Population Division, 'World Contraceptive Use 2010' (POP/DB/CP/Rev2010). Female sterilisation is far more common than male sterilisation (19% compared to 2.4%).

[146] Davidson R Gwatkin, 'Political Will and Family Planning: The Implications of India's Emergency Experience' (1979) 5 *Population and Development Review* 29.

[147] A more recent context includes involuntary sterilisation of indigent women in Latin American countries: see, eg, Rebecca J Cook and Bernard M Dickens, 'Voluntary and Involuntary Sterilization: Denials and Abuses of Rights' (2000) 68 *International Journal of Gynecology and Obstetrics* 61, 62.

[148] See, eg, Angus McLaren, *Our Own Master Race: Eugenics in Canada, 1885–1945* (Toronto, McClelland and Stewart, 1990); Roberta Cepko, 'Involuntary Sterilisation of Mentally Disabled Women' (1993) 8 *Berkeley Women's Law Journal* 122; Timothy Caulfield and Gerald Robertson, 'Eugenic Policies in Alberta: From the Systematic to the Systemic?' (1996) 35 *Alberta Law Review* 59; Gail Rodgers, 'Yin and Yang: The Eugenic Policies of the United States and China: Is the Analysis that Black and White?' (1999) 22 *Houston Journal of International Law* 129. Dorothy Roberts and Jennifer Malat have also noted the racialised application of eugenics policies (Roberts (n 27) 56–103; Jennifer Malat, 'Racial Differences in Norplant Use in the United States' (2000) 50 *Social Science & Medicine* 1297, 1298).

[149] And compensation successfully sought in relation to how some such laws were applied: see, eg, *Muir v The Queen in Right of Alberta*, 179 AR 321, 132 DLR (4th) 695 (1996) (ABQB); *E(D) (Guardian Ad Litem of) v British Columbia*, 2005 BCCA 134, (2005) BCJ No 492.

[150] In the vast majority of situations in which sterilisation is proposed for an intellectually-disabled individual, that individual is a woman (Susan M Brady and Sonia Grover, *The Sterilisation of Girls and Young Women in Australia: A Legal, Medical and Social Context* (Sydney, Human Rights and Equal Opportunity Commission, 1997). There is also a 2001 update to the Report (Susan Brady, John Britton and Sonia Grover, *The Sterilisation of Girls and Young Women in Australia: Issues and Progress* (Sydney, Human Rights and Equal Opportunity Commission, 2001). As Mason and Laurie point out, it is perhaps not surprising that this is the case, as 'The only bases for intentional, non-consensual, non-therapeutic sterilisation of a man would be punitive or eugenic, which is what all would agree should be avoided' (J Kenyon Mason and Graeme T Laurie, *Mason and McCall Smith's Law and Medical Ethics*, 8th edn (Oxford, Oxford University Press, 2011) 308).

A. Law and non-consensual birth control

Courts in Canada, the US, the UK and Australia have all had occasion to wrestle with the difficult issues presented by applications seeking guidance on the permissibility of the non-therapeutic sterilisation of persons who lack the capacity to consent, including children and adults with disabilities. With one exception, the results have been remarkably consistent – UK, US and Australian courts have all held that even in the absence of enabling legislation, they possess the jurisdiction to authorise such procedures. Canada is an outlier as the only jurisdiction in which the highest court has held that sterilisation 'should never be authorised for non-therapeutic purposes under the *parens patriae* jurisdiction'.[151]

The US (like Canada) has a history of State-sponsored eugenics policies that included legislation authorising sterilisation of the 'feebleminded' and other social undesirables.[152] There is no recent authority on the question of non-consensual, non-therapeutic sterilisation from the US Supreme Court; the cases that the Court has considered date from 1927[153] and 1942.[154] In the first, *Buck v Bell*, the Court upheld as constitutionally valid a Virginia statute. The law permitted the involuntary sterilisation of 'inmates' of certain state institutions who were 'afflicted with hereditary forms of insanity, imbecility, etc, on complying with the very careful provisions by which the act protects the patients from possible abuse'.[155] The case is the source of Justice Oliver Wendell Holmes's now infamous statement 'Three generations of imbeciles are enough,'[156] leaving no mystery as to the Court's view as to the desirability of procreation by certain classes of individuals.

Fifteen years later, in *Skinner v Oklahoma*, the Court struck down legislation that permitted the sterilisation of particular classes of criminals on the basis that the State had 'no rational basis . . . for distinguishing between the classes of criminals to be sterilized'.[157] The Court did not take the opportunity in *Skinner v Oklahoma* to overrule *Buck v Bell*, and has not since had (or taken) another opportunity to do so.

The legal position in the US with respect to sterilisation of persons with developmental disabilities has been described as creating 'a confusing and contradictory array of restrictions'.[158] American courts asked to consider authorising the sterilisation of those who are not competent to consent to treatment refer to a 'heavy presumption' against sterilisation, particularly in the case of minors. But most courts, when faced with an application of this nature, find in favour of having jurisdiction to grant it.[159] Courts have in some instances held that they have jurisdiction on the basis of an enabling statute, in

---

[151] *E (Mrs) v Eve* [1986] 2 SCR 388, [1986] SCJ No 60, 431 (cited to SCR).

[152] Rodgers (n 148) 135–36; Jeff Goldhar, 'The Sterilization of Women with an Intellectual Disability – A Lawyer Looks at the Medical Aspects' (1990–91) 10 *University of Tasmania Law Review* 157.

[153] *Buck v Bell*, 274 US 200 (1927).

[154] *Skinner v Oklahoma*, 316 US 535 (1942).

[155] *Buck v Bell* (n 153) 206.

[156] *Ibid* 207.

[157] Cepko (n 148) 123.

[158] American Academy of Pediatrics, Committee on Bioethics, 'Sterilization of Minors with Developmental Disabilities' (1999) 104 *Pediatrics* 337. For a discussion of ethical issues respecting the sterilisation of adult women with intellectual or mental disabilities, see, eg, American College of Obstetricians and Gynecologists, 'ACOG Committee Opinion No 371: Sterilization of Women, Including those with Mental Disabilities' (2007) 110 *Obstetrics & Gynecology* 217.

[159] See, eg, *Re Hayes*, 608 P 2d 635 (Wash 1980); *Re Terwilliger*, 450 A 2d 1376 (Pa Super Ct 1982) (jurisdiction *parens patriae*).

some cases broadening the purview of the statute to include categories of persons not evidently contemplated by the legislation.[160] But even in the absence of enabling legislation, courts have nevertheless held that they have the authority to determine these matters on the basis of their general jurisdiction or their jurisdiction *parens patriae*.[161]

While not precluding involuntary non-therapeutic sterilisation, American courts have sought to protect persons who may be subject to involuntary sterilisation by way of strict procedural requirements. In its decision in *Re Hayes*,[162] the Supreme Court of Washington articulated a standard for procedural requirements that has been followed in other American jurisdictions.[163] According to *Re Hayes*, the person sought to be sterilised must be represented by a 'disinterested' litigation guardian, the court must receive independent advice respecting medical, social and psychological aspects of the individual's life, and the court must, 'to the greatest extent possible,' take the views of the individual into consideration.[164] The court must find that the person is incapable to make her own decision as regards sterilisation, and that she is unlikely to become capable to do so in the foreseeable future. Further, there must be a need for contraception, and the court must find that there is no reasonable alternative to sterilisation.[165]

Concerns around coerced birth control have also arisen in the US in relation to long-acting (but non-permanent) contraceptive methods.[166] In 1990, the FDA approved Norplant, an implantable contraceptive device consisting of six plastic rods containing levonorgestrel. The drug is released slowly and the implants can provide effective contraception for up to five years; upon removal, fertility is restored within days.[167] A few days after the device was approved for use in the US, an editorial writer for the *Philadelphia Inquirer* suggested that poor women could be offered cash incentives to use Norplant; in turn, this could help to break the 'cycle of poverty'.[168] The idea quickly became more than the controversial suggestion of an editorialist, as several states considered legislation that would either encourage or, in some cases, require poor women to

[160] See, eg, *Ruby v Massey*, 452 F Supp 361 (D Conn 1978), where the Court held that a statute restricting court-ordered sterilisation to incompetent minors in state institutions violated the equal protection rights of the parents of non-institutionalised incompetent minors. Cepko notes that the statute in question in *Ruby v Massey* was later repealed and replaced with a statute applying only to incompetent adults (Cepko (n 148)). She notes that the courts on occasion refer to the existence of a fundamental right to procreate, then proceed to ignore that right in their reasoning and permit the sterilisation procedure to be carried out (*ibid* 133–34).

[161] Cepko (n 148) 145–59. In *Stump v Sparkman*, 435 US 349 (1978) 351, the Court was faced with a liability claim against an Indiana judge based on his decision to authorise the sterilisation of a 15-year-old girl whose mother alleged that she was 'somewhat retarded'. The Court held that Indiana law gave circuit courts 'original exclusive jurisdiction in all cases at law and in equity' and jurisdiction over 'all other causes, matters and proceedings where exclusive jurisdiction thereof is not conferred by law upon some other court, board or officer'. The Court did not interpret the absence of legislation authorising sterilisation as indicating a 'clear absence of all jurisdiction' to authorise the procedure. Rodgers notes that since this decision, lower courts have been more likely to find that they have jurisdiction to authorise non-therapeutic sterilisation procedures (Rodgers (n 148) 150).

[162] *Re Hayes* (n 159).

[163] Barry R Furrow *et al*, *Health Law: Cases, Materials and Problems*, 3rd edn (St Paul, MN, West Group, 1997) 930.

[164] *Re Hayes* (n 159).

[165] *Ibid* 641.

[166] See above (n 27).

[167] Population Council, *Norplant, Levonorgestrel Implants: A Summary of Scientific Data* (New York, The Population Council, 1990).

[168] Donald Kimmelman, 'Poverty and Norplant: Can Contraception Reduce the Underclass?', *Philadelphia Inquirer*, 12 December 1990, A18.

have Norplant inserted.[169] Some judges also took up the idea, ordering Norplant use as a condition of probation for women convicted of child abuse.[170] In the end, none of the proposed legislation was passed, and the judicial attempts to impose the use of Norplant as a condition of probation or in sentencing were overturned on appeal,[171] but questions remained about potentially coercive or oppressive practices.[172] Norplant has been withdrawn from the US and UK markets, but remains available in the developing world.

Australian courts, like their counterparts in the US (and the UK), have held that while parents may consent to medically necessary (or therapeutic) sterilisation procedures in respect of their minor children who are intellectually disabled,[173] a court order is required for non-therapeutic sterilisation to proceed lawfully.[174] In *Marion's Case*, the High Court of Australia held that consent to non-therapeutic sterilisation of an intellectually-disabled minor child is beyond the scope of parental competence. Such procedures can be lawfully carried out only where authorised by the Family Court. The majority held that the role of the Court in this context is to 'decide whether, in the circumstances of the case, [sterilisation] is in the best interests of the child'.[175] While declining to formulate a rule as to when, precisely, sterilisation is in the child's best interests, the Court referred to sterilisation as a 'step of last resort'.[176] The Court indicated that this entails the failure of all other 'less invasive' procedures, or the certainty that 'no other procedure or treatment will work'.[177] In affirming the centrality of the welfare of the child in cases of this nature, the Court clarified that such procedures would not be authorised by the courts where the intention is 'eugenic or entirely for the convenience of others'.[178]

Some Australian states have legislation granting the authority to make sterilisation decisions to a specialised tribunal. In *Marion's Case*, the High Court had noted the potential for jurisdictional conflict, but did not find it necessary to address the issue in that case.[179] In a later case, *P v P*,[180] the parents of an intellectually-disabled 16-year-old young woman sought authorisation to have their daughter undergo a hysterectomy to prevent pregnancy and menstruation. Here, the jurisdictional question arose to be considered as a result of relevant New South Wales legislation.[181] The matter was brought before the High Court of Australia[182] to determine whether the Family Court could

---

[169] Andrew R Davidson and Debra Kalmuss, 'Topics For Our Times: Norplant Coercion – An Overstated Threat' (1997) 87 *American Journal of Public Health* 550.

[170] See, eg, Malat (n 148) 1298; K Ravi Srinivas and K Kanakamala, 'Introducing Norplant: Politics of Coercion' (1992) 29 *Economic and Political Weekly* 1531.

[171] Davidson and Kalmuss (n 169).

[172] Malat (n 148).

[173] The Court specified that parental consent for sterilisation is limited to circumstances in which sterilisation results from surgery 'appropriately carried out to treat some malfunction or disease' (*Secretary, Department of Health and Community Services v JWB and SMB (Marion's Case)* (1992) 175 CLR 218, 250).

[174] See, eg, *Marion's Case* (n 173); *P v P* (1994) 181 CLR 583 (HCA); *In the Matter of: P Appellant and P Respondent and Legal Aid Commission of New South Wales Separate Representative and Human Rights and Equal Opportunity Commission Intervener* [1995] Fam CA 44; (1995) 19 Fam LR 1 (Fam Ct Australia).

[175] *Marion's Case* (n 173) 259.

[176] *Ibid.*

[177] *Ibid.*

[178] Ian Kennedy and Andrew Grubb, *Medical Law*, 3rd edn (London, Butterworths, 2000) 1172.

[179] *Marion's Case* (n 173) 263.

[180] *P v P* (HCA) (n 174).

[181] The former Children (Care and Protection) Act 1987 (NSW) (applicable to those under 16 years of age) and Guardianship Act 1987 (NSW) (applicable to those 16 years and older). For the new legislation respecting children, see Children and Young Persons (Care and Protection) Act 1998 (NSW), s 175.

[182] *P v P* (HCA) (n 174).

authorise non-therapeutic sterilisation of an intellectually-disabled minor. New South Wales law permits the NSW Guardianship Board to authorise a sterilisation procedure in such a case only where needed to 'prevent serious damage to [the child's] health'.[183] The Commonwealth Family Law Act 1975 (from which the Family Court acquires juris-diction), in contrast, requires consideration of each case in accordance with the 'best interests' test and the principles set out by the High Court in *Marion's Case*. Given that the test employed by the Family Court could conceivably yield different results than the mandate of the Guardianship Tribunal would permit, the concern arose that the State guardianship legislation might impede the Family Court's jurisdiction to make such orders. The High Court held that state legislation such as the NSW Guardianship Act cannot operate to frustrate or interfere with the jurisdiction of the Family Court. To the extent that state law is more restrictive than the criteria established in *Marion's Case*, it is invalid.[184] Put another way, the two decision-making bodies exercise concurrent juris-diction, but once the Family Court has either granted or refused an order authorising sterilisation, there is no role for the state legislation or state tribunal to play.[185]

Following the High Court decision, the application was heard and dismissed by Moore J of the Family Court of Australia.[186] Moore J concluded that she could not 'be satisfied to the requisite standard, that the proposed procedure would increase [the minor's] capacity for enjoyment of life. Nor could [she] be satisfied that there is a pres-ent need for it.'[187] On appeal to the Full Court of the Family Court, Moore J's decision was reversed and the sterilisation procedure was authorised.[188] In the course of provid-ing reasons, the Family Court set out guidelines to be considered in applications of this nature.[189] The guidelines mandate consideration of the condition of the child, the nature of the treatment or procedure being proposed, the reason for the suggested treatment, the alternative approaches available and a number of other matters.[190]

The Family Court has been criticised in relation to its approach to applications to authorise sterilisation procedures.[191] Two significant worries articulated by commentators

---

[183] Danny Sandor, 'Sterilisation and Special Medical Procedures on Children and Young People: Blunt Instrument? Bad Medicine?' in Ian R Freckelton and Kerry Anne Petersen (eds), *Controversies in Health Law* (Sydney, Law Federation Press, 2000) 2, 11.

[184] *P v P* (HCA) (n 174).

[185] Similar legislation exists in South Australia (Guardianship and Administration Act 1993 (SA), ss 58, 61), Tasmania (Guardianship and Administration Act 1995 (Tas), ss 3, 6, 36, 45, 46) and Queensland (Guardianship and Administration Act 2000 (Qld), ss 68, 70; ss 80A–80D re children). All three statutes prescribe the circum-stances in which the relevant tribunal may consent to sterilisation on behalf of a child, or an adult with cogni-tive impairment.

[186] Moore J's decision is not reported but is quoted at length by the Family Court in its decision on the appeal of Moore J's decision (*In the Matter of: P Appellant and P Respondent* (Fam Ct Australia) (n 174).

[187] *Ibid* 10 (quoting Moore J).

[188] *Ibid*.

[189] See Sandor (n 183) 7, for description and comments on the guidelines. Since the decisions in *Marion's Case* (n 173) and *P v P* (HCA) (n 174), the Family Law Act 1975 (Cth) has been amended. It now includes a provision (s 67zc(2)) that specifies that the court has jurisdiction to make orders relating to the welfare of chil-dren and that in making such decisions, 'a court must regard the best interests of the child as the paramount consideration' thus enshrining the decision of the High Court in *Marion's Case*.

[190] *In the Matter of: P Appellant and P Respondent* (Fam Ct Australia) (n 174) 26.

[191] See Sandor (n 183) 16, for a brief outline of some of these criticisms. See also Jennifer Ford, 'The Sterilisation of Young Women with an Intellectual Disability: A Comparison Between the Family Court of Australia and the Guardianship Board of New South Wales' (1996) 10 *Australian Journal of Family Law* 236; Nick O'Neill, 'Sterilisation of Children with Intellectual Disabilities' (1996) 2 *Australian Journal of Human Rights* 262.

are the indeterminacy of the 'best interests' test and the uncertainty of the distinction between therapeutic sterilisations (which can be authorised by parents or guardians) and non-therapeutic procedures (which require authorisation by the Court).[192] But of even greater concern in Australia is a 1997 Report[193] finding that 'Courts and tribunals have authorized a total of 17 sterilizations of girls since *Marion's Case*. Meanwhile, data collated by the Health Insurance Commission shows that at least 1045 girls have been sterilised over the same period . . .'[194] The authors go on to note that, given the rarity of disease of the reproductive organs in women under 20 years of age, they were unable to avoid the conclusion that 'most were sterilised unlawfully'.[195]

There has been ongoing discussion of this issue in Australia, including debate around the numbers cited in the 1997 Human Rights and Equal Opportunity Commission (HREOC) Report. In responding to the Report, the Minister for Health claimed that the actual number of sterilisations performed on female minors was 200, not the 1,045 claimed in the HREOC Report.[196] In 2000, a report was tabled in the Senate by the Minister for Family and Community Services and the Minister Assisting the Prime Minister for the Status of Women.[197] That report indicated an even lower number of sterilisation procedures – 22 sterilisations between 1993–99, and 11 for the fiscal years 1996/97–1998/99. As Brady, Briton and Grover note in their 2001 follow-up Report, coming to a firm conclusion about the number of sterilisation procedures performed on young women is extremely challenging due to the lack of consistency among various databases in terms of how the information is coded and recorded.[198] They also note that the number of sterilisation procedures performed according to the Senate Report is lower than the number authorised by the Family Court and State Guardianship Tribunals for the relevant time frames.[199] Lastly, they point to the anecdotal information from women, parents and parent groups, community groups, healthcare providers and statutory agencies about the reality of unauthorised sterilisation.[200]

Since the 1997 HREOC Report, there have been calls for law reform in Australia. In the early 2000s it appeared that progress was being made on this front, although the process has since ground to a halt. In 2003, the Standing Committee of Attorneys-General (SCAG) agreed to pursue a nationally consistent approach to authorisation procedures to be utilised in applications respecting the sterilisation of minors with a 'decision making disability'.[201] In 2006, the SCAG released a draft bill for consultation.[202] Two years later, however, the SCAG reported that further research into the issues revealed a fall in the

[192] See, eg, Ford (n 191); Natasha Cica, 'Sterilising the Intellectually Disabled: The Approach of the High Court of Australia in *Department of Health v J.W.B. and S.M.B*' (1993) 1 *Medical Law Review* 186.

[193] Brady and Grover (n 150).

[194] *Ibid.*

[195] *Ibid.*

[196] See, eg, Sandor (n 183); Brady, Britton and Grover (n 150) 14.

[197] Commonwealth Department of Family and Community Services, 'Sterilisation of Women and Young Girls with an Intellectual Disability – Report to the Senate' (Women With Disabilities Australia, 6 December 2000), at <www.wwda.org.au/senate.htm>.

[198] Brady, Britton and Grover (n 150) 15–18.

[199] *Ibid* 16.

[200] *Ibid* 19.

[201] Standing Committee of Attorneys-General, 'Issues Paper on the Non-Therapeutic Sterilisation of Minors with a Decision-Making Disability' (Women With Disabilities Australia, 2004), at <www.wwda.org.au/scag-pap1.htm>.

[202] Standing Committee of Attorneys-General, 'Draft 17 Children with Intellectual Disabilities (Regulation of Sterilisation) Bill 2006' (Women With Disabilities Australia, 2006), at <www.wwda.org.au/sterbill06.pdf>.

number of procedures relative to the numbers indicated in the 1997 HREOC Report.[203] In addition, it appeared that physicians and hospitals had a clearer understanding of their legal obligations, and that alternatives to sterilisation are progressively more available and successful. Moreover, given that each jurisdiction within the country had a process in place to authorise sterilisation procedures (and these processes seemed to be working effectively), developing model legislation would be of 'limited benefit'.[204] Accordingly, the SCAG decided to remove this item from its agenda.[205] It seems, for the moment at least, that significant legal and policy change in Australia is unlikely, in spite of pressure by organisations such as Women with Disabilities Australia and the United Nations.[206]

As in Australia, courts in the UK can authorise non-therapeutic sterilisation of at least certain groups of persons who lack the capacity to make the decision for themselves. The High Court, Family Division, may authorise the sterilisation of a minor who is mentally incompetent; applications for authorisation may be made either under relevant legislation[207] or pursuant to the court's inherent jurisdiction.

The court has no common law jurisdiction to authorise non-therapeutic sterilisation of adults, but has held that the involvement of the court in such matters is 'highly desirable as a matter of good practice'.[208] A declaration that the procedure can be lawfully carried out in the case of an adult is required only where the procedure is not incidental to required medical or surgical treatment. This is also true in Canada and Australia; indeed, this is the distinction Mr Justice La Forest sought to make in *E (Mrs) v Eve* between therapeutic and non-therapeutic procedures.[209] The courts have consistently reaffirmed that the sole justification for sterilisation of a person who lacks capacity is that the procedure is in the person's 'best interests'.[210] Although the Court's articulation of the 'best interests' test in *Re F (Mental Patient) (Sterilisation)* was not very specific or detailed, the test evolved over time to become 'a more sophisticated conception of best interests'[211] that encompasses not only medical interests, but emotional and 'all other welfare issues'.[212] The test has been characterised by Thorpe LJ as requiring the judge to evaluate the best interests of a person respecting whom a declaration in favour of sterilisation is sought, in

---

[203] The SCAG noted that those 1997 numbers were the 'trigger' for the issue being placed on its agenda (Standing Committee of Attorneys General, 'Communiqué' (Property Law Reform Alliance, 28 March 2008) 6, at <www.plra.com.au/News/SCAG_article.pdf>).

[204] *Ibid* 7.

[205] *Ibid.*

[206] See, eg, 'United Nations Calls on Australia to Prohibit Non-therapeutic Sterilisation of Girls with Disabilities' (Women With Disabilities Australia, March 2011), at <www.wwda.org.au/UNsterilise2011.pdf>. One point that WWDA has asserted many times in its work on this issue is that sterilisation is a 'question for adulthood not childhood' (Carolyn Frohmader and Women With Disabilities Australia, 'Policy & Position Paper: The Development of Legislation to Authorise Procedures for the Sterilisation of Children with Intellectual Disabilities' (Women With Disabilities Australia, June 2007), at <www.wwda.org.au/polpapster07.htm>).

[207] Children Act 1989 (UK), s 8(1).

[208] *Re F (Mental Patient: Sterilisation)* [1991] UKHL 1, [1990] 2 AC 15. The judgment includes a detailed explanation as to why the courts no longer have inherent jurisdiction over adults. See also *Practice Note (Official Solicitor: declaratory proceedings: medical and welfare decisions for adults who lack capacity)* [2001] 2 FCR 569.

[209] *Re SL (Adult Patient)(Medical Treatment)* [2000] 2 FCR 452. If there is uncertainty as to whether the sterilisation is therapeutic, it should be referred to the court (*ibid* 469).

[210] See eg, *Re F* (n 208); *Re B (A Minor) (Wardship: Sterilisation)* [1988] AC 199; *Re A (Medical Treatment: Male Sterilisation)* [2000] 1 FCR 193.

[211] Mary Donnelly, 'Best Interests, Patient Participation and the Mental Capacity Act 2005' (2009) 17 *Medical Law Review* 1, 4.

[212] *Re A* (n 210) 200.

effect, to create a 'balance sheet' contrasting the benefits and burdens of the procedure to the patient. Once all of the effects, positive and negative, are listed, the judge should compare the two lists, with a view to striking

> a balance between the sum of the certain and possible gains against the sum of the certain and possible losses. Obviously only if the account is in relatively significant credit will the judge conclude that the application is likely to advance the best interests of the claimant.[213]

The common law approach has been continued under the statutory regime introduced in 2005. Since the adoption of the Mental Capacity Act 2005, applications for a declaration of the lawfulness of a proposed sterilisation procedure on an adult who lacks capacity are to be brought before the Court of Protection.[214] The Act sets out several underlying principles, two of which are relevant in the context of decision making for adults who lack capacity.[215] The first provides that any act done or decision made for or on behalf of a person who lacks capacity must be done or made in the person's best interests.[216] The second requires that in making a decision or taking action, the decision maker must have regard to whether the objective sought to be achieved could equally be realised in a way that is 'less restrictive of the person's rights and freedom of action'.[217] Section 4 of the Act details the steps to be taken and the circumstances which must be considered in reaching a decision as to 'best interests'. These factors include consideration of whether the person is likely to regain capacity to make the decision in question, as well as 'the person's past and present wishes and feelings . . . the beliefs and values that would be likely to influence his decision if he had capacity, and . . . the other factors that he would be likely to consider if he were able to do so'.[218] The individual who lacks capacity is also to be encouraged to participate in decision making.[219]

One important issue that has arisen in relation to the Mental Capacity Act is the test to be employed in assessing whether an individual is indeed capable of making her own decision as to the use of contraception. In *A Local Authority v A*, the Court of Protection faced this question for the first time.[220] The local authority applied to the Court of Protection for a declaration that Ms A lacked capacity to decide whether or not to use contraception. It argued that the test for capacity requires that the individual be able to appreciate the wider consequences of the decision, including what is involved in caring for a child.[221] The Court declined to adopt the broad test urged by the local authority, noting that such a test risks 'blurring the line between capacity and best interests'.[222] The

---

[213] *Ibid* 206. This 'balance sheet' approach is also included in the Official Solicitor's Practice Note regarding declaratory proceedings for medical and welfare decisions for adults who lack capacity (*Practice Note* (n 208) para 7).

[214] Mental Capacity Act 2005 (UK). The Mental Capacity Act Code of Practice notes that cases involving proposed non-therapeutic sterilisation should be brought before a court, consistent with the common law position (Department for Constitutional Affairs, *Mental Capacity Act 2005 Code of Practice* (London, The Stationery Office, 2007) 8.18).

[215] Mental Capacity Act (n 214), s 1.

[216] *Ibid* s 1(5).

[217] *Ibid* s 1(6). This section sets out an approach that mirrors the common law, as can be seen in *Re SL* (n 209), where the Court held that insertion of a levonorgestrel-releasing IUD was a more appropriate first step for pregnancy prevention than was surgical sterilisation, as it would be effective in preventing pregnancy and less invasive than the permanent option of surgical sterilisation.

[218] Mental Capacity Act (n 214), s 4(6).

[219] *Ibid* s 4(4).

[220] *A Local Authority v A* [2010] EWHC 1549 (COP), [2011] 1 Fam 61.

[221] *Ibid* para 56.

[222] *Ibid* para 61.

Court held that the issues to be considered in this context are medical issues related to contraceptive decision making. These include the following:

(a) whether the individual has the capacity to understand the reason for using contra-
    ception and its effects, including the likelihood of pregnancy if it is not used;
(b) the types of contraceptives available, and the methods, advantages, disadvantages
    and side-effects of each type;
(c) the ease of changing from one type of contraception to another; and
(d) the effectiveness of each type.[223]

Scotland also has legislation dealing with, *inter alia*, issues related to medical care of adults who lack capacity to make healthcare-related decisions. The Adults with Incapacity (Scotland) Act[224] permits medical practitioners primarily responsible for the care of an adult who lacks capacity 'to do what is reasonable in the circumstances, in relation to the medical treatment in question, to safeguard or promote the physical or mental health of the adult'[225] except where specified otherwise by regulations.[226] The regulations[227] set out certain types of treatment which must be authorised by the Court of Session, provided that it is satisfied 'that the treatment will safeguard or promote the physical or mental health of the adult and that the adult does not oppose the treatment,' and that the adult will not resist the treatment being carried out. One such type of treat-ment is 'Sterilisation where there is no serious malfunction or disease of the reproductive organs'.[228]

Like its UK counterpart, the Scots legislation sets out foundational principles. These principles focus on the benefit to be gained as a result of intervening in an incapacitated adult's affairs,[229] and require that the least restrictive option consistent with the purpose of the intervention be adopted.[230] Interestingly, the phrase 'best interests' does not appear in the legislation. The Act has been described as '[steering] the decision-maker away from the best interest standards and towards the use of substituted judgment'.[231] Given the inherent difficulty of determining either the 'best interests' of a specific individual, or what the individual himself or herself would choose in the circumstances, it is difficult to say what difference the distinct approaches will ultimately make in practice.

As noted earlier, Canadian law on non-consensual, non-therapeutic sterilisation is clear. A third party may not authorise the non-therapeutic sterilisation of an individual who is incapable of consenting for himself or herself, nor may the court do so under its *parens patriae* jurisdiction.[232] In *E (Mrs) v Eve*, the mother of Eve, a 24-year-old woman

---

[223] *Ibid* para 64.
[224] Adults with Incapacity (Scotland) Act 2000, asp 4.
[225] *Ibid* s 47(2).
[226] Section 48(2) states that the regulations may 'specify medical treatment, or a class or classes of medical treatment, in relation to which the authority conferred by section 47(2) shall not apply'. Section 48(3) provides that 'Regulations made under subsection (2) may provide for the circumstances in which the specified medical treatment or specified class or classes of medical treatment may be carried out.'
[227] Adults with Incapacity (Specified Medical Treatments) (Scotland) Regulations (Scot SI 2002/208), reg 3.
[228] *Ibid* Sch 1. Also, reg 3(2) provides that the Court shall give the 'opportunity to any person having an inter-est in the personal welfare of the adult to make representations in respect of it'.
[229] Adults with Incapacity (Scotland) Act (n 224), s 1(2).
[230] *Ibid* s 1(3).
[231] Gary Scot Stevenson, Tracy Ryan and Susan Anderson, 'Principles, Patient Welfare and the Adults with Incapacity (Scotland) Act 2000' (2009) 32 *International Journal of Law and Psychiatry* 120, 125.
[232] *E (Mrs) v Eve* (n 151).

with severe expressive aphasia,[233] sought judicial approval for contraceptive sterilisation for her daughter. The purpose of the proposed procedure was purely contraceptive; Mrs E was concerned that her daughter would become pregnant and, given that Eve was unable to care for a child, that the burden of raising such a child would fall to her. Mr Justice La Forest concluded that the courts lack the jurisdiction to authorise sterilisation for non-therapeutic purposes. As he explained:

> The grave intrusion on a person's rights and the certain physical damage that ensues from non-therapeutic sterilization without consent, when compared to the highly questionable advantages that can result from it, have persuaded me that it can never safely be determined that such a procedure is for the benefit of that person.[234]

Only by way of statutory intervention granting the courts (or perhaps a designated third party, such as a guardian) the power to authorise non-therapeutic sterilisation, or a subsequent case in which the decision is explicitly overruled, could such a procedure be authorised.[235]

The decision in *E (Mrs) v Eve* has been harshly criticised in both academic and judicial opinion. In *Re B*, Lord Hailsham referred to Justice La Forest's decision in unforgiving terms:

> I find, with great respect, their conclusion . . . that the procedure of sterilisation should never be authorised for non-therapeutic purposes totally unconvincing and in startling contradiction to the welfare principle which should be the first and paramount consideration in wardship cases. Moreover, for the purposes of the present appeal I find the distinction they purport to draw between "therapeutic" and "non-therapeutic" purposes of this operation in relation to the facts of the present case above as totally meaningless, and, if meaningful, quite irrelevant to the correct application of the welfare principle. To talk of the "basic right" to reproduce of an individual who is not capable of knowing the causal connection between intercourse and childbirth, the nature of pregnancy, what is involved in delivery, unable to form maternal instincts or to care for a child appears to me wholly to part company with reality.[236]

---

[233] Expressive aphasia is a neurological condition in which one's ability to convey information through speech or writing is impaired. It is difficult to know whether there are concomitant disorders of thought or intelligence because of the difficulty the person has in expressing himself or herself using language (*E (Mrs) v Eve* (n 151) 394 (cited to SCR)).

[234] *Ibid* 431.

[235] See, eg, *Re EMH*, 130 Sask R 281, [1995] SJ no 220 (SKQB). But see Jackie Smith, 'Burden of Care v Burden of Proof', *National Post* (Don Mills, 1 June 2002) A23; Mindelle Jacobs, 'Sterilization Issue in Court's Hands', *Edmonton Sun*, 2 June 2002, 27; Alastair Jamieson, 'Parents Wrestling with Sterilization Issues Deserve Compassion', *Vancouver Sun*, 5 June 2002, A15; Helen Henderson, 'Case Reignites Debate on Forced Sterilization', *Toronto Star*, 8 June 2002, M15; W Gifford Jones, 'Sterilization Can Be Decision of a Loving Mother', *Halifax Daily News*, 8 October 2002, 28. These media reports refer to a case where the public trustee of British Columbia threatened to sue a number of individuals involved in the non-consensual castration of a 25-year-old man with learning disabilities. In a number of Canadian jurisdictions, legislation that permits the appointment of a healthcare proxy in a healthcare directive excludes non-therapeutic sterilisation from the proxy's authority unless it is expressly permitted in the directive. In some cases, the legislation states that it does not affect the law relating to consent to non-therapeutic sterilisation. See, eg, Health Care Directives Act, CCSM, c H-27, s 14(b); Advance Health Care Directives Act, SNL 1995, c A-4.1, s 5(3)(b); Health Care (Consent) and Care Facility (Admission) Act, RSBC 1996, c 181, s 2(d); Health Care Consent Act 1996, SO 1996, c 2, Sch A, s 6; Consent to Treatment and Health Care Directive Act, RSPEI 1998, c C-17.2, s 12(b); Personal Directives Act, RSA 2000, c P-6, s 15(b).

[236] *Re B* (n 210) 203–04. In this case, the House of Lords authorised the sterilisation of a mentally-disabled 17-year-old, holding that the procedure was in her 'best interests'.

In view of the critique directed at the Supreme Court's decision, at least one author has raised questions about its continued persuasiveness.[237] But the foundation for the Supreme Court's decision is clear, when viewed in the context of a legal system that permitted eugenic sterilisations (and in which abuses of power to authorise such procedures are well-documented[238]). Moreover, as illustrated by the concerns that have arisen in Australia related to sterilisation of mentally-disabled children (in particular), Mr Justice La Forest's fears appear to have been well founded.

B. Non-consensual birth control and reproductive autonomy

In its decision in *E (Mrs) v Eve*, the Supreme Court of Canada refers to the grave intrusion on individual rights and the physical damage that results from non-consensual sterilisation, making it clear that bodily integrity was an important consideration for the Court. Yet bodily integrity is also jealously guarded in the law of other jurisdictions, including the UK, Australia and the US, and none has taken a similarly restrictive approach to non-consensual sterilisation. Indeed, the UK House of Lords has been extremely critical of the Canadian Court's decision in *E (Mrs) v Eve*. Kristin Savell has noted this divergence in approach in the Canadian and UK courts; she suggests that fundamentally, the disagreement rests on 'competing constructions of body, sexuality, and community'.[239] In her view, when the court's primary 'concern is the question of how to contain the sexuality of a learning disabled person perceived as "out of control" or "vulnerable to seduction", sterilization is cast as a just and humane solution that will advance the welfare of the individual concerned'.[240] In contrast, where the court's primary aim is to 'preserve the integrity of a law committed to the principle of equality, sterilization is thought to be a violation of the bodily integrity of the person'.[241]

Savell's observations are significant in relation to the reproductive autonomy of those whose autonomy may be diminished by reason of an intellectual disability or mental illness. Where there is no therapeutic purpose for the procedure, non-consensual sterilisation is clearly not permitted in Canada. But 'non-therapeutic' is a vague term subject to varying interpretations.[242] And, given evolving contraceptive technologies, there are

---

[237] Dwight Newman, 'An Examination of Saskatchewan Law on the Sterilization of Persons with Mental Disabilities' (1999) 62 *Saskatchewan Law Review* 329, 336–37: 'When combined with the criticism it faces in Canadian academic and law reform writing, the judgment is of rather uncertain persuasive force. While the case may articulate a rule, one might wonder to what extent this rule can stand in its present form when it has been the subject of such criticism.'

[238] See above (nn 147 and 148). See also Cook and Dickens (n 147); Ellen I Picard and Gerald B Robertson, *Legal Liability of Doctors and Hospitals in Canada*, 4th edn (Toronto, Thomson Carswell, 2007) 118–19.

[239] Kristin Savell, 'Sex and the Sacred: Sterilization and Bodily Integrity in English and Canadian Law' (2004) 49 *McGill Law Journal* 1093, 1141.

[240] *Ibid* 1141. Savell notes that 'legal and cultural discourses' that perceive the sexuality of those with learning disabilities in this way adopt and promote norms around women's behaviour in pregnancy and childbirth, and are rife with moral unease around the fitness of such persons to parent. She suggests that, in this context, there is no conflict with the courts' recognition of the significance of bodily integrity and their willingness to approve non-consensual sterilisation, 'because sterilization is understood as protecting the bodily integrity and enhancing the freedom of the learning disabled woman'.

[241] *Ibid.*

[242] In her empirical study of the sexuality of learning-disabled women, Michelle McCarthy investigated contraceptive use in her subjects (Michelle McCarthy, *Sexuality and Women with Learning Disabilities* (London, Jessica Kingsley, 1999)). As she notes (*ibid* 224): 'The reason for prescribing contraception to women with learning disabilities is not always a straightforward matter of preventing an unwanted pregnancy in a

methods of ensuring long-term (albeit arguably not permanent) fertility control that require little to no 'active user participation'[243] and that lead virtually to the same result as surgical sterilisation. Sterilising women with intellectual or cognitive disabilities is thus not the only effective way to prevent pregnancy, meaning that in most cases, sterilisation is quite probably not necessary. It is also almost surely not the 'least restrictive' method to prevent pregnancy, and it certainly is not the 'method of choice' for young women who do not have an intellectual disability and can make their own contraceptive choices.[244] In turn, the inevitable consequence is that women can be prevented from becoming mothers in ways that are legally acceptable and that do not require any review or oversight by a neutral authority. Thus, while a prohibition on non-consensual non-therapeutic sterilisation might serve an important symbolic function in relation to the bodily integrity and rights of those with disabilities, its importance in practice might not be as significant.

A key issue in the context of non-consensual sterilisation is capacity to make health-care-related decisions. Capacity is widely considered to be a functional (as opposed to global) matter,[245] meaning that while a person may not have the requisite capacity to make all healthcare decisions, he or she may well be capable of making some such decisions. In relation to sterilisation, the relevant issue is whether the individual is capable of understanding the nature and effect of agreeing to or refusing the procedure, and the risks involved in accepting or refusing treatment.[246] The fluidity of capacity is one of the complicating factors with respect to sterilisation of those with intellectual or mental disabilities.[247] The courts that have granted authorisation for sterilisation of intellectually-disabled women and girls do not seem to have given much consideration to the fact that capacity is a slippery concept, and that an individual's ability to make reproductive decisions may well change over time.[248]

Arguably, the nature of capacity itself warrants more attention than it appears to have received, particularly given the permanence of sterilisation and the development of safe and effective new technologies which permit good fertility control while not foreclosing

sexually active woman of childbearing age. Many times when I have questioned why a woman with learning disabilities who was not sexually active was on the Pill I have been told by staff and carers that it is because of heavy or painful periods. . . . Whilst not dismissing these as genuine concerns, I must say that it does seem to be a *very* common problem for women with learning disabilities, to the point where I cannot help wondering whether staff and carers are not exaggerating it in order to justify being able to use the Pill or, indeed, other methods of contraception, as a long-term strategy to avoid any possibility of pregnancy for the whole of a woman's reproductive life. The very long-term use of the Pill and the ways in which IUDs and Depo-Provera are used with women with learning disabilities, combined with a lack of attention to side-effects and after-effects, suggests that less importance is placed on their health and future fertility than on other women's.'

[243] Michelle McCarthy, 'Contraception and Women with Intellectual Disabilities' (2009) 22 *Journal of Applied Research in Intellectual Disabilities* 363, 368.

[244] AJ Stansfield, AJ Holland and ICH Clare, 'The Sterilisation of People with Intellectual Disabilities in England and Wales During the Period 1988 to 1999' (2007) 51 *Journal of Intellectual Disability Research* 569, 577.

[245] See, eg, Gerald B Roberston, *Mental Disability and the Law*, 2nd edn (Toronto, Carswell, 1984) 3–4, 467–69; Erin Nelson, 'The Fundamentals of Consent' in Jocelyn Downie, Timothy Caulfield and Colleen M Flood (eds), *Canadian Health Law and Policy*, 2nd edn (Markham, Butterworths, 2002) 122.

[246] See, eg, H Archibald Kaiser, 'Mental Disability Law' in Downie *et al* (eds) (n 245) 298.

[247] In the past, another complicating factor has been the complex jurisdictional issues that may arise in this context: see, eg, *Re F* (n 208); *Marion's Case* (n 173). Courts have first to determine whether they have jurisdiction to authorise sterilisation and then determine whether they ought to do so.

[248] Indeed, in *Re Eve*, 115 DLR (3d) 283, [1980] PEIJ No 92 (PECA) the courts do not seem to have given much consideration to whether Eve did or did not have capacity.

the possibility of future child-bearing.[249] Clearly, a balance needs to be struck between the potential advantages and disadvantages of the various methods of contraception and the desire to preserve an individual's fertility, particularly when there may be no real likelihood that it will ever matter to her whether or not she can bear children.

But not all individuals who have intellectual disabilities or who are mentally ill entirely lack the capacity to make autonomous decisions. Moreover, in light of cases such as that of Leilani Muir,[250] who was sterilised at the age of 11 by a Eugenics Board that failed to follow the legislative standards that governed its decisions, a restrictive approach seems far preferable to one which might permit sterilisation in anticipation of problems that may never materialise.[251] On application by a third party for authority to perform a sterilisation procedure, the court can assess capacity (and capacity potential) in only a very limited way. And, as Jonathan Montgomery eloquently explains, judicial interpretation of facts is not a purely objective enquiry, and there is a real risk that the court will be swayed to a pessimistic view of the factual background in a case of this nature.[252] Citing the *Re B* case, Montgomery asserts that the decision to permit sterilisation was made 'not so much at the stage when the court asked what was best for her but when they were persuaded to take so pessimistic a view of the facts'.[253]

The risk of adopting pessimistic views of the potential meaning of reproduction to those who are intellectually disabled or mentally ill, combined with negative assumptions about the sexual lives of those with disabilities, means that we must approach the question of limiting reproduction by these individuals with extreme caution. The State must remain neutral on the question of who should or should not reproduce (unless there is evidence of a danger posed to the individual himself or herself, or to others) by refraining from the provision of incentives to poor or disabled men and women in order to discourage them from procreating.

In her empirical study of the sexual lives of women with learning disabilities, Michelle McCarthy investigated the use of contraception among the 17 women whom she interviewed in the course of her research. Fifteen of the women McCarthy interviewed either had used or were using contraception. When asked who had decided that they should use contraception at all, and what form of contraception they should employ,

> [s]even said that doctors had decided, two said that their parents had decided . . . two said that staff had decided and three did not know or could not remember. Only one had made the decision for herself, a shocking fact given the relatively high levels of ability of the whole group.[254]

All of the women in McCarthy's study used (or had used) either oral contraceptive pills, or Depo-Provera[255] or an IUD – methods that require minimal (or no) 'active user

---

[249] Such as, eg, lower-dose oral contraceptives, contraceptive patches, vaginal contraceptive rings, injectable contraceptives (combined estrogen and progesterone, or progestin only), progestin implants and IUDs. For a detailed description of efficacy rates, safety, side-effects and contraindications of these methods of contraception, see Amanda Black *et al*, 'SOGC Clinical Practice Guideline No 143: Canadian Contraception Consensus, Part 2 of 3' (2004) 26 *Journal of Gynecology and Obstetrics Canada* 219.

[250] Leilani Muir was sterilised pursuant to Alberta's Sexual Sterilization Act, SA 1928, c 37 (repealed by the Sexual Sterilization Repeal Act, SA 1972, c 87). She later successfully sued the Government of Alberta for wrongful sterilisation on the basis that the Eugenics Board that ordered her sterilisation failed to follow the legislative standards (*Muir v The Queen in Right of Alberta* (n 149)).

[251] Sandor (n 183) 16.

[252] Jonathan Montgomery, 'Rhetoric and "Welfare"' (1989) 9 *OJLS* 395, 397–99.

[253] *Ibid* 398.

[254] McCarthy (n 242) 195–96.

[255] A long-acting injectable hormonal contraceptive.

participation'.[256] McCarthy notes that the reliance on these particular contraceptive methods 'assumes that women with learning disabilities are incapable or unreliable when it comes to managing their own fertility'.[257]

While some women with learning disabilities are no doubt unable to make their own choices about contraception, or to manage the use of some contraceptive methods, McCarthy points out that many women are simply not provided with the information and support they need in order to make these decisions for themselves.[258] She also indicates that a number of the women she spoke with expressed a desire to have children,[259] and were dissatisfied with the method of birth control that had been selected for them by others. Again, while it is clear that some learning-disabled women would not be capable of coping with the demands of parenting, it is by no means clear that this is universally, or even generally, the case.[260] Moreover, it is certainly not the case for many learning-disabled women who could potentially raise children with the provision of appropriate support. Savell notes that in considering whether women with intellectual disabilities are 'fit to parent', courts tend to consider the woman's capacity to marry[261] – her prospects of attracting a competent partner who could help her to raise children. They do not acknowledge that parenting need not take place within a traditional heterosexual family form, and that other forms of support might equally enable some intellectually-disabled women to parent.[262]

Some commentators have argued that to focus on all of the reasons why sterilisation might be inappropriate is to fail to acknowledge the possibility that carers might be led to 'sexually segregate' intellectually-disabled women because of fears about pregnancy. Such an approach would deny these women the ability to have a satisfying sex life, and if that is the case then we need to consider carefully whether sterilisation is indeed a preferable approach.[263] Of course, unwanted pregnancy is not the only negative outcome that can arise from sexual activity, and the avoidance of pregnancy might not be the only reason to seek to prevent women with intellectual disabilities from being sexually active.

One consideration that seems rarely to feature in discussions around non-consensual sterilisation of those with developmental or learning disabilities is their capacity to consent to sexual relations at all. Where individuals are not capable of giving consent to sexual contact then such contact is sexual assault, and sterilisation is not the answer to that problem. An English study[264] of referrals to the Official Solicitor's office for sterilisations between 1988 and 1999 found that of the 73 individuals in respect of whom referrals were made, 55 were not in a relationship of any kind at the time of the referral and were noted to be 'probably unlikely ever to enter a long-term heterosexual relationship'.[265] The study authors note that most of the women in respect of whom referrals were made were single, living at home and not thought likely to be sexually active; most seemed to

---

[256] McCarthy (n 242) 221.

[257] *Ibid.*

[258] *Ibid* 222.

[259] *Ibid* 219–20.

[260] Neither, as some have argued, is it necessarily clear that the inability to parent should be a factor in a decision about sterilisation (Ruth Howard and Steve Hendy, 'The Sterilisation of Women with Learning Disabilities – Some Points for Consideration' (2004) 50 *British Journal of Developmental Disabilities* 133).

[261] See, eg, *Re Eve* (n 248) paras 16–17 (cited to DLR).

[262] Savell (n 239) 1137–38.

[263] See, eg, Mason and Laurie (n 150) 313; *In the matter of Lee Ann Grady*, 426 A 2d 467 (NJ 1981) 486; Raanan Gillon, 'On Sterilising Severely Mentally Handicapped People' (1987) 13 *Journal of Medical Ethics* 59.

[264] Stansfield *et al* (n 244).

[265] *Ibid* 574.

have a 'severe' intellectual disability.[266] In light of the fact that most of the women in question had had severe intellectual disabilities and were thought incapable of consenting to sterilisation, it is odd that no mention is made by anyone of their ability (or lack of ability) to consent to sexual relations. Moreover, as the authors point out, if these women did have a significant or severe intellectual disability, they would need high levels of support and supervision, including 24-hour care. As they explain:

> In such situations, there is both a responsibility, through education and support, to enable consensual and non-abusive relationships that are acceptable to, and wanted by, both partners and also a duty to prevent harm. Under such circumstances, contraception could be planned and appropriate supervision would minimize the risk of abuse.[267]

In considering whether the decisions to approve the applications for sterilisation really did respond to the 'best interests' of the person in respect of whom the application was made, the authors noted that for most of these women there was no reason to imagine that a 'mutually enjoyable sexual relationship was a likely eventuality'. Neither had there been any behaviour that would lead to the conclusion that this was likely;[268] indeed, not even one-third of the women had partners. The authors reasoned that rather than being based on the best interests of the intellectually-disabled individual, these requests may reflect diverse factors, including 'fear of the risks associated with the person's transition to adulthood, parental contraceptive attitudes, the requirement for a permanent solution to potential pregnancy and concern about who would care for any grandchild'.[269] In some of the cases, the request appears to have been motivated by past sexual abuse and, as the authors explain, sterilisation is not an appropriate response to that concern.[270]

Reproductive autonomy is only partially respected by a legal stance prohibiting non-therapeutic sterilisation of those who may lack capacity to consent. A contextualised approach to reproductive autonomy takes a much more inclusive look at coercive practices, noting that direct forcible intervention is far from the only form of coercion. Appropriate respect for reproductive autonomy requires not only that persons with intellectual disabilities not be sterilised if they are not capable of making that decision autonomously, but also that they be permitted to make their own reproductive decisions in so far as their capacity permits. Such an approach insists that women who may be capable of participating in decisions about the form of contraception they wish to use be given the information and support they need in order to do so. It also looks at the notion of the capacity to parent through a wider lens, and demands that persons not be precluded from reproducing because they may not be in a position to form a traditional family.

Stansfield and her co-authors eloquently capture what is at stake in deliberations about intellectual disability and reproductive autonomy:

> The integration of people with ID fully into community life and the societal acceptance of their right to a full and satisfying life, including sexual relationships and the benefits and risks that that entails, requires that the issues of sexuality are considered in an holistic way. An approach, such as . . . sterilisation, which only results in the reduction of one risk (pregnancy) but not others (e.g. sexual abuse, sexually transmitted diseases), cannot be an acceptable option.[271]

[266] *Ibid* 577.
[267] *Ibid.*
[268] *Ibid.*
[269] *Ibid.*
[270] *Ibid.*
[271] *Ibid* 578.

5

Abortion

ABORTION REGULATION IS a polarising political issue that is not amenable to resolution or compromise. Although it was not always so politically contentious, abortion is an 'age-old' practice; it is believed to date back to prehistory,[1] and records exist describing abortion techniques from as far back as 3000 BCE.[2] From a medical standpoint, abortion is a simple, safe and effective procedure.[3] Indeed, 'legal abortion in industrialised nations has emerged as one of the safest procedures in contemporary medical practice'.[4] Where abortion services are not legally available or where access is highly restricted, the story is quite different. Unsafe abortion persists in jurisdictions where law restricts the availability of abortion services, because although the legality of the procedure has little to do with whether women seek abortion services, it has a great deal to do with whether the procedure is done safely.[5] This point must be underlined: the lowest rates of abortion are found in countries with liberal abortion laws and where abortion is readily accessible, whereas regions with the most restrictive abortion laws tend to have the highest abortion rates.[6]

There are some important similarities in abortion law and policy among Canada, the US, the UK and Australia, but all handle abortion in distinct ways. In the UK, abortion remains a criminal offence, yet it is nevertheless quite readily available for most women, provided that two physicians agree that to continue the pregnancy would pose a risk to the woman's mental or physical health.[7] In the United States, women have a constitutional right to terminate a pregnancy. Yet access to abortion can be a significant challenge, as many states attempt to impede access and to regulate abortion as tightly as possible without stepping over the line into impermissible regulation. Canada, in contrast to both of these jurisdictions, has no formal law (neither a statutory regime nor a constitutional right) regulating the provision of abortion services. Regulation is instead accomplished by pro-

---

[1] Christopher Tietze and Sarah Lewit, 'Abortion' (1969) 220 *Scientific American* 21, 21. Methods of pregnancy termination in early societies were variable, and included 'physical exertion . . . the application of heat or skin irritants . . . or the insertion of a variety of instruments into the uterus'.

[2] Janet Hadley, *Abortion: Between Freedom and Necessity* (Philadelphia, PA, Temple University Press, 1996) 34.

[3] Maureen F. Paul *et al*, 'Early Surgical Abortion: Efficacy and Safety' (2002) 187 *American Journal of Obstetrics & Gynecology* 407.

[4] David A Grimes *et al*, 'Unsafe Abortion: The Preventable Pandemic' (2006) 368 *The Lancet* 1908, 1908.

[5] As the World Health Organization has noted, abortion-related maternal mortality is higher in regions with restrictive abortion laws (Department of Reproductive Health and Research, World Health Organization, *Unsafe Abortion: Global and Regional Estimates of the Incidence of Unsafe Abortion and Associated Mortality in 2008*, 6th edn (Geneva, World Health Organization, 2011)).

[6] *Ibid*. See also Gilda Sedgh *et al*, 'Induced Abortion: Incidence and Trends Worldwide from 1995 to 2008' (2012) 379 *The Lancet* 625, 630.

[7] Abortion Act 1967 (UK), s 1(1).

fessional medical regulators, and by provincial regulation of funding and delivery of healthcare. In Australia, abortion law is state-based. Most states have a statutory regime in which, like the UK system, women's ability to obtain abortion services is mediated by their physician.

Law and policy around abortion have clear implications for reproductive autonomy. Failing to respect a woman's decision to terminate her pregnancy – either by prohibiting abortion, or by impeding access to the procedure – constrains reproductive autonomy in a fundamental way. Abortion fits within the nucleus of the reproductive autonomy model, as restricting a woman's ability to terminate a pregnancy deeply implicates her bodily integrity.

Access to timely and safe abortion services is an essential component of reproductive autonomy, and resides at the heart of the bodily integrity model. The ability to decide whether or not to continue a pregnancy obviously engages women's bodily integrity and, as a result, whether cast as a right or not, must be accorded strong respect. It is not enough to permit access either by repealing criminal laws that prohibit abortion, or by creating defences to what is otherwise criminal activity. State measures designed to restrict access to abortion obviously fail to respect reproductive autonomy. But so too do State failures to provide meaningful access – including failure to fund abortion services, failure to provide access to medical abortion as an option and failure to clarify the law around provider conscientious objection to ensure that the duty to refer is clearly spelled out.[8]

In this chapter, I first discuss the legal and moral status of the fetus, given the significance of that issue to a discussion of abortion rights. I then examine current law on abortion in all four jurisdictions. Due to the distinct legal approaches adopted by the various jurisdictions, I deal with each separately before commenting on the implications of the various legal approaches for reproductive autonomy. Next, I consider the policy dimensions of several barriers to access that are not necessarily created by abortion law per se. In the last section of the chapter, I briefly discuss some special cases in abortion regulation: second-trimester abortion and selective abortion.

I. ABORTION AND THE STATUS OF THE FETUS

This is not a book about the fetus or about intrauterine life. But in discussing reproductive autonomy and its implications for law and policy around reproductive decision making, particularly abortion decision making, the question of the status of the fetus cannot be avoided.[9] The legal treatment of the fetus (and embryo) has significant potential effects on other legal and policy considerations around reproductive autonomy. If a fetus is a person, women's ability to make decisions about their own health and

---

[8] That this is particularly urgent is borne out by studies that show that physicians and even medical students may not have a clear understanding of what the law (and their professional ethical obligations) permits: see, eg, Ryan E Lawrence and Farr A Curlin, 'Physicians' Beliefs about Conscience in Medicine: A National Survey' (2009) 84 *Academic Medicine* 1276; Sophie LM Strickland, 'Conscientious Objection in Medical Students: A Questionnaire Survey' (2012) 38 *Journal of Medical Ethics* 22.

[9] For purposes of this discussion, the fetal stage of development begins at approximately eight weeks after fertilisation (Roy G Farquharson, Eric Jauniaux and Nick Exalto, 'Updated and Revised Nomenclature for Description of Early Pregnancy Events' (2005) 20 *Human Reproduction* 3008).

well-being may be limited by the rights of the fetus.[10] The implications for abortion rights are stark.

No jurisdiction under consideration here grants legal status or legal personhood to the fetus.[11] The fetus has no rights while it is within a woman's body; only once a child is born alive, having completely exited its mother's body, does the law recognise it as a person and grant it the full array of legal rights.[12] This means, for example, that a fetus (or a person acting on its behalf) cannot prevent a pregnant woman from terminating the pregnancy (thereby ending the fetus's life);[13] it also means that a fetus cannot sue another person for damages suffered pre-natally.[14] But while none of these jurisdictions recognises fetal personhood, all offer some legal protections. For example, a child who was not born at the time of a testator's death is deemed to have been alive at the time in order to facilitate the testator's wishes, and a child in utero at the time of a motor vehicle collision is deemed to have been alive at the time, in order to ensure that the child may claim compensation for injuries suffered.[15]

Where courts have faced the question of the legal status of the fetus in the context of abortion rights, they have largely refused to confront the issue directly.[16] Although quite prepared to accept that the fetus can be treated as a legal person for some purposes, when abortion rights are in issue, the general approach is to avoid the question and assert that there is no need for the court to settle the 'philosophical and theological debates about whether or not a foetus is a person'.[17] Yet in spite of the assertion that they need not take on the issue of fetal personhood, as Caitlin Borgmann has argued, some courts have done so by implication, as in the case of American courts that have reaffirmed the essential

[10] Where issues arise in relation to other reproductive autonomy-related issues, they will be mentioned specifically; eg, issues of coercive treatment of pregnant women and tort duties owed by pregnant women to their fetuses.

[11] This means, at a minimum, that no legal action can be brought by a fetus, or by anyone else on behalf of a fetus in Australia (*In the Marriage of F* (1989) 13 Fam LR 189, following *Paton v British Pregnancy Advisory Service Trustees* [1979] QB 276). The Australian High Court affirmed an earlier decision of the Supreme Court of Queensland that the father's rights begin only when the baby is born (*AG (ex-rel Kerr) v T* (1983) 46 ALR 275). Similar case law exists in the UK, Canada and the US: see, eg, *Paton* (above) (a husband tried to obtain an injunction to prevent his wife's abortion; the Court held that a fetus becomes a legal person upon being born alive and therefore any rights are contingent on live birth); *Tremblay v Daigle* [1989] 2 SCR 530, (1989) 62 DLR (4th) 634; *Diamond v Hirsch* [1989] MJ No 377 (QB) (wherein the Manitoba Court of Queen's Bench refused to issue an order prohibiting Ms Hirsch from obtaining an abortion); *Roe v Wade*, 410 US 113 (1973). See also John A Robertson, *Children of Choice: Freedom and the New Reproductive Technologies* (Princeton, NJ, Princeton University Press, 1994) 57.

[12] *Paton* (n 11); *Winnipeg Child and Family Services (Northwest Area) v G (DF)* [1997] 3 SCR 925, 152 DLR (4th) 193.

[13] *Paton* (n 11); *Tremblay v Daigle* (n 11).

[14] Once the child is born, however, it can maintain such a claim, as the claim 'crystallises' at birth: see, eg, *Montreal Tramways v Léveillé* [1933] SCR 456, [1933] 4 DLR 337; *Bonbrest v Kotz*, 65 F Supp 138 (DDC 1946); *Duval v Seguin* [1972] 2 OR 686, 26 DLR (3d) 418 (Ont HCJ); *Watt v Rama* [1972] VR 353; *Burton v Islington Health Authority* [1993] QB 204 (it should be noted that the law on this point is governed in the UK (except Scotland) by the Congenital Disabilities (Civil Liability) Act 1976 (UK)).

[15] See, eg, *Montreal Tramways v Léveillé* (n 14); *Duval v Seguin* (n 14); *Watt v Rama* (n 14).

[16] In *Vo v France* (2005) 40 EHRR 12, the European Court of Human Rights also distanced itself from the question of fetal personhood, in the context of a claim that Art 2 ECHR requires States to impose criminal sanctions on those who negligently cause fetal death. In *Vo*, the fetus died after the physician negligently ruptured the amniotic membrane while attempting to remove an IUD from the wrong patient, a patient who was pregnant and at the clinic for a routine pre-natal visit. The Grand Chamber classified the case as one relating to abortion and held that the question of imposing criminal penalties in such circumstances is one for the national legislative body to decide.

[17] *Tremblay v Daigle* (n 11) 552 (cited by SCR).

validity of *Roe v Wade*.[18] As the Court plainly indicated in *Roe v Wade*, the conclusion that a fetus is a legal person would decisively settle the abortion question.[19]

Though it acknowledges fetal interests in certain circumstances and for certain purposes, the law is relatively clear: the fetus is not a legal person. The moral status of the fetus is another matter entirely. As courts and commentators have noted, views as to fetal status are strongly held and not amenable to argument.[20] One's view of the fetus and its moral worth will obviously play an important part in shaping one's views about the morality and legality of abortion. If a fetus has the same moral worth as a person then killing it is morally unjustifiable and abortion cannot be permitted. If one sees the fetus as human, but not as a person with the same moral worth as (for example) the pregnant woman, it is possible to justify terminating a pregnancy to protect the interests of the pregnant woman in favour of those of the fetus.

The debate about personhood and the moral status of the fetus is irresolvable, and it is neither useful nor necessary to dwell on the question at any length here. I think it is helpful, however, briefly to state my own views around fetal moral status. I subscribe to what has been labeled the 'gradualist' perspective of fetal moral status. Margaret Little has described the position in these terms:

> [E]ven at early stages of pregnancy, developing human life has an important value worthy of respect; its status grows as it does, increasing gradually until, at some point late in pregnancy, the fetus is deserving of the very strong moral protection due newborns.[21]

There are many who see the question of moral status in stark terms: either the embryo is a full moral person from the moment of conception, or the embryo (and later, fetus) is an entity with no (or very limited) moral value. But the nuanced perspective embraced by the gradualist view is likely consistent with the majority view, given that most view abortion as permissible in at least some circumstances.[22] It is also in keeping with the legal and moral position around decision making for extremely premature or severely-ill newborns, where parents are entitled to decide how to proceed and are not required to accept all possible medical treatment even if there is a chance that the newborn's life could be saved.[23] The gradualist perspective also seems very well aligned with the

---

[18] Caitlin E Borgmann, 'The Meaning of "Life": Belief and Reason in the Abortion Debate' (2009) 18 *Columbia Journal of Gender and Law* 551, 562–63. Borgmann's point also applies to the decisions *Tremblay v Daigle* (n 11) and *R v Morgentaler* [1988] 1 SCR 30, 63 OR (2d) 281.

[19] Similarly, in *Roe v Wade*, the Court acknowledged that full fetal personhood has never been accepted in the law, and that if it were, 'the fetus' right to life would then be guaranteed specifically' by the Constitution (*Roe v Wade* (n 11) 157).

[20] See, eg, Borgmann (n 18); Margaret O Little, 'Abortion and the Margins of Personhood' (2007/08) 39 *Rutgers Law Journal* 331; Sara Fovargue and José Miola, 'The Legal Status of the Fetus' (2010) 5 *Clinical Ethics* 122.

[21] Little (n 20) 332. See also Rosamund Scott, *Rights, Duties and the Body: Law and Ethics of the Maternal–Fetal Conflict* (Oxford, Hart Publishing, 2002).

[22] See, eg, Michelle Grattan, 'Poll Backs Abortion Laws', *The Age* (Melbourne, 11 January 2006), at <www.theage.com.au/news/National/Poll-backs-abortion-laws/2005/02/15/1108230007300.html>; 'Canadians Uphold Abortion Policy, Split on Health Care System's Role' (*Angus Reid Public Opinion*, 20 June 2008), at <www.angus-reid.com/wp-content/uploads/archived-pdf/2008.06.20_Abortion.pdf>; 'Half of Britons Say NHS Should Only Fund Abortions in Emergency Cases' (*Angus Reid Public Opinion*, 13 January 2010), at <www.angus-reid.com/polls/40182/half-of-britons-say-nhs-should-only-fund-abortions-in-emergency-cases/>; 'Americans Split on Covering Abortion in Insurance Plans that Use Federal Subsidies' (*Angus Reid Public Opinion*, 14 January 2010), at <www.ekospolitics.com/wp-content/uploads/full_report_april_11.pdf>; 'Canadians Decisively Pro-Choice on Abortion' (*EKOS Politics*, 1 April 2010), at <www.ekospolitics.com/wp-content/uploads/full_report_april_11.pdf>.

[23] Lachlan J de Crespigny and Julian Savulescu, 'Pregnant Women with Fetal Abnormalities: The Forgotten People in the Abortion Debate' (2008) 188 *Medical Journal of Australia* 100.

approach many pregnant women take in valuing the developing life within their own bodies.[24] It is a view of fetal moral worth that resonates with the approach I take to reproductive autonomy, which focuses on the context of women's lives and the situations in which they find themselves. Ultimately, it is a view that trusts women to make decisions about fetal worth based on their own values and convictions, and one that affords respect for their interest in so doing.

II. ABORTION IN THE LAW

The late 1960s and early 1970s proved to be a watershed in terms of abortion law. Abortion laws were liberalised in the UK,[25] Canada[26] and in parts of Australia[27] through a process of statutory reform, and in the US[28] (and two Australian states[29]) through judicial decisions. Only in the US was the end result of the liberalisation process the grant of a constitutional right to abortion. The US is also the site of the most frequent – in fact, relentless – attempts to limit the scope of the abortion right and to reduce access to abortion services.

This section briefly touches on the history of abortion regulation in Canada, the US, the UK and Australia, and then proceeds to outline the current state of regulation in these jurisdictions. It bears mention that in the US in particular, attempting to set down current law feels like a losing proposition, given the fevered regulatory activity in many states.

A. Canada

As in many countries, Canadian law and policy on pregnancy termination, though arguably settled, remains deeply contested. Though not as explosively political as in the US, the Canadian abortion context has involved picketing and demonstrations near private abortion facilities, as well as attempts on the lives of abortion providers.[30] In spite of the contested nature of abortion law and policy in this country, Canada currently has no formal legal regulation delineating restrictions on the provision of abortion services.[31]

---

[24] Catriona Mackenzie, 'Abortion and Embodiment' (1992) 70 *Australasian Journal of Philosophy* 136.

[25] Abortion Act 1967.

[26] Criminal Law Amendment Act, SC 1968–69, c 38.

[27] The first Australian jurisdiction to liberalise abortion law through statutory reform was South Australia in January 1970 (Farhat Yusuf and Dora Briggs, 'Legalized Abortion in South Australia: The First 7 Years' Experience' (1979) 11 *Journal of Biosocial Science* 179, 180).

[28] *Roe v Wade* (n 11).

[29] In Victoria, what is referred to as the Menhennitt Ruling was made in *R v Davidson* [1969] VR 667. This approach was adopted by the NSW courts in *R v Wald* (1971) 3 NSWDCR 25.

[30] See, eg, K Bolan, 'Shootings of 3 Abortion MDs are Linked, Police Suspect', *Vancouver Sun*, 13 November 1997, 1; David Spurgeon, 'Abortion Doctor Suffers Second Attack in Six Years' (2000) 321 *British Medical Journal* 197; Sanda Rodgers, 'The Legal Regulation of Women's Reproductive Capacity in Canada' in Jocelyn Downie, Timothy Caulfield and Colleen M Flood (eds), *Canadian Health Law and Policy*, 2nd edn (Markham, Butterworths, 2002) 331, 341. See also the British Columbia Access to Abortion Services Act, RSBC 1996, c 1, enacted to prohibit demonstrations, protests and harassment designed to hinder access to abortion services.

[31] On occasion Canadian politicians have attempted to reignite the abortion debate by proposing legal measures designed to restrict access to abortion, or to debate related matters. Most recently, an Ontario Member of Parliament introduced a motion that would see the creation of a special Parliamentary Committee to discuss the definition of 'human being' in the Criminal Code, RSC 1985, c C-46, s 223 (Laura Beaulne-

As in several other jurisdictions, abortion was criminalised in Canada in the nineteenth century.[32] In 1969, the abortion provisions in the Criminal Code were modified to make it possible for women to obtain legal abortions.[33] Section 251 of the Criminal Code permitted therapeutic abortions where the woman received the approval of a hospital therapeutic abortion committee (made up of three physicians), on the basis that continuation of the pregnancy would endanger her life or health. [34] While permitting abortion in some circumstances, the provisions instituted a rigid administrative structure which could impede a woman's ability to obtain abortion services. Pro-choice advocates therefore continued to lobby for legislative change.[35]

In 1988, section 251 of the Criminal Code was struck down by the Supreme Court of Canada in *R v Morgentaler*,[36] on the ground that it violated women's constitutionally enshrined right to security of the person. The abortion provision was found to violate section 7 of the Canadian Charter of Rights and Freedoms,[37] not because it prohibited abortion in all but limited circumstances, but because the administrative process that it put into place could deprive women of security of the person in a manner that did not accord with the principles of fundamental justice.[38] In other words, the Court struck down the law not because criminal prohibition of abortion is impermissible under the Charter, but because the law created an arbitrary and unfair decision-making process.[39]

One year after the *R v Morgentaler* decision, the Federal Government introduced a new restrictive abortion Bill;[40] the Bill recriminalised abortion except in circumstances where a woman's physician believed that her life or health would be in danger should the pregnancy continue.[41] The Bill was passed in the House of Commons, but was defeated by one vote in the Senate. Since then, no new federal law governing abortion has been introduced, although several provinces have enacted legislation or regulations that purport to govern the provision of abortion services.

Stuebing, 'Backbench Tory Poised to Trigger Abortion Debate in Parliament', *Globe and Mail* (Toronto, 25 April 2012), at <www.theglobeandmail.com/news/politics/backbench-tory-poised-to-trigger-abortion-debate-in-parliament/article2414177/>). The text of the motion may be found at <www.parl.gc.ca/HousePublications/Publication.aspx?Language=E&DocId=5437818>.

[32] Prior to the 19th century, expertise around pregnancy and childbirth rested with midwives, usually women. In the 19th century, as part of the drive to wrest control over obstetrical care from midwives, physicians campaigned to criminalise abortion: see, eg, Janine Brodie, Shelley AM Gavigan and Jane Jenson, *The Politics of Abortion* (Toronto, Oxford University Press, 1992); Reva Siegel, 'Reasoning from the Body: A Historical Perspective on Abortion Regulation and Questions of Equal Protection' (1992) 44 *Stanford Law Review* 261.

[33] Criminal Law Amendment Act (n 26).

[34] Criminal Code, RSC 1970, c C-34.

[35] Rodgers (n 30) 334–35. For an itemisation of concerns with the provision, see Department of Justice, *Report of the Committee on the Operation of the Abortion Law* (Ottawa, Minister of Supply and Services, 1977).

[36] *R v Morgentaler* (1988) (n 18).

[37] Canadian Charter of Rights and Freedoms, Part I of the Constitution Act, 1982, being Schedule B to the Canada Act 1982 (UK), 1982, c 11.

[38] *R v Morgentaler* (1988) (n 18).

[39] Eg, different committees took different approaches to the interpretation of what constituted a threat to a woman's health. Some hospitals did not have therapeutic abortion committees, which meant that some jurisdictions did not have any legal access to abortion (*ibid*).

[40] Bill C-43, *An Act Respecting Abortion*, 2nd Sess, 34th Parl, 1989 (defeated in the Senate 31 January 1991). See also Rodgers (n 30) 331.

[41] Health was defined to include mental, physical and psychological health.

Canada is a federal jurisdiction, meaning that different levels of government have regulatory responsibility over distinct areas of law. The criminal law power rests exclusively with the Federal Government and (although not specifically enumerated in the Constitution) the power to make laws respecting health largely rests with the provincial governments.[42] Most of the provincial statutes described below have been found to be ultra vires provincial jurisdiction (or beyond the scope of their parent legislation) and therefore unconstitutional, in general because they are seen as attempts by provinces to make criminal laws.

Provincial legislative attempts to restrict the availability of abortion have generally either sought to limit funding for abortion services to those provided in hospitals, or to preclude the provision of abortion outside a hospital setting. British Columbia, for example, passed a regulation pursuant to its former Medical Services Act,[43] which provided that the only insured abortion services were those provided in a hospital in cases where continuing the pregnancy posed a significant threat to a woman's life; the regulation was struck down as ultra vires the province.[44] The Province of New Brunswick amended its medical professional regulatory statute[45] to provide the penalty of licence suspension for any physician who performed (or was likely to perform) abortion services outside a hospital. The amendment was found to be ultra vires the Province.[46] New Brunswick has since amended the legislation and regulations to remove the penalty of licence suspension for the performance of abortions in private clinics, but maintains the prohibition on paying for clinic abortions. The prohibition is not a straightforward refusal to fund clinic abortions. Instead, the regulation in issue states that abortion is not an 'entitled service' under the Medical Services Payment Act,[47]

> unless the abortion is performed by a specialist in the field of obstetrics and gynaecology in a hospital facility approved by the jurisdiction in which the hospital facility is located and two medical practitioners certify in writing that the abortion was medically required . . .[48]

---

[42] Constitution Act 1867 (UK), 30 & 31 Vict, c 3, ss 91(27) (criminal law), 92 (7), (13) (establishment, maintenance, and management of hospitals and asylums in and for the province; property and civil rights in the province).

[43] Medical Services Act, RSBC 1979, c 255; BC Reg 54/1988. The Act has since been repealed.

[44] *British Columbia Civil Liberties Assn v British Columbia (Attorney General)* [1988] BCJ No 373, 24 BCLR (2d) 189 (BCSC). In Manitoba, a regulation excluding non-hospital abortions from the Province's health insurance plan was also ruled ultra vires (*Lexogest Inc v Manitoba (Attorney General)*, 85 Man R (2d) 8, 101 DLR (4th) 523 (1993) (Man CA)).

[45] Then the Medical Act, SNB 1985, c 76.

[46] *Morgentaler v New Brunswick (Attorney General)*, 156 NBR (2d) 205, [1995] NBJ No 40 (NBCA).

[47] Medical Services Payment Act, RSNB 1973, c M-7.

[48] NB Reg 1984-20, Sch 2 (a.1). This prohibition was challenged by Dr Henry Morgentaler, a champion of women's reproductive rights and an extremely controversial figure (Nick Rockel, 'Henry Morgentaler Fought a Long Battle to Decriminalize Abortion in Canada', *Globe and Mail* (Toronto, 26 October 2010), at <www.theglobeandmail.com/report-on-business/henry-morgentaler-fought-a-long-battle-to-decriminalize-abortion-in-canada/article1216155/>). In its Statement of Defence to this latest lawsuit initiated by Dr Morgentaler, the Province of New Brunswick asserted that Dr Morgentaler did not have standing to bring the claim. The New Brunswick courts have declared that Dr Morgentaler does indeed have public interest standing to challenge the regulation. The Province has said that it will not appeal this decision and that the claim, which was commenced in July 2003, will continue to go forward ('N.B. Will Not Appeal Morgentaler Decision', *CBC News*, 18 August 2009, at <www.cbc.ca/canada/new-brunswick/story/2009/08/18/nb-morgentaler-appeal-206.html>; *Morgentaler v New Brunswick*, 2008 NBQB 258, [2008] NBJ No 279, affd *Province of New Brunswick v Morgentaler*, 2009 NBCA 26, [2009] NBJ No 139). Nova Scotia enacted legislation creating significant penal sanctions for anyone providing healthcare services outside a hospital; this, too, was struck down as ultra vires (*R v Morgentaler* [1993] 3 SCR 463, [1993] SCJ No 95).

Utilising a slightly different tactic, the Province of Prince Edward Island (PEI) enacted regulations under the Health Services Payment Act[49] that permitted coverage by the Province's healthcare insurance plan only for those abortions performed in a hospital, and only where a committee of five doctors authorised the abortion. The PEI Court of Appeal upheld these regulations as being authorised by the Health Services Payment Act.[50] As Sanda Rodgers notes, this case is anomalous and is arguably wrongly decided.[51] Also seeking to discourage clinic abortions, between 1999 and 2005, the Province of Québec required women to pay for part of the cost of abortion procedures performed in private clinics. Recently, the Québec Superior Court ordered the Province to pay $13 million to reimburse these women.[52]

In spite of these attempts at instating legal limits on the availability of abortion, there is no criminal (or other direct governmental) control over the provision of abortion services in Canada. Under current Canadian law, a woman may have an abortion at any time, for any reason. As will be discussed in section IV. below, however, the absence of criminal prohibitions on abortion has not translated into readily accessible abortion services for all Canadian women. Currently, pregnancy termination is governed in diverse ways across the country, with significant variations among jurisdictions. Timing, site and methods of pregnancy termination are governed in part by provincial physician regulatory bodies,[53] and (as explained above) provincial governments control access to and funding for abortion services pursuant to their jurisdiction over the delivery of healthcare. The implication of this approach to regulation of abortion services is enormous variation in the accessibility of these services across the country.

B. United States

Abortion has been and continues to be a defining political issue in the US. The current starting point for a look at US abortion law is the 1973 US Supreme Court decision in *Roe v Wade*.[54] Prior to this landmark case, abortion was generally illegal in the US, having been criminalised in the nineteenth century,[55] although legislation permitted abortion in limited circumstances. In some states, abortion was available only to preserve the life of a pregnant woman; in others, an abortion could be obtained where necessary to protect a woman's life or health.[56]

---

[49] Health Services Payment Act, RSPEI 1988, c H-2; Health Services Payment Act Regulation, PEI Reg EC 453/96, s 1(d)(iv).

[50] *Morgentaler v Prince Edward Island (Minister of Health and Social Services)* [1996] PEIJ No 75, 139 DLR (4th) 603 (PEI SCAD).

[51] Rodgers (n 30) 341.

[52] *Association pour l'accès à l'avortement c Québec (Procureur général)*, 2006 QCCS 4694, [2006] JQ no 8654. The Government of Québec did not appeal the decision.

[53] See, eg, College of Physicians and Surgeons of Alberta, 'Non-Hospital Surgical Facilities – Termination of Pregnancy: Standards and Guidelines' (February 2008), at <www.cpsa.ab.ca/Libraries/Pro_QofC_Non-Hospital/NHSF_-_Termination_of_Pregnancy.sflb.ashx>; College of Physicians and Surgeons of British Columbia 'Professional Standards and Guidelines; Abortion' (rev September 2009), at <www.cpsbc.ca/files/u6/Abortion.pdf>.

[54] *Roe v Wade* (n 11).

[55] Siegel (n 32).

[56] *Ibid*.

Roe v Wade seemed to settle the abortion question, holding that a pregnant woman has a right to privacy (pursuant to the 14th Amendment of the US Constitution[57]), which includes the right to terminate a pregnancy. The Court did not recognise an absolute right to abortion, instead acknowledging that the State has an interest in the protection of potential life, an interest that increases in strength as the pregnancy progresses. In *Roe v Wade*, the Court created a 'trimester framework'[58] to mirror the growing importance of the State interest in protecting fetal life (and the reduced safety of the abortion procedure itself) as pregnancy advances. The *Roe v Wade* framework permitted abortion without restriction in the first trimester of pregnancy; in the second trimester, the State was permitted to regulate some aspects of abortion (in essence, where the procedure can be performed, and by whom). Finally, in the third trimester of pregnancy, States were free to prohibit abortion except where necessary to preserve the life or health of the pregnant woman. Fetal viability (the stage at which a fetus is theoretically capable of sustained life outside of the pregnant woman's body) was the point at which the State's interest in protecting potential life became 'compelling'.[59]

Since 1973, the abortion right has remained profoundly contentious, with opponents of abortion continuing to attempt to circumscribe (or even abrogate) the right articulated in *Roe v Wade*. The challenges to *Roe v Wade* have come primarily in the form of state legislation that limits women's ability to exercise the right to terminate a pregnancy. The continued attempts to legislate such limits have meant that the issue of abortion rights has returned to the US Supreme Court on a number of occasions. These legislative efforts have had variable results; although the Court has not resiled from the basic holding in *Roe v Wade*, the continued attacks on that decision (and the partial successes its opponents can claim) make it clear that abortion rights in the US cannot be taken for granted.

In *Planned Parenthood of Southeastern Pennsylvannia v Casey*, an important post-*Roe v Wade* case, the constitutionality of several provisions of a Pennsylvania law was disputed.[60] The impugned provisions included a requirement that a woman's spouse be notified of her plan to terminate her pregnancy, a mandatory 24-hour wait between a first consultation respecting abortion and the procedure itself, mandatory informed consent provisions and a parental consent requirement where a minor sought abortion services.[61] In its decision in *Casey*, the Court abandoned the trimester framework set out in *Roe v Wade*,[62] holding that the state has a legitimate interest in fetal life from the beginning of pregnancy and that this interest becomes compelling at viability. The *Casey* decision means that there is no longer an unqualified right to terminate a pregnancy in the first trimester[63] and that the state may regulate the provision of abortion services throughout pregnancy, provided

---

[57] US Const amend XIV.

[58] This phrase was adopted subsequent to *Roe v Wade*, in *Planned Parenthood of Pennsylvannia v Casey*, 505 US 833 (1992).

[59] *Roe v Wade* (n 11) 163.

[60] *Casey* (n 58).

[61] Pennsylvania Abortion Control Act of 1982, 18 Pa Cons Stat §§ 3205 (informed consent, 24-hour wait), 3206 (parental consent), 3209 (spousal notification) (1990).

[62] Referring to it as an 'elaborate but rigid construct' (*Casey* (n 58) 872).

[63] The vast majority of abortions are performed in the first trimester. According to data from the Centers for Disease Control and Prevention, well over half (62.8%) of abortions reported by centres that include information about gestational age were carried out during the first eight weeks of pregnancy, and 91.4% were performed at or before 13 weeks' gestation (Centers for Disease Control and Prevention, 'Abortion Surveillance – United States, 2008' (2011) 60(15) *Morbidity and Mortality Weekly Report* 1, 6).

that the regulation does not amount to an 'undue burden' on women's right to choose abortion.[64] The question for the court in making this determination is whether the law in question 'has the purpose or effect of placing a substantial obstacle in the path of a woman seeking an abortion of a nonviable fetus'.[65] In the end, the *Casey* Court upheld all of the disputed provisions save the spousal notification requirement.

Most recently, the US Supreme Court has considered state and federal legislation banning so-called 'partial-birth abortion'.[66] The federal statute at issue in *Carhart v Gonzales*[67] was nearly identical to a state statute struck down by the Supreme Court in *Stenberg v Carhart*.[68] Two elements of the state statute were found to be unconstitutional in *Stenberg*: its vague description of 'partial birth abortion', which relied on non-medical terminology and could foreseeably have been applied to other abortion techniques, including pre-viability abortions; and its failure to include a 'health' exception to the ban.[69] Neither of these flaws was remedied in the federal legislation, yet that statute was upheld by a majority of the US Supreme Court in 2007.[70]

The law at issue in *Carhart v Gonzales* was the federal Partial-Birth Abortion Ban Act,[71] which bans any abortion procedure that involves the intentional delivery of a living fetus until the fetal head is entirely outside the woman's body, or (in the case of a feet-first presentation) until the fetus's body is delivered past the navel.[72] The procedure targeted by the legislation is colloquially known as 'partial-birth abortion'; more accurately, it is a procedure known as 'intact dilation and extraction'.[73] The law does not apply if fetal death occurs prior to the fetus's removal from the woman's body.

The Supreme Court upheld the Act, in spite of the absence of an exception for maternal health, holding that the sole concern for the court is whether the legislation places a 'substantial obstacle' in the way of a woman's ability to exercise her right to a pre-viability abortion.[74] In the Court's view, the prohibition of a particular method (or group of methods) of abortion is permissible in order to promote 'respect for the dignity of human life'.[75] The Court rejected the argument that the prohibitions placed too little weight on women's health, noting that 'There is documented medical disagreement whether the Act's prohibition would ever impose significant health risks on women'.[76] In short, the prohibition of one among several alternative methods for a second-trimester abortion did not place an undue burden on women's abortion rights.

---

[64] *Casey* (n 58) 877.

[65] *Ibid*.

[66] Partial-Birth Abortion Ban Act, 18 USC § 1531 (2007).

[67] *Gonzales v Carhart*, 550 US 124 (2007).

[68] *Stenberg v Carhart*, 530 US 914 (2000).

[69] In *Roe v Wade* (n 11), the Court held that states may proscribe post-viability abortions as long as they include an exception where abortion is necessary to preserve the life or health of the pregnant woman (Melissa C Holsinger, 'The Partial Birth Abortion Ban Act of 2003: The Congressional Reaction to *Stenberg v Carhart*' (2002/2003) 6 *New York University Journal of Legislation and Public Policy* 603).

[70] *Gonzales v Carhart* (n 67). See also *National Abortion Federation v Aschcroft*, 330 F Supp 2d 436 (SDNY 2004); *Planned Parenthood Federation of America v Aschcroft*, 320 F Supp 2d 957 (ND Cal 2004).

[71] Partial-Birth Abortion Ban Act (n 66).

[72] *Ibid*.

[73] Bonnie Scott Jones and Tracy A Weitz, 'Legal Barriers to Second-Trimester Abortion Provision and Public Health Consequences' (2009) 99 *American Journal of Public Health* 623, 624 ('Partial-birth abortion . . . is not the name of any known medical procedure . . .').

[74] *Gonzales v Carhart* (n 67) 156.

[75] *Ibid* 157.

[76] *Ibid* 162.

Justice Ginsburg wrote a scathing dissent, referring to the majority's reasons as offering 'flimsy and transparent justifications'[77] for upholding a ban with no health-related exception. She stated:

> Today's decision is alarming. It refuses to take *Casey* and *Stenberg* seriously. It tolerates, indeed applauds, federal intervention to ban nationwide a procedure found necessary and proper in certain cases by the American College of Obstetricians and Gynecologists (ACOG). It blurs the line, firmly drawn in *Casey*, between previability and postviability abortions. And, for the first time since *Roe*, the Court blesses a prohibition with no exception safeguarding a woman's health.[78]

Pro-choice supporters expressed a great deal of concern in the wake of the decision, both in terms of its potential political implications and its implications for medical practice.[79] Of particular concern was the lack of an exception to the ban for reasons related to maternal health, meaning that physicians are limited in their choice of procedure even where the banned procedure is or could be necessary to safeguard the woman's health.[80] Arguably, since the decision, not much has changed in either the political or the medical practice context – David Garrow claims that the decision has had 'far more modest consequences than many critics and commentators initially proclaimed'.[81] The real risk, in his view, is that the decision opens the door to state legislation that, in turn, will give 'prosecutors the statutory authority to prosecute, or persecute, reputable physicians who perform second-trimester abortions'.[82]

i. Contemporary trends in US abortion law

Since the Supreme Court decided *Roe v Wade*, and particularly following the decision in *Casey*, many states have adopted legal measures that impede access to abortion services. Several have also attempted to go well beyond the degree of regulation permitted by the decision in *Casey*. As noted, one example of legislation seeking to restrict women's ability to access abortions services is the banning of 'partial-birth abortion', as was in issue in *Carhart v Gonzales*. Although the states' attempts have not been wholly successful, abortion opponents have made significant inroads. State laws seeking to restrict women's ability to exercise their right to choose abortion include the following:[83]

– laws requiring mandatory parental involvement (either parental notification or parental consent laws[84]) where minors seek abortion services;

---

[77] *Ibid* 181.

[78] *Ibid* 170–71.

[79] See, eg, Jones and Weitz (n 73) 626; George J Annas, 'The Supreme Court and Abortion Rights' (2007) 356 *New England Journal of Medicine* 2201, 2205–06; David J Garrow, 'Significant Risks: Gonzales v Carhart and the Future of Abortion Law' (2007) 1 *The Supreme Court Review* 1, 28–30.

[80] 'The Bush Administration's Federal Abortion Ban' (*NARAL Pro-Choice America*, 1 January 2011), at <www.prochoiceamerica.org/media/fact-sheets/abortion-bans-federal-abortion-ban.pdf>.

[81] Garrow (n 79) 2.

[82] *Ibid* 47.

[83] See Rachel Benson Gold and Elizabeth Nash, 'Troubling Trend: More States Hostile to Abortion Rights as Middle Ground Shrinks' (2012) 15(1) *Guttmacher Policy Review* 14.

[84] States are free to require parental consent for minors who seek abortion services, as long as the statute does not create a veto power, and as long as it permits the minor to seek a judicial hearing as to whether she is mature and may make the decision without parental involvement, or allows the court to decide that the abortion is in her best interests (*Bellotti v Baird*, 443 US 622 (1979)). State policies vary as to whether there is a parental notification requirement only, or whether parental consent is also required. There are also differences

- laws that mandate pre-procedure counselling[85] (in some cases, with the state specifying the information to be provided);
- laws setting out extended waiting periods between the consultation and the procedure (requiring, in effect, two separate clinic visits);
- laws mandating the performance of an ultrasound prior to abortion;
- laws prohibiting Medicaid funding for abortion services unless the pregnant woman's life is endangered, or the pregnancy is the result of rape or incest;[86]
- laws restricting coverage of abortion in private insurance plans;
- laws restricting the availability of medical abortion;
- laws placing onerous facility requirements (that are not related to patient safety) on abortion clinics;
- laws banning some pre-viability abortions; and
- laws that would immediately ban all abortions in the event that the decision in *Roe v Wade* is overturned.[87]

In terms of the sheer volume of abortion-related legislative activity in the states, 2011 has been called 'a year for the record books',[88] as the states saw unprecedented levels of activity in the general area of reproductive health and rights. Specifically,

> legislators in all 50 states introduced more than 1,100 provisions related to reproductive health and rights. At the end of it all, states had adopted 135 new reproductive health provisions – a dramatic increase from the 89 enacted in 2010 and the 77 enacted in 2009. Fully 92 of the enacted provisions seek to restrict abortion, shattering the previous record of 34 abortion restrictions in 2005 . . .[89]

The types of abortion restrictions included in the most recent wave of legislative action range from the familiar – such as mandatory ultrasound laws, restrictions on insurance

among states in terms of whether both parents must be notified or must provide consent, or whether an adult relative other than the parent(s) may be involved in the decision. Thirty-seven states have a parental involvement requirement, and only one (Utah) fails to provide an alternative procedure, such as a judicial bypass procedure (Guttmacher Institute, 'State Policies in Brief: Parental Involvement in Minors' Abortions' (1 August 2012), at <www.guttmacher.org/statecenter/spibs/spib_PIMA.pdf>). The Guttmacher Institute notes that although most states require some level of parental involvement, the majority make exceptions in certain circumstances, such as for medical emergencies and situations of abuse, assault, incest or neglect.

[85] Most states (35) have legislation requiring counselling for women seeking abortion services; often these statutes require the provision of specific information to women before an abortion can be performed (this is the case in 26 states). In addition, most of the states that require counselling also stipulate a waiting period after the counselling session and before provision of the abortion. Nine states currently require 'in person' counselling, and all nine specify a significant waiting period (the lowest being 18 hours) post-counselling. South Dakota's law, which is currently enjoined, requires a 72-hour wait period post-counselling (Guttmacher Institute, 'State Policies in Brief: Counseling and Waiting Periods for Abortion' (1 August 2012), at <www.guttmacher.org/statecenter/spibs/spib_MWPA.pdf>).

[86] *Harris v McRae*, 448 US 297 (1980), upholding the Hyde Amendment to the Medicaid Act. Medicaid is a joint state-federal program that provides health insurance to those who meet the eligibility criteria; eligibility is based on factors in addition to inability to afford health insurance. See, generally, Barbara S Klees, Christian J Wolfe and Catherine A Curtis, *Brief Summaries of Medicare & Medicaid: Title XVIII and XIX of the Social Security Act* (Washington, DC, Centers for Medicare and Medicaid Services, Department of Health and Human Services, 2010).

[87] These laws have been characterised as 'major abortion restrictions' by Gold and Nash (Gold and Nash (n 83) 14–15). They note that some of their categories blend together more than one kind of restriction; they state that taken together, the categories comprise 19 separate abortion restrictions.

[88] *Ibid* 16.

[89] *Ibid*.

coverage, expanded wait times or counselling periods[90] – to such novel restrictions as banning abortion after 22 weeks' gestation[91] based on the assertion that a fetus can feel pain at that point.[92] Another new type of restriction seen in this time frame is a prohibition on the use of telemedicine for medical abortion, by requiring that the prescribing physician be in the same room as the patient when the medication is prescribed.[93]

These examples are part of a trend in the US wherein several states that have traditionally been in the 'middle-ground' as far as restricting access to abortion have become 'hostile' to abortion rights. Nash and Gold describe the dwindling middle ground, noting that not much more than a decade ago, 19 states could be described as being in the 'middle-ground', while 13 could be described as 'hostile' to abortion rights.[94] As they explain: 'By 2011 . . . that picture had shifted dramatically: 26 states were hostile to abortion rights, and the number of middle-ground states had cut in half, to nine.'[95] The 26 'hostile' states are responsible for almost all of the restrictions enacted in 2011. The number of states that have traditionally been supportive of abortion rights has also decreased, from 18 in 2000 to 15 in 2011.[96]

The intense legislative activity continued at least into the early part of 2012: between January and April 2012, legislators introduced over 900 provisions 'related to reproductive health and rights. Half of these provisions would restrict abortion access.'[97] Like many of the provisions passed in 2011, legislators have targeted ultrasound requirements, limiting access to medical abortion and gestational limits.[98] Several states are also contemplating allowing employers to refuse to provide contraception coverage.[99]

Legislation introduced in the 2012 wave includes laws requiring ultrasound prior to abortion, even in the case of early abortion. Some of these laws specify that certain fetal characteristics must be visualised on ultrasound. While none of these laws explicitly mandates transvaginal ultrasound,[100] there is no other way to ensure that the specified

---

[90] *Ibid.*

[91] The ban is actually framed in post-fertilisation terms, with a ban on abortion at 20 weeks post-fertilisation translating into 22 weeks' gestation (gestational age is based on the date of the woman's last menstrual period (LMP), which is roughly two weeks before fertilisation takes place). Nebraska's 2010 law provides a model for some of these new provisions (Neb Rev Stat § 28-3, 102–111 (enacted 2010)). Other statutes refer to fetal pain around 20 weeks post-fertilisation (Ind Code § 16-34-2-1.1 (2011); GA HB 89 (introduced 21 January 2011)). Ohio law requires viability testing for abortions at 20 weeks' (or more) gestation (Oh Rev Code § 2919.18(B)(2011)).

[92] I Glenn Cohen and Sadath Sayeed, 'Fetal Pain, Abortion, Viability, and the Constitution' (2011) 39 *Journal of Law, Medicine & Ethics* 235.

[93] Five states currently have such a requirement (Guttmacher Institute, 'State Policies in Brief: Medication Abortion' (1 August 2012), at <www.guttmacher.org/statecenter/spibs/spib_MA.pdf>).

[94] Gold and Nash (n 83) 17.

[95] *Ibid.*

[96] *Ibid.* The authors note that Arizona went from supportive to hostile when the Democratic Governor (Janet Napolitano) left office, as she had repeatedly vetoed provisions that would limit access. Two other states that are no longer 'supportive' are Alaska and Minnesota (now both are described as middle-ground states). Eight states that continue to support abortion rights (California, Connecticut, Hawaii, New Jersey, New Mexico, Oregon, Vermont and Washington) have not enacted any of the types of restrictions included in this study.

[97] By mid-April 2012, '75 abortion restrictions [had] been approved by at least one legislative chamber, and nine [had] been enacted' (Guttmacher Institute, 'State Policy Trends: Abortion and Contraception in the Crosshairs' (13 April 2012), at <www.guttmacher.org/media/inthenews/2012/04/13/index.html>).

[98] *Ibid.*

[99] *Ibid.*

[100] Transvaginal ultrasound involves the insertion of the ultrasound probe into the woman's vagina. The technique is used in early pregnancy as the uterus is not high enough in the abdomen for abdominal ultrasound to permit visualisation of the fetus (Gregory T Fossum, V Davajan and OA Kletzky, 'Early Detection of Pregnancy with Transvaginal Ultrasound' (1988) 49 *Fertility and Sterility* 788).

characteristics can be seen in early pregnancy.[101] Thus, these laws de facto require the use of an invasive medical procedure, one that some commentators have likened to sexual assault.[102] More states introduced laws that limit access to medical abortion by requiring the prescribing physician to be in the same room as the patient, and a number of states have introduced laws which require medical abortion to be carried out in compliance with the current FDA protocol (an older protocol that is less widely used and more complicated than new ones).[103] Lastly, several more states have introduced legislation that would ban some pre-viability abortions (between 18 and 25 weeks after fertilisation, or 20 and 27 weeks' gestation).[104]

Other legislative efforts to restrict abortion include regulations aimed specifically at abortion providers and facilities. A new Mississippi law, for example, requires that all physicians associated with abortion clinics must have local admitting privileges.[105] There is at present only one clinic in the state, and none of the physicians currently meets this requirement (only one of the four lives in the state).[106] Several other states have similar requirements,[107] but Mississippi is the only one in which the law could have the effect of requiring the closure of the sole abortion clinic in the state. State legislators insist that the aim of this law is to safeguard women's health, in that the provider would be able to follow up if a patient seeks hospital care for complications – but several are hopeful that the clinic will indeed have to close.[108]

In addition to all of the above-described policy initiatives, laws purporting to protect 'unborn victims of violence' have also come under criticism in respect of their potential effects on pregnant women. Such laws are aimed at recognising the additional crime involved in harming a pregnant woman in a way also intended to harm the fetus she is carrying; they recognise a separate offence where bodily injury or death of a fetus occurs in the course of the commission of specific crimes. The legislation defines a 'child in

---

[101] Guttmacher Institute (n 97). In February 2012, a Texas law (an Act 'relating to informed consent to an abortion' HB 15, 82nd Leg Reg Sess (Tex 2011)) requiring ultrasound prior to abortion was upheld by a US District Court (*Texas Medical Providers Performing Abortion Services v Lakey*, 667 F 3d 570 (5th Cir 10 Jan 2012)). Virginia also recently enacted a similar law (*A BILL to amend and reenact § 18.2-76 of the Code of Virginia, relating to ultrasound requirement as part of informed consent for abortion*, HB 462, 2012 Sess (Virginia 2012)). Both of these laws also mandate that women who live within 100 miles of the abortion clinic or facility have the ultrasound at least 24 hours before the termination.

[102] See, eg, Nicholas D Kristof, 'When States Abuse Women', *New York Times*, 3 March 2012, at <www. nytimes.com/2012/03/04/opinion/sunday/kristof-when-states-abuse-women.html>.

[103] Guttmacher Institute (n 97).

[104] *Ibid*. See also Guttmacher Institute, 'State Policies in Brief: State Policies on Later Abortions' (1 August 2012), at <www.guttmacher.org/statecenter/spibs/spib_PLTA.pdf>. Georgia's law bans abortion after 22 weeks' gestation unless the woman's life is endangered or there is a possible 'substantial and irreversible physical impairment of a major bodily function', or the fetus has a fatal abnormality (GA12 HB 954/AP). The Act also refers to 'medically futile pregnancy' as follows: 'medically futile' means that, in reasonable medical judgement, the unborn child has a profound and irremediable congenital or chromosomal anomaly that is incompatible with sustaining life after birth.'

[105] An Act to amend section 41-75-1, Mississippi Code of 1972, to require that all physicians who perform abortions in abortion facilities must have admitting privileges at a local hospital and must be board certified in obstetrics and gynecology; and for related purposes, HB 1390.

[106] Campbell Robertson, 'Mississippi's Only Abortion Clinic at Risk as Law Nears', *New York Times*, 22 June 2012, at <www.nytimes.com/2012/06/23/us/mississippis-only-abortion-clinic-is-at-risk-as-new-law-nears. html>. As Robertson points out, if in the end the clinic does have to close, Mississippi will be the only state without a single abortion clinic.

[107] Gold and Nash (n 83); Guttmacher Institute, 'State Center: Monthly State Update: Major Developments in 2012' (1 August 2012), at <www.guttmacher.org/statecenter/updates/index.html#HospitalPrivileges>.

[108] See, eg, Robertson (n 106); Elizabeth Waibel, 'Abortion Clinic Stays Open, For Now', *Jackson Free Press*, 20 June 2012, at <www.jacksonfreepress.com/news/2012/jun/20/abortion-clinic-stays-open-for-now/>.

utero' as a 'member of the species homo sapiens, at any stage of development, who is carried in the womb'.[109] Critics view such legislation as an attempt at an 'end run' around *Roe v Wade*. They point out that there are many measures that could be adopted to prevent and punish the commission of violent crimes against pregnant women that do not create a potential threat to abortion rights and other reproductive autonomy-based interests.[110] There is an argument to be made, however, that a gradualist view of fetal status could make space for recognition of the additional injury that occurs when a violent act harms both the pregnant woman herself and the fetus.[111]

In addition to legislation aimed at limiting the scope of the right to abortion, conservative politicians have also sought to make Supreme Court appointments with a view to an ultimate victory – the possibility that *Roe v Wade* could be overturned by a differently composed court, meaning that abortion regulation would be placed back in the hands of the states.[112]

C. Australia

As in Canada and the US (and, as will be seen below, the UK), abortion was criminalised in the various Australian states and territories in the nineteenth century.[113] Abortion law in Australia is left to the jurisdiction of individual states. Though none of the states currently has a legal regime that allows for 'abortion on demand',[114] law reform in two states seems to provide just that, perhaps in all but name. In both the Australian Capital Territory (ACT)[115] and Victoria, abortion has been decriminalised, and each of these two states has reformed the law such that abortion is in essence available upon request by a pregnant woman seeking to end her pregnancy. In the ACT, abortion is not a criminal offence when carried out by a physician in an approved facility.[116] Gestational limits

---

[109] Unborn Victims of Violence Act of 2004 (Laci and Conner's Law), Pub L 108-212, 118 Stat 568, s 2(D)(d). In the absence of similar legislation, the English House of Lords considered the question of whether a charge of unlawful homicide may be brought against the perpetrator of a violent act that causes a fetus to be born alive and then subsequently die from its injuries (*AG's Reference (No 3 of 1994)* [1998] AC 245). In this case, the baby was born very prematurely after its mother was stabbed numerous times, including in the abdomen. After its birth, it was discovered that the baby had also been injured. The House of Lords held that while a murder charge may not be brought in such circumstances, a charge of manslaughter is possible. This issue has also been considered by the European Court of Human Rights in *Vo v France* (n 16). In this case, physician negligence led to the death of a 20–21-week-old fetus, and the argument was made that in failing to provide a criminal punishment for this act, French law failed to protect the fetus's right to life under Art 2 ECHR. The European Court of Human Rights found that Art 2 ECHR does not oblige States to impose criminal penalties for this type of conduct.

[110] See, eg, Sheryl McCarthy, 'Abortion Foes Exploit a Murder to Kill Roe v Wade', *Newsday* (New York, 9 June 2003), at <advocatesforpregnantwomen.org/issues/abortionfoes.htm>. Others have questioned the commitment of jurisdictions that pass such legislation to the well-being of women and children, given the lack of action on other fronts that might actually do more to protect fetal health (Joni Seager, '"Protectors" of Unborn Put Them in Peril', *Baltimore Sun*, 7 April 2004, at <www.commondreams.org/views04/0407-01.htm>).

[111] Aurora Plomer, 'A Foetal Right to Life? The Case of *Vo v France*' (2005) 5 *Human Rights Law Review* 311.

[112] Jeffrey A Segal, Richard J Timpone and Robert M Howard, 'Buyer Beware? Presidential Success Through Supreme Court Appointments' (2000) 53 *Political Research Quarterly* 557.

[113] See, eg, Victorian Law Reform Commission, *Law of Abortion: Final Report*, No 15 (Melbourne, Victorian Law Reform Commission, 2008).

[114] Kirsty Morris, Kristin Savell and Christopher J Ryan, 'Psychiatrists and Termination of Pregnancy: Clinical, Legal and Ethical Aspects' (2012) 46 *Australian and New Zealand Journal of Psychiatry* 18, 19.

[115] Crimes (Abolition of Offence of Abortion) Act 2002 (ACT).

[116] Health Act 1993 (ACT), ss 81, 82.

are not specified, but there is an offence of child destruction within the Crimes Act[117] that could potentially be applicable in the case of late-term or post-viability abortion.

Until 2008, Victorian abortion law was based on the common law Menhennitt Ruling, which (in very general terms) holds that abortion is not unlawful if it is 'necessary'.[118] In 2008, a law reform process[119] culminated with the passage of legislation aimed at clarifying abortion law in Victoria and abolishing the criminal offence of abortion.[120] The Victorian legislation provides that 'a registered medical practitioner may perform an abortion on a woman who is not more than 24 weeks pregnant'.[121] After 24 weeks' gestation, abortion is permissible only on the basis of a reasonable belief 'that abortion is appropriate in all the circumstances' and where a second medical practitioner agrees with that assessment.[122]

Abortion law has also been reformed in Western Australia, although not to the same extent as in the ACT and Victoria. According to Western Australian law, abortion is not a criminal offence where performed by a physician, in good faith with reasonable care and skill, and where the woman provides informed consent and is not more than 20 weeks pregnant.[123] After the 20-week gestational limit, abortion may be legally performed only where two physicians who are members of a government-appointed committee are of the view that the woman or the fetus has a 'severe medical condition that, in the clinical judgment of those 2 medical practitioners, justifies the procedure'.[124] The legislation contains informed consent provisions that require counselling by a physician who will not be involved in the procedure about the medical risks of termination of pregnancy, and that require the offer of counselling about 'matters relating to termination of pregnancy and carrying a pregnancy to term'.[125] In the case of a dependent minor (defined as a woman under the age of 16 who is being supported by a custodial parent or parents[126]), the informed consent requirement is met only where a custodial parent has been informed that abortion is being considered and has been afforded the opportunity to participate in the consultation process.[127]

In the remaining Australian jurisdictions, abortion is a criminal offence, although the existence of common law or statutory defences means that the procedure is available without the threat of criminal sanctions if carried out in circumstances that render it 'lawful'.[128] In South Australia, for example, abortion is permissible where two physicians, after examining the pregnant woman, form the bona fide opinion that 'the risk of

---

[117] Crimes Act 1900 (ACT), s 42.

[118] *R v Davidson* (n 29). This is discussed in more detail in the context of Queensland and NSW law, below.

[119] Victorian Law Reform Commission (n 113). The Commission noted that abortion law in Victoria was unclear and that the abortion provisions in that state had not been judicially considered since the Menhennitt Ruling in 1969 (*R v Davidson* (n 29)).

[120] Abortion Law Reform Act 2008 (Vic).

[121] *Ibid* s 4.

[122] *Ibid* s 5.

[123] Health Act 1911 (WA), s 334.

[124] *Ibid* s 334(7)(a). Section 334(7)(b) also provides that the abortion must then be performed in an approved facility. One author notes that between May 1998 and 31 December 2003, approximately 0.5% of all induced abortions in Western Australia involved pregnancies of over 20 weeks' gestation (Jan E Dickinson, 'Late Pregnancy Termination within a Legislated Medical Environment' (2004) 44 *Australia and New Zealand Journal of Obstetrics and Gynaecology* 337).

[125] Health Act 1911 (WA), s 334(5), (6).

[126] *Ibid* s 334(8)(b).

[127] *Ibid* s 334(8)(a).

[128] South Australia's legislation is modeled on the UK's Abortion Act 1967 (n 7) (Yusuf and Briggs (n 27) 180–81).

continuing the pregnancy is more dangerous to the woman's physical and mental health than a termination,' or that there is a substantial risk that the child, if born, would suffer from serious mental or physical abnormalities.[129] In determining whether the pregnancy would pose a greater risk to the woman's health than would termination, the physicians are entitled to take into account the woman's 'actual or reasonably foreseeable environment'.[130] The abortion must take place in a prescribed hospital, and is not specifically time-limited, but is impermissible where the fetus is 'capable of being born alive'[131] unless done in good faith only to preserve the life of the 'mother'.[132] The statute presumes that a child is capable of being born alive at 28 weeks' gestation.[133]

Abortion law in the Northern Territory is very similar in approach to that in South Australia, but abortion is permissible only on the basis of maternal or fetal health up to 14 weeks' gestation,[134] and at least one of the physicians involved must be a gynaecologist or obstetrician.[135] After 14 weeks' gestation (and only up to 23 weeks), an abortion is permissible only where the two physicians are of the opinion that 'termination of the pregnancy is immediately necessary to prevent grave injury to [the pregnant woman's] physical or mental health'.[136] Abortion is permissible without regard to the stage of a pregnancy where its sole purpose is to preserve the pregnant woman's life.[137] The Northern Territory statute also makes reference to the need for consent from the 'appropriate person'. In most instances this is the woman herself, but if she is under 16 years of age or incapable of consenting, consent must be obtained from her legal guardian.[138]

Abortion is also a matter for the criminal law in New South Wales and Queensland. In New South Wales (NSW), it is an offence 'unlawfully' to use or administer an instrument or drug with the intention of procuring a miscarriage.[139] With the adoption of the Menhennitt Ruling into NSW law in *R v Wald*, however, the courts have taken the view that an abortion is not unlawful if it is 'necessary'.[140] The defence of necessity applies (and abortion is lawful) where the doctor honestly believes, on reasonable grounds, that the abortion is necessary in order to prevent serious danger to the pregnant woman's life or physical or mental health, and where, in the circumstances, the risk posed by the procedure is not 'out of proportion' to the risk to be avoided.[141] In other words, to prosecute

---

[129] Criminal Law Consolidation Act 1935 (SA), ss 82A(1)(a)(i) (maternal health), 82A(1)(a)(ii) (fetal abnormality). See also Kerry Petersen, 'Abortion Laws and Medical Developments: A Medico-Legal Anomaly in Queensland' (2011) 18 *Journal of Law and Medicine* 594.

[130] Criminal Law Consolidation Act 1935 (SA), s 82A(3).

[131] *Ibid* s 82A(7).

[132] *Ibid.*

[133] *Ibid* s 82A(8). Hospital ethics committees play a role in considering requests for terminations between 24 and 28 weeks' gestation (Morris, Savell and Ryan (n 114) 21).

[134] Medical Services Act 1982 (NT), s 11.

[135] *Ibid* s 11(2). This requirement may be dispensed with if it is 'not reasonably practicable'.

[136] *Ibid* s 11(3).

[137] *Ibid* s 11(4).

[138] *Ibid* s 11(5). Tasmania's abortion law similarly provides that abortion is lawful if two physicians certify in writing that continuing the pregnancy would pose a greater risk of injury to the woman's life or health than terminating it would, and provided that the woman has given her informed consent to the termination (Criminal Code Act 1924 (Tas), s 164). Informed consent is given a specific statutory definition that refers to the woman having been counselled by a medical practitioner (*ibid* s 164(9)).

[139] Crimes Act 1900 (NSW), ss 82–84.

[140] See, eg, *R v Davidson* (n 29); *R v Wald* (n 29); *CES v Superclinics (Australia) Pty Ltd* (1995) 38 NSWLR 47. For detailed discussions of the common law defence of necessity, see Victorian Law Reform Commission (n 113) 18–21; Kate Gleeson, 'The Other Abortion Myth – The Failure of the Common Law' (2009) 6 *Journal of Bioethical Inquiry* 69, 70–71.

[141] *R v Davidson* (n 29); *R v Wald* (n 29).

a physician successfully for unlawful abortion, the prosecution must prove that the accused physician did not honestly believe *either* that the abortion was necessary to prevent serious danger to the woman's life or health, *or* that terminating the pregnancy was a proportionate response to the danger posed by continuing the pregnancy.[142]

The defence of necessity has been interpreted broadly by the NSW courts. In *R v Wald*, Levine J held that the 'reasonable grounds' on which the physician must rely could include 'any economic, social or medical ground or reason' that at any time during the pregnancy could lead to serious danger to the woman's life or health.[143] This reasoning was accepted by the NSW Court of Appeal in *CES v Superclinics*, and was extended to encompass the period 'after the birth of the child'.[144] The *Wald* test also arose in *R v Sood*,[145] a case in which a physician was prosecuted under section 83 of the Crimes Act. Dr Sood was convicted of unlawfully procuring a miscarriage because she failed to counsel or examine the pregnant woman in order to determine whether abortion was 'necessary'. Once again, in *R v Sood*, the broad interpretation of the necessity defence was accepted.

The law in Queensland is similar to that in NSW, although it is based on statutory offences and (it appears) both common law and statutory defences. The offences and the statutory defence are found in the Criminal Code.[146] In essence, abortion is lawful if carried out in good faith and with reasonable care and skill to preserve the mother's life, and provided that the treatment was 'reasonable, having regard to the patient's state at the time and to all the circumstances of the case'.[147] The Menhennitt Ruling on the defence of necessity articulated in *R v Davidson* is applicable in Queensland,[148] but the extended version of the defence adopted by the courts in NSW does not appear to apply.[149]

Section 225 of Queensland's Criminal Code prohibits the self-administration of 'any poison or other noxious thing' by a woman with the aim of procuring her own miscarriage. In 2010, 21-year-old Tegan Leach was charged under this section of the Criminal Code (and her partner was charged under section 226, which prohibits the supply of 'anything whatever knowing that it is intended to be unlawfully used to procure the miscarriage of a woman') when she ingested mifepristone and misoprostol to end her pregnancy.[150] Because they are not readily available in Australia, the medications were obtained by the woman through her partner's sister who sent them from Ukraine. Both the woman and her partner were acquitted by the jury 'following a direction from the trial judge that "noxious" was to be determined by reference to whether it was noxious to Leach as opposed to any fetus she might have been carrying'.[151] But as Morris, Savell and Ryan explain, the Criminal Code sections refer to the procurement of a miscarriage by 'any other means whatever,' and so even if mifepristone is not a 'noxious thing' as defined by the trial judge, the abortion could still have been treated as unlawful.[152]

---

[142]   Morris, Savell and Ryan (n 114) 20.
[143]   *R v Wald* (n 29) 29.
[144]   *CES v Superclinics* (n 140) 60.
[145]   *R v Sood* [2006] NSWSC 1141.
[146]   Criminal Code 1899 (Qld), ss 224–226, 282.
[147]   *Ibid* s 282(1)(b).
[148]   *R v Bayliss and Cullen* [1986] 9 Qld Lawyer Reps 8.
[149]   *Ibid*.
[150]   *R v Brennan and Leach* [2010] QDC 329 (Judge Everson, 27 August 2010).
[151]   Morris, Savell and Ryan (n 114) 21.
[152]   *Ibid*. The authors explain that this argument was not pursued by the prosecutors.

D. United Kingdom

Until the nineteenth century, abortion was regulated in the UK through both ecclesiastical and common law. There is some dispute about the legality of abortion at common law, although John Keown claims that the 'weight of available authority supports the view that the common law prohibited abortion, at least after the fetus had become "quick" or "animated"'.[153] In 1803, abortion was brought within the purview of the criminal law with the passage of Lord Ellenborough's Act.[154] Over the years, abortion law has been reformed by statute and by the common law.

Under the Offences Against the Person Act 1861, abortion was a criminal offence in all circumstances,[155] as was the supply of 'any poison or other noxious thing, or any instrument' with the knowledge that the poison or instrument would be used to procure an abortion.[156] The Act makes reference to 'unlawful' administration of a poison or noxious substance, or the 'unlawful' use of any instrument with the intent to procure a miscarriage. The Act is silent as to timing, making no mention of the point in pregnancy at which the abortion was carried out, and makes no exceptions for termination of pregnancy for therapeutic purposes.

In 1929, the Infant Life (Preservation) Act was enacted in order to make it a crime to destroy a child during the birthing process.[157] As Sally Sheldon explains, the killing of a child while it was emerging from its mother's body was caught neither by the Offences Against the Person Act (which speaks to procuring a miscarriage), nor by the law of murder, as until the child is born, he or she is not a 'person in being'.[158] The Infant Life (Preservation) Act 1929 establishes a criminal offence for the commission of a wilful act that 'with intent to destroy the life of a child, capable of being born alive, . . . [causes] a child to die before it has an existence independent of its mother' except where done in good faith to preserve the life of the mother.[159] The statute presumes that a child born at 28 weeks' gestation (or later) is capable of being born alive.[160] Read together with the Offences Against the Person Act 1861, the law was understood to permit abortions carried out for the purpose of preserving the life of the pregnant woman.

In 1938, Dr Aleck Bourne was charged with breaching section 58 of the Offences Against the Person Act 1861when he performed an abortion on a 15-year-old girl who had been raped by a group of soldiers.[161] He insisted that the abortion was not 'unlawful' within the meaning of the statutory provision, and that the abortion was necessary in order to preserve his patient's health. In his charge to the jury, Macnaghten J explained that the Crown has the burden of proving 'beyond reasonable doubt that the defendant did not procure the miscarriage of this girl in good faith for the purpose only of preserving her life'.[162] He

---

[153] John Keown, *Abortion, Doctors and the Law: Some Aspects of the Legal Regulation of Abortion in England from 1803 to 1982* (Cambridge, Cambridge University Press, 1988) 3. See also Bernard M Dickens, *Abortion and the Law* (Bristol, MacGibbon & Kee, 1966) 23.
[154] Lord Ellenborough's Act 1803 (43 Geo 3 c 53).
[155] Offences Against the Person Act 1861 (UK), s 58.
[156] *Ibid* s 59.
[157] Infant Life (Preservation) Act 1929 (UK).
[158] Sally Sheldon, *Beyond Control: Medical Power and Abortion Law* (London, Pluto Press, 1997) 15.
[159] Infant Life (Preservation) Act 1929, s 1(1). See also Scott (n 21) 153.
[160] Infant Life (Preservation) Act 1929, s 1(2).
[161] *R v Bourne* [1939] 1 KB 687.
[162] *Ibid* 691.

then considered the meaning of the phrase 'for the purpose of preserving the life of the mother' within the Infant Life (Preservation) Act 1929, concluding as follows:

> As I have said, I think those words ought to be construed in a reasonable sense, and, if the doctor is of opinion, on reasonable grounds and with adequate knowledge, that the probable consequence of the continuance of the pregnancy will be to make the woman a physical or mental wreck, the jury are quite entitled to take the view that the doctor who, under those circumstances and in that honest belief, operates, is operating for the purpose of preserving the life of the mother.[163]

Thus, at common law, as long as the physician was acting in good faith and on the basis of an honestly-held belief, abortion could be considered legal where necessary to preserve the life or health of the pregnant woman.[164]

Abortion services in most of the UK were formally liberalised in 1967, with the passage of the Abortion Act 1967. The Act creates statutory defences to the offences of 'procuring a miscarriage, and destroying a viable fetus'.[165] Currently, based on the Abortion Act 1967 as amended by the Human Fertilisation and Embryology Act 1990 (HFE Act 1990), abortion is legally permitted up to 24 weeks' gestation, when performed by a physician, 'if two registered medical practitioners are of the opinion, formed in good faith' that to continue the pregnancy would threaten injury to the woman's physical or mental health (or that of any of her existing children).[166] If the pregnancy has advanced beyond 24 weeks, abortion is lawful only if the two physicians believe that termination is necessary to prevent 'grave permanent injury to the physical or mental health of the pregnant woman,' that continuing the pregnancy would pose a risk to the pregnant woman's life greater than that posed by the termination, or that there is a 'substantial risk' that the child, if born, would 'suffer from such physical or mental abnormalities as to be seriously handicapped'.[167] In all cases, the abortion must be approved by two doctors (or, in the case of emergency, by only one doctor[168]) and must be carried out by a doctor in an approved hospital or clinic facility.[169]

It has been noted that prior to the amendment of the Abortion Act 1967 by the HFE Act 1990, there was no explicit time limit on abortion in the UK. However, when the Abortion Act 1967 was read together with the Infant Life (Preservation) Act 1929, it was generally thought that 'a child capable of being born alive' indicated 28 weeks' gestation.[170] As noted, it is now clear that the gestational limit on legal abortion is 24 weeks, except where necessary to prevent 'grave permanent injury' to the woman's physical or mental health or to prevent the birth of a child who will be 'seriously handicapped'.[171]

---

[163] *Ibid* 693–94.

[164] Later cases confirmed the view that the physician's opinion about the risk to the woman's health entailed by pregnancy must be honestly held, even if mistaken see *R v Bergmann and Ferguson* [1948] 1 BMJ 1008, cited by Sheldon (n 158) 16.

[165] Emily Jackson, *Regulating Reproduction: Law, Technology and Autonomy* (Oxford, Hart Publishing, 2001) 77.

[166] The 24-week gestational limit is based on the Abortion Act 1967, s 1(1), as amended by the HFE Act 1990 (UK), s 37. Originally, the Abortion Act 1967 permitted abortions up to 28 weeks' gestation. Jackson (n 165) 82.

[167] Abortion Act 1967, s 1(1).

[168] *Ibid* s 1(4).

[169] *Ibid* s 1(3).

[170] Sheldon (n 158) 108.

[171] In 2011, 91.1% of abortions for women resident in England and Wales were performed before 13 weeks' gestation; 77.7% were carried out before 10 weeks' gestation (Department of Health, 'Abortion Statistics,

In the UK, then, there is no 'abortion right' as such (just as is the case in Canada and Australia); rather, the law provides a defence (to physicians) to what would otherwise constitute an unlawful act. Indeed, as Sally Sheldon points out,[172] in the Parliamentary debates surrounding the passage of the Abortion Act 1967, the legislators and medical governing bodies took care to ensure that the statute did not contain language which might be construed as granting women such a right.

The Abortion Act 1967 is applicable in England and Wales and in Scotland. Northern Ireland is excluded from the Act and, as such, is the only part of the UK that remains subject to the more restrictive regulation of abortion that was in place throughout the UK prior to 1967.[173] In Northern Ireland, abortion law is based on sections 58 and 59 of the Offences Against the Person Act 1861, the Criminal Justice Act (Northern Ireland) 1945[174] and the decision in *R v Bourne*.[175] Abortion is presumptively prohibited in Northern Ireland, but may lawfully be carried out in certain circumstances.[176] As long as the physician who terminates a pregnancy does so in good faith and only for the purpose of preserving the life of the pregnant woman, the abortion is legal. Based on judicial interpretation, the 'life' of the pregnant woman includes her physical and mental health. Thus,

> a termination will therefore be lawful where the continuance of the pregnancy threatens the life of the woman or would adversely affect her physical or mental health. The adverse effect on her physical or mental health must be a 'real and serious' one, and must also be permanent or long-term.[177]

Northern Irish law is silent as to gestational age limits for pregnancy termination.

England & Wales: 2011' (May 2012) 9, at <www.wp.dh.gov.uk/transparency/files/2012/05/Commentary1. pdf>). That same year, 146 abortions were performed at or after 24 weeks' gestation (accounting for 0.1% of the total abortion procedures performed that year).

[172] Sheldon (n 158) 27–28.

[173] Abortion law is even more restrictive in the Republic of Ireland, where the Constitution recognises a right to life for unborn children ('the State acknowledges the right to life of the unborn and, with due regard to the equal right to life of the mother, guarantees in its laws to respect, and, as far as practicable, by its laws to defend and vindicate that right' (Constitution of Ireland 1937, Art 40.3.3)). The Irish courts have held that the Constitution permits abortion to save the life of the pregnant woman, but there has been no statutory reform to reflect the Supreme Court's decision on this point (see *Attorney-General v X* [1992] IESC 1). A recent decision of the European Court of Human Rights (Grand Chamber) awarded damages to a woman living in Ireland on the basis that the lack of availability of information respecting legal abortion (in a situation where her pregnancy could have been life-threatening) violated her Art 8 ECHR rights to private life (*A, B and C v Ireland* [2010] ECHR 2032). Two other claimants were denied relief on the basis of the margin of appreciation conferred on States. The Irish Government commissioned an expert report to advise as to how to implement the Grand Chamber's decision. Just days before the report was issued, Savita Halappanavar died as a result of septicemia caused by an incomplete miscarriage and the refusal of her physicians to perform an abortion (Kitty Holland, 'Savita Halappanavar asked for termination, staff confirm' *Irish Times*, 18 January 2013 at <www. irishtimes.com/newspaper/frontpage/2013/0118/1224329001402.html>). It is to be hoped that the pressure generated by the 2010 case and Ms Halappanavar's tragic death might lead to real reform of Irish abortion law.

[174] The Criminal Justice Act (Northern Ireland) 1945, s 25(1) is identical to the Infant Life (Preservation) Act 1929 (n 157), s 1.

[175] *R v Bourne* (n 161).

[176] *Society for the Protection of Unborn Children's Application* [2009] NIQB 92.

[177] Department of Health, Social Services and Public Safety, 'Guidance on the Termination of Pregnancy: The Law and Clinical Practice in Northern Ireland' (Northern Ireland Department of Health, March 2009), para 1.3(iii), at <http://news.bbc.co.uk/2/shared/bsp/hi/pdfs/20_03_09_ninursing.pdfv>. This was held to be an accurate statement of the law in *Society for the Protection of Unborn Children's Application* (n 176). For revised Guidance, in draft form, see the Department's website at <http://www.dhsspsni.gov.uk/guidance_on_ the_termination_of_pregnancy__the_law_and_clinical_practice_in_northern_ireland.pdf>.

It is difficult to obtain information about abortion practice in Northern Ireland. In 2009, the Department of Health, Social Services and Public Safety issued Guidance on law and practice respecting termination of pregnancy in Northern Ireland.[178] The Guidance was issued in response to a 2004 decision of the Court of Appeal in Northern Ireland.[179] Very quickly after being issued, the Guidance was challenged in the courts when the Society for the Protection of Unborn Children brought an application for judicial review. The Society sought a declaration that the Guidance was unlawful, and an order requiring that it be publicly rescinded and removed from the Department's website or, alternatively, an order requiring the Department to vary the guidance as directed by the Court.[180] While rejecting most of the Society's arguments, the Court found some aspects of the Guidance to be 'misleading' and ordered its withdrawal 'with a view to . . . being reconsidered by the Department taking account of the contents of this judgment'.[181]

As a result of the very limited availability of abortion in Northern Ireland, most women must travel (often to England or Wales) for abortion services. In 2011, 16.4 per cent of the 6,151 abortions on non-English or Welsh women carried out in England or Wales were done on Northern Irish women (roughly 1,007 in 2011).[182]

As is clear from the foregoing, access to abortion in the UK remains very much under the control of medical practitioners. In the more than 40 years since the law was reformed via the Abortion Act 1967, advocates have continued to push for meaningful reform, particularly with a view to recognising the decisional autonomy of women seeking abortion services.[183] The most recent opportunity for a debate on potential reform arose in 2008, when the HFE Act 1990 was under review. Several amendments were proposed to the 1990 Act which would have amended the provisions of the Abortion Act 1967. However as a result of the Government's decision to change the order for discussion of proposed changes to the Act, there was no opportunity for debate on these particular amendments.[184] Among the proposed amendments were suggestions for the extension of the Abortion Act 1967 to Northern Ireland, removal of the need for approval by two physicians for abortions earlier than 12 weeks' gestation, and the provision of increased choice for women as to where and by whom abortion procedures may be performed.[185]

III. LAW, ABORTION AND REPRODUCTIVE AUTONOMY

A model of reproductive autonomy that places women's interests in autonomy and bodily integrity at its core demands that women have access to safe, legal abortion. It is beyond

---

[178] The Family Planning Association of Northern Ireland had applied to the Northern Irish courts 'seeking a declaration that the respondent [Minister for Health Social Services and Public Safety] has acted unlawfully in failing to issue advice and/or guidance to women of child-bearing age and to clinicians in Northern Ireland on the availability and provision of termination of pregnancy services in Northern Ireland' (*Family Planning Association of Northern Ireland v Minister For Health Social Services and Public Safety* [2004] NICA 39 para 3).

[179] *Ibid.*

[180] *Society for the Protection of Unborn Children's Application* (n 176).

[181] *Ibid* para 48.

[182] 'Abortion Statistics, England & Wales' (n 171) 36.

[183] See, eg, Jackson (n 165); Sheldon (n 158); Marie Fox, 'The Human Fertilisation and Embryology Act 2008: Tinkering at the Margins' (2009) 17 *Feminist Legal Studies* 333.

[184] See, eg, Fox (n 183) 336; Sally Sheldon, 'A Missed Opportunity to Reform an Outdated Law' (2009) 4 *Clinical Ethics* 3.

[185] Fox (n 183). The proposed amendments were also based on recommendations made by the House of Commons Science and Technology Committee in a report to Parliament (House of Commons Science and Technology Committee, *Scientific Developments Relating to the Abortion Act 1967* (HC 2006-07, 1045-I)).

reasonable dispute that restricting access to abortion through criminal prohibitions is ineffective in reducing the incidence of abortion. It is effective, instead, in generating high rates of illegal, unsafe abortion.[186] Of the four jurisdictions under study here, only Canadian law succeeds in demonstrating appropriate respect for reproductive autonomy – albeit for reasons other than a deliberate commitment to the importance of abortion rights for women. All of the other jurisdictions fail properly to respect reproductive autonomy in maintaining unnecessary legal limits on abortion services.

In the US, the law permits generous access to abortion – in theory, at any rate – but the ongoing political battle to erode the right articulated in *Roe v Wade* means that women's legal ability to access abortion is constantly under threat. State action that places ridiculous and pointless limits on providers (including regulations relating to examination-room temperature[187]), and that requires women to hear inaccurate and misleading information designed to discourage them from going ahead with an abortion,[188] not only fails to respect reproductive autonomy but actively undermines women's autonomy. Requiring women to submit to unnecessary invasive procedures such as transvaginal ultrasound in order to access a safe, legal healthcare service is an egregious violation of autonomy and bodily integrity. Insisting that women under the age of majority inform their parents of their plans to abort an unwanted pregnancy (and in some cases, seek their parents' permission to do so) also clearly fails to respect reproductive autonomy. It would be one thing if these women were not capable of providing consent on their own, but these laws apply to all minors, regardless of their age or capacity to consent to medical care.[189] It is shocking and alarming to be writing – in 2012 – about the frenzied legislative activity in many US states, the objective of which is slowly but surely to chip away at women's right to terminate an unwanted pregnancy, for it suggests that the notion of meaningful respect for reproductive autonomy in that country is absolutely unattainable.

The common law approach taken in most of Australia certainly permits many women to access abortion, in spite of the fact that statutory provisions related to abortion have not been (in most cases) fundamentally reformed. Likewise, UK law permits liberal access to legal abortion services, at least for women in England, Wales and Scotland. But both approaches fail to respect women's reproductive autonomy as I understand and describe that concept. Laws such as those in the UK and in Australia leave a great deal of control over abortion in the hands of medical practitioners, which may mean that women are denied abortion services by physicians who are concerned about the adequacy of their reasons for terminating their pregnancy.[190]

[186] Department of Reproductive Health and Research, World Health Organization (n 5); Grimes *et al* (n 4); Sedgh *et al* (n 6).

[187] Laws aimed specifically at abortion providers and abortion facilities are collectively known as Targeted Regulation of Abortion Providers (TRAP) laws, and include a variety of restrictions that are unrelated to medical care or patient safety. For descriptions of the various types of TRAP laws, see Tracy A Weitz, 'What Physicians Need to Know About the Legal Status of Abortion in the United States' (2009) 52 *Clinical Obstetrics and Gynecology* 130; Marshall H Medoff, 'State Abortion Politics and TRAP Abortion Laws' (2012) 33 *Journal of Women, Politics & Policy* 239.

[188] Currently, as part of their 'informed consent' requirements, several states require women to be told that abortion causes breast cancer (in spite of the scientific consensus that it does not), and several also require that women be informed that the fetus can feel pain at a particular point in gestation, in spite of a lack of evidence that this is the case (Weitz (n 187) 134).

[189] Carol Sanger, 'Regulating Teenage Abortion in the United States: Politics and Policy' (2004) 18 *International Journal of Law, Policy and the Family* 305.

[190] This point is made in a study surveying obstetrician-gynaecologists' views about conscientious objection and referral in the US context (Lisa H Harris *et al*, 'Obstetrician-Gynecologists' Objections to and Willingness to Help Patients Obtain an Abortion' (2011) 118 *Obstetrics & Gynecology* 905, 909).

It is certainly preferable to make abortion available, even on limited terms, than severely to restrict its availability. Fundamentally, though, laws that mediate women's decision making through practitioners are unquestionably a flawed way to demonstrate respect for women's reproductive autonomy. It is perhaps easier to take the view that the concessions that have been made have by and large improved access to abortion services and so we should be careful not to be too critical. The problem with that attitude is that the continued role of the criminal law leaves women and physicians open to political whim and prosecutorial discretion. That women are exposed to significant legal risk is clear from *R v Brennan and Leach*,[191] which is a good example of the potential dangers women face when 'obsolete' abortion laws are left in place.[192] Such legal risks are, of course, in addition to the physical risks to which women are subject when abortion is difficult to access and they have to seek self-help remedies or unsafe abortion. As explained above, *R v Brennan and Leach* involved the prosecution of a young couple under sections 225 and 226 of the Queensland Criminal Code.[193] Although both were acquitted, the case illustrates the urgent need for abortion law reform in Queensland.[194] As Kerry Petersen puts it, 'The state of Queensland has put two young people through an unnecessary and gruelling criminal trial because of obsolete abortion laws which lack regulatory legitimacy'.[195] In response to concerns raised in relation to the prosecution, the government of Queensland has indicated that no amendments are planned to Queensland's abortion laws in the near term at least, leaving the state with what have been referred to as 'antiquated' laws.[196]

Even where there is only a very small chance of a conviction for abortion-related offences, the fact that the risk exists at all is difficult to accept from the perspective of respect for reproductive autonomy. The very fact that abortion remains on the books as a criminal offence perpetuates the idea that seeking to terminate a pregnancy is something of which to be ashamed, or something that rightly brings social disapprobation. It also does nothing to make it more likely that new, safer and more effective technologies or methods of abortion will be made available to women – the example of medical abortion in Australia is a case in point.

The bottom line is this: framing abortion as a decision for physicians to make about women, instead of one for women to make for themselves, reveals distrust for women's capacity to make these decisions. That stance is essentially at odds with an ethic of respect for reproductive autonomy, in that it suggests that women cannot make these decisions autonomously but must be helped through them by their physicians. It is not enough to have a law that allows a superficial exercise of reproductive autonomy – as we have seen, the effects of such an approach leave much to be desired.

Legal restrictions on abortion access tell only part of the story in terms of women's ability to access timely and safe abortion services. In the next section, I consider how policy positions can affect access to abortion. The three main areas of focus are funding for abortion services, availability of medical abortion and provider conscientious objection.

---

[191] *R v Brennan and Leach* (n 150).
[192] Petersen (n 129) 600.
[193] *R v Brennan and Leach* (n 150).
[194] Petersen (n 129) 600.
[195] *Ibid*.
[196] Caroline M de Costa, Darren B Russell and Michael Carrette, 'Correspondence: Abortion in Australia: Still to Emerge from the 19th Century' (2010) 375 *The Lancet* 804. de Costa and her co-authors also note that abortions are now done in public hospitals only where the pregnant woman's life is at risk.

IV. ACCESS TO ABORTION SERVICES

As far as can be determined from available data, abortion is a common procedure in Canada, the US, the UK and Australia, but is relatively rare in those jurisdictions in comparison with other countries.[197] The best statistical data are available in the UK, where physicians who perform abortions are required by law to notify the appropriate Chief Medical Officer of the abortion within 14 days' of its occurrence.[198] In 2011 (the most recent year for which statistics are available), there were 196,082 abortions in England and Wales,[199] with 189,931 carried out on residents of England and Wales.[200] The age-standardised abortion rate was 17.5 per 1,000 resident women aged 15–44,[201] and the rate was highest for women aged 20.[202] The teenage abortion rate was very low, and reflects small decreases over the prior year and over the same measure taken a decade earlier in 2001.[203] The vast majority (91 per cent) of abortions were carried out earlier than 13 weeks' gestation.[204] Most abortions in the UK are surgical abortions, but the medical abortion rate continues to rise. In 2011, medical abortions represented 47 per cent of the total number of abortions, a slight increase over 2010, and a remarkable increase of 30 per cent relative to 2001.[205] Complications are very rare, the complication rate being roughly one in every 700 procedures.[206]

The incidence of abortion in the US is higher than that in the UK, at 19.6 abortions per 1,000 women aged 15–44.[207] On an annual basis, 22 per cent of pregnancies end in abor-

---

[197] In 2008, the worldwide abortion rate was 28 per 1,000 women aged 15–44. The highest regional abortion rate worldwide was 43 per 1,000, in Eastern Europe, and the lowest was 12 per 1,000, in Western Europe (Sedgh *et al* (n 6) 629).

[198] The Abortion (Amendment) (England) Regulations 2002 (SI 2002/887), reg 4. The reporting requirement applies to pregnancy terminations that take place in NHS hospitals or approved independent (private) facilities, and whether or not the woman accessing services is a UK resident.

[199] 'Abortion Statistics, England & Wales' (n 171) 6. Statistics for Scotland are kept separately (Information Services Division Scotland, 'Abortion Statistics: Year Ending 31 December 2011' (29 May 2012), at <www.isd-scotland.org/Health-Topics/Sexual-Health/Publications/2012-05-29/2012-05-29-Abortions-Report-2011.pdf?69610232115>). Minimal statistical information is kept in Northern Ireland; based on the data available on the Department of Health, Social Services and Public Safety website, it appears that 43 abortions took place in Northern Ireland in 2011/12 (Department of Health, Social Services and Public Safety, 'Audit of Northern Ireland Termination of Pregnancy Statistics' (2012), at <www.dhsspsni.gov.uk/index/stats_research/hospital-stats/inpatients/terminations_of_pregnancy.htm>). The total number of abortions performed in England and Wales for non-residents was 6,151, which is the lowest annual number since 1969. The majority of the non-resident women who sought abortion services in England and Wales were from Northern Ireland (16% of the 6,151) and the Republic of Ireland (67%) ('Abortion Statistics, England & Wales' (n 171) 36).

[200] Of the total, 2,307 (or 1% of) abortions were carried out under the ground provided by s 1(1)(d) of the Abortion Act 1967, which provides that abortion is permissible where 'there is a substantial risk that if the child were born it would suffer from such physical or mental abnormalities as to be seriously handicapped' ('Abortion Statistics, England & Wales' (n 171) 8).

[201] *Ibid* 7.

[202] The rate for 20-year-old women was 33 per 1,000 (*ibid* 3).

[203] For women under 16 years, the abortion rate was 3.4 per 1,000 women; the under 18 rate was 15.0 per 1,000 women (*ibid* 7).

[204] In addition, 78% of abortions took place at under 10 weeks (*ibid* 9).

[205] *Ibid* 10. In addition, 60% of abortions carried out at nine weeks' gestation or less were medical abortions; this is a huge increase in comparison with 2001, when the proportion was 20%.

[206] *Ibid* 22. Complications include haemorrhage, uterine perforation and sepsis, up to time of discharge from place of termination.

[207] Rachel K Jones and Kathryn Kooistra, 'Abortion Incidence and Access to Services In the United States, 2008' (2011) 43 *Perspectives on Sexual and Reproductive Health* 41. The abortion rate is based on 2008 data. To put the abortion rate in perspective, the highest abortion rate historically reported in the US was 29.3 per

tion, and each year 2 per cent of women of reproductive age (between 15 and 44 years of age) have an abortion.[208] In 2008, medical abortions accounted for 17 per cent of all non-hospital terminations, and approximately 25 per cent of terminations before nine weeks' gestation.[209] In terms of safety, abortion is very safe in the US, with a complication rate of less than 0.3 per cent (for complications requiring hospitalisation).[210]

Australia does not keep abortion statistics in such a way as to make them readily available and reliable. There is no single database in which information about induced abortion is maintained, and though it is possible to estimate the number and rate of abortions in Australia based on existing data, it is difficult to be confident in these estimates.[211] One concern is that there is no Medicare code specific to induced abortion, and the codes that might be used to refer to induced abortion could also relate to any other 'abortive outcome' of a pregnancy, including miscarriage.[212] In addition, several states have no abortion reporting requirements.[213] That said, the incidence of abortion in Australia has been estimated at between 80,000 to 85,000 procedures annually,[214] for a rate of 17.7 per 1,000 women aged 15–44.[215]

In Canada, as in Australia, the available data are neither accurate nor reliable. Most recently, the Canadian Institute for Health Information reported that there were 64,641 abortions in Canada in 2010, but noted that the figures do not include Québec and that data relating to clinic abortions in British Columbia are incomplete.[216] The total number of

---

1,000 in 1981 (Guttmacher Institute, 'In Brief: Facts on Induced Abortion in the United States' (August 2011), at <www.guttmacher.org/pubs/fb_induced_abortion.html>). It should be noted that according to the Centers for Disease Control (CDC), the abortion rate in 2008 was 16 per 1000 (Centers for Disease Control and Prevention (n 63) 8). The CDC data are based on voluntary reporting by the states; for 2008, data were received from 49 of the 52 areas from which it was requested (*ibid* 1). The CDC notes that because reporting requirements are established by the states themselves, data collection is variable and the CDC is not able to obtain accurate data on the total number of abortions performed in the US. The CDC notes that during the 1999–2008 period, 'the total annual number of abortions recorded by CDC was 65%–69% of the number recorded by the Guttmacher Institute, which uses numerous active follow-up techniques to increase the completeness of the data obtained' (*ibid* 10).

[208] Jones and Kooistra (n 207) 43.

[209] *Ibid* 46.

[210] 'In Brief: Facts on Induced Abortion in the United States' (n 207). For first trimester abortion, the risks of long-term complications (such as infertility, ectopic pregnancy, miscarriage, birth defect or pre-term delivery/low birth weight) are so low as to be almost non-existent. Serious complications are also very rare, although they can occur. There is one death per million for abortions at/before eight weeks, one per 29,000 at 16–20 weeks, and one per 11,000 at 21+ weeks.

[211] See, eg, Narelle Grayson, Jenny Hargreaves and Elizabeth A Sullivan, *Use of Routinely Collected National Data Sets for Reporting on Induced Abortion in Australia AIHW Cat No PER 30* (Sydney, Australian Institute of Health and Welfare, National Perinatal Statistics Unit, 2005); Children by Choice, 'Briefing Paper: The Sexual and Reproductive Health of Australian Women', at <www.childrenbychoice.org.au/info-a-resources/facts-and-figures/briefing-paper-the-sexual-and-reproductive-health-of-australian-women>.

[212] See, eg, Grayson *et al* (n 211) 20; Doreen Rosenthal *et al*, *Understanding Women's Experiences of Unplanned Pregnancy and Abortion: Final Report* (Melbourne, The Key Centre for Women's Health In Society, Melbourne School of Population Health, University of Melbourne, 2009) 6.

[213] Grayson *et al* (n 211) 1.

[214] See, eg, *ibid* 32 (this estimate is applicable to 2003); Victorian Law Reform Commission (n 113) 32.

[215] Grayson *et al* (n 211) 33 (again, this applies to 2003).

[216] Canadian Institute for Health Information, 'QuickStats: Induced Abortions Performed in Canada in 2010' (2010), at <www.cihi.ca/CIHI-ext-portal/pdf/internet/TA_10_ALLDATATABLES20120417_EN>. As Québec reported 27,139 abortions in 2009 (and that only included publicly-funded abortions), it is clear that the total for 2010 is much lower than the actual number (Canadian Institute for Health Information, 'QuickStats: Induced Abortions Performed in Canada in 2009' (2009), at <www.cihi.ca/CIHI-ext-portal/pdf/internet/TA_09_ALLDATATABLES20111028_EN>).

abortions in 2009 was reported at 93,775.[217] Complication rates (reported for hospital abortions only) represent a low number of the total (649 complications in 27,576 procedures, or 2.3 per cent).[218] A study published in 2012 indicates that Canada's abortion rate (as of 2004) is approximately 14.5 per 1,000 women aged 15–44.[219] As in other countries, the rate is highest for women in their 20s.[220] It appears that, like the US and the UK, the vast majority of abortions in Canada take place early, although the data are incomplete.[221]

Based on these numbers, it appears that women have ready access to abortion services in all four jurisdictions. For the most part, that is true. However, there are a number of barriers to accessing abortion services, and these likely affect women who are poor or otherwise marginalised more so than they do women who have the means to pay for abortion services as well as the knowledge as to where services can be accessed. In addition to limited funding for abortion services, limited access to medical abortion and provider objection, barriers to access include the need to travel outside one's community to access services;[222] the lack of availability of information about abortion services; long waiting periods (particularly in the public system); hospital gestational limits on abortion services; and anti-choice 'counselling' centres.[223]

A. Abortion funding

In Canada, funding for abortion services is determined by provincial policy, and there is significant variation across the country. For example, although seven provinces have free-standing abortion clinics, only six of these provinces cover the cost of clinic abortions.[224]

---

[217] 'Quickstats' (2009) (n 216).

[218] 'QuickStats' (2010) (n 216) 10. Complications that are counted include any complications during initial admission as well as transfers or readmissions over a 28-day period post-procedure. This is significantly more inclusive than the statistics on complications kept in England and Wales.

[219] Wendy V Norman, 'Induced Abortion in Canada 1974–2005: Trends Over the First Generation with Legal Access' (2012) 85 *Contraception* 185, 187.

[220] The rate for women aged 20–24 is 27 per 1,000, and for women aged 25–29, it is 20 per 1,000. Women aged 15–19 had an abortion rate of 15 per 1,000 in 2004 (*ibid*).

[221] 'QuickStats' (2010) (n 216) 6. The CIHI report indicates that 70.7% of abortions took place in the first 12 weeks of pregnancy, but there is a significant proportion of abortions for which gestational age is unknown (17.8%).

[222] See Canadian Abortion Rights Action League, *Protecting Abortion Rights in Canada: A Special Report to Celebrate the 15th Anniversary of the Decriminalization of Abortion* (Ottawa, CARAL, 2003). See also Laura Eggertson, 'News: Abortion Services in Canada: A Patchwork Quilt with Many Holes' (2001) 164 *Canadian Medical Association Journal* 847; Christabelle Sethna and Marion Doull, 'Far From Home? A Pilot Study Tracking Women's Journeys to a Canadian Abortion Clinic' (2007) 27 *Journal of Obstetrics and Gynaecology Canada* 640; Ingrid Peritz, 'Despite Being Legal, Abortions Still Not Accessible For All Canadians', *Globe and Mail* (Toronto, 18 June 2010), at <www.theglobeandmail.com/news/national/abortion-access-unequal-across-country/article1215524/>. In PEI, women must travel outside their home jurisdiction in order to obtain abortion services (Jessica Shaw, *Reality Check: A Close Look at Accessing Abortion Services in Canadian Hospitals* (Ottawa, Canadians for Choice, 2006) 32).

[223] Shaw (n 222).

[224] British Columbia, Alberta, Manitoba, Ontario, Québec, and Newfoundland and Labrador (Eggertson (n 222)). In Manitoba and Québec, full funding for non-hospital abortion services is now paid as a result of successful litigation. For Manitoba, see *Jane Doe 1 v Manitoba*, 2004 MBQB 285, [2004] MJ No 456 (granting the applicants' motion for summary judgment and declaring the offending provision of the Manitoba Health Services Insurance Act (CCSM c H35, s 116(1)(g) and (h), Excluded Services Regulation, Man Reg 46/93 s 2(28)) of no force and effect). The case was later reversed in part by the Manitoba Court of Appeal and the applicant's motion for leave to appeal to the Supreme Court of Canada was denied (*Doe 1 v Manitoba* [2005] 2005 MBCA 109, MJ No 335 (allowing the Government's appeal from the summary judgment in favour of the plaintiffs); *Jane Doe 1 v Manitoba* [2005] SCCA No 513 (SCC)). The *Jane Doe 1 v Manitoba* case differs from

Three provinces and all three territories lack non-hospital abortion facilities,[225] and the number of hospitals that provide abortion services appears to continue to decline. A 2003 report by the Canadian Abortion Rights Action League (CARAL) noted that only 17.8 per cent of Canadian hospitals performed abortion services,[226] while a similar report issued by Canadians For Choice (CFC) in 2006 puts the figure at 15.9 per cent.[227] In addition to the declining availability of abortion in Canadian hospitals, the exclusion of therapeutic abortion services from the interprovincial reciprocal billing agreement creates a further constraint on access for women who are temporarily living away from their home province (such as university students), or those who live in an area where the nearest abortion provider is in a different province.[228] In 2001, the executive director of the CARAL noted the significant implications of funding policy on the availability of abortion services: 'Ironically, it seems to be getting worse rather than better since the Morgentaler decision in 1988. There are a number of barriers and the [number is increasing].'[229]

In the US, as with most healthcare services, coverage for abortion services depends heavily on whether one is relying on public or private insurance. In spite of recognising a constitutional right to abortion services in *Roe v Wade*, the US Supreme Court has held that states are entitled to express 'a value judgment favoring childbirth over abortion, and to implement that judgment by the allocation of public funds'.[230] Medicaid funding for abortion is limited by the Hyde Amendment, which permits funding of abortions only where they are medically necessary, as defined in the Amendment to mean abortions following rape or incest, or those needed to save the life of the pregnant woman.[231] Federal funds cannot be used to pay for abortion services unless they are medically necessary as narrowly defined above, and generally states are free to refuse to fund non-therapeutic abortions.

States can provide public funding for abortion services more widely, although they must use state funds to do so. Currently, 32 states and the District of Columbia provide Medicaid funding for abortion in cases of rape, incest or where the continuation of the pregnancy would endanger the woman's life.[232] Two (Mississippi, Virginia) also provide funding for abortions for fetal abnormality, and three others (Indiana, Utah and Wisconsin) also provide funding for abortions that are needed to protect the physical health of the pregnant woman.[233] South Dakota funds only those abortions that are

Lexogest Inc v Manitoba (n 44), in that the Charter issues were not decided in *Lexogest Inc v Manitoba*. For Québec, see *Association pour l'accès à l'avortement c Québec* (n 52).

[225] Saskatchewan, Nova Scotia and Prince Edward Island. See National Abortion Federation, 'Access to Abortion in Canada: Abortion Coverage by Region', at <www.prochoice.org/canada/regional.html>.

[226] Canadian Abortion Rights Action League (n 222)

[227] Shaw (n 222).

[228] The agreement means that Canadians who receive healthcare services outside of their home province are covered by their provincial healthcare insurance plan. The provider will bill the patient's insurance plan rather than require payment directly from the patient (Canadian Institute for Health Information, 'Have Health Card, Will Travel: Out-of-Province/-Territory Patients' (March 2010), at <https://secure.cihi.ca/free_products/out_of_province_aib_201003_e.pdf>). Abortion services are excluded from the agreement (*Reciprocal Billing Report, Canada, 2004–2005, Revised August 2007* (Ottawa, Canadian Institute for Health Information, 2007) F-1).

[229] Eggertson (n 222) 847.

[230] *Maher v Roe*, 432 US 464 (1977) 474.

[231] The Hyde Amendment was challenged, but was upheld by the US Supreme Court (*Harris v McRae* (n 86)).

[232] Guttmacher Institute, 'State Policies in Brief: State Funding of Abortion Under Medicaid' (1 August 2012), at <www.guttmacher.org/statecenter/spibs/spib_SFAM.pdf>.

[233] *Ibid.*

necessary to protect the life of the pregnant woman (and is thus in violation of the federal Medicaid law). Seventeen states fund 'all or most medically necessary abortions'; four do so voluntarily, the others do so pursuant to court orders.[234]

Even where women have private insurance coverage for abortion, most often they pay for the procedure in some other way.[235] The new US healthcare law (the Affordable Care Act) has been lauded as a major improvement for women and women's health, as it will increase the availability of healthcare insurance coverage for women, and will specifically improve contraceptive coverage, but there are significant restrictions on abortion coverage in health plans that will be offered by states under the new law.[236]

Although abortion is funded through the NHS in the UK, coverage varies by region, as does the method of service provision. In 2001, the Royal College of Obstetricians and Gynaecologists (RCOG) conducted an audit of abortion services. The RCOG noted large regional variations in the availability of publicly-funded abortion, finding that in only a minority of health authorities in England and Wales, 90 per cent of abortion procedures were covered, while in many other health authorities, under 75 per cent of procedures were covered.[237] It is not clear whether the regional variation remains this pronounced, but the most recent RCOG Guidelines indicate that regional variation persists, both with respect to access to abortion services and access to NHS-funded abortion.[238] In 2011, 96 per cent of abortions were publicly funded, with 61 per cent of publicly-funded procedures taking place in the private sector under NHS contract.[239] Abortion services may also be obtained privately;[240] in 2011, 4 per cent of such procedures took place in the private system.[241]

---

[234] *Ibid.*

[235] It has been speculated that women may choose not to rely on insurance as a result of either lack of knowledge of coverage, or because they are concerned about confidentiality (Rachel K Jones and Lawrence B Finer, 'Who Has Second-trimester Abortions in the United States?' (2012) 85 *Contraception* 544, 549).

[236] *Ibid.* See also Rachel Benson Gold, 'Insurance Coverage and Abortion Incidence: Information and Misinformation' (2010) 13(4) *Guttmacher Policy Review* 7, 9.

[237] See, eg, Royal College of Obstetricians and Gynaecologists, Clinical Effectiveness Support Unit, *National Audit of Induced Abortion 2000: Report of England and Wales* (London, Royal College of Obstetricians and Gynaecologists, September 2001) 2; Royal College of Obstetricians and Gynaecologists, *The Care of Women Requesting Induced Abortion: Evidence Based Clinical Guideline Number 7* (London, Royal College of Obstetricians and Gynaecologists, November 2011) 28.

[238] Royal College of Obstetricians and Gynaecologists, *The Care of Women Requesting Induced Abortion* (n 237) 28. According to Emily Jackson, one of the reasons for regional variation in coverage of abortion services is the lack of clarity in the law around conscientious objection (Jackson (n 165) 85–86). The Abortion Act permits physicians to refuse to participate in abortion procedures, but it is not clear whether providing a referral for a patient seeking such services amounts to 'participation' such that it is also covered by the conscientious objection provisions. As Jackson explains, this reality has significant implications for women who cannot afford the fees for abortion services in the private sector.

[239] This figure is slightly higher than in 2010, when it was 59%, and markedly higher than 1981, when 2% of abortions were done in the private sector with NHS funding ('Abortion Statistics, England & Wales' (n 171) 8).

[240] Costs in the private system are variable, but generally range from £400 (for a medical abortion up to nine weeks' gestation) to £800 (for surgical termination, up to 19 weeks, with a general anaesthetic) (Private Healthcare UK, 'Termination of Pregnancy, Sterilisation, Vasectomy: What Does it Cost?', at <www.privatehealth.co.uk/hospitaltreatment/find-a-treatment/contraception/whatdoesitcost/>). The British Pregnancy Advisory Service (BPAS) current price list indicates a range of £535 (for a medical abortion up to nine weeks) to £1,660 (for a surgical abortion between 19–24 weeks). Surgical abortions at up to 14 weeks' gestation cost roughly £605 (British Pregnancy Advisory Service, 'Prices' (*Abortion*, 1 April 2012), at <www.bpas.org/bpaswoman/prices>).

[241] This represents a significant change over time. In 2001, Jackson noted that abortion was the most commonly privately-funded procedure (Jackson (n 165) 85).

Abortion in Australia is theoretically available both publicly[242] and privately, but in practice public availability is marginal.[243] Out-of-pocket costs for abortions obtained in the private system range from $200–$500 for those with a Medicare card (Medicare provides a partial rebate). The cost can be much higher for those without a Medicare card.[244] It is much more difficult to obtain abortion services without delay in the public system, so large numbers of women travel to jurisdictions with private abortion clinics, incurring additional costs, time away from work and stress.[245]

Respect for reproductive autonomy demands that women have access to abortion services. As noted earlier, restrictive or prohibitive laws are only one way to limit access, and the absence of criminal prohibitions does not necessarily translate into meaningful opportunities for women to exercise this fundamental reproductive choice. An inclusive and contextual understanding of reproductive autonomy demands that the State must take positive steps to ensure that abortion services are available and accessible.

Abortion services should be readily available and funded by the public healthcare system, regardless of whether the services are obtained in hospital or in a private clinic. It is perhaps not surprising to see limited public coverage for abortion in the US, given the structure of the American healthcare system. But even in Canada, the UK and Australia, where public funding is the norm for most healthcare services, abortion services tend to be treated differently, meaning that access to publicly-funded abortion varies markedly from one region to another. In Canada, few hospitals provide abortion services, not all provinces have clinics and in one province the cost of clinic abortions is not covered.[246] In Australia, abortion services are subsidised by the public system, but out-of-pocket costs can still be high.[247] Although the UK system provides extensive public access, availability of abortion services can vary by region and could be improved.[248] All of these jurisdictions thus fail, to a greater or lesser extent, to respect reproductive autonomy in terms of making abortion services accessible.

[242] Abortion is listed as a medical service on the Medical Benefits Schedule (Kerry Petersen, 'Criminal Abortion Laws: An Impediment to Reproductive Health?' in Ian Freckelton and Kerry Petersen (eds), *Controversies in Health Law* (Sydney, The Federation Press, 1999) 28, 29).

[243] A national report published in 1997 indicated that 87% of abortions are carried out in private clinics (*ibid* 31). The report (*An Information Paper on Termination of Pregnancy in Australia* (Canberra, National Health and Medical Research Council, 1997)) was withdrawn from sale the following year (Australian Government, National Health and Medical Research Council, *Report of the 126th Session Canberra, 10 March 1998* (NHMRC, 1998), at <www.nhmrc.gov.au/guidelines/publications/sess126>).

[244] In the Australian system, privately-obtained procedures are subsidised by the public system and may be eligible for a partial Medicare rebate. Sections 20 and 20A of the Health Insurance Act 1973 (Cth) provide for the Medicare rebate for privately-obtained services. Prices also vary considerably from state to state, and depending on gestational age: see, eg, Jenna Price, 'High Cost of Abortion Hurts Young Women', *Canberra Times*, 8 May 2012, at <www.canberratimes.com.au/opinion/high-cost-of-abortion-hurts-young-women-20120508-1yalr.html>; Children by Choice, 'How Much Will an Abortion Cost?' (2012) at <www.childrenby-choice.org.au/if-youre-pregnant/im-considering-an-abortion/termination-costs-in-queensland>.

[245] See, eg, Petersen (n 242) 31; Rosenthal *et al* (n 212) 7.

[246] As noted above (n 224), only six Canadian provinces (British Columbia, Alberta, Manitoba, Ontario, Québec and Newfoundland) cover the full cost of abortion services where they are obtained in a free-standing clinic.

[247] Above (n 244).

[248] Above (n 238).

B. Medical abortion

Medical abortion – where pregnancy is terminated as a result of the ingestion of pharmaceutical agents – is an option that many women prefer over surgical abortion.[249] Studies from France and the UK show that when given the choice, more than half of women opt for medical rather than surgical abortion.[250] Medical abortion using mifepristone (the only medication approved for this indication) and misoprostol 'can make abortion earlier, more accessible, safer, less traumatic, less medicalised and less expensive'.[251] Up to nine weeks' gestation, medical abortion can take place at home if the woman prefers that option to waiting in the clinic, and need involve only two visits to the clinic.[252] There is evidence of its safety, efficacy and acceptability as an alternative to surgical abortion, at least in the early part of pregnancy.[253]

Medical abortion is available in the UK and the US, as both countries have approved mifepristone (although, as noted earlier, there are restrictions on access to medical abortion in many US states).[254] In the UK, although medical abortion is available, access could be improved. As noted earlier, when the HFE Act 1990 was amended in 2008, the UK Parliament had an opportunity to amend the Abortion Act 1967. One of the proposed amendments would have liberalised access to medical abortion, in that it would have permitted women to take the second medication (misoprostol) at home, rather than at an approved facility as is required by the legislation.[255] None of the proposed amendments passed. In 2011, in order to pilot a new protocol for early medical abortion (EMA), the British Pregnancy Advisory Service sought a declaration from the High Court that 'it would be lawful, under the Abortion Act 1967, 'to pilot and if successful adopt, subject to regulation, a process of providing "early medical abortion" (EMA)

---

[249] There is also some preliminary evidence suggesting that the incidence of miscarriage and post-partum hemorrhage in the next pregnancy is significantly lower after first-trimester medical (as opposed to surgical) abortion: see, eg, Changping Gan *et al*, 'The Influence of Medical Abortion Compared with Surgical Abortion on Subsequent Pregnancy Outcome' (2008) 101 *International Journal of Gynecology & Obstetrics* 231.

[250] Victoria Jane Davis, 'SOGC Clinical Practice Guideline No 184: Induced Abortion Guidelines' (2006) 28 *Journal of Obstetrics and Gynaecology Canada* 1014, 1018. See also Ellen Wiebe *et al*, 'Comparison of Abortions Induced by Methotrexate or Mifepristone Followed by Misoprostol' (2002) 99 *Obstetrics & Gynecology* 813.

[251] Marge Berer, 'Medical Abortion: Issues of Choice and Acceptability' (2005) 13(26) *Reproductive Health Matters* 25, 26.

[252] Janice Raymond has argued that medical abortion using mifepristone and misoprostol is highly medicalised, time-consuming and painful (Janice G Raymond, 'RU486: Progress or Peril'? in Joan C Callahan (ed), *Reproduction, Ethics, and the Law: Feminist Perspectives* (Bloomington, Indiana University Press, 1995) 284). As Marge Berer points out, however, it need not be so highly medicalised – as with surgical abortion, there need only be two clinic visits: one to prescribe the drug and give instructions on use as well as on complications, and one follow-up visit to ensure that the abortion is complete and that there are no complications (Berer (n 251) 29). This is identical to the clinical schedule with surgical abortion. Berer also notes that most women who have experienced medical abortion have been satisfied with the procedure and would choose it again (*ibid* 26).

[253] In the US, concerns have been voiced about the safety of mifepristone, but the data indicate that medical abortion is a safe and effective option: see, eg, Jillian T Henderson *et al*, 'Safety of Mifepristone Abortions in Clinical Use' (2005) 72 *Contraception* 175; Association of Reproductive Health Professionals, 'What You Need to Know: Mifepristone Safety Overview' (updated April 2008), at <www.arhp.org/uploadDocs/mifepristone-factsheet.pdf>; Susan Dudley and Stephanie Mueller, 'Fact Sheet: What is Medical Abortion?' (Washington, DC, National Abortion Federation, 2008); Eric Schaff, 'Mifepristone: Ten Years Later' (2010) 81 *Contraception* 1.

[254] Above (nn 93, 103).

[255] Sheldon (n 184) 4.

whereby part of the treatment is self-administered by the woman at home'.[256] The declaration was refused on the basis that the administration of a drug intended to induce abortion falls within the meaning of 'any treatment for the termination of pregnancy' in section 1(3) of the Abortion Act 1967, and therefore may be carried out only in an approved facility.[257]

Mifepristone has not been approved in either Canada or Australia, and it is therefore difficult to access medical abortion in these two countries.[258] Another medication, methotrexate, can be and is used for medical abortion, but this use is 'off-label' in that the drug has not been approved for the termination of pregnancy. Medical abortion is somewhat accessible in both Canada and Australia using the methotrexate and misoprostol combination, but this is not a suitable alternative to the mifepristone and misoprostol regime. Although it is an effective abortifacient, methotrexate abortions take longer to complete than those induced using mifepristone.[259] In addition, methotrexate may pose a risk of fetal malformation if the pregnancy is not terminated successfully.[260]

In the Canadian context, the Society of Obstetricians and Gynaecologists of Canada has urged Health Canada to work with industry and with professional organisations to ensure the availability of mifepristone in Canada, and has noted that 'The antiprogesterone steroid mifepristone has been developed, tested, and approved for use in several European countries and the United States. The use of such medication for terminating early pregnancy constitutes a significant medical and public health gain.'[261] Canadian regulatory policy provides for a process whereby Canadian physicians can apply for access to unapproved drugs on behalf of their patients; but because the process requires a separate application for each patient seeking access to the drug, this is not an appropriate route for improving access to medical abortion for Canadian women.[262]

There has been little movement toward improving access to medical abortion in Canada. In Australia, although there has been some activity, access remains significantly constrained. In order to be approved (and therefore generally available) in Australia, a drug must be registered on the Australian Register of Therapeutic Goods (ARTG). To have a drug registered on the ARTG, a sponsor company needs to apply to the Therapeutic Goods Administration (TGA), which will then evaluate the 'quality, safety

---

[256] *British Pregnancy Advisory Service v Secretary of State for Health* [2011] EWHC 235 (Admin), [2011] 3 All ER 1012, para 3.

[257] *Ibid* para 35.

[258] See, eg, Society of Obstetricians and Gynaecologists of Canada, 'SOGC Policy Statement No 237: Mifepristone' (2009) 31 *Journal of Obstetrics and Gynaecology Canada* 1180; Kerry A Petersen, 'Early Medical Abortion: Legal and Medical Developments in Australia' (2010) 193 *Medical Journal of Australia* 26.

[259] See, eg, Wiebe *et al* (n 250); Joanna N Erdman, Amy Grenon and Leigh Harrison-Wilson, 'Medication Abortion in Canada: A Right-to-Health Perspective' (2008) 98 *American Journal of Public Health* 1764, 1767.

[260] In other words, if the abortion is incomplete or unsuccessful and the pregnancy continues, the use of methotrexate poses a risk to the health of the fetus (Marge Berer, 'Medical Abortion: A Fact Sheet' (2005) 13 *Reproductive Health Matters* 20, 20).

[261] Society of Obstetrics and Gynaecologists of Canada (n 258). It bears mention here that Mifepristone is listed on the WHO model list of essential medicines (and has been since 2006) (*WHO Model List of Essential Medicines*, 16th edn (Geneva, World Health Organization, 2010); Performance Assessment Tool for Quality Improvement in Hospitals (PATH), World Health Organization, United Nations Population Fund, *Essential Medicines for Reproductive Health: Guiding Principles for their Inclusion on National Medicines List* (Seattle, WA, PATH, 2006)).

[262] Erdman *et al* (n 259) 1768; Health Canada, Health Products and Food Branch, *Guidance Document For Industry and Practitioners – Special Access Programme for Drugs* (Ottawa, Health Canada, 2008).

and efficacy of the medication'.[263] Until 2006, as a result of the Harradine Amendment,[264] Australian law required personal approval by the Minister of Health – in addition to the TGA process – in order for mifepristone to be imported into or used in Australia. The Amendment was repealed in 2006 after a Private Member's Bill was introduced and a conscience vote held,[265] but to date no sponsor has applied to have mifepristone approved in Australia.[266]

Mifepristone has become available in a very limited way in Australia, through a special TGA authorisation process.[267] Doctors with the appropriate training and expertise can be allowed to prescribe unapproved drugs 'for a specified class of patients suffering from a life-threatening or otherwise serious illness or condition'.[268] Medical practitioners who seek authorisation from the TGA must provide medical reasons for their request, as well as 'evidence about the seriousness of the condition, and the justification for using the unregistered product in preference to other available treatments'.[269]

Obstetrician Caroline de Costa and her colleagues published an article outlining their experience as Authorised Prescribers of mifepristone under the TGA scheme.[270] As they explain, the TGA will give its approval only for 'clinical indications that are "life-threatening or otherwise serious"'.[271] The authors received numerous inquiries from physicians and women (600 requests) during the 12 months after receiving TGA approval. Between July 2006 and April 2007, they performed 10 EMAs using mifepristone and misoprostol on women with medical indications including

> severe hypertension, severe pre-eclampsia/eclampsia in a previous pregnancy, thromboembolic disease requiring long-term anticoagulation, polycystic kidneys with recurrent urinary tract infections, previous ruptured uterus in pregnancy, severe depression requiring antidepressant therapy, recent major breast and pelvic floor surgery, and history of major fetal anomaly in a previous pregnancy. Most women had more than one indication.[272]

Although 12 other women sought early medical termination in this same time frame, the indications (while in compliance with Queensland abortion law) did not seem to reach the level of the requirements of the TGA scheme (presumably these were not life-threatening or otherwise serious indications).

Ultimately, the TGA scheme is not an appropriate way to improve access for Australian women in general, but it does show that 'the TGA has concluded from the evidence provided that the drug is sufficiently safe and effective to be available for at least some

---

[263] Petersen (n 258) 27.

[264] Therapeutic Goods Amendment Act 1996 (Cth).

[265] Therapeutic Goods Amendment (Repeal of Ministerial Responsibility for approval of RU 486) Act 2006 (Cth); Petersen (n 258) 27; Christopher Zinn, 'Health Minister is Stripped of his Right to Veto Use of Abortion Pill' (2006) 332 *British Medical Journal* 441.

[266] Erdman, Grenon and Harrison-Wilson point to two main reasons for the fact that no application has been made for approval of mifepristone in Canada: the limited financial potential of the drug and the political concerns that will inevitably arise if such an application is made (Erdman, Grenon and Harrison-Wilson (n 259) 1767).

[267] Therapeutic Goods Act 1989 (Cth), ss 18, 19(1), (4), (5). These sections require the TGA 'to authorise the use of unapproved medicines not registered on the ARTG . . . and one pathway for this is the TGA's Authorised Prescribers scheme' (Petersen (n 258) 27).

[268] Therapeutic Goods Act 1989 (Cth), ss 19(5), 31B(3); Therapeutic Goods Regulations 1990 (Cth), reg 12B.

[269] Petersen (n 258) 27.

[270] Caroline M de Costa *et al*, 'Early Medical Abortion in Cairns, Queensland: July 2006–April 2007' (2007) 187 *Medical Journal of Australia* 171.

[271] *Ibid* 171.

[272] *Ibid* 172.

Australian women'.[273] Dr de Costa and colleagues point out that the publicity around the 'cross-party vote' to get rid of the Harradine Amendment, together with the fact that the amendment was repealed, shows widespread support for the idea that Australian women should have access to medical abortion. However, at time of writing, only a small number of women in only one part of the country have been able to gain access. According to *The Age* newspaper, in 2009, 61 Australian physicians were authorised prescribers.[274]

As is clear from the foregoing, in order successfully to access medications through the TGA Authorised Prescriber's scheme, physicians must meet several requirements. These include having the ongoing support of their hospital ethics committee or 'appropriate specialist college', as well as ensuring a process to 'obtain written informed consent from each patient (or the legal guardian) after advising the patient that the drug is not approved in Australia'.[275] They must also be in compliance with relevant laws in the state or territory in which they practise. Given the current state of abortion law in Australia, this may be considerably more challenging than it sounds. After Queensland proceeded to prosecute Tegan Leach and Sergei Brennan under the existing abortion provisions in that state, de Costa and her colleagues decided to cease provision of the drug because of the risks to both patients and providers resulting from the lack of clarity in the law.[276]

Access to medical abortion is an area in urgent need of improvement, particularly in Canada and Australia. Medical abortion is superior to surgical abortion in very early pregnancy (up to seven weeks' gestation) because surgical abortion is often incomplete at that stage.[277] Up to nine weeks' gestation, medical abortion may take place at home if the woman prefers, and need involve only two visits to the clinic.[278] Medical abortion may not be an option desired by a majority of women, but there is evidence of its safety, efficacy and acceptability as an alternative to surgical abortion, at least in the early part of pregnancy. In line with appropriate respect for reproductive autonomy, it should be readily available to women who wish to use it. Beverly Winikoff and Anne Davis explain:

> The development of accessible and simple methods of early abortion is a social and humanitarian good from almost every point of view. Expansion of access to early medical abortion is a humane approach that benefits both women and their societies. In some places, such treatment allows women to access abortion services that are otherwise not available. In all places, improved technology will allow more women to have abortions earlier in pregnancy.[279]

Respect for reproductive autonomy requires that women have the opportunity to make meaningful reproductive choices. In the context of access to abortion services, this entails providing medical abortion as an option. It is an option that has the potential to

---

[273] *Ibid.*

[274] Nick Miller, 'Abortion Pill to be Widely Available', *The Age* (Melbourne, 10 August 2009), at <www.theage.com.au/national/abortion-pill-to-be-widely-available-20090809-ee9i.html>.

[275] Petersen (n 258) 27.

[276] Caroline de Costa and Michael Carrette, 'Legal Issues Lead Cairns Doctors to Cease Medical Abortion', *Crikey* (Melbourne, 2 June 2009), at <www.crikey.com.au/2009/06/02/legal-issues-lead-cairns-doctors-to-cease-medical-abortion/>.

[277] Petersen (n 258) 27. While it is likely often the case that women do not know they are pregnant at this very early stage, for those who are aware and who wish to terminate the pregnancy, the option of doing so immediately with a medical approach seems far superior to having to wait for some number of weeks for surgical abortion.

[278] As explained above (n 252).

[279] Beverly Winikoff and Anne Rachel Davis, 'Comment: Abortion is for Women' (2007) 369 *The Lancet* 1904, 1905.

improve access to early abortion; in turn, this could lead to reduced waiting times and improvements in access more generally. Abortion is legally permitted in both Canada and (at least in some circumstances) Australia, and there is no legitimate reason to fail to provide medical abortion as an option.

The history of the treatment of medical abortion in some jurisdictions makes it clear that a move toward approval of mifepristone will provoke opposition and controversy. This is particularly likely given that the approval process will have to be instigated by government. But respect for reproductive autonomy demands that these governments take action. There is no reason, other than political concern, for failing to do what is needed to ensure that mifepristone is an option for those women who would choose medical abortion. In the meantime, women in Australia and Canada continue to face a more limited array of options, and risk harm, and in some cases prosecution, if they seek to obtain mifepristone through unregulated channels or from abroad. For far too long, women's needs and interests have taken second place to concerns about the political risks inherent in improving access to abortion. The governments of Canada and Australia must make it a priority to afford women this option.

C. Provider conscientious objection

Another barrier to access faced by women seeking abortion services relates to the availability of healthcare providers able and willing to perform the procedure. Refusal laws (also referred to as conscience laws) have been in place in the US since weeks after the decision in *Roe v Wade* was released by the Supreme Court.[280] In the UK, a conscientious objection provision is included within the Abortion Act 1967, and several of the Australian abortion provisions include a clause related to conscientious refusal to participate in the provision of abortion services. There is no Canadian case law or legislation that clearly delineates the rights or responsibilities of providers who object to abortion for moral or religious reasons, but concerns have been raised about both the insufficiency of training in abortion procedures offered by medical schools[281] and the scope of conscientious objection to the provision of abortion services.[282]

In the UK, the conscientious objection provision found in the Abortion Act 1967 states:

---

[280] See, eg, Church Amendment to the Public Health Service Extension Act of 1973, Pub L No 93-45, Tit IV, § 401, 87 Stat 95 (codified at 42 USC § 300a-7); Thaddeus Mason Pope, 'Legal Briefing: Conscience Clauses and Conscientious Refusal' (2010) 21 *Journal of Clinical Ethics* 163.

[281] See, eg, Eggertson (n 222) 848; Laura Shanner, 'Pregnancy Intervention and Models of Maternal–Fetal Relationship: Philosophical Reflections on the *Winnipeg C.F.S.* Dissent' (1998) 36 *Alberta Law Review* 751, 764; Bonnie Steinbock, 'Symposium: Opening Remarks' (1999) 62 *Albany Law Review* 805, 806; Abortion Rights Coalition of Canada, 'Position Paper # 6: Training of Abortion Providers/Medical Students for Choice' (October 2005), at <www.arcc-cdac.ca/postionpapers/06-Training-Abortion-Providers-MSFC.PDF>; Atsuko Koyama and Robin Williams, 'Abortion in Medical School Curricula' (2005) 8 *McGill Journal of Medicine* 157.

[282] See, eg, Bernard M Dickens and Rebecca J Cook, 'The Scope and Limits of Conscientious Objection' (2000) 71 *International Journal of Gynecology & Obstetrics* 71, 73; Bernard M Dickens, 'Informed Consent' in Jocelyn Downie, Timothy Caulfield and Colleen M Flood (eds), *Canadian Health Law and Policy*, 2nd edn (Markham, Butterworths 2002) 148; Sanda Rodgers and Jocelyn Downie, 'Guest Editorial: Abortion: Ensuring Access' (2006) 175 *Canadian Medical Association Journal* 9.

Subject to subsection (2) of this section, no person shall be under any duty, whether by contract or by any statutory or other legal requirement, to participate in any treatment authorised by this Act to which he has a conscientious objection:

Provided that in any legal proceedings the burden of proof of conscientious objection shall rest on the person claiming to rely on it.[283]

The conscience clauses found in Australian legislation offer varying degrees of protection for provider conscience. Victoria's legislation contains a provision mandating an objecting provider to notify the woman of his or her conscientious objection, and to refer her to a different provider whom he or she 'knows does not have a conscientious objection to abortion'.[284] The South Australian statute also makes provision for conscientious objection, except where the procedure is 'necessary to save the life, or to prevent grave injury to the physical or mental health' of the pregnant woman.[285] In the Northern Territory, those who conscientiously object are entitled to refrain from participating in the procedure or the disposal of an aborted fetus.[286]

Conscience laws in the US are far more expansive, and in general also provide protection to facilities or institutions, such that hospitals cannot be required to provide abortion services and medical schools cannot be forced to provide abortion training in their post-graduate programs. There are both federal and state laws dealing with conscientious objection. Federal law precludes courts and government agencies from insisting that individuals or facilities provide abortion or sterilisation services where the individual or facility has a moral objection to such services.[287] It also prohibits discrimination against providers who object to participating in training for the provision of abortion or sterilisation services on the basis of moral objections.[288] Most states have similar policies in place at the state level.[289]

Although conscience laws have long been in place, over the past decade attempts have been made to enlarge their reach. In 2012, the Scottish Court of Session heard a petition by two midwives working as 'labour ward co-ordinators' who sought a declaration that the right to conscientious objection extended to the delegation, supervision and support of staff involved in directly providing care for women undergoing termination of pregnancy.[290] Neither midwife was asked to participate in the direct care of women who

---

[283] Abortion Act 1967, s 4(1). Section 4(2) limits the protection of conscientious objection, making it inapplicable to situations where the abortion 'is necessary to save the life or to prevent grave permanent injury to the physical or mental health of a pregnant woman'.

[284] Abortion Law Reform Act 2008 (Vic) s 8(1)(b). The section also provides that objecting medical practitioners and registered nurses are under a duty to perform or assist in an abortion 'in an emergency where the abortion is necessary to preserve the life of the pregnant woman' (*ibid* s 8(3), (4)).

[285] Criminal Law Consolidation Act 1935 (SA), s 82A(5), (6). Tasmania law also provides for conscientious objection, on the same grounds and in the same circumstances as in South Australia (Criminal Code Act 1924, (Tas) s 164(7)).

[286] Medical Services Act (NT) s 11(6).

[287] Church Amendment to the Public Health Service Extension Act of 1973 (n 280).

[288] Public Health Services Act, 42 USC § 238n, s 245; Omnibus Appropriations Act of 2009, Pub L No 111-8, § 508.

[289] Currently, 46 states allow providers to refuse to participate in abortion services and 44 states allow at least some healthcare institutions to refuse to provide such services (Guttmacher Institute, 'State Policies in Brief: Refusing to Provide Health Services' (1 August 2012), at <www.guttmacher.org/statecenter/spibs/spib_RPHS.pdf>).

[290] *Doogan and another v Greater Glasgow and Clyde Health Board* [2012] CSOH 32 para 27. The petitioners also argued unsuccessfully that their rights to freedom of conscience and religion under Art 9 ECHR required a broad reading of the statutory language.

were on the ward because they were terminating their pregnancies, but they argued that their conscience rights extended far enough that neither could they be required to delegate to, supervise or support their staff who were involved in providing care to these women. The outcome turned on the meaning of 'participate in any treatment' within section 4 of the Abortion Act 1967. The Court concluded that the section itself makes it clear that the right to object is not absolute,[291] and does not entitle those who work in a supervisory capacity in a labour ward to refuse to have any involvement with staff members who are directly providing treatment aimed at terminating a pregnancy.

As noted above, refusal clauses found in US law (at both state and federal levels) are cast more widely than the provision in the UK legislation. Nevertheless, there have been many attempts to extend them even further. Federal initiatives have included the publication of Department of Health and Human Services (DHHS) Regulations interpreting the federal refusal laws[292] to preclude federal funding of any healthcare entity that failed to accommodate employees who refused to provide certain kinds of healthcare for moral or religious reasons. The Regulations were extraordinarily broad, essentially allowing 'everyone connected to health care . . . [to] opt out of a wide range of activities, from discussions about birth control to referrals for vaccinations'.[293] The DHHS Regulations have since been replaced by new regulations[294] that rescind almost all of the original rules.

Many states have also been active in extending existing conscience provisions to permit objecting providers to refuse to refer patients for abortion services, or even to provide information about the availability of such services.[295] Most states legally protect providers who conscientiously object to participation in particular services, but the laws seek to strike a balance between protection of provider conscience and patient rights to access services by imposing an obligation to refer and a duty to treat in an emergency.[296] Although most providers agree that they are obliged to refer patients to non-objecting providers, some insist that their right to refuse extends as well to the right to refuse to refer.[297] The right to refuse has also been extended beyond the traditional providers (physicians and nurses) to pharmacists who object to providing contraception (particularly emergency contraception).[298]

[291] As does judicial interpretation of the section (*Janaway v Salford Area Health Authority* [1989] AC 537).

[292] Department of Health and Human Services, *Final Rule: Ensuring that Department of Health and Human Services Funds Do Not Support Coercive or Discriminatory Policies or Practices in Violation of Federal Law*, 73 Federal Register 78072 (19 December 2008).

[293] See, eg, Julie D Cantor, 'Conscientious Objection Gone Awry – Restoring Selfless Professionalism in Medicine' (2009) 360 *New England Journal of Medicine* 1484; Robert Card, 'Federal Provider Conscience Regulation: Unconscionable' (2009) 35 *Journal of Medical Ethics* 471. As Cantor explains, the Regulations went so far as stating that employees whose responsibility it was to clean medical or surgical instruments used in a procedure would be viewed as assisting in that procedure.

[294] Department of Health and Human Services, Regulation for the Enforcement of Federal Health Care Provider Conscience Protection Laws 45 CFR § 88 (2011).

[295] See, eg, Fla Stat Ann § 390.0111(8); NY Civ Rights Law § 79-I (Enacted 1971); NY Comp Codes R & Regs tit 10 § 405.9; NC Gen Stat Ann § 14-45.1(e), (f); Utah Code Ann § 76-7-306. A similar Arizona law was challenged but ultimately upheld by the state's appellate court (*Planned Parenthood Arizona, Inc v American Association of Pro-Life Obstetricians and Gynecologists*, 257 P 3d 181 (Ariz Ct of Appeals 2011)).

[296] Pope (n 280).

[297] Lawrence and Curlin (n 8) 1281.

[298] Provider conscientious objection to provision of contraceptives is discussed in ch 4, section II.C. The vast majority of states have conscience clauses related to abortion services, while far fewer have similar protections relating to contraception and sterilisation.

In Canada, a Private Member's Bill aimed at protecting 'conscience rights' was introduced to Parliament in 2008.[299] The Bill sought to '[protect] the right of health care practitioners and other persons to refuse, without fear of reprisal or other discriminatory coercion, to participate in medical procedures that offend a tenet of their religion, or their belief that human life is inviolable'.[300]

The Bill defined human life as beginning at fertilisation, and made it a criminal offence to refuse to employ or promote, or to dismiss, healthcare practitioners who refuse to participate in medical procedures that offend their religion or their belief that human life is inviolable. Similarly, it would be a criminal offence under this Bill to refuse to admit to study, to grant accreditation to or to refuse to admit (or exclude from membership) a healthcare practitioner to a professional association on this basis. The Bill generated significant discussion and debate; due to the dissolution of Parliament in September 2008, it did not get past first reading stage.[301]

As discussed in the previous chapter, it seems clear that the law of negligence demands that providers are at least obligated to refer their patients to non-objecting practitioners.[302] Nevertheless, there appears to be significant opposition to this claim within the Canadian medical profession. In response to a *Canadian Medical Association Journal* guest editorial[303] which stated that physicians who 'fail to provide appropriate referrals . . . are committing malpractice and risk lawsuits and disciplinary proceedings,' the CMA provided a 'clarification' of its own policy on induced abortion.[304] This clarification suggests that physicians are not obligated to provide referrals where participating in the termination of a pregnancy violates their moral beliefs.[305] The CMA policy does not explicitly require referrals to an abortion provider. It does, however, state that the risk of complications from abortion is minimised in early pregnancy, that 'early diagnosis of pregnancy and determination of appropriate management should be encouraged' and that 'There should be no delay in the provision of abortion services'.[306]

The College of Physicians and Surgeons of Alberta published its Health Professions Act Standards of Practice in 2010.[307] The Standards preclude physicians from withholding 'information about the existence of a procedure or treatment because providing that procedure or giving advice about it conflicts with their moral or religious beliefs'.[308] They further provide:

> When moral or religious beliefs prevent a physician from providing or offering access to information about a legally available medical or surgical treatment or service, that physician must

---

[299] Bill C-537, *An Act to amend the Criminal Code (protection of conscience rights in the health care profession)*, 2nd Sess, 39th Parl, 2008 (Introduction and First Reading in the House of Commons 16 April 2008).

[300] *Ibid.*

[301] To date, the Bill has not been reintroduced.

[302] See ch 4, section II.C., discussing *Zimmer v Ringrose*, 28 AR 69, [1981] 4 WWR 75. See also Rebecca J Cook and Bernard M Dickens, 'Access to Emergency Contraception' (2003) 25 *Journal of Obstetrics and Gynaecology Canada* 914.

[303] See Rodgers and Downie (n 282).

[304] Jeff Blackmer, 'Letter: Clarification of the CMA's Position Concerning Induced Abortion' (2007) 176 *Canadian Medical Association Journal* 1310.

[305] See, eg, Dickens (n 282); Dickens and Cook (n 282). Dickens notes that fiduciary law also protects patients from their physician's failure to disclose options or to refer due to the provider's moral convictions.

[306] *CMA Policy: Induced Abortion* (Ottawa, Canadian Medical Association, 1988) (reviewed 2007).

[307] College of Physicians & Surgeons of Alberta, 'Health Professions Act Standards of Practice' (2010), at <www.cpsa.ab.ca/Libraries/Res_Standards_of_Practice/HPA_Standards_of_Practice_Consolidatation_Issued_Jan_1_2010.pdf>.

[308] *Ibid* Moral or Religious Beliefs Affecting Medical Care: Standard 26.

ensure that the patient who seeks such advice or medical care is offered timely access to another physician or resource that will provide accurate information about all available medical options.[309]

When the Standards of Practice were circulated to physicians in draft form, they met with the same kind of opposition that arose in response to the guest editorial.[310]

Whether or not physician codes of ethics or standards of practice clearly articulate a requirement to refer, respect for reproductive autonomy demands that providers make appropriate referrals when they refuse to participate in procedures on the basis of moral or religious objection. As Bernard Dickens puts it:

> The equilibrium between physicians' rights and those of patients is maintained through objecting physicians' legal and ethical duty to refer their patients who request lawful services to physicians who do not object. Religiously based claims of complicity in procedures, conducted by physicians to whom patients are referred, have neither legal nor ethical substance. Referral does not constitute participation in any discussions that referred physicians have with patients, or in any procedures upon which such physicians and patients agree. Physicians do not share in any fees paid to the physicians to whom they refer their patients, nor in any liability that physicians may incur for any form of malpractice.[311]

The state must ensure that women have meaningful access to abortion services. This cannot be achieved if objecting providers can frustrate women's ability to access a necessary healthcare service. Ideally, providers should be free to refrain from participation in procedures that are at odds with their personal moral or religious views, but the importance of reproductive autonomy means that providers' right to object cannot be absolute. If both provider and patient rights cannot be respected, priority must go the patient.

V. SPECIAL CONSIDERATIONS: SECOND-TRIMESTER ABORTION AND SELECTIVE ABORTION

A. Second-trimester abortion

The vast majority of abortions take place in the first trimester, and ensuring that pregnancy termination takes place as early as possible is a goal shared by many commentators and policy makers. Second-trimester abortion creates far more discomfort than does abortion earlier in pregnancy, even among abortion providers who do offer late terminations.[312] But in spite of the preference for abortion earlier in pregnancy rather than later, it will always be the case that some women will need to access second-trimester abortion. Second-trimester abortions occur for a variety of reasons. Selective abortions tend to occur in the second trimester because information about fetal sex and disability is in general not available until late in the first trimester or early in the second

---

[309] *Ibid* 26(4).

[310] 'Edmonton Physician Opposes Mandatory Referrals for Abortion', *CBC News*, 23 February 2009, at <www.cbc.ca/canada/edmonton/story/2009/02/22/edm-abortion-referrals.html>.

[311] Bernard M Dickens, 'Conscientious Objection and Professionalism' (2009) 4 *Expert Review of Obstetrics & Gynecology* 97, 97. See also Bernard M Dickens, 'Legal Protection and Limits of Conscientious Objection: When Conscientious Objection is Unethical' (2009) 28 *Medicine and Law* 337.

[312] Lisa H Harris, 'Second Trimester Abortion Provision: Breaking the Silence and Changing the Discourse' (2008) 16(31 Supp) *Reproductive Health Matters* 74.

trimester.[313] There are other reasons for second-trimester abortions as well, some of which have to do with delays in accessing abortion services,[314] but many of which have to do with women themselves. Some women do not recognise that they are pregnant until several weeks into pregnancy. By the time they confirm the pregnancy with a pregnancy test, make the decision to terminate the pregnancy and seek and obtain abortion services, the pregnancy has advanced to the second trimester.[315]

Second-trimester abortion can be difficult to access. Few providers are prepared to provide abortion services late in pregnancy,[316] some because of personal discomfort with the procedures themselves,[317] others because of the uncertain legal terrain around the limits on legal abortion. This latter issue is particularly of concern in Australia, where abortion remains subject in some states to criminal prohibitions and where the law in most states does not clearly spell out gestational time limits.[318] Coupled with the existence of child destruction laws of uncertain applicability in the abortion context, these laws give rise to significant doubt about the legal permissibility of second-trimester abortion.[319] As such, it is not surprising that many physicians are concerned about the legal implications of providing late-term abortion services.[320]

Perhaps because of the lower level of comfort around late termination, second-trimester abortion has been an important focus for opponents of abortion rights. In *Carhart v Gonzales*, the US Supreme Court addressed a statutory prohibition of a specific second-trimester abortion procedure, known medically as 'intact D&E' and referred to by many anti-abortion advocates as 'partial-birth abortion'.[321] Justice Kennedy (writing for the majority) took it as a given that women must regret their abortion choice and that their regret must be more profound in cases where the technique used elicits unease. As he articulated it:

> Respect for human life finds an ultimate expression in the bond of love the mother has for her child. The Act recognizes this reality as well. Whether to have an abortion requires a difficult

[313] This may change in the future, as scientists are working to create clinically useful testing procedures whereby the fetal genome may be determined via a maternal blood test in early pregnancy: see, eg, H Christina Fan *et al*, 'Non-invasive Prenatal Measurement of the Fetal Genome' (2012) 487 *Nature* 320; Jacob O Kitzman *et al*, 'Noninvasive Whole-genome Sequencing of a Human Fetus' (2012) 4(137) *Science Translational Medicine* 137ra76. A blood test that identifies a number of chromosomal abnormalities is already being marketed in the US (Roger Collier, 'Surge in Down Syndrome Prenatal Testing Anticipated' (2012) 184 *Canadian Medical Association Journal* E449).

[314] See, eg, Lawrence B Finer *et al*, 'Timing of Steps and Reasons for Delays in Obtaining Abortions in the United States' (2006) 74 *Contraception* 334, 343–44 (noting that delay can also be caused by the need to raise the money for the procedure); Roger Ingham *et al*, 'Reasons for Second Trimester Abortions in England and Wales' (2008) 16(31 Supp) *Reproductive Health Matters* 18, 26–27.

[315] See, eg, Finer *et al* (n 314) 343–44; Harris (n 312); Ingham *et al* (n 314) 23–26.

[316] Harris (n 312) 74–76. According to the Guttmacher Institute, 23% of providers offer abortion at 20 weeks' gestation and only 11% at 24 weeks ('In Brief: Facts on Induced Abortion in the United States' (n 207)). According to the National Abortion Federation, abortion services are available in Canada past 16 weeks' gestation in only four provinces (British Columbia, Alberta, Ontario and Québec). Only Ontario offers abortion services as late as 24 weeks ('Access to Abortion in Canada' (225)).

[317] See, eg, Harris (n 312); M Habiba *et al*, 'Late Termination of Pregnancy: A Comparison of Obstetricians' Experience in Eight European Countries' (2009) 116 *BJOG: An International Journal of Obstetrics and Gynaecology* 1340.

[318] As discussed above (n 117 and accompanying text).

[319] de Crespigny and Savulescu (n 23).

[320] To add to the potential confusion, it seems inconsistent to rule out late-term abortion but yet permit parents to decide to withhold life-saving medical care to a neonate that is born prematurely at the same point in gestation (*ibid* 102–03).

[321] See discussion in section II.B. above.

and painful moral decision. . . . While we find no reliable data to measure the phenomenon, it seems unexceptionable to conclude some women come to regret their choice to abort the infant life they once created and sustained. . . . Severe depression and loss of esteem can follow. . . . The State has an interest in ensuring so grave a choice is well informed. . . . It is a reasonable inference that a necessary effect of the regulation and the knowledge it conveys will be to encourage some women to carry the infant to full term, thus reducing the absolute number of late-term abortions. The medical profession, furthermore, may find different and less shocking methods to abort the fetus in the second trimester, thereby accommodating legislative demand. The State's interest in respect for life is advanced by the dialogue that better informs the political and legal systems, the medical profession, expectant mothers, and society as a whole of the consequences that follow from a decision to elect a late-term abortion.[322]

Justice Kennedy's comments were motivated by the expressions of regret in affidavits filed by many women who had terminated past pregnancies. He came under fire for his comments and for his reliance on the women's statements, in part because the literature suggests that most women who terminate a pregnancy do not experience adverse psychological consequences.[323] As David Garrow points out, however, 'No jurist ought to be denounced for considering real women's real testimonies with the utmost seriousness while judging an abortion case'.[324] A view of reproductive autonomy that places women's interests at its centre must also take women's testimonies seriously. But taking women's statements of regret seriously does not lead to the conclusion that abortion rights should be restricted in order to prevent the possibility of regret. Autonomous persons make decisions in accordance with their own values. Values can change, and regret may arise, but limiting choice is not an appropriate response.[325]

In *Carhart v Gonzales*, Justice Kennedy focused on one particular dimension of regret – that experienced by some women who have had an abortion. Yet what of the regret experienced by some women who choose to have a child in abusive or adverse circumstances? What about the profound regret experienced by some women who relinquish a child for adoption?[326] Or the regret of some parents who decide to bear a child with a serious disability, only to watch him or her suffer?[327] A reproductive autonomy analysis based on the contextual approach I advocate suggests that a much wider lens needs to be applied to consideration of the emotional and psychological effects of particular reproductive decisions.

[322] *Gonzales v Carhart* (n 67) 159–60.
[323] See, eg, Brenda Major *et al*, 'Psychological Responses of Women After First-Trimester Abortion' (2000) 57 *Archives of General Psychiatry* 777; Brenda Major *et al*, 'Abortion and Mental Health: Evaluating the Evidence' (2009) 64 *American Psychologist* 863; Trine Munk-Olsen *et al*, 'Induced First-Trimester Abortion and Risk of Mental Disorder' (2011) 364 *New England Journal of Medicine* 332.
[324] Garrow (n 79) 23.
[325] Indeed, experiencing regret when one realises that one's values have shifted or that one has acted contrary to one's deeply-held values is arguably part of the process of developing autonomy competency.
[326] See, eg, Anne B Brodzinsky, 'Surrendering an Infant for Adoption: The Birthmother Experience' in David M Brodzinsky and Marshall D Schechter (eds), *The Psychology of Adoption* (New York, Oxford University Press, 1990) 295; Merry Bloch Jones, *Birthmothers: Women Who Have Relinquished Babies for Adoption Tell Their Stories* (Chicago, IL, Chicago Review Press, 1993); Ann Fessler, *The Girls Who Went Away: The Hidden History of Women Who Surrendered Children for Adoption in the Decades Before* Roe v Wade (New York, Penguin Press, 2006).
[327] See, eg, Joan Lalor, Cecily M Begley and Eoin Galavan, 'Recasting Hope: A Process of Adaptation Following Fetal Anomaly Diagnosis' (2009) 68 *Social Science & Medicine* 462 (noting the need for further study of this group of parents who decide to proceed with the pregnancy after a diagnosis of fetal anomaly); Charlotte Wool, 'Systematic Review of the Literature: Parental Outcomes After Diagnosis of Fetal Anomaly' (2011) 11 *Advances in Neonatal Care* 182.

More importantly, it is essential to understand the contribution law makes to the creation of feelings of regret. To describe abortion itself as causally implicated in regret, and to focus on a particular abortion procedure as exacerbating regret, is to ignore the reality that for some women, in the absence of State support for the choice to bear and raise their child,[328] abortion is their only option. As Susan Appleton explains:

> In sum, *Gonzales*'s promise that the law can rescue the vulnerable among us from feelings of regret fails to acknowledge the role of both law and culture in creating reasons why we experience such feelings in the first place, just as it fails to acknowledge how the abortion options that remain often present greater risks and trauma than the procedure proscribed.[329]

Reproductive autonomy demands that women be able to make choices about whether to continue or terminate a pregnancy. It would overstate the case to insist that reproductive autonomy requires the availability of specific procedures in order to give women the widest possible scope for decision making, but it is troubling from an autonomy standpoint that the US Supreme Court was prepared to uphold a ban that includes no maternal health exception and that leaves no room for physician discretion to do what is best for the woman herself. As one physician who used the intact D&E procedure has explained: 'Once you decide the uterus must be emptied, you then have 100% allegiance to maternal risk. There's no justification to doing a more dangerous procedure because somehow this doesn't offend your sensibilities as much.'[330]

But even if reproductive autonomy does not sustain an interpretation that all procedures must be available so that women have the widest possible choice, it certainly demands an ethic that declines to interfere with decision making about abortion by a woman and her doctor. Regulation of abortion, to the extent that reproductive autonomy would allow, should be directed at safeguarding women's health, ensuring informed consent and protecting a sphere of decision making from State interference. While there is nothing wrong in principle with the State expressing a preference for women to make one choice rather than another, there is no justification for ruling out specific medical procedures on the basis that they inspire discomfort, or even revulsion or disgust.

B. Selective abortion

Selective abortion is an issue for abortion rights in respect of several intersecting themes. It most often takes place later in pregnancy (usually in the second trimester), giving rise to unease (as discussed above) around the procedures involved, even for strong advocates of abortion rights. A decision to abort selectively is also, to some, a decision that expresses views about which people should or should not be in the world, and therefore a decision about which lives are worth living.

Selective abortion is abortion in the context of an otherwise wanted pregnancy because of a particular fetal characteristic: either the fetus has a congenital or genetic

---

[328] For arguments as to how child support could be envisioned as a responsibility of the State, see Martha Albertson Fineman, *The Autonomy Myth: A Theory of Dependency* (New York, The New Press, 2004); Anne L Alstott, 'Private Tragedies? Family Law as Social Insurance' (2010) 4 *Harvard Law and Policy Review* 3. See ch 2 and ch 3 for discussion on autonomy generally.

[329] Susan Frelich Appleton, 'Reproduction and Regret' (2011) 23 *Yale Journal of Law and Feminism* 255, 318.

[330] Dr James T McMahon, quoted by Diane M Gianelli, 'Shock-Tactic Ads Target Late-Term Abortion Procedure', *American Medical News*, 5 July 1993, 3.

abnormality, or it is the 'wrong' sex. This choice seems to present a special case, in that many who support abortion rights in general are hesitant when it comes to selective abortion, fearing that social acceptance of pregnancy termination for reasons of fetal disability or ill-health expresses a lack of respect for the lives of persons with disabilities.[331] Likewise, sex-selective abortion suggests a negative evaluation of what it means to be a member of the sex selected against; most often, selective abortion targets the female fetus.

Selective abortion in the case of fetal disability or genetic abnormality is widespread, and has become increasingly common as screening for fetal anomalies has become a routine part of pregnancy. Certainly in all of the jurisdictions under consideration here, selective abortion for reasons of fetal disability is available, and (as is discussed in chapter seven) the failure to provide information that will enable women to choose to terminate a pregnancy in such circumstances can lead to provider liability.

Sex selection is far less familiar in these jurisdictions, although it is widespread in countries with strong inclinations toward 'son preference'. These cultures have long had practices that devalue girl children and result in high rates of female mortality,[332] but the sex ratio imbalance has become increasingly skewed in the past two to three decades.[333] In general, the sex ratio imbalance grows with increased birth order, so that while it might be within normal limits for a first birth, ratios for second and third births can be much less balanced.[334] South and East Asian countries in particular have struggled with sex-selective abortion since the combination of ultrasound and abortion technologies have permitted women and couples to learn the sex of their fetus early enough in pregnancy that they can terminate pregnancies where the fetus is female.[335] Several Asian countries have attempted to address the problem of sex ratio imbalances in part by precluding the use of pre-natal technologies to determine fetal sex and by banning sex-selective abortion.[336] Although such laws do make it impossible to determine the actual prevalence or frequency of sex-selective abortion, they do not solve the problem of the

[331] See, eg, Marsha Saxton, 'Born and Unborn: The Implications of Reproductive Technologies for People with Disabilities' in Rita Arditti, Renate Duelli Klein and Shelley Minden (eds), *Test-Tube Women: What Future for Motherhood?* (London, Pandora Press, 1984) 298; Deborah Kaplan, 'Prenatal Screening and Diagnosis: The Impact on Persons with Disabilities' in Karen H Rothenberg and Elizabeth J Thomson (eds), *Women and Prenatal Testing: Facing the Challenges of Genetic Technology* (Columbus, Ohio State University Press, 1994) 49; Adrienne Asch, 'Prenatal Diagnosis and Selective Abortion: A Challenge to Practice and Policy' (1999) 89 *American Journal of Public Health* 1649; Emily Jackson, 'Abortion, Autonomy and Prenatal Diagnosis' (2000) 9 *Social & Legal Studies* 467; Erik Parens and Adrienne Asch, *Prenatal Testing and Disability Rights* (Washington, DC, Georgetown University Press, 2000); Rosamund Scott, 'Prenatal Testing, Reproductive Autonomy, and Disability Interests' (2005) 14 *Cambridge Quarterly of Healthcare Ethics* 65.

[332] See, eg, Amartya Sen, 'Women's Survival as a Development Problem' (1989) 43 *Bulletin of the American Academy of Arts and Sciences* 14; Ansley J Coale, 'Excess Female Mortality and the Balance of the Sexes in the Population: An Estimate of the Number of "Missing Females"' (1991) 17 *Population and Development Review* 517.

[333] See, eg, Qu Jian Ding and Therese Hesketh, 'Family Size, Fertility Preferences, and Sex Ratio in China in the Era of the One Child Family Policy: Results from National Family Planning and Reproductive Health Survey' (2006) 333 *British Medical Journal* 371; Bela Ganatra, 'Maintaining Access to Safe Abortion and Reducing Sex Ratio Imbalances in Asia' (2008) 16(31 Supp) *Reproductive Health Matters* 90; Prabhat Jha *et al*, 'Trends in Selective Abortion of Girls in India: Analysis of Nationally Representative Birth Histories from 1990 to 2005 and Census Data from 1991 to 2011' (2011) 377 *The Lancet* 1921.

[334] See, eg, Doo-Sub Kim, 'Missing Girls in South Korea: Trends, Levels and Regional Variations' (2004) 59 *Population* (English Edition) 865, 869; Therese Hesketh, Li Lu and Zhu Wei Xing, 'The Effect of China's One-Child Family Policy After 25 Years' (2005) 353 *New England Journal of Medicine* 1171, 1173.

[335] Kim (n 334); Hesketh *et al* (n 334).

[336] Ganatra (n 333) 92.

sex ratio imbalance. The sex ratio disparity in several of these countries continues to grow, and the explanation for this phenomenon seems to be found in the practice of sex-selective abortion.[337]

Sex ratios are not similarly imbalanced in Europe or North America in general, but trends similar to those seen in South and East Asia are found within those continents among groups of South and East Asian immigrants. Data from Canada,[338] the US[339] and the UK[340] show that son preference and related practices (including sex-selective abortion) may remain a part of life for some groups of immigrants. In Canada, for example, first generation South and East Asian immigrants have a relatively normal sex ratio[341] for first births (108 boys to 100 girls). But for third births to Chinese, Vietnamese and Korean immigrant families with two daughters, the sex ratio is 139 boys to 100 girls; for Indian families, it is 190 boys to 100 girls.[342]

In both Canada and the US, these data have raised alarm, and have led to calls for bans on sex-selective abortion (in the US[343]) and on revealing fetal sex after ultrasound until late in pregnancy (in Canada).[344] Predictably, and quite legitimately, the proposed US legislation was viewed with suspicion by pro-choice commentators who saw it as a thinly-veiled attack on abortion rights more generally.[345] The sponsor of the US Bill, Congressman Trent Franks, is a vocal opponent of abortion rights and has acknowledged that the wider agenda behind his proposal to ban sex-selective abortion is to protect children of all sexes and races from abortion on demand.[346]

While the motivations for banning sex-selective abortion, or for attempting to prevent

---

[337] See, eg, *ibid*; Jha *et al* (n 333).

[338] Douglas Almond, Lena Edlund and Kevin Milligan, *O Sister, Where Art Thou? The Role of Son Preference and Sex Choice: Evidence from Immigrants to Canada* National Bureau of Economic Research Working Paper No 15391 (Cambridge, MA, National Bureau of Economic Research, 2009).

[339] See, eg, Douglas Almond and Lena Edlund, 'Son-Biased Sex Ratios in the 2000 United States Census' (2008) 105 *Proceedings of the National Academy of Sciences* 5681; Jason Abrevaya, 'Are There Missing Girls in the United States? Evidence from Birth Data' (2009) 1(2) *American Economic Journal: Applied Economics* 1.

[340] Sylvie Dubuc and David Coleman, 'An Increase in the Sex Ratio of Births to India-born Mothers in England and Wales: Evidence for Sex-Selective Abortion' (2007) 33(2) *Population and Development Review* 383.

[341] The normal sex ratio in industrialised countries is between 103 and 107 boys to 100 girls, or 1.03 to 1.07 (Hesketh *et al* (n 334) 1172).

[342] Almond *et al* (n 338) 38.

[343] Prenatal Nondiscrimination Act (PRENDA) of 2012, HR 3541, 112th Cong, 2d sess, Report No 112–496. The Bill was defeated by Congress in May 2012 (Cheryl Wetzstein, 'Dems Succeed in Sinking Bill Against Sex Selection Abortion', *Washington Times*, 31 May 2012, at <www.washingtontimes.com/news/2012/may/31/dems-succeed-sinking-bill-against-sex-selection-ab/?page=1>).

[344] Rajendra Kale, 'Editorial: "It's a Girl!" – Could be a Death Sentence' (2012) 184 *Canadian Medical Association Journal* 387.

[345] See, eg, Sneha Barot, 'A Problem-and-Solution Mismatch: Son Preference and Sex-Selective Abortion Bans' (2012) 15(2) *Guttmacher Policy Review* 18; Soraya Chemaly, '160 Million Missing Females: PRENDA and Misogyny', *Huffington Post*, 1 June 2012, at <www.huffingtonpost.com/soraya-chemaly/gender-selection-sex-discrimination-abortion_b_1559405.html>.

[346] Lauren Vogel, 'Sex Selective Abortions: No Simple Solution' (2012) 184 *Canadian Medical Association Journal* 286. The original proposal would have banned both sex-selective abortion and abortion motivated by racial selection, but the latter was omitted from the Bill that was voted on in May 2012. The rationale for the proposal to ban race-selective abortion was Congressman Franks's concern that higher abortion rates among women of colour meant that abortion providers were 'targeting' these women: see, eg, Barot (n 345) 20; Carole Joffe and Willie J Parker, 'Editorial: Race, Reproductive Politics and Reproductive Health Care in the Contemporary United States' (2012) 86 *Contraception* 1. See also Susan A Cohen, 'Abortion and Women of Color: The Bigger Picture' (2008) 11(3) *Guttmacher Policy Review* 2. As Cohen points out, it is indeed the case that the abortion rate is far higher among black women in the US, but so is the rate of unintended pregnancy among black women.

women from learning the sex of the fetus until the pregnancy is too far advanced for abortion to be available, are laudable, such measures are poorly aimed. Evidence from India, China, Vietnam and other countries that ban both pre-natal sex determination and sex-selective abortion illustrates that such laws are ineffective and likely impossible to enforce. India has had laws in place to prevent sex-selective abortion for well over a decade, and these laws have proven to be utterly ineffective, as in many regions of the country the sex ratio disparity continues to increase.[347] It is already difficult in many jurisdictions for women to obtain second-trimester abortion services, even in cases of fetal abnormalities that are likely to be lethal, as few providers offer such services.[348] In the end, all that a prohibition on sex-selective abortion can realistically accomplish is to impede access to safe abortion services.[349] In part, this is achieved by creating uncertainty among clinicians about the legal risks they face should they offer abortion services later in pregnancy.

Eliminating sex discrimination and son preference are important objectives that require an integrated approach in law and policy. South Korea's sex ratio at birth reached a height of 115 boys per 100 girls around 1990, but has since dropped to 106 boys per 100 girls, which is within a normal range.[350] A whole host of factors have played a role in this shift, including greater urbanisation and improved educational and employment opportunities for women,[351] with restrictions on testing for fetal sex being only one aspect of an integrated approach.

Some commentators have characterised the concerns raised by those who oppose selection against disability (known generally as the disability rights critique) and by those who oppose sex selection as necessarily conflicting with reproductive autonomy.[352] But viewing reproductive autonomy through the lens of a contextualised approach belies that characterisation. Disability rights advocates who raise concerns around selective abortion in general do not claim that women should be precluded from making this choice. Rather, their claim is that the clinical interaction and informed consent processes paint a primarily medical, and overly negative, picture of life with a disabled child, thus failing to provide prospective parents with any real opportunity to imagine what their lives would be like were they to welcome such a child in their family.[353] Far from being a rejection of reproductive autonomy, this argument acknowledges the difficult reality created by the need for such decisions. Further, it demands that sufficient information be

[347] Jha *et al* (n 333).
[348] Harris (n 312).
[349] As is discussed in more detail in ch 9, concerns have been raised about legal prohibitions on embryo sex selection where there are no parallel prohibitions related to selection of embryos to exclude disability. The worry is that prohibiting sex selection, but not precluding selection against disability, sends a particularly harmful message about the value of persons with disabilities.
[350] Christophe Z Guilmoto, 'The Sex Ratio Transition in Asia' (2009) 35 *Population and Development Review* 519, 525.
[351] Ganatra (n 333) 94–95.
[352] See, eg, Robertson (n 11); John Harris, 'Rights and Reproductive Choice' in John Harris and Søren Holm (eds), *The Future of Human Reproduction: Ethics, Choice and Regulation* (Oxford, Clarendon Press, 1998) 5; John Harris, 'Is There a Coherent Social Conception of Disability?' (2000) 26 *Journal of Medical Ethics* 95; Julian Savulescu, 'Procreative Beneficence: Why We Should Select the Best Children' (2001) 15 *Bioethics* 413; Julian Savulescu, 'Editorial: Is There a "Right Not to be Born"? Reproductive Decision Making, Options and the Right to Information' (2002) 28 *Journal of Medical Ethics* 65; John A Robertson, 'Procreative Liberty in the Era of Genomics' (2003) 29 *American Journal of Law & Medicine* 439.
[353] See, eg, Asch (n 331) 1651; Adrienne Asch and Erik Parens, 'The Disability Rights Critique of Prenatal Genetic Testing: Reflections and Recommendations' in Erik Parens and Adrienne Asch, *Prenatal Testing and Disability Rights* (Washington, DC, Georgetown University Press, 2000) 3.

provided to those who are faced with making such difficult decisions, so as to ensure that these decisions are, in fact, autonomous. As Adrienne Asch and Erik Parens explain, parental decisions around pre-natal diagnosis 'will be truly informed – those exercises of liberty will be authentic – only when people in our society come to learn what disability really does and does not mean for individuals and their families'.[354]

In terms of sex selection more specifically, as a woman, I have significant personal concerns about the practice of sex-selective abortion. That said, I can reach no other conclusion but that respect for reproductive autonomy requires that we respect women's decisions to terminate their pregnancies, regardless of their reasons. Women must be trusted to make their own 'mortal decisions'[355] and respect for reproductive autonomy demands that they be given the space to do so. Opponents of abortion, and even many of those who are generally supportive of abortion rights, often cite the example of a woman who seeks to terminate a pregnancy for reasons of 'convenience'[356] or because it will throw a wrench into her upcoming holiday plans.[357] As I have argued elsewhere, this concern stems from the failure of society (and law) to trust women's capacity to make their own procreative decisions.[358]

As I see it, meaningful respect for reproductive autonomy rules out legal restrictions on abortion for specific reasons, such as sex selection or disability selection. In fact, it rules out most restrictions on abortion. There is no way to respect reproductive autonomy fully and at the same time bracket that respect by prohibiting abortion in some circumstances or for some reasons. That some women will terminate pregnancies in circumstances that are generally considered morally objectionable is undeniable, and regrettable. But in liberal democratic societies, moral views around the propriety of certain abortions should not be translated into legal restrictions.

The only legitimate restriction on abortion is one based on timing, in keeping with a gradualist view of fetal personhood that sees the protection due a late gestation fetus as approaching the protection due a neonate. And even to the extent that time limits could be imposed to prohibit abortion in late pregnancy, respect for reproductive autonomy seems to preclude an approach that makes abortion categorically impermissible at or

---

[354] Asch and Parens (n 353) 38. Similarly, Tom Shakespeare acknowledges the complexity of decisions about abortion due to fetal disease or disability, noting that there are reasons to terminate such pregnancies that have nothing to do with discrimination against persons with disabilities (Tom Shakespeare, 'Choices and Rights: Eugenics, Genetics and Disability Equality' (1998) 13 *Disability and Society* 665). He suggests that the 'obvious disability equality answer . . . is to argue for better provision of welfare services and financial benefits to parents of disabled children, in order to make it easier for parents to choose to . . . continue such a pregnancy' (*ibid* 672).

[355] See, eg, Marie Ashe, 'Zig-Zag Stitching and the Seamless Web: Thoughts on "Reproduction" and the Law' (1989) 13 *Nova Law Review* 355. As Ashe puts it (*ibid* 383): 'I want a law that will let us be – women. That, recognizing the violence inherent in every regulation of female "reproduction," defines an area of non-regulation, within which we will make, each of us, our own "mortal decisions."'

[356] Or, indeed, at the 'whim' of the pregnant woman: see, eg, Brian C Melton, 'Loopholes and Health Threats: The Deus ex Machina of American Abortion' (*Capitol Hill Coffee House*, 26 May 2005), at <http://capitolhillcoffeehouse.com/archives/chch_news_149.htm>. See also Justice White's dissenting reasons in *Doe v Bolton*, 410 US 179 (1973) 221, wherein he claims that the majority's decision in *Roe v Wade* demonstrates that 'during the period prior to the time the fetus becomes viable, the Constitution of the United States values the convenience, whim, or caprice of the putative mother more than the life of the fetus'.

[357] See, eg, Sally Sheldon, '"Who is the Mother to Make the Judgment?" The Constructions of Woman in English Abortion Law' (1993) 1 *Feminist Legal Studies* 3; Leslie Cannold, *The Abortion Myth: Feminism, Morality, and the Hard Choices Women Make* (St Leonard's, NSW, Allen & Unwin,1998) 96–97.

[358] Erin Nelson, 'Reconceiving Pregnancy: Expressive Choice and Legal Reasoning' (2004) 49 *McGill Law Journal* 593, 623.

after a certain point in pregnancy. There will always be a need for an exception where the woman's life or health is at risk. It is sometimes suggested by anti-abortion advocates that Canada's lack of any law stipulating gestational limits means that abortion can take place at any time prior to birth.[359] In practice, the absence of a legal time limit for abortion does not imply that a woman can terminate her pregnancy at full term. As noted, late abortion is not readily accessible, and in spite of the absence of legal restrictions, the latest a Canadian woman can obtain abortion services is 24 weeks (and, in most provinces, abortion is available only much earlier in pregnancy).[360]

I have argued in favour of law and policy that allows women liberal access to safe abortion services, based on the demands of a contextualised approach to reproductive autonomy. I want to note here as well that this approach to reproductive autonomy equally insists that support be available to women making a decision about terminating or proceeding with a pregnancy. Women need to have authentic choices about pregnancy and abortion. Although leaving the decision in women's hands is necessary to demonstrate respect for reproductive autonomy, it is not sufficient to tell women that the decision is theirs and leave it at that. Good pre-natal, perinatal and post-natal care must be available, as must support services for women who choose to bear children in difficult circumstances. Only then will women be able to exercise genuine autonomy in reproductive decision making.

[359] See, eg, Cassie Farrell, 'Hey Joyce, Get Your Outdated Views Off my Body', *Huffington Post*, 31 May 2012, at <www.huffingtonpost.ca/cassie-farrell/abortion-pro-life_b_1556088.html>.
[360] Above (n 316). In addition, the Canadian Medical Association's guidance on Induced Abortion specifies that induced abortion means 'the active termination of a pregnancy before fetal viability' and that viability may be possible at 20 weeks post-fertilisation (or 22 weeks' gestation, measured from the date of the woman's last menstrual period). The guidance also states that post-viability abortion 'may be indicated under exceptional circumstances' (*CMA Policy: Induced Abortion* (n 306)).

Part Three

Controlling Reproductive Outcomes

6

Law, Medicine and Pregnancy: Maternal Liability and Intervention in the Lives of Pregnant Women

DECISION MAKING IN pregnancy involves everything from the everyday to the extraordinary. Women must consider and decide what foods to consume or avoid and how much to exercise, and may also face the question of whether to have invasive pre-natal testing that will potentially reveal that the fetus is affected by a condition that will be fatal within hours or days of birth. Along this entire continuum, women face intense social pressure to act as good mothers and to subordinate their own needs and desires to the interests of the fetus. In addition to social norms that dictate how pregnant women should behave, the law has come to be employed in an attempt to compel appropriate behaviour by those women who cannot or will not comply with social norms. Most often, the law's power is exercised against women who are marginalised (sometimes in multiple ways) or who for some reason do not fit with the normative image of the good mother. In these cases, rather than seeing the pregnant woman as a partner in maximising fetal health and well-being, the State seems to imagine the pregnant woman as a factor or variable that must be controlled and managed in order to secure a positive outcome.

The perception that the outcome of pregnancy can be controlled or determined by maternal behaviour depends heavily on the medicalised context in which pregnancy and pre-natal care take place. My first task in this chapter is to explain the phenomenon of the medicalised pregnancy and its implications. I then explore three contexts in which law has been used in an attempt to address the perceived conflict between maternal and fetal interests: tort liability for pre-natal conduct; coercive medical treatment during pregnancy; and the use of child welfare and criminal laws to control and punish women for their choices and behaviour during pregnancy.

I. MEDICALISATION AND PREGNANCY

Modern pregnancy is, for most women, a highly medicalised phenomenon.[1] Medicalisation is not new in pregnancy and childbirth,[2] nor is it unique to pregnancy.[3] But the incredible pace of technological change in pre-natal care and childbirth has led – in a relatively short time frame[4] – to a profound level of involvement of medical care and medical technology in the context of a normal, healthy life event.

Medicalisation in pregnancy is a complex development and is contributed to by several factors. One justification commonly offered to explain the medicalisation of pregnancy is the simultaneous dramatic reduction of infant and maternal morbidity and mortality in the twentieth century, ostensibly in parallel with increasing medical involvement in pregnancy.[5] The claim is that the phenomenon of medicalisation simply reflects an acknowledgement of the efficacy of pre-natal care in improving outcomes for mothers and babies. But as several authors have noted, this explanation does not stand up to scrutiny. Kristin Barker explains that 'the significant fall in maternal mortality during the twentieth century [pre-dated] the widespread use of prenatal care, [and] even the modest fall in mortality since the 1950's has not been convincingly linked to prenatal care'.[6] The same is true of infant mortality.[7] The story of the evolution of medicalisation in pregnancy is in reality more complex, and includes improvements in healthcare for women and children, as well as interventions that do not benefit women and might actually increase the risks they face.[8]

An important contributor to medicalisation is the fear of potential liability; specifically, concerns about liability when things go wrong during labour and delivery. In some ways, perhaps, modern obstetrical care is a victim of its own success, in that the public have come to expect that with high quality, error-free care, it is possible to prevent all

---

[1] See, eg, Carole H Browner and Nancy Press, 'The Production of Authoritative Knowledge in American Prenatal Care' (1996) 10(2) *Medical Anthropology Quarterly* 141; Kristin K Barker, 'A Ship Upon a Stormy Sea: The Medicalization of Pregnancy' (1998) 47 *Social Science & Medicine* 1067; Amy Mullin, *Reconceiving Pregnancy and Childcare: Ethics, Experience, and Reproductive Labor* (New York, Cambridge University Press, 2005).

[2] Emily Jackson notes that the first description of a Caesarean section appears in a text dating from 1305 (Emily Jackson, *Regulating Reproduction: Law, Technology and Autonomy* (Oxford, Hart Publishing, 2001) 119). It is certainly the case that childbirth became medicalised before pre-natal care did: Barker has estimated that fewer than 'five percent of pregnant women had any contact with a physician prior to delivery in the first two decades of the [twentieth] century' (Barker (n 1) 1068).

[3] There are numerous examples of medicalisation in the social sciences literature, including alcoholism, homosexuality, obesity, anorexia, premenstrual and menstrual discomfort, sadness, sexuality, aging and death: see, eg, Peter Conrad, 'Medicalization and Social Control' (1992) 18 *Annual Review of Sociology* 209; 'Special Issue on Medicalisation' (2002) 324 *British Medical Journal* 859.

[4] Barker notes that '[w]hile almost no women saw physicians prior to delivery in the early century, almost all pregnant women receive such care today' (Barker (n 1) 1068).

[5] Barker (n 1); Marjorie Tew, *Safer Childbirth? A Critical History of Maternity Care*, 3rd edn (London, Free Association Books, 1998) 1–5.

[6] Barker (n 1) 1068. See also Richard W Wertz and Dorothy C Wertz, *Lying-In: A History of Childbirth in America* (New York, Schocken Books, 1979) 161–64; Jo Murphy-Lawless, *Reading Birth and Death: A History of Obstetric Thinking* (Bloomington, Indiana University Press, 1998) 190–96; Tew (n 5) 270–86.

[7] Barker (n 1) 1068.

[8] See, eg, Anne Drapkin Lyerly *et al*, 'Risk and the Pregnant Body' (2009) 39(6) *Hastings Center Report* 34, 37–38; Richard Johanson, Mary Newburn and Alison Macfarlane, 'Has the Medicalisation of Childbirth Gone Too Far?' (2002) 324 *British Medical Journal* 892.

maternal deaths and all stillbirths.[9] This, of course, is not the case; risk is inevitable in pregnancy and childbirth.[10] In reality, maternal deaths are exceptional in developed nations,[11] and although stillbirth rates in wealthy countries remain a concern, the vast majority of neonatal deaths and stillbirths occur in developing nations[12] where access to high quality obstetrical care is far less frequent.[13] Even though poor outcomes may be (and likely most often are) the result of causes other than provider negligence, it is rare that a case would 'reach the courts . . . because of "unnecessary intervention"'.[14] In other words, the risk of liability to an obstetrician for intervening is far less than the risk of standing by out of concern that the intervention itself might be harmful.

A. Pre-natal care and reproductive autonomy

Medical technologies are used throughout the pregnancy continuum. Pre-natal screening and diagnostic testing directed at ascertaining fetal health and well-being, although relatively speaking quite new, have become routine aspects of pregnancy in the developed world, where virtually all pregnant women will be offered most, if not all, of these forms of testing at some point in pregnancy. [15]

---

[9] See, eg, Lyerly *et al* (n 8) 40; Steven L Clark *et al*, 'Maternal Death in the 21st Century: Causes, Prevention, and Relationship to Cesarean Delivery' (2008) 199(1) *American Journal of Obstetrics & Gynecology* 36e1 (estimating that 28% of the maternal deaths that occur in the US each year are preventable); Haywood Brown and Maria Small, 'The Role of the Maternal–Fetal Medicine Subspecialist in Review and Prevention of Maternal Deaths' (2012) 36 *Seminars in Perinatology* 27; Gwyneth Lewis, 'Saving Mothers' Lives: The Continuing Benefits for Maternal Health from the United Kingdom (UK) Confidential Enquires into Maternal Deaths' (2012) 36 *Seminars in Perinatology* 19.

[10] Lyerly *et al* (n 8) 40 ('In birth, no less than in life itself, there is an irreducible element of risk').

[11] According to the World Health Organization (WHO), maternal mortality ratios are estimated as follows: Canada, 12 maternal deaths per 100,000 live births; Australia, 7; UK, 12; US, 21 (World Health Organization, *Trends in Maternal Mortality 1990–2010: WHO, UNICEF, UNFPA and The World Bank Estimates* (Geneva, World Health Organization, 2012)). There are discrepancies in the maternal mortality ratios estimated by the WHO and other studies. Margaret Hogan and colleagues reported the following ratios in 2010: Canada, 7; Australia, 5; UK, 8; US, 17 (Margaret C Hogan *et al*, 'Maternal Mortality for 181 Countries, 1980–2008: A Systematic Analysis of Progress Towards Millennium Development Goal 5' (2010) 375 *The Lancet* 1609). There is a concern that maternal mortality is rising in Canada, the UK and the US, and has been gradually climbing since 1990, but it is not clear whether these are real increases or just reflect changes in how these deaths are coded and determined (Sarka Lisonkova *et al*, 'Temporal Trends in Maternal Mortality in Canada I: Estimates Based on Vital Statistics Data' (2011) 33 *Journal of Obstetrics and Gynaecology Canada* 1011; Sarka Lisonkova *et al*, 'Temporal Trends in Maternal Mortality in Canada II: Estimates Based on Hospitalization Data' (2011) 33 *Journal of Obstetrics and Gynaecology Canada* 1020).

[12] And among minority and disadvantaged groups in many developed nations as well (Vicki Flenady *et al*, 'Stillbirths: The Way Forward in High-Income Countries' (2011) 377 *The Lancet* 1703, 1704). The authors note that in Canada's northern areas, where most of Canada's Inuit population is found, stillbirth rates are three times higher than the national average. In the US, African-American women suffer stillbirth at twice the rate of white women (and this is also the case for Australia's indigenous population when compared to the non-indigenous population). In the UK and New Zealand, stillbirth rates are relatively higher in populations that are socio-economically deprived.

[13] Ninety-eight per cent of stillbirths occur in low and middle-income nations (Zoë Mullan and Richard Horton, 'Comment: Bringing Stillbirths out of the Shadows' (2011) 377 *The Lancet* 1291). In most high-income nations, the stillbirth rate (as of 2009) is between 2.5 and 4 per 1,000 births (Flenady *et al* (n 12) 1704; Vicki Flenady *et al*, 'Major Risk Factors for Stillbirth in High-Income Countries: A Systematic Review and Meta-analysis' (2011) 377 *The Lancet* 1331).

[14] Johanson *et al* (n 8) 893.

[15] See, eg, Royal College of Obstetricians and Gynaecologists, 'Guideline: Ultrasound Screening' (2000), at <www.rcog.org.uk/womens-health/clinical-guidance/ultrasound-screening>; Royal Australian and New Zealand College of Obstetricians and Gynaecologists, 'College Statement C-Obs 03b: Routine Antenatal Assessment in

Most pregnant women will be offered a significant array of pre-natal tests, including ultrasound, pre-natal screening (blood testing, plus ultrasound in some cases),[16] testing for gestational diabetes, chromosomal testing (amniocentesis, chorionic villus sampling) and testing for specific genetic disorders. Screening tests provide risk information, and diagnostic tests can identify a specific concern with fetal health or development. Aneuploidy screening is a technique used to identify women who are at higher risk of giving birth to a child with an abnormal number of chromosomes (usually an extra chromosome, referred to as a 'trisomy', to reflect the three copies of the chromosome in question). The most common chromosomes to be affected are 21 (trisomy 21 is Down Syndrome), 18 and 13.[17] There are various methods of screening, based on, for example, maternal age, biochemical serum markers and ultrasound screening for nuchal translucency.[18] Women and couples who are told that their screening test results are positive, meaning that the fetus is at an increased risk for a particular chromosomal disorder, are offered diagnostic testing to confirm whether or not the fetus is affected by a chromosomal disorder. All that a screening test can provide, in other words, is risk information. The diagnostic tests were developed first; the screening tests in use today have been available for less than three decades, and have continued to evolve and be refined over that period.[19] Nevertheless, they are now a routine part of pre-natal care, and recommendations from professional societies and regulators in Canada, the US, the UK and Australia indicate that they should be offered to all pregnant women.[20]

Ultrasound has a longer history of use in obstetrics than pre-natal screening and diagnostic testing for genetic and chromosomal abnormalities, and has for some time been a

the Absence of Pregnancy Complications' (2009), at < http://www.ranzcog.edu.au/womens-health/statements-a-guidelines/college-statements-and-guidelines.html?showall=&start=1>; American College of Obstetricians and Gynecologists, 'ACOG Practice Bulletin No 101: Ultrasonography in Pregnancy' (2009) 113 *Obstetrics and Gynecology* 451; Yvonne Cargill and Lucie Morin, 'SOGC Clinical Practice Guideline No 223: Content of a Complete Routine Second Trimester Obstetrical Ultrasound Examination and Report' (2009) 31 *Journal of Obstetrics and Gynaecology Canada* 272.

[16] See, eg, David Chitiyat, Sylvie Langlois and R Douglas Wilson, 'SOGC Clinical Practice Guideline No 261: Prenatal Screening for Fetal Aneuploidy in Singleton Pregnancies' (2011) 33 *Journal of Obstetrics and Gynaecology Canada* 736; American College of Obstetricians and Gynecologists, 'ACOG Practice Bulletin No 77: Screening for Fetal Chromosomal Abnormalities' (2007) 109 *Obstetrics & Gynecology* 217; Royal Australian and New Zealand College of Obstetricians and Gynaecologists, 'College Statement C-Obs 4: Prenatal Screening Tests for Trisomy 21 (Down Syndrome), Trisomy 18 (Edwards Syndrome) and Neural Tube Defects' (2007), at < http://www.ranzcog.edu.au/womens-health/statements-a-guidelines/college-statements-and-guidelines.html?showall=&start=1>; Royal Australian and New Zealand College of Obstetricians and Gynaecologists, 'College Statement C-Obs 3b' (n 15). The ACOG has also recommended that invasive pre-natal testing, including amniocentesis and chorionic villus sampling, should be available to all pregnant women, regardless of age (American College of Obstetricians and Gynecologists, 'ACOG Practice Bulletin No 88: Invasive Prenatal Testing for Aneuploidy' (2007) 110 *Obstetrics & Gynecology* 1459).

[17] Trisomy 18 is also referred to as Edwards Syndrome; trisomy 13 is known as Patau Syndrome (Deborah A Driscoll and Susan Gross, 'Prenatal Screening for Aneuploidy' (2009) 360 *New England Journal of Medicine* 2556, 2557). Fewer than 10% of children born with either of these trisomies live past the first year of life.

[18] Nuchal translucency refers to the amount of fluid at the back of the fetal neck; this can be measured using ultrasound. Increased nuchal translucency in the first trimester of pregnancy is associated with a variety of chromosomal, structural and genetic abnormalities in the fetus (*ibid*; American College of Obstetricians and Gynecologists, 'ACOG Practice Bulletin No 77' (n 16) 218).

[19] American College of Obstetricians and Gynecologists, 'ACOG Practice Bulletin No 77' (n 16) 217–18.

[20] See sources cited in nn 15 and 16.

routine part of pregnancy.[21] Not only has ultrasound given expectant parents an opportunity to see the fetus,[22] the technology has also allowed the public to see into the womb;
this has had significant implications in obstetrical care, and in relation to public scrutiny
of pregnancy and pregnant women.[23] Most recently, concerns have arisen about the
application of ultrasound outside of the medical context,[24] the argument being that this
technology belongs in the medical realm.

Medical technology continues to play a role at the point of labour and delivery. As
obstetricians have increasingly become involved in normal pregnancies and deliveries,
women are more likely to have one of several interventions, including electronic fetal
monitoring (which is routinely used to monitor the fetal heart rate during labour[25]),
delivery in the lithotomy position and surgical delivery.[26] Other interventions are possible as well, including induction, epidural or other pain relief, and operative vaginal
delivery (vacuum extraction or forceps).[27]

As outlined in chapter three, the increasing medicalisation of pregnancy has become
cause for concern, particularly among feminists. The feminist critique of medicalisation
includes concern about the normalisation of technology in pregnancy and childbirth and
about increasing rates of intervention in pregnancy, particularly in labour and delivery,
given that the routine application of these technologies can cause significant harm, both
to pregnant women and to the fetus.[28] Caesarean section has been a focal point for critics

---

[21] A 2010 study notes that 'nearly one in five women now undergo four or more ultrasound examinations
during the second and third trimesters' (John J You *et al*, 'Proliferation of Prenatal Ultrasonography' (2010)
182 *Canadian Medical Association Journal* 143, 143).

[22] And, some argue, bond with the fetus: see, eg, John C Fletcher and Mark I Evans, 'Maternal Bonding in
Early Fetal Ultrasound Examinations' (1983) 308 *New England Journal of Medicine* 392; Judith Lumley,
'Through a Glass Darkly: Ultrasound and Prenatal Bonding' (1990) 17 *Birth* 214.

[23] See, eg, Rosalind Pollack Petchesky, 'Fetal Images: The Power of Visual Culture in the Politics of Reproduction'
(1987) 13 *Feminist Studies* 263; Barbara Duden, *Disembodying Women: Perspectives on Pregnancy and the
Unborn* (Lee Hoinacki tr, Cambridge, MA, Harvard University Press, 1993) 11–15, 51–52; Janet Gallagher,
'Collective Bad Faith: "Protecting" the Fetus' in Joan C Callahan (ed), *Reproduction, Ethics, and the Law:
Feminist Perspectives* (Bloomington, Indiana University Press, 1995) 343, 347; Sozos J Fasouliotis and Joseph G
Schenker, 'Maternal–Fetal Conflict' (2000) 89 *European Journal of Obstetrics & Gynecology, and Reproductive
Biology* 101; Nathan Stormer, 'Seeing the Fetus: The Role of Technology and Image in the Maternal–Fetal
Relationship' (2003) 289 *Journal of the American Medical Association* 1700.

[24] Frank A Chervenak and Laurence B McCullough, 'An Ethical Critique of Boutique Fetal Imaging: A Case
for the Medicalization of Fetal Imaging' (2005) 192 *American Journal of Obstetrics & Gynecology* 31;
Bioeffects and Safety Committee on Behalf of the Board of the International Society of Ultrasound in
Obstetrics and Gynecology (ISUOG), 'ISUOG Statement on the Non-Medical Use of Ultrasound, 2009' (2009)
33 *Ultrasound in Obstetrics and Gynecology* 617.

[25] Electronic fetal monitoring is used routinely in labour in spite of uncertainty as to its utility and predictive
value: see, eg, George A Macones *et al*, 'The 2008 National Institute of Child Health and Human Development
Workshop Report on Electronic Fetal Monitoring: Update on Definitions, Interpretation, and Research
Guidelines' (2008) 37 *Journal of Obstetric, Gynecologic and Neonatal Nursing* 510; David A Grimes and
Jeffrey F Peipert, 'Electronic Fetal Monitoring as a Public Health Screening Program: The Arithmetic of
Failure' (2010) 116 *Obstetrics & Gynecology* 1397.

[26] Johanson *et al* (n 8).

[27] *Ibid*; Lyerly *et al* (n 8).

[28] Susan Sherwin, 'Normalizing Reproductive Technologies and the Implications for Autonomy' in Rosemary
Tong, Gwen Anderson and Aida Santos (eds), *Globalizing Feminist Bioethics: Crosscultural Perspectives* (Boulder,
CO, Westview Press, 2001) 96; Sylvia Burrow, 'On the Cutting Edge: Ethical Responsiveness to Cesarean Rates'
(2012) 12(7) *American Journal of Bioethics* 44.

of medicalisation, who note that rates of surgical delivery are rising,[29] and that many of these procedures are unnecessary and can themselves cause harm.[30]

All of these medical technologies call for decision making on the part of the pregnant woman, making the pre-natal care context an important site for consideration of reproductive autonomy. The primary worry from the perspective of reproductive autonomy is what happens when pregnant women are faced with choices about which tests or interventions to accept and which to forgo. Traditional liberal views of reproductive autonomy tend to see this in a straightforward manner – respect for reproductive autonomy requires that women and couples be informed about the availability of testing and permitted to decide which test(s) they will accept.[31] The main concern is whether a woman's consent to a particular test or procedure was sufficiently informed as to represent a genuine instance of informed choice. But a more contextualised view of reproductive autonomy is concerned with additional questions, including the extent to which the routinisation of the tests and interventions makes it difficult for women to navigate a space in which to make autonomous decisions.[32] It has been argued that in the context of a medicalised approach to pregnancy and childbirth, the offer of certain tests to women by their physicians, particularly when the tests are characterised as routine aspects of pre-natal care, is laden with the sense that the only appropriate response is acceptance.[33] Sociologists Carole Browner and Nancy Ann Press note that the way information about a particular test (alpha-fetoprotein screening) is provided can be seen to encourage women to agree to have the test, as opposed to simply informing them about its availability. Browner and Press cite a number of examples to illustrate this point, the most striking of which is as follows: a nurse informs a patient, 'This is a screening test we're doing on all women that the state requires, but you have to read the booklet and sign it

---

[29] Caesarean section rates in Canada, the UK and Australia are in the range of 20–25%, while the most recent data out of the US show a rate of 34% in that country. There is variation among Canadian provinces, from a low of 5% in Nunavut to a high of 23% in Newfoundland and Labrador (Canadian Institute for Health Information, *Health Care in Canada 2010* (Ottawa, Canadian Institute for Health Information, 2010) 26–30). For UK data, see National Collaborating Centre for Women's and Children's Health for the National Institute for Health and Clinical Excellence, *Caesarean Section Clinical Guideline* (London, Royal College of Obstetricians and Gynaecologists Press, 2011) 38; for Australian data, see Australian Government, Department of Health and Ageing, *Improving Maternity Services in Australia: A Discussion Paper from the Australian Government* (Barton, Commonwealth of Australia, 2008) 5) (noting a 30.3% rate in 2005). In the US, the average rate is 34%, and the range is from 22.5% to 38.6% ('Health Grades 2011 Obstetrics & Gynecology in American Hospitals' (*Health Grades*, 2011), at <www.healthgrades.com/business/img/HealthGrades2011ObstetricsandGynecologyinAmericanHospitalsReport.pdf>).

[30] See, eg, Johanson *et al* (n 8) 892–93; Veronique Bergeron, 'The Ethics of Cesarean Section on Maternal Request: A Feminist Critique of the American College of Obstetricians and Gynecologists' Position on Patient-Choice Surgery' (2007) 21 *Bioethics* 478; Cecilia Benoit *et al*, 'Medical Dominance and Neoliberalisation in Maternal Care Provision: The Evidence from Canada and Australia' (2010) 71 *Social Science & Medicine* 475, 475–76.

[31] See, eg, John A Robertson, 'Procreative Liberty and Human Genetics' (1990) 39 *Emory Law Journal* 697; Robert J Boyle and Julian Savulescu, 'Prenatal Testing for "Minor" Genetic Abnormalities is Ethical' (2003) 3(1) *American Journal of Bioethics* 60.

[32] See, eg, Rayna Rapp, *Testing Women, Testing the Fetus: The Social Impact of Amniocentesis in America* (New York, Routledge, 2000); Erik Parens and Adrienne Asch, 'The Disability Rights Critique of Prenatal Genetic Testing: Reflections and Recommendations' in Erik Parens and Adrienne Asch (eds), *Prenatal Testing and Disability Rights* (Washington, DC, Georgetown University Press, 2000) 3.

[33] See, eg, Barbara Katz Rothman, *The Tentative Pregnancy: Prenatal Diagnosis and the Future of Motherhood* (New York, Viking, 1986); Nancy Press and Carole H Browner, 'Why Women Say Yes to Prenatal Diagnosis' (1997) 45 *Social Science & Medicine* 979; Nancy Press, 'Assessing the Expressive Character of Prenatal Testing: The Choices Made or the Choices Made Available?' in Parens and Asch (eds) (n 32) 214.

in the back and we keep the signed copy in the chart.'[34] Likewise, concerns have been raised about opt-out pre-natal HIV screening programs, in which pregnant women are routinely screened for HIV infection unless they specifically choose to forgo testing, in that such programs may lead to testing even where there has not been true 'informed consent'.[35]

It bears mention here again that medicalisation is not a unidirectional phenomenon in which medical technology has been applied contrary to women's wishes. Indeed, part of the explanation for the increasing medicalisation of pregnancy and pre-natal care may be found in women's desire to access (at least some) of these technologies.[36]

B. Medicalisation and the 'maternal–fetal conflict'

Medical technology in pregnancy has played a key role in shaping the response of both healthcare providers and the public to pregnancy and women's decision making therein. Based on what technology can tell them, providers often claim 'knowledge which is perceived as more quantifiable, more valid, than the woman's experiential knowledge'.[37] Providers also see the fetus differently because of and through technology; the fetus is understood and displayed as a being separate from the pregnant woman, with its own medical needs and interests. The routine use of technology that allows a 'window into the womb' permits this construction of the fetus as separate from the pregnant woman.[38] Once the separation is effected, it becomes possible for the pregnant woman to be obscured from view as care and interventions are focused on the fetus. The perception thus becomes that there are two patients in each pregnant woman: the woman herself and the developing fetus.[39] The result of the separation of pregnant woman and fetus is the construction of the idea of maternal–fetal conflict – the problem that arises when the interests of pregnant woman and fetus diverge and physicians are faced with a situation that seems to call for the prioritisation of either maternal or fetal interests.[40]

As feminist writers have long argued, the maternal–fetal relationship is unique among human relationships. There is quite simply no parallel. In pregnancy, in fact and in law, there are temporarily two beings in one person. The fetus and the pregnant woman are

---

[34] Carole H Browner and Nancy Ann Press, 'The Normalization of Prenatal Diagnostic Screening' in Faye D Ginsburg and Rayna Rapp (eds), *Conceiving the New World Order: The Global Politics of Reproduction* (Berkeley, University of California Press, 1995) 307, 315.

[35] Ronald Bayer and Amy L Fairchild, 'Changing the Paradigm for HIV Testing – The End of Exceptionalism' (2006) 355 *New England Journal of Medicine* 647; American Civil Liberties Union, 'Increasing Access to Voluntary HIV Testing: The Importance of Informed Consent and Counseling in HIV Testing' (2007), at <http://www.aclu.org/files/images/asset_upload_file473_30248.pdf>.

[36] See discussion in ch 3, section I.A.

[37] Michael Thomson, *Reproducing Narrative: Gender, Reproduction and Law* (Aldershot, Ashgate, 1998) 213.

[38] See sources cited above (n 23).

[39] See, eg, Fasouliotis and Schenker (n 23); Gallagher (n 23); Janet Gallagher, 'Fetus as Patient' in Sherrill Cohen and Nadine Taub (eds), *Reproductive Laws for the 1990s* (Clifton, NJ, Humana Press, 1989) 185; Jeffrey P Phelan, 'The Maternal Abdominal Wall: A Fortress Against Fetal Health Care?' (1991) 65 *Southern California Law Review* 461, 464; Frank A Chervenak and Asim Kurjak, *Current Perspectives on the Fetus as a Patient* (New York, Parthenon, 1996); Laurence B McCullough and Frank A Chervenak, 'A Critical Analysis of the Concept and Discourse of "Unborn Child"' (2008) 8(7) *American Journal of Bioethics* 34.

[40] Michelle Oberman, 'Mothers and Doctors' Orders: Unmasking the Doctor's Fiduciary Role in Maternal–Fetal Conflicts' (1999–2000) 94(2) *Northwestern University Law Review* 451; Lisa H Harris, 'Rethinking Maternal–Fetal Conflict: Gender and Equality in Perinatal Ethics' (2000) 96 *Obstetrics & Gynecology* 786.

interconnected,[41] they are 'not-one-but-not-two'.[42] The pregnant woman is all there, but 'she is not all that is there'.[43] Although the technology has changed and now allows us to imagine the fetus as a separate being, a patient in its own right, the biological facts of pregnancy have not altered, and there is no way to the fetus other than through the pregnant woman.

The idea of 'fetus as patient' creates interesting tensions in law and ethics. Laurence McCullough and Frank Chervenak can be credited with the idea that the fetus should be conceived of as a separate patient to whom physicians owe legal and ethical duties of care.[44] Specifically, they claim that the fetus is owed beneficence-based duties and that physicians must respect the fetus' future autonomy.[45] McCullough and Chervenak emphasise that the obligations owed to the fetus are grounded in its dependent (as opposed to independent) moral status, and that the use of the ethical concept of fetus as patient does not entail rights claims on behalf of the fetus.[46] The authors are primarily concerned with the duties owed by physicians to the viable fetus; a pre-viable fetus can become a patient only if and when the pregnant woman autonomously confers that moral status on the fetus by deciding to continue the pregnancy to viability.[47] The duties owed to the fetus must be weighed against the autonomy- and beneficence- based duties owed by physician to pregnant woman, but the authors assert that pregnant women are obliged to accept reasonable '[risks] to themselves – to protect the fetal patient'.[48]

As others have argued, the 'fetus as patient' construct presents several problematic conflicts. It might encourage physicians and other healthcare providers to conceive of the fetus as a separate being, 'obscuring the physical and social relationship between pregnant woman and fetus, the ways that maternal and fetal physiologies and welfare are linked, and perhaps most problematically, the woman herself'.[49] In addition, the normative designation of 'patient' carries with it legal duties of the highest order – fiduciary duties – and could lead to a tendency of healthcare providers to view the duties to these two patients as equal.[50] Lastly, concerns arise about the extent to which 'society . . . may impose burdens upon a pregnant woman's liberty interests'.[51]

---

[41] As Robin West puts it: 'Women are not essentially, necessarily, inevitably, invariably, always, and forever separate from other human beings: women, distinctively, are quite clearly "connected" to another human life when pregnant.' (Robin West, 'Jurisprudence and Gender' (1988) 55 *University of Chicago Law Review* 1, 2) See also Mary B Mahowald, 'As If There Were Fetuses Without Women: A Remedial Essay' in Joan C Callahan (ed), *Reproduction, Ethics and the Law: Feminist Perspectives* (Bloomington, Indiana University Press, 1995) 199, 200–01.
[42] John Seymour, *Childbirth and the Law* (Oxford, Oxford University Press, 2000) 199–202.
[43] Catharine MacKinnon, 'Reflections on Sex Equality Under Law' (1991) 100 *Yale Law Journal* 1281, 1316.
[44] McCullough and Chervenak (n 39); Frank A Chervenak and Laurence B McCullough, 'Perinatal Ethics: A Practical Method of Analysis of Obligations to Mother and Fetus' (1985) 66 *Obstetrics & Gynecology* 442; Laurence B McCullough and Frank A Chervenak, *Ethics in Obstetrics and Gynecology* (New York, Oxford University Press, 1994).
[45] McCullough and Chervenak (n 39); Chervenak and McCullough 'Perinatal Ethics' (n 44); McCullough and Chervenak, *Ethics in Obstetrics* (n 44).
[46] McCullough and Chervenak (n 39) 37.
[47] *Ibid.*
[48] *Ibid* 38.
[49] Anne Drapkin Lyerly, Margaret Olivia Little and Ruth R Faden, 'A Critique of the "Fetus as Patient"' (2008) 8(7) *American Journal of Bioethics* 42, 43.
[50] *Ibid.*
[51] Stephen D Brown, 'The "Fetus as Patient": A Critique' (2008) 8(7) *American Journal of Bioethics* 47, 49.

C. Law and the maternal–fetal conflict

Medicalisation helps to shape not only social, but also legal responses to choice in pregnancy. McCullough and Chervenak sought to introduce the concept of fetus as patient to provide an alternative to the construction of 'conflict' between maternal and fetal rights.[52] In spite of this, the law has come to be used (with increasing frequency) in attempts to handle the perceived maternal–fetal conflict. In part, this is due to the considerable influence of medical knowledge on legal decision making, with courts demonstrating a willingness to defer to medical knowledge, particularly in urgent, critical matters.[53] Judicial deference to technologically-derived medical knowledge is not unique to pregnancy,[54] but is perhaps even more likely in this context because of the perceived high stakes of conceding maternal autonomy.

II. TORT LAW: MATERNAL LIABILITY FOR PRE-NATAL CONDUCT

Although the link between owing tort law duties to one's fetus and reproductive autonomy is not direct or immediate, it inheres in the potential ability of the interests of the fetus (or the threat of liability) to dictate how pregnant women may behave.[55]

The common law has long recognised the ability of a child to claim damages from a third party whose negligence injured the child while *en ventre sa mère*,[56] and the courts have had opportunities to consider whether children can sue their parents for personal injuries caused by parental negligence (in general finding that such claims can be maintained).[57] The question that seems naturally to follow is whether a child can sue his or her mother for injuries allegedly caused by her negligent conduct during pregnancy. Perhaps surprisingly, the courts have not had occasion to consider this question until relatively recently. Not surprisingly, these cases have had interesting results.

The US, Canada and Australia have dealt with the question of maternal tort liability for antenatal conduct primarily through the common law (although one Canadian province has legislation on point). By contrast, the UK has legislation on point. The common law and statutory regimes will be discussed in turn.

---

[52] Harris (n 40) 787.

[53] Thomson (n 37) 213. See also Vangie Bergum, *A Child on Her Mind: The Experience of Becoming a Mother* (Westport, CT, Bergin & Garvey, 1997) 58.

[54] See, eg, William M Sage, 'Over Under or Through: Physicians, Law and Health Care Reform' (2009) 53 *Saint Louis University Law Journal* 1033, 1037–38.

[55] As put in *Chenault v Huie*, '[f]or example, would a woman cast in the role of a "reasonable pregnant woman" be forced to endure pain and suffering or even forego critical medical treatment because of potentially adverse effects the treatment may have on her fetus? Should a woman be forced to consider whether a jury would find her decision "reasonable" before she decides to accept or reject medical treatment?' (*Chenault v Huie*, 989 SW 2d 474 (Tex App 1999) 477–78).

[56] *Bonbrest v Kotz*, 65 F Supp 138 (DDC 1946); *X and Y (By Her Tutor X) v Pal* (1991) 23 NSWLR 26; *de Martell v Merton and Sutton Health Authority* [1993] QB 204; *Burton v Islington Health Authority* [1993] QB 204. See also, Congenital Disabilities (Civil Liability) Act 1976 (UK); *Montreal Tramways v Léveillé* [1933] SCR 456, [1933] 4 DLR 337; *Duval v Seguin* [1972] 2 OR 686, 26 DLR (3d) 418 (Ont HCJ); *Watt v Rama* [1972] VR 353.

[57] *Young v Rankin* [1934] SC 499; *Deziel v Deziel* [1953] 1 DLR 651, [1952] OJ No 529 (Ont HCJ); Martin J Rooney and Colleen M Rooney, 'Parental Tort Immunity: Spare the Liability, Spoil the Parent' (1990–91) 25 *New England Law Review* 1161.

A. Common law

In the common law jurisdictions, the courts that have been faced with claims alleging that a woman owes a duty of care to her child in respect of her conduct while pregnant have approached the problem from one of two opposing perspectives. In the cases where a duty of care has been imposed, the courts have taken a narrow view of the issue. These courts have analysed the duty question from the standpoint that a pregnant woman owes the same duty of care to her fetus as she owes to all others in the same circumstances (this is typical in the driving cases), or that the pregnant woman is no differently situated vis-à-vis potential liability to the child for pre-natal harm than is any third party. By contrast, in the cases where courts have refused to impose a duty of care, the refusal is based on the uniqueness of the maternal–fetal relationship and the implications of the biology of pregnancy for women's privacy and autonomy interests.

Before discussing the cases on maternal tort liability, it is important to note the existence and significance of the parental immunity doctrine in the US. Unlike the situation in Canada,[58] England[59] and Australia,[60] the American common law includes a concept of parental immunity, which prohibits children from suing their parents.[61] The doctrine developed out of public policy concerns related to the potential for disruption of family relationships, and the belief that recourse to a legal remedy might 'undermine parental authority and control over their children, and that easy availability of legal remedy might encourage people to go too quickly into an adversarial arena rather than attempting in good faith to work out their differences'.[62]

Most American jurisdictions have by now strictly limited or abolished the doctrine of parental immunity.[63] To an extent at least, legal consideration of the question of maternal liability for pre-natal conduct in the US has been governed by the rise and fall of parental immunity. At one time, the question of maternal (or indeed, paternal) liability to one's fetus or born-alive child was largely irrelevant, as most such lawsuits were prohibited on the basis of parental immunity.[64] But as the doctrine continues to erode, state courts have come to face the question of maternal liability for pre-natal negligence, a question they are ill-equipped to address given the absence of clearly articulated principles on point.[65] Indeed, one author makes the alarming observation that the US courts

---

[58] See, eg, *Deziel v Deziel* (n 57).

[59] See, eg, *Surtees v Kingston-upon-Thames* [1992] PIQR P101, 123–24; *XA v YA* [2010] EWHC 1983 (QB), [2011] PIQR P1, para 140. The English courts have noted that 'the court should be wary in its approach to holding parents in breach of a duty of care owed to their children' (*Surtees v Kingston-upon-Thames*, 123–24). See also *Young v Rankin* (n 57) (Scotland)).

[60] *Hahn v Conley* (1971) 126 CLR 276, 283–84; *Harriton v Stephens* [2006] HCA 15 (2006) 226 CLR 52, para 129.

[61] For a detailed discussion of the parental immunity doctrine, see Gail D Hollister, 'Parent–Child Immunity: A Doctrine in Search of Justification' (1982) 50 *Fordham Law Review* 489.

[62] Deborah R Mathieu, *Preventing Prenatal Harm: Should the State Intervene?* 2nd edn (Washington, DC, Georgetown University Press, 1996) 141. See also Ron Beal, '"Can I Sue Mommy?" An Analysis of a Woman's Tort Liability for Prenatal Injuries to her Child Born Alive' (1984) 21 *San Diego Law Review* 325, 333–57.

[63] Beal (n 62).

[64] Benjamin Shmueli, 'Love and the Law, Children Against Mothers and Fathers: Or, What's Love Got To Do With It?' (2010) 17 *Duke Journal of Gender Law & Policy* 131.

[65] In *Chenault v Huie*, the Texas Court of Appeals pointed out the mistake in this approach: 'We note that both *Grodin* and *Bonte* focus almost entirely on the application of the parental immunity doctrine, which when applicable prevents the imposition of liability on a parent. But application of an immunity from liability and the recognition of a legal duty that is the prerequisite to a civil cause of action are two entirely separate issues

have '[u]nconsciously . . . established the opportunity for litigation between mother and child'.[66]

There are few US appellate level cases considering the potential tort liability of a woman for her conduct during pregnancy, and the decisions are not uniform in either outcome or analysis. Of the handful of appellate decisions, four have allowed maternal liability claims to proceed. Of these, two limit their reasoning around maternal liability to negligence in operating a motor vehicle. Both courts held that while there are public policy reasons that might lead the common law to decline to recognise a general duty of care with respect to maternal conduct during pregnancy, these policy reasons do not apply in the context of negligent driving.[67] Australian courts have taken largely the same approach as the US cases concerning negligent driving.[68] The courts chose to construe the liability question narrowly, as involving nothing more than the question of maternal liability in the context of operating a motor vehicle. As Clarke JA put it in *Lynch v Lynch*:

> [T]he question with which this Court is concerned is a narrow one and does not, in my opinion, involve far reaching questions of policy. That question is whether a mother can be liable to her child, who was born with disabilities, in respect of injury caused to that child while a foetus by the mother's negligent driving of a motor vehicle.[69]

The two other US appellate level cases that approve the possibility of maternal liability deal with conduct outside of the motor vehicle accident context. In *Grodin v Grodin*,[70] a mother was sued by her son for damages resulting from her negligent use of prescription medication during her pregnancy. Mrs Grodin had taken tetracycline during her

... Immunity presupposes a legal duty and corresponding liability when the duty is breached. If a legal duty does not exist, the possible application of an immunity never becomes an issue. A court's decision whether to create a legal duty involves complex considerations of public policy including social, economic, and political questions.' (*Chenault v Huie* (n 55) 476)

[66] Deborah M Santello, 'Maternal Tort Liability for Prenatal Injuries' (1988) 22 *Suffolk University Law Review* 747, 748. See also Beal (n 62) 326: 'The potential legal framework for lawsuits by children born alive for prenatal injuries caused by the negligent conduct of their mothers has been unknowingly created by the state courts.'

[67] In *National Cas Co v Northern Trust Bank*, the Court adopted the reasoning of the trial judge, who stated: 'The Court recognizes that there may be [an] argument that the mother's decision relating to privacy issues or personal health decisions could be impacted by this ruling. However, based on the narrow facts involved in this lawsuit, it is the Court's ruling that there is no public policy against finding a cause of action of the [child] against the mother for simple automobile negligence up to the limits of the insurance coverage. It is the Court's ruling that under these limited circumstances, there is no invasion of the mother's decision-making relating to any privacy issue, nor is there any violation of the mother's right to decision-making relating to her health as well as the fetus.' (*National Cas Co v Northern Trust Bank*, 807 SO 2d 86 (Fla Dist Ct App 2002) 87) Similarly, in *Tesar v Anderson*, the Wisconsin Supreme Court 'emphasize[d] that no reader of this opinion should surmise that we are weighing in on whether women should be held liable for other negligent acts that harm fetuses' (*Tesar v Anderson*, 329 Wis 2d 240, (WI App 2010) 259–60). In this case, the Court noted that Wisconsin law adopts the approach to duty of care outlined by Andrews J (in dissent) in *Palsgraf v Long Island RR Co*, 248 NY 339 (1928). This conception of duty of care holds that 'everyone owes to the world at large the duty of refraining from those acts which may unreasonably threaten the safety of others' (*ibid* 350). This approach to the duty of care was crucial from the perspective of the Court's willingness to hold that pregnant women owe a duty to the fetus in the context of negligent driving.

[68] There are two Australian cases on point; both are driving cases: *Lynch v Lynch* (1991) 25 NSWLR 411; 14 MVR 521, 523; *Bowditch (by his next friend John Stanley Bowditch) v McEwan and Others* [2001] QSC 448, affd [2002] QCA 172 (this case was decided after the Canadian case *Dobson (Litigation Guardian of) v Dobson* [1999] 2 SCR 753, 214 NBR (2d) 201, and the Queensland Supreme Court explicitly declined to follow the Canadian court's reasoning).

[69] *Lynch v Lynch* (n 68) 523.

[70] *Grodin v Grodin*, 102 Mich App 396 (1980).

pregnancy, causing her son's teeth to become discoloured. The court approached the issue as an extension of the concept of third party liability for injuries caused in utero, and found that Mrs Grodin's decision to continue taking the medication while pregnant could be assessed for its reasonableness.[71] Similar reasoning was adopted by the Supreme Court of New Hampshire in *Bonte v Bonte*, which involved an allegation of negligence by a child against his mother for failing to exercise reasonable care while crossing the road.[72] The Court noted that New Hampshire authority permitted a child to sue a third party for harm caused prior to birth, and that the parental immunity rule had been abandoned in the state. It was a straightforward move, from these propositions, to find that women can owe tort duties of care to their children in respect of their conduct during pregnancy. In response to the defendant's argument from public policy, the Court stated that a child has

> a cause of action against his or her mother for negligence that occurred after birth and that caused injury to the child, [and that] it is neither logical, nor in accord with our precedent, to disallow that child's claim against the mother for negligent conduct that caused injury to the child months, days, or mere hours before the child's birth.[73]

The Court refused to acknowledge that the unique character of the maternal–fetal relationship had any bearing on the decision as to whether a duty of care should be imposed, dismissing the defendant's assertion that its 'decision . . . deprives a mother of her right to control her life during pregnancy'.[74] In the court's view, its decision simply confirms that a pregnant woman 'is required to act with the appropriate duty of care, as we have consistently held other persons are required to act, with respect to the fetus'.[75]

As noted above, there are conflicting authorities in the US on the question of maternal liability. Turning now to the cases in which the courts have declined to impose a duty of care on a woman for her alleged negligence during pregnancy, it is clear that the unique character of the maternal–fetal relationship plays a defining role in the judicial approach to these claims. In *Stallman v Youngquist*,[76] a case involving injuries resulting from a motor vehicle accident, the Illinois Supreme Court held that a child could not bring an action against its mother for unintentional infliction of pre-natal injuries. The Court considered the reasoning in *Grodin v Grodin*, finding it unconvincing. The Court noted that the effect of the approach taken in *Grodin* is to treat 'a pregnant woman as a stranger to her developing fetus,'[77] and asserted that the *Grodin* court utterly failed to

---

[71] *Ibid*. The Court of Appeals reversed the decision of the Circuit Court (which granted the mother's motion for summary judgment) and remanded the case to the Circuit Court for a determination as to the 'reasonableness' of the mother's conduct in continuing to take the medication. It is interesting to note that this case commenced as a suit brought by the child against his mother's physician. During the discovery process, the physician claimed that he had cautioned the mother to stop taking the medication. In order to avert the possibility that a jury might find the mother to be liable for the child's injuries and refuse to award damages against the physician, the complaint was amended to include the mother as a defendant. As one commentator has noted, '[b]ut for the existence of a homeowner's policy with broad coverage, the suit against the mother would not have been filed' (John A Robertson, 'Procreative Liberty and the Control of Conception, Pregnancy and Childbirth' (1983) 69 *Virginia Law Review* 405, 441–42, fn 114).

[72] *Bonte v Bonte*, 616 A 2d 464 (NH 1992).

[73] *Ibid* 466.

[74] *Ibid*.

[75] *Ibid*.

[76] *Stallman v Youngquist*, 125 Ill 2d 267 (1988).

[77] *Ibid* 274.

address 'any of the profound implications'[78] which flow from its decision. The notion that a fetus might have a right 'assertable after birth against its mother would have serious ramifications for all women and their families, and for the way in which society views women and women's reproductive abilities'.[79] Because of the intimate and unique relation of woman to fetus, the imposition of a duty of care in the antenatal context would mean that any action taken by a pregnant woman could potentially be a basis for liability to her later-born child. The Court saw clearly that imposing a legal duty in this context would amount to acknowledging that the rights of a fetus prevail over those of its mother, and reasoned that to recognise

> [a] legal right of a fetus to begin life with a sound mind and body assertable against a mother would make a pregnant woman the guarantor of the mind and body of her child at birth. A legal duty to guarantee the mental and physical health of another has never before been recognized in law. Any action which negatively impacted on fetal development would be a breach of the pregnant woman's duty to her developing fetus. Mother and child would be legal adversaries from the moment of conception until birth.[80]

The Court went on to explain the problems inherent in any attempt to articulate a judicial standard of behaviour during pregnancy. These include the difficulty of imposing objective standards on everything the pregnant woman does or omits to do, and the spectre of juries basing liability on 'prejudicial and stereotypical beliefs'[81] about how pregnant women ought to behave.

Similar comments are found in other American authorities reaching the same conclusion on the duty-of-care question. The Texas Court of Appeals has held that the conclusion that no legal duty is owed by a pregnant woman to her fetus or later-born child is 'compelled by the unique relationship between a mother and her fetus, and ... the inherent differences between imposing a duty on entirely separate individuals and imposing the same duty on a person biologically joined to the injured party'.[82] The Supreme Judicial Court of Massachusetts has echoed this reasoning, noting that the unique maternal–fetal context allows for the drawing of a 'bright line' to distinguish between the conduct of a pregnant woman in relation to her later-born child and the issue of maternal liability to an existing child for negligence in the automobile accident context.[83]

Canadian law around maternal tort liability is governed primarily by case law, although one province has legislation on point, as is discussed in section II.B. below. In *Dobson (Litigation Guardian of) v Dobson*,[84] a child brought a claim against his mother (or, more accurately, his mother's insurer) for her allegedly negligent driving. Ms Dobson was involved in a collision, and her fetus was delivered prematurely that same day; Ryan Dobson was born with permanent mental and physical impairments, including cerebral palsy. The case advanced to the Supreme Court of Canada on the preliminary question of whether a pregnant woman owes a tort law duty of care to her fetus, meaning that there was no trial of the issues, nor were any factual findings made.

---

[78] *Ibid.*

[79] *Ibid* 275.

[80] *Ibid* 276.

[81] *Ibid* 278.

[82] *Chenault v Huie* (n 55) 476. The facts in *Chenault v Huie* are quite different from those in any of the other cases under discussion here. In this case, the child sought damages from her mother on the basis that her mother's use of alcohol and illegal narcotics during her pregnancy caused her to be born with cerebral palsy.

[83] *Remy v MacDonald*, 440 Mass 675 (2004) 683.

[84] *Dobson* (n 68).

The lower courts followed the reasoning articulated in the American cases (*Grodin v Grodin* and *Bonte v Bonte*), as well as in the Australian case *Lynch v Lynch*.[85] Like these courts, they took the approach that the narrow issue requiring consideration in this case was the potential liability of a pregnant woman for negligent driving causing injuries to her born-alive child.[86] Therefore, any policy considerations that might arise in cases involving negligence in 'lifestyle choices'[87] were irrelevant.[88] The Court of Appeal concluded that the duty of a pregnant woman toward her unborn fetus in the context of driving a motor vehicle is a part of her 'general duty to drive carefully', and that if a child suffers injury as a result of the mother's negligent driving during pregnancy, the child should be able to sue for compensation.[89] To hold otherwise would constitute a partial exception to a pregnant woman's general duty to drive with care.

A majority of the Supreme Court of Canada allowed Cynthia Dobson's appeal, holding that 'The public policy concerns raised in this case are of such a nature and magnitude that they clearly indicate that a legal duty of care cannot, and should not, be imposed by the courts upon a woman towards her foetus or subsequently born child'.[90] The policy concerns articulated by the Court fall into two categories: those relating to the privacy and autonomy rights of women,[91] and those relating to the difficulties inherent in articulating a judicial standard of conduct for pregnant women. With respect to the privacy and autonomy rights of women, the Court refused to impose a duty of care upon pregnant women, because 'To do so would result in very extensive and unacceptable intrusions into the bodily integrity, privacy and autonomy rights of women'.[92]

The Supreme Court's decision in *Dobson* was not unanimous. The dissent found that the two central objections to recognising the child plaintiff's right of action against his mother for pre-natal injuries – the uniqueness of the maternal–fetal relationship and the policy reasons in opposition to imposing a duty on a pregnant woman toward her fetus – are easily overcome in this case. For the dissent, this case was about the right of a born-alive child to sue his or her mother for pre-natally caused injuries. The parties to the action

---

[85] *Lynch v Lynch* (n 68).

[86] *Dobson (Litigation Guardian of) v Dobson*, 189 NBR (2d) 208, 148 DLR (4th) 332 (1997) (NBCA), revd *Dobson* (n 68).

[87] By this, Hoyt CJNB seems to have meant such things as cigarette smoking, consumption of alcohol and other legal or illegal substances, and the taking of or refusal to take medication.

[88] The Court made reference to the fact that this distinction has been employed in legislation in the UK: the Congenital Disabilities (Civil Liability) Act 1976 (n 56). The Act provides that mothers cannot be sued by their children for pre-natal injuries, with the exception of injuries caused by motor vehicle accidents. The specific reason for this exception is the existence of a mandatory insurance regime with respect to motor vehicles; the UK Law Commission that recommended the enactment of this legislation was of the view that permitting recovery by the child (to the extent of the policy limits) in this situation would decrease the anxiety pregnant women feel in relation to driving (Law Commission, *Report on Injuries to Unborn Children* (Law Com No 60, 1974)).

[89] The Court of Appeal found support for its decision in an Australian case (*Lynch v Lynch* (n 68)) and in some of the American jurisprudence.

[90] *Dobson* (n 68) para 76 (cited to SCR).

[91] *Ibid* para 78 (cited to SCR). While Cory J refers at length in his decision to such 'privacy and autonomy rights', which he refers to at one point as 'fundamental rights' (para 30), he does not explain the derivation or character of those rights.

[92] *Ibid* para 23 (cited to SCR). Although the facts of the case related solely to the question of negligent driving during pregnancy, the Court was concerned about the broader implications of any decision it might make, given the common law process; as Cory J noted, 'There is no rational and principled limit to the types of claims which may be brought if such a . . . duty of care were imposed upon pregnant women' (*ibid* para 28).

are two separate legal entities: a born-alive child and the child's mother. Neither the fetus as an entity, nor any rights or interests it may have are relevant. The dissent acknowledged the policy concerns that exist in this context,[93] but argued that the same concerns do not apply in this case, where the sole issue is the duty of a woman to another legal person – her child born alive. The decision is not whether the court can abrogate the rights of pregnant women in favour of the fetus, an entity with no legal rights of its own; rather, the question for the court is whether there are compelling policy reasons to extinguish the right of a child to sue for injuries caused by the negligence of his or her mother. The autonomy interests of pregnant women are not at issue in this context.[94] The fact that a pregnant woman owes a duty of care in respect of her driving to other users of the road precludes the argument that imposing a duty of care toward her fetus would limit the woman's freedom of action any more than it is already limited. This distinction – between acts which involve a duty of care to third parties and those that do not – restricts the potential liability of pregnant women to their fetuses and subsequently-born children, thereby alleviating the policy concerns that animated the majority.

B. Statutory jurisdictions

In its reasons in *Dobson*, the Supreme Court of Canada emphasised that the common law is not well suited to creating a circumscribed duty of care as was urged in this case, and invited legislative intervention in this area of private law. At least one province has taken up that invitation.[95] In November 2005, the Alberta Legislature passed the *Maternal Tort Liability Act*,[96] which provides:

> 4. A mother may be liable to her child for injuries suffered by her child on or after birth that were caused by the mother's use or operation of an automobile during her pregnancy if, at the time of that use or operation, the mother was insured under a contract of automobile insurance evidenced by a motor vehicle liability policy.

Section 5(1) of the Act provides that the liability created by section 4 is limited in quantum to the automobile insurance policy limits.

In introducing the Bill to the legislature, the Government indicated that its intent was to create a limited exception to the common law position set out in *Dobson*.[97] As the Member of Parliament presenting the Bill stated, 'The proposed provision relates only to motor vehicle accidents and does not change tort law in any way other than to provide for a narrow statutory exception to the common law concept of maternal tort immunity'.[98] Further, the Government's stated objective in passing this legislation was to

[93] Such as was the case in *Winnipeg Child and Family Services (Northwest Area) v G (DF)* [1997] 3 SCR 925, 152 DLR (4th) 193.
[94] As he put it, 'She was not legally free to operate a motor vehicle without due care. She did not have the freedom to drive carelessly. Therefore, it cannot be said that the imposition of a duty of care to her born alive child would restrict her freedom to drive' (*Dobson* (n 68) para 113 (cited to SCR)).
[95] 'However, unlike the courts, the legislature may, as did the Parliament of the United Kingdom, enact legislation in this field, subject to the limits imposed by the *Canadian Charter of Rights and Freedoms*' (*ibid* para 76 (cited to SCR)).
[96] Maternal Tort Liability Act, SA 2005, c M-7.5.
[97] *Dobson* (n 68).
[98] Alberta, Legislative Assembly, *Hansard* 26th Leg, 1st Sess, No 44 (16 November 2005) 1681 (Mr Oberle).

provide a means of accessing insurance funds to benefit the child, the mother and the family as a whole.[99]

Likewise, in much of the UK, maternal liability for pre-natal negligence is governed by statute: the Congenital Disabilities (Civil Liability) Act 1976[100] provides that third parties may be liable to a born child for pre-natal injuries,[101] and that, aside from one exceptional situation, mothers cannot be sued by their children for pre-natal injuries. The lone exception to maternal immunity is set out in section 2 of the Act:[102]

> A woman driving a motor vehicle when she knows (or ought reasonably to know) herself to be pregnant is to be regarded as being under the same duty to take care for the safety of her unborn child as the law imposes on her with respect to the safety of other people; and if in consequence of her breach of that duty her child is born with disabilities which would not otherwise have been present, those disabilities are to be regarded as damage resulting from her wrongful act and actionable accordingly at the suit of the child.

The 1976 Act was the result of a study by the Law Commission.[103] In light of the concerns raised by pending thalidomide litigation, the Commission was asked to advise Parliament 'what the nature and extent of civil liability for ante-natal injury should be'.[104] The Law Commission had initially argued that there should be no distinction made between pre-natal injury claims against third parties and against the child's mother. The consultation process led the Commissioners to reverse this opinion and to instead propose that the recommended legislation should exclude maternal liability for pre-natal conduct, but also carve out an exception to this general statutory immunity in respect of motor vehicle accidents to ensure that 'the child whose pre-natal injury was

---

[99] *Ibid.* The Government's reasons for proceeding with the Maternal Tort Liability Act are intriguing. In addressing the Bill, the Government stated that situations requiring legislation of this nature arise infrequently. Why, then, did the Government decide to pursue this route? In the spring of 2004, a Private Bill was introduced to the Private Bills Committee of the Alberta Legislature in an attempt to create an exception to the applicability of the *Dobson* case for Brooklyn Rewega. Brooklyn was born blind and suffering from cerebral palsy, allegedly as a result of a motor vehicle accident caused by her mother, who was five months pregnant with Brooklyn at the time (Alberta, Legislative Assembly, 'Private Bills Committee Transcripts' (20 April 2004), at <www. assembly.ab.ca/ISYS/LADDAR_files/docs/committees/pb/legislature_25/session_4/20040420_1200_01_pb. pdf>). Before the Private Bills Committee made a decision about whether to introduce the Bill to the Legislature, an election was called and the Legislature dissolved. In November 2005, both the Maternal Tort Liability Act (n 96) and the Brooklyn Hannah George Rewega Right of Civil Action Act, SA 2005, c 51, were debated and passed by the Alberta Legislature. In his comments on the Maternal Tort Liability Act, the Minister of Justice and Attorney General of Alberta stated that the Private Bill relating to Brooklyn Rewega addressed an issue of public policy, and that a private bill was not the appropriate place to deal with issues of public policy (Alberta, Legislative Assembly, *Hansard* 26th Leg, 1st Sess, No 47 (21 November 2005) 1772 (Mr Stevens)).

[100] The legislation applies in England, Wales and Northern Ireland, but not in Scotland (J Kenyon Mason and Graeme T Laurie, *Mason and McCall Smith's Law and Medical Ethics*, 8th edn (Oxford, Oxford University Press, 2011) 369).

[101] Congenital Disabilities (Civil Liability) Act 1976, s 1(1) provides that 'If a child is born disabled as a result of . . . an occurrence before its birth . . . and a person (other than the child's own mother) is under this section answerable to the child in respect of the occurrence, the child's disabilities are to be regarded as damage resulting from the wrongful act of that person and actionable accordingly at the suit of the child'.

[102] *Ibid* s 2.

[103] The Scottish Law Commission also considered and reported on the question of liability for antenatal injury, and concluded that the existing law was adequate to provide a remedy to a child injured while in utero (Scottish Law Commission, *Liability for Antenatal Injury* (Scot Law Com No 30, 1973)). It is clear in Scotland that a child can sue a third party for injuries caused in the pre-natal period (*Hamilton v Fife Health Board* (1993) SC 369), but the question of maternal liability for injuries caused during pregnancy has not been addressed.

[104] Law Commission, *Report on Injuries to Unborn Children* (n 88) para 1.

caused by his own mother's negligence should not be singled out as the one class of blameless victims of negligent road accidents to be unentitled to compensation'.[105]

C. Tort liability and reproductive autonomy

It is noteworthy that none of the courts that have *imposed* a duty of care in relation to the antenatal conduct of a pregnant woman has done so after a full consideration of the relevant policy considerations. The court that has come closest to doing so is the Wisconsin Supreme Court in *Tesar v Anderson*[106] – and there the Court was at pains to note the distinct legal approach taken by Wisconsin courts to the larger question of the duty of care and the implications of this approach for its decision on maternal liability.[107] Instead, the courts have limited their reasoning to the specific factual context, and left for another day the significant public policy issues related to the wider question of whether a child should be able to sue its mother for harms alleged to result from her choices and actions during pregnancy.

The context of decision making in pregnancy is complex, as is alluded to in the discussion around medicalisation in section I. above. Other contextual factors are important here as well, including society's approach to risk and to individual responsibility for health and well-being. Ours has been referred to as a 'risk society',[108] not because we face a higher level of danger or hazard, but because of our increasing anxiety about the future and about safety.[109] The paradoxical nature of this anxiety is captured in the fact that we live longer, healthier lives than at any point in the past, and that we also worry more about our health than did previous generations.[110] Concern about risk and health is fuelled in part by our access to vast amounts of information about risk, much of which is contradictory and unclear.[111]

What *is* clear is that in pregnancy, women are expected to do everything in their power to control risk and to minimise the possibility of harm to the fetus.[112] The volume of information available to pregnant women is immense, and expert recommendations are made, seemingly on a daily basis, on every conceivable aspect of a woman's behaviour during pregnancy: whether to consume alcohol, how much to exercise, which foods

---

[105] *Ibid* para 60. There are no cases on point in the UK; the legislation was enacted in anticipation of such litigation.

[106] *Tesar v Anderson* (n 67).

[107] As noted above (n 67), Wisconsin common law has adopted an approach to the duty of care that asks whether the defendant's carelessness subjects anyone to a risk of harm. If it does, then a duty is owed unless the court decides to rely on public policy reasons to dismiss the claim. The approach taken in Wisconsin is to hold that 'liability is the rule and relief for public policy reasons is the exception' (*Tesar v Anderson* (n 67) 250, quoting from *Cormican v Larrabee*, 171 Wis 2 d 309 (Ct App 1992) 318).

[108] Ulrich Beck, *Risk Society: Towards a New Modernity* (London, Sage Publications, 1992).

[109] Anthony Giddens, 'Risk and Responsibility' (1999) 62 *MLR* 1.

[110] See, eg, Keith J Petrie *et al*, 'Thoroughly Modern Worries: The Relationship of Worries about Modernity to Reported Symptoms, Health and Medical Care Utilization' (2001) 51 *Journal of Psychosomatic Research* 395; Keith J Petrie and Simon Wessely, 'Modern Worries, New Technology, and Medicine' (2002) 324 *British Medical Journal* 690.

[111] I have written about this in more detail in Erin Nelson, 'Informed Consent: Reasonableness, Risk and Disclosure' in Jocelyn Downie and Elaine Gibson (eds), *Health Law at the Supreme Court of Canada* (Toronto, Irwin Law, 2007) 145, 156.

[112] See, eg, Mullin (n 1) 75–76; Rebecca Kukla, *Mass Hysteria: Medicine, Culture, and Mother's Bodies* (Lanham, MD, Rowman and Littlefield, 2005) 19–21.

should and should not be included in a pregnant woman's diet, whether sexual activity should be avoided or may be engaged in safely.[113] There is virtually no aspect of pregnancy that has not been the subject of recommendations as to what pregnant women should do or refrain from doing, in order to protect the health of the fetus.

A contemporary tendency that runs in tandem with the increasing availability of information about health promotion and prevention of illness and disease is the notion of personal or individual responsibility for health. The expectation is that we will all use this information to improve and safeguard our own health.[114] In the case of pregnant women, this applies with even more force – the woman is responsible not only for her own health, but also for the health and well-being of her future child.[115] Ironically, perhaps, most women self-impose this responsibility, often to the extent of agreeing to invasive, risky procedures solely for the benefit of the fetus, and they feel guilty and blameworthy when things go wrong.[116] They read books, participate in online forums, enlist advice from their physicians, female friends, mothers and grandmothers.[117] It would be both inaccurate and unfair to claim that the burden of expectations that pregnant women perceive themselves to carry comes solely from external sources, but certainly the social expectation is that pregnant women will act as 'good mothers'.[118]

It is one thing for society to expect us to avoid health risks and take ownership over our own well-being, perhaps using the power of social norms to encourage individual responsibility and asserting that women owe beneficence-based moral duties to the fetus.[119] But does law have a role to play here? Women may choose to regulate and modify their own conduct during pregnancy, but should law participate in that project by assigning liability for bad outcomes perceived to result from women's conduct during pregnancy? If so, to what extent is a pregnant woman's choice of activities circumscribed by the fact of her decision to reproduce? Is she free to engage in risky conduct, such as driving, while pregnant? Or, if she chooses to do so, could she be held liable for injuries suffered by her child (once born) due to her negligent conduct while pregnant?

The question of tort liability to one's later-born child for potentially harmful conduct during pregnancy is related to reproductive autonomy in that recognition of such liability creates the potential for the fact of pregnancy (or, the decision to reproduce) to constrain a

---

[113] Deborah Lupton, 'Risk and the Ontology of Pregnant Embodiment' in Deborah Lupton (ed), *Risk and Sociocultural Theory: New Directions and Perspectives* (Cambridge, Cambridge University Press, 1999) 59, 64; Karalyn McDonald, Lisa H Amir and Mary-Ann Davey, 'Maternal Bodies and Medicines: A Commentary on Risk and Decision-Making of Pregnant and Breastfeeding Women and Health Professionals' (2011) 11 (Supp 5) *BioMed Central Public Health* S5.

[114] See, eg, Robert Steinbrook, 'Imposing Personal Responsibility for Health' (2006) 355 *New England Journal of Medicine* 753; Michelle M Mello and Meredith B Rosenthal, 'Wellness Programs and Lifestyle Discrimination – The Legal Limits' (2008) 359 *New England Journal of Medicine* 192; Harald Schmidt, Kristin Voigt and Daniel Wikler, 'Carrots, Sticks, and Health Care Reform – Problems with Wellness Incentives' (2010) 362 *New England Journal of Medicine* e3.

[115] Lupton refers to the pregnant woman being perceived as 'doubly at risk and . . . portrayed as doubly responsible, for two bodies' (Lupton (n 113) 63).

[116] See, eg, McDonald *et al* (n 113) 2; Bernie Reid *et al*, 'A Meta-Synthesis of Pregnant Women's Decision-Making Processes with Regard to Antenatal Screening for Down Syndrome' (2009) 69 *Social Science & Medicine* 1561. Kukla (n 112) notes that this notion of maternal responsibility for pregnancy has a long history.

[117] Pam Lowe *et al*, '"Making it all Normal": The Role of the Internet in Problematic Pregnancy' (2009) 19 *Qualitative Health Research* 1476.

[118] See, eg, *ibid*; Mullin (n 1) 76.

[119] See, eg, Lyerly *et al* (n 49); McCullough and Chervenak, 'A Critical Analysis' (n 39).

woman's behaviour. The threat of liability does not permit the exercise of immediate or direct control over a pregnant woman's behaviour.[120] But the prospect of facing litigation for decisions taken during pregnancy might lead a pregnant woman to police her behaviour, leading to much the same result. Activities that are ordinarily irrelevant to private law obligations – such as agreeing to medical treatment or testing, engaging in exercise, deciding what to eat and drink – become relevant only because a woman is pregnant.

Arguably, maternal liability in the limited context of operating a motor vehicle does not raise the same implications for autonomy, given that pregnant women are subject to a duty of care to others when they drive, regardless whether their later-born child may have a claim against them as well. The assumption that grounds this argument is that the only time a woman might be liable to her child for her negligence in the operation of a motor vehicle is in a situation in which she would also (potentially, at least) be liable to others. But it is worth questioning this assumption. Although intended to apply narrowly to the motor vehicle context,[121] the Alberta legislation could lead to the imposition of liability in cases where the legislature arguably did not intend it to. For example, the question of what constitutes 'use' of an automobile for purposes of liability is subject to interpretation.[122] Could travelling as a passenger in a car count as 'use'? Could a woman be liable to her child for injuries suffered in utero because of her careless decision to drive with a third party whom she knows to be a less than adequate driver, or who had too much to drink at a party and then drove home? What if a pregnant woman drives a motorcycle, or an all-terrain vehicle, or some similarly more 'risky' form of transport than a car? Will she be liable for using a less safe mode of transport while pregnant, even if she operates that vehicle with reasonable care?

Tort liability for her conduct during pregnancy clearly has the potential to infringe on a woman's bodily integrity; as such, it should be approached from a perspective of strong respect for reproductive autonomy. Imposing liability on a woman based on her nutritional habits or exercise regime (too much or not enough) clearly engages her ability to decide for herself what will be done with and to her body. Liability for one's conduct in the use or operation of an automobile may be an exception to the inclusion of tort duties within the bodily integrity aspect of reproductive autonomy, as restricting one's freedom to drive carelessly (or ride with certain other drivers) does not necessarily or clearly implicate bodily integrity. Some aspects of tort liability for conduct during pregnancy thus fall within the core of the model, and others slightly outside the core. Either way, respect for reproductive autonomy demands that we think carefully about

---

[120] Adrian Whitfield asserts that 'There is an important distinction between exercising control, which is an infringement of individual rights, and allowing freedom of action but making the actor pay for it if he or she breaks a duty to others' (Adrian Whitfield, 'Common Law Duties to Unborn Children' (1993) 1 *Medical Law Review* 28, 51).

[121] Not as narrowly drafted as the UK statute, which specifies that liability relates to '*driving* a motor vehicle' (Congenital Disabilities (Civil Liabilities) Act 1976, s 2 (emphasis added)). The Alberta statute, by contrast, refers to '*use or operation of* an automobile' (Maternal Tort Liability Act (n 96) s 4 (emphasis added)).

[122] In *Herbison v Lumbermens Mutual Casualty Co*, 76 OR (3d) 81, 255 DLR (4th) 75 (2006) (Ont CA), a more questionable 'use' of a motor vehicle was found by the Ontario Court of Appeal to be a use within the meaning of motor vehicle insurance legislation. In this case, a hunter (Wolfe) negligently shot and injured his hunting companion (Herbison). At the time of the shooting, Wolfe was not in his car, but the headlights were on and the vehicle was running. At issue was whether damages could be sought by Herbison from Wolfe's automobile insurer. Herbison was unsuccessful at trial, but the Ontario Court of Appeal ordered the insurer to indemnify Herbison. The Supreme Court of Canada allowed the insurer's appeal (*Lumbermen's Mutual Casualty Co v Herbison* 2007 SCC 47, [2007] 3 SCR 393).

imposing private obligations on women for their actions while pregnant, and that we turn our attention to the broader implications of imposing such obligations.

While tort law has not become a popular means of regulating women's conduct in pregnancy,[123] some American legal scholars nonetheless advocate broad duties of care in (and in some cases, prior to) pregnancy.[124] Kate Wellington has commented on the position that Australian law ought to take on the question of maternal liability for pre-natal conduct. She suggests that imposing such liability, not just in respect of motor vehicle accidents but in general, is in keeping with 'well-established principles of tort law'.[125] Should public opinion be opposed to the imposition of liability, legislation can override the common law and resolve the concern. The argument, put succinctly, is that tort law principles are capable of dealing with the policy concerns (including maternal autonomy). There is little, if any, risk of constraining women's behaviour unduly simply by permitting compensation for children who are harmed by their mother's conduct during pregnancy.[126] The argument is captured well in the following excerpt:

> The dangers to an unborn child of its mother smoking, drinking, putting excessive strain on her body or engaging in unprotected sex are well known in the community. Further, in assessing the calculus of negligence, there are simple and inexpensive alternatives to each activity: abstaining from smoking and drinking, doing light exercise, and having protected sex. The question of why *should* a mother be liable for damage caused by such activities could easily become: why *shouldn't* she? Every person has the right to make choices about their daily life when those choices affect only the person who makes them. But when those choices are negligently made and cause injury to a person with recognised legal rights, the principles of tort law assign responsibility to the person who makes the choice . . .[127]

As with Justice Major's dissenting reasons in *Dobson* (and it is worth noting that even he did not appear to agree that maternal liability should extend to contexts of women's lives where they do not owe a corresponding duty of care to others), this description adeptly elides the context in which the pregnant woman/tortfeasor finds herself. Major J says that a lawsuit brought by a child against his or her mother for the consequences of her behaviour while pregnant has nothing to do with pregnancy. And Wellington's assertions – that the smoker should simply stop smoking, for example – seem to suggest an approach that similarly ignores reality. To her claim that it is well known in the com-

---

[123] Mathieu describes tort law as a 'relatively new and untested way of responding to prenatal harm after the fact' (Mathieu (n 62) 139).

[124] See, eg, Robertson (n 71) 438, where Robertson asserts that 'Although [a woman] is under no obligation to invite the fetus in or to allow it to remain, once she has done these things she assumes obligations to the fetus that limit her freedom over her body'. For Robertson, these obligations 'may require [a pregnant woman] to avoid work, recreation, and medical care choices that are hazardous to the fetus. They also obligate her to preserve her health for the fetus' sake or even allow established therapies to be performed on an affected fetus. Finally, they require that she undergo prenatal screening where there is reason to believe that this screening may identify congenital defects correctable with available therapies.' (*ibid* 450) See also Margery W Shaw, 'The Potential Plaintiff: Preconception and Prenatal Torts' in Aubrey Milunsky and George J Annas (eds), *Genetics and the Law II*, 2nd edn (New York, Plenum Press, 1980); Douglas E Carroll, 'Parental Liability for Preconception Negligence: Do Parents Owe a Legal Duty to their Potential Children?' (1986) 22 *California Western Law Review* 289; John A Robertson, *Children of Choice: Freedom and the New Reproductive Technologies* (Princeton, NJ, Princeton University Press, 1994).

[125] Kate Wellington, 'Maternal Liability for Prenatal Injury: The Preferable Approach for Australian Law?' (2010) 18 *Tort Law Review* 89, 89.

[126] The suggestion being that not all restrictions on a pregnant woman's behaviour are undue; that it is indeed legitimate to constrain, by the threat of liability, at least some aspects of pregnant women's behaviour.

[127] Wellington (n 125) 94.

munity that smoking is dangerous to the fetus, one could point out that it is equally well known in the community that it can be very difficult indeed to give up a substance to which one has become addicted. Who are the mothers in the imagination of the judges and commentators? Is it being assumed that these pregnant women simply do not care how their actions affect their future children? Or that they are selfishly pursuing their own interests and cannot be bothered to consider how it might affect the fetus?

It is worth noting here as well the limited utility of this use of the private law. From a practical perspective, the imposition of tort obligations in this context is pointless vis-à-vis the family unit unless there is insurance to cover the claim.[128] The likelihood that potential liability would be more important in influencing a woman's behavior than her concern for both her own well-being and that of the fetus is slim. The only outcome, in the absence of insurance, would be to transfer funds from the mother's bank account to an account held in trust for the child, to be administered by the mother, father or other guardian(s) for the benefit of the child. Arguably, all that is achieved by this approach is the formalising of blame. It hardly seems worth the costs (both of litigation and of potentially disrupting the family). A more appropriate response to the needs of children with special needs, whether injured in utero or not, is to consider how we can provide resources and support to families who need them.

III. INTERVENTION IN THE LIVES OF PREGNANT WOMEN

In the previous section, I considered the use of private law in responding to women's decisions during pregnancy; in this section, the focus is on State action that threatens the ability of pregnant women autonomously to refuse recommended medical treatment, and on State responses to reproduction by certain classes of women.[129]

Two types of State action are of concern here. First is the legal imposition of medical care or other treatment intended to protect the fetus from the actions or decisions of the pregnant woman. Where a pregnant woman refuses medically-recommended care, State intervention can take the form of court-ordered medical treatment. Second is the use of public law, including child welfare law and criminal law, to control the behaviour of pregnant women who are engaging in practices alleged to be harmful to the fetus. Most often, this arises where a pregnant woman is addicted to a substance that is (or is believed to be) harmful to the fetus. The interventions in question are potentially wide-ranging

---

[128] As noted by the Bar Council in its submission to the Law Commission regarding pre-natal injuries, families will often not be in a position to pay compensation to one child without causing hardship to other family members. See Law Commission, *Report on Injuries to Unborn Children* (n 88) para 55, quoting from the Bar Council's submission.

[129] A number of commentators have noted that State intervention in the lives of pregnant women is almost exclusively directed at women who are addicted to drugs, at poor women and women of colour: see, eg, Dorothy E Roberts, 'Punishing Drug Addicts Who Have Babies: Women of Color, Equality, and the Right of Privacy' (1991) 104 *Harvard Law Review* 1419; Dorothy E Roberts, 'Racism and Patriarchy in the Meaning of Motherhood' (1993) 1 *American University Journal of Gender & the Law* 1; Françoise Baylis, 'Dissenting with the Dissent: *Winnipeg Child and Family Services (Northwest Area) v G (DF)*' (1998) 36 *Alberta Law Review* 785; Lynn M Paltrow, 'Punishment and Prejudice: Judging Drug-Using Pregnant Women' in Julia E Hanigsberg and Sara Ruddick (eds), *Mother Troubles: Rethinking Contemporary Maternal Dilemmas* (Boston, MA, Beacon Press, 1999) 59; Sanda Rodgers, 'The Legal Regulation of Women's Reproductive Capacity in Canada' in Jocelyn Downie, Timothy Caulfield and Colleen M Flood (eds), *Canadian Health Law and Policy*, 2nd edn (Markham, Butterworths, 2002) 331.

and can include criminal prosecution, sentencing practices intended to restrict the woman's access to the substance to which she is addicted, and the use of child welfare or mental health legislation to attempt to confine or otherwise constrain the behaviour of pregnant addicts.

All forms of State intervention in pregnancy purportedly serve the same aim – to protect the fetus who may suffer harm as a result of the pregnant woman's behaviour, whether that consists of refusing recommended medical interventions or ingesting a potentially feto-toxic substance. Commendable though that objective may be, all of these interventions involve, to a greater or lesser degree, violations of the pregnant woman's bodily integrity and reproductive autonomy. If a woman is required to submit to a Caesarean section because, in her physician's opinion, the baby cannot be safely delivered otherwise, the violation is particularly profound. The same goes for detention in a healthcare facility or incarceration. But even in the case of less invasive measures, it must be borne in mind that the woman's bodily integrity is implicated. Respect for women's reproductive autonomy in this context thus requires that the State proceed with great caution.

A. Compelling medical intervention in pregnancy

Coercive medical intervention in pregnancy occurs when a woman's physician, hospital or healthcare team seeks a court order compelling her to undergo a procedure to which she has withheld her consent. Procedures for which orders have been sought in the past include Caesarean sections,[130] blood transfusions[131] and intrauterine transfusions,[132] but as Lisa Ikemoto has noted, the same reasoning used in these cases 'could be used to support other court-ordered fetal therapies'.[133] Another way in which the law can frustrate a woman's attempt to make her own decisions about the course of her medical care is by the invalidation of advance healthcare directives by operation of law during preg-

---

[130] See, eg, *Jefferson v Griffin Spalding County Hospital Authority*, 274 SE 2d 457 (Ga 1981); *Re Madyun*, 114 Daily Washington L Rptr 2233 (DC Sup Ct 1986); *Re AC*, 533 A 2d 611 (DC App 1987) revd 573 A 2d 1235 (DC App 1990); *Re Baby R*, 30 BCLR (2d) 237, 53 DLR (4th) 69 (1988) (BCSC); *Re Baby Boy Doe*, 632 NE 2d 326 (Ill App Ct 1994); *Pemberton v Tallahassee Memorial Regional Medical Center, Inc*, 66 F Supp 2d 1247 (Fla Dist Ct 1999). See also Veronika EB Kolder, Janet Gallagher and Michael T Parsons, 'Court-Ordered Obstetrical Interventions' (1987) 316 *New England Journal of Medicine* 1192.
[131] See, eg, *Re President and Directors of Georgetown College Inc*, 331 F 2d 1010 (DC Cir 1964); *Raleigh Fitkin Paul Morgan Memorial Hospital v Anderson*, 201 A 2d 537 (NJ Sup Ct 1964); *Re Jamaica Hospital*, 491 NYS 2d 898 (Sup Ct 1985); *Crouse Irving Memorial Hospital Inc v Paddock*, 485 NYS 2d 443 (Sup Ct 1985); *Re Fetus Brown*, 689 NE 2d 397 (Ill App Ct 1997).
[132] Kolder *et al* (n 130).
[133] Lisa C Ikemoto, 'The Code of Perfect Pregnancy: At the Intersection of the Ideology of Motherhood, the Practice of Defaulting to Science, and the Interventionist Mindset of Law' (1992) 53 *Ohio State Law Journal* 1205, 1251. Ikemoto notes that there have also been cases involving forced cerclage (a surgical procedure used to keep the cervix closed during pregnancy in women at high risk of miscarriage or premature delivery due to incompetent cervix). The same reasoning could also theoretically apply with respect to pre-natal testing and even in utero fetal therapies (Robertson, *Children of Choice* (n 124) 161 ('[a]lthough the original high expectations for in utero surgery have not been borne out, more effective operations can be expected in the future'); Barbara Katz Rothman, *Recreating Motherhood: Ideology and Technology in a Patriarchal Society* (New York, Norton, 1989) 167; Rosalind Pollack Petchesky, *Abortion and Woman's Choice: The State, Sexuality, and Reproductive Freedom* (Boston, MA, Northeastern University Press, 1990) 356–57; Krista L Newkirk, 'State-compelled Fetal Surgery: The Viability Test is Not Viable' (1998) 4 *William and Mary Journal of Women and the Law* 467, 470–71; Maggie Jones, 'A Miracle and Yet', *New York Times Magazine*, 15 July 2001, 39).

nancy.[134] Such statutory provisions also fall within the scope of coercive medical treatment, as they permit the provision of treatment in spite of a clear and relevant advance directive instructing otherwise.

Canadian, British and American courts have all faced applications requesting that a pregnant woman be compelled to submit to some type of obstetrical care (most often a Caesarean section in spite of her express refusal to consent to the procedure. Many (if not all) of these cases follow a predictable pattern – the procedure is authorised by the lower court, and the authorisation is later (usually too late) reversed by an appellate court.

A number of American courts have considered the legitimacy of compelled medical treatment during pregnancy. The appellate level courts that have heard cases of this nature have uniformly held that a competent refusal of treatment by a pregnant woman must be respected – although some have left open the possibility that, in the right case, treatment for the benefit of the fetus could take place in spite of a refusal by a competent pregnant woman.[135] In spite of this relative consistency among jurisdictions at the appellate level,[136] lower courts have continued to permit medical intervention, and it is important to keep in mind that the reported cases on point may only be the 'tip of the iceberg'.[137] It is also essential to acknowledge that these cases are often heard on an urgent basis, meaning that there may not be time to explore and consider the relevant appellate authorities.[138]

The American cases begin with *Re AC*, almost certainly the most well-known of the forced Caesarean section cases.[139] In *Re AC*, the lower court authorised the performance of a Caesarean section on a woman at 26 weeks' gestation. She had been in remission from osteosarcoma when she became pregnant, but after she experienced some trouble breathing at 25 weeks' gestation, a metastatic tumour was found on her lung. Given the poor prognosis for a fetus born that early, the pregnant woman (Angela Carder) emphasised to her physicians that her comfort should be the priority, and she agreed to a course of palliative treatment. Her condition deteriorated very rapidly, and it became apparent that she did not have much longer to live. The hospital administrators successfully applied for a court order to permit delivery of the fetus by Caesarean section. When Angela was told of the court order, she initially agreed to the surgery, but then revoked her consent. The surgery went ahead; the fetus lived for approximately two and a half hours; Angela for two days.

---

[134] See, eg, Susan E Hickman *et al*, 'The POLST (Physician Orders for Life-Sustaining Treatment) Paradigm to Improve End-of-Life Care: Potential State Legal Barriers to Implementation' (2008) 36 *Journal of Law, Medicine and Ethics* 119; Charles P Sabatino, 'The Evolution of Health Care Advance Planning Law and Policy' (2010) 88 *Milbank Quarterly* 211, 221. This seems to be a uniquely American phenomenon. I am not aware of similar provisions in any Canadian advance directive legislation. For discussion of these provisions, see Katherine A Taylor, 'Compelling Pregnancy at Death's Door' (1997) 7 *Columbia Journal of Gender and Law* 85; Amy Lynn Jerdee, 'Breaking Through the Silence: Minnesota's Pregnancy Presumption and the Right to Refuse Medical Treatment' (2000) 84 *Minnesota Law Review* 971.

[135] See, eg, *Re AC* (1990) (n 130); *Re Baby Boy Doe* (n 130); *Re Fetus Brown* (n 131).

[136] In *Burton v Florida*, 49 SO 3d 263 (Fla App 2010), the Court noted that Florida law provides for the possibility of overriding this right where the state has an interest, sufficiently compelling in nature, to warrant that extraordinary step.

[137] Rachel Roth, *Making Women Pay: The Hidden Costs of Fetal Rights* (Ithaca, NY, Cornell University Press, 2000) 95.

[138] *Re Baby Boy Doe* (n 130) 329–30.

[139] *Re AC* (1990) (n 130).

On appeal, the DC Court of Appeals held that where a competent pregnant woman refuses recommended medical treatment, her decision will control 'in virtually all cases'.[140] Although it did not rule out the possibility that a state interest could 'ever prevail over the interests of a pregnant patient,'[141] the Court noted

> that it would be an extraordinary case indeed in which a court might ever be justified in overriding the patient's wishes and authorizing a major surgical procedure such as a caesarean section. Throughout this opinion we have stressed that the patient's wishes, once they are ascertained, must be followed in 'virtually all cases,' . . . unless there are 'truly extraordinary or compelling reasons to override them' . . . Indeed, some may doubt that there could ever be a situation extraordinary or compelling enough to justify a massive intrusion into a person's body, such as a caesarean section, against that person's will. Whether such a situation may someday present itself is a question that we need not strive to answer here.[142]

Although the door is left open (in theory at least) to a future case where the outcome would be different, *Re AC* is widely considered to establish a strong precedent in favour of a pregnant woman's right to determine the course of her own medical treatment.[143]

The Illinois Appellate Court has also considered whether a woman can be forced to submit to medical treatment for the benefit of the fetus. In the context of the refusal of both a Caesarean section[144] and, later, a blood transfusion, the Court upheld the pregnant woman's decisional authority in relation to her medical care. In *Re Fetus Brown*,[145] Ms Brown had surgery to remove a urethral mass when she was approximately 34½ weeks pregnant. She lost more blood than expected during the surgery and her haemoglobin level dropped to a precarious level, endangering her life as well as that of her fetus. At the state's request, temporary custody of the fetus was granted to the administrator of the hospital and blood transfusions were administered. Ms Brown later gave birth to a healthy baby. Although the factual issues were moot by the time of the appellate hearing (as was the case in *Re AC*), the Court nonetheless agreed to hear the case.[146] In concluding that the lower court erred in granting the petition, the Court held that 'the State may not override a pregnant woman's competent treatment decision, including refusal of recommended invasive medical procedures, to potentially save the life of the viable fetus'.[147]

In spite of what appear to be clear and important authorities holding that medical treatment may not be forced on pregnant women who refuse it, these cases continue to surface in the US. In 1996, Laura Pemberton, a Florida mother, was compelled by court order to submit to a Caesarean section despite her refusal to consent. Ms Pemberton had had a previous Caesarean delivery in which a vertical incision was used, meaning that the risk of uterine rupture in a subsequent labour was significantly higher than would be

---

[140] *Ibid* 1237.

[141] *Ibid* 1252.

[142] *Ibid* 1252.

[143] The Court's refusal to rule out any possibility that a case might arise in which fetal interests might prevail over those of the pregnant woman's has been described as leaving only a 'theoretical possibility' that such a case might arise (Howard Minkoff and Anne Drapkin Lyerly, 'Samantha Burton and the Rights of Pregnant Women Twenty Years after *Re A.C.*' (2010) 40(6) *Hastings Center Report* 13, 14).

[144] *Re Baby Boy Doe* (n 130).

[145] *Re Fetus Brown* (n 131).

[146] On the basis that the 'remaining legal issue [satisfied] the public policy exception to the Illinois mootness doctrine' (*ibid* 400).

[147] *Ibid* 405.

the case for a typical Caesarean incision. Ms Pemberton was unable to find a physician who would agree to allow her to attempt to deliver her second child vaginally, but did manage to find a midwife who would attend her home labour. During the course of her labour, Ms Pemberton went to the emergency room of Tallahassee Memorial Regional Medical Center, seeking intravenous (IV) fluids as she was becoming dehydrated. Once the hospital staff became aware of the situation, Ms Pemberton was advised that she needed a Caesarean section. She refused, saying she wished to have IV fluids and to return home to deliver the baby. She and her husband left the hospital shortly thereafter, against medical advice. In the meanwhile, the hospital had initiated a legal process that ultimately resulted in Ms Pemberton being returned to the hospital against her wishes and undergoing a court-ordered Caesarean section.[148]

In January 2004, a Pennsylvania court granted an order permitting a local hospital to 'force a woman to deliver a baby via Caesarean section against her will'.[149] The surgical delivery was recommended because of concerns about fetal macrosomia.[150] When the medical team could not persuade Amber Marlowe to consent to a Caesarean, they sought a court order to grant the hospital guardianship over the fetus. Ms Marlowe, who had left the hospital prior to the order being obtained, went on to deliver a healthy baby (her seventh) vaginally at another hospital.[151] In 2009, a Florida woman who was 25 weeks pregnant and was showing signs of premature labour was confined to hospital when her obstetrician successfully sought a court order compelling her to 'submit to any medical treatment deemed necessary by the attending obstetrician, including detention in the hospital for enforcement of bed rest, administration of intra-venous medications, and anticipated surgical delivery of the fetus'.[152] Again, the lower court's order was reversed on appeal. The Court noted, however, that if the state had shown that the fetus was viable (there was no evidence before the lower court on this point), it would have been open to the court to find that the state's interest in a viable fetus was sufficiently compelling 'to override the pregnant woman's constitutional right to the control of her person, including her right to refuse medical treatment'.[153]

American state prosecutors have stepped in to the medical treatment arena as well: Melissa Rowland was charged with murder when one of her twins was stillborn after she refused to undergo a Caesarean section.[154] The murder charge was ultimately dropped, but

---

[148] *Pemberton v Tallahassee* (n 130). This judgment is a trial level judgment in the lawsuit Ms Pemberton brought against the Tallahassee Memorial Regional Medical Center; the proceedings that led to the lawsuit are described in the reasons.

[149] David Weiss, 'Court Delivers Controversy' *The Times Leader* (Wilkes-Barre, 16 January 2004) 1A.

[150] Macrosomia is sometimes defined as synonymous with 'large for gestational age' and sometimes on the basis of absolute standards (birthweight over 4,000g/8 lbs 13 oz) (RA Sack, 'The Large Infant: A Study of Maternal, Obstetric, Fetal, and Newborn Characteristics; Including a Long-Term Pediatric Follow-up' (1969) 104 *American Journal of Obstetrics & Gynecology* 195; Ira M Golditch and Kathryn Kirkman, 'The Large Fetus: Management and Outcome' (1978) 52 *Obstetrics & Gynecology* 26; Mark E Boyd, Robert H Usher and Frances H McLean, 'Fetal Macrosomia: Prediction, Risks, Proposed Management' (1983) 61 *Obstetrics & Gynecology* 715).

[151] After Ms Marlowe left the hospital, an order was granted to permit the hospital to act as guardian of the fetus and deliver the baby by Caesarean section should she return to the hospital (Weiss (n 149)).

[152] *Burton v Florida* (n 136).

[153] *Ibid* 266. The court noted that the state would also have to satisfy it that the method through which the state interest was to be pursued is the least intrusive means.

[154] Lynn M Paltrow, 'Coercive Medicine' (*National Advocates for Pregnant Women*, 21 March 2004), at <http://advocatesforpregnantwomen.org/file/Coercive_Medicine.pdf>.

Rowland entered guilty pleas to two charges of child endangerment for 'using drugs during pregnancy';[155] ultimately she was sentenced to 18 months' probation.[156]

Cases involving forced medical treatment have also been brought before the English courts. Some of the early cases suggest that there may be instances in which a woman's right to make her own treatment decisions could be abrogated during pregnancy.[157] In one of the early cases, *Tameside & Glossop Acute Services Unit v CH*,[158] the Court authorised a Caesarean delivery pursuant to section 63 of the Mental Health Act 1983 (should the procedure become necessary and the pregnant woman refuse to give consent), on the basis that the surgery was routine 'treatment' for the woman's paranoid schizophrenia.[159] In *Norfolk and Norwich NHS Trust v W*,[160] the pregnant woman arrived at the hospital in a state of arrested labour, denying that she was pregnant. While she was not found to be suffering from a mental disorder, the examining psychiatrist could not conclude that she was capable of balancing the information given to her in arriving at a decision about whether to accept or refuse treatment. Johnson J held that the pain and emotional distress of labour, combined with W's 'particular mental history,' rendered her 'incapable of weighing up the considerations that were involved'.[161]

During the hearing of *Norfolk and Norwich NHS Trust v W*, Johnson J was asked to decide a similar application – *Rochdale Healthcare NHS Trust v C*.[162] In spite of having no opportunity to meet or speak with Ms C, and after a very brief *ex parte* hearing that included no psychiatric opinion as to Ms C's capacity, he 'overruled [Ms C's] obstetrician's finding of competence'.[163] Ms C had previously undergone a Caesarean section, and told the obstetrician that she would rather die than have the surgery again.[164] Johnson J held that

> [t]he patient was in the throes of labour with all that is involved in terms of pain and emotional stress. I concluded that a patient who could, in those circumstances, speak in terms which seemed to accept the inevitability of her own death, was not a patient who was able properly to weigh-up the considerations that arose so as to make any valid decision, about anything of even the most trivial kind, surely still less one which involved her own life.[165]

---

[155] Katha Pollitt, 'Pregnant and Dangerous' (26 April 2004) 278(16) *The Nation* 9.

[156] KaiserNetwork.org, 'Woman Who Gave Birth to Stillborn Infant After Allegedly Refusing C-Section Sentenced to 18 Months of Probation' (*Illinois Federation for Right to Life*, 30 April 2004), at <http://ifrl.org/IFRLDailyNews/040430/2/>.

[157] In *Re T (Adult: Refusal of Treatment)* [1992] EWCA Civ 18, [1993] Fam 95, Lord Donaldson concluded that a competent patient is entitled to make his or her own treatment choices, however ill-advised the choice might seem. He allowed, however, that there exists a 'possible qualification' where 'the choice may lead to the death of a viable fetus. That is not this case and, if and when it arises, the courts will be faced with a novel problem of considerable legal and ethical complexity.' (*ibid* para 3) In *Re S (Adult) (Refusal of Medical Treatment)* [1993] Fam 123, the Family Division of the English High Court (Sir Stephen Brown) ordered that a Caesarean section be carried out in spite of the refusal of the pregnant woman. In this case, the woman had been in labour for more than two days, and the fetus was in a transverse lie, with its elbow projecting through the woman's cervix. The medical evidence accepted by the court was that the situation of both woman and fetus was extremely grave, and that both could die if the surgery was not performed.

[158] *Tameside & Glossop Acute Services Unit v CH* [1996] Fam Law 353.

[159] In order to assert jurisdiction to grant the order, the trial judge felt it necessary to fit the proposed treatment within the Mental Health Act, which meant that the treatment had to be treatment for the woman's mental disorder.

[160] *Norfolk and Norwich NHS Trust v W* [1996] 2 FLR 613.

[161] *Ibid* 616.

[162] *Rochdale Healthcare NHS Trust v C* [1997] 1 FCR 274.

[163] Jackson (n 2) 137.

[164] *Rochdale NHS Trust v C* (n 162) 275.

[165] *Ibid.*

Despite the early case law, the English Court of Appeal has now clearly articulated that

> a competent woman who has the capacity to decide may, for religious reasons, other reasons, for rational or irrational reasons or for no reason at all, choose not to have medical intervention, even though the consequence may be the death or serious handicap of the child she bears, or her own death.[166]

In *Re MB*, the Court of Appeal noted that English law on this point is clear, and is contrary to the views expressed in earlier cases.[167] *Re MB* involved a judicially-authorised Caesarean section; the authorisation was upheld by the Court of Appeal on the basis that Ms MB was not competent to refuse the procedure because she had a needle phobia that rendered her temporarily incompetent. Ms MB had initially consented to the surgery, but refused to consent to the administration of anaesthetic. The Court took the view that the medical evidence established that what was preventing Ms MB from giving consent at the point at which the procedure was to be performed was her abnormal fear of needles, which caused her to panic. As the physician explained:

> I had no doubt at all that she fully understood the need for a caesarian section and consented to it. However in the final phase she got into a panic and said she could not go on. If she were calmed down I thought she would consent to the procedure. At the moment of panic, however, her fear dominated all . . . It seemed to me that at the actual point she was not capable of making a decision at all, in the sense of being able to hold information in the balance and make a choice. At that moment the needle or mask dominated her thinking and made her quite unable to consider anything else . . .[168]

The fact that Ms MB understood the need for and gave her consent to the procedure itself was a critical consideration for the Court. In reviewing the case law on point, Lady Butler-Sloss noted that, with one exception,[169] in all of the cases where the courts have been asked to authorise a Caesarean section over the objections of the pregnant woman, the court found that the woman 'lack[ed] the capacity to consent to or refuse treatment'.[170] Likewise, in *Re MB*, the Court concluded that Ms MB 'was incapable of making a decision at all . . . she was temporarily incompetent'.[171]

In its most recent decision on point,[172] the English Court of Appeal confirmed its decision in *Re MB*. The Court concluded that a competent pregnant woman is entitled to make her own healthcare decisions, and that a surgical procedure such as a Caesarean section should not be carried out absent her consent. Ms S had arrived at a physician's office in order to register as a patient. She was 36 weeks pregnant at the time, and had not received any obstetrical care during her pregnancy. She was diagnosed with pre-eclampsia, and was informed that she required urgent attention (including immediate induction of labour), without which her health and life, and the health and life of her baby, were in real danger. Ms S understood the risks and the medical advice, but declined to seek the recommended treatment, as she wanted her baby to be born without such intervention. Ms S was

---

[166] *Re MB (An Adult: Medical Treatment)* [1997] EWCA Civ 3093 para 30, [1997] 2 FLR 426, 434.
[167] See, eg, *Re S* (n 157); *Re T* (n 157).
[168] *Re MB* (n 166) paras 11, 12.
[169] As Lady Butler-Sloss noted in *Re MB* (*ibid* para 28), capacity was not in issue in *Re S* (n 157).
[170] *Re MB* (n 166) para 28.
[171] *Ibid* para 30.
[172] *St George's Healthcare NHS Trust v S* [1999] Fam 26.

seen by a social worker and psychiatrist, and was admitted to a mental health facility against her will.[173] After her admission, Ms S recorded in writing her '"extreme objection" to *any* medical or surgical intervention, and stated that she would consider any such intervention 'an assault on [her] person'.[174] Later that night, she was transferred to St George's Hospital. An *ex parte* application was made on behalf of the hospital for an order dispensing with the need for her consent to a Caesarean section.[175] The order was granted and the surgery was performed several hours later. The Court of Appeal held:

> In our judgment while pregnancy increases the personal responsibilities of a woman it does not diminish her entitlement to decide whether or not to undergo medical treatment. Although human, . . . an unborn child is not a separate person from its mother. Its need for medical assistance does not prevail over her rights. She is entitled not to be forced to submit to an invasion of her body against her will, whether her own life or that of her unborn child depends on it. Her right is not reduced or diminished merely because her decision to exercise it may appear morally repugnant.[176]

Canadian courts have also had occasion to hear applications concerning coercive medical treatment in pregnancy, although there are few reported decisions.[177] In Canada, the cases have usually been grounded in child welfare law, even where they concern medical treatment or assessment of the pregnant woman. In *Re Children's Aid Society of City of Belleville, Hastings County and T et al*,[178] for example, the Ontario Provincial Court held that a fetus can be a 'child in need of protection' under the Child and Family Services Act[179] where a pregnant woman refuses obstetrical care. Accordingly, the court granted an order making the 'child' a ward of the Children's Aid Society for a period of three months. The court also issued an order under the Mental Health Act, for assessment of the pregnant woman by a physician, on the basis that her behaviour posed a danger to both herself and the 'child'.[180]

In *Re Baby R*, the Superintendent of Child and Family Services apprehended a fetus during labour after the pregnant woman refused to consent to delivery via Caesarean section. Ms R was never notified of the apprehension and, ultimately, consented to the surgery 'practically at the door of the operating room'.[181] The child was apprehended immediately following its birth, and the Provincial Court judge held that the apprehension was justified. On appeal by the mother, the British Columbia Supreme Court overturned the order of the Provincial Court, on the basis that the Family and Child Service Act gave the Superintendent the power to apprehend only 'living children that have been delivered'.[182]

---

[173] Mental Health Act 1983 (UK), s 2.

[174] *St George's Healthcare* (n 172) 37.

[175] Although Ms S had instructed solicitors, they were not notified of the application; neither was the judge who heard the application informed that Ms S had instructed counsel.

[176] *St George's Healthcare* (n 172) 50.

[177] Although similar issues were raised in *Winnipeg Child and Family Services* (n 93), as will be discussed below. But see Roth (n 137) 94–95 (noting that it is not possible to ascertain the full extent of court-ordered medical intervention in pregnancy. Roth's work suggests that by no means all such cases are reported in law reports (or elsewhere, for that matter)).

[178] *Children's Aid Society of City of Belleville, Hastings County and T et al (Re)*, (1987) 59 OR (2d) 204 (Ont Prov Ct).

[179] Then Child and Family Services Act, SO 1984, c 55, s 37. The current legislation is Child and Family Services Act, RSO 1990, c C 11, s 37.

[180] Above (n 178).

[181] *Re Baby R* (n 130) 73 (cited to BCLR).

[182] *Re Baby R* (n 130) 80 (cited to BCLR).

In *Re A*, the Children's Aid Society of Hamilton-Wentworth sought an order subjecting Mrs A's fetus to the supervision of the Society, and requiring Mrs A to seek pre-natal care from a physician whose name was to be provided to the Society. In addition, the Society asked the court to order Mrs A to make 'immediate plans' for a hospital birth, to advise the Society of the name of the hospital and to attend at the hospital for the child's birth.[183] The Society also requested that the court grant a further order 'requiring P.A. to be detained in hospital until the birth of the child and to undergo all necessary medical procedures for the well-being of the unborn child' in the event that Mrs A refused to comply with the original order.[184] The order was sought on the basis of the court's jurisdiction under the Child and Family Services Act or, in the alternative, its jurisdiction *parens patriae*.[185] The court concluded, albeit 'reluctantly,'[186] that it had no jurisdiction to make an order that would require the forcible confinement of the pregnant woman in order to protect the fetus.[187]

Australia is exceptional among these jurisdictions, in that there are no reported cases concerning forced medical treatment during pregnancy in that country.[188] The Supreme Court of New South Wales has, however, decided a case involving similar considerations. In *Re ELM*,[189] the Director of Community Services (DOCS) applied to the court for various declaratory orders concerning a pregnant woman who was HIV positive and due to give birth within two weeks of the court application. Although she had initially agreed to take anti-retroviral medication during her pregnancy, she had stopped taking the drugs some months earlier based on her belief that God had cured her illness. She had indicated that she would not agree to a Caesarean section, neither would she consent to anti-retroviral therapy for her baby upon its birth. She did not intend to breastfeed the baby. The DOCS, uncertain whether the child welfare legislation would permit him to authorise prophylactic therapy without the mother's consent, applied to the courts on an urgent *ex parte* basis. The orders sought included a declaration clarifying whether the DOCS could consent to treatment for the child, upon its birth, even though the mother would be retaining her parental rights. In addition to the declaration respecting the DOCS's power to consent to treatment for the child, injunctions were requested to prevent the mother from breastfeeding the child and from removing him from the hospital without written approval to do so. In explaining his decision to grant the orders, Brereton J noted that the Court was

> not being asked to authorise any intervention in or invasion of the rights of the defendant, but simply to declare the effect and extent of what has already been authorised by the legislature. The short and long-term health and well-being, if not the life, of a child soon to be born is at stake.[190]

---

[183] *Re A (In Utero)*, 75 OR (2d) 82, 72 DLR (4th) 722 (1990) (Ont UFC) 723–24 (cited to DLR).

[184] *Ibid*.

[185] *Ibid*.

[186] *Ibid* 728. The court thus overruled *Children's Aid Society v T* (n 178).

[187] There are also three Canadian cases in which a post-birth apprehension under child welfare legislation was justified on the basis of the conduct of the child's mother during her pregnancy; these are discussed in section III.B.i below (*Re Children's Aid Society for the District of Kenora and JL*, 134 DLR (3d) 249, [1982] WDFL 390 (Ont Prov Ct); *M(J) v Superintendent of Family and Child Services* [1983] 4 CNLR 41, (1983) 35 RFL (2d) 364 (BCCA) (*sub nom Re Superintendent of Family and Child Services and McDonald*) affing 37 BCLR 32, 135 DLR (3d) 330 (1982) (BCSC); *Ackerman v McGoldrick* [1990] BCJ no 2832 (Prov Ct)). Sanda Rodgers discusses these cases as well (Rodgers (n 129) 343–45).

[188] This does not necessarily mean that no such cases have been brought before the courts, as anecdotal reports suggest that these cases might be brought but not come to public attention.

[189] *Re ELM* [2006] NSWSC 1137, (2006) 36 Fam LR 257.

[190] *Ibid* para 25.

The Court noted the unusual nature of the proceedings, in that they were brought without notice to the pregnant woman whose parental rights were in issue. The reason given for proceeding in this fashion was the concern that the pregnant woman would not present herself to the hospital to give birth. The decision to grant the requested injunctions in advance was aimed at 'preventing wrongs to the child: the provision of breast milk which may carry HIV, or the removal of the child from medical treatment essential to life and health'.[191] While the *ex parte* nature of the proceedings and the injunction against breastfeeding and leaving the hospital without permission seem extraordinary,[192] it is noteworthy that the question of whether the woman could have been compelled to have medical treatment (here, a Caesarean section or anti-retroviral drugs) does not appear to have been raised at all.

i. Compelled medical intervention and reproductive autonomy

It is beyond dispute that forcing a pregnant woman to undergo medical treatment or testing against her wishes is a profound interference with her reproductive autonomy and her bodily integrity.[193] As such, the question of decision making about medical treatment during pregnancy belongs in the centre of the model of reproductive autonomy I describe in this book. Indeed, this has been the position universally adopted by the appellate courts that have had the opportunity to address the issue.

It is tempting to read the judicial pronouncements around the centrality of respect for women's autonomy to make their own healthcare decisions as resolving the issue decisively, but the story is more complex. Alasdair MacLean has pointed out that the English Caesarean cases ultimately conclude that the competent pregnant woman's right to refuse treatment is no different from that of any other adult. But it is only in the cases 'where the woman could be declared incompetent, or where the fetus had already been delivered, that the court made strong statements supporting self-determination'.[194] In all of the cases where the life of the fetus remained at risk, the court was prepared to grant the requested order permitting the Caesarean section against the objections of the pregnant woman. The tendency of lower courts to grant such requests is not surprising, given that 'at some level the judicial outcome will be influenced by the expert evidence as to which treatment affords the best chance of the happy announcement that both mother and baby are doing well'.[195] And, as noted earlier, in spite of what appears to be a strong precedent out of the DC Court of Appeals in 1990, as well as additional authorities decided by appellate level courts over the years, these cases continue to come before American courts.

The forced Caesarean cases seem to epitomise the maternal–fetal conflict, in that the pregnant woman's right to refuse medical treatment is cast against the clear need for

---

[191] *Ibid* para 23.

[192] Mainly because of the common law position that a fetus does not have standing and protective orders therefore cannot be granted in favour of a fetus (*Winnipeg Child and Family Services* (n 93); *Re F (in utero)* [1988] 1 Fam 122). These cases are not referred to in the Court's reasons, and in the context of an urgent *ex parte* application, it is entirely possible that this matter was not drawn to the Court's attention.

[193] There is a rich literature on women's autonomy and forced medical treatment during pregnancy, and I have made this argument in more detail as well. See sources cited at n 199 below.

[194] Alasdair MacLean, 'Advance Directives and the Rocky Waters of Anticipatory Decision-Making' (2008) 16 *Medical Law Review* 1, 4.

[195] Lord Justice Thorpe, 'The Caesarean Section Debate' (1997) 27 *Family Law* 663, 663–64.

intervention on the part of the fetus. The sentiment is captured well by John Robertson, who explains that

> [t]he behavioral restrictions on pregnant women and the arguments for mandating fetal therapy and prenatal screening illustrate an important limit on a woman's freedom to control her body during pregnancy. She is free not to conceive, and free also to abort after conception and before viability. But once she chooses to carry the child to term, she acquires obligations to assure its well-being. These obligations may require her to avoid work, recreation, and medical care choices that are hazardous to the fetus. They also obligate her to preserve her health for the fetus' sake or even allow established therapies to be performed on an affected fetus. Finally, they require that she undergo prenatal screening where there is reason to believe that this screening may identify congenital defects correctable with available therapies.[196]

When examined more closely, however, it becomes clear that the real conflict is between the pregnant woman and the physician or healthcare team,[197] based on concerns around the risks of failing to intervene.[198]

A great deal has been written about the multiple ways in which women's reproductive autonomy is implicated by the forced medical treatment cases.[199] Even if one were to agree with the premise that intervention is justified because of the potential harm to the fetus if nothing is done, it is difficult to dispute the profound violation of the pregnant woman's autonomy and bodily integrity. Indeed, the Canadian Royal Commission on New Reproductive Technologies considered the issue of judicial intervention in pregnant women's lives. It concluded that the interference with women's autonomy and bodily integrity is so great that the appropriate State response is the explicit recognition of forcible medical treatment or 'other interferences . . . with the physical autonomy of pregnant women' as criminal assault within the Criminal Code.[200]

ii. Caesarean delivery on maternal request

I want to turn now to a newer concern around decision making and Caesarean section, as women's decision making about Caesarean section provides an extremely interesting lens through which to reflect on reproductive autonomy. At the same time as alarms are being raised about rising Caesarean section rates and the lack of necessity for many of these surgical deliveries, the suggestion is also being made that women should be free to

---

[196] Robertson (n 71) 450.

[197] Oberman (n 40).

[198] Lyerly *et al* (n 8).

[199] See, eg, George J Annas, 'Forced Cesareans: The Most Unkindest Cut of All' (1982) 12(3) *Hastings Center Report* 16; Nancy Rhoden, 'The Judge in the Delivery Room: The Emergence of Court-Ordered Cesareans' (1986) 74 *California Law Review* 1951; Cheryl E Amana, 'Maternal–Fetal Conflict: A Call for Humanism and Consciousness in a Time of Crisis' (1992) 3 *Columbia Journal of Gender and Law* 351; Nancy Ehrenreich, 'The Colonization of the Womb' (1993) 43 *Duke Law Journal* 492; Eric M Levine, 'The Constitutionality of Court-Ordered Cesarean Surgery: A Threshold Question' (1994) 4 *Albany Law Journal of Science and Technology* 229; Joan C Callahan (ed), *Reproduction, Ethics, and the Law: Feminist Perspectives* (Bloomington, Indiana University Press, 1995); Martha Fineman and Isabel Karpin (eds), *Mothers in Law: Feminist Theory and the Legal Regulation of Motherhood* (New York, Columbia University Press, 1995); Julia E Hanigsberg and Sara Ruddick (eds), *Mother Troubles: Rethinking Contemporary Maternal Dilemmas* (Boston, MA, Beacon Press, 1999); Erin Nelson, 'Reconceiving Pregnancy: Expressive Choice and Legal Reasoning' (2004) 49 *McGill Law Journal* 593.

[200] Royal Commission on New Reproductive Technologies, *Proceed with Care: Final Report of the Royal Commission on New Reproductive Technologies*, vol 2 (Ottawa, Supply and Services Canada, 1993) 965.

elect surgical delivery as an alternative equally legitimate to vaginal delivery.[201] The state of the science is such that it is not possible to point to either vaginal or surgical delivery as clearly best.[202] Most professional obstetrics organisations that have commented or issued guidelines on point have expressed some level of concern with the practice of Caesarean delivery on maternal request (CDMR). While none of these organisations endorses the provision of surgical delivery for non-medical reasons, the vague language adopted in some of the policies leaves open the possibility of CDMR in a potentially wide range of cases. The International Federation of Gynecology and Obstetrics states that 'surgical intervention without a medical rationale . . . [falls] outside the bounds of best professional practice [and] . . . should be undertaken only when indicated to enhance the well-being of mothers and babies and improve outcomes'.[203] The Society of Obstetricians and Gynaecologists of Canada (SOGC) opines that surgical delivery 'should be reserved for pregnancies in which there is a threat to the health of the mother and/or baby'.[204] The American College of Obstetricians and Gynecologists (ACOG) has taken a somewhat neutral stance, noting the 'limitations of data regarding the relative short- and long-term risks and benefits' of Caesarean and vaginal delivery and outlining a deliberative process for physicians faced with such requests.[205]

Although CDMR has been presented by some as a clear means of augmenting women's autonomy in reproductive matters, the reality is arguably much more complex.[206] If autonomy can be equated with an expanding number of choices, then offering surgical

[201] See, eg, Rothman (n 33); George B Feldman and Jennie A Frieman, 'Prophylactic Cesarean Section at Term?' (1985) 312 *New England Journal of Medicine* 1264; Howard Minkoff and Frank A Chervenak, 'Elective Primary Cesarean Delivery' (2003) 348 *New England Journal of Medicine* 946; Robin B Kalish, Laurence B McCullough and Frank A Chervenak, 'Decision-making About Caesarean Delivery' (2006) 367 *The Lancet* 883.

[202] See, eg, Howard Minkoff, 'The Ethics of Cesarean Section by Choice' (2006) 30 *Seminars in Perinatology* 309; Victoria H Coleman-Cowager *et al*, 'Current Practice of Cesarean Delivery on Maternal Request Following the 2006 State-of-the-Science Conference' (2010) 55 *Journal of Reproductive Medicine* 25. But see Cesar G Victora and Fernando C Barros, 'Beware: Unnecessary Caesarean Sections may be Hazardous' (2006) 367 *The Lancet* 1796; José Villar *et al*, 'Caesarean Delivery Rates and Pregnancy Outcomes: The 2005 WHO Global Survey on Maternal and Perinatal Health in Latin America (2006) 367 *The Lancet* 1819.

[203] International Federation of Gynecology and Obstetrics, 'FIGO Statement on Caesarean Section' (January 2007), at <www.figo.org/Caesarean>.

[204] The SOGC policy is a joint one, involving other perinatal healthcare providers (Society of Obstetricians and Gynaecologists of Canada, Association of Women's Health, Obstetric and Neonatal Nurses of Canada, Canadian Association of Midwives, College of Family Physicians of Canada and the Society of Rural Physicians of Canada, 'Joint Policy Statement on Normal Childbirth' (2008) 30 *Journal of Obstetrics and Gynaecology Canada* 1163, 1164).

[205] American College of Obstetricians and Gynecologists, 'ACOG Committee Opinion No 395: Surgery and Patient Choice' (2008) 111 *Obstetrics & Gynecology* 243, 246. In Australia, the Royal Australian and New Zealand College of Obstetricians and Gynaecologists says that 'When a woman requests elective delivery by caesarean section in the absence of medical indication, the obstetrician should acknowledge the legitimacy of the request and explore the reasons underlying it,' and then choose from three options, one of which is to agree to perform the requested Caesarean section (Royal Australian and New Zealand College of Obstetricians and Gynaecologists, 'College Statement C-Obs 39: Caesarean Delivery on Maternal Request (CDMR)' (2010), at <www.ranzcog.edu.au/womens-health/statements-a-guidelines/college-statements-and-guidelines. html?showall=&start=1>). The most recent NICE Guideline states that if, after discussing the matter with the pregnant woman, she continues to request the procedure, the obstetrician should either offer the procedure, or refer her to another practitioner (National Collaborating Centre for Women's and Children's Health for the National Institute for Health and Clinical Excellence (n 29)102).

[206] See, eg, Burrow (n 28); Rebecca Kukla *et al*, 'Finding Autonomy in Birth' (2009) 23 *Bioethics* 1; Suze Berkhout, 'Relational Autonomy on the Cutting Edge' (2012) 12(7) *American Journal of Bioethics* 59; Kavita R Shah, 'Increasing Cesarean Rates: The Balance of Technology, Autonomy, and Beneficence' (2012) 12(7) *American Journal of Bioethics* 58.

delivery as an alternative to vaginal delivery would indeed increase women's autonomy. But adding options to the list does not necessarily create space for meaningful exercise of autonomy,[207] and a longer list of choices may well not be experienced by those making the choice as autonomy-enhancing.[208] In the highly medicalised context of modern pregnancy and childbirth, some have argued that the very idea of CDMR might diminish, rather than enhance, women's autonomy in childbirth.[209] At the very least, we must acknowledge that a longer menu of choices does not straightforwardly translate into increased autonomy for the women making such decisions. In addition, we currently lack the empirical data to help us know for sure whether CDMR is, on balance, beneficial or harmful to women and their children. As one group of authors has eloquently explained:

> We . . . believe that it is too early to be 'for' or 'against' women's access to cesarean delivery in the absence of traditional medical indications – and indeed, that a simple pro- or con- position is never going to do justice to the subtlety of the issue. The right question is not whether women ought to be 'allowed to choose' their delivery approach, but rather, taking the value of a woman's autonomy in decision-making around birth as a given, what sorts of guidelines, practices, and conversations will best promote and protect women's full inclusion in a safe and positive birth process.[210]

This coincides precisely with the point I seek to make about a rich, contextualised understanding of reproductive autonomy. At one end of the spectrum are arguments around whether women can be legally compelled to undergo surgical delivery in spite of their competent refusal to consent. At the other are claims that it is unethical to agree to provision of CDMR. Medicalisation plays an important role in our (legal and ethical) approach to Caesarean section, and again, the bidirectional nature of medicalisation is revealed. In some cases, the end result is the product of women's desires to have the technology made available. But not all women wish to avail themselves of the technology; some comply, and some resist. And some feminists argue that those who comply are acting non-autonomously[211] (or are suffering from false consciousness), as there appears to be no other basis for a request for unnecessary and potentially harmful surgery. This is exactly why we need a robust feminist conception of reproductive autonomy – to preserve the space in which each woman can make her reproductive decisions for herself.

Sylvia Burrow has written about CDMR and attempts to reduce Caesarean section rates.[212] She comments on the many factors that influence Caesarean section rates, noting that one factor that might play a role is CDMR. She also notes that physician preferences have an important role in this context as well, and argues that physicians must ensure that they support women's decisional autonomy in deliberating about method of delivery.

I have no quarrel with any of this. But where I do become concerned is with Burrow's approach to CDMR in particular and to the question of whether maternal request for Caesarean section is or can be autonomous. Although she does not rule out the possibility

---

[207] As discussed in ch 2 section III, III.A. See also Berkhout (n 206); Burrow (n 28).

[208] See, eg, Barry Schwartz, *The Paradox of Choice: Why More is Less* (New York, Harper Perennial, 2004) 99–103; Simona Botti, Kristina Orfali and Sheena S Iyengar, 'Tragic Choices: Autonomy and Emotional Responses to Medical Decisions' (2009) 36 *Journal of Consumer Research* 337; Sheena Iyengar, *The Art of Choosing* (New York, Twelve, 2010).

[209] See, eg, Bergeron (n 30); Burrow (n 28); Kukla *et al* (n 206).

[210] Kukla *et al* (n 206) 8.

[211] Burrow (n 28).

[212] *Ibid.*

that such a request could reflect an autonomous choice, she takes the view that a request for Caesarean delivery is probably not compatible with autonomous decision making. Burrow says that while it may appear that adding the option of CDMR increases women's autonomy, this is a 'limited view' of autonomy.[213] Her argument about why CDMR decisions are not (or may not be) autonomous is based on two main factors. Her first concern relates to the availability of information and patient awareness of the risks and benefits of CDMR. Her premise here is that the ACOG does not oblige physicians to present CDMR as an option. Thus, she says, patients may proceed to choose CDMR without a discussion of risks and benefits. Moreover, she explains, we lack sufficient evidence about elective Caesarean and its relative risks and benefits to permit an autonomous decision on this matter.[214]

These arguments are clearly flawed. First, in saying that physicians are not obliged to raise the possibility of a maternal request for unnecessary surgery, the ACOG is not also saying that if a patient requests Caesarean section, doctors have no obligation to explain the risks and benefits. In fact, the ACOG requires physicians to discuss the risks and benefits with patients if the topic is raised.[215] Secondly, all healthcare decisions involve uncertainty, and in many instances we lack sufficient evidence to enable optimal conditions for autonomous decision making. Surely Burrow is not suggesting that all healthcare decisions are fundamentally non-autonomous because of the impossibility of knowing for certain which choice is best.

As I explain in the context of reproductive autonomy in theory,[216] Burrow's more problematic argument is the second autonomy-compromising factor she identifies – that 'Social pressures can influence the desire to have a cesarean in a way that undermines rather than fosters autonomy'.[217] I have already articulated my concern with this line of reasoning, but I think it is helpful to note it again in the context of this specific example. When, on Burrow's reasoning, can a choice ever be autonomous? The end result of this argument is to suggest that only when a woman's reproductive choices conform to the intuitions of (certain) feminists as to what is appropriate will they be considered autonomous.

B. Coercion by the State: controlling the pregnant woman

i. Child welfare law

Not only have physicians and hospitals sought to control the behaviour of pregnant women by seeking judicial enforcement of medical advice. State agents (including child welfare authorities and prosecutors) have also sought to exploit the power of law to constrain pregnant women's freedom of action, as well as to punish pregnant women and new mothers for their conduct during pregnancy.

The earliest cases in which child welfare laws were engaged in an effort to protect a fetus from its mother were those involving substance abuse by pregnant women. While

---

[213] *Ibid* 45.
[214] *Ibid* 45–46.
[215] 'ACOG Committee Opinion No 395: Surgery and Patient Choice' (n 205).
[216] See ch 2, section III.A.
[217] Burrow (n 28) 46.

these cases arose out of the moral panic related to crack cocaine,[218] the cases are not exclusively about cocaine consumption.[219]

The connection between cases concerning substance abuse by pregnant women and autonomous decision making is perhaps not readily apparent. Women who use illicit substances because they are addicted to those substances are in all likelihood impaired in their ability to make autonomous decisions in relation to this aspect of their behaviour.[220] But when we consider broader questions around lifestyle choices and behaviour during pregnancy, and about socio-economic status and its power to constrain behaviour and determine health – and the relation of both to pregnancy – we begin to expose the link between reproductive autonomy and these cases, as examples of attempts to control the behaviour of pregnant women.

Child welfare (or child protection) proceedings have arisen in Canada and England as well as the US. As discussed above, in some instances, child welfare laws have been invoked in an attempt to force women to comply with medical advice.[221] Child welfare laws have also been used to punish women for being addicted to drugs and bearing children.

The US has seen the most activity in this area, with a number of states passing legislation to address various aspects of the problem of substance abuse by pregnant women. Measures include defining substance use during pregnancy as child abuse, mandating reporting of suspected pre-natal drug use and, in some cases, mandating priority access for pregnant women in drug treatment programs.[222] The various state statutes may loosely be categorised as focusing on either education and treatment, or 'punishment and surveillance'.[223] A number of states consider substance abuse during pregnancy to be child abuse, and in three states pregnant women are liable to civil committal for drug abuse.[224] Some of the states have adopted comprehensive policies, addressing aspects of both treatment and child neglect in their statutes.[225]

Canadian lawmakers have not passed legislation to address substance abuse by pregnant women, but there is a handful of Canadian cases in which a woman's drug-related behaviour was used in an attempt to justify either her detention and drug treatment

---

[218] See, eg, Craig Reinarman and Harry Gene Levine (eds), *Crack in America: Demon Drugs and Social Justice* (Berkeley, University of California Press, 1997); Drew Humphries, *Crack Mothers: Pregnancy, Drugs, and the Media* (Columbus, State University Press, 1999); Wendy Chavkin, 'Cocaine and Pregnancy – Time to Look at the Evidence' (2001) 285 *Journal of the American Medical Association* 1626; Jeanne Flavin and Lynn M Paltrow, 'Punishing Pregnant Drug-Using Women: Defying Law, Medicine, and Common Sense' (2010) 29 *Journal of Addictive Diseases* 231, 233–34.

[219] See, eg, *Winnipeg Child and Family Services* (n 93) (glue sniffing). Other cases are cited above at n 187.

[220] See, eg, Carolyn McLeod, 'Women's Autonomy and the "G" Case' (May 1998) 3 *Canadian Bioethics Society Newsletter* 6.

[221] See section III.B.i.

[222] Roth notes that 'between 1973 and 1992 two-thirds of the states . . . (thirty-three and the District of Columbia) passed legislation on women's drug and alcohol abuse during pregnancy' (Roth (n 137) 163).

[223] *Ibid*. For a detailed discussion of the various state statutes, see *ibid* 163–83; Lynn M Paltrow, David S Cohen and Corrine A Carey, *Year 2000 Overview: Governmental Responses to Pregnant Women Who Use Alcohol or Other Drugs* (Philadelphia, PA, Women's Law Project, 2000). A more recent description of state policies is found in Janet W Steverson, 'Prenatal Drug Exposure: The Impetus for Overreaction by the Legal Community or a Serious Problem Needing a Serious Solution?' (2008) 28(4) *Children's Legal Rights Journal* 41.

[224] Guttmacher Institute, 'State Policies in Brief: Substance Abuse During Pregnancy' (1 August 2012), at <www.guttmacher.org/statecenter/spibs/spib_SADP.pdf>.

[225] *Ibid*.

during pregnancy, or apprehension of a newborn because the child's mother used illicit drugs during her pregnancy.[226]

In *Children's Aid Society for the District of Kenora and JL*,[227] the child suffered from fetal alcohol syndrome as a result of the mother's alcohol abuse during her pregnancy. The Ontario Provincial Court held that a fetus was entitled to protection under the Child Welfare Act.[228] In *M(J) v Superintendent of Family and Child Services*,[229] a baby born addicted to methadone (whose mother had been advised by her physician to continue to take methadone during pregnancy) was apprehended, and an order of permanent custody was made in favour of the child welfare authorities. In upholding the order, Madame Justice Proudfoot stated that 'it would be incredible to come to any other conclusion than that a drug-addicted baby is born abused'.[230]

In *Winnipeg Child and Family Services v G (DF)*,[231] the Supreme Court of Canada considered the broader question of whether there is any foundation in law to support the detention of a pregnant woman for the purpose of protecting her fetus. When Ms G was five months pregnant with her fourth child,[232] and addicted to sniffing glue, Winnipeg Child and Family Services sought an order for mandatory detention so that Ms G could be kept at a place of safety (and required to undergo treatment for her addiction). The order was granted by the Manitoba Court of Queen's Bench, which held that both the Mental Health Act and the court's inherent jurisdiction could be invoked in support of the order.[233] The Manitoba Court of Appeal struck down the order, holding that Ms G was not incompetent (a condition that must exist before the issuance of an order under the Mental Health Act), and concluding that the lower court erred in relying on the *parens patriae* jurisdiction.[234] In spite of the invalidity of the court order, Ms G voluntarily remained at the Winnipeg Health Sciences Centre until her discharge a number of weeks later. Ultimately, she gave birth to a healthy baby who remained in her custody for some period of time.

The Supreme Court of Canada heard an appeal from the Manitoba Court of Appeal's decision. A majority of the Court ultimately concluded that an order of the type granted in this case could not be supported by statute, tort law or the court's inherent jurisdic-

---

[226] In one of these cases (*Ackerman v McGoldrick* (n 187)), a baby apprehended after her father absconded with her was returned to her mother's care, as there was no evidence that she was in need of protection. The baby's mother had ingested drugs on one or two occasions during her pregnancy, but at the time of the hearing the baby was developing normally. See also *Joe v Yukon Territory (Director, Family and Children Services, Director)*, 1 YR 169, 5 BCLR (2d) 267 (1986) (YTSC), striking down a provision of the Yukon *Children's Act*, SYT 1984, c 2. Section 134(1) of the Act permitted the Director of Family and Children Services who – acting on reasonable and probable grounds – believed that a fetus was at 'serious risk of suffering from foetal alcohol syndrome or some other congenital injury attributable to the pregnant [woman's consumption of] addictive or intoxicating substances', – '[to] apply to a judge for an order requiring the woman to participate in such reasonable supervision or counselling as the order specifies in respect of her use of addictive or intoxicating substances'. The section was found to be unconstitutionally vague. In spite of this ruling, the section remained on the books in the *Children's Act*, RSY 2002, c 31, as s 135(1).

[227] *Re Children's Aid Society* (n 187).

[228] *Ibid.*

[229] *M(J) v Superintendent of Family and Child Services* (BCCA) (n 187) para 20 (cited to RFL).

[230] *Ibid* 335.

[231] *Winnipeg Child and Family Services* (n 93).

[232] Her three children were all wards of the state.

[233] *Winnipeg Child and Family Services (Northwest Area) v G (DF)*, 111 Man R (2d) 219, 138 DLR (4th) 238 (1996) (Man QB).

[234] *Winnipeg Child and Family Services (Northwest Area) v G (DF)*, 113 Man R (2d) 3, 138 DLR (4th) 254 (1996) (Man CA).

tion *parens patriae*. The Court noted the significant policy issues that arise in the context of contemplating the extension of the common law in this way.[235] In particular, the Court noted the dramatic impact on women's fundamental liberties that would result from extending the common law to permit an order for the detention and treatment of a pregnant woman to prevent harm to the fetus, as well as the ramifications of such a change for other areas of tort law.[236] As in the case of tort law duties of pregnant women, the Supreme Court took the view that 'The changes to the law sought on this appeal are best left to the wisdom of the elected legislature'.[237]

In dissent, Justices Major and Sopinka held that the fact that Ms G could have terminated her pregnancy permits the state to intervene to safeguard the 'child's' health.[238] As Major J put it:

> Once the mother decides to bear the child the state has an interest in trying to ensure the child's health. What circumstances permit state intervention? The 'slippery slope' argument was raised that permitting state intervention here would impose a standard of behaviour on all pregnant women. Questions were raised about women who smoked, who lived with a smoker, who ate unhealthy diets, etc. In response to the query of where a reasonable line should be drawn it was submitted that the pen should not even be lifted. This approach would entail the state to stand idly by while a reckless and/or addicted mother inflicts serious and permanent harm on to a child she had decided to bring into the world.[239]

Characterising the long-standing 'born alive' rule as a rule of evidence the utility of which is questionable in light of medical advances, Major J had no difficulty finding that the Court's *parens patriae* jurisdiction can be exercised in favour of a fetus, just as it can in favour of a child in need of protection.[240] On this view, state intervention is justified in circumstances 'where the conduct of the mother has a reasonable probability of causing serious irreparable harm to the unborn child'.[241]

There are no reported cases on point in Australia or the UK, although there are some English authorities that address similar concerns. In *Re D (A Minor)*,[242] the local authority commenced child protection proceedings in respect of a baby born to drug-addicted parents. The mother had used drugs during her pregnancy and the child was born suffering from withdrawal symptoms. Although Lord Goff stated that he could see 'no reason why the magistrates should not be entitled to have regard to events which occurred before the child was born,'[243] he noted that the legislation under which

[235] *Winnipeg Child and Family Services* (n 93) paras 30–45 (cited to SCR).
[236] *Ibid* paras 18–57 (cited to SCR).
[237] *Ibid* para 59 (cited to SCR) in n 238. Indeed, McLachlin J refers repeatedly to the possibility of legislative action throughout her judgment.
[238] *Ibid* para 95 (cited to SCR) in 239.
[239] *Ibid.*
[240] *Ibid* paras 104–20 (cited to SCR) in n 240.
[241] *Ibid* para 121 (cited to SCR) in 241. Major J set out the following test to be used to determine whether or not intervention is justified (*ibid* para 96): '(1) The woman must have decided to carry the child to term; (2) Proof must be presented to a civil standard that the abusive activity will cause serious and irreparable harm to the foetus; (3) The remedy must be the least intrusive option; (4) The process must be procedurally fair.' Major J's reasoning has been heartily criticised: see, eg, Baylis (n 129); Timothy Caulfield and Erin Nelson, '*Winnipeg Child and Family Services (Northwest Area) v DFG*: A Commentary on the Law, Reproductive Autonomy and the Allure of Technopolicy' (1998) 36 *Alberta Law Review* 799; FC DeCoste, '*Winnipeg Child and Family Services (Northwest Area) v DFG*: The Impossibility of Fetal Rights and the Obligations of Judicial Governance' (1998) 36 *Alberta Law Review* 725.
[242] *Re D (A Minor)* [1987] AC 317.
[243] *Ibid* 350.

the care order was sought was concerned with an ongoing state of affairs rather than solely with past behaviour. The reason for granting a care order was not the mother's drug use during pregnancy, but the fact that both she and the child's father were drug addicts; the care order was needed in order to prevent avoidable harm to the child's health and ongoing development. To illustrate his point, Lord Goff posited a hypothetical case in which

> a mother conceives a child when she is an alcoholic and is unable at first to give up drinking, despite the fact that she knows that this may have an adverse effect upon her unborn child. Shortly before the child is born, the full effect of her conduct is brought home to her; and she becomes a confirmed teetotaller. The child is born. Its proper development has indeed been prevented, or its health has indeed been impaired, by its mother's drinking. But if the case then came before the magistrates, I do not think that they could properly conclude that, at the time when they were asked to make the order, the child's proper development was then *being* avoidably prevented, or that its health was then *being* avoidably impaired.[244]

Thus in spite of Lord Goff's comments about the court's ability to take into account the mother's conduct during pregnancy, he did not adopt the view that the child welfare legislation is concerned with punishing women for their conduct during pregnancy.

In *Re F (in utero)*,[245] a local authority sought to make a fetus a ward of the court. The pregnant woman had suffered from significant mental illness for many years. She had lived a nomadic existence, travelling between the UK and other parts of Europe over the years. During her pregnancy, she had attended some pre-natal care appointments, but then missed several appointments and could not be located by her family or the local authority. The authority sought to make the child a ward of the court in order 'to protect the unborn child'. The order was refused, both at first instance and in the Court of Appeal, on the basis that the wardship jurisdiction of the courts does not extend to 'a child who is yet unborn'.[246] As Hollings J (the trial judge) explained,

> wardship can only apply to a living child. For it to apply to a child still within the body of the child's mother, very serious considerations must arise with regard to the welfare of the mother . . . one can well imagine that there would be a repugnance on the part of a right thinking person in certain instances to think of applying the principle of paramountcy in favour of the child's welfare at the expense of the welfare and interests of the mother.[247]

All three members of the Court of Appeal agreed with Hollings J, noting that 'the only purpose of extending the jurisdiction to include a foetus is to enable the mother's actions to be controlled'.[248] In short, the Court held that its wardship jurisdiction is not available to control the behaviour of pregnant women.

ii. Criminal law

As with many of the topics discussed in this book, the US is an outlier in its treatment of pregnant women, particularly those with addictions. The US has the distinction of

[244] *Ibid* 351.
[245] *Re F* (n 192).
[246] *Ibid* 129 (Hollings J).
[247] *Ibid* 131.
[248] *Ibid* 143 (Balcombe LJ).

taking a unique approach to the use of the criminal law in an attempt to control and punish pregnant women. Unlike the situation in the other jurisdictions under study here, the American courts have heard a considerable number of cases involving criminal prosecution of women for their behaviour during pregnancy. Typically, these cases involve the attempted use of criminal offences in ways that the offences were not intended to be construed. Although courts of first instance occasionally accept the arguments, the higher level and appellate courts have almost uniformly rejected them.[249] Lynn Paltrow has long been an advocate for pregnant women facing prosecution and child welfare proceedings; her organisation (National Advocates for Pregnant Women) has followed 'hundreds of known cases in at least 40 states' in which drug-using and drug-addicted pregnant women have been arrested.[250] In spite of the large number of criminal charges that have been brought before the courts, only one state (South Carolina) has upheld a conviction of this type.[251]

The first known case involving criminal prosecution of a woman for using illicit drugs during pregnancy is *Reyes v Superior Court*.[252] Ms Reyes was charged with two counts of felony child endangerment when her twins were born addicted to heroin. The appellate court held that the statute under which Ms Reyes had been charged had no application to fetuses, and dismissed the charges. In the late 1980s and early 1990s, a number of similar prosecutions were undertaken against pregnant women or women who had just given birth. In *People of California v Jaurigue*,[253] a woman was unsuccessfully prosecuted for murder when her baby was stillborn allegedly as a result of her ingestion of drugs while pregnant. In 1992, Pamela Rae Stewart was charged on the basis of a 1926 statute for the offence of wilfully omitting to furnish necessary medical attention to a child; Stewart was also charged with failing to follow her doctor's orders.[254] Ms Stewart's baby died shortly after his birth due to massive brain damage sustained during gestation. The charges against Stewart were ultimately dismissed; the court held that the intent of the statute under which she was charged was to require fathers to pay child support.[255]

As mentioned above, South Carolina is the only state in which convictions of pregnant women have been upheld. In *State of South Carolina v Whitner*,[256] a woman was charged with endangering the life of her unborn child by smoking crack cocaine during pregnancy. After pleading guilty to child neglect charges, Whitner was sentenced to an eight-year

---

[249] A Kentucky appellate court upheld a charge, but the ruling was overturned by the state Supreme Court (*Commonwealth v Cochran*, No 2006-CA-001561 (Ky App 2008) rev'd 315 SW 3d 325 (Ky Supreme Ct 2010)).

[250] Flavin and Paltrow (n 218) 233. Similar figures have been cited by others: see, eg, Roth (n 137) 146 (noting that by 'mid-1992, there were more than 150 documented cases of women who faced unprecedented criminal charges for using drugs or alcohol during pregnancy'); Linda C Fentiman, 'Pursuing the Perfect Mother: Why America's Criminalization of Maternal Substance Abuse is Not the Answer – A Comparative Legal Analysis' (2009) 15 *Michigan Journal of Gender and Law* 389, 398.

[251] *Whitner v State*, 492 SE 2d 777 (SC 1097). See further below.

[252] *Reyes v Superior Court*, 75 Cal App 3d 214 (1977).

[253] Roth (n 137) 135–36.

[254] Ms Stewart had been advised to seek medical attention immediately if she began bleeding. She was also advised to abstain from drug use and sexual intercourse. After having intercourse with her husband, Ms Stewart began to haemorrhage, but waited several hours before seeking medical care. There was also evidence of a substance in her blood that was consistent with the use of street drugs (and also apparently consistent with the use of an over-the-counter antihistamine) (Michelle Oberman, 'Sex, Drugs, Pregnancy, and the Law: Rethinking the Problems of Pregnant Women Who Use Drugs' (1992) 43 *Hastings Law Journal* 505, 505–06).

[255] Roth (n 137) 145–46.

[256] *Whitner v State* (n 251).

prison term.[257] In *State v McKnight*,[258] another South Carolina woman was convicted of homicide by child abuse after her child was stillborn. The state claimed that Ms McKnight's cocaine use led to the stillbirth, though there is no evidence linking cocaine use and still-birth. Ms McKnight was sentenced to serve 12 years of a 20-year sentence.[259] She later filed a motion for post-conviction relief, and in 2008, the South Carolina Supreme Court reversed her conviction, holding that her counsel was ineffective in failing to prepare an adequate defence. Her counsel had called an expert witness whose testimony undermined the defence position, had failed to call an expert whose evidence would support the defence position, and had failed to ensure that the trial judge gave proper instructions to the jury.[260] Ms McKnight pled guilty to a reduced charge of involuntary manslaughter in order to avoid a new trial, and to secure her release from prison.[261]

A discussion of policies targeting the behaviour of pregnant women would be incom-plete without some attention to the extraordinary approach adopted in South Carolina. That state is an outlier (even within the US) in its treatment of pregnant women who are addicted to harmful substances.[262] Beginning in 1989, the Medical University Hospital of South Carolina developed a policy for screening pregnant women for evi-dence of cocaine use and reporting those who tested positive to authorities who would then arrest the women. The hospital essentially agreed to cooperate with penal authori-ties in prosecuting women for using drugs during pregnancy. In 2001, the US Supreme Court held that testing pregnant women for evidence of use of illicit substances without a warrant or consent violated the women's right to be free from unreasonable search and seizure, pursuant to the Fourth Amendment of the US Constitution.[263] The case was remanded for determination as to whether consent to the testing had been obtained from these women. The US Court of Appeals, 4th Circuit, concluded that the testing was not done for medical purposes, that the consent forms presented to patients were not adequate to establish informed consent to urinalysis for purposes of law enforce-ment and that most of the women did not consent to the testing for law enforcement purposes.[264]

Questionable criminal prosecutions are not the only tool in the states' arsenal in rela-tion to substance abuse by pregnant women. Women have also been sentenced more harshly than a man or a non-pregnant woman would have been. In *United States v Vaughn*,[265] a pregnant woman was convicted of forgery and, because she had a history of

---

[257] Whitner's lawyer had advised her to plead guilty to the charges, and promised that she would then be able to obtain treatment for her addiction (Dorothy Roberts, *Killing the Black Body: Race, Reproduction, and the Meaning of Liberty* (New York, Pantheon Press, 1997) 150). Whitner later applied for 'post-conviction relief'. Her petition was granted by the Circuit Court, but reversed by the South Carolina Supreme Court on appeal by the state. The Court held that a viable fetus is a 'child' within the meaning of the child abuse and endanger-ment statute, and that, therefore, Whitner could legitimately be charged under the statute for her ingestion of crack cocaine during the third trimester of her pregnancy (*Whitner v State* (n 251) 780–81).

[258] *State v McKnight*, 576 SE 2d 168 (SC 2003).

[259] *Ibid*. The jury's verdict was affirmed on a direct appeal to the South Carolina Supreme Court.

[260] *McKnight v State*, 661 SE 2d 354 (SC 2008).

[261] Barry Lester and Sue Veer, 'A Measure of Justice for Regina McKnight', *The State* (Columbia, 1 July 2008).

[262] See also *State v Peppers*, 552 SE 2d 288 (Sup Ct SC 2001) (Peppers pleaded guilty to 'unlawful conduct toward a child' for ingesting drugs during her pregnancy. Her plea and sentence were later vacated by the state Supreme Court as the plea was conditional and therefore constitutionally impermissible).

[263] *Ferguson v Charleston*, 532 US 67 (2001).

[264] *Ferguson v City of Charleston*, 308 F 3d 380 (4th c 2002).

[265] *United States v Vaughn*, Daily Washington Reporter, 7 March 1989, 441, 446–47.

drug use, was ordered to take a drug test after informing the judge of her pregnancy. Ms Vaughn tested positive and was sentenced to a 180-day jail term, 'to ensure that she would remain confined for the duration of her pregnancy'.[266] In justifying the sentence imposed, the judge noted, 'it is true that the defendant has not been treated the same as if she were a man in this case . . . She has also not been treated the same as a non-pregnant woman. But Ms Vaughn became pregnant and chose to bear the baby'.[267]

The failure of the vast majority of attempts to criminalise the behaviour of pregnant women does not seem to have deterred American prosecutorial enthusiasm. In 2007, an Oklahoma woman, Theresa Hernandez, was charged with first-degree murder when she delivered a stillborn infant. The basis for the charge was Ms Hernandez's use of methamphetamine. In spite of the lack of scientific evidence linking methamphetamine use to stillbirth,[268] Ms Hernandez pled guilty to second-degree murder and was sentenced to a term of imprisonment. She was released after serving one year of her sentence.[269] The State of Mississippi has pursued the murder prosecution of 15-year-old Rennie Gibbs, who delivered a stillborn infant at 36 weeks' gestation. The murder charge is based on the fact that Gibbs had a 'cocaine habit', although there is no evidence tying the stillbirth to drug use.[270] In 2010, Bei Bei Shuai was pregnant and living with her boyfriend, with plans to be married. In December 2010, she learned that he was already married and he abandoned her. She became severely depressed and attempted suicide by swallowing rat poison. She was found by friends and taken to hospital where she was successfully treated. The 33-week-old fetus was delivered by Caesarean section, but the baby died a few days after her birth. In March 2011, Ms Shuai was charged with murder and attempted feticide, and was incarcerated; she remained in prison for more than a year before being released in May 2012.[271] And in Alabama, over 60 women have been prosecuted under a 'chemical endangerment' statute that was passed with a view to protecting children from exposure to the dangers of methamphetamine production.[272] The law makes no mention of exposure to controlled substances during pregnancy, neither does

---

[266] Roth (n 137) 152.

[267] *United States v Vaughn* (n 265) 447. In *People v Zaring*, Ms Zaring pleaded guilty to possession of heroin and being under the influence of heroin (*People v Zaring*, 8 Cal App 4th 362 (Cal App 5 Dist 1992)). Her sentence included a 5-year term of probation, a condition of which was that she 'not get pregnant during the term of her probation' (*ibid* 365). The sentencing judge stated (*ibid* 368–69): 'I want . . . to make it clear that one of the reasons I am making this order is you've got five children. You're thirty years old. None of your children are in your custody or control. Two of them on AFDC. And I'm afraid that if you get pregnant we're going to get a cocaine or heroin addicted baby. So come in and report to the Court on the first day of November. Make sure that you comply with the terms and conditions. If you get pregnant, I'm going to send you to prison in large part because I want to protect the un-born child. But more importantly – that's the most important reason, but second of all, because you have violated a term and condition of your probation. Do you understand that?'

[268] See Flavin and Paltrow (n 218) 233; Robert M Silver *et al*, 'Work-up of Stillbirth: A Review of the Evidence' (2007) 196 *American Journal of Obstetrics & Gynecology* 433.

[269] See, eg, Flavin and Paltrow (n 218) 233–34; Jay F Marks, 'OKC Meth Mom Wins Early Release', *NewsOK, Oklahoma City* (20 November 2008).

[270] Ed Pilkington, 'Outcry in America as Pregnant Women Who Lose Babies Face Murder Charges' *Guardian*, 24 June 2011, at <www.guardian.co.uk/world/2011/jun/24/america-pregnant-women-murder-charges>.

[271] Ed Pilkington, 'Indiana Prosecuting Chinese Woman for Suicide Attempt that Killed her Foetus', *Guardian*, 30 May 2012, at www.guardian.co.uk/world/2012/may/30/indiana-prosecuting-chinese-woman-suicide-foetus; David Orentlicher and Nada Stotland, 'Danger for Pregnant Women', *Indianapolis Star*, 14 July 2011, at <www.indystar.com/apps/pbcs.dll/article?AID=2011107150318>.

[272] Chemical Endangerment of a Child, § 26-15-3.2 Ala Code 1975. The section provides that the 'crime of chemical endangerment' is committed by a 'responsible person' who '[k]nowingly, recklessly, or intentionally causes or permits a child to be exposed to, to ingest or inhale, or to have contact with a controlled substance, chemical substance, or drug paraphernalia'.

it purport to extend its reach to 'unborn children'. Two women who have been convicted of chemical endangerment for ingesting illicit drugs during pregnancy await the decision of the Alabama Supreme Court as to whether the statute can legitimately be applied in such circumstances.[273]

iii. Reproductive autonomy and State intervention

While the prevailing view in legal and ethical scholarship is that forcing pregnant women to undergo unwanted medical treatment, or using the criminal law to punish pregnant women, is the wrong approach, this is far from a universal view. And even some who advocate respect for reproductive autonomy are prepared to concede that in some cases, coercion or punishment might be justified.[274] It is not difficult to understand the frustration and concern over a pregnant woman's behaviour and its potential to harm the fetus. Proudfoot JA's comments in *M(J) v Superintendent of Family and Child Services*, to the effect that a child born addicted to drugs is 'born abused,'[275] are quite probably representative of the sentiments of numerous Canadians, and many no doubt feel that the law should be able to respond to such cases. But, as with so many of the topics and themes relevant to reproductive decision making, the reality is far more complex. In *M(J)*, the child was born addicted to methadone because the mother had continued her methadone therapy during her pregnancy on the advice of her physician. A recent obstetrics guideline notes that opioid detoxification is 'not advisable' during pregnancy, primarily because of the increased likelihood of relapse; instead, opiate substitution therapy (such as methadone maintenance) is considered the standard of care for treatment of opioid addiction in pregnancy.[276] While this 2011 guideline was clearly not available to the British Columbia Court of Appeal in 1982, methadone maintenance has been the preferred approach in treating pregnant opiate addicts since the 1970s.[277]

Intervention in pregnancy, as currently practised, is disrespectful of reproductive autonomy and is bad public policy. But State intervention in the lives of pregnant women can take a variety of forms. Arguably, and depending heavily on what such involvement entails, involvement by the State in the lives of pregnant women might sometimes be very desirable. If it means, for example, a positive commitment by the State to seek out and help those pregnant women who need assistance with pre-natal care, addiction treatment, nutrition, care of other children or protection from a violent spouse, then there clearly is an important role for intervention. If, on the other hand, we take it to mean what it seems to mean now – forced obstetrical treatment, incarceration, detention or other forms of punishment – intervention in pregnancy is misguided and unlikely to further the alleged goal of healthy mothers and healthy children.[278]

As explained earlier, the purported aim of State intervention – protection of the fetus at risk of harm as a result of the conduct of the pregnant woman – is laudable. But it

---

[273] Ada Calhoun, 'The Criminalization of Bad Mothers', *New York Times Magazine*, 25 April 2012, MM30; Jonathan Wolfe, 'APA Condemns Prosecution of Pregnant Drug Abusers' (2012) 47(9) *Psychiatric News* 12a.

[274] See, eg, Phelan (n 39); Robertson, *Children of Choice* (n 124) 173–94; Robertson (n 71) 450.

[275] *M(J) v Superintendent of Family and Child Services* (BCSC) (n 187).

[276] Suzanne Wong *et al*, 'SOGC Clinical Practice Guideline No 256: Substance Use in Pregnancy' (2011) 33 *Journal of Obstetrics and Gynaecology Canada* 367, 375.

[277] Joan Ellen Zweben and J Thomas Payte, 'Methadone Maintenance in the Treatment of Opioid Dependence: A Current Perspective' (1990) 152 *Western Journal of Medicine* 588, 592.

[278] See Rodgers (n 129); Seymour (n 42) 230, 238.

cannot be disputed that State intervention, at least in the forms it has taken to date, constitutes a profound interference with women's bodies and their lives. As such, it is fundamentally at odds with respect for reproductive autonomy. In the case of medical treatment, respect for reproductive autonomy clearly requires that women's decisions about what medical treatment they will or will not accept must be deferred to, even where it appears that this decision might lead to a less than desirable outcome for the pregnant woman and the fetus. Healthcare providers may attempt to persuade a woman to change her mind about treatment, they may advise her about all of the concerns they have for her potential child should she refuse the treatment, but they may not coerce her to agree to the procedure, either physically or through the use of threats.

But what about the pregnant drug addict? Is she capable of exercising autonomy? If not, do her decisions deserve respect? The situation of substance-addicted pregnant women is complex. A contextualised account of reproductive autonomy reminds us that true or complete autonomy is unachievable; persons are neither fully autonomous nor non-autonomous. It also asks us to attend to the fact that even those who live in oppressive conditions can exhibit a degree of autonomy. Addictions undeniably have great potential to interfere with autonomy.[279] But to treat addicts as being completely incapable of exercising autonomy is misguided. As McLeod and Sherwin explain:

> Treating any patient whose autonomy and self-trust are reduced because of her oppression is a complex matter. It must begin with understanding the political nature of oppression and recognising the importance of finding ways to empower patients by helping to restore their autonomy, in addition to dealing with their physical symptoms. Much of this work is beyond the scope of health-care providers; it requires broadscale social and political change. . . . If health-care providers are to respond effectively to these problems, however, they must understand the impact of oppression on relational autonomy and make what efforts they can to increase the autonomy of their patients and clients.[280]

A contextualised account of reproductive autonomy approaches this problem from the perspective of the woman in her full social and personal context, instead of narrowly focusing on two current facts of her life – her pregnancy and her addiction. In the *Winnipeg Child and Family Services* case, there was evidence that Ms G had sought treatment earlier in her pregnancy but was turned away because of the unavailability of addiction treatment programs appropriate for pregnant women.[281] She expressed an interest in getting help for her addiction and agreed to enter a treatment facility. When the social worker returned to accompany Ms G to the treatment centre, Ms G was high and refused to go. Instead of waiting until Ms G was sober, Winnipeg Child and Family Services sought an order compelling Ms G to remain 'in a place of safety' and requiring treatment for her addiction.[282]

These facts illustrate that, if not completely (or even significantly) capable of making an autonomous decision, Ms G was nonetheless capable of exercising some degree of autonomy, at least while not under the influence of the addictive substance. Her decision not to accompany the social worker to the treatment centre was made while her capacity

[279] See, eg, McLeod (n 220).
[280] Carolyn McLeod and Susan Sherwin, 'Relational Autonomy, Self-Trust and Health Care for Patients who are Oppressed' in Catriona Mackenzie and Natalie Stoljar (eds), *Relational Autonomy: Feminist Perspectives on Autonomy, Agency, and the Social Self* (Oxford, Oxford University Press, 2000) 259, 275–76.
[281] *Winnipeg Child and Family Services* (n 93) para 5 (cited to SCR).
[282] *Ibid.*

to exercise autonomy was significantly impaired,[283] but seeking a court order to compel her to enter addiction treatment shows absolute contempt for the minimal degree of autonomy Ms G was capable of exercising. This, together with her initial agreement to seek treatment, suggests that respect for Ms G's autonomy (and that of women in like circumstances) requires the commitment of resources necessary to create conditions in which treatment is available and is most likely to be successful. At the very least, it seems that Ms G's autonomy could have been respected by making a further attempt to enrol her into a treatment program once she was sober, instead of seeking a court order for her mandatory detention and treatment. Rather than focusing solely on the immediate need for addiction treatment, this account of autonomy is concerned with putting into place the resources and supports needed in order for pregnant addicts to overcome their addictions and to care for their children and themselves in the long term. In other words, a contexualised account of reproductive autonomy favours State intervention to the extent that it involves positive involvement by the State in the lives of pregnant women who need support in order to exercise reproductive autonomy (even only to a limited extent), and whose capacity for autonomy will be increased by the provision of such support and assistance.

[283] This is borne out by her decision to remain in the addiction treatment program even after order of the Manitoba Court of Queen's Bench mandating treatment was stayed two days later, pending appeal (*ibid*).

7

Law, Medicine and Pregnancy: Provider Liability for Pre-natal Torts

I. INTRODUCTION

IN THE PREVIOUS chapter, I examined the issues of maternal liability for pre-natal conduct and State intervention in the lives of pregnant women. In this chapter, I turn to considering provider liability to women, couples and children for acts or omissions during or prior to pregnancy. Continuing with the theme of medicalisation from the foregoing chapter, here the focus is on the physician–patient relationship in a unique context where technological imperatives play a role in shaping law's reaction to medical practice in pregnancy. In this chapter, we move from a focus on control over women's behaviour during pregnancy to considering the question of legal recourse when women's desire to control whether they will have children (and if so, when and how many, and which ones) is frustrated.

Though it might appear that the issue of provider liability is an ill fit within a discussion of reproductive autonomy, I think it is clear that judicial and legislative treatment of these types of cases raise issues that are centrally relevant to reproductive autonomy.

As reproductive technology has become increasingly sophisticated, expectations about the level of control we can exercise over our reproductive capacity have shifted. Women and couples now routinely seek to control the number and timing of their children, as well as the health and developmental attributes of the children they bear. When these aims are frustrated by medical negligence, parents may seek compensation for costs related to the pregnancy and birth, including costs of child-rearing. Children who are born with disabilities resulting from medical negligence may also seek compensation for their injuries. Parental claims are variously referred to as wrongful conception (or sometimes wrongful pregnancy) and wrongful birth claims,[1] while the label 'wrongful life' is applied to the claim by a child that 'but for' the physician's negligence he or she would not have been born. The claims are typically based on unwanted pregnancy after failure of a sterilisation procedure, loss of an opportunity to terminate an otherwise wanted pregnancy because of a physician's failure to provide accurate medical information or advice, or physical harm to the fetus as a result of a medical procedure during pregnancy.[2]

---

[1] See Ellen I Picard and Gerald B Robertson, *Legal Liability of Doctors and Hospitals in Canada*, 4th edn (Toronto, Thomson Carswell, 2007) 260–67.

[2] This list of potential factual scenarios is based on that articulated by Low J in *Krangle (Guardian Ad Litem of) v Brisco*, 55 BCLR (3d) 23, 154 DLR (4th) 707 (BCSC) para 60, affd 2002 SCC 9, [2002] 1 SCR 205. He also includes unwanted birth following an unsuccessful abortion procedure.

In spite of the differing terminology used in these cases, it is clear that these are all negligence claims where the injury relates to the birth of a child. The distinct taxonomy applied to these cases seems to capture the judicial discomfort and uncertainty around these claims. Indeed, it has been argued that the very fact of the distinctive vocabulary used to depict these claims indicates the unwillingness of judges to recognise and compensate women's losses related to child-bearing and child-rearing. As Sanda Rodgers has noted, 'Tort actions . . . for wrongful birth, wrongful pregnancy and wrongful life, show a remarkably unsettled, variable and fundamentally resistant jurisprudential and legislative life both in common law and in civil law jurisdictions'.[3]

The wrongful life, birth and conception cases are multi-faceted and fascinating to analyse, from a variety of perspectives. Here, the purpose is to consider some aspects of these claims as they relate to reproductive autonomy, rather than to focus in depth on the wider legal and policy issues or on the soundness of these kinds of cases from the standpoint of tort and contract law. As such, I shall touch on examples from the US, the UK, Australia and Canada, and highlight issues that are relevant to reproductive decision making.

I begin the chapter with a discussion of the wrongful life claim, and after outlining the law on point in the US, the UK, Canada and Australia, I turn to considering the points of connection between the judicial handling of wrongful life claims and reproductive autonomy. I then discuss wrongful conception and wrongful birth claims, again by outlining the legal treatment of these claims in the four jurisdictions. I conclude the chapter with a discussion of the relevance of wrongful conception and wrongful birth claims to reproductive autonomy, including consideration of the disability rights critique of these claims and their effect on both those with disabilities and on society as a whole. I close with the suggestion that some of the more contemporary cases demonstrate a more reflective judicial appreciation of the harm done by the legal reluctance to fully accept these claims.

II. WRONGFUL LIFE

Of the tort claims for wrongful conception, wrongful birth and wrongful life, the action for wrongful life is the least relevant to reproductive autonomy, as it is brought by the child rather than the parents. But the law on wrongful life is nevertheless instructive because of what it tells us about the common law's views around harm to actual and potential children, and that, in turn, has implications for the legal treatment of reproductive autonomy.

From a descriptive perspective, wrongful life cases are perhaps the easiest of the three claims to dispense with – except for three American states,[4] none of the jurisdictions under consideration here permits wrongful life claims.[5] Indeed, few jurisdictions inter-

---

[3] Sanda Rodgers, 'A Mother's Loss Is the Price of Parenthood: The Failure of Tort Law to Recognize Birth as Compensable Reproductive Injury' in Sanda Rodgers, Rakhi Ruparelia and Louise Bélanger-Hardy (eds), *Critical Torts* (Markham, LexisNexis Canada, 2009) 161, 162.

[4] California, New Jersey and Washington (see below, nn 13–16).

[5] Ten states have statutorily precluded wrongful life actions: Arizona (Ariz Rev Stat § 12-719 (2012); Idaho (Idaho Code § 5-334 (1986)); Indiana (Ind Code Ann § 34-12-1); Michigan (Mich Comp Laws Ann § 600.2971 (West 2001)); Minnesota (Minn Stat Ann § 145.424(1), (2) (1993)); Missouri (Mo Rev Stat § 188.130 (1992)); North Dakota (ND Cent Code § 32-03-43 (1993)); Pennsylvania (41 Pa Cons Stat § 8305 (1993)); South Dakota

nationally recognise such actions.[6] As explained above, wrongful life claims are those brought by the child himself or herself (through a litigation guardian), alleging that, but for the provider's negligent failure to inform the child's mother of the risk that he or she would suffer from disease or disability, he or she would not have been born and would not now be suffering from the effects of the disease or disability. The claim is for damages associated with the pain and suffering involved in living with a disability, as well as for costs of past and future medical and day-to-day care.

In general, the view taken of these cases is that birth is the injury complained of; that the child's claim, properly understood, is that he or she would have been better off having not been born at all. This has created one of the major difficulties for courts faced with such claims, and it has been argued that the child's claim is perhaps better understood as one for 'diminished life'.[7]

Courts and lawmakers have raised several public policy-based objections to permitting wrongful life claims. These range from arguments about the potential social implications of such claims (such as the possibility that they will lead providers to encourage abortion so as to avoid liability),[8] to concerns about the difficulty of the judicial task involved in assessing damages, which requires comparing the value of life with a disability against the value of non-existence.[9] Some have asserted that as a matter of public policy, life is always preferred to non-existence.[10]

In spite of the apparent judicial contempt for wrongful life claims, several commentators have argued that there is no principled basis for refusing such claims, particularly given the recognition of wrongful birth claims.[11] These authors assert that wrongful life claims satisfy the basic elements of a traditional negligence action and should therefore be recognised as such. As Mark Strasser notes:

> Very few jurisdictions are willing to recognize wrongful life claims, although the rationales for that refusal often involve specious arguments and, in any event, are unpersuasive. Each of the elements of the tort claim can plausibly be established in at least some wrongful life cases, and the reasoning employed to nonetheless preclude recognition of those claims would

---

(SD Codified Laws Ann §§ 21-55-1 & 21-55-2 (1987)); and Utah (Utah Code Ann § 78-11-24 (1993)). For a discussion of statutory bars against wrongful life and wrongful birth claims, see Christine Intromasso, 'Reproductive Self-Determination in the Third Circuit: The Statutory Proscription of Wrongful Birth and Wrongful Life Claims as an Unconstitutional Violation of *Planned Parenthood v Casey*'s Undue Burden Standard' (2003) 24 *Women's Rights Law Reporter* 101.

[6] Cases recognising a wrongful life action have been upheld in France (*X v Mutuelle d'Assurance du Corps Sanitaire Français et al (Perruche)* (2000) JCP 2293), the Netherlands (*X v Y*, The Hague, Court of Appeals, 26 March 2003) and Israel (*Zeitzov v Katz* [1986] 40(2) PD 85). In the wake of public reaction to the *Perruche* case, the French Parliament passed legislation invalidating wrongful life claims in 2002 (Loi no 2002-303 relative aux droits des malades et à la qualité du système de santé, 04/03/2002, *Journal Officiel* 05/03/2002).

[7] J Kenyon Mason, *The Troubled Pregnancy: Legal Wrongs and Rights in Reproduction* (Cambridge, Cambridge University Press, 2007) 237–40.

[8] *McKay v Essex Area Health Authority* [1982] QB 1166.

[9] See, eg, *ibid*; *Jones (Guardian Ad Litem of) v Rostvig*, (1999) 44 CCLT (2d) 313; [1999] BCJ No 647.

[10] See, eg, *McKay* (n 8) 1180, 1188; *Harriton (by her tutor) v Stephens; Waller (by his tutor) v James & Anor; Waller (by his tutor) v Hoolahan* [2004] NSWCA 93, para 24; *Procanik v Cillo*, 478 A 2d 755 (NJ 1984) 772 (Schreiber J dissenting in part).

[11] See, eg, Anthony Jackson, 'Wrongful Life and Wrongful Birth: The English Conception' (1996) 17 *Journal of Legal Medicine* 349 (Jackson suggests not only that English courts should allow wrongful life claims, but that they should *not* recognise wrongful birth claims); Amos Shapira, '''Wrongful Life' Lawsuits for Faulty Genetic Counselling: Should the Impaired Newborn be Entitled to Sue?' (1998) 24 *Journal of Medical Ethics* 369; Mark Strasser, 'Wrongful Life, Wrongful Birth, Wrongful Death and the Right to Refuse Treatment: Can Reasonable Jurisdictions Recognize All But One?' (1999) 64 *Missouri Law Review* 29.

seem to have important implications for the continued recognition of other existing tort claims.[12]

As noted above, a minority of American states have recognised wrongful life claims. In *Curlender v Bioscience Laboratories*,[13] the child plaintiff was born with Tay-Sachs disease, and the California courts awarded general damages for pain and suffering, as well as damages for pecuniary losses suffered as a result of his condition. The basic premise supporting recovery was upheld in a later California case (where the child was born deaf after an older sibling's deafness was incorrectly diagnosed as not being hereditary).[14] The child's claim for the additional expenses caused by his impairment was allowed, but the Court rejected the approach taken in *Curlender* and declined to award general damages. Two other state courts have recognised wrongful life claims: New Jersey and Washington. In *Procanik v Cillo*,[15] the New Jersey courts awarded special damages (for medical expenses incurred due to his disability) to a child born with congenital rubella syndrome, but rejected the additional claim in general damages for pain and suffering and 'diminished childhood'. Similarly, in *Harbeson v Parke-Davis*,[16] the Washington Court awarded damages but confined the award to special damages associated with the extraordinary costs referable to the plaintiff's disability.

These few exceptions aside, the vast majority of American states have rejected the claim for wrongful life,[17] relying primarily on arguments concerning the impossibility of comparing life with a disability to no life at all.[18] As will be seen below, this reasoning is echoed by courts in other jurisdictions.[19]

Courts in England have also refused to allow wrongful life claims. In *McKay v Essex Area Health Authority*,[20] the English Court of Appeal rejected a damages claim brought by a child born with disabilities as a result of his mother becoming infected with rubella early in her pregnancy.[21] The Court of Appeal held that to recognise such a claim

> would . . . make a further inroad on the sanctity of human life which would be contrary to public policy. It would mean regarding the life of a handicapped child as not only less valuable than the life of a normal child, but so much less valuable that it was not worth preserving . . .[22]

---

[12] Strasser (n 11) 75.

[13] *Curlender v Bioscience Laboratories*, 106 Cal App 3d 811 (1980).

[14] *Turpin v Sortini*, 643 P 2d 954 (Cal 1982).

[15] *Procanik v Cillo* (n 10).

[16] *Harbeson v Parke-Davis*, 656 P 2d 483 (Wash 1983).

[17] See, eg, *Lininger v Eisenbaum*, 764 P 2d 1202 (Colo 1988); *Kassama v Magat*, 767 A 2d 348 (Md 2001).

[18] For a list of the cases in the 26 states which have rejected this cause of action, see Penelope Watson, 'Legal and Ethical Issues in Wrongful Life Actions' (2002) 26 *Melbourne University Law Review* 736, fn 39.

[19] See, eg, Strasser (n 11) 30, fn 2; Brent W Herrin, 'Tort Law – *Etkind v Suarez*: When Do the Joys of Being a Parent Become a Burden?' (1999) 23 *American Journal of Trial Advocacy* 481.

[20] *McKay* (n 8). A recent case from Northern Ireland deals with a fascinating wrongful life claim. Here, twins were born via IVF involving the use of donor sperm. The parents were white, and the twins (although their skin colour was not identical) both had much darker-coloured skin than the parents. The defendant Trust had mistakenly used sperm from a donor that was labeled 'Caucasian (Cape Coloured)' rather than from a 'white' or 'Caucasian' donor. The Trust admitted liability to the parents, but contested the separate claim for damages brought by the children. The twins' claims were ultimately rejected (*A (a minor) and B (a minor) by C (their mother and next friend) v A Health and Social Services Trust* [2010] NIQB 108, affd [2011] NICA 28). For a comment on the case, see Sally Sheldon, 'Only Skin Deep? The Harm of Being Born a Different Colour to One's Parents' (2011) 19 *Medical Law Review* 657.

[21] The mother was tested but was negligently informed that she did not have rubella and that she could safely continue the pregnancy (*McKay* (n 8)).

[22] *Ibid* 1180.

In his reasons in *McKay*, Stephenson LJ also expressed concern that wrongful life claims would lead to potential liability for medical practitioners even where the child suffers from only minor disabilities.[23] Further, he speculated that recognition of such claims would expose *mothers* to wrongful life claims for failing to terminate the pregnancy in spite of becoming aware of the likelihood that the child would be born with disabilities.[24] He also noted the extreme difficulty that would arise in attempting to assess damages in such a case: 'Even if a court were competent to decide between the conflicting views of theologians and philosophers and to assume an "after life" or non-existence as the basis for the comparison, how can a judge put value on the one or the other[?]'[25]

The decisive rejection of wrongful life cases in the UK might be linked to the view that these claims are barred by the Congenital Disabilities (Civil Liability) Act 1976. Indeed, this was the unanimous view of the Court of Appeal in *McKay*. Sections 1(1) and (2)(b) of the Act provide as follows:

(1) If a child is born disabled as the result of such an occurrence before its birth as is mentioned in subsection (2) below, and a person (other than the child's own mother) is under this section answerable to the child in respect of the occurrence, the child's disabilities are to be regarded as damage resulting from the wrongful act of that person and actionable accordingly at the suit of the child.

(2) An occurrence to which this section applies is one which –

. . .

(b) affected the mother during her pregnancy, or affected her or the child in the course of its birth, so that the child is born with disabilities which would not otherwise have been present.

According to the Court in *McKay*, the section specifically precludes wrongful life claims in that it contemplates that 'but for the occurrence giving rise to a disabled birth, the child would have been born normal and healthy – not that it would not have been born at all'.[26] A number of legal scholars have disputed this interpretation: Anthony Jackson has argued that, at best, the Act is 'neutral in its attitude toward the wrongful life claim,'[27] and J Kenyon Mason has also disagreed with the Court's interpretation.[28] It is difficult to disagree with Jackson and Mason in their assertions that this section does not preclude a wrongful life action,[29] as the wording of the legislation appears to be inapplicable to wrongful life claims. In any event, Mason notes that the decision in *McKay* resolved the issue 'with such determination that, Act or no Act of Parliament, no similar case has since been allowed to proceed'.[30]

---

[23] *Ibid* 1181.

[24] *Ibid*. The California Court of Appeals took this concern one step further, stating that parents should be liable in such circumstances: 'we see no sound public policy which should protect those parents from being answerable for the pain, suffering and misery which they have wrought upon their offspring' (*Curlender v Bioscience Laboratories* (n 13) 829). The California Legislature responded by passing legislation to preclude such claims (Cal Civ Code § 43.6 (West 2003)).

[25] *McKay* (n 8) 1181.

[26] *McKay* (n 8) 1186–87.

[27] Jackson (n 11) 366.

[28] Noting that while it may be unwise to question the Court's unanimous reasoning, he is unable to accept their view (Mason (n 7) 212).

[29] See also Jane ES Fortin, 'Is the "Wrongful Life" Action Really Dead?' (1987) 9 *Journal of Social Welfare Law* 306, who suggests that perhaps the reason for this error in interpretation rests with the Court of Appeal's awareness that the Law Commission had argued that such claims should be prohibited.

[30] Mason (n 7) 205.

In spite of the treatment of these claims in the case law,[31] there arguably remains a live question about whether wrongful life claims may be brought in the UK as a result of the interaction of the Human Fertilisation and Embryology 1990 (HFE Act 1990)[32] and the Congenital Disabilities (Civil Liability) Act 1976. The 1976 Act permits a child who is 'born disabled' as a result of the wrongful act of a third party during his or her mother's pregnancy or in the course of birth to sue the third party and recover damages for his or her injuries.[33] The child's right crystallises at birth, and is derivative in that it depends upon the defendant being potentially liable to one or both of the child's parents.[34] Section 1A of the Congenital Disabilities (Civil Liability) Act 1976, which was included as a result of the passage of the HFE Act 1990, provides that where a person fails to exercise due care 'in the course of the selection . . . of the embryo' and the child is as a result born with disabilities, 'the child's disabilities are to be regarded as damage resulting from the wrongful act of that person and actionable accordingly at the suit of the child'.[35] As Anthony Jackson points out, 'The nature of the claim is that if the physician had exercised due care, a different embryo would have been selected and the child would never have been born'.[36] Thus, 'It seems that with this legislation the English Parliament is recognising wrongful life claims in certain circumstances'.[37]

The UK and US approaches to wrongful life have been established since the earliest days of wrongful life claims. In Canada and Australia, by contrast, these issues have been dealt with much more recently. These cases deserve a bit more time and attention here than some of the older authorities from the UK and the US. In part, this is because they are more recently decided and have had less scholarly attention, but more importantly because they deal with the legal issues in a way that makes them more relevant for consideration from the standpoint of reproductive autonomy. The Canadian cases in particular need some detailed analysis because they adopt a very different approach from that seen to date in other jurisdictions.

Like the UK and most American courts, the Australian High Court has held that the common law does not recognise a claim for wrongful life. Two cases came before the High Court in 2005: *Harriton v Stephens*[38] and *Waller v James*.[39] Alexia Harriton was born with what Kirby J referred to as 'catastrophic disabilities' as a result of exposure to the rubella virus in utero,[40] after her mother was wrongly advised that she did not have rubella during the first trimester of her pregnancy. Keeden Waller was born with a blood disorder (AT3 deficiency) passed on to him by his father.[41] Keeden's parents claimed that had they known that the AT3 deficiency was genetic and could be passed to their child, they would either have deferred IVF until a test was available, or used donor sperm to conceive a child.[42]

---

[31] *Ibid* 213.

[32] Human Fertilisation and Embryology Act 1990, s 44(1).

[33] Congenital Disabilities (Civil Liability) Act 1976, s 1(1).

[34] *Ibid* s 1(3).

[35] *Ibid* s 1A(1).

[36] Jackson (n 11) 370.

[37] MJ Howlett, Denise Avard and Bartha Maria Knoppers, 'Physicians and Genetic Malpractice' (2002) 21 *Medicine and Law* 661, 671.

[38] *Harriton v Stephens* [2006] HCA 15, (2006) 226 CLR 52.

[39] *Waller v James* [2006] HCA 16, (2006) 226 CLR 136.

[40] *Harriton* (n 38) para 20.

[41] *Waller v James* (n 39) paras 9–14.

[42] *Ibid*. See also *Bannerman v Mills* (1991) Aust Torts Reports ¶81-079 (NSWSC); *Edwards v Blomeley* [2002] NSWSC 460 (as a result of an unsuccessful vasectomy, a child was born with 'cri du chat' syndrome, which results from a deletion or translocation of material from chromosome 5).

Though the two appeals dealt with distinct facts they were heard together, and the reasons in *Harriton v Stephens* contain the details of the Court's approach to wrongful life claims. The claims were denied at first instance[43] (as well as in the Court of Appeal and the High Court), for largely the same reasons as those that have been expressed by US courts and by the English Court of Appeal in *McKay*.

Crennan J wrote the lead judgment for the High Court. Put concisely, she denied the claim because in her view the plaintiffs had suffered no legally cognisable harm. If no legally relevant harm is suffered, no legal duty of care can arise. The claims advanced by both Alexia Harriton and Keeden Waller, according to Crennan J, centred on the assertion that it would be preferable if they had not been born, and this, in turn,

> raises the difficult question of whether the common law could or should recognise a right of a foetus to be aborted, or an interest of a foetus in its own termination, which is distinct from the recognised right of a foetus not to be physically injured whilst *en ventre sa mère* . . .[44]

Crennan J acknowledged that a physician owes a duty of care to the fetus;[45] in her view, however, the creation of a duty to the fetus that entails advising the mother of the condition of the fetus so that she can 'terminate a pregnancy in the interest of the foetus in not being born' would potentially 'introduce conflict, even incoherence, into the body of relevant legal principle'.[46]

Turning to the question of damage (which, as noted, she perceived to be intimately linked with the recognition of a duty of care), Crennan J agreed with the view expressed in *McKay* that the true comparison for the purpose of assessing damage in wrongful life cases is the difference between life with disabilities and 'non-existence', and that this comparison is impossible.[47] To the suggestion that, instead of comparing life with disability and non-existence, the appropriate comparison is between life as a healthy child and life with disability,[48] Crennan J responded that this is an 'awkward, unconvincing and unworkable legal fiction'.[49] Put simply, the majority position in *Harriton v Stephens* is that 'Life with disabilities, like life, is not actionable'.[50]

The lone dissenting opinion in the High Court was offered by Kirby J, who began by stating that the language of 'wrongful life' is inapposite and misleading.[51] In his view, the label itself implies disrespect for human life, and as such 'has caused judges to recoil from affording remedies in "wrongful life" cases'.[52] Kirby J expressed particular concern about the majority's denial of a duty of care because of the perception that the plaintiffs could not show legally cognisable harm. In his view, the existing duty owed by healthcare

---

[43] The cases proceeded by way of 'preliminary determination' of specific questions, rather than by way of a trial. The preliminary questions were (i) if the respondents failed to exercise reasonable care in their management of the appellants' parents, and, but for that failure, the appellants would not have been born, do the appellants have a cause of action against the respondents? And (ii) if so, what categories of damages are available? As the first question was answered in the negative by Studdert J in the New South Wales Supreme Court, as well as by a majority in both the Court of Appeal and the High Court, there was never a full trial of the issues (Harriton (n 38) para 22).

[44] *Harriton* (n 38) para 245.

[45] A duty 'which may be mediated through the mother' (*ibid* para 249).

[46] *Ibid.*

[47] *Ibid* para 252.

[48] As was done by the Supreme Court of Israel in *Ziestzov v Katz* (n 6).

[49] *Harriton* (n 38) para 276.

[50] *Ibid* para 277.

[51] *Ibid* paras 8–14.

[52] *Ibid* para 13.

providers to employ reasonable care to avoid causing injury to the fetus is sufficient in scope to lead to the imposition of a duty in a wrongful life case.[53] Moreover, the refusal to recognise a duty in these circumstances results in conferring an 'exceptional immunity' on physicians and providers.[54]

Kirby J also took issue with the 'conflicting duties' argument raised by the majority, noting that the issue of conflicting obligations is more properly a matter for consideration in relation to the standard of care. He noted that the 'conflicting duties' argument 'would logically apply to exclude the duty owed by medical practitioners to unborn children in respect of pre-natal injuries. Such a duty has the same potential in every case to conflict with the duty owed to the mother.'[55]

Turning to the majority's assertion that damage in such cases is unquantifiable, Kirby J pointed out that with respect to special damages, this argument is simply not maintainable. The loss suffered by the plaintiff in this regard is fully the responsibility of the negligent defendant. As to general damages, Kirby J stated that courts are frequently required to 'assign monetary values to . . . intangible injuries and nebulous losses,' including pain and suffering and loss of expectation of life,[56] and that difficulty in assessing damages does not relieve the court of its duty to award compensation to a plaintiff who has suffered actionable damage.[57]

Finally, Kirby J turned his attention to the policy arguments that have been raised (and accepted) in many wrongful life cases. As he explained:

> It remains for me to consider whether any policy reasons exist that would warrant rejecting wrongful life actions although they are consistent with established tort doctrine. Numerous policy arguments have been suggested in the courts below and in other cases. None of these arguments is convincing. Some of them are premised on a misunderstanding of the tort of negligence. Most depend upon what I regard as a distorted characterisation of wrongful life claims. A number seem to rest on religious beliefs rather than on the application of legal doctrine in a secular community. In today's world a steady adherence to secularism in the law is more important to a mutually respectful civil society than before. Judges have no right to impose their religious convictions (if any) on others who may not share those convictions.[58]

In keeping with courts in Australia and the UK, and most American courts, to date, no Canadian court has recognised a wrongful life claim. Indeed, in the few cases in which such a claim has been advanced, usually together with a wrongful birth claim brought by the child's parents, the courts have dismissed this aspect of the case, citing public policy reasons.[59]

The first Canadian appellate court to consider a wrongful life claim was the Manitoba

---

[53]   *Ibid* para 71.
[54]   *Ibid* para 72.
[55]   *Ibid* para 75.
[56]   *Ibid* para 83.
[57]   *Ibid* paras 83–84.
[58]   *Ibid* para 110.
[59]   See, eg, *Jones v Rostvig* (n 9); *Cataford v Moreau* [1978] CS 933, (1979) 7 CCLT 241 (QCSC); *Mickle v Salvation Army Grace Hospital Windsor Ontario* (1998) 166 DLR (4th) 743, [1998] OJ No 4683 (Ont Gen Div); *Patmore (Guardian Ad Litem of) v Weatherston* [1999] BCJ No 650, 86 ACWS (3d) 981 (BCSC); *Lacroix (Litigation Guardian of) v Dominque* (1999) 141 Man R (2d) 1, [1999] 12 WWR 38 (QB) affd 156 Man R (2d) 262, (2001) 202 DLR (4th) 121 (MBCA), leave to appeal to SCC denied [2001] SCCA No 477, (2001) 289 NR 202.

Court of Appeal in *Lacroix (Litigation Guardian of) v Dominique*.[60] Donna Lacroix was born with physical and developmental disabilities as a result of her mother's ingestion of medication to control her epilepsy. Her parents claimed that they had not been informed by their physicians of the risks to the fetus of ingestion of this medication during pregnancy.[61] The Court noted that claims made by children born with disabilities may be characterised as falling into one of two categories. The first – cases in which the disabilities or injuries were caused by the wrongful act or omission of a third party – have long been considered valid claims,[62] while claims in the second category – cases in which the negligence did not cause the injury, but led to the birth of the child – have been labelled wrongful life claims and uniformly rejected.[63]

In two recent judgments, the Ontario Court of Appeal has raised doubt about the above-described approach to cases in which a child born with disabilities brings a negligence claim against a physician.[64] Arguably, neither was a typical wrongful life case, which most often involve failure by a healthcare provider to identify the existence of a condition affecting the fetus and to inform the pregnant woman that the only way to avoid the consequences of that condition is to terminate the pregnancy.[65] One of the Ontario cases involved the question of informed consent to treatment with the fertility drug Clomid, and the other concerned prescription of Accutane (a teratogenic drug used in treating acne) to a woman who became pregnant during the course of treatment.

In *Paxton v Ramji*, based on the framework articulated in *Lacroix*, the trial judge considered and rejected the possibility that the claim was one for wrongful life.[66] Instead, she concluded that the child's claim was more properly framed as being based on the defendant physician's duty not to prescribe Accutane to a woman of childbearing potential. The claim was ultimately unsuccessful because in the view of the trial judge, the defendant met the standard of care and thus did not breach his duty to the infant plaintiff. In other words, it was clear to the trial judge that the defendant

---

[60] *Lacroix* (MBCA) (n 59). Perhaps more accurately, the Manitoba Court of Appeal is the first Canadian appellate court to acknowledge that it was deciding a wrongful life claim. See *Cherry (Guardian Ad Litem of) v Borsman*, 70 BCLR (2d) 273, [1992] 6 WWR 701 (BCCA) para 71 (cited to BCLR), where the British Columbia Court of Appeal stated: 'The first thing that must be said here is that in our opinion this is not a "wrongful life" case . . .' Arguably, it is indeed a wrongful life case. See Mason (n 7) 225; Picard and Robertson (n 1) 269.

[61] The parents also asserted a wrongful birth claim, but their claim was brought after the expiry of the limitation period and could not proceed.

[62] See, eg, *Montreal Tramways v Léveillé* [1933] SCR 456, [1933] 4 DLR 337; *Duval v Seguin* [1972] 2 OR 686, 26 DLR (3d) 418 (Ont HCJ).

[63] See, eg, *Cataford v Moreau* (n 59); *Jones v Rostvig* (n 9); *Lacroix* (MBCA) (n 59); *Mickle v Salvation Army Grace Hospital Windsor Ontario* (n 59); *Patmore v Weatherston* (n 59). In a few such cases, courts have denied the defendant's motion for summary judgment on the basis that it is not plain and obvious that the claim discloses no reasonable cause of action: see, eg, *Bartok v Shokeir*, 168 Sask R 280, [1998] SJ No 645 (SKCA); *Petkovic v Olupona*, 30 CCLT (3d) 266, [2002] OJ No 3411 (Ont SCJ); *McDonald-Wright (Litigation Guardian of) v O'Herlihy*, 75 OR (3d) 261, [2005] OJ No 135 (Ont SCJ).

[64] *Paxton v Ramji*, [2006] OJ No 1179 (Ont SCJ) affd 2008 ONCA 697, 299 DLR (4th) 614, leave to appeal refused [2008] SCCA No 508; *Bovingdon v Hergott*, 2008 ONCA 2, 290 DLR (4th) 126, leave to appeal refused [2008] SCCA No 92.

[65] Wrongful life claims also involve situations where conception of the child would have been avoided had the provider properly identified the risk of a heritable condition (*Waller v James* (n 39) is such a case). *Bovingdon* (n 64), while not a typical wrongful life scenario, could certainly be viewed as such, in that had the physician not been negligent in advising his patient about the risk of multiple gestation posed by Clomid, the patient would not have taken the medication and the children would not have been born. The harm to the twins was related to their premature birth, which is a significant risk of multiple pregnancy.

[66] *Paxton* (Ont SCJ) (n 64).

physician owed a duty of care to the child plaintiff; he avoided liability because he discharged the duty.

The Court of Appeal, while agreeing with the result reached by the trial judge, did not
endorse the approach she adopted. The Court held that the framework articulated in
Lacroix fails to provide a sufficiently rigorous starting point for the analysis in the pre-
natal negligence context. In both *Lacroix* and this case, the provider's negligence could
have been characterised either as harm caused by the prescription of a particular medication during early pregnancy, or as the failure to prevent conception of the child (to
prevent the harm that would be caused to the fetus by the woman's ingestion of the
drug). The Court stated that in 'asking whether or not the claim before the court should
be characterized as one for wrongful life, Canadian courts have asked the wrong
question'.[67] Instead, according to Feldman JA, the appropriate analysis in such a case is
a first-principles duty of care analysis based on the reasoning of the House of Lords in
Anns v Merton London Borough Council,[68] and expounded upon by the Supreme Court
of Canada in several negligence cases.[69]

The duty of care analysis undertaken by the Court of Appeal requires consideration of
questions of foreseeability, proximity (including policy considerations relevant to the
relationship between plaintiff and defendant) and policy.[70] In *Paxton*, the Court declined
to impose a duty of care, primarily because of its 'proximity' analysis, which demands
consideration of whether the defendant doctor and the future child are in such a 'close
and direct relationship' that the court would be justified in imposing a duty of care on
the doctor. The primary reason the Court gave for declining to impose a duty of care
was the potential for the physician to owe conflicting duties to 'a female patient and to
her future child (whether conceived or not yet conceived)'.[71] The worry is that such a
conflict could have 'an undesirable chilling effect on doctors,' in that they might 'offer
treatment to some female patients in a way that might deprive them of their autonomy
and freedom of informed choice in their medical care'.[72]

The fact that the Court of Appeal thought the *Anns* analysis necessary here is itself
difficult to comprehend, given the long line of cases in the labour and delivery context,
where it has never been suggested that a physician does not owe a duty of care to an
unborn child.[73] Moreover, it is settled law in Canada (and elsewhere) that third parties

---

[67]   *Paxton* (ONCA) (n 64) para 29.

[68]   *Anns v Merton London Borough Council* [1978] AC 728.

[69]   See, eg, *Kamloops (City) v Nielsen* [1984] 2 SCR 2, [1984] 5 WWR 1; *Cooper v Hobart*, 2001 SCC 79,
[2001] 3 SCR 537; *Edwards v Law Society of Upper Canada*, 2001 SCC 80, [2001] 3 SCR 562; *Childs v
Desormeaux*, 2006 SCC 18, [2006] 1 SCR 643; *Syl Apps Secure Treatment Centre v D(B)*, 2007 SCC 38, [2007]
3 SCR 83; *Holland v Saskatchewan*, 2008 SCC 42, [2008] 2 SCR 551. The *Anns* analysis is reserved for cases in
which the courts are faced with a novel claim, or a case of first impression, where the duty alleged is not analo-
gous to another recognised duty of care (*Cooper v Hobart* (n 69) paras 36–39; Lewis N Klar, *Tort Law*, 5th edn
(Toronto, Thompson Carswell, 2012) 179; Allen M Linden and Bruce Feldthusen, *Canadian Tort Law*, 9th edn
(Markham, LexisNexis Canada, 2011) 304–05). As Linden and Feldthusen explain, the analysis is intended for
use in rare cases, not as a means of revisiting existing or already recognised duties of care.

[70]   Specifically, residual policy considerations that would justify a refusal to recognise a duty of care (*Paxton*
(ONCA) (n 64) paras 77–85).

[71]   *Ibid* para 76.

[72]   *Ibid* para 68.

[73]   See, eg, *Crawford (Litigation Guardian of) v Penney*, 14 CCLT (3d) 60, [2003] OJ No 89 (Ont SCJ), affd
[2004] OJ No 3669, 26 CCLT (3d) 246 (Ont CA); *Commisso (Litigation Guardian of) v North York Branson
Hospital*, (2003) 48 OR (3d) 484.

owe a duty of care to a child *en ventre sa mère*.[74] But if the Court of Appeal's recourse to a full duty of care analysis in these cases is unexpected, its conclusion – that no duty of care is owed by a physician to a child not yet *born or conceived* at the time of the negligent act – is astonishing.

Because of the Court's references to the child being 'conceived or not yet conceived' at the time of the physician's negligent act, the Ontario Court of Appeal's reasoning in *Paxton* (and *Bovingdon v Hergott*) immediately gave rise to concern about the long line of cases in which it had always been assumed that a duty of care is owed by physicians (and other healthcare providers) to an unborn child. The so-called 'labour and delivery' cases[75] follow the reasoning of the early cases that held that a child, once born alive, may sue a third party for damages caused by negligence while the child was *'en ventre sa mère'*.[76] The use of the words 'conceived or not yet conceived' and 'not yet conceived or born' in the Court of Appeal's reasons understandably led to uncertainty about the potential scope of the decision and its impact on what was thought to be settled law. The Ontario Court of Appeal has since clarified its comments in *Paxton* and *Bovingdon v Hergott*, noting that:

> We do not read those passages as governing the issue raised on this appeal. In accordance with the tradition of the common law and the doctrine of precedent, *Paxton* and *Bovingdon* must be read in the light of their precise facts, the issues they addressed, and in a proper legal context . . . In our view, the authority of the labour and delivery cases remains intact and is unaffected by *Bovingdon* and *Paxton*.[77]

The Court of Appeal's comments are welcome to the extent that they foreclose any doubt about whether a physician owes a duty of care to a fetus in the labour and delivery context. But as alluded to above, there is more than just this to be concerned about in the reasoning of the Court in these wrongful life cases. Even if *Paxton* and *Bovingdon v Hergott* are confined to their particular facts, the reasoning in both cases is flawed. There is much to dispute in the Ontario Court of Appeal's approach to reasoning about wrongful life cases and the duty of care; much of this critique relates to tort law principles more generally and will not be dealt with here. Instead, I shall focus on the implications of the Court's reasoning in relation to reproductive autonomy.

In raising the concern about conflicting duties, the Court of Appeal drew on the Supreme Court's decision in *Syl Apps Secure Treatment Centre v D(B)*,[78] where the parents of a child apprehended under Ontario's child welfare law sued a treatment centre involved in the child's care.[79] Given the vast factual differences between *Syl Apps* and

---

[74] See *Duval v Seguin* (n 62); *Montreal Tramways v Léveillé* (n 62); *Bonbrest v Kotz*, 65 F Supp 138 (DDC 1946); *Watt v Rama* [1972] VR 353; *X and Y (By Her Tutor X) v Pal* (1991) 23 NSWLR 26; *de Martell v Merton and Sutton Health Authority* [1993] QB 204; *Burton v Islington Health Authority* [1993] QB 204.

[75] See, eg, *Commisso (Litigation Guardian of) v North York Branson Hospital* (Ont CA) (n 73); *Crawford (Litigation Guardian of) v Penney* (Ont CA) (n 73).

[76] See, eg, *Duval v Seguin* (n 62); *Montreal Tramways v Léveillé* (n 62).

[77] *Liebig (Litigation Guardian of) v Guelph General Hospital*, 2010 ONCA 450, 263 OAC 180, para 13.

[78] *Syl Apps* (n 69).

[79] The lawsuit claimed that various parties involved in treating the child had been negligent, and that their negligence resulted in the permanent disruption of the relationship between the child and her family. The Supreme Court, in holding that the Centre did not owe a private law duty of care to the child's family, based its decision largely on the worry about the potential for conflicting obligations. The Centre's 'transcendent' statutory duty is to look after the child's best interests; imposing a private duty of care to the child's family (whose interests would often be distinct from those of the child) would mean that the Centre might be unable to fulfill this primary obligation (*ibid* para 41).

Paxton, it is difficult to understand Feldman JA's reliance on the former in considering whether a duty should be imposed in *Paxton*. In any situation in which a physician might owe a duty of care to a fetus, the duty is mediated through the pregnant woman. No intervention undertaken to further the interests of the fetus can occur without involving the pregnant woman. To compare the healthcare provider's duty to a fetus on the one hand and an adolescent on the other is peculiar, to say the least.

Moreover, in the child welfare context, the 'paramount purpose' of the statutory regime is to 'promote the best interests, protection and well being of children'.[80] In so far as the legislation has *any other* purpose, that purpose must be compatible with the objective of furthering the best interests of the child.[81] Physicians who care for pregnant women are faced with working to promote the best interests of both the pregnant woman and the fetus, but in situations where the interests of one of those 'entities' must yield, it is clear that the paramount obligation is to the pregnant woman.[82]

What about the concern around conflicting duties raised by the Ontario Court of Appeal and by Crennan J in the Australian High Court? There are unquestionably instances in which a physician caring for a pregnant woman feels conflicted in his or her ability to look after the best interests of both the woman and the fetus she carries. While most pregnant women do everything they can to ensure that their child is born healthy and free from disability,[83] there are times when the interests of the pregnant woman and that of the fetus are poorly aligned. When, for example, a pregnant woman is diagnosed with cancer, her interests in obtaining prompt treatment may conflict with the best interests of the fetus in avoiding exposure to potentially harmful medications. The woman's life may depend on a treatment that threatens the health or viability of the fetus, but even if the physician owes a duty to the fetus, that duty (and the potential conflict it gives rise to) does not override the physician's duty to the pregnant woman.[84] The fact that the *interests* of the pregnant woman and fetus are in conflict does not mean that the physician owes conflicting *duties*. As explained by Holmes J of the British Columbia Supreme Court, to the extent any such conflict exists,

> it is answered by the simple reality that mothers make decisions – both as to medical care and in other areas – for their unborn children. As to the conflict of interests (mother's versus unborn child's) implicated in that decision, it is for the mother, and not the physician, to resolve.[85]

[80] See, eg, Child and Family Services Act, RSO 1990, c C-11, s 1(1).
[81] *Ibid* s 1(2).
[82] See, eg, Mason (n 7) 79; Picard and Robertson (n 1) 334; American College of Obstetricians and Gynecologists, 'Committee Opinion No 321: Maternal Decision Making, Ethics and the Law' (2005) 106 *Obstetrics & Gynecology* 1127; Royal College of Obstetricians and Gynaecologists, 'Ethics Committee Guideline No 1: Law and Ethics in Relation to Court-Authorised Obstetric Intervention' (London, Royal College of Obstetricians and Gynaecologists, September 2006). See also *Tameside & Glossop Acute Services Unit v CH* [1996] 1 FLR 762; *Re MB (An Adult: Medical Treatment)* [1997] EWCA Civ 3093, [1997] 2 FLR 426; *St George's Healthcare NHS Trust v S* [1999] Fam 26, [1998] 3 All ER 673. These cases are further discussed in ch 6, section III.A.
[83] As discussed in ch 6, section II.C.
[84] Another example might be HIV treatment, where anti-retroviral drugs are used to reduce the risk of maternal–fetal transmission of HIV, but where that treatment during pregnancy may actually make later treatment of the woman's condition more difficult. See Alice Grey, '*Harriton v Stephens*: Life, Logic and Legal Fictions' (2006) 28 *Sydney Law Review* 545, 555.
[85] *Ediger (Guardian Ad Litem of) v Johnston*, 2009 BCSC 386, 65 CCLT (3d) 1, para 186. Justice Holmes declined to find that *Paxton* and *Bovingdon* 'require reconsideration of the law in this province that a physician's duty of care to a pregnant woman encompasses her fetus' (para 213). The case was overturned on appeal, but the Court of Appeal agreed with Justice Holmes on this point (*Ediger v Johnston*, 2011 BCCA 253, 19 BCLR (5th) 60 paras 30–33). Justice Holmes's reasoning has been followed in other BC cases: see, eg, *Cojocaru (Guardian*

The physician's duty extends to informing the pregnant woman about treatment options and the risks to her and to the fetus of either accepting or refusing treatment. Having done that, the physician will have discharged her duty and it will fall to the woman to make a decision about how to proceed. While there may be a conflict of interests, there is no conflict in the duty owed by the physician – there is a single duty, and that is to provide the pregnant woman with the information she needs in order to make a decision.

As Kirby J noted in *Harriton v Stephens*,[86] the potential problem of conflicting duties, to the extent that it arises in the context of wrongful life claims, also arises in any situation where a physician or healthcare provider might owe a duty of care to avoid negligently injuring the fetus.[87] Indeed, had Ms Paxton been pregnant when she consulted Dr Ramji about Accutane, it seems clear (or would have seemed so, prior to the decisions in *Paxton* and *Liebig v Guelph General Hospital*) that he would not have been able to prescribe it without being liable in negligence for harm caused to the child. How could it be said to be reasonable for a physician to prescribe a contraindicated, teratogenic drug to a pregnant woman for the treatment of a non life-threatening condition? But, as Kirby J notes, this is an issue relevant to whether the physician has met the standard of care, rather than to whether a duty exists to begin with.[88]

A. Wrongful life and reproductive autonomy

While the wrongful life cases do not implicate reproductive autonomy directly, the comments made by the Australian High Court and the Ontario Court of Appeal about conflicting duties are interesting in that they demonstrate an awareness of the need to respect pregnant women's 'autonomy and freedom of informed choice' in medical care. It is particularly noteworthy that these comments are made in the larger context of a line of cases in which women's reproductive autonomy is largely, if not completely, disregarded.

The concern about conflicting duties raised in *Paxton* seems to be based in part on the fact that in Canada, mothers are immune from liability for their conduct during pregnancy.[89] The court seems to have understood maternal immunity to imply the necessity of a similar immunity for physicians, lest women be deprived of their ability to make autonomous decisions about their own healthcare during pregnancy. But as has been explained, the conflict, if any, is resolved by providing the pregnant woman with the information she needs in order to make an informed choice.

Ad Litem of) v British Columbia Women's Hospital, 2009 BCSC 494, 65 CCLT (3d) 75; affd on this point *Cojocaru (Guardian Ad Litem of) v British Columbia Women's Hospital and Health Centre*, 2011 BCCA 192, 81 CCLT (3d) 183 para 104. The Supreme Court of Canada heard appeals in both of these cases in December 2012 (*Eric Victor Cojocaru, an infant by his Guardian Ad Litem, Monica Cojocaru et al v British Columbia Women's Hospital and Health Center et al*, 2011 CanLII 75132 (SCC) – 2011-11-24); *Steinebach (Litigation Guardian of) v Fraser Health Authority*, 2010 BCSC 832, [2010] BCJ No 1129, vard 2011 BCCA 302, 19 BCLR (5th) 92. For an interesting discussion of *Paxton* and *Bovingdon*, see Richard Halpern, 'Birth Trauma and the Duty of Care' (*Thomson Rogers*, 26 April 2010), at <www.thomsonrogers.com/birth-trauma-and-duty-care>.

[86] *Harriton* (2006) (n 38) paras 73, 75.
[87] *Ibid* para 75.
[88] As Kirby J noted in his reasons (*ibid* paras 74–75).
[89] *Dobson (Litigation Guardian of) v Dobson* [1999] 2 SCR 753, 214 NBR (2d) 201. See discussion in ch 6, section II.A.

Crennan J in the Australian High Court also raised the conflicting duties issue,[90] albeit not in relation to concerns about maternal immunity. Crennan J's concern seems to relate to the potential for an actual conflict between the physician's duty to avoid harming the fetus and a duty (also owed to the fetus) to advise the mother to terminate the pregnancy. Although Crennan J did not frame it in this way, the question of autonomy in making reproductive decisions during pregnancy is front and centre. The account of reproductive autonomy that I adopt here places decision making about whether to continue or terminate a pregnancy in the hands of the pregnant woman, and no one else. The obligation of the physician is to inform the woman of facts that may bear on that decision.

Perhaps, in part, what the courts are concerned about here is the potential extension of liability to women who choose not to terminate a pregnancy after learning that the fetus has a disease or disability that might lead to pain and suffering. In Canada and in some parts of the US, this question has been answered in the case law; *Dobson (Litigation Guardian of) v Dobson* holds that mothers do not owe a duty of care to their children for their behaviour during pregnancy.[91] In any event, in the wrongful birth cases, courts have not been prepared to accept the argument that failure to have an abortion is unreasonable.[92] It strikes me as quite clear that a woman's decision not to terminate a pregnancy simply cannot be equated with negligent failure to inform a woman that she might wish to consider doing so. The confusion here seems to be in relation to the distinction between owing a duty of care and being found liable for breaching that duty. In providing information about the condition of the fetus to the pregnant woman, the physician discharges the duty and will not be liable for the woman's decision to proceed with the pregnancy.

Another point relevant to considerations around reproductive autonomy and wrongful life claims is worth exploring here. In *Liebig* the Court held that no duty of care can exist in relation to preconception harm.[93] The Court refers to claims by infants 'yet to be conceived at the time the alleged negligence occurred'[94] as cases that have been characterised as 'wrongful life' cases, citing *Lacroix* and *McKay* as examples. Once again, the reasoning is flawed. First, *McKay* clearly does not involve a case of preconception negligence – the negligent failure to diagnose rubella in Mrs McKay occurred after conception. Likewise, as explained by Feldman JA in *Paxton*, one need not conclude that *Lacroix* was a case of preconception negligence; it could equally be characterised as an instance of negligence in prescribing a contraindicated medication during early pregnancy.[95]

But even if *Paxton* and *Bovingdon v Hergott* are legitimately cases of preconception negligence, should that fact lead decisively to their rejection on the basis that no duty of care can be owed by a physician to a potential child? Should a claim that involves negligence that took place prior to the conception of a child mean that the child, once born, cannot sue the negligent actors? There is authority in the US and Australia to the effect

---

[90] *Harriton* (2006) (n 38) para 249.

[91] *Dobson* (n 89).

[92] As is discussed below, section V.

[93] As the Court of Appeal stated in *Liebig* (n 77) para 11: 'Both *Bovingdon* and *Paxton* hold that there is no duty of care to a future child if the alleged negligence by a health care provider took place prior to conception.'

[94] *Ibid.*

[95] *Paxton* (ONCA) (n 64) paras 49–52.

that preconception negligence can lead to liability to a later-born child,[96] based on the same reasoning as in the case of liability for causing injury to a fetus in utero. The Court of Appeal may be right in the end, and perhaps it is necessary strictly to limit or to rule out preconception negligence, due to concerns about indeterminacy as to the extent and timing of potential liability. But surely we should await a case with an appropriate factual context in which the court can consider and explain why this is a suitable dividing line, rather than simply asserting that it is.[97]

One area where preconception negligence causing harm to a later-born child might come before the courts in the near future is in the assisted reproduction context. Without wishing to spend too much time speculating about the various circumstances in which preconception liability might arise, I do think it is necessary to at least mention this concern, given the potential impact of such judicial reasoning on reproductive autonomy.

Women's options during pregnancy are in many ways already constrained by the potential for provider liability. In the US, vaginal birth after Caesarean (VBAC) is rarely an option for pregnant women, because of the risk of uterine rupture, which can lead to perinatal morbidity and mortality.[98] Physicians are, for the most part, unwilling to risk liability should things go wrong. And it seems fairly obvious that pregnant women are not going to be given the choice of being treated with a teratogenic medication for a non-life threatening condition, even though that arguably limits their ability to choose among treatment options. The context of assisted reproduction is another one in which women's reproductive choices might realistically be constrained because of concerns about provider liability. For example, a woman's wish to transfer multiple embryos might be met with resistance from her provider due to the potential for harm to the resulting children as a result of high order multiple pregnancy.[99] I want to be clear that I am not

---

[96] See, eg, *Renslow v Mennonite Hospital*, 367 NE 2d 1250 (Ill 1977); *Bergstresser v Mitchell*, 577 F 2d 22 (8th Cir 1978) (negligence in performing a Caesarean section in one pregnancy led to uterine rupture during the next pregnancy, resulting in the need for an emergency Caesarean and leading to brain damage in the second child); *Empire Casualty Co v St Paul Fire & Marine Insurance Co*, 764 P 2d 1191 (Colo 1988) (physician liability for preconception negligence involving Rh incompatibility of a future child); *X and Y (By Her Tutor X) v Pal* (1991) 23 NSWLR 26 (failure to diagnose and treat the mother's syphilis led to a finding of liability to a later-conceived child). But see *Albala v City of New York*, 429 NE 2d 786 (NY 1981) (negligence in performing an abortion caused perforation of the uterus, leading to brain damage in the child of the woman's next pregnancy); *Hegyes v Unjian Enterprises, Inc*, 286 Cal Rptr 85 (Cal Ct App 1991) (a driver who injured the mother in a motor vehicle collision was not liable for injuries caused to her later-conceived child). For an in-depth discussion of the American cases, see Julie A Greenberg, 'Reconceptualizing Preconception Torts' (1997) 64 *Tennessee Law Review* 315; Matthew Browne, 'Preconception Tort Law in an Era of Assisted Reproduction: Applying a Nexus Test for Duty' (2001) 69 *Fordham Law Review* 2555.

[97] Other authors have used the example of products intended for use with infants and have asked why, assuming the product was negligently manufactured, it would make any sense to relieve the manufacturer of liability because the item was made prior to the injured child's conception: see, eg, Browne (n 96); 'Preconception Tort as a Basis for Recovery' (1982) 60 *Washington University Law Quarterly* 275.

[98] See, eg, EA Rybak, 'Hippocratic Idea, Faustian Bargain and Damocles' Sword: Erosion of Patient Autonomy in Obstetrics' (2009) 29 *Journal of Perinatology* 721; Clarissa Bonanno, Marilee Clausing and Richard Berkowitz, 'VBAC: A Medicolegal Perspective' (2011) 38 *Clinics in Perinatology* 217.

[99] Arguments have also been made that the woman or couple should also bear liability for making such choices (Kirsten Rabe Smolensky, 'Creating Children with Disabilities: Parental Tort Liability for Preimplantation Genetic Interventions' (2008) 60 *Hastings Law Journal* 299 (arguing that parents should be liable for choices relating to the use of pre-implantation genetic diagnosis and pre-implantation genetic manipulation); Jaime King, 'Duty to the Unborn: A Response to Smolensky' (2008) 60 *Hastings Law Journal* 377 (arguing that Smolensky's claim could be extended to more choices in assisted reproduction); Michele Goodwin, 'A View from the Cradle: Tort Law and the Private Regulation of Assisted Reproduction' (2010) 59 *Emory Law Journal* 1039).

suggesting that such choices as taking teratogenic medications during pregnancy or insisting on transferring 10 in vitro embryos into a woman's uterus during an IVF cycle are choices that should be open to women to make. I simply wish to urge that we attend to the potential points of connection between judicial reasoning in some of these wrongful life and preconception negligence claims and women's freedom to make reproductive decisions.

III. WRONGFUL CONCEPTION

As noted earlier, wrongful conception and wrongful birth claims are brought by the parents of an unplanned or planned but disabled child, respectively, and are generally claims for the costs of child-rearing. While the two types of claims are often referred to collectively as 'wrongful birth' claims, there are some significant distinctions between the two, and they are best conceptualised and considered independently (I shall consider their relevance to reproductive autonomy after going through both types of claims). Wrongful conception and wrongful birth cases may be differentiated generally on the basis that wrongful conception cases usually concern healthy, able-bodied children born as a result of negligence related to contraception or sterilisation (for example, negligent tubal ligation, or inaccurate advice regarding the effectiveness of a vasectomy), whereas wrongful birth cases involve claims relating to provider negligence in the provision of information that would have led to the termination of the pregnancy. The two claims relate to distinct decision points – wrongful conception cases are about avoiding having children (or more children) and wrongful birth cases are about avoiding having a child with a specific characteristic.

Unlike the claim for wrongful life, parental claims for wrongful birth and wrongful conception are fairly well established in Canada, Australia, the UK and the US,[100] with the notable exception of a handful of American states that refuse to recognise the wrongful birth claim.[101]

The genesis of the claims for wrongful birth and wrongful conception is found in American jurisprudence. The first wrongful conception case was brought in Minnesota in 1934.[102] The early cases were unsuccessful; the claims were denied on the basis that they were contrary to public policy around the nature of family and the purpose of marriage. The initial reluctance to acknowledge wrongful conception claims was relatively

---

[100] See, eg, *Colp v Ringrose* (1976) 3 L Med Q 72 (Alta TD); *Doiron v Orr*, 20 OR (2d) 71, 86 DLR (3d) 719 (1978) (Ont SC); *Pozdzik (Next friend of) v Wilson*, 2002 ABQB 351, 311 AR 258.

[101] Most states have recognised the wrongful conception claim (Wendy F Hensel, 'The Disabling Impact of Wrongful Birth and Wrongful Life Actions' (2005) 40 *Harvard Civil Rights – Civil Liberties Law Review* 141, 153; Michael T Murtaugh, 'Wrongful Birth: The Courts' Dilemma in Determining a Remedy for a "Blessed Event"' (2007) 27 *Pace Law Review* 241, 277). Wrongful birth claims are prohibited in some states, either by statute or common law. States with statutes prohibiting the claim are Arizona, Michigan (but the claim is permitted if the physician has been grossly negligent), Minnesota, Missouri, Pennsylvania, Idaho, South Dakota and Utah (see citations of these statutes above (n 5)). States where the common law prohibits the claim are Georgia, Kentucky, North Carolina, Michigan and Missouri (*Azzolino v Dingfelder*, 337 SE 2d 528 (NC 1985); *Wilson v Kuenzi*, 751 SW 2d 741 (Mo 1988); *Etkind v Suarez*, 519 SE 2d 210 (Ga Sup Ct 1999); *Taylor v Kurapati*, 600 NW 2d 670 (Mich Ct App 1999); *Grubbs ex rel Grubbs v Barbourville Family Health Center PSC*, 120 SW 3d 682 (Ky Sup Ct 2003)).

[102] *Christensen v Thornby*, 255 NW 2d 620 (1934).

short-lived, and now the vast majority of states recognise these claims.[103] As in most other jurisdictions that accept these claims, however, there remains intense disagreement as to the appropriate measure of damages.

The damages question that has proven most difficult to resolve is whether a woman or couple can recover the full costs of rearing the 'unplanned' child, or only the costs associated with pregnancy and childbirth (such as pain and suffering for the woman, loss of consortium for her partner, and loss of income during pregnancy and after childbirth). In general, there are four possible approaches to assessing damages in wrongful conception cases. These may be described as follows:

(a) *No recovery.* The basis for this approach seems to be that although the child was unplanned or initially unwanted, the birth of a child is a blessing for the family, not a circumstance which can or should result in an award of damages.

(b) *Total recovery.* The full costs of raising the child are included in the damages award, with no 'offset' for the benefits that accrue to the parents as a result of the child's presence in the family.

(c) *Offset-benefits.* Here, the damages ostensibly include the costs of child-rearing, but these costs are offset by the benefits that the parents gain by the birth of the child.

(d) *Limited damages.* This approach permits recovery only of costs associated with the pregnancy, childbirth and the initial adjustments related to the presence of the newborn.[104]

The state of play for wrongful conception cases in American jurisdictions is as follows: a small minority of jurisdictions hold that parents may recover all costs of child-rearing.[105] A second minority approach is to permit recovery of all damages, but with a deduction 'for the benefits, including . . . the services, love, joy and affection that parents will receive by virtue of having and raising the child'.[106] The majority of American jurisdictions permit the parents to claim expenses related to pregnancy and childbirth, but not those attributable to child-rearing.[107]

In the UK, although the jurisprudence has arguably been settled since the House of Lords decision in *McFarlane v Tayside Health Board*,[108] a number of interesting issues

[103] For a detailed review of the wrongful pregnancy and wrongful birth jurisprudence in the US, see Murtaugh (n 101) 244–45. As Murtaugh notes, after the US Supreme Court decisions in *Griswold v Connecticut*, 381 US 479 (1965) and *Roe v Wade*, 410 US 113 (1973) acknowledged the existence of a constitutional right to privacy that encompassed such intimate decisions as the avoidance of procreation through the use of birth control or the termination of pregnancy, it was no longer possible to deny wrongful pregnancy claims on the basis that they are contrary to the purpose of marriage or because the birth of a child is necessarily a blessing to its family. See also Hensel (n 101).

[104] See, eg, *Roe v Dabbs* [2004] BCSC 957, 31 BCLR (4th) 158. There is also arguably a fifth approach – that of permitting rearing costs where the child suffers from some type of disability: see, eg, *Parkinson v St James and Seacroft University Hospital NHS Trust* [2001] EWCA Civ 530, [2002] QB 266. This approach is operative in a few Australian states as a result of statutory reform in the wake of the High Court's decision in *Cattanach v Melchior* [2003] HCA 38, (2003) 215 CLR 1 (see the discussion in the text at nn 119–123 below).

[105] See, eg, *Custodio v Bauer*, 59 Cal Rptr 463 (Cal Ct App 1967); *Marciniak v Lundborg*, 450 NW 2d 243 (Wis 1990); *Lovelace Med Ctr v Mendez*, 805 P 2d 603 (NM 1991); *Zehr v Haugen*, 871 P 2d 1006 (Ore Sup Ct 1994).

[106] *Chaffee v Seslar*, 786 NE 2d 705 (Ind SC 2003) 707–08, in which the Supreme Court of Indiana clearly and concisely explains the state of play in American jurisdictions. For cases adopting this approach, see, eg, *Sherlock v Stillwater Clinic*, 260 NW 2d 169 (Minn 1977); *Ochs v Borrelli*, 187 Conn 253 (1982); *Univ of Arizona Health Sciences Ctr v Superior Court,* 136 Ariz 579 (1983).

[107] For a list of cases, see *Chaffee v Seslar* (n 106) 708.

[108] *McFarlane v Tayside Health Board* [2000] 2 AC 59.

remain to be considered. In *McFarlane*, the Law Lords reversed more than a decade of case law to the contrary and held that the costs of raising a healthy child are not recoverable in wrongful conception claims. The facts in *McFarlane* are similar to those in other wrongful conception cases: Mr McFarlane had a vasectomy and was afterward informed that his sperm count was 'negative', and that he and his wife need no longer rely on contraceptives. On the basis of this advice, the couple dispensed with contraception, following which Mrs McFarlane became pregnant with her fifth child, Catherine. The speeches in *McFarlane* have been analysed at length and need not be revisited here in detail.[109] Briefly, the Law Lords held that Mrs McFarlane's claim for damages related to the pregnancy and the birth of the child would succeed (Lord Millett dissented on this point), but that the costs of raising Catherine could not be recovered from the negligent defendants.[110] All five of their Lordships reached the same conclusion, albeit by different routes.[111] In essence, all five seem to have concluded that it was not 'fair, just and reasonable' to impose liability on the defendant physicians to indemnify the McFarlanes for all of the costs associated with rearing Catherine.

Academic reaction to the House of Lords decision in *McFarlane* has been overwhelmingly negative, on the basis that the decision is an unjustifiable departure from principle and that it demonstrates contempt for reproductive autonomy.[112] Nevertheless, the decision was reaffirmed several years later in *Rees v Darlington Memorial Hospital NHS Trust*.[113] In that case the plaintiff was a woman with a severe visual disability. Because of her disability, she did not feel capable of caring for a child and therefore underwent an elective tubal ligation. The procedure was negligently performed and failed to completely occlude Ms Rees' fallopian tubes. Ms Rees was not aware of the failure of the procedure,[114] and a year after her surgery she conceived a child. At the time of the decision of the House of Lords the child would have been six years old; he is apparently healthy and able-bodied.

Ms Rees sued the Darlington Memorial Hospital NHS Trust, claiming the costs associated with her son's rearing and maintenance. The claim included the ordinary costs of child maintenance that would be incurred by any parent, as well as the additional costs specific to Ms Rees due to her visual impairment. She was unsuccessful in the High Court on the preliminary question of the recoverability of child-rearing costs, on the basis of *McFarlane*. On appeal, the Court of Appeal held that *McFarlane* did not address the question of the recoverability of exceptional costs incurred in raising a child when the *parent* has a disability; accordingly, a majority allowed the appeal and awarded Ms Rees 'those "extra" costs involved in discharging . . . her responsibility to bring up a healthy child which are attributable to and incurred as a result of the fact of the parent's

---

[109] See, eg, Mason (n 7) 112–25; J Ellis Cameron Perry, 'Return of the Burden of the "Blessing"' (1999) 149 *New Law Journal* 1887; Alasdair Maclean, 'McFarlane v Tayside Health Board: A Wrongful Conception in the House of Lords?' (2000) 3 *Web Journal of Current Legal Issues*, at <webjcli.ncl.ac.uk/2000/issue3/maclean3.html#Heading7>; Emily Jackson, *Regulating Reproduction: Law, Technology and Autonomy* (Oxford, Hart Publishing, 2001) 30–37; Laura CH Hoyano, 'Misconceptions about Wrongful Conceptions' (2002) 65 *MLR* 883.

[110] *McFarlane* (n 108).

[111] Indeed, in a later case, most members of the Appellate Committee noted that the reasoning adopted by each of the Law Lords in *McFarlane* differed, and Lord Steyn actually commented that he did 'not propose to undertake the gruesome task of discussing the judgments in *McFarlane*.' (*Rees v Darlington Memorial Hospital NHS Trust* [2003] UKHL 52, [2004] 1 AC 309, para 28).

[112] See sources cited at n 109.

[113] *Rees* (n 111).

[114] *Ibid* para 22. The Defendant NHS Trust admitted that the surgery was performed negligently.

disability'.[115] The House of Lords allowed the NHS Trust's appeal by a 4:3 margin, affirming its commitment to *McFarlane*. But to the surprise of many, the majority substituted an award for £15,000 as a conventional sum, intended to recognise the legal wrong done and the deprivation of the appellant's freedom to limit the size of her family.[116]

The idea of awarding a conventional sum was first raised by Lord Millett in *McFarlane* (though in that case, he suggested the amount be £5,000); none of the other Law Lords agreed with his suggestion. In *Rees*, Lords Hope and Steyn were highly critical of this approach, Lord Steyn referring to the decision to award a conventional sum as exceeding the 'limits [of] permissible creativity for judges' and constituting a 'backdoor evasion of the legal policy enunciated in *McFarlane*'.[117] But as Lord Bingham explained,

> the fact remains that the parent of a child born following a negligently performed vasectomy or sterilisation, or negligent advice on the effect of such a procedure, is the victim of a legal wrong. . . . I can accept and support a rule of legal policy which precludes recovery of the full cost of bringing up a child in the situation postulated, but I question the fairness of a rule which denies the victim of a legal wrong any recompense at all beyond an award immediately related to the unwanted pregnancy and birth. The spectre of well-to-do parents plundering the National Health Service should not blind one to other realities: that of the single mother with young children, struggling to make ends meet and counting the days until her children are of an age to enable her to work more hours and so enable the family to live a less straitened existence; the mother whose burning ambition is to put domestic chores so far as possible behind her and embark on a new career or resume an old one. Examples can be multiplied. *To speak of losing the freedom to limit the size of one's family is to mask the real loss suffered in a situation of this kind. This is that a parent, particularly (even today) the mother, has been denied, through the negligence of another, the opportunity to live her life in the way that she wished and planned.* I do not think that an award immediately relating to the unwanted pregnancy and birth gives adequate recognition of or does justice to that loss.[118]

Thus although the Law Lords did not resile in *Rees* from their decision in *McFarlane*, the majority appears to have recognised the harshness and potential unfairness of a rule that awards nothing beyond damages for the unwanted pregnancy and birth in a situation where the wrong done may have considerable implications for the woman who wished to avoid having a family at all, or who sought to limit the size of her family.

In contrast to the UK jurisprudence and most of the American states, the Australian High Court has held that the costs of raising a healthy child are recoverable.[119] In *Cattanach v Melchior*, the female plaintiff had a tubal ligation to prevent future pregnancy. Prior to undergoing the procedure, she informed Dr Cattanach that she had an appendectomy when she was 15 years old and that her right ovary and fallopian tube had been removed at that time. During the procedure, Dr Cattanach was unable to visualise the right fallopian tube and applied a clip only to the left fallopian tube. Approximately four years after

---

[115] *Ibid* para 25.

[116] *Ibid* (Lord Bingham) paras 8–10. As Mason explains ((n 7) 176): 'This 'conventional award' provides possibly the most complex and controversial aspect of the *Rees* judgment – indeed, it is hard to find a commentator who does not, at this point, start to scratch his or her head.' See also Samatha Singer, '*Rees v Darlington Memorial Hospital NHS Trust* [2004] 1 AC 309' (2004) 26 *Journal of Social Welfare and Family Law* 403, 414.

[117] *Rees* (n 111) para 46.

[118] *Ibid* para 8 (emphasis added).

[119] Specifically, costs of child-rearing to the age of majority (*Cattanach v Melchior* (HCA) (n 104)). Other wrongful conception cases in Australia are *Dahl v Purnell* (1992) 15 Queensland Lawyer Reps 33; *CES v Superclinics (Australia) Pty Ltd* (1995) 38 NSWLR 47.

her tubal ligation, Mrs Melchior became pregnant. Contrary to what she believed and had told Dr Cattanach, her right fallopian tube had not been removed during her appendectomy. The lower courts found Dr Cattanach to have been negligent:

(a) for failing to advise Mrs Melchior that she could undergo testing to rule out the presence of the right fallopian tube (a hysterosalpingogram would have shown the presence of the tube); and

(b) for failing to warn her that if she was mistaken about the tube having been removed, there was a much greater risk of future conception than would ordinarily be the case following a tubal ligation.[120]

The policy arguments embraced by the House of Lords in *McFarlane* – including the claim that the birth of a healthy child is a benefit that outweighs the burdens associated with its care and upbringing, and the notion that it would harm a child to discover that his or her parents sought damages as a result of his or her birth – were not persuasive in the Australian courts. The trial judge awarded damages to the plaintiffs for pregnancy and birth, loss of consortium and costs of rearing and maintaining the child.[121] The decision was appealed only with respect to the award for child-rearing costs, and the decision was upheld in the Queensland Court of Appeal[122] and (by a slim majority) in the High Court. The majority dismissed the policy arguments against full recovery, noting that these arguments depend upon values which are described as (or asserted to be) widely-held but which are unsupported by evidence, and thus difficult to analyse and critique.[123]

The decision in *Cattanach v Melchior* has now been overtaken by statute in three jurisdictions.[124] The New South Wales and Queensland statutes were enacted within months of the High Court decision, and all three statutes appear to permit the recovery of damages for additional rearing costs attributable to disability in the wrongful birth context.

In contrast to the common law in the UK and Australia, Canadian jurisprudence on damage assessment in wrongful conception cases remains (apparently hopelessly) unsettled. This is due, in part at least, to the fact that the Supreme Court of Canada has to date not heard a wrongful conception claim. The trial level and appellate decisions,

---

[120] *Cattanach v Melchior* (n 104) para 46.
[121] *Melchior v Cattanach* [2000] QSC 285.
[122] *Melchior v Cattanach* [2001] QCA 246.
[123] *Cattanach v Melchior* (n 104) *per* Kirby J at para 152: 'In short, if the application of ordinary legal principles is to be denied on the basis of public policy, it is essential that such policy be spelt out so as to be susceptible of analysis and criticism. Desirably, it should be founded on empirical evidence, not mere judicial assertion. Yet this was not attempted in the present case, whether at trial or on appeal.' See also Callinan J at para 296, noting that judicial distaste for such claims cannot override legal principle.
[124] Civil Liability Act 2002 (NSW), ss 70, 71. Section 71 provides:

'(1) In any proceedings involving a claim for the birth of a child to which this Part applies, the court cannot award damages for economic loss for:

(a) the costs associated with rearing or maintaining the child that the claimant has incurred or will incur in the future, or

(b) any loss of earnings by the claimant while the claimant rears or maintains the child.

(2) Subsection (1) (a) does not preclude the recovery of any additional costs associated with rearing or maintaining a child who suffers from a disability that arise by reason of the disability.'

See also Civil Liability Act 1936 (SA) s 67; Civil Liability Act 2003 (Qld) ss 49A, 49B.

although heavily influenced by the House of Lords decision in *McFarlane*, are inconsistent, and it is difficult to identify general principles with any degree of precision.

The early Canadian cases did not permit recovery of damages related to the birth of a healthy, albeit initially unwanted, child. The case law later evolved to permit recovery of damages, but not for the costs of child-rearing (although there was authority for awarding the costs of rearing where the child was born with disabilities[125]). In the early to mid-1990s, the Québec and Ontario courts addressed the issue of wrongful conception and took distinct approaches. In *Suite v Cooke*, the Québec Court of Appeal permitted recovery of the costs of raising a healthy child, but held that these costs should be evaluated against the potential for future financial support from the child, and the 'joys and the comfort which this same child will bring'.[126] In the early Ontario decision (*Kealey v Berezowski*[127]) Lax J teased out the distinctions between the various 'birth torts' cases (wrongful life, wrongful birth and wrongful conception) and examined the diverse approaches taken in respect of damages in wrongful conception cases. Ultimately, she concluded that the costs of raising a healthy child could be recovered in wrongful conception, but only where the parents' decision to seek a permanent end to their fertility was based on financial considerations.[128] As the facts in *Kealey v Berezowski* did not show finances to be the primary reason for the decision not to have more children, Lax J did not award rearing costs in that case.

Only five years after the decision in *Kealey v Berezowski*, a factually similar case came before the Ontario courts.[129] After considering the reasons in both *Kealey v Berezowski* and *McFarlane*, Forestell J decided to follow the latter. And one year later, the Alberta courts had occasion to consider two wrongful conception cases, both of which concerned failed tubal ligations. The two trial judges came to opposite conclusions as to whether child-rearing costs may be recovered in such cases (although neither judge found the defendant physician to have been negligent, both went on to assess damages in the event that they might be found to have erred in this conclusion).[130]

Most recently, the British Columbia Supreme Court has held that in spite of the considerable array of options articulated by the courts, none of the various approaches to damages assessment adopted to date is adequate to the task. Instead, the 'appropriate method of assessment is one that treats the damages as essentially non-pecuniary in

---

[125] See, eg, *Cherry v Borsman* (n 60); *Joshi (Guardian Ad Litem of) v Woolley*, (1995) 4 BCLR (3d) 208, [1995] BCJ No 113 (BCSC).

[126] *Suite v Cooke* [1995] RJQ 2765, [1995] JQ No 696 (CA) (as cited in *Kealey v Berezowski*, 30 OR (3d) 37, [1996] OJ No 2460 (Ont Gen Div) para 57).

[127] *Kealey v Berezowski* (n 126).

[128] More specifically, Lax J characterised costs of child-rearing as pure economic loss and held that such costs may be recoverable in certain circumstances, where the birth of the child causes prejudice to the parents (*ibid*).

[129] *Mummery v Olsson*, 102 ACWS (3d) 815, [2001] OJ No 226 (Ont SCJ).

[130] *MS v Baker*, 2001 ABQB 1032, 309 AR 1. Following the reasoning in *Kealey v Berezowski* (n 126), Moreau J would have awarded the costs of child-rearing because the parents' decision to proceed with sterilisation was motivated by financial considerations. In *MY v Boutros*, 2002 ABQB 362, 313 AR 1, Rawlins J disagreed with the approach adopted in *Kealey v Berezowski* and in *MS v Baker*, and instead followed *McFarlane*, although it is not clear on what basis she did so. She found that the Law Lords were unanimous in declining to award the costs of raising a healthy child, although all five arrived at this result for different reasons; as she put it, 'Notwithstanding their differing approaches, I do not disagree with any of the approaches taken by the House of Lords in *McFarlane* and I accept the result' (*ibid* para 147). Rawlins J then went on to consider the 'offset-benefits' approach to the question whether damages for child-rearing should be awarded, and concluded that although this approach was not adopted in *McFarlane*, she 'accept[ed] that the benefits a child brings to a family outweigh the costs of that child to a family' (*ibid* para 157).

nature'.[131] In *Bevilaqua v Altenkirk*, Groberman J held that factors relevant to determination of the appropriate measure of non-pecuniary damages include such matters as the parents' reasons for wanting to limit their family size and 'their actual circumstances both at the time of the sterilization, and at the time of the pregnancy and childbirth'.[132] In both of the British Columbia cases, the judges were careful to distance themselves from the 'conventional sum' award approved by the House of Lords in *Rees*, stating that this approach is contrary to principle, as damages awards are to be compensatory and 'must be tailored to meet the circumstances of the individual plaintiffs. A purely conventional sum fails to accomplish these goals.'[133]

As the Supreme Court of Canada has not yet agreed to hear a wrongful conception case, the bewildering array of lower court cases persist as relevant authorities. It remains to be seen whether the approach to damage assessment outlined in the British Columbia cases will be followed, or whether one of the several other methods of assessment will eventually prevail.

IV. WRONGFUL BIRTH

As in the case of wrongful life and wrongful conception claims, wrongful birth suits originated in the US.[134] Although the overall trend has been to recognise the claim, the evolution of the common law on point has not been uncontroversial. Indeed, 'Virtually every aspect of the wrongful birth concept has been the focus of controversy, including whether the claim should have constitutional protection, and whether it fits within traditional tort principles'.[135]

Currently, a majority of American states recognise wrongful birth claims; in a minority of states the claim is barred either at common law[136] or by statute.[137] Although the courts tend to characterise the wrong in such cases as the deprivation of the parents' opportunity to make a meaningful and informed choice to terminate the pregnancy or to give birth to a child with disabilities,[138] Wendy Hensel points out that this characterisation is belied by a careful examination of the cases and the approach they adopt to causation. In wrongful birth cases, the American courts require the mother of the child to establish that if she had been made aware during pregnancy of the illness or disability that the child would suffer after birth, she would have terminated the pregnancy. Thus,

---

[131] *Bevilacqua v Altenkirk* [2004] BCSC 945, 35 BCLR (4th) 281, para 182. See also *Roe v Dabbs* (n 104) para 216.

[132] *Bevilacqua v Altenkirk* (n 131) para 194.

[133] *Ibid* para 181. And in any case, Groberman J did not feel that it was open to the court to create 'such an unprecedented approach to damages'.

[134] The first such claim was made – unsuccessfully – in *Gleitman v Cosgrove*, 227 A 2d 689 (NJ 1967). Like the *Gleitman* court, the New York Court of Appeals denied the wrongful life claim raised in *Becker v Schwartz*, 386 NE 2d 807 (NY 1978). The Court did, however, accept the parents' wrongful birth claim in that case.

[135] Jeffrey R Botkin and Maxwell J Mehlman, 'Wrongful Birth: Medical, Legal, and Philosophical Issues' (1994) 22 *Journal of Law, Medicine & Ethics* 21, 22.

[136] Georgia (*Etkind v Suarez* (n 101)); Kentucky (*Grubbs v Barbourville Family Health Center PSC* (n 101)); Michigan (*Taylor v Kurapati* (n 101)); Missouri (*Wilson v Kuenzi* (n 101)); and North Carolina (*Azzolino v Dingfelder* (n 101)).

[137] Arizona, Idaho, Indiana, Michigan, Minnesota, Missouri, North Dakota, Pennsylvania, South Dakota and Utah (see above (n 5)).

[138] *Siemieniec v Lutheran General Hospital*, 512 NE 2d 691 (Ill 1987) 703. See also *Haymon v Wilkerson*, 535 A 2d 880 (DC 1987) 882; *Coleman v Dogra*, 812 NE 2d 332 (Ohio Ct App 2004) 337–38.

it appears clear that the harm the woman is being compensated for is the birth of the disabled child, rather than the loss of opportunity to make an informed choice.[139]

As noted above, not all US jurisdictions recognise the validity of wrongful birth claims. Where US courts have rejected wrongful birth claims, the reasons vary – some courts object on the basis of public policy,[140] while others assert that ordinary tort law principles are inapposite and that recognition of these claims requires legislative action.[141]

The US aside, wrongful birth claims have been accepted without much controversy. In Australia, they are grouped with wrongful conception cases, and there are few reported cases on point.[142] In the UK, wrongful birth claims have been readily accepted,[143] though since the decision in *McFarlane*, the costs of raising a healthy child are deducted from the award of damages so that the only rearing costs parents can recover are those additional costs attributable to the child's disability or illness.[144]

Damages do not seem to pose the same moral difficulty – at least in so far as the courts are concerned – in wrongful birth cases as they do in the wrongful conception context. Disability rights scholars, however, have argued that these claims (together with wrongful life claims) embody harmful attitudes toward the lives of persons with disabilities, and that their judicial acceptance entrenches those attitudes in law.[145]

The jurisprudence in the UK has been vigorously criticised on this front. As has been explained, the law on recoverability of rearing costs for healthy children is settled in the UK: damages for child-rearing are not recoverable. However, the question of whether parents can claim the extraordinary costs associated with raising a child with disabilities remains unsettled. All of the wrongful birth cases decided in England since *McFarlane* have held that *McFarlane* does not bar a claim for the extraordinary costs involved in raising a child with disabilities,[146] including the English Court of Appeal decision in *Parkinson v St James and Seacroft University Hospital NHS Trust*.[147] From a disability

---

[139] Hensel (n 101) 164–67.

[140] See, eg, *Etkind v Suarez* (n 101) 213–14; *Grubbs ex rel Grubbs v Barbourville Family Health Center PSC* (n 101) 690.

[141] *Azzolino v Dingfelder* (n 101) 536–37. Maine has enacted legislation to allow such claims (Me Rev Stat Ann tit 24, § 2931(3)).

[142] *Veivers v Connnolly* [1995] 2 Qd R 326; *Murray v Whiting* [2002] QSC 257.

[143] See, eg, *Salih v Enfield Health Authority* [1991] 3 All ER 400; *Anderson v Forth Valley Health Board* 1998 SLT 588; *McLelland v Greater Glasgow Health Board* 2001 SLT 446.

[144] See, eg, *Hardman v Amin* [2000] Lloyd's Rep Med 498; *Rand v East Dorset Health Authority* [2000] Lloyd's Rep Med 181; *Lee v Taunton & Somerset NHS Trust* [2001] 1 FLR 419. Damages are to be assessed on the basis of the child's needs (J Kenyon Mason and Graeme T Laurie, *Mason and McCall Smith's Law and Medical Ethics*, 8th edn (Oxford, Oxford University Press, 2011) 356).

[145] See, eg, Hensel (n 101); Adrienne Asch, 'Disability Equality and Prenatal Testing: Contradictory or Compatible?' (2003) 30 *Florida State University Law Review* 315; Nicolette Priaulx, 'Joy to the World! A (Healthy) Child is Born! Reconceptualizing 'Harm' in Wrongful Conception' (2004) 13 *Social & Legal Studies* 5; Nicolette M Priaulx, 'Damages for the "Unwanted" Child: Time for a Rethink?' (2005) 73 *Medico-Legal Journal* 152.

[146] See, eg, *Hardman v Amin* (n 144); *Lee v Taunton & Somerset NHS Trust* (n 144); *Rand v East Dorset Health Authority* (n 144). In *Hardman v Amin* and *Rand v East Dorset Health Authority*, the courts held that the decision in *McFarlane* means that only extra costs of rearing related to special needs may be claimed, while the decision in *Lee v Taunton & Somerset NHS Trust* states that the entire costs of maintenance are recoverable, 'subject . . . to a causation test as to whether the parents would have ordinary upbringing costs anyway, by conceiving again after the hypothetical termination' (Hoyano (n 109) 896).

[147] *Parkinson v St James and Seacroft University Hospital NHS Trust* (n 104). In *Rees* (n 111), the most recent House of Lords case to consider the damages issue, most of the Law Lords considered this question in their speeches even though *Rees* did not involve such a claim. The lack of agreement among the Law Lords is remarkable, given the agreement in the lower courts. Lords Steyn, Hope and Hutton all stated their agreement

rights perspective, these cases are particularly problematic, as they appear to suggest very strongly that while the birth of a healthy child is an occasion for celebration and cannot be viewed as an injury, the birth of a child with disabilities is, from the standpoint of the law, such a grievous event that it warrants legal acknowledgement as a harm necessitating compensation.[148]

In the Canadian jurisprudence around wrongful birth, the more challenging issue is causation.[149] The Canadian courts have tended to approach wrongful birth claims as a species of informed consent claim, meaning that the plaintiff has to establish, first, that the physician negligently failed to provide her with relevant information and, secondly, that had this information been provided, she would have terminated the pregnancy.[150]

Arndt v Smith is credited as establishing the wrongful birth claim in Canada. Ms Arndt's daughter Miranda was born with congenital varicella syndrome, which led to multiple disabilities. Ms Arndt had become infected with chicken pox in the twelfth week of her pregnancy and was not informed by her physician, Dr Smith, of the potentially serious risks to the fetus, including developmental disability and cortical atrophy.[151] At trial, Hutchinson J accepted the validity of wrongful birth claims in Canadian law, but denied Ms Arndt's claim on the basis that causation had not been made out. In spite of her testimony to the contrary, Hutchinson J found that even had Ms Arndt been made aware of the risks, she would not have terminated the pregnancy.[152] The British Columbia Court of Appeal allowed the appeal, holding that the trial judge had misdirected himself in applying the causation test.[153] The trial judge did not assess damages,

---

with the result in *Parkinson v St James and Seacroft University Hospital NHS Trust*, while Lord Bingham asserted that *McFarlane* applies even where the child is born with disabilities. Lord Millett noted that it was not necessary for the disposition of the appeal in *Rees* to reach a conclusion on this question, and stated that he would 'wish to keep the point open' (*Rees* (n 111) para 112). Lastly, Lord Scott agreed that there was no need to resolve the question of recovery for the additional costs of raising a disabled child, but considered that where the avoidance of disability is the parents' very motivation for seeking sterilisation, a distinction may need to be made. However, *Parkinson v St James and Seacroft University Hospital NHS Trust* was not such a case and so the rule in *McFarlane* would apply.

[148] Above (n 145, 146).

[149] In Canada, two wrongful birth cases have reached the Supreme Court (*Krangle v Brisco* (SCC) (n 2); *Arndt v Smith* [1997] 2 SCR 539, [1997] SCJ No 65). *Krangle v Brisco* dealt solely with the question of whether the child's parents could receive damages for the costs of caring for their disabled child after he reached adulthood; the Court's decision turned on its interpretation of relevant family law legislation.

[150] See also Erin Nelson and Timothy Caulfield, 'You Can't Get There From Here: A Case Comment on *Arndt v Smith*' (1998) 32 *University of British Columbia Law Review* 353.

[151] Dr Smith's rationale for failing to inform Ms Arndt of these risks was that she did not wish to 'unduly worry an expectant mother about an improbable risk and one for which she would not advise therapeutic abortion' (*Arndt v Smith*, 93 BCLR (2d) 220, (1994) 21 CCLT (2d) 66 (BCSC) para 59) (cited to BCLR). This concern around 'unduly worrying' an expectant mother is actually something of a delicate issue. Obviously, a robust approach to reproductive autonomy would recognise the significance of the pregnant woman having this information. Without it, she is not in a position to decide whether or not to continue the pregnancy, to risk having a severely, multiply disabled child (which, in turn, will have immense significance for her own life). Yet it is not entirely clear that informing a pregnant woman that she runs a minimal risk of her child being born with multiple, severe disabilities and health issues is helpful to a woman's ability to make choices. See Barbara Katz Rothman, *The Tentative Pregnancy: Prenatal Diagnosis and the Future of Motherhood* (New York, Viking, 1986) 180–81: 'The whole thing about the new technology that they are offered is that it gives choice. That is what it is all about, after all, the opening up of new reproductive choices. But for most women the choices are all so dreadful that trying to find one she can live with is terribly hard. Taking the least awful choice is not experienced as "choosing" . . .'

[152] *Arndt v Smith* (n 151).

[153] *Arndt v Smith*, 61 BCAC 57, (1995) 6 BCLR (3d) 201. The British Columbia Court of Appeal ordered a new trial.

and the issue of damages was not argued at the Court of Appeal. The Supreme Court of Canada granted leave to appeal; the sole issue on appeal was causation.[154] As one judge has since put it, 'Thus the claim for wrongful birth slipped quietly into Canadian tort law simply as a type of medical malpractice case without any fundamental analysis or delineation of the extent of such a claim'.[155]

Since the decision in *Arndt v Smith*, a number of wrongful birth cases have come before Canadian courts.[156] In some of the more recent Canadian cases, the defendants have alleged contributory negligence on the part of the mother. In *Patmore v Weatherston*, the child was born with a neural tube defect.[157] The mother asserted that her physician was negligent for not referring her for an ultrasound. The trial judge concluded that the physician had not been negligent in failing to order an ultrasound given that such testing would ordinarily be done between 16 and 18 weeks' gestation, and the plaintiff did not return for a pre-natal visit until she was 19 weeks pregnant. Because he did not find the physician liable, it was not strictly necessary for the trial judge to apportion liability, but he noted that if he had reached a different conclusion as to the physician's liability, he would have split liability equally between the parties, as 'It was the plaintiff who deprived herself of the standard, routine ultrasound shortly after 16 weeks'[158] as a result of her failure to attend for any pre-natal visits between eight and 19 weeks' gestation.[159]

---

[154] This decision, as well as the decision in *Mickle v Salvation Army Grace Hospital Windsor Ontario* (n 59), illustrates one of the significant difficulties that courts have in wrongful birth cases – some reasonable women might choose to carry a pregnancy to term, in spite of warnings of possible problems with the fetus; other reasonable women might choose to terminate the pregnancy in those circumstances. The test for causation in Canadian common law is whether a reasonable person in the position of the patient, having been properly informed of the risks, would have taken a different approach with respect to treatment. Given that two equally reasonable choices exist, the test seems unworkable in these circumstances. In its decision in *Arndt v Smith*, the British Columbia Court of Appeal specifically invited the Supreme Court of Canada to deal with this point, but the decision of the Supreme Court does not address the issue. See Nelson and Caulfield (n 150). See also Vaughan Black and Dennis Klimchuk, 'Case Comment: *Hollis* v *Dow Corning*' (1996) 75 *Canadian Bar Review* 355, 363 (explaining problems with the test for causation).

[155] *Mickle v Salvation Army Grace Hospital Windsor Ontario* (n 59) 748 (cited to DLR). The parents of a child born with CHILD syndrome (which causes serious skin and limb abnormalities on one side of her body) sued the ultrasound technologist and radiologist who respectively performed and evaluated a routine second-trimester ultrasound and detected no abnormalities in the fetus. Zuber J found in favour of the defendants on the basis that the plaintiffs had not established that the defendants acted negligently. He went on to state, however, that even had he concluded that the defendants were negligent, the plaintiffs would have failed to establish causation because the reasonable woman in Kelly Mickle's position would not have terminated the pregnancy.

[156] In the genetics context, the cases have dealt with negligence in failing to provide or to refer parents for genetic counselling, resulting in the birth of two children with Duchenne muscular dystrophy (*H(R) v Hunter*, 22 OTC 204, (1996) 32 CCLT (2d) 44 (Ont Gen Div)), and negligence in failing to inform parents of the availability of pre-natal genetic testing, resulting in the birth of a child with Down Syndrome (*Jones v Rostvig* (n 9); *Krangle v Brisco* (SCC) (n 2)).

[157] *Patmore v Weatherston* (n 59).

[158] *Ibid* para 26.

[159] See also *Zhang v Kan*, 2003 BCSC 5, (2003) 15 CCLT (3d), where the British Columbia Supreme Court assessed the plaintiff's contributory negligence at 50%. The plaintiff sought a referral for amniocentesis from the defendant physician; he informed her that it was too late in her pregnancy for amniocentesis, even though she was only 17 weeks pregnant at the time. The Court noted that the plaintiff doubted the defendant's advice, but did not seek a second opinion, or seek to have testing elsewhere.

V. WRONGFUL CONCEPTION, WRONGFUL BIRTH AND
REPRODUCTIVE AUTONOMY

Wrongful birth and wrongful conception claims are a mechanism through which an individual may seek compensation for the denial of his or her freedom to make reproductive choices autonomously. When a healthcare provider fails to inform a pregnant woman of genetic testing options, or of risk factors her fetus may face for genetic disease or disabilities, he or she denies the woman the ability to make an informed decision about whether to continue the pregnancy.[160] Similarly, in failing to convey accurate information about sperm counts post-vasectomy, or in negligently performing a tubal ligation procedure, the physician removes the choice about avoiding pregnancy from the individuals who have sought that very end in undergoing the procedure in the first place. Arguably, from a strictly legal point of view, there is no reason why wrongful conception and wrongful birth claims should be treated in a way different from any other medical malpractice claim.[161] The elements of malpractice all exist in such cases, and even though the assessment of damages might prove difficult, there are no legally sound reasons for rejecting such claims.

In spite of the reasons in favour of awarding the full measure of damages – including child-rearing costs – in wrongful conception cases, only the Australian High Court[162] and a small minority of American courts have adopted this approach. Yet while the courts struggle with the propriety of characterising the birth of a child as a compensable injury, and with the potential consequences to the healthcare system of such potentially large awards,[163] the rejection of claims for the costs of child-rearing largely relieves the defendant physician of the consequences of his or her negligence.

Various policy arguments have been deployed in rationalising the departure from principle marked by the refusal to award the full measure of damages to parents who

---

[160] For an interesting discussion of the complexities of wrongful birth, see Elizabeth Weil, 'A Wrongful Birth?' *New York Times Magazine*, 12 March 2006, 52.

[161] Like some others, I would also include wrongful life claims: see, eg, A Jackson (n 11); Shapira (n 11); Strasser (n 11).

[162] As noted above, some Australian states have passed legislation to preclude the claim for child-rearing costs in spite of the decision in *Cattanach v Melchior* (HCA) (n 104). It is tempting to read the statutory override of *Cattanach v Melchior* as revealing contempt for reproductive autonomy, but these statutes must be placed in the broader context of tort law reform in Australia, where the ability to recover damages in medical malpractice claims has in recent years been generally limited by statute. Thomas Faunce and Susannah Jefferys note that since 2002, all Australian jurisdictions have passed legislation aimed at minimising the cost of public liability and medical malpractice insurance by restricting plaintiffs' ability to sue for negligence (Thomas Faunce and Susannah Jefferys, 'Abandoning the Common Law: Medical Negligence, Genetic Tests and Wrongful Life in the Australian High Court' (2007) 14 *Journal of Law and Medicine* 469, 473). Another issue in the Australian context has been the characterisation of damages for child-rearing as either pure economic loss or loss consequential upon personal injury. The characterisation is important, because the limitation periods for the different damage claims vary in different jurisdictions. See Clare Lake, 'The Kid and the Cash: Categorising Damage in Wrongful Birth and Wrongful Pregnancy' (2009) 17 *Torts Law Journal* 55.

[163] This is especially the case in the UK, where the NHS would, in some cases at least, be required to pay the damages. See E Jackson (n 109) 36–37, noting that one 'underlying reason' for the House of Lords' decision in *McFarlane* is a concern about the effect on the public health system in the UK. In Canada, this would occur only where a hospital is liable. Physician liability is dealt with through the Canadian Medical Protective Association, which is funded by physicians themselves, and operated on a not-for-profit basis. For a more detailed discussion of the Canadian medical malpractice system, see Colleen M Flood and Bryan Thomas, 'Canadian Medical Malpractice Law in 2011: Missing the Mark on Patient Safety' (2011) 86 *Chicago-Kent Law Review* 1053.

have established provider negligence leading to the birth of an (at least initially) unwanted child. These include concerns about what message it sends to the individual child who is the claimant or subject of his or her parents' claim, including whether there are negative psychological consequences to children who advance such claims, or whose parents do.[164]

Most of these arguments boil down to essentially the same premise – that 'it is morally offensive to regard a normal, healthy baby as more trouble and expense than it is worth'.[165] Less troubling to courts is the reality that this approach leaves parents – especially women – who have been negligently deprived of their right to limit the size of their family without compensation for the most significant part of their loss.[166]

These claims raise complex questions about reproductive autonomy. Appropriate respect for reproductive autonomy seems to demand that the courts tackle the complex questions raised by such cases, instead of simply concluding that the benefits of having children outweigh any associated costs, or asserting that the difficulty in assessing damages means that the parents' interests simply cannot be protected. The issue of mitigation of damages has also been raised in some of the wrongful conception cases, the suggestion being that parents could have avoided the costs of child-rearing by terminating the pregnancy or by seeking to place the child with another family through adoption.[167] For the most part, the mitigation argument has been unsuccessful, and as Lord Steyn put it in *McFarlane*, it is difficult to 'conceive of any circumstances in which the autonomous decision of the parents not to resort to even a lawful abortion could be questioned'.[168]

An important issue in wrongful birth is the assertion that the very existence of such lawsuits is irreconcilable with the values of an inclusive society.[169] Concerns about pre-natal testing and selective abortion and the messages they send to society (and, in particular, those living with disabilities) are not new.[170] But the disability rights critique has increasingly become interested in private law's approach to disability as harm. Critics focus on the legal conception of disability, arguing that it is based on the medical model, which focuses on specific biological traits rather than a whole person with

---

[164] *Cattanach v Melchior* (HCA) (n 104) paras 372–402; *CES v Superclinics (Australia) Pty Ltd* (n 119); *Udale v Bloomsbury Health Authority* [1983] All ER 522, 531. See also Dean Stretton, 'The Birth Torts: Damages for Wrongful Birth and Wrongful Life' (2005) 10 *Deakin Law Review* 319, 340.

[165] Lord Millet in *McFarlane* (n 108) 114.

[166] See, eg, Priaulx, 'Joy to the World!' (n 145); Ben Golder, 'From *McFarlane* to *Melchior* and Beyond: Love, Sex, Money and Commodification in the Anglo-Australian Law of Torts' (2004) 12 *Torts Law Journal* 1; Elizabeth Adjin-Tettey, 'Claims of Involuntary Parenthood: Why the Resistance?' in Jason W Neyers, Erika Chamberlain and Stephen GA Pitel (eds), *Emerging Issues in Tort Law* (Oxford, Hart Publishing, 2007) 85.

[167] The Canadian cases that have alluded to this issue are *Kealey v Berezowski* (n 126) and *Keats v Pearce* (1984) 48 Nfld & PEIR 102, [1984] NJ No 271 (NFSC). In *Emeh v Kensington, Chelsea and Fulham Area Health Authority* [1984] 3 All ER 1044, the notion that a woman's decision to carry the pregnancy to term is the 'cause' of the child's birth (as opposed to the negligence of the physician) was rejected. This potential argument was also rejected by Lord Slynn in *McFarlane* (n 108) 74.

[168] *McFarlane* (n 108) 81. And indeed, it is not clear that abortion would be lawful in such circumstances in some jurisdictions. Abortion law is discussed in ch 5 (see esp section II).

[169] Hensel (n 101).

[170] Asch, 'Disability Equality' (n 145); Erik Parens and Adrienne Asch, 'The Disability Rights Critique of Prenatal Genetic Testing: Reflections and Recommendations' in Erik Parens and Adrienne Asch (eds), *Prenatal Testing and Disability Rights* (Washington, DC, Georgetown University Press, 2000) 3; Marsha Saxton, 'Why Members of the Disability Community Oppose Prenatal Diagnosis and Selective Abortion' in Adrienne Asch and Erik Parens (eds), *Prenatal Testing and Disability Rights* (Washington, DC, Georgetown University Press, 2000) 147.

multiple characteristics, and envisions persons with disabilities as 'patients' who 'suffer' from their disabilities.[171] A better approach is one based on the social model or minority rights model of disability, both of which adopt the perspective that what creates suffering in the disability context is the fact that our society is preoccupied with normalcy, afraid of disability and unwelcoming of difference. Importantly, from the standpoint of wrongful birth actions, these scholars argue that it is disingenuous to speak of choice and autonomy in the context of a society that views abortion as the 'reasonable' response to potential disability or impairment in a fetus.[172] From this perspective, wrongful birth actions in particular constrain rather than facilitate reproductive autonomy, as the 'unpopular' choice to continue with the pregnancy and welcome the child into one's life is not equally an option for parents.

The disability rights perspective is also concerned with the way in which wrongful birth cases have to be presented, from the standpoint of causation. In some jurisdictions, courts have alluded to the need for the disability to be sufficiently serious to warrant recovery.[173] Parents must (for the most part) claim that had they been made aware of the disability or illness the child would have, they would have either avoided conceiving or terminated the pregnancy.[174]

While I agree with many of the concerns raised by scholars who embrace the disability rights critique – in particular that the two choices are not really considered equally acceptable – I am not prepared to agree that social justice demands that such claims not be recognised. Wendy Hensel has argued that

> [t]ort law should not serve as a tool of injustice under the guise of benevolent intervention on behalf of individuals with disabilities. Because relief to individual litigants in wrongful birth and wrongful life actions is purchased at a cost to society as a whole, neither action should be recognized by state legislatures or the courts.[175]

In theory, it is possible to reconcile the disability rights view with support for reproductive autonomy, and several scholars who adopt the disability rights view also claim to be pro-choice.[176] But ruling out wrongful birth claims would fail to respect reproductive autonomy, given the potential effect of ruling out recovery of damages in such cases on women's lives.

In some Canadian cases,[177] recovery has been refused even where the mother has testified that she would have terminated the pregnancy had she known of the risk of serious

---

[171]   Asch, 'Disability Equality' (n 145); Parens and Asch (n 170); Saxton (n 170).

[172]   Hensel (n 101) 172–73 .

[173]   *Ibid* 169–70.

[174]   *Ibid* 171–73.

[175]   *Ibid* 145.

[176]   Parens and Asch, 'The Disability Rights Critique' (n 170); Adrienne Asch, 'Reproductive Technology and Disability' in Sherrill Cohen and Nadine Taub (eds), *Reproductive Laws for the 1990s* (Clifton, NJ, Humana Press, 1989) 69, 89; Marsha Saxton, 'Disability Rights and Selective Abortion' in Rickie Solinger (ed), *Abortion Wars: A Half Century of Struggle, 1950 to 2000* (Berkeley, University of California Press, 1998) 374; Tom Shakespeare, 'Choices and Rights: Eugenics, Genetics and Disability Equality' (1998) 13 *Disability and Society* 665.

[177]   *Arndt v Smith* (SCC) (n 149); *Mickle v Salvation Army Grace Hospital Windsor Ontario* (n 59). In *Arndt v Smith*, it is clear that the plaintiff testified that she would have terminated the pregnancy had she been made aware of fetal abnormalities; but in *Mickle v Salvation Army Grace Hospital Windsor Ontario*, the judgment does not indicate if there was testimony on point. The trial judge concerned himself with whether the reasonable woman would have done so, on the basis of the modified objective test used in Canada for informed consent claims.

disability. In some ways, the Canadian approach to causation suggests (in contrast to the claims of disability rights critique) that the continuation of a pregnancy in the face of a disabling diagnosis is very much a reasonable option. But it seems shockingly disrespectful, from the perspective of reproductive autonomy, to find – in spite of testimony to the contrary – that a woman would have chosen to continue the pregnancy. In such circumstances some reasonable women would elect to terminate the pregnancy, while other reasonable women would not. A thoughtful approach to reproductive autonomy requires that we grapple with this very question and attend to the woman's ability to make such choices on the basis of her own values.

But perhaps a more creative approach can be found to wrongful birth and wrongful conception claims. Instead of focusing on the costs of child-rearing as the damage in such cases, it might be wise to consider an approach that considers the loss of autonomy as the violation of a process right.

Aaron Twerski and Neil Cohen have argued that informed choice in the healthcare context should not be approached through traditional negligence principles applicable to personal injury claims. Instead, the denial of a person's right to participate in his or her own healthcare decisions should be viewed as an actionable wrong, capable of sounding in damages in its own right.[178] This kind of approach would mean that the courts were in fact awarding damages for the loss of opportunity to make a meaningful, informed choice, rather than for the harm of bearing an impaired child. The House of Lords, in *Rees*,[179] awarded what the Law Lords referred to as a 'modest solatium' or conventional sum of £15,000 to recognise the legal wrong done to the plaintiff by the physician who negligently performed a tubal ligation procedure, as well as to acknowledge that the physician's negligence deprived the plaintiff of her ability to determine for herself the size of her family. The sum awarded is probably not significant enough, neither is the language of 'solatium' strong enough, to achieve the aims suggested by Twerski and Cohen – they claim that any award based on the violation of process rights would have to be significant enough to deter the conduct complained of – but it might be a step in the right direction.[180]

Shawn Harmon and Graeme Laurie have noted a tendency toward recognition of a right to autonomy (distinguishable from a right based on autonomy) in order to permit recovery by plaintiffs who have lost an opportunity to make an autonomous choice.[181] The examples they draw on include *McFarlane*[182] and *Rees*, as well as two other medical law cases.[183] They view this inclination with some concern, noting that without 'well

---

[178] See, eg, Aaron D Twerski and Neil B Cohen, 'Informed Decision-Making and the Law of Torts: The Myth of Justiciable Causation' (1988) *University of Illinois Law Review* 607. Twerski and Cohen's position is that causation in informed consent cases is simply not justiciable, and the traditional informed consent negligence analysis should therefore be abandoned. The two authors do differ on the question of whether wrongful birth claims, because they involve moral values rather than simply an analysis of risk information, should be handled similarly (*ibid* 661–63).

[179] *Rees* (n 111).

[180] Interestingly, Twerski and Cohen themselves suggest that the one 'informed consent' scenario in which causation can possibly be realistically determined is that of wrongful birth, because it is a moral decision as opposed to a strictly information-based risk calculation, which we know we are notoriously bad at making (Twerski and Cohen (n 178) 656–58, 662–63).

[181] Shawn HE Harmon and Graeme T Laurie, '*Yearworth v North Bristol NHS Trust*: Property, Principles, Precedents and Paradigms' (2010) 69 *Cambridge Law Journal* 476.

[182] Where general damages were awarded, even though child-rearing damages were not.

[183] *Chester v Afshar* [2004] UKHL 41, [2005] 1 AC 134; *Yearworth v North Bristol NHS Trust* [2009] EWCA Civ 37, [2010] 1 QB 1.

conceived foundations and well articulated limits, such an outcome-oriented approach will become deeply problematic in practice'.[184] The reservations articulated by Harmon and Laurie, including increased unpredictability in the law, as well (possibly) as harm to the healthcare system and to those who are served by it,[185] are well founded. If the courts do pursue an approach to damages for wrongful life and wrongful birth cases that skirts the boundaries of established legal principles, they must do so thoughtfully and with care.

It is starkly apparent that the law around wrongful life, wrongful birth and wrongful conception claims is (with a few exceptions) unsettled, confusing and a source of wasteful litigation. It is frankly astounding that this level of uncertainty persists after more than three decades of jurisprudence. Perhaps, though, this is merely a symptom of the fact that there are few cases dealing with these issues, meaning that the courts have not been faced with the issues on a sufficiently frequent basis to engage in developing a clear jurisprudence.

While the continuing uncertainty around these claims is disappointing, it is encouraging to note the shift in judicial thinking about the meaning of these claims for the lives of parents – particularly mothers – who find themselves caring for an unplanned child or one with serious disabilities. In the earliest Canadian case considering wrongful conception claims, the very idea of the claim was said to be 'grotesque'.[186] More recently, the language used to describe these claims has illustrated that the courts are coming around to the notion of reproductive autonomy and are prepared to acknowledge the gendered distribution of harms to reproductive autonomy. As Lord Bingham expressed it in *Rees*, the 'real loss suffered in a situation of this kind . . . is that a parent, particularly (even today) the mother, has been denied, through the negligence of another, the opportunity to live her life in the way that she wished and planned'.[187] And Lady Justice Hale's reasons in *Parkinson v St James and Seacroft University Hospital NHS Trust* are even more pointed. She notes that

> their Lordships [in *McFarlane*] did not go into detail about what is entailed in the invasion of bodily integrity caused by conception, pregnancy and child birth. But it is worthwhile spelling out the more obvious features. Some will sound in damages and some may not, but they are all the consequence of that fundamental invasion. They are none the less an invasion because they are the result of natural processes. They stem from something which should never have happened. And they last for a great deal longer than the pregnancy itself. Whatever the outcome, happy or sad, a woman never gets over it.[188]

Among these features, Lady Justice Hale notes, are 'profound physical changes,' psychological changes, including the 'development of deep feelings for the new life as it grows within one,' and the 'severe curtailment of personal autonomy' that is entailed in the assumption of continuous responsibility for another life, that begins with conception and does not end until the child is able to care for his or her own needs.[189] It is to be hoped that these judicial comments will eventually sound in real recognition of the harm done by provider negligence in infringing reproductive autonomy.

---

[184] Harmon and Laurie (n 181) 490.
[185] *Ibid*.
[186] *Doiron v Orr* (n 100) para 32.
[187] *Rees* (n 111) para 8.
[188] *Parkinson v St James and Seacroft University Hospital NHS Trust* (n 104) para 63.
[189] *Ibid* paras 64–71.

Part Four

Assisting Reproduction

8

Regulating Assisted Reproductive Technologies: Governance and Access to Treatment

I. INTRODUCTION

ASSISTED REPRODUCTION HAS been a feature of reproductive healthcare for over three decades, with some forms of treatment having been used for far longer.[1] In the past, the practice was cloaked in secrecy and was highly stigmatised. Over the years, the number of individuals and couples seeking to form families using assisted reproductive technologies (ARTs) has increased dramatically. In 2010, over 18,000 assisted reproduction cycles were performed in Canada, resulting in 5,633 pregnancies.[2] In the US, close to 150,000 treatment cycles were performed.[3] Worldwide, over five million babies had been born through in vitro fertilisation (IVF) by mid-2012.[4] This is truly remarkable, given that the first IVF birth took place only 34 years ago.[5]

The pace of growth and change in the world of ARTs over the past three decades has been incredible, and policy makers have struggled to keep up with the changing

---

[1] See, eg, Robin Marantz Henig, *Pandora's Baby: How the First Test Tube Babies Sparked the Reproductive Revolution* (Boston, MA, Houghton Mifflin, 2004) 26–27 (describing donor insemination by Dr William Pancoast in 1884).

[2] This is the number of intrauterine pregnancies (Canadian Fertility and Andrology Society, 'Canadian Assisted Reproductive Technologies Register (CARTR): 2010 Pregnancy Outcomes' (2010), at <www.cfas.ca/index.php?option=com_content&view=article&id=1130&Itemid=670)>. In 2009, 16,315 ART cycles were performed, resulting in 4,412 live births (Joanne Gunby, 'Assisted Reproductive Technologies (ART) in Canada: 2009 Results from the Canadian ART Register' (Canadian Fertility and Andrology Society, 2009), at <www.cfas.ca/images/stories/pdf/CARTR_2009.pdf>).

[3] 'Clinic Summary Report' (SART Cors Online, 2012), at <www.sartcorsonline.com/rptCSR_PublicMultYear.aspx?ClinicPKID=0>. The Centers for Disease Control (CDC) data indicate that 146,244 cycles were performed, and that there were 45,870 live births (60,190 infants born, in total) in 2009 (Centers for Disease Control and Prevention, American Society for Reproductive Medicine, Society for Assisted Reproductive Technology, *2009 Assisted Reproductive Technology Success Rates: National Summary and Fertility Clinic Reports* (Atlanta, US Department of Health and Human Services, 2011) 65). In the UK, 57,652 IVF treatment cycles were performed in 2010, up from approximately 54,250 in 2009 (Human Fertilisation and Embryology Authority, 'Latest UK IVF Figures: 2009 and 2010' (2012), at <www.hfea.gov.uk/ivf-figures-2006.html>). In 2009, 12,714 babies were born after IVF. In Australia and New Zealand, 2009 statistics indicate that 70,541 ART treatment cycles were undertaken, and 12,127 live births took place, resulting in the birth of 13,114 infants (Yueping A Wang *et al*, *Assisted Reproductive Technology in Australia and New Zealand 2009* (Canberra, Australian Institute of Health and Welfare, 2011) 4).

[4] European Society of Human Reproduction and Embryology, 'World's Number of IVF and ICSI Babies Has Now Reached a Calculated Total of 5 Million', *ScienceDaily*, 1 July 2012, at <www.sciencedaily.com/releases/2012/07/120702134746.htm>.

[5] Patrick C Steptoe and Robert G Edwards, 'Birth After the Reimplantation of a Human Embryo' (1978) 2 *The Lancet* 366.

technologies and with evolving societal perceptions about their appropriate uses. While the science of assisted reproduction continues to drive forward, concerns have been expressed by those with religious and socially conservative views about the potential of these technologies radically to alter our views about parenthood, family and embryonic human life, as well as about the potential negative effects of commodifying reproduction. Some of these same anxieties have been raised by feminist scholars and activists, albeit from the perspective of the potential harms to women that can result from the application of ARTs. Perhaps the most salient challenge posed by ARTs for feminist thought is the tricky question of how to secure women's needs, interests and bodily integrity, while at the same acknowledging that the desires of infertile women who wish to access assisted reproduction are legitimate and demand respect.

Legal regulation of ARTs intersects with reproductive autonomy in a number of ways. Laws around which reproductive technologies may be used have clear implications for autonomous reproductive choice; the State may limit autonomy by putting some technologies out of bounds. Restricting access to reproductive technologies (for example, to married couples) also limits reproductive autonomy, as individuals and unmarried couples (both heterosexual and homosexual) may wish to use various reproductive technologies in order to have children. In addition, the provision (or withholding) of public funding has a significant effect on access to treatment, given the expense attendant on such services.

The fundamental question of whether or not particular ARTs can be used at all, or whether they can be used for specific applications, does not directly engage women's interest in bodily integrity. While a blanket prohibition on the use of IVF might threaten the psycho-social integrity of individual infertile women, it would not threaten their bodily integrity per se. Most applications of ARTs, however, do engage women's bodily integrity in various ways. In vitro fertilisation itself entails hormonal stimulation, egg retrieval and embryo or blastocyst implantation, all of which are invasive techniques. Egg donation, for either reproductive or research purposes, clearly implicates women's bodily integrity. Pre-implantation genetic diagnosis (PGD) involves IVF, and in that way affects women's bodies; but prohibiting PGD might also indirectly affect women's bodily integrity, if such a prohibition leads women to conceive and then pursue pre-natal diagnosis and selective abortion.

The fact that regulation of ART use only indirectly affects women's bodily integrity suggests that ART applications, in general, fall outside the core of reproductive autonomy, and therefore do not demand the highest level of respect from the State. But some regulatory decisions around ART use clearly have the potential to impact women's bodily integrity, and regulation therefore requires exceptional care and attention to women's interests.

I have argued that abortion and contraception fall within the core of reproductive autonomy and that they must be State-funded in order to be readily accessible. The conclusion that IVF and related ARTs fall outside of this core suggests that the State would not fail to respect reproductive autonomy by declining to fund these interventions and procedures.[6] There are arguments for and against State funding of ART services. Probably first among the arguments against State funding is the reality that healthcare budgets form

---

[6] Assuming, of course, that the decision to deny funding is made on the basis of fair and relevant reasons: see, eg, Emily Jackson, *Regulating Reproduction: Law, Technology and Autonomy* (Oxford, Hart Publishing, 2001) 201.

the largest proportion of provincial government expenditures,[7] and there are many medically beneficial services that are not funded as a result of fiscal constraints.[8] In spite of such financial impediments, in my view, ART services should be selectively funded, with funding tailored, in so far as this is possible, to evidence of efficacy.[9] Provision of funding for IVF could actually lead to reduced spending elsewhere in the healthcare system, in that those who cannot afford IVF are more likely to opt for fertility drugs that can lead to high order multiple pregnancies, with their accompanying risks and costs.[10] Even if IVF is funded, however, there are other urgent priorities in reproductive health, including (among other things) research into the causes of infertility.[11]

My focus in this chapter is on law and policy around the governance of ART practice generally, and on questions of access to ART treatment. After briefly describing some of the most common ARTs, I discuss how ART practice is currently regulated in the US, Australia, the UK and Canada. I then consider the implications of reproductive autonomy for the choice of regulatory or governance approach. In particular, I reflect on the question of whether regulation should be left to the medical profession, or whether the State should also play a role in regulation. In the final section of the chapter, I discuss regulation and access to treatment from the standpoint of respect for reproductive autonomy; here I focus on eligibility criteria that spell out who may access ART services, and on the relationship between funding for ART services and accessibility of treatment.

II. INFERTILITY AND TECHNIQUES USED IN ASSISTING CONCEPTION

Infertility is clinically defined as the failure to conceive after 12 months of unprotected heterosexual intercourse in the fertile phase of the woman's menstrual cycle.[12] Infertility can also be understood non-medically, where a person is 'infertile' or unable to conceive because he or she lacks a heterosexual partner with whom to attempt conception. A variety of methods and technologies may be used to assist conception in those who are unable to conceive naturally. These include:

---

[7] See, eg, William Lahey, 'Medicare and the Law: Contours of an Evolving Relationship' in Jocelyn Downie, Timothy Caulfield and Colleen M Flood (eds), *Canadian Health Law and Policy* 4th edn (Markham, LexisNexis Canada, 2011) 1, 8.

[8] Including prescription drugs (in most provinces), dental services and some expensive cancer drugs (again, this varies by province).

[9] In keeping with the trend toward evidence-based medicine, it is essential to look at success rates of IVF and other ART treatments in various age groups, as well as with reference to the cause of infertility for the particular couple. The Canadian Royal Commission that studied this issue, too, was concerned about efficacy and the evidentiary foundation for the provision of various ARTs (Royal Commission on New Reproductive Technologies, *Proceed with Care: Final Report of the Royal Commission on New Reproductive Technologies*, vol 2 (Ottawa, Minister of Supply and Services Canada, 1993) 70–73, 517, 538–44) [Baird Commission].

[10] Jeff Nisker, 'Socially Based Discrimination Against Clinically Appropriate Care' (2009) 181 *Canadian Medical Association Journal* 764. Funding for IVF and related ARTs is discussed more fully in section V.B. below.

[11] It should be noted that infertility prevention might, in an increasing number of cases, be as simple as creating laws and policies that make it possible for women to have children earlier without jeopardising their career prospects: see, eg, BC Dunphy et al, 'Female Age, the Length of Involuntary Infertility Prior to Investigation and Fertility Outcome' (1989) 4 *Human Reproduction* 527; Chih-Chi Chuang et al, 'Age is a Better Predictor of Pregnancy Potential Than Basal Follicle-stimulating Hormone Levels in Women Undergoing In Vitro Fertilization' (2003) 79 *Fertility and Sterility* 63.

[12] C Gnoth et al, 'Definition and Prevalence of Subfertility and Infertility' (2005) 20 *Human Reproduction* 1144; American Society for Reproductive Medicine, *Infertility: An Overview: A Guide for Patients* (Birmingham, AL, American Society for Reproductive Medicine, 2012) 3.

(a) *Assisted insemination (AI):* sperm is placed into the woman's reproductive tract by a means other than intercourse. Assisted insemination may be done using the woman's partner's sperm, or donor sperm (in which case it is usually referred to as donor insemination, or DI). Depending upon where in the woman's reproductive tract the sperm are deposited, the label can vary. Intrauterine insemination (IUI) is a form of AI in which the sperm are deposited directly into the uterus, while intra-vaginal insemination involves the deposit of sperm into the vagina. These methods are usually excluded from the definition of ARTs because they do not involve manipulation of both ova and sperm, neither do they involve surgical procedures to retrieve oocytes.[13]

(b) *Gamete intrafallopian transfer (GIFT):* egg and sperm are placed in the woman's fallopian tube, in the hope that fertilisation and, later, implantation will take place. Zygote intrafallopian transfer (ZIFT) involves the transfer of a fertilised oocyte (or zygote) into the fallopian tube.[14]

(c) *In vitro fertilisation (IVF):* this involves several steps, including ovarian stimulation, egg retrieval (eggs are surgically removed from the woman's ovaries (or from a donor's ovaries)), fertilisation and transfer back to the woman's uterus. Here, conception takes place outside the woman's body, and may include additional techniques, such as intracytoplasmic sperm injection and assisted hatching. In vitro fertilisation may also involve diagnostic techniques, such as pre-implantation genetic diagnosis.[15]

(d) *Intracytoplasmic sperm injection (ICSI):* a variation on IVF used in cases of male factor infertility (insufficient numbers of sperm, insufficient sperm motility), where a single sperm cell is injected into the egg to attempt to ensure fertilisation.[16]

(e) *Assisted hatching (AH):* prior to the embryo(s) being transferred back to the uterus, a hole is made in the outer membrane of the egg/embryo, known as the *zona pellucida*, in the hope that this will facilitate 'hatching' of the embryo and subsequent implantation into the woman's uterus.[17]

(f) *Pre-implantation genetic diagnosis (PGD):* after embryos are created for use in IVF, one cell is removed from the embryo for the purposes of genetic testing. This technique was first used in an attempt to avoid the transmission of sex-linked disorders, but is now available for a wide variety of genetic conditions, and for human-leucocyte-antigen (HLA) testing, to determine whether an embryo is a match for an ill sibling.[18] Pre-implantation genetic screening (PGS) is used to screen embryos for aneuploidy (a condition of having more or less than the usual complement of chromosomes).[19]

---

[13] Fernando Zegers-Hochschild *et al*, 'International Committee for Monitoring Assisted Reproductive Technology (ICMART) and the World Health Organization (WHO) Revised Glossary of ART Terminology, 2009' (2009) 92 *Fertility and Sterility* 1520.

[14] Bradley J Van Voorhis, 'Outcomes from Assisted Reproductive Technology' (2006) 107 *Obstetrics & Gynecology* 183, 184.

[15] *Ibid*; Steptoe and Edwards (n 5).

[16] Gianpiero Palermo *et al*, 'Pregnancies After Intracytoplasmic Injection of a Single Spermatozoa into an Oocyte' (1992) 340 *The Lancet* 17.

[17] Jacques Cohen, 'Assisted Hatching of Human Embryos' (1991) 8 *Journal of In Vitro Fertilization and Embryo Transfer* 179.

[18] Alan H Handyside *et al*, 'Pregnancies from Biopsied Human Preimplantation Embryos Sexed by Y-specific DNA Amplification' (1990) 344 *Nature* 768; Yury Verlinsky *et al*, 'Preimplantation Diagnosis for Fanconi Anemia Combined With HLA Matching' (2001) 285 *Journal of the American Medical Association* 3130; Karen Sermon, André Van Steirteghem and Inge Liebaers, 'Preimplantation Genetic Diagnosis' (2004) 363 *The Lancet* 1633.

[19] Sebastiaan Mastenbroek *et al*, 'In Vitro Fertilization with Preimplantation Genetic Screening' (2007) 357 *New England Journal of Medicine* 9.

III. GOVERNANCE OF ARTS: REGULATORY STRUCTURES

Assisted reproductive technologies burst onto the world scene in the late 1970s, with the birth of Louise Brown in 1978 marking the beginning of a process of debate and regulation that continues to evolve today.[20] In the wake of the first few births to result from IVF, many governments established committees to study the legal, ethical and social issues posed by the reality of assisted reproduction.[21] After studying the issues, governments in various jurisdictions adopted distinct approaches to governance of ARTs. The purpose of this section is to outline the differing approaches to regulation taken in the US, the UK, Canada and Australia, using broad brush-strokes, before focusing in on issues related to access to treatment; specifically eligibility criteria and funding.

Australia, Canada and the UK have adopted (or more accurately in the case of Canada, attempted to adopt) regulatory regimes that have aspects in common with one another, and that are all distinct from the American regulatory approach (such as it is) to ARTs.[22] The discussion that follows will first examine regulation in the US, and then consider how Australia, the UK and Canada have set out to govern the use of ARTs.

A. United States

The regulatory climate in the US has been likened to the 'wild west',[23] given the lack of regulation of the assisted reproduction industry. Some have objected to this characterisation, noting that there is a significant level of regulation around ART practice (and related research) in the US,[24] but it would be misleading to speak of a 'regulatory structure', as regulation is extremely piece-meal and fragmented. It is indeed the case that

---

[20] Steptoe and Edwards (n 5).

[21] See, eg, Royal Commission on New Reproductive Technologies (n 9); Warnock Committee, *Report Of The Committee Of Inquiry Into Human Fertilisation And Embryology* (Cmnd 9314, 1983); Australia, Family Law Council, *Creating Children: A Uniform Approach to the Law and Practice of Reproductive Technology in Australia* (Canberra, Family Law Council, 1985); Ontario Law Reform Commission, *Report on Human Artificial Reproduction and Related Matters* (Toronto, The Commission, 1985); New South Wales Law Reform Commission, *Report 49 (1986): Artificial Conception: Human Artificial Insemination* (Sydney, The Commission, 1986); Select Committee of the Legislative Council, *Report of the Select Committee of the Legislative Council on Artificial Insemination by Donor, In-Vitro Fertilisation and Embryo Transfer Procedures and Related Matters in South Australia* (Adelaide, Government Printer, 1987); New South Wales Law Reform Commission, *Discussion Paper 15 (1987): Artificial Conception: In Vitro Fertilisation* (Sydney, The Commission, 1988); New South Wales Law Reform Commission, *Report 60 (1988): Artificial Conception: Surrogate Motherhood* (Sydney, The Commission, 1988); Victoria Committee to Consider the Social, Ethical and Legal Issues Arising from In Vitro Fertilization, *Consolidated Reports of the Victorian Inquiry into IVF and Related Issues, 1982–1984* (Melbourne, Committee to Consider the Social, Ethical and Legal Issues Arising from In-vitro Fertilisation, 1990); Law Reform Commission of Canada, *Medically Assisted Procreation (Working Paper 65)* (Ottawa, Minister of Supply and Services Canada, 1992).

[22] Debora L Spar, *The Baby Business: How Money, Science, and Politics Drive the Commerce of Conception* (Boston, MA, Harvard Business School Press, 2006) 50–67.

[23] See, eg, Rebecca Dresser, 'Regulating Assisted Reproduction' (2000) 30(6) *Hastings Center Report* 26, 26; Mark V Sauer, 'Italian Law 40/2004: A View from the "Wild West"' (2006) 12 *Reproductive Biomedicine Online* 8, 9; Nanette R Elster, 'Book Review of *Test Tube Families: Why the Fertility Market Needs Legal Regulation*' (2009) 119 *Journal of Clinical Investigation* 3501; John Robertson, 'The Octuplet Case – Why More Regulation is Not Likely' (2009) 39(3) *Hastings Center Report* 26, 27.

[24] David Adamson, 'Regulation of Assisted Reproductive Technologies in the United States' (2002) 78 *Fertility and Sterility* 932.

there are numerous laws in the US touching on various aspects of ART practice, including insurance coverage, success rate reporting, surrogacy, parentage and certification of diagnostic testing facilities. That said, in general terms, there is limited direct government regulation (at either the federal or state levels) of ART services. The regulatory picture in the US includes measures directed at various aspects of ARTs at both state and federal levels, but neither jurisdiction deals with all aspects of ARTs, nor does the sum of federal and state regulation cover the entire field.

Federal regulation of ART practices is accomplished by two federal statutes (the Clinical Laboratories Improvement Amendments of 1988[25] (CLIA) and the Fertility Clinic Success Rate and Certification Act[26]) and the Food and Drug Administration's (FDA's) regulatory jurisdiction over some aspects of ART practice.[27] This jurisdiction covers ovulation stimulating drugs, culture media used to grow embryos in vitro, and other drugs and devices used in ART practice.[28]

Pursuant to CLIA, ART laboratories that carry out diagnostic testing on semen or blood must be certified. Regulations have been issued by the Centers for Medicare and Medicaid Services (CMS) – the group responsible for administration of the CLIA program – which address quality control and quality assurance, educational and professional qualifications for centre staff, and procedures for inspection and enforcement (including the potential imposition of sanctions for non-compliance).[29] While the regulations developed under CLIA clearly apply to ART laboratories involved in diagnostic procedures,[30] the CMS has taken the position 'that PGD is not covered by CLIA' because it involves the 'assessment of a product' and is therefore within the FDA's jurisdiction over reproductive tissues and cells.[31]

The second federal statute, the Fertility Clinic Success Rate and Certification Act, has two primary purposes: first, to provide information to consumers about the efficacy of ART services;[32] and, secondly, to develop a model certification program for use by states in developing their own programs for certifying embryo laboratories.[33]

The FDA does not have jurisdiction to regulate 'the practice of medicine',[34] and it therefore has limited authority over ARTs as medical services. The FDA does, however, have authority to regulate certain aspects of the ART process, including any drugs or

[25] Clinical Laboratories Improvement Amendments of 1988, PL 100–578, 102 Stat 2903 (1988) (codified at 42 USC § 263a *et seq*).

[26] Fertility Clinic Success Rate and Certification Act, PL 102–493, 106 Stat 3146 (1992) (codified at 42 USC § 263a-1 *et seq*).

[27] Federal Food, Drug and Cosmetic Act, 21 USC § 301 (1938).

[28] David Adamson, 'Regulation of Assisted Reproductive Technologies in the United States' (2005–06) 39 *Family Law Quarterly* 727, 735–36.

[29] CLIA Regulations, 42 CFR Part 493.

[30] It should be noted, however, that the CLIA Regulations do not apply 'when these tests are performed as an adjunct to the provision of ART services' (President's Council on Bioethics, *Reproduction and Responsibility: The Regulation of New Biotechnologies* (Washington, DC, The President's Council on Bioethics, 2004) 77).

[31] Susannah Baruch, David Kaufman and Kathy L Hudson, 'Genetic Testing of Embryos: Practices and Perspectives of US In Vitro Fertilization Clinics' (2008) 89 *Fertility and Sterility* 1053, 1056. See also President's Council on Bioethics (n 30).

[32] Clinics offering ART services are to report annually to the CDC for each ART procedure initiated. The CDC post the data in reports (*2009 Assisted Reproductive Technology Success Rates* (n 3)). Appendix C to the report lists 'nonreporting clinics' (which are clinics that perform ART services but either did not provide data or did not verify the accuracy of the tabulated success rates, as required by the CDC for publication).

[33] President's Council on Bioethics (n 30) 47–51. The model program was issued in 1999, but it is not clear whether any states have used the model as a basis for developing their own guidelines.

[34] *Ibid* 60.

devices involved in the provision of ART services.[35] The FDA has also asserted regulatory authority over reproductive tissues, as a part of its comprehensive strategy for regulating 'human cells, tissues, and cellular and tissue-based products'.[36]

State laws also play a role in regulating ARTs. Several states have legislation dealing with issues around the disposition, use and storage of frozen embryos,[37] surrogacy, gamete donation and embryo research.[38] At least two states have comprehensive legislation governing surrogacy (Virginia and New Hampshire[39]), and a number of other states have legislation that touches on some aspect(s) of ARTs. Some, for example, have laws that mandate insurance coverage of some aspects of infertility treatment.[40] States are also responsible for the regulation of the status of children born as a result of ART procedures, and a number of states have adopted legislation governing at least some aspects of parentage in the ART context.[41]

In addition to state and federal governance, professional organisations play a role in governance in the US. In particular, the American Society for Reproductive Medicine (ASRM) (together with its affiliated society, the Society for Assisted Reproductive Technology (SART)) provides guidelines for its members on the various aspects of infertility treatment services,[42] including gamete and embryo donation,[43] pre-implantation genetic testing,[44] the number of embryos transferred,[45] and even 'child-rearing ability

---

[35] As the President's Council on Bioethics explains, the FDA 'regulates some of the *articles* used in assisted reproduction, but it does not, as a general matter, oversee the *practice* of assisted reproduction' (*ibid* 54–55).

[36] *Ibid* 58. For a detailed discussion on this point, see *ibid* 56–62.

[37] This is discussed in more detail in ch 9, section II. California, Colorado, Florida, Louisiana, North Dakota, Oklahoma, Texas, Washington and Wyoming (for more detail and for citations to the relevant legislation, see National Conference of State Legislatures, 'Embryo and Gamete Disposition Laws' (July 2007), at <www.ncsl.org/programs/health/embryodisposition.htm>). Case law exists in other jurisdictions concerning related issues: see, eg, *Kass v Kass*, 696 NE 2d 174 (NY 1998); *AZ v BZ*, 725 NE 2d 1051 (Mass 2000); *JB v MB*, 783 A 2d 707 (NJ 2001); *Re the Marriage of Litowitz v Litowitz*, 48 P 3d 261 (Wash 2002).

[38] For a detailed discussion of the state-based approaches to the regulation of ARTs, see Charles P Kindregan Jr and Maureen McBrien, *Assisted Reproductive Technology: A Lawyer's Guide to Emerging Law and Science*, 2nd edn (Chicago, IL, American Bar Association, 2011). There are also a number of states with legislation relating to therapeutic and/or reproductive cloning. Most of the states that regulate cloning ban human reproductive cloning (Arizona and Missouri ban only the use of public funds for cloning), while some permit and some prohibit therapeutic cloning. Some states also prohibit state funding of research involving cloning. For a discussion of cloning prohibitions, see Steven Goldberg, 'Cloning Matters: How *Lawrence v Texas* Protects Therapeutic Research' (2004) 4 *Yale Journal of Health Policy, Law, and Ethics* 305.

[39] See, eg, VA Code Ann § 20-156 (2004); NH Rev Stat § 168-B (2004). See also Erik Parens and Lori P Knowles, 'Reprogenetics and Public Policy: Reflections and Recommendations' (July 2003) Special Supplement *Hastings Center Report* S1, S12.

[40] These laws are not uniform. Legislation in some states requires insurers to offer infertility treatment coverage, but does not require employers to pay for this coverage (California, Connecticut and Texas); in other states, insurers are required to cover infertility treatment (ie coverage must be provided in every insurance policy) (Arkansas, Hawaii, Illinois, Louisiana, Maryland, Massachusetts, Montana, New Jersey, New York, Ohio, Rhode Island, Texas, West Virginia). These laws are discussed in more detail below (section V.B.).

[41] Parentage in assisted reproduction is discussed in ch 9, section IV.

[42] American Society for Reproductive Medicine Practice Committee, 'Guidelines for the Provision of Infertility Services' (2004) 82 (Supp 1) *Fertility and Sterility* 24, 24–25.

[43] American Society for Reproductive Medicine Practice Committee and Society for Assisted Reproductive Technology Practice Committee, '2008 Guidelines for Gamete and Embryo Donation: A Practice Committee Report' (2008) 90 (Supp 3) *Fertility and Sterility* S30.

[44] Society for Assisted Reproductive Technology Practice Committee and American Society for Reproductive Medicine Practice Committee, 'Preimplantation Genetic Testing: A Practice Committee Opinion' (2008) 90 (Supp 3) *Fertility and Sterility* S136.

[45] American Society for Reproductive Medicine Practice Committee and Society for Assisted Reproductive Technology Practice Committee, 'Guidelines on Number of Embryos Transferred' (2009) 92 *Fertility and Sterility* 1518.

and the provision of fertility services'.[46] These guidelines are just that – professional guidelines that are 'developed to assist physicians with clinical decisions regarding the care of their patients. They are not intended to be a protocol to be applied in all situations, and cannot substitute for the individual judgment of the treating physicians . . .'[47] The ASRM and SART are not professional regulatory authorities and do not play a role in centre accreditation; as a result, the guidelines do not have the force of law. Physicians who do not follow the guidelines may be removed from the membership of ASRM, but cannot be prevented from practising medicine unless the regulatory authority (state medical board) revokes the physician's licence.[48]

Another area of regulatory oversight in the US is research involving human embryos. This area of regulation has been described as having a 'long and tortuous history in the United States'.[49] Although there is no federal legislation governing research on human embryos, since 1996, federal law has prohibited the use of federal funds to create human embryos for research purposes or to conduct research resulting in the destruction of human embryos.[50] But as the federal law restricts only the uses to which federal funds may be put, the US regulatory landscape is extremely variable, with some states banning human embryonic stem-cell research and others seeking to create an entire industry around it. California, for example, has been a leader on the embryonic stem-cell research front, creating the California Institute for Regenerative Medicine in 2004.[51] A number of other states have laws aimed at encouraging stem-cell research, yet others forbid all research on human embryos.[52] It is difficult to describe the regulatory picture in any thematic way other than to note the enormous influence of abortion politics or, more specifically, the questions of the moral status of the embryo and fetus on the regulation of embryo research.[53]

---

[46] American Society for Reproductive Medicine Ethics Committee, 'Child-rearing Ability and the Provision of Fertility Services' (2009) 92 *Fertility and Sterility* 864.

[47] American Society for Reproductive Medicine, 'Practice Committee Documents', at <www.asrm.org/Guidelines/>.

[48] After the birth of octuplets to Nadya Suleman (known in the press as 'octomom'), the physician who carried out the IVF procedure (in which 12 embryos were transferred to Ms Suleman's uterus) had his licence suspended by the Medical Board of California (Shaya Tayefe Mohajer, 'Octomom's Doctor Has License Revoked For "Mega-Birth"', *Huffington Post*, 1 June 2011, at <www.huffingtonpost.com/2011/06/01/octomoms-doctor-license-revoked_n_869991.html>).

[49] Adamson (n 28) 729.

[50] *Ibid*; John A Robertson, 'Embryo Stem Cell Research: Ten Years of Controversy' (2010) 38 *Journal of Law, Medicine & Ethics* 191. The legislation in question is known as the Dickey-Wicker Amendment; since 1996, the Amendment has been added to appropriations legislation each year. The original amendment can be found in the NIH budget legislation from 1996 (Balanced Budget Downpayment Act, I, Public Law No 104-99 § 128, 110 Stat 26, 34).

[51] California Health & Safety 2004 Proposition 71 §§ 123440, 24185, 12115-7, 125300-320.

[52] States in which human embryonic stem-cell research is encouraged include Connecticut, Illinois, Maryland, Massachusetts, New Jersey and New York. States with restrictive embryo research laws include South Dakota (which prohibits all research on human embryos), Louisiana, Arkansas and Kansas. Several states also have policies relating to cloning, for either reproductive or research purposes (National Conference of State Legislatures, 'Stem Cell Research' (January 2008), at <www.ncsl.org/issues-research/health/embryonic- and-fetal-research-laws.aspx>).

[53] For a discussion of the history and politics of embryo research in the US, see Herbert Gottweiss, 'The Endless hESC Controversy in the United States: History, Context, and Prospects' (2010) 7 *Cell Stem Cell* 555.

B. Australia

Australia's regulatory picture, like that in the US, involves both national and state regulation. Australia is a federal jurisdiction with separate central and regional governments; jurisdiction over health rests with state (rather than the central) governments. Governance of ART research and practice is accomplished through a complex, sometimes duplicative, regulatory structure that includes elements of both national and state oversight.[54] In addition to the division of responsibility into national and state components, clinical practice and research are separately regulated in Australia, and prohibitions on research and clinical uses of gametes and embryos are often found in legislation separate from that which regulates clinical practice of ARTs.

As a result of the division of powers among the Commonwealth and state governments, Australia's system is somewhat fragmented, although given the impediments to nationalised policy in Australia the degree of consistency that has been achieved on some fronts is noteworthy.[55] At the Commonwealth level, ART governance arises out of a combination of national ethics guidelines and professional regulation.[56] The National Health and Medical Research Council (NHMRC) has issued three sets of Guidelines specific to assisted reproduction; in the first (issued in 1996),[57] the NHMRC expressed the view that social issues concerning the use of ARTs (such as access to services, surrogacy and posthumous use of gametes) should be addressed in legislation.[58] As will be discussed below, some of these issues have now been dealt with in legislation in at least some jurisdictions. Although the most recent version of the NHMRC Guidelines again adverts to a recommendation for legislation in all states and territories of Australia,[59] both the 2004 and 2007 versions incorporate guidelines concerning some of the matters that were shied away from in 1996, including posthumous use of gametes,[60] pre-implantation genetic diagnosis, surrogacy, and storage of gametes and embryos.[61] The Guidelines do note that most Australian

---

[54] A national approach to regulation was recommended by the Family Law Council of Australia; this would have included the establishment of a regulatory or oversight body (*Creating Children* (n 21); Linda Martin, 'Reproductive Rights and New Technologies: Lessons from Law Reform' (1986) 58 *The Australian Quarterly* 375, 379).

[55] Dave Snow and Ranier Knopff, 'Assisted Reproduction Policy in Federal States: What Canada Should Learn from Australia' (2012) 5(12) *School of Public Policy Research Papers* 1. Given the failure of Canada's attempt at regulation, perhaps we shall see some use of the strategies employed in Australia, as described by Snow and Knopff.

[56] See, eg, Australian Government, National Health and Medical Research Council, *Ethical Guidelines on the Use of Assisted Reproductive Technology in Clinical Practice and Research 2007* (Canberra, Commonwealth of Australia, 2007 (NHMRC Guidelines 2007)); Fertility Society of Australia, Reproductive Technology Accreditation Committee, 'Code of Practice for Assisted Reproductive Technology Units' (Fertility Society of Australia, revised October 2010), at <www.fertilitysociety.com.au/wp-content/uploads/201011201-final-rtac-cop.pdf>; Fertility Society of Australia Reproductive Technology Accreditation Committee, 'Certification Scheme' (Fertility Society of Australia, October 2010), at <www.fertilitysociety.com.au/wp-content/uploads/201011201-final-rtac-scheme.pdf>.

[57] Australian Government, National Health and Medical Research Council, *Ethical Guidelines on Assisted Reproductive Technology* (Canberra, Commonwealth of Australia, 1996). The guidelines were revised in 2004 and again in 2007 (NHMRC Guidelines 2007 (n 56)).

[58] NHMRC Guidelines 1996 (n 57). See also Helen Szoke, 'Regulation of Assisted Reproductive Technology: The State of Play in Australia' in Ian Freckelton and Kerry Petersen (eds), *Controversies in Health Law* (Sydney, Federation Press, 1999) 240.

[59] NHMRC Guidelines 2007 (n 56) 5. It is noted that at the time of preparation of these Guidelines, uniform legislation had not been enacted.

[60] *Ibid* s 6.15.

[61] *Ibid* ss 8 (storage of gametes and embryos), 12 (pre-implantation genetic diagnosis), 13 (surrogacy).

jurisdictions have passed uniform legislation prohibiting human cloning (and other practices[62]) and regulating human embryo research.[63]

In terms of clinical practice, the Guidelines cover many of the ethical and practice issues that arise in the context of assisted reproductive services, including the use and storage of gametes and donated embryos, counselling and consent, training and quality assurance, and record keeping. In addition to specific guidance on these issues, the Guidelines include a section articulating ethical principles for clinical practice.[64] A separate section deals with research involving human gametes and embryos. In an appendix to the Guidelines, the NHMRC has briefly summarised arguments in favour of and opposing three 'controversial' issues in ART practice – genetic technologies,[65] sex selection[66] and surrogacy[67] – which it feels require further community debate and discussion, as well as 'consideration by elected governments'.[68]

The professional regulation aspect of national ART governance is accomplished through accreditation requirements and practice guidelines issued under the auspices of the Fertility Society of Australia (FSA), a professional organisation that represents ART providers (including physicians, nurses and counsellors), scientists and consumers of ART services in Australia and New Zealand. Accreditation of assisted reproduction treatment programs is the responsibility of the FSA's Reproductive Technology Accreditation Committee (RTAC). The accreditation regime and national ethics guidelines are mutually complementary, in that the NHMRC Guidelines require that all organisations providing ART services be accredited by the RTAC;[69] in turn, accreditation is contingent on compliance with NHMRC Guidelines.[70]

The RTAC was established by the FSA in 1987. Its terms of reference require the RTAC to develop a Code of Practice for ART centres, as well as to accredit ART centres

[62] Prohibition of Human Cloning for Reproduction Act 2002 (Cth). Other offences include: placing a human embryo clone in the human body or body of an animal (s 9); creating a human embryo for a purpose other than achieving pregnancy in a woman (s 12); creating or developing a human embryo by fertilisation containing genetic material provided by more than two persons (s 13); developing a human embryo outside the body of a woman for more than 14 days (s 14); heritable alterations to genome (s 15); collecting a viable human embryo from the body of a woman (s 16); creating a chimeric embryo or developing a hybrid embryo (ss 17, 18); placing a human embryo in an animal or in a part of a woman's body other than the reproductive tract, or placing an animal embryo in the body of a human for 'any period of gestation' (s 19); importing, exporting or placing a prohibited embryo (s 20); commercial trading in human eggs, human sperm or human embryos (s 21). The legislation also lists practices which are permitted only if authorised by a licence (including creating a human embryo other than by fertilisation, or developing such an embryo (s 22); using precursor cells from a human embryo or a human fetus to create a human embryo, or developing such an embryo (s 23A); creating a hybrid embryo (s 23B).

[63] See, eg, Prohibition of Human Cloning for Reproduction Act 2002 (Cth); Research Involving Human Embryos Act 2002 (Cth); Human Cloning and Embryo Research Act 2004 (ACT); Prohibition of Human Cloning for Reproduction Act 2003 (SA); Research Involving Human Embryos Act 2003 (SA); Research Involving Human Embryos and Prohibition of Human Cloning for Reproduction Act 2003 (Qld); Prohibition of Human Cloning for Reproduction Act 2008 (Vic); Research Involving Human Embryos Act 2008 (Vic).

[64] NHMRC Guidelines 2007 (n 56) s 5 (21–23).

[65] *Ibid* app C2 (90–91).

[66] *Ibid* s 11 (prohibits non-medical sex selection).

[67] *Ibid* s 13, and app C4 (at 92–93). The Guidelines state that clinics must not undertake or facilitate commercial surrogacy, and that clinics must not facilitate non-commercial surrogacy unless 'every effort' has been made to ensure that all parties understand the 'ethical, social and legal implications' of the arrangement and that all parties have received counselling as to the social and psychological significance of surrogacy arrangements for the parties involved and the child born as a result (*ibid* 57).

[68] *Ibid* app C1 (89).

[69] *Ibid* s 1.2 (5).

[70] *Ibid*.

and set and monitor practice standards.[71] The RTAC Code of Practice[72] provides guidance around compliance with statutory and other regulatory requirements, as well as guidance related to practice matters such as staff and resources, patient information, consent, laboratory services, treatment methods, records, ethics and research. One matter of particular concern to the RTAC is multiple pregnancy resulting from infertility treatment. The Code of Practice is explicit on this point, directing centres to 'minimise the incidence of multiple pregnancy'.[73] To this end, centres must provide evidence of the implementation and review of policies and procedures relating to the number of embryos transferred in each cycle.[74]

As noted above, the national ethics guidelines and accreditation standards are supplemented in some Australian states by specific legislation. All Australian states and territories other than the Northern Territory have legislation banning human reproductive cloning,[75] and laws relating to surrogacy.[76] Most jurisdictions also have legislation governing research on human embryos; these laws prohibit many research practices, including the use of human embryos that are not 'excess ART embryos' for any reason other than ART treatment.[77] In other words, embryos cannot be created for purposes other than use in assisted reproduction. Research on excess ART embryos is permitted, but only if carried out pursuant to a licence granted by the NHMRC.[78]

In addition to statutes regulating surrogacy and ART-related research, four Australian states have adopted legislation governing ART practice more generally.[79] In these states, the legislative provisions override the NHMRC Guidelines and RTAC accreditation standards.[80] Other than in these four states, there is no formalised regulatory approach to ARTs, meaning that there is significant variation in terms of how ART practice is governed throughout Australia.[81]

---

[71] The RTAC is also responsible for providing feedback to centres with a view to quality improvement, and for publishing a list of accredited ART centres, annual reports and recommendations for changes to the Code of Practice (Reproductive Technology Accreditation Committee, 'Terms of Reference' (*Senate Parliament of Australia*, 2008), at <https://senate.aph.gov.au/submissions/comittees/viewdocument.aspx?id>).

[72] Fertility Society of Australia, Reproductive Technology Accreditation Committee, 'Code of Practice for Assisted Reproductive Technology Units' (n 56).

[73] *Ibid* 11.

[74] *Ibid*.

[75] This was accomplished by state mirroring of Commonwealth legislation. See above (n 63). The Northern Territory is the only jurisdiction that has not passed mirroring legislation.

[76] Surrogacy laws are discussed in more detail in ch 9, section III.

[77] Research Involving Human Embryos Act 2002 (Cth) s 11. Other prohibited practices include the creation of embryos other than by fertilisation of an egg by a sperm (in other words, somatic cell nuclear transfer), and the creation of hybrid embryos for use in testing sperm quality (*ibid* ss 10A, 10B).

[78] *Ibid*. The only jurisdictions without 'mirrored' legislation on this issue are Western Australia and the Northern Territory; Western Australia's attempt to pass legislation to mirror the new Commonwealth legislation was defeated. Western Australia does have rules on the uses of surplus embryos (initially created for reproductive use) in its ART legislation; see below (n 79).

[79] See, eg, South Australia (Assisted Reproductive Treatment Act 1988 (SA)); Western Australia (Human Reproductive Technology Act 1991 (WA)); New South Wales (Assisted Reproductive Technology Act 2007 (NSW)); Victoria (Assisted Reproductive Treatment Act 2008 (Vic)). Several Australian states also have legislation addressing surrogacy and all have laws on the legal status of children born following the use of assisted reproduction. These are discussed in ch 9.

[80] R Thorpe *et al*, 'New Assisted Reproductive Technology Laws in Victoria: A Genuine Overhaul or Just Cut and Paste?' (2011) 18 *Journal of Law and Medicine* 835, 840.

[81] Other states and territories have legislation that deals with surrogacy, but not with reproductive technology generally, see, eg, Surrogacy Contracts Act 1993 (Tas) (makes it an offence to seek surrogacy arrangements); Parentage Act 2004 (ACT) (allows altruistic surrogacy, involving no commercial arrangements and no soliciting of candidates); Surrogacy Act 2010 (Qld).

All of the states that have legislation relating to ART practice have taken distinct approaches to various aspects of regulation. The one common thread running through all four Australian statutory jurisdictions is the inclusion of either a registration or a licensing mechanism for providers wishing to offer ART treatment services.[82] In most other respects, there are variations (some slight, some more pronounced) among the four statutory jurisdictions.

Two of the four Australian states with ART legislation (Victoria and Western Australia) have created oversight bodies responsible for executing the regulatory function.[83] In general terms, the regulatory bodies in Victoria and Western Australia have similar responsibilities, including licensing or registration of providers, information collection, standards of practice and the like. South Australia also had a regulatory authority when it first enacted legislation governing ART treatment, but the authority was dissolved when South Australia's legislation was amended in 2009. In presenting the amending statute to the House of Assembly in late 2008, the South Australian Minister for Health explained that the Reproductive Technology Act 1988 was put in place at a time when assisted reproduction was in its infancy, and that the framework created by the Act is not in keeping with a modern approach to ART regulation. As he put it:

> Assisted reproductive treatment . . . is no longer considered novel. It is now an accepted means of family formation. South Australia's legislation does not accommodate or respond to advances in infertility treatment, emerging public health challenges or shifts in social attitudes. The act has constrained assisted reproductive medicine services and the code has further complicated practice. Advances and discoveries in assisted reproductive treatment since the 1980s have made the present legislative scheme difficult to interpret and apply.[84]

Although all four states that have legislation on point have explicitly set out the guiding principles or purposes on which regulation is to be based, there are differences among the statutes on this front as well. In Victoria, for example, the Act includes guiding principles which make the welfare of the child the paramount consideration.[85] The Western Australian statute also refers to the importance of the welfare of the child,[86] but includes a number of other objectives as well, such as permitting 'beneficial developments in reproductive technology, but . . . discourag[ing], and if required . . . prohibit[ing], developments or procedures that are not both proper and suitable'.[87] In addition, the Preamble to the Act emphasises

[82] Assisted Reproductive Treatment Act 1988 (SA), ss 5–14; Human Reproductive Technology Act 1991 (WA), ss 6, 27–30; Assisted Reproductive Technology Act 2007 (NSW), ss 6–9; Assisted Reproductive Treatment Act 2008 (Vic), ss 7, 74.

[83] Victoria's regulatory body is referred to as a regulator (the Victorian Assisted Reproductive Treatment Authority, or VARTA) (Assisted Reproductive Treatment Act 2008 (Vic), s 100), and Western Australia's is a statutory council (the Western Australian Reproductive Technology Council). The Council's role includes the development and review of a Code of Practice, advising the Minister of Health as to applications for and compliance with licences, advising the Minister on issues related to ART services, the promotion of informed public debate on these issues, and the facilitation of research into human infertility and the social and public health implications of ART procedures (Human Reproductive Technology Act 1991 (WA), s 14).

[84] South Australia, *Parliamentary Debates*, House of Assembly, 26 November 2008, 1111 (JD Hill, Minister for Health, Minister for the Southern Suburbs, Minister Assisting the Premier in the Arts).

[85] Assisted Reproductive Treatment Act 2008 (Vic), s 5. Other guiding principles are: (i) non-exploitation of reproductive capacities of men, women or children born as a result of treatment procedures; (ii) the right of children born through the use of donated gametes to information about their genetic origins; (iii) the protection of the health of those undergoing treatment procedures; and (iv) non-discrimination against those seeking to undergo treatment procedures on the basis of sexual orientation, marital status or religion.

[86] Human Reproductive Technology Act 1991 (WA), s 4.

[87] *Ibid* s 4(c).

that the primary purpose and only justification for the creation of a human embryo in vitro is to assist persons who are unable to conceive children naturally due to medical reasons or whose children are otherwise likely to be affected by a genetic abnormality or a disease, to have children, and this legislation should respect the life created by this process.[88]

By contrast, the objectives of the New South Wales (NSW) legislation are simply to prevent the commercialisation of human reproduction and to protect the interests of those involved in ART treatment (including gamete donors, women receiving treatment and persons born as a result of ART treatment).[89]

Statutory eligibility criteria also vary among the states.[90] The NSW statute does not include eligibility criteria, while the other three state statutes do restrict access to treatment to some extent. All three initially limited access to treatment to heterosexual couples (married or, in some cases, 'de facto'), and all three have now changed their eligibility provisions so that they no longer refer explicitly to sexual orientation or marital status.[91] In South Australia and Western Australia eligibility is still restricted, but the restrictions are now based on medical infertility or on the risk that the individual might pass on a genetic disease or abnormality to the child. While the explicit (and clearly discriminatory) limits on eligibility have been removed, access remains limited in practice to those who meet the medical criteria for treatment.

The Victorian statute makes a noteworthy change on the eligibility front from its predecessor legislation in that it enables lesbian and single women who do not meet a medical definition of infertility to seek ART treatment.[92] It also introduces a new constraint on access, whereby women seeking treatment (and their partners) must submit to a criminal records and child protection order check prior to treatment being commenced. If either member of the couple has a criminal record disclosing violent or sexual offences, or if either has had a child removed from his or her custody or guardianship, a 'presumption against treatment' applies and ART treatment may not be provided.[93] The Act establishes a Patient Review Panel, which hears applications related to presumptions against treatment, as well as other eligibility-related matters, including applications for treatment where the ART provider is concerned about the well-being of a child that might be born as a result of ART treatment, and applications for treatment where the applicant does not meet the legislative criteria for treatment.[94]

New South Wales' ART legislation[95] is the most recently-developed state law in Australia, and it is distinct from the other Australian state laws in a number of ways.[96] The aim of the government in passing the legislation was to complement the existing national framework rather than to duplicate it, though as one author has noted, this

---

[88]   *Ibid* Preamble.
[89]   Assisted Reproductive Technology Act 2007 (NSW), s 3.
[90]   As do provisions dealing with donor anonymity, which are discussed in more detail in ch 9, section I.D.
[91]   In both Victoria and South Australia, the criteria were challenged on the basis of anti-discrimination laws. Eligibility criteria are discussed in more detail in section V. below.
[92]   Assisted Reproductive Treatment Act 2008 (Vic), s 10(1), (2).
[93]   *Ibid* ss 11, 12, 14.
[94]   *Ibid* s 85. The criteria for treatment are found in s 10(2). The Patient Review Panel can also consider applications related to surrogacy, posthumous use of gametes and embryos, and extensions of the storage period for gametes and embryos.
[95]   Assisted Reproductive Technology Act 2007 (NSW).
[96]   The NSW statute has been described as a 'light touch' (Malcolm Smith, 'Reviewing Regulation of Assisted Reproductive Technology in New South Wales: The Assisted Reproductive Technology Act 2007 (NSW)' (2008) 16 *Journal of Law and Medicine* 120).

objective does not appear to have been met in full, in that there is some duplication of NHMRC Guidelines in the Act, as well as some gaps that arguably should be addressed (including regulation of PGD).[97]

C. United Kingdom

The UK has been a pioneer in both ART practice and regulation. The first step in the UK regulatory process was the appointment of the Committee on Human Fertilisation and Embryology, chaired by Dame Mary Warnock. The Warnock Committee took the view that regulatory oversight of ARTs and embryo research was required to protect the public, and that the regulatory function should be played by an expert body, independent of government.[98] To that end, the Warnock Committee recommended the creation of a statutory licensing authority to regulate both research and clinical activity in this area.[99]

Based on the Committee's recommendations, clinical and research uses of assisted reproductive technologies, and embryo research generally, are comprehensively regulated under the Human Fertilisation and Embryology Act 1990 (HFE Act 1990).[100] The Act establishes a permissive licensing scheme whereby a central non-governmental body – the Human Fertilisation and Embryology Authority (HFEA) – is established and delegated authority to licence and monitor facilities that perform reproductive technologies and related research, including IVF, donor insemination and human embryo research. There is no statutory purpose or formal articulation of objectives within the HFE Act 1990, though it is widely noted that the legislation rests upon an ethical foundation that acknowledges the primary importance of the 'twin pillars' of consent and the welfare of the child.[101]

The Act assigns the HFEA the power to grant licences to facilities that wish to carry out ART practice, upon application by the facilities. In general, the HFEA may grant licences for any conceivable application of reproductive technologies, except those that are specifically prohibited by the legislation. These include research involving the use of embryos 'older' than 14 days,[102] placing non-human[103] or artificially or genetically modified gametes or embryos in a woman,[104] and reproductive cloning.[105]

With respect to the regulator itself, the Warnock Committee recognised the need for medical and scientific expertise in the membership of the Authority, but also explicitly advocated for substantial lay representation, including the recommendation that the chair of the board must be a layperson.[106] Although not formally included in its recom-

---

[97] *Ibid* 125, 131.

[98] Warnock Committee (n 21) para 13.3.

[99] *Ibid.*

[100] Human Fertilisation and Embryology Act 1990 (UK).

[101] See, eg, Marie Fox, 'The Human Fertilisation and Embryology Act 2008: Tinkering at the Margins' (2009) 17 *Feminist Legal Studies* 333, 334; Sally Sheldon, '*Evans v Amicus Health Care; Hadley v Midland Fertility Services* – Revealing Cracks in the "Twin Pillars"?' (2012) 16 *Child and Family Law Quarterly* 437.

[102] HFE Act 1990 (as amended), ss 3(3)(a), 3(4).

[103] *Ibid* s 4A(1).

[104] *Ibid* s 3(2) limits gametes and embryos which can be 'placed in a woman' to permitted embryos, which in turn are defined in s 3ZA(2), (3) and (4).

[105] *Ibid* s 3ZA(4). The Act also grants the Secretary of State for Health the power to make regulations respecting changes to the prohibitions or mandatory conditions for licences, but only if such regulations are laid before and approved by both Houses of Parliament in draft form (HFE Act 1990, s 45(4)).

[106] Warnock Committee (n 21) para 13.4.

mendations, the Committee also elaborated on its vision for the mandate of the statutory Authority, which included both advisory and executive functions. The executive function of the Authority would relate to licensing of ART-related treatment, as well as research involving human gametes and embryos.[107] The Authority's advisory role, as envisaged by the Committee, would extend to the issuing of guidelines respecting good practice 'in infertility service provision and on the types of research which, without prejudice to its view of any individual project, it finds broadly ethically acceptable'.[108]

The recommendation respecting the advisory function of the Authority translated into, in part, section 25 of the HFE Act 1990, which requires the HFEA to maintain a *Code of Practice*, 'giving guidance about the proper conduct of activities carried on in pursuance of a licence under this Act'.[109] The *Code of Practice* is to be approved by the Secretary of State for Health, after which it is to be laid before Parliament.[110] The *Code of Practice*, now in its eighth iteration,[111] provides detailed guidance regarding all of the matters within the HFEA's remit, which covers everything from the qualifications and responsibilities of staff employed by licenced centres, to procedures and considerations relevant to assessments of the 'welfare of the child'[112] and of persons seeking treatment.[113]

The HFEA has broad discretion in fulfilling its regulatory mandate. This has led on occasion to legal challenges from organisations and individuals who dispute a specific policy decision and assert that the HFEA's interpretation of the Act is flawed. Such challenges have occurred in relation to a variety of matters over the years. The first was brought by Diane Blood, when the HFEA refused her request to use sperm obtained from her deceased husband in order to conceive a child.[114] The sperm had been obtained without consent, there having been no opportunity to obtain consent prior to Mr Blood's death. The Authority's policy around the permissibility of using PGD and tissue typing

---

[107] *Ibid* para 13.6.

[108] *Ibid* para 13.5.

[109] HFE Act 1990, s 25(1).

[110] HFE Act 1990, s 26 (for purposes of information and formal publication). The Act also specifies that if the Secretary of State does not approve the *Code of Practice*, he is to provide reasons to the Authority (*ibid* s 26(3)).

[111] Human Fertilisation and Embryology Authority, *Code of Practice*, 8th edn (London, HFEA, 2009 (revised April 2012)).

[112] The HFE Act 1990 required treatment providers to take account 'of the welfare of any child who may be born as a result of the treatment' prior to the provision of services (HFE Act 1990, s 13(5)). Section 25(2) requires that guidance on this issue be included in the *Code of Practice*. The HFEA conducted a review of its guidance on this issue in 2004/05; its report was published in late 2005 (Human Fertilisation and Embryology Authority, 'Tomorrow's Children: Report of the Policy Review of Welfare of the Child Assessments in Licensed Assisted Conception Clinics' (2005), at <www.hfea.gov.uk/docs/TomorrowsChildren_consultation_doc.pdf>). The HFEA's guidance on point has also been changed since the passage of the HFE Act 2008 reforms, to reflect the removal of the specific requirement that centres have regard to 'the need of that child for a father'. For more on this point, see below. For a critical perspective on the legislative requirement that the welfare of the child be considered prior to the provision of infertility treatment, see Emily Jackson, 'Conception and the Irrelevance of the Welfare Principle' (2002) 65 *MLR* 176.

[113] The *Code* also provides guidance related to assessment and screening of potential gamete donors; provision of information to donors and to service recipients; consent; counselling; use, storage and handling of gametes and embryos; research; records and confidentiality; complaints; pre-implantation testing; witnessing clinical and laboratory procedures; and intra-cytoplasmic sperm injection (*Code of Practice* (n 111)).

[114] *R (Blood) v Human Fertilisation and Embryology Authority* [1997] EWCA Civ 3092 (holding that the HFEA could not prevent a woman from exporting sperm obtained from her husband in contravention of the Act). A similar case arose to be decided in 2008 (David Josiah-Lake, 'Posthumous Retrieval of Gametes: a Response' (1 December 2008) 486 *BioNews*, at <www.bionews.org.uk/page_38035.asp>; Alan Doran, 'Posthumous Retrieval of Gametes: a Response From the HFEA' (12 December 2008) 488 *BioNews*, at <www.bionews.org.uk/page_38039.asp>).

to create a 'saviour sibling' has also been challenged,[115] as has its approach to questions related to the destruction of embryos upon the withdrawal of consent by one of the gamete donors,[116] and around donor anonymity.[117]

A major element of the HFEA's role is to inform the public about ART practice and research, and the Authority undertakes public consultation as a significant part of its ongoing educational and advisory function. Updates to policy and HFEA advice are readily accessible through public documents and the HFEA's website. The Authority's approach creates a significant level of transparency, a key ingredient to successful regulation.

The HFE Act 1990 has been amended with the passage of the HFE Act 2008.[118] Though some of the amendments are significant, the basic structure of the Act has not been changed, meaning that the two statutes must be read together, along with other earlier amending statutes. The result has been described as 'a rather clumsy and convoluted mass of legislation'.[119]

Several significant changes to the HFE Act 1990 have come out of the 2008 reform process, but in spite of the importance of many of these amendments, it must be acknowledged that the process was one involving revisions to existing law, rather than 'a thorough and fundamental rethinking of the kind of regulation which might best suit this area or the ethical principles which should underpin it'.[120] In essence, the process asked which aspects of the existing legislation required alteration in light of scientific advances and shifting social attitudes toward reproductive technologies and embryo research.

A number of notable changes were made, including the removal from the child welfare provisions of the requirement that providers must consider 'the need of [the potential future] child for a father'.[121] The new section directs providers to consider the potential child's need for 'supportive parenting'.[122] The 'need for a father' provision was the focus of much criticism,[123] and its repeal was no doubt welcomed by its critics, but it is difficult to know what the change will mean in practice, as the direction to have regard for the welfare of the child prior to providing assisted reproduction treatment to a woman vests a good deal of discretion in providers.[124] The Act's status provisions (relating to parentage) were also amended, as were provisions relating to surrogacy arrangements, the information collected by the HFEA, the use and storage of gametes and

---

[115] *Quintavalle, R (on the application of) v Human Fertilisation and Embryology Authority* [2003] EWCA 667, [2004] QB 168, affd [2005] UKHL 28, [2005] 2 WLR 1061 (challenging the HFEA's authority to permit the use of pre-implantation genetic diagnosis and tissue typing).

[116] *Evans v Amicus Healthcare Limited & Others* [2004] EWCA Civ 727, [2005] Fam 1.

[117] *Rose and Another v Secretary of State for Health* [2002] EWHC 1593 (Admin), [2002] 2 FLR 962. The HFEA has also been involved in legal disputes about whether embryos created by cell nuclear replacement (as opposed to fertilisation) are within its remit (*Quintavalle, R* (2005) (n 115)) and in relation to gamete mix-ups (*Leeds Teaching Hospital NHS Trust v A and others* [2003] EWHC 259 (QB), [2003] 1 FLR 412).

[118] Human Fertilisation and Embryology Act 2008 (UK).

[119] Fox (n 101) 334. See also Julie McCandless and Sally Sheldon, 'The Human Fertilisation and Embryology Act (2008) and the Tenacity of the Sexual Family Form' (2010) 73 *MLR* 175, 180. For a detailed, section-by-section analysis of the new legislation, see Dewinder Birk, *Human Fertilisation and Embryology: The New Law* (Bristol, Jordan Publishing, 2009).

[120] McCandless and Sheldon (n 119) 180.

[121] HFE Act 1990, s 13(5).

[122] HFE Act 1990 (as amended), s 13(5) or HFE Act 2008, s 14(2)(b).

[123] See, eg, Jackson (n 6); Michael Thomson, 'Legislating for the Monstrous: Access to Reproductive Services and the Monstrous Feminine' (1997) 6 *Social and Legal Studies* 401; Margaret Brazier, 'Liberty, Responsibility, Maternity' (1999) 52 *Current Legal Problems* 359.

[124] This is considered at more length below (section V.A.i.).

embryos (particularly research using human embryos), and the use of particular technologies (PGD).[125]

Another significant feature of the 2008 Act is the inclusion of provisions relating to embryo selection. These statutory changes are in alignment with existing HFEA policy on sex selection[126] and the use of PGD and tissue typing aimed at the conception of a child that would be a tissue match for an ill sibling,[127] but their inclusion in the statute (along with directions to the HFEA as to factors to be considered in granting licences)[128] has the effect of limiting the HFEA's discretion to make policy around these issues.

In general terms, the 2008 Act preserves the existing regulatory structure in the UK, whereby the HFEA is granted considerable authority to control the provision of ART services and the conduct of research on embryos, among other matters, including directing medical practice in this area to a significant degree. A much more significant change may be yet to come, with the passage of a law that permits the Government to transfer the functions of the HFEA to another regulatory body.

This is not the first time that the continued existence of the HFEA has been placed into doubt. In 2006, the UK Department of Health proposed to merge the HFEA with another existing regulatory body (the Human Tissue Authority, or HTA) and create the Regulatory Authority for Tissue and Embryos (RATE). The idea was to merge the two existing authorities with the regulator responsible for blood and blood products (Medicines and Healthcare products Regulatory Agency), making RATE the

> single Competent Authority under the EU Blood and Tissue and Cells Directives, the purpose of which is to secure the safety and quality of blood and tissue and cells used for transplantation, and the sole body responsible for regulatory oversight of activities relating to the use of human bodily material.[129]

The Government's draft legislation to amend the HFE Act 1990 (introduced in 2007[130]) included its proposal to merge these three regulators into the RATE. Parliament established a Joint Committee on the Human Tissue and Embryos (Draft) Bill; its terms of reference were to study and report on the Draft Bill presented by the Minister of Health.[131] Based on what it termed 'overwhelming and convincing' evidence against this

---

[125] The various changes are discussed in more detail in the relevant sections of this and the following chapter.

[126] HFE Act 1990 (as amended), s 13(10). That section prohibits testing an embryo to determine the sex of the embryo, except where there is a 'particular risk' of a serious gender-related illness, disability or medical condition. Pre-existing HFEA policy similarly banned sex selection for non-medical reasons (Human Fertilisation and Embryology Authority, 'Sex Selection: Options for Regulation: A Report on the HFEA's 2002–03 Review of Sex Selection Including a Discussion of Legislative and Regulatory Options' (2003), at <www.hfea.gov.uk/docs/Final_sex_selection_main_report.pdf>). For a critical view on this policy, see John Harris, 'Sex Selection and Regulated Hatred' (2005) 31 *Journal of Medical Ethics* 291.

[127] HFE Act 1990 (as amended), Sch 2, s 1ZA(1)(d). Again, this is consistent with HFEA policy already in place: Human Fertilisation and Embryology Authority, 'Human Fertilisation and Embryology Authority Report: Preimplantation Tissue Typing' (2004), at <www.hfea.gov.uk/docs/PolicyReview_PreimplantationTissueReport.pdf>.

[128] HFE Act 1990 (as amended), Sch 2, s 1ZA(2), (3) (respecting embryo testing); para 1ZB(4) (respecting sex selection).

[129] Human Fertilisation and Embryology Authority, 'New Chair of Human Tissue Authority and Human Fertilisation and Embryology Authority Appointed' (20 December 2006), at <www.hfea.gov.uk/551.html>.

[130] Department of Health, *Human Tissue and Embryos (Draft) Bill*, Cm 7087 (London, The Stationery Office, 2007).

[131] Joint Committee on the Human Tissue and Embryos (Draft) Bill, *Human Tissue and Embryos (Draft) Bill* (2006–07, HL 169-1, HC 630-1) para 1.

proposed merger, the Joint Committee recommended that the Government abandon its plans to merge the regulators. The Government accepted the Committee's recommendation.[132] More recently, the Government has again announced plans to reassign the role and functions of the HFEA. This time, the proposal arises out of a broadly-based plan that would see the number of public bodies (known colloquially as quasi-autonomous non-governmental organisations, or 'quangos') radically reduced. After considering 901 public bodies as part of its review, the Government proposed to disband 192 such bodies, and merge another 118.[133] The HFEA is one of the bodies that will be cut; its functions related to clinical ART practice are to be assigned to the Care Quality Commission, while the licensing of embryo research will be undertaken by a proposed new entity that will regulate medical research.[134]

When initially proposed, the plan to eliminate the HFEA met with significant concern and opposition.[135] The Government's approach to the review process also met with much criticism.[136] The Public Bodies Act[137] received Royal Assent in December 2011, and though advocacy efforts managed to spare some of the public bodies that were set to be abolished by the original government proposal, the HFEA was not one of them.[138] It is difficult to predict the actual outcome of this process; although the way has now been cleared for the Government to pass legislation transferring the functions of the HFEA to another public body, in light of a recent report highlighting concerns about the ability of the Care Quality Commission to take on these functions, the Department of Health has agreed to a full consultation process before making further decisions about the future of the HFEA.[139]

D. Canada

Canada's ART regulation story begins like that in the UK, with the appointment of a commission to inquire into and make recommendations about legal regulation of assisted reproduction. The Royal Commission on New Reproductive Technologies reported in 1993, after spending four years and approximately $30 million studying the

---

[132] Department of Health, *Government Response to the Report from the Joint Committee on the Human Tissue and Embryos (Draft) Bill*, Cm 7209 (London, The Stationery Office, 2007) paras 14–17.

[133] Public Administration Select Committee, *Smaller Government: Shrinking the Quango State* (HC 2010-11, 537) 7.

[134] Department of Health, 'Liberating the NHS: Report of the Arm's-Length Bodies Review' (26 July 2010) 41, at <www.dh.gov.uk/prod_consum_dh/groups/dh_digitalassets/@dh/@en/@ps/documents/digitalasset/dh_118053.pdf>.

[135] See, eg, Clare Dyer, 'New Life for the HFEA?' (2011) 342 *British Medical Journal* 258; Sarah Guy, 'The End of the HFEA: Are We Throwing the Baby out with the Bathwater?' (24 January 2011) 592 *BioNews*, at <www.bionews.org.uk/page_87217.asp>.

[136] Public Administration Select Committee (n 133) 3. The Committee states that the 'review was poorly managed. There was no meaningful consultation, the tests the review used were not clearly defined and the Cabinet Office failed to establish a proper procedure for departments to follow'.

[137] Public Bodies Act 2011 (UK).

[138] Sandy Starr, 'New Law Empowers UK Government to Transfer HFEA's Functions' (19 December 2011) 638 *BioNews*, at <www.bionews.org.uk/page_115729.asp>.

[139] House of Commons Committee of Public Accounts, *The Care Quality Commission: Regulating the Quality and Safety of Health and Adult Social Care* (HC 2010-12, 1779), at <www.publications.parliament.uk/pa/cm201012/cmselect/cmpubacc/1779/1779.pdf>; Tamara Hirsch, 'NHS Watchdog Not Up to Taking on HFEA's Role' (2 April 2012) 651 *BioNews*, at <www.publications.parliament.uk/pa/cm201012/cmselect/cmpubacc/1779/1779.pdf>.

issues.[140] Based on the Commission's recommendations, several attempts at passing legislation were made, but it was not until a decade later that the Federal Government finally passed legislation aimed at comprehensively regulating research and practice in the ART context.[141] The legislation was only partially implemented and, due to the success of a legal challenge to its validity, has been radically reduced in scope.[142] Thus, unlike the UK, Canada has not succeeded in implementing a comprehensive approach to ART regulation.

While the Assisted Human Reproduction Act (AHR Act) as passed is now of primarily historical interest, it is helpful briefly to explain the original structure and aims of the legislation to provide some context for the Canadian regulatory picture. Very generally, the AHR Act created categories of prohibited and controlled activities, regulated privacy and access to information, established the Assisted Human Reproduction Agency of Canada ('Assisted Human Reproduction Canada', or 'AHRC'), and set out provisions relating to administration, inspection and enforcement of the provisions of the AHR Act and Regulations.[143] In short, the AHR Act designated ART-related activities as either prohibited or controlled; the majority of the Act was devoted to the regulation of the controlled activities. Several sections of the AHR Act (those concerning prohibited and controlled activities[144]) came into force upon the passage of the legislation in 2004. The remaining sections (the majority of the Act) were to be gradually developed and implemented over a period of three years.[145]

The legislative objectives upon which the AHR Act is based are found in a declaratory section referring to overriding principles.[146] These principles refer to the paramountcy of the health and well-being of children born through ART procedures, and assert that the benefits of ARTs can best be secured by taking appropriate measures to safeguard human health, safety, dignity and rights in the use of ARTs in practice and research. The principles also acknowledge that ART practice affects women more 'directly and significantly'

---

[140] Royal Commission on New Reproductive Technologies (n 9); Alison Harvison Young and Angela Wasunna, 'Wrestling with the Limits of Law: Regulating New Reproductive Technologies' (1998) 6 *Health Law Journal* 239.

[141] Assisted Human Reproduction Act, SC 2004, c 2.

[142] The challenge was instigated when the Government of Québec referred the legislation to the Québec Court of Appeal for an opinion as to the Act's constitutional validity. The Québec Court of Appeal found the impugned sections of the Act ultra vires; the Federal Government then referred the law to the Supreme Court of Canada (*Renvoi fait par le gouvernement du Québec en vertu de la Loi sur les renvois à la Cour d'appel, LRQ ch R-23, relativement à la constitutionnalité des articles 8 à 19, 40 à 53, 60, 61 et 68 de la Loi sur la procréation assistée, LC 2004, ch 2 (Dans l'affaire du)*, 2008 QCCA 1167, 298 DLR (4th) 712; *Reference re Assisted Human Reproduction Act*, 2010 SCC 61, [2010] 3 SCR 457).

[143] According to s 66 of the AHR Act, the Minister of Health must present proposed regulations to both the House of Commons and the Senate. The 'appropriate committee' of each House will then have an opportunity to consider and report on the regulations, and the Minister is to take into account these reports. In the event that the regulations are not modified to incorporate recommendations of the committees, the Minister 'shall lay before that House a statement of the reasons for not incorporating [them]' (*ibid*, s 66(4)). The only exceptions to the requirement of presenting proposed regulations to Parliament are found in s 67, and occur: (i) where the changes made by the regulations to existing regulations are, in the opinion of the Minister, 'so immaterial or insubstantial that section 66 should not apply in the circumstances' (*ibid* s 67(1)(a)); and (ii) in situations where the regulations must be made immediately 'to protect the health or safety of any person' (*ibid* s 67(1)(b)).

[144] Prior to the coming into force of the Act, a voluntary moratorium was put in place to deal with concerns around the prohibited activities (Health Canada, 'A Chronology of the *Assisted Human Reproduction Act*' (January 2008), at <www.hc-sc.gc.ca/hl-vs/reprod/hc-sc/general/chronolog-eng.php>).

[145] *Ibid*.

[146] AHR Act, s 2.

than it does men, and that measures must be taken to ensure the protection of women's health and well-being. The importance of informed consent is noted, as is the importance of non-discrimination in the provision of ART services (with particular reference to marital status and sexual orientation). The principles also outline a rationale for the prohibition of commercialisation of reproductive capacity, and state that human diversity and individuality and the integrity of the human genome must be protected.

Although heavily influenced by that taken in the UK, Canada's approach is markedly distinct from that adopted in the UK in the sheer number of prohibited activities within the regulatory legislation.[147] A significant number of ART-related clinical and research practices are prohibited by the AHR Act; maximum penalties for the commission of prohibited activities are a fine of $500,000 or a 10-year term of imprisonment, or both.[148] Prohibited activities include cloning,[149] creating an embryo for research purposes (other than the narrow research purpose of improving or providing instruction in ART procedures),[150] commercial surrogacy[151] and sex selection for non-medical purposes.[152]

Arguably, the most significant feature of the Canadian legislation was the creation of the regulatory body, AHRC.[153] AHRC was intended to operate at arm's length from the Federal Government, but be accountable to Parliament through the Minister of Health.[154] The objectives of AHRC centred on the protection and promotion of the health, safety, human dignity and human rights of Canadians, and the fostering of the application of ethical principles in relation to ART practice.[155] Under the AHR Act, AHRC was empowered comprehensively to regulate ART techniques used both in the clinical and research settings. Its mandate included powers in relation to licensing,[156] inspection and enforcement,[157] and the provision of advice to the Minister of Health on matters integral to the AHR Act.[158] AHRC was also charged with monitoring and evaluating national and international developments in ART practice,[159] consulting with persons and organisations both within and outside Canada,[160] and collecting, analysing and maintaining health-reporting information relating to controlled activities.[161] The Agency was also to play a dissemination role in providing information to the public and relevant professions respecting ART prac-

---

[147] In Australia, by contrast, the prohibited activities tend to be found (where they are found at all) in separate legislation; see, eg, Prohibition of Human Cloning for Reproduction Act 2002 (Cth).

[148] AHR Act, s 60.

[149] *Ibid* s 5(1)(a).

[150] *Ibid* s 5(1)(b).

[151] *Ibid* s 6. This includes prohibitions on payment to the surrogate mother herself or an intermediary, and also prohibits the acceptance of payment by an intermediary.

[152] *Ibid* s 5(1)(e). Other prohibitions under s 5 are: creating an embryo from an embryo or fetus (s 5(1)(c)); maintaining an embryo in vitro for more than 14 days (s 5(1)(d)); germ line alteration (s 5(1)(f)), transfer of non-human gametes, embryos or fetuses into a human being (s 5(1)(g)); use (for reproductive purposes) of any human reproductive material that is or was transplanted into a non-human animal (s 5(1)(h)); creation of a chimera or hybrid (s 5(1)(i)); and advertising (s 5(2)) or paying (s 5(3)) for the performance of prohibited activities. Additional prohibitions in the Act are purchase of gametes or embryos (s 7) and use of reproductive material without consent (s 8).

[153] *Ibid* s 21.

[154] Assisted Human Reproduction Canada, 'All About AHRC: Organizational Structure' (April 2011), at <www.ahrc-pac.gc.ca/v2/aaa-app/wwa-qsn/structure-structure-eng.php>.

[155] AHR Act (n 141), s 22.

[156] *Ibid* s 24(1)(a).

[157] *Ibid* s 24(1)(g).

[158] *Ibid* s 24(1)(b).

[159] *Ibid* s 24(1)(c).

[160] *Ibid* s 24(1)(d).

[161] *Ibid* s 24(1)(e).

tice and regulation, and risk factors for infertility.[162] The Board of Directors was to be made up of members reflecting 'a range of backgrounds and disciplines relevant to the Agency's objectives,'[163] and could not include a licensee or applicant for a licence, or a director, officer, shareholder or partner of a licensee or applicant.[164]

As is clear from this brief overview, the AHR Act had both criminal law and regulatory elements, with an emphasis on regulation. Canada is a federation with a Constitution that divides powers between the federal and provincial/territorial jurisdictions, with residuary powers allocated to the Federal Government.[165] The criminal law power is within federal jurisdiction,[166] while power over health is generally seen to reside with the provinces and territories.[167] The Royal Commission on New Reproductive Technologies urged the implementation of a comprehensive, national regulatory strategy, although it did acknowledge that jurisdictional issues could prove to be a challenge.[168] The Federal Government decided to pursue the Commission's recommendation for a national approach, and sought to ground the legislation in the criminal law power in spite of the fact that most of the law was aimed at regulating, rather than prohibiting, ART-related research and practice. Before the legislation could be fully implemented, it was challenged by the Province of Québec on the basis that much of the Act covered matters that fall within provincial, not federal, jurisdiction.[169] The Québec Court of Appeal agreed with the Province's argument.[170]

The Government of Canada appealed the decision to the Supreme Court of Canada, which heard arguments in April 2009 and rendered its decision more than 18 months later, in late December 2010.[171] The reasons reveal a deeply divided Court, which might explain the lengthy interval between the hearing and the release of the reasons. The Court split 4:4:1, with Justice Cromwell's vote determining the majority. Chief Justice McLachlin, writing for one of the groups of four justices, would have upheld the AHR Act as a valid exercise of the federal criminal law power, stating that 'Taken as a whole, the Act seeks to avert serious damage to the fabric of our society by prohibiting practices that tend to devalue human life and degrade participants'.[172] Justices LeBel and Deschamps, who authored the reasons for the other group of four, found all of the impugned provisions to be ultra vires Parliament on the basis that the regulation of clinical uses of ARTs and related research activities falls within provincial jurisdiction.[173] Justice Cromwell agreed with Justices LeBel and Deschamps as to their charac-

[162] *Ibid* s 24(1)(f).

[163] *Ibid* s 26(2).

[164] *Ibid* s 26(8).

[165] Constitution Act, 1982, being Schedule B to the Canada Act 1982 (UK), 1982, c 11, s 91.

[166] *Ibid* s 91(27).

[167] Health is not specifically enumerated in the division of powers, but is generally thought to fall within provincial jurisdiction (*Reference re Assisted Human Reproduction Act* (n 142) paras 52, 260, 287).

[168] Royal Commission on New Reproductive Technologies (n 9) 16–21.

[169] *Orders in Council Reference to the Court of Appeal re Assisted Human Reproduction Act*, OC 1177-2004, December 15, 2004, GOQ 2005.II.62; *Amendment to Order in Council 1177-2004 concerning a Reference to the Court of Appeal re the Assisted Human Reproduction Act*, OC 73-2006, February 14, 2006, GOQ 2006. II.1290, made pursuant to the *Court of Appeal Reference Act* RSQ, c R-23. The impugned sections are ss 8–19, 40–53, 60–68.

[170] *Renvoi fait par le gouvernement du Québec en vertu de la Loi sur les renvois à la Cour d'appel* (n 142).

[171] *Reference re Assisted Human Reproduction Act* (n 142).

[172] *Ibid* para 61.

[173] In particular, provincial jurisdiction over hospitals, property and civil rights in the province and matters of a merely local nature (*ibid*).

terisation of the majority of the impugned sections of the Act, stating that these provisions are aimed at 'regulation of virtually every aspect of research and clinical practice in relation to assisted human reproduction'.[174] He did uphold several sections of the Act, however, on the basis that they fall within the 'traditional ambit of the federal criminal law power'[175] or are sufficiently related to sections of the Act that are constitutionally valid.

Not until almost 18 months after the decision did its practical impact become clear. The Federal Government, after showing no interest in taking any steps on this issue for some time, finally announced its intentions with respect to the Act and the statutory regulator in omnibus budget legislation introduced in the Spring of 2012.[176] The regulator, AHRC, was wound down at the end of the 2012 budget year, and the AHR Act is substantially reduced in scope. What remains is a statute that criminalises the originally prohibited activities and that grants the federal Minister of Health powers to inspect facilities in order to enforce the Act. The Act also has a minimal regulatory aspect in relation to the testing of gametes to be used in assisted reproduction, and the reimbursement of expenditures related to gamete donation and surrogacy services.[177]

Few who are familiar with the history of ART regulation in Canada were surprised by the decision to wind down AHRC. Like its parent legislation, the Agency was beleaguered by controversy and opposition. The President and Board of Directors of AHRC were appointed in December 2006, in a process that commenced under the Liberal Government and concluded after the election of a Conservative Government in January 2006. Concerns were raised at the time about the lack of broad representation on the Board of Directors; the absence of stem-cell researchers, obstetrician-gynaecologists and patient representatives was particularly notable.[178] Not only was the initial appointment process of the Board problematic; in 2010, several members of the Board of Directors resigned their positions.[179] One of those who resigned apparently did so because of unease related to the Agency's 'prudence and diligence in managing public funds'.[180] Another 'cited "Group dynamics" on the board, limits on the expert advice provided to directors and a lack of regulations'[181] as factors leading to her resignation. In addition to these criticisms, one Member of Parliament had urged the closure of AHRC because of its lack of action and output, in spite of having an annual budget of $10 million.[182] Fertility experts also began to suggest that the prohibitions in

---

[174]   *Ibid* para 285.

[175]   *Ibid* para 291.

[176]   Jobs, Growth and Long-Term Prosperity Act, SC 2012, c 19.

[177]   The regulation-making power also remains, meaning that we could see further action by the Federal Government in the area.

[178]   Laura Eggertson, 'New Reproductive Technology Board Belies Expert Selection Process' (2007) 176 *Canadian Medical Association Journal* 611. See also Sam Solomon, 'Reproduction Agency Appointments Spark Controversy' (2007) 4(2) *National Review of Medicine*, at <www.nationalreviewofmedicine.com/issue/2007/01_30/4_policy_politics02_2.html> (Ms Irene Ryll, a patient/consumer representative, was later appointed to the Board of Directors).

[179]   See Antony Blackburn-Starza, 'Another Member Leaves Canada's AHRC' (7 June 2010) 561 *BioNews*, at <www.bionews.org.uk/page_62469.asp>.

[180]   Tom Blackwell, 'Fertility Spending at Issue: Letter', *The National Post* (Don Mills, 2 June 2010) A5.

[181]   *Ibid.*

[182]   Gabrielle Samuel, 'Canada's Fertility-Industry Watchdog Under Scrutiny Again' (21 June 2010) 563 *BioNews*, at <www.bionews.org.uk/page_64674.asp>.

the Act, which had been in force since 2004, were being ignored by some fertility clinics.[183]

It is difficult to be optimistic about the future of the regulation of assisted human reproduction in Canada at this point, given the history of the legislation, the problems at the AHRC and the Federal Government's apparent lack of interest in taking action. More globally, the Supreme Court's decision raises a number of concerns. It is beyond the scope of this work to examine in depth broader questions about how the Supreme Court understands the federal criminal law power, but LeBel and Deschamps JJ are exactly right in pointing out that many advances in medical technology and practice give rise to concerns around 'ethics, morality, safety and public health'[184] but that this alone does not justify regulation of those technologies on the basis of the federal criminal law power.[185] While it may be very desirable to have national standards for regulating clinical and research uses of ARTs, it seems fairly clear that the Federal Government simply does not have the constitutional authority to legislate such standards.[186]

Unfortunately, we are now left with a great deal of uncertainty as to the future regulatory landscape for assisted reproduction in Canada. The provinces do have legislative authority to regulate in this area, but it is highly doubtful that all provinces (or even most) will do so. Alberta, for example, has two fertility treatment clinics, and a number of other provinces have only one clinic. Does it make sense for those provinces to expend the time, energy and political capital demanded by a full debate and discussion of assisted reproduction to create laws that will be relevant to such a narrow group of medical practitioners? How will data on outcomes be collected in Canada in absence of the AHR Act's data collection requirements? On a more optimistic note, perhaps we shall now see cooperation among provinces, or better yet between government and the professions, in crafting a regulatory regime for ARTs.[187]

[183] Tom Blackwell, 'Fertility Law Leaves us in Limbo, Doctors Say: Oversight of Burgeoning Industry a "Farce"', *The National Post* (Don Mills, 30 April 2010) A1; Alison Motluk, 'The Human Egg Trade: How Canada's Fertility Laws Are Failing Donors, Doctors, and Parents', *Walrus Magazine*, April 2010, at <www.walrusmagazine.com/articles/2010.04-health-the-human-egg-trade/>.

[184] *Reference re Assisted Human Reproduction Act* (n 142) para 255.

[185] Another concern respecting the Court's reasoning (and this applies particularly to McLachlin CJC's reasons) is the role of or need for evidence of a legitimate criminal law purpose. The Chief Justice's reasons are replete with comments about the 'public health evils' sought to be avoided by the AHR Act: see, eg, *ibid* paras 32, 47, 90, 113–18. Here is one example of the Chief Justice's concerns (*ibid* para 100): 'These developments raise the prospect of novel harms to society, as the Baird Report amply documents. The "commodification of women and children" (p 718); sex-selective abortions (p 896); cross-species hybrids; ectogenesis with the potential to "dehumanize motherhood"; "baby farms" (p 637); saviour siblings (a child whose primary purpose is to cure another child suffering from a genetic disorder); devaluation of persons with disabilities; discrimination based on ethnicity or genetic status (p 28); and exploitation of the vulnerable – these are but some of the moral concerns raised in the Report. While the ethical acceptability of these techniques is, of course, debatable . . . it cannot be seriously questioned that Parliament is able to prohibit or regulate them.' It is troubling to see the extent to which concerns – many of which were completely speculative – that were raised in a Report published 18 years earlier are being relied on to justify current criminal prohibitions and regulation of a widely-used medical technology. I do not mean to suggest that none of these concerns was then (or is now) valid, simply that it is a mistake to rely on the Baird Commission's articulation of these worries without explaining or expanding on the current status of these issues.

[186] Arguably, this was acknowledged by the Baird Commission, which noted that the provinces have broad legislative jurisdiction over health. The Commission asserted, however, that the regulation of reproductive technologies could be accomplished by the federal Government pursuant to the federal power to legislate for peace, order and good government, as the matter is one of 'genuine national concern' (Royal Commission on New Reproductive Technologies (n 9) 18–22).

[187] The Alberta medical regulator has put in place minimal regulatory standards as part of its responsibility to regulate Non-Hospital Surgical Facilities (College of Physicians and Surgeons of Alberta, 'Standards &

Even when originally enacted, the AHR Act did not completely occupy the field in regulating reproductive technologies. The Canadian regulatory picture outside of the federal legislation involves some regulation of ARTs, but regulation is neither comprehensive nor integrated, nor is it uniformly applied or enforced.[188]

A number of Canadian jurisdictions have legislation concerning the status of children born as a result of ARTs,[189] but in most provinces the common law governs on this issue.[190] Processing, testing and distribution of semen for donor insemination[191] had been governed by the Food and Drugs Act,[192] but in light of the 2012 amendments to the AHR Act, regulations concerning gametes and embryos will ultimately be made pursuant to the AHR Act itself. In addition, all provinces have human tissue legislation.[193]

There are also professional guidelines and policies in place to help guide medical practice involving some aspects of assisted human reproduction. In particular, the Society of Obstetricians and Gynecologists of Canada (SOGC) and the Canadian Fertility and Andrology Society (CFAS) have produced a joint policy statement on ethical issues in assisted reproduction,[194] which sets out ethical guidelines in relation to sperm sorting for non-medical reasons, preconception arrangements, oocyte donation, disposition of frozen embryos, research on human embryos, ICSI, PGD, social screening and participation in reproductive technologies, and medical and genetic screening of gamete and embryo donors.[195]

Guidelines: In Vitro Fertilization (IVF)' (December 2011), at <www.cpsa.ab.ca/Libraries/Pro_QofC_Non-Hospital/NHSF_IVF_Standards_-_December_2011.sflb.ashx>).

[188] Including, eg, the status of gametes and embryos: see, eg, Roxanne Mykitiuk and Albert Wallrap, 'Regulating Reproductive Technologies in Canada' in Jocelyn Downie, Timothy Caulfield and Colleen M Flood (eds), *Canadian Health Law and Policy*, 2nd edn (Markham, Butterworths, 2002) 399. See also *C(C) v W(A)*, 2005 ABQB 290, 50 Alta LR (4th) 61 (where Sanderman J treats embryos and gametes as property). More recently, the British Columbia Supreme Court drew on *C(C) v W(A)*, and on *Yearworth v North Bristol NHS Trust* [2009] EWCA Civ 37, [2010] 1 QB 1, to conclude that remaining frozen sperm purchased by a lesbian couple were to be treated as the property of the couple and divided between the two women after their relationship broke down (*JCM v ANA*, 2012 BCSC 584, 214 ACWS 3d 499).

[189] This is discussed in greater detail in ch 9, section IV.A.

[190] For a discussion of the case law on point, see, eg, Roxanne Mykitiuk, 'Beyond Conception: Legal Determinations of Filiation in the Context of Assisted Reproductive Technologies' (2001) 39 *Osgoode Hall Law Journal* 771, 791–814; Angela Campbell, 'Conceiving Parents Through Law' (2007) 21 *International Journal of Law, Policy and the Family* 242. See also Simon R Fodden, *Family Law* (Toronto, Irwin Law, 1999) chs 5–6.

[191] Processing and Distribution of Semen for Assisted Conception Regulations, SOR/96-254, as am.

[192] Food and Drugs Act, RSC 1985, c F-27.

[193] Eg, Human Tissue and Organ Donation Act, SA 2006, c H-14.5. While the Alberta legislation specifies that the Act does not apply to zygotes, oocytes, embryos, sperm, semen and ova (s 2(c)), some such statutes, although they deal generally with organ transplantation, do not define 'tissue' narrowly, and therefore could be involved in the regulation of some aspects of ARTs: see, eg, Human Tissue Act, RSNWT 1988, c H-6; Human Tissue Gift Act, RSS 1978, c H-15; Human Tissue Gift Act, RSBC 1996, c 211.

[194] Canadian Fertility and Andrology Society/ Society of Obstetricians and Gynaecologists of Canada, 'Joint Policy Statement: Ethical Issues in Assisted Reproduction' (1999) 21 *Journal of Obstetrics and Gynaecology Canada* 1. See also Erin Nelson, Roxanne Mykitiuk and Jeff Nisker, 'SOGC Clinical Practice Guideline No 215: Informed Consent to Donate Embryos for Research Purposes' (2008) 30 *Journal of Obstetrics and Gynaecology Canada* 824; Jason K Min, Paul Claman and Ed Hughes, 'Joint SOGC-CFAS Clinical Practice Guideline, Elective Single Embryo Transfer Following In Vitro Fertilization' (2010) 32 *Journal of Obstetrics and Gynaecology Canada* 363.

[195] The 1999 CFAS / SOGC 'Joint Policy Statement' (n 194) is very dated, and a joint project between the Canadian Medical Association (CMA), the CFAS and the SOGC is currently underway to develop policy (Marie-Claude Léveillé, 'A Message From the President' (Spring 2012) *CFAS Newsletter*, at <www.cfas.ca/images/stories/pdf/spring_newsletter_cfas_2012.pdf>).

Lastly, research involving ARTs is governed by the *Tri-Council Policy Statement: Ethical Conduct for Research Involving Humans*,[196] which has rules in place as to ethically appropriate uses of human genetic material, gametes, embryos and fetuses. In general, these rules echo (and refer to) the AHR Act provisions respecting the use of gametes and embryos.[197] The *Tri-Council Policy Statement* also notes that the AHR Act prohibits the creation of human embryos specifically for use in research[198] and certain activities related to the creation of hybrids and chimeras.[199]

IV. REGULATING ARTS AND REPRODUCTIVE AUTONOMY

One of the most challenging aspects of regulating reproductive technologies is to strike a balance between protecting women's interests and ensuring that their autonomy is taken seriously. The narrative of Canada's attempt at regulating ART research and practice is an illustration of this very challenge. Canada's AHR Act[200] acknowledges the central place of women's interests in the ART context, from the perspective that women's 'health and well-being . . . must be protected in the application'[201] of ARTs. Although the emphasis on women's health and well-being is welcome, the view of women's interests adopted here is cause for concern. Women's 'health and well-being' is not some uniform, neatly calculable quantity. An approach that serves the needs and interests of some women in their own 'health and well-being' might leave the needs of others unmet. The well-being of an infertile woman might be best fostered by facilitating unrestricted access to all ARTs, while that of a potential egg-donor might demand a more restricted approach.

The AHR Act's declaratory statement with respect to women's health and well-being is also dubious in that it seems to envisage that someone other than the woman herself is best situated to determine what is needed in order to protect her health and well-being. While there are references to human dignity, human rights and the need for informed consent in section 2 of the AHR Act, there is no commitment anywhere in the Act to the

---

[196] Canadian Institutes of Health Research, Natural Sciences and Engineering Research Council of Canada and Social Sciences and Humanities Research Council of Canada, *Tri-Council Policy Statement: Ethical Conduct for Research Involving Humans* (Ottawa, Interagency Advisory Panel on Research Ethics, December 2010).

[197] Ch 13 of the *Tri-Council Policy Statement* (*ibid*), which governs human genetic material, refers to the prohibition on germ-line genetic alteration found in the AHR Act (n 141) and notes that the issue of germ-line alteration is addressed in s 5(1)(f) of the AHR Act. Ch 12 of the *Tri-Council Policy Statement*, which considers ethical issues involving human biological (including reproductive) materials, states that commercially obtained human reproductive materials shall not be used in research (*Tri-Council Policy Statement* (n 196) Art 12.6(b)).

[198] The use of embryos created for reproductive (or other permitted) purposes is permitted once the embryos are no longer needed for the original purpose, provided that the following conditions are met: '(a) the ova and sperm from which they were formed are obtained in accordance with Article 12.7; (b) consent was provided by the gamete donors; (c) embryos exposed to manipulations not directed specifically to their ongoing normal development will not be transferred for continuing pregnancy; and (d) research involving human embryos will take place only during the first 14 days after their formation by combination of the gametes, excluding any time during which embryonic development has been suspended' (*ibid* Art 12.8). Art 12.10 directs that researchers who use embryos 'to derive or use pluripotent stem cells shall follow the *Guidelines for Human Pluripotent Stem Cell Research* [www.cihr-irsc.gc.ca/e/42071.html], as amended from time to time' (*Tri-Council Policy Statement* (n 196)).

[199] *Tri-Council Policy Statement* (n 196) Art 12.10 refers researchers to the AHR Act for prohibitions on the use of chimeras and hybrids (see AHR Act (n 141)).

[200] AHR Act (n 141).

[201] *Ibid* s 2(c).

principle of reproductive autonomy, or to the importance of individual choice in reproductive decision making. As a result, the declaration about women's health and well-
being adopts a potentially paternalistic stance, as an oversight body could conceivably
take the view that women's health and well-being is best safeguarded by a restrictive
regulatory approach, and thereby harm the health and well-being of infertile women
under the guise of protecting those very interests. In addition, the section places paramount importance on the health and well-being of the children born as a result of
assisted reproduction. This language prioritises the interests of *potential* children over
those of *actual* women.

Many feminists are suspicious of ARTs and their potential negative effects on women.
Women who choose to attempt conception using ARTs are told that consent to infertility treatment is a myth,[202] that to choose to have treatment is to yield to the socially created 'need' to be a mother and that the technologies merely reinforce the notion of
maternity as 'woman's destiny'.[203] Critics also express concern about the desperation of
women and couples who undergo treatment, and the strain of infertility treatment on
women.[204] As others have noted, such characterisations of the women who seek infertility treatment and of their motivations for so doing seem to ignore (or worse, actively
silence) the voices of infertile women[205] and deny infertile women's autonomy.[206]
Margarete Sandelowski's research with infertile couples arguably shows that if anything, the decisions of those facing infertility are exactly the sort of decisions we should
conceive of as autonomous, given the reflective, considered way in which they are
made.[207]

While feminists who are critical of ARTs often claim that the use of such technologies
to have genetically related children valorises the genetic connection above all else,
Barbara Berg points out that those who choose to use ARTs also wish to experience
other aspects of parenting, including pregnancy and childbirth. Berg takes issue with the
feminist equation of adoption and biological parenthood, noting that, from an objective
perspective, the two appear roughly equal, but that there is nonetheless a universal preference for biological parenthood.[208] In any case, she suggests that the importance of a
genetic linkage between parents and children can be viewed in a more neutral, or even
positive, light than the negative way in which it has been portrayed by many feminist
commentators.[209] Like Berg, Barbara Katz Rothman has argued: 'The treatment of infertility needs to be recognized as an issue of self-determination. It is as important an issue

---

[202] See, eg, Susan Sherwin, *No Longer Patient: Feminist Ethics and Health Care* (Philadelphia, Pa, Temple
University Press, 1992) 128–29; Joan C Callahan and Dorothy E Roberts, 'A Feminist Social Justice Approach
to Reproduction-Assisting Technologies: A Case Study on the Limits of Liberal Theory' (1996) 84 *Kentucky
Law Journal* 1197, 1227.

[203] See, eg, Callahan and Roberts (n 202) 1211; Sherwin (n 202); April L Cherry, 'Choosing Substantive
Justice: A Discussion of "Choice", "Rights", and the New Reproductive Technologies' (1997) 11 *Wisconsin
Women's Law Journal* 431, 439.

[204] See, eg, Gena Corea, *The Mother Machine: Reproductive Technologies from Assisted Insemination to
Artificial Wombs* (New York, Harper & Row, 1985); Sarah Franklin, *Embodied Progress: A Cultural Account
of Assisted Conception* (London, Routledge, 1997).

[205] Barbara J Berg, 'Listening to the Voices of the Infertile' in Joan C Callahan (ed), *Reproduction, Ethics,
and the Law: Feminist Perspectives* (Bloomington, Indiana University Press, 1995) 80.

[206] Jody Lynée Madeira, 'Woman Scorned?: Resurrecting Infertile Women's Decision-Making Autonomy'
(2012) 71 *Maryland Law Review* 339.

[207] Margarete Sandelowski, 'Fault Lines: Infertility and Imperiled Sisterhood' (1990) 16 *Feminist Studies* 33.

[208] Berg (n 205) 81.

[209] Ibid 82–84.

for women as access to contraception and abortion, and freedom from forced sterilization.'[210]

Although I take a view that is disputed by many feminists – that ART regulation should be respectful of reproductive autonomy – some of the feminist concerns around ARTs must be acknowledged. One of the principal reasons for feminists' misgivings about infertility treatment is the fact that the technologies were introduced into clinical practice without ever being subjected to comprehensive safety and efficacy studies.[211] A robust approach to reproductive autonomy recognises that women should be able to decide for themselves whether to take health risks by using ARTs, but if the health risks are unknown and unstudied, women's ability to make informed decisions is compromised. Autonomous decision making requires information, and if the information is unavailable because of the introduction of an unevaluated technology, we should be concerned about women's health. Respect for reproductive autonomy demands that we attempt to seek that elusive balance between fostering women's autonomy and protecting them from harm.

Turning now to consider the shape of a regulatory model, it is evident from the foregoing discussion that there are many different ways to implement regulation of assisted reproduction. Various considerations are involved in choosing a regulatory model, including constitutional constraints and healthcare system structure. From a perspective of respect for reproductive autonomy, how should we regulate – or at least develop regulatory policy in respect of – ARTs?

A number of biotechnology policy models have emerged in the past two decades. Bartha Knoppers characterises the models as follows: the human rights model, the legislation-specific approach, the administrative/regulatory model and the market-driven/professional practices model.[212] As she notes, all four tend to be relied upon to different degrees in different jurisdictions, and all have unique strengths and weaknesses. In the legal and ethical literature around the regulation of ARTs, it is common to see strong arguments in favour of the market-driven/professional practices approach.[213] The claim is that this model best safeguards reproductive autonomy, because it involves the least State interference and leaves most decisions in the hands of patients and professionals. But the sentiment that reproductive autonomy is best protected by State disengagement depends on a liberal reading that views reproductive autonomy simply as freedom from interference with one's reproductive decisions. A contextualised approach to reproductive autonomy demands much more of the State. Such a conception recognises that leaving individuals alone to make their own reproductive decisions quite often fails to respect the richer conception of autonomy that grounds a contextual approach.

---

[210] Barbara Katz Rothman, *Recreating Motherhood: Ideology and Technology in a Patriarchal Society* (New York, Norton, 1989) 140.

[211] Sherwin (n 202) 128; Raymond D Lambert, 'Safety Issues in Assisted Reproduction Technology: The Children of Assisted Reproduction Confront the Responsible Conduct of Assisted Reproductive Technologies' (2002) 17 *Human Reproduction* 3011, 3013 (noting that based on research ethics guidelines, 'the transfer of multiple IVF embryos should have not even reached phase I in the clinical trials, much less should it have become a widely accepted medical practice').

[212] Bartha Maria Knoppers, 'Reflections: The Challenge of Biotechnology and Public Policy' (2000) 45 *McGill Law Journal* 559, 564–65. See also Bartha M Knoppers and Rosario M Isasi, 'Regulatory Approaches to Reproductive Genetic Testing' (2004) 19 *Human Reproduction* 2695.

[213] See, eg, John A Robertson, 'Procreative Liberty and Harm to Offspring in Assisted Reproduction' (2004) 30 *American Journal of Law & Medicine* 7.

Two broad questions emerge in thinking about how to regulate ARTs while manifesting respect for reproductive autonomy. The first relates to the type of regulatory structure that should be employed, including the body or bodies responsible for regulation. The second asks how restrictively we ought to regulate. My focus in this section is on the question of how a regulatory approach should be structured; the second will be considered in section V. below on controlling access to treatment, as well as in the following chapter, in relation to several key concerns around ART practice.

A. Public or professional regulation?

As soon as it became clear that assisted reproduction was scientifically and clinically possible, concerns were raised about whether and how the technologies should be regulated. All medical technologies and services are subject to regulatory control, often through a combination of professional and State regulation. As is evident from the above discussion, in Canada, the UK and Australia, there is significant State or public control over the use of reproductive technologies, achieved either through prohibitions on certain uses of the technologies or through regulatory measures that require considerable oversight of ARTs. In the US there is a far smaller role for State-based regulation, and much of the regulatory enterprise is left to the medical profession.

The question of where regulatory authority over ARTs should lie has been much discussed and debated. Legitimate concerns have been raised around State regulation of reproduction,[214] given its potential to interfere with autonomy in reproductive decision making,[215] and the possible chilling effect such regulation might have on, for example, ART research and practice. But I agree with Emily Jackson on this point.[216] It would not only be unwise to leave research and clinical practice in ARTs unregulated by the State, it is also unrealistic. Whatever one's views about the necessity of regulation, the reality is that reproductive technologies of all types must be accessed through a gatekeeper of sorts – in some cases, individual physicians, in others, professional organisations or the State itself. Regulation, whether accomplished publicly or privately, is inevitable. And in whatever manner regulation is effected, reproductive autonomy is implicated.

Regulation of ARTs solely (or even primarily) by individual professionals and by professional associations is not a viable option, for a number of reasons. First, a variety of highly specialised professions are involved in the delivery of reproductive healthcare. Far from encouraging a comprehensive, integrated approach to regulation, this diversity of professional interests will only intensify the current incoherent and fragmentary approach to regulation of reproduction. Secondly, the decisions of professionals and professional organisations are not transparent, nor, in most cases, should they be. Individual professionals are obligated to protect their patients' confidences; this is an essential element of the provision of safe and effective medical care. But such duties cannot coexist with the need to regulate the use of these technologies in the interests of patients and the wider pub-

---

[214] See, eg, John A Robertson, *Children of Choice: Freedom and the New Reproductive Technologies* (Princeton, NJ, Princeton University Press, 1994); Julian Savulescu, 'Sex Selection: the Case For' (1999) 171 *Medical Journal of Australia* 373.

[215] One need only look to the history of sterilisation laws in Canada and the US to recognise the source of such concern.

[216] Jackson (n 6).

lic. Healthcare providers also owe fiduciary duties to their patients,[217] meaning that the providers must focus on the needs and interests of their patients, not their own, and not those of outsiders to the relationship.[218] It seems inappropriate, then, to ask these providers to consider the wider societal implications of the decisions that they make in conjunction with individual patients and in specific circumstances.

Professional associations and societies have a number of disparate functions, including the provision of professional and ethical guidance to their membership. These organisations are also in place to regulate their profession, and to promote their profession and its activities, aims which may be incompatible with crafting sound legal and policy approaches to the regulation of reproduction.[219] In addition, transparency of processes and decision making is not achievable when regulation is carried out by professional organisations – these are not public bodies and as such are under no obligation to seek public input on their decisions, except to the extent that there are public members on their governing councils.

Entrusting the regulation of reproductive health services and technologies to the professions that deliver those services also gives rise to serious concerns about potential conflicts of interest. As Debora Spar notes:

> What complicates this particular area of the baby market . . . is the fine line it walks between commerce and medicine, between treatment for an illness and purchase of a much-desired good. In other realms with similar characteristics – the market for donor kidneys, for example, or cancer treatments – the state traditionally has intervened to establish guidelines. . . . In the fertility trade, by contrast, private rules reign. The fertility centers themselves set the rules that guide their conduct, working under the auspices of the ASRM . . .[220]

Even absent a full-blown conflict of interest, the professional role itself leaves little room for consideration of how regulation should be approached from a detached, indifferent point of view. Those involved in the provision of ART services surely must be of the view that the technologies themselves are beneficial and ethically appropriate; this view, in turn, will necessarily shape their views relative to how such technologies ought to be regulated.

Granting regulatory authority to professional regulatory bodies or associations is also problematic because of the voices that are thereby left out of the process. There is no reason to assume that healthcare providers are especially competent to recognise and grapple with ethical (let alone legal and policy) issues. Indeed, leaving these decisions in the hands of a privileged few is probably a guarantee that significant ethical concerns

---

[217] A number of Canadian cases have recognised the fiduciary nature of the physician–patient relationship: see, eg, *McInerney v MacDonald* [1992] 2 SCR 138, 126 NBR (2d) 271; *Norberg v Wynrib* [1992] 2 SCR 226, 92 DLR (4th) 449, 271 (cited to SCR):'But perhaps the most fundamental characteristic of the doctor–patient relationship is its fiduciary nature. All the authorities agree that the relationship of physician to patient also falls into that special category of relationships which the law calls fiduciary.'

[218] See, eg, Moe M Litman, 'Fiduciary Law and For-Profit and Not-For-Profit Health Care' in Timothy A Caulfield and Barbara von Tigerstrom (eds), *Health Care Reform and the Law in Canada: Meeting the Challenge* (Edmonton, University of Alberta Press, 2002) 85, 85–86. Litman notes that physicians' fiduciary duties entail stringent duties of loyalty to their patients, and that loyalty is threatened by current pressures for healthcare reform that require physicians to take into account 'considerations other than the best interests of their patients' (*ibid* 86).

[219] See, eg, Tracey Epps, 'Regulation of Health Care Professionals' in Jocelyn Downie, Timothy Caulfield and Colleen M Flood (eds), *Canadian Health Law and Policy*, 4th edn (Markham, LexisNexis Canada, 2011) 75, 76–79.

[220] Spar (n 22) 51.

will be overlooked. Medical and allied health professionals are highly educated and scientifically literate, and have, as a result, a specific perspective on science and its possibilities. Clearly, these individuals must be involved in the regulatory process, but they ought not to be exclusively involved.

There are also limits to what professional regulation can achieve. In section V.B. below, I discuss funding and access to ART services. Funding is a critical aspect of the overall regulatory picture in the ART context, because the high price of most infertility treatment precludes access to treatment for a great many individuals. Professional regulators may advocate in favour of funding for treatment, but as they do not control the public purse, they are not in a position to do more than encourage governments to fund ART treatement.

Not only is professional regulation of ART research and practice not feasible, it does not ensure appropriate respect for reproductive autonomy. It might be the case that the reproductive choices of certain groups or individuals are well served by a professional regulatory approach, but it is clear that the least powerful (socially and economically) will not benefit in the same way, just as is the case in respect of all other aspects of healthcare.[221]

In spite of the understandable worries that arise in connection with State regulation of reproduction,[222] it is essential that the State play a role. Ideally, regulation should be independent (of both the State itself and the professions) and centralised. The responsibility of the State is to create a regulatory structure that incorporates expertise and vision, and that is permitted to function independently.

B. Independent regulator or government regulation?

Public regulation of ARTs can take place in a variety of ways – the government itself can regulate, it can appoint a public body with the power to regulate, or it can take on part of the regulatory function and delegate other aspects to a public body or bodies.[223] While concerns have been raised in relation to public regulation and its likely (negative) impact

---

[221] See, eg, Louise Séguin *et al*, 'Effects of Low Income on Infant Health' (2003) 168 *Canadian Medical Association Journal* 1533; Eddy van Doorslaer, Cristina Masseria and Xander Koolman, 'Inequalities in Access to Medical Care by Income in Developed Countries' (2006) 174 *Canadian Medical Association Journal* 177.

[222] This is most notably the case in the US. The explosive nature of abortion politics in the US, and the readiness of some administrations (notably the George W Bush administration) to interfere in the work of various departments that deal with reproductive health issues, gives me considerable pause. Two examples that come readily to mind are the recent decision of the FDA respecting emergency contraception and the Bush administration's abstinence-only policy: see, eg, Adrienne Germain, 'Playing Politics with Women's Lives' (2004) 305 *Science* 17; Alastair JJ Wood, Jeffrey M Drazen and Michael F Greene, 'A Sad Day for Science at the FDA' (2005) 353 *New England Journal of Medicine* 1197; Tracy Hampton, 'Abstinence-Only Programs Under Fire' (2008) 299 *Journal of the American Medical Association* 2013, 2014. But while I can sympathise with the worry that a State presence in regulating reproduction is dangerous given the ideologically-driven 'politics of life,' I think that the only way an integrated, coherent scheme of regulation can be achieved is by an independent, centralised oversight agency.

[223] As Roger Brownsword explains, the House of Lords decision in *Quintavalle, R* (2005) (n 115) 'boils down' to a choice between two competing regulatory structures: 'One design is that favoured by the House of Lords, under which the Authority has a broad discretion to deal with a wide range of controversial reproductive choices subject to Parliamentary reserve powers, the other design is one that confers upon the Authority a limited licensing discretion with Parliament having to expressly authorise each significant extension of the Authority's remit.' (Roger Brownsword, 'Happy Families, Consenting Couples, and Children with Dignity: Sex Selection and Saviour Siblings' (2005) 17 *Child and Family Law Quarterly* 435, 464)

on reproductive autonomy, particularly in the UK and the US, regulation need not necessarily be restrictive. Although the HFEA has been criticised for failing to respect reproductive autonomy appropriately,[224] in general terms the UK regulatory regime is permissive and does seek to respect reproductive autonomy.

The primary tension that arises in contemplating whether regulation is best accomplished by direct government control or by the delegation of regulatory activity to an independent body is accountability, which is a fundamental tension in questions around public decision making.[225] There are advantages to regulation by agencies that are separate from but accountable to the executive and legislative branches of government; these include the ability to involve experts in their membership, more flexible and responsive policy making, and the fact that these entities are 'insulated against political pressures'.[226] The primary disadvantage of such institutions, from the point of view of those who advocate for democratic decision making, is that the body is not elected and therefore not directly accountable to the public.

This tension comes across very plainly in the report of the UK House of Commons Select Committee on Science and Technology.[227] In October 2003, the Committee embarked on a review of the legal regime in place with respect to reproductive technologies (in other words, the HFE Act 1990 and the HFEA), having apparently become frustrated with the Department of Health's failure to review the Act.[228] In its Report the Select Committee called for greater powers for Parliament 'to debate and amend legislation,' arguing that 'a larger role for our democratically accountable Parliament would give the public greater confidence that the big ethical issues of the day are being given adequate attention'.[229]

It seems fairly clear that what is desired by both advocates for arm's-length agencies and those who urge a greater role for Parliament is accountability, transparency and respect for public opinion.[230] The disagreement primarily centres on how best to achieve those aims.[231] While there are benefits and disadvantages to both systems, as I have argued elsewhere, in my view the benefits weigh in favour of an independent regulator, for a number of reasons.[232] Independent regulators can include members with appropriate expertise on complex legal, ethical and medical issues, they can be flexible and

---

[224] See, eg, Harris (n 126); Julian Savulescu, 'The HFEA has Restricted Liberty Without Good Cause', *Guardian*, 7 February 2011, at <www.guardian.co.uk/commentisfree/belief/2011/feb/07/hfea-reproductive-technology-research>.

[225] Although a detailed discussion of issues and concerns related to the various roles filled by administrative agencies generally is beyond the scope of this project, the issue of accountability does merit brief discussion.

[226] Science and Technology Committee, *Human Reproductive Technologies and the Law* (HC 2004–05, 7-I) paras 355, 356.

[227] *Ibid*.

[228] *Ibid* para 2. The Department of Health ultimately completed its own review (Department of Health, *Review of the Human Fertilisation and Embryology Act: Proposals for revised legislation (including establishment of the Regulatory Authority for Tissue and Embryos)* Cm 6989 (London, The Stationery Office, 2006)).

[229] Science and Technology Committee (n 226) paras 82, 87.

[230] See, eg, Science and Technology Committee, *Human Reproductive Technologies and the Law* (HC 2004–05, 7-II, Oral and Written Evidence), Ev 84, Ev 95, Ev 215, Ev 221, Ev 242, Ev 246, Ev 272; House of Commons Standing Committee on Health, *Assisted Human Reproduction: Building Families* (Ottawa, Public Works and Government Services Canada, 2001).

[231] Of course, there are those who suggest that State regulation of ARTs itself is misguided: see, eg, Robertson (n 214); Judith Daar, 'Regulating Reproductive Technologies: Panacea or Paper Tiger' (1997) 34 *Houston Law Review* 609.

[232] Erin L Nelson, 'Comparative Perspectives on the Regulation of Assisted Reproductive Technologies in the United Kingdom and Canada' (2006) 43 *Alberta Law Review* 1023, 1033–38.

responsive in respect of new scientific developments, and they are somewhat 'insulated against political pressures'[233] because they are not concerned about re-election. This last benefit is extremely significant in an area as sensitive and controversial as ART-related research and practice. Policy making in this area is fraught with difficulty, given the strong views held by various segments of society on embryonic life,[234] the propriety of embryo research and the acceptability of various genetic technologies in the assisted reproduction context.[235] As can be seen by simply perusing the list of witnesses and stakeholders that have appeared before the various commissions of inquiry and parliamentary bodies that have examined the issue of assisted reproduction, an enormous number and range of groups feel that they have an important stake in framing any decision-making process that will govern applications of ARTs: religious groups, medical and other health professionals (and related voluntary associations), legal professionals, specific ethnic and national communities, and individuals and groups representing those affected by infertility or those who wish to access specific technologies. Each of these groups has its own interests in and positions on various aspects of regulatory oversight, all of which demand respect and consideration. But at the end of the day, no matter where decision making takes place, some of these parties will be disappointed with the end result.

The importance of democratic accountability should not be discounted, particularly given the individual and social implications raised by the regulation of assisted reproduction. But most, if not all, of the accountability-related concerns can be addressed. In short, simply creating an arm's-length body to make these important decisions need not mean that there will be no accountability. Compulsory public consultation, combined with a mandate to educate and inform the public about the agency's business, will ensure that decision making remains transparent.[236] Further, it is possible to create an independent entity with some policy-making role *and* with significant parliamentary oversight.

The benefits of public regulation in the area of reproductive technologies include quality control,[237] public knowledge, accountability and transparency of processes,[238] and facilitation of the transition of various technologies from research to practice.

---

[233] Science and Technology Committee (n 226) para 356.

[234] The conflict around which, as Jackson notes, is simply not amenable to consensus (Jackson (n 6) 1).

[235] See, eg, Timothy Caulfield, 'Too Heavy a Hand on Science', *Globe and Mail* (Toronto, 3 June 2003), at <http://health.groups.yahoo.com/group/StemCellInformation/message/2302> (noting that the Parliamentary debates on the AHR Act were 'dominated [by] political rhetoric on the moral status of the embryo'). See also Science and Technology Committee (n 230) Ev 113; *House of Commons Debates*, 37th Parl, 3rd Sess, No 048 (29 January 2003) 2858 (Mr David Anderson), 2862–63 (Mrs Elsie Wayne); *House of Commons Debates*, 37th Parl, 3rd Sess, No 049 (30 January 2003) 2973 (Mr Richard Harris), 2978 (Mr Philip Mayfield), 2982 (Mr Ken Epp); *House of Commons Debates*, 37th Parl, 3rd Sess, No 053 (5 February 2003) 3191 (Miss Deborah Grey), 3192 (Mrs Elsie Wayne), 3196 (Mr Leon Benoit); *House of Commons Debates*, 37th Parl, 3rd Sess, No 057 (11 February 2003) 3399 (Mr Réal Ménard), 3403 (Mr Gerry Ritz), 3405 (Mr Reed Elley); *House of Commons Debates*, 37th Parl, 3rd Sess, No 047 (28 February 2003) 2778 (Mr Jason Kenney), 2811 (Mr Chuck Strahl), 2816 (Mr Ken Epp), 2819 (Mr Jim Karygiannis).

[236] See, eg, National Health Law and Family Law Sections, Canadian Bar Association, 'Submission on Draft Legislation on Assisted Human Reproduction' (2001) 10 *Health Law Review* 25, 27; Timothy Caulfield, 'Bill C-13: The Assisted Human Reproduction Act: Examining the Arguments Against a Regulatory Approach' (2002) 11 *Health Law Review* 20, 23 (fn 30).

[237] See, eg, Jackson (n 6); Don P Wolf, 'An Opinion on Regulating the Assisted Reproductive Technologies' (2003) 20 *Journal of Assisted Reproduction and Genetics* 290.

[238] See, eg, Caulfield, 'Bill C-13' (n 236); Harvison Young and Wasunna (n 140); Timothy Caulfield, 'Clones, Controversy, and Criminal Law: A Comment on the Proposal for Legislation Governing Assisted Human Reproduction' (2001) 39 *Alberta Law Review* 335; Françoise Baylis, 'Human Cloning: Three Mistakes and an Alternative' (2002) 27 *Journal of Medicine and Philosophy* 319.

Clearly, a number of these functions are beyond the scope of a Ministry of Health (or any other government department) acting alone. A material benefit specifically related to the existence of an independent regulatory agency is its potential role as a focal point for public debate and discussion of the ethical issues to which the use of reproductive technologies gives rise.[239] An especially important advantage of having a regulatory system in place is the ability to collect data about practices.[240] It can also allow public debate and discussion as part of the policy-making process – the only meaningful way for the public to have input into the uses of reproductive technologies is for the public to be aware of current practice.[241] In addition to being of benefit specifically in relation to ARTs, a regulatory system that focuses some attention on issues in assisted reproduction might also help to bring reproductive health-related issues more generally into focus. Many of these benefits are directly related to reproductive autonomy, in that a transparent, accountable regulator is best placed to ensure that access to ART services is not denied on discriminatory grounds, and given that the data-collection function is essential to informed decision making on the use of reproductive technologies.

There are, then, some good reasons to favour a regime that creates a centralised, independent oversight agency that is accountable to government. In addition, the public body should also have an explicit mandate to respect reproductive autonomy.[242] In this way, we can achieve the beneficial aims of public regulation without tying up too much in the way of parliamentary resources on a single issue, and we can, it is hoped, prevent the repeated revisiting of intractable questions, such as the moral status of the embryo – an issue that has characterised so much of the legislative debate on research and practice in assisted human reproduction.[243] A contextualised account of reproductive autonomy demands a regulatory regime that entails a comprehensive and considered view of assisted reproduction and the concerns it raises. Comprehensive reproductive regulation can of course be restrictive of reproductive autonomy. It is not enough simply to have

[239] Timothy Caulfield, Lori Knowles and Eric M Meslin, 'Law and Policy in the Era of Reproductive Genetics' (2004) 30 *Journal of Medical Ethics* 414.

[240] Data collection is needed to permit future research into issues such as the health of offspring conceived using ARTs, the health of women who use ARTs and those who donate oocytes for clinical or research use, as well as family and psycho-social implications raised by the use of reproductive technologies: see, eg, S Baruch et al, 'Preimplantation Genetic Diagnosis: A Discussion of Challenges, Concerns, and Preliminary Policy Options Related to the Genetic Testing of Human Embryos' (Report) (*Genetics & Public Policy Center*, 2004), at <www.dnapolicy.org/pub.reports.php?action=detail&report_id=8>.

[241] *Ibid.*

[242] And, in keeping with my argument that regulation of reproduction should be coherent and purposeful, I would recommend the creation of an independent, national body charged with developing and implementing a national strategy for reproductive health. Regulation of ART research and practice would be one aspect of the body's mandate.

[243] This is particularly true of the stem-cell research debate in Canada: see, eg, Timothy Caulfield and Tania Bubela, 'Why a Criminal Ban? Analyzing the Arguments Against Somatic Cell Nuclear Transfer in the Canadian Parliamentary Debate' (2007) 7(2) *American Journal of Bioethics* 51; Tania Bubela and Timothy Caulfield, 'When Human Dignity is Not Enough: Embryonic Stem Cell Research and Human Cloning in Canada' in Edna F Einsiedel (ed), *Emerging Technologies: From Hindsight and Foresight* (Vancouver, University of British Columbia Press, 2008) 161. What is most frustrating about this situation is that many feminist thinkers and women's health advocates continue to insist that the restrictions on embryo research are in place to protect women's health. A look at the Parliamentary debates shows almost no mention of women's health, but the issue of the moral status of the fetus features prominently. In insisting that the restrictions are aimed at safeguarding women's interests, these commentators essentially allow the women's health issues to disappear from the debate. See Diana Backhouse and Maneesha Deckha, 'Shifting Rationales: The Waning Influence of Feminism on Canada's Embryo Research Restrictions' (2009) 21 *Canadian Journal of Women and Law* 229; Mavis Jones and Brian Salter, 'Proceeding Carefully: Assisted Human Reproduction Policy in Canada' (2010) 19 *Public Understanding of Science* 420.

such an approach; care must also be taken to ensure that the regulatory regime is structured in such a way as to ensure respect for reproductive autonomy.

The UK experience suggests that public regulation of ARTs can be achieved effectively by way of an independent regulatory agency with a policy-making role. Admittedly, the HFEA has been criticised on many fronts and by many players, but as a number of commentators have pointed out, criticism is not surprising given the HFEA's mandate to '[seek] to regulate in an area where people hold strong but incompatible views'.[244] In spite of the HFEA's very vocal critics, by and large it seems that the UK's ART regulatory system is well regarded. The UK system has influenced developments in Australia and France, in addition to having made a significant impression on Canada's Royal Commission.[245] An expert working group has made recommendations for regulation of ARTs in the US that are based on an HFEA-like model.[246]

The HFEA has proved to be responsive, flexible and willing to modify its approach when warranted. It has been required to deal with complex and ethically challenging issues, has taken its public consultation role seriously,[247] and has fostered a facilitative approach to ART research and practice that has allowed the UK to become an international leader in ART-related science. As one fertility expert has said:

> [O]verall I would commend the Authority for maintaining an up-to-date, common sense approach to its complex role. It is easy to criticise the HFEA, but the organisation serves to deflect many of the ethical and political difficulties that would otherwise bedevil day-to-day clinical care, to define what may and may not be done, and to act as an interface between a rapacious news media, a concerned public, a reactive and frequently reactionary Parliament and those of us involved in clinical practice in IVF.[248]

The one improvement that could be made to the UK approach is the inclusion of a larger role for the professions involved in providing ART services. Australia's blended model, which includes a significant role for professional regulation in combination with public regulation through the NHMRC (and, in some states, legislation), seems superior in that it permits the benefits of both public and professional regulation to be realised, while at the same time minimising the potential negative aspects of both regulatory models on their own. A key ingredient of Australia's model is the mutually reinforcing nature of the professional and public elements of regulation.[249] This combined professional and public approach is not only the most practical means of accomplishing thoughtful and appropriate regulation of ARTs, it also seems the most likely contender for a regulatory model that will properly respect reproductive autonomy.

Legal regulation of reproductive technologies is fraught with ethical complexity. Decision making about embarking on parenthood involves choices of a most intimate

---

[244] Angus Dawson, 'The Human Fertilisation and Embryology Authority: Evidence Based Policy Formation in a Contested Context' (2004) 12 *Health Care Analysis* 1, 5. See also Derek Morgan, 'Ethics, Economics and the Exotic: The Early Career of the HFEA' (2004) 12 *Health Care Analysis* 7, 10; William Leigh Ledger, 'Regulation of Reproduction in the UK' (2005) 8 *Human Fertility* 65, 67.

[245] See, eg, Parens and Knowles (n 39); Science and Technology Committee (n 230) Ev 225, Ev 280, Ev 362, Ev 399.

[246] Parens and Knowles (n 39) S15–16, S18–21.

[247] Some would say too seriously: see, eg, Dawson (n 244) 3; Harris (n 126) 291.

[248] Ledger (n 244) 67.

[249] As explained above, the RTAC accreditation process requires compliance with the NHMRC Guidelines, and the Guidelines in turn require that organisations providing ART services be accredited by the RTAC. See above section III.B.

and private nature, including choices about whether and how to use reproductive technologies. Yet the research and treatment implications of these technologies have very public dimensions as well, particularly in States with public healthcare systems where the State funds some aspects of assisted reproduction. And because reproductive technologies cannot be accessed without professional assistance, there is necessarily a gatekeeper involved in the use of the technologies, whether that comprises individual physicians, professional organisations or the State itself.

Public regulation of ARTs is also controversial from a political philosophy perspective – should government regulate personal morality in matters of reproduction? A full exploration of that question is beyond the scope of this work, but even if one feels strongly that government has no role in policing morality, there is still a role for State regulation of research and clinical practice in ARTs. As noted earlier, numerous benefits arise from public regulation of ARTs, including quality control, public knowledge, accountability and data collection.

A regulatory system such as that found in the UK (even if modified to grant professional organisations a larger role) will certainly not satisfy all participants in the debate over appropriate forms of regulation. Nonetheless, State regulation should not be dismissed as an alternative simply because of fears that such a system might dampen research and practice involving reproductive technologies. Both the US and Canada have had, to date, a complex web of regulatory approaches for reproductive technologies, and no central oversight agency, but practices in the two nations have developed very differently; there is much more work being done in the reproductive medicine arena in the US than in Canada. The UK, by contrast, has a comprehensive system and has remained on the leading edge of research into reproductive technologies. Some years ago, the UK became the first jurisdiction to permit scientists to attempt to isolate stem cells from cloned early human embryos, thus attesting to the fact that the existence of a coherent regulatory scheme need not be viewed solely as a barrier to progress.[250] The difficult task for policy makers lies in striking a balance that is appropriately respectful of a number of pressing social goals, including private decision making, scientific inquiry and ethical uses of new technologies.

C. ART regulation and reproductive tourism

As a result of uneven local, regional and national laws on access to fertility treatment, the practice of 'fertility tourism' has arisen. This phenomenon is one manifestation of globalisation and a dimension of the wider category of medical tourism;[251] it appears to be fairly common in Australia, and has been noted as well in other jurisdictions, including Europe and North America.[252]

---

[250] Human Fertilisation and Embryology Authority, 'HFEA Grants the First Therapeutic Cloning Licence for Research' (11 August 2004), at <www.hfea.gov.uk/758.html>.

[251] See, eg, Anne Donchin, 'Reproductive Tourism and the Quest for Global Justice' (2010) 24 *Bioethics* 323; YY Brandon Chen and Colleen M Flood, 'Moving Beyond Hype and Rhetoric: An Evidence-Based Examination of the Implications of Medical Tourism for Health Care Access and Global Equity' (2012) *Journal of Law, Medicine & Ethics* (in press); I Glenn Cohen, 'How To Regulate Medical Tourism (And Why It Matters For Bioethics)' (2012) 12 *Developing World Bioethics* 9.

[252] Guido Pennings, 'Legal Harmonization and Reproductive Tourism in Europe' (2004) 19 *Human Reproduction* 2689; Guido Pennings *et al*, 'Cross Border Reproductive Care in Belgium' (2009) 24 *Human Reproduction* 3108; Françoise Shenfield *et al*, 'Cross Border Reproductive Care in Six European Countries' (2010) 25 *Human Reproduction* 1361.

In the broader medical tourism context, the rationale for seeking out-of-country care is more likely that the procedure is inaccessible in one's home jurisdiction, as opposed to being legally prohibited. I shall discuss fertility tourism in more detail in the context of the international trade in surrogacy services, but it also requires brief mention in the context of regulation and autonomy. Guido Pennings has argued that reproductive tourism is a phenomenon to be viewed as a 'safety valve that avoids moral conflict, and as such, contributes to a peaceful coexistence of different ethical and religious views in Europe'.[253] Whether or not one agrees with Pennings' view, it is clear that reproductive tourism is an important consideration in the context of national regulation.[254]

The scope of reproductive tourism is largely unknown, although some data are beginning to emerge. According to Françoise Shenfield and colleagues, roughly one-third of patients who participated in their study cited more than one reason to seek reproductive health services outside their home jurisdiction, but legal barriers to treatment at home appear to be a 'major factor' in patient decision making.[255] Price is the other main driver of reproductive tourism.[256] In the case of surrogacy services in particular, the variation in price from one jurisdiction to another can be immense. It has been estimated that the cost of surrogacy in the US can range from $59,000 to $80,000, whereas in India, the range is $10,000 to $35,000 (USD).[257]

As will be discussed in more detail in the following chapter, some Australian states have attempted to criminalise commercial surrogacy, even when undertaken outside of Australia.[258] Is this a legitimate response? In part the answer to this question depends on how one characterises reproductive autonomy – both what it means and what it demands. If respect for reproductive autonomy means that it is not legitimate to restrict ART practice, then clearly banning cross-border care is out of bounds. But even if it is considered legitimate to prohibit or restrict practices within a jurisdiction, the legitimacy of prohibitions on seeking care outside one's home jurisdiction is highly questionable, for reasons of both principle and practicality. Such prohibitions are not only disrespectful of autonomy; it is unlikely that they can effectively be enforced.

V. CONTROLLING ACCESS TO TREATMENT: ELIGIBILITY CRITERIA AND FUNDING

Access to ART treatment is mediated by the imposition of eligibility criteria and by the availability of insurance coverage or other financial assistance in meeting treatment costs. These issues will be considered separately, but it is essential to bear in mind their close relatedness. Even if eligibility criteria permit (or mandate) access for all who might wish to use ART treatment, financial constraints may effectively prevent it. In some

---

[253] Pennings, 'Legal Harmonization and Reproductive Tourism in Europe' (n 252) 2694.

[254] Eric Blyth and Abigail Farrand, 'Reproductive Tourism – a Price Worth Paying for Reproductive Autonomy?' (2005) 25 *Critical Social Policy* 91.

[255] Shenfield *et al* (n 252) 1365–66.

[256] Usha Rengachary Smerdon, 'Crossing Bodies, Crossing Borders: International Surrogacy Between the United States and India' (2008) 39 *Cumberland Law Review* 15, 32–33; Casey Humbyrd, 'Fair Trade International Surrogacy' (2009) 9 *Developing World Bioethics* 111; Lisa Ikemoto, 'Reproductive Tourism: Equality Concerns in the Global Market for Fertility Services' (2009) 27 *Law and Inequality* 277.

[257] Smerdon (n 256) 32–33; Andrea Whittaker, 'Cross-border Assisted Reproduction Care in Asia: Implications for Access, Equity and Regulations' (2011) 19(37) *Reproductive Health Matters* 107.

[258] See discussion in ch 9, section III.

cases, access to funding for treatment is directly tied to 'eligibility for funding' criteria. Where financial barriers prevent a person from obtaining treatment, these rules can have the same impact as restrictions on eligibility.

The issue of access to treatment is one of the general questions related to ART governance more broadly and as such will be considered here. More specific questions around reproductive materials and services, and particularly the involvement of third parties in the ART context, will be considered in the next chapter.

A. Access to treatment and eligibility criteria

Eligibility criteria are conditions spelling out which individuals or groups can (or cannot) access infertility treatment. As is clear from the above discussion of ART regulation in Canada, the US, the UK and Australia, law and policy relevant to ARTs (including eligibility criteria) may be found in multiple locations, including legislation, professional regulatory standards, practice guidelines and ethical guidelines. Eligibility for treatment is also subject to restriction on the basis of physician practice, even in the absence of legal or policy restrictions.

One of the most significant social concerns related to ART treatment is its potential to disrupt traditional ideas of parenthood and family. Early in the history of ARTs, public concern around moral and social issues led in some cases to the adoption of eligibility rules designed to minimise this potential and to reassure the public. In order to respond to the widespread worries about the future of the family and of society as a whole, many jurisdictions sought to prevent or limit the use of ARTs to form non-traditional families by restricting eligibility to heterosexual married couples. In addition to worries about single women and gay or lesbian couples seeking access to ART treatment in order to create their families, social concern around access to ARTs by post-menopausal women was also pronounced,[259] and there is no shortage of criticism even to this day in response to stories of babies being born to women in their 50s and 60s.[260]

All of the original versions of ART legislation in Australia employed eligibility criteria to limit access to treatment. The original Victorian ART legislation restricted access to ART services to married and 'de facto heterosexual couples'.[261] The eligibility criteria in the original Victorian legislation were held to be unenforceable,[262] as they

[259] Jackson (n 6) 202–05.
[260] William Saletan, 'Fertile Old Ladies: Is it OK to impregnate a 60-year-old woman?', *Slate Magazine*, 30 July 2009, at <www.slate.com/articles/health_and_science/human_nature/2009/07/fertile_old_ladies.html>; Allison Pearson, 'Deluded and Selfish – World's Oldest Mum Made a Mockery of Motherhood', *Daily Mail*, 1 September 2009, at <www.dailymail.co.uk/femail/article-1200267/ALLISON-PEARSON-Deluded-selfish--worlds-oldest-mum-mockery-motherhood.html>; Arthur L Caplan and Pasquale Patrizio, 'Are You Ever Too Old to Have a Baby? The Ethical Challenges of Older Women Using Infertility Services' (2010) 28 *Seminars in Reproductive Medicine* 281.
[261] Szoke (n 58) 246. The legislation was the Infertility Treatment Act 1995 (Vic).
[262] *Re McBain* (2002) 209 CLR 372 (HCA). The Australian Catholic Bishops Conference was included in the Federal Court litigation concerning the validity of the eligibility provisions as *amicus curiae*, not as a party to the proceedings. As a result, the Bishops Conference had no right of appeal from the Federal Court decision. Instead, the Bishops Conference sought to have the High Court overturn the decision of Sundberg J in the Federal Court, on the basis that Sundberg J erred in law in concluding that the eligibility provisions of the Infertility Treatment Act 1995 (Vic) were invalid. The High Court did not address the substantive issues concerning equality of access to ART services and the ambit of the Sex Discrimination Act 1984 (Cth). For a discussion of the substantive issues, see *McBain v Victoria* (2000) 99 FCR 116.

contravened Commonwealth anti-discrimination legislation.[263] In Western Australia, the original version of section 23 of the Act restricted access to IVF and related services to infertile, heterosexual couples.[264] The explicit restrictions related to marital status and sexual orientation have been removed,[265] and the provision now permits women who are medically infertile or at risk of having a child with a genetic abnormality or disease to access ART services.[266] The woman's age must not be the reason for her infertility.[267] South Australia's legislation imposes similar eligibility criteria through conditions on provider registration. Eligibility for ART services is limited to women or couples who are or appear to be infertile[268] (defined as the inability to carry a pregnancy to term, or inability to achieve pregnancy after 12 months of unprotected sexual intercourse[269]), or those at risk of passing on a serious genetic defect, disease or illness to the child.[270]

As a result of the concerns around discriminatory limits on access to ART treatment, eligibility criteria have been refined, and no longer refer explicitly to marital status or sexual orientation. Instead, contemporary restrictions around eligibility for treatment (where they exist) may be grouped into two main types:

(a) those based on medical definitions of infertility (as in the case of Victoria, Western Australia and South Australia); and
(b) those based on welfare-orientated concerns.

But even where eligibility criteria have been refined or altered to respond to concerns about discrimination, the effect of the eligibility criteria arguably remains the same. Where infertility is defined in strictly medical terms, those who are unable to conceive for social reasons are implicitly excluded.

Welfare-based justifications are also a foundation upon which regulators (be they governmental actors, professional societies or individual providers) limit access to treatment. Sometimes the two approaches are used in combination. In South Australia and Western Australia, for example, clinicians must make decisions about eligibility for

---

[263] Sex Discrimination Act 1984 (Cth). Kristen Walker has noted that the Australian Government threatened to amend the Sex Discrimination Act and override the decision in *McBain v Victoria* (2000) (n 262) (Kristen Walker, 'The Bishops, The Doctor, His Patient and the Attorney-General: The Conclusion of the McBain Litigation' (2002) 30 *Federal Law Review* 507, 508).

[264] Szoke (n 58) 249.

[265] Western Australian Reproductive Technology Council, 'Acts Amendment (Lesbian and Gay Law Reform) Act 2002 – Amendment of the Human Reproductive Technology Act 1991 and the Artificial Conception Act 1985', at <www.rtc.org.au/clinics/docs/Info-Gay_and_Lesbian.pdf>.

[266] Human Reproductive Technology Act 1991 (WA), s 23. The medical reason for the infertility can pertain, in the case of a married woman or a woman in a de facto relationship with a man, to the infertility of the male partner.

[267] Human Reproductive Technology Act 1991 (WA), s 23(d). The Act does not extend this restriction to AI, meaning that a fertile single woman or a fertile woman in a same-sex relationship is free to attempt to conceive using AI.

[268] Assisted Reproductive Treatment Act 1988 (SA), s 9(1)(c). While this does not explicitly preclude treatment of single women or those in a same-sex relationship, the requirement that the woman seeking treatment must be medically infertile in effect restricts access in practice.

[269] Government of South Australia, 'Fact Sheet One: Access to ART at a Registered Clinic in South Australia' (*South Australia Health*), at <www.sahealth.sa.gov.au/wps/wcm/connect/public+content/sa+health+internet/health+services/womens+health/pregnancy+and+fertility/fertility+treatment/art+treatment>.

[270] Assisted Reproductive Treatment Act 1988 (SA), s 9(1)(c)(iii).

treatment on the basis of medical eligibility criteria *and* with regard to the paramount principle of the welfare of the child.[271]

The original eligibility criteria were finally removed from Victorian legislation almost a decade after the High Court held that they were impermissibly discriminatory. The change came about with the passage of the Assisted Reproductive Treatment Act 2008, which substituted new welfare-based restrictions on access to treatment. The 'presumption against treatment' provisions prohibit treatment where either the woman to be treated or her partner has a criminal record disclosing a conviction for a violent or sexual offence, or where either partner has had a child removed from his or her custody or guardianship.[272] The Victorian government introduced these requirements (contrary to the recommendations of the Victorian Law Reform Commission) in order to reassure the public that although the new legislation liberalises access to ART services, the government had adopted a 'balanced approach' that requires some evidence of the ability of treatment seekers to be good parents, but that does not discriminate on the basis of 'race, gender, religion or sexuality'.[273]

In the UK, access to infertility treatment has never been formally limited through statutory eligibility criteria, but the legislation as originally passed did contain a potentially restrictive welfare-based limitation on access to treatment. The question of whether eligibility for infertility treatment should be limited was strongly contested during debates on the HFE Act 1990.[274] A proposed amendment that would have limited the provision of ART services to married couples was defeated by one vote in the House of Lords.[275] The issue was also forcefully debated in the House of Commons, and what was ultimately agreed upon was the compromise that was enshrined in section 13(5) of the HFE Act 1990. The section provided that it is a condition of every licence granted to authorise the provision of ART treatment that

> [a] woman shall not be provided with treatment services unless account has been taken of the welfare of any child who may be born as a result of the treatment (including the need of that child for a father), and of any other child who may be affected by the birth.

As noted in section III.C. above, the 2008 amendments to the HFE Act 1990 substituted the phrase 'including the need for supportive parenting' for the requirement to consider the child's need for a father, although this change surprisingly became very contentious as well.[276]

Canada's AHR Act enshrines a commitment to non-discrimination that specifically refers to the impermissibility of discrimination on the basis of sexual orientation and marital status.[277] It also provides that 'the health and well-being of children born through the application of assisted human reproductive technologies must be given priority in all

---

[271] *Ibid* s 4A. In Western Australia's legislation, the language differs slightly, requiring providers to consider the welfare and interests of 'any child likely to be born as a result of the procedure' (Human Reproductive Technology Act 1991 (WA), s 23(e)).

[272] See above (n 93 and accompanying text). Women who are denied treatment on this basis are entitled to appeal to the Patient Review Panel for a review of the decision (Assisted Reproductive Treatment Act 2008 (Vic), s 15).

[273] Parliament of Victoria, Legislative Council Legislation Committee, *Report on the Consideration in Detail of the Assisted Reproductive Treatment Bill 2008* (Melbourne, Government Printer, 2008) 20.

[274] HL Deb 6 February 1990, vol 515, cols 788–804.

[275] *Ibid* col 804.

[276] HL Deb 19 November 2007, vol 696, cols 674–75; HC Deb 12 May 2008, vol 475, cols 1070–72, 1125–31.

[277] AHR Act (n 141), s 2(e).

decisions respecting their use'.[278] As the Canadian legislation never came fully into force, and the AHRC did not issue a single licence to treatment providers, it is not possible to comment on the Canadian approach to balancing those two potentially conflicting aims. It seems clear, however, that the prioritisation of the welfare of the potential child could justify limits on access to treatment. In addition to the statutory mandate to place priority on the welfare of the child, Canadian professional guidelines advert to the necessity of evaluating the potential welfare of the child. Although the guidelines state that access to ART services should not be denied on the basis of age or other social (ie non-medical) characteristics, they also expressly contemplate the exercise of discretion by indicating that providers should refuse to offer treatment where they are concerned that the person seeking treatment 'is . . . a potentially incapable parent'.[279]

Given the lack of comprehensive government regulation in the US, professional guidelines play an important role in the governance of ART service provision in that country.[280] The ASRM Ethics Committee has addressed this issue in a guideline dealing with access to treatment for single persons and gays and lesbians, as well as in a report on access to treatment for persons who are seropositive for human immunodeficiency virus (HIV).[281] The Ethics Committee asserts that 'Offspring welfare is a valid consideration that fertility programs may take into account in selecting patients and providing services as long as they do not discriminate on the basis of disability or other impermissible factor'.[282] Providers are not under an obligation to withhold treatment unless they are concerned that 'significant harm to future children is likely'.[283] Although it draws on welfare-based justifications for refusal to provide treatment, the report does appear to take reproductive autonomy as a starting point, stating that 'Because of the importance of reproduction to persons, judgments to deny treatment should be made only when there is a strong and substantial basis for doing so'.[284]

The ASRM guideline is explicit in stating that the Americans with Disabilities Act precludes the denial of services to persons with disabilities, 'if the denial is based on ill-founded doubts or stereotypes about their ability to rear and parent'.[285] With respect to HIV-infected persons, the Ethics Committee concludes that fertility clinics should offer services where the individual is or couple are 'willing to use risk-reducing therapies' such as antiretroviral therapy and delivery by Caesarean section to limit the risk of transmission to offspring.[286]

i. Eligibility criteria and reproductive autonomy

Clearly, statutory restrictions that preclude access to ART services for certain individuals and groups constitute a profound interference with reproductive autonomy, one that

---

[278] *Ibid* s 2(a).

[279] 'Joint Policy Statement' (n 194) 37.

[280] Some states do regulate aspects of ART practice, and although no state imposes eligibility criteria as to who is entitled to access ART treatment, a few states have laws mandating insurance coverage of ARTs in some circumstances; these laws are discussed in the following section.

[281] American Society for Reproductive Medicine Ethics Committee, 'Human Immunodeficiency Virus and Infertility Treatment' (2010) 94 *Fertility and Sterility* 11.

[282] American Society for Reproductive Medicine Ethics Committee (n 46) 867.

[283] *Ibid.*

[284] *Ibid* 866.

[285] *Ibid.*

[286] American Society for Reproductive Medicine Ethics Committee (n 281) 11.

cannot be justified from the standpoint of respect for reproductive autonomy on the contextualised view that I adopt. Frankly, in my view, such a stance cannot be justified on the basis of a less inclusive view of reproductive autonomy. Even when framed as being based on welfare-orientated concerns, rules that deny access to treatment to particular groups or individuals are cause for concern from the perspective of reproductive autonomy.

As Natalie Gamble has noted, some who opposed the removal of 'the need for a father' provision from the HFE Act 1990 argued that the law was not discriminatory. Opponents of the amendment claimed that the section was primarily concerned with the welfare of children born via ART treatment and that it 'applied equally to same-sex and opposite-sex couples'.[287] While it is indeed the case that the law applied equally to heterosexual and homosexual couples, the argument that the section did not seek to treat single women and same-sex couples differently is, as Gamble notes, unsustainable. She uses stronger language, stating that the claim is 'quite clearly ludicrous . . . The duty to consider the need for a father was always quite clearly (and in 1990 quite openly) targeted at excluding single and lesbian women' from eligibility for ART treatment.[288]

Gamble has pointed out that the shift in attitudes over time is obvious when various editions of the HFEA *Code of Practice* are compared.[289] As she explains, the first edition of the *Code of Practice* states that

> [c]entres are required to have regard to the child's need for a father and should pay particular attention to the prospective mother's ability to meet the child's needs throughout his or her childhood, and where appropriate whether there is anyone else within the prospective mother's family and social circle . . . who is willing and able to share the responsibility for meeting those needs.[290]

Several years later, in the seventh edition of the *Code of Practice*, the guidance on the obligation to consider the need for a father reads as follows:

> Where the child will have no legal father, the centre should assess the prospective mother's ability to meet the child's/children's needs and the ability of other persons within the family or social circle willing to share responsibility for those needs.[291]

While the 'need for a father' condition did not explicitly preclude the provision of ART services to single or lesbian women, it did grant wide discretion to clinicians, many of whom refused to treat single and lesbian women.[292] When initially proposed, the 2008 amendments sought simply to remove the phrase 'need for a father' from the child welfare provision, but this became controversial after early debates in the House of Lords.[293] What made the resistance so surprising was its inconsistency with the shift in attitudes and in practice that had taken place since the passage of the 1990 Act. As is clear from the above excerpts, the HFEA *Code of Practice* changed over the years to reflect that section 13(5) did not legally bar ART providers from treating single or lesbian women.

---

[287] Natalie Gamble, 'Considering the Need for a Father: The Role of Clinicians in Safeguarding Family Values in UK Fertility Treatment' (2009) 19 (Supp 1) *Reproductive Biomedicine Online* 15, 17.

[288] *Ibid.*

[289] *Ibid.*

[290] Human Fertilisation and Embryology Authority, *Code of Practice* (London, HFEA, 1991) para 3.16(b).

[291] Human Fertilisation and Embryology Authority, *Code of Practice*, 7th edn (London, HFEA, 2007) para G3.3.3.

[292] Gamble (n 287) 16.

[293] HL Deb 2007 (n 276).

Significant social changes, including the passage of legislation prohibiting discrimination on the basis of sexual orientation,[294] and the move toward equality for same-sex couples both as partners[295] and as parents,[296] also meant that the obligation to consider the child's need for a father had to be firmly situated in a context of respect for equal rights.

There appears to be no basis upon which legitimately to assume that statutory requirements such as those found in the UK and Australian legislation do indeed protect the welfare and interests of children who may be born as a result of ART treatment.[297] As Ian Thorpe explains, it appears that the Victorian government has taken the view that fairness to those in need of assistance in reproduction must yield to the need to '[reassure] the wider community that ART is strongly regulated'.[298] But such broadly-worded aspirational provisions by no means ensure the involvement of regulators or government in strictly controlling access to ART services. They do, however, give providers wide discretion to make decisions about to whom they will offer treatment. This is also true of the New South Wales legislation, which does not specify eligibility criteria for ART treatment.[299] Kerry Petersen is critical of this approach, noting that the result is to leave a great deal of discretion in the hands of ART providers and that this, in turn, might lead to an approach that limits the availability of treatment to those with medical, rather than social, needs for treatment.[300] Petersen notes that where statutes create narrow eligibility criteria, the limits may be challenged on the basis of anti-discrimination laws, but where 'gate-keeping is left to clinics and medical practitioners, it can be difficult to obtain the evidence necessary to challenge'[301] these decisions. Just as in the case of abortion law, giving physicians a gatekeeping function can render discriminatory or other inappropriate refusals of treatment largely invisible.[302]

The same concerns raised by Petersen apply where regulation is accomplished by way of clinical practice guidelines or professional ethics guidelines. Such guidelines explicitly permit professionals to act as gatekeepers to treatment on the basis of social as well as medical factors. These providers, however, have no particular expertise or training that would give them any special insight into who should or should not be a parent.[303] And indeed, as we have seen in the context of involuntary sterilisation, there is a case to be made that physicians might take a narrow and pessimistic view of a patient's potential abilities as a parent.[304] Moreover, physicians are not necessarily well placed to know

---

[294] Equality Act 2006 (UK).

[295] Civil Partnership Act 2004 (UK).

[296] Adoption and Children Act 2002 (UK). In addition, the changes to the parentage provisions in the 2008 amendments reflected this liberalisation.

[297] Thorpe *et al* (n 80) 850.

[298] *Ibid.*

[299] Assisted Reproductive Technology Act 2007 (NSW).

[300] Smith (n 96) 126–29. See also Kerry Petersen, 'The Regulation of Assisted Reproductive Technology: A Comparative Study of Permissive and Prescriptive Laws and Policies' (2002) 9 *Journal of Law and Medicine* 483, 484–85.

[301] Petersen (n 300) 484–85.

[302] *Ibid*; Jackson (n 6) 194–95. A recent example of discriminatory gatekeeping by a physician arose in California, where two physicians refused to provide AI to a lesbian woman seeking to have children with her long-time partner. The California Supreme Court ultimately held that California's anti-discrimination law precludes discrimination on the basis of sexual orientation and that the physicians' refusal to treat the plaintiff amounted to impermissible discrimination (*North Coast Women's Care Medical Group, Inc et al v SC (Benitez)*, 189 P 3d 959 (Cal 2008)).

[303] Jackson (n 112).

[304] This is discussed in ch 4, section III.

what their patients' social circumstances are – for example, whether they live within a caring and supportive environment in which children might do very well.

Access to fertility treatment may determine whether a woman or couple can become parents. No one would disagree that the welfare of children conceived using ARTs is an important concern, as is the welfare of all children. But appropriate respect for reproductive autonomy demands that concern for the welfare of a not-yet-conceived (and possibly never-to-be-conceived) child must not be permitted to disqualify from access those who wish to use fertility treatment to become parents. Potential parents who do not require assistance to conceive are not subject to restrictions on the basis of welfare considerations, and it is legitimate to ask why those who do require assistance should be subject to such limits.[305]

Emily Jackson has made a compelling argument that the welfare principle enshrined in the HFE Act 1990 is 'hopelessly incoherent,' and that appeals to the welfare of potential children cannot properly be invoked to limit access to ART treatments. Glenn Cohen has made this argument as well, although his claims are more sweeping, in that they implicate the regulation of reproduction more generally. Cohen claims that the 'best interests' test, when transposed from consideration of the needs and interests of existing children to the case of potential children, is 'empty and misleading,' yet it is used to justify much regulatory activity in the context of reproduction.[306] He asserts that most regulation of reproductive activity cannot be defended on any legitimate basis. I have argued here that regulation is needed in order to safeguard reproductive autonomy, and while I am not prepared to go so far as to say that the interests of potential children are irrelevant to questions of ART regulation, I do have sympathy for Cohen's fundamental concern in the context of eligibility criteria for access to ART services. Indeed, I agree with his central argument that we lack a well-thought-out foundation for regulating reproduction. This is one of the most significant challenges we face in regulating ARTs. When the potential implications of ARTs first began to be contemplated, moral concerns were in the forefront, and regulation was justified on the basis of appeals to morality. Over time, and based on liberal arguments about the impermissibility of morals-based regulation in pluralistic societies, the justification for regulating has shifted toward regulation based on health, safety and individual and social welfare. But the substitution of welfare considerations for moral considerations seems to have occurred without sufficient attention to whether welfare-based justifications can do the work we want them to do. Perhaps this is one of the reasons why reproductive autonomy arguments are often met with resistance in the debates around ART law and policy. If appeals to welfare cannot justify regulation to limit autonomy-based arguments in favour to access to treatment, then how (if at all) can we limit individual autonomy?

B. Treatment costs, funding and access to ART treatment

Infertility treatment is expensive. The cost of a fresh embryo transfer cycle ranges from a high of over $12,000 in the US to $5,645 in Australia, with Canada ($8,500) and the UK ($6,534) falling between those two extremes.[307] In one study, the estimated costs of

---

[305] Jackson (n 112); I Glenn Cohen, 'Beyond Best Interests' (2012) 96 *Minnesota Law Review* 1187.
[306] Cohen (n 305).
[307] Georgina M Chambers *et al*, 'The Economic Impact of Assisted Reproductive Technology: A Review of Selected Developed Countries' (2009) 91 *Fertility and Sterility* 2281, 2288.

'successful outcomes' (defined as delivery, or ongoing pregnancy at the end of the study) were even higher, at $61,377 for a successful outcome following IVF treatment.[308] The cost of a successful outcome is of course highly dependent upon the type of treatment involved. For treatment cycles involving medication only, the cost estimate was $5,894, while for a successful outcome after IVF using donor eggs it was $72,642.[309] Another way of framing infertility treatment costs is to consider the cost per live birth. In the various jurisdictions under study here (based on 2003 data), the cost per live birth ranges from a low of $25,843 in Australia to a high of $41,132 in the US.[310]

Treatment costs can have an enormous influence on access to ARTs, as many treatment seekers are not in a position to pay thousands of dollars for treatment. As a result, the availability of insurance coverage or public funding for infertility treatment can have a substantial effect on access to ART services, and in many cases likely plays a decisive role in a woman's or couple's ability to pursue treatment. Canada, the US, the UK and Australia have all taken different approaches to funding ART treatment. In part, these distinctions reflect the differences in the healthcare systems in these jurisdictions,[311] but the variations reflect other factors as well, including treatment success rates and the relative novelty of ARTs as a medical treatment for infertility.

Insurance coverage for infertility treatment in the US is dealt with on a state-by-state basis. At present, 14 states have laws requiring insurers to provide or offer coverage for diagnosis and treatment of infertility.[312] Two of these states (California and Texas) require that coverage be offered; the remainder require that coverage be provided. Two states (California and New York) require offer of coverage (California) or coverage (New York) for all techniques except IVF.[313] Even in the states where coverage for infertility treatment is mandatory, there is significant variation as to what is covered. Some state statutes require coverage for IVF; others exclude IVF. Some state laws cover diagnostic procedures only, some cover a defined number of cycles, others are comprehensive.[314]

As noted in the previous section, some of the state statutes restrict insurance coverage to those who meet medical or other eligibility criteria. Arkansas law, for example, mandates coverage for those who have either a two-year history of unexplained infertility, or a medical diagnosis of infertility such as blocked or absent fallopian tubes (not due to

---

[308] Patricia Katz *et al*, 'Costs of Infertility Treatment: Results from an 18-month Prospective Cohort Study' (2011) 95 *Fertility and Sterility* 915. This is the first prospective study to 'examine costs across the full range of infertility treatments' (*ibid* 920).

[309] *Ibid*.

[310] In the UK, the cost per live birth was $40,364, and in Canada, the cost was $33,183 (Chambers *et al* (n 307) 2290). These amounts reflect 2006 USD.

[311] The healthcare systems of the various jurisdictions are discussed briefly in ch 4, section II.B. Australia, the UK and Canada all have universal public systems that cover most or all of the cost of many healthcare services. The US, by contrast, has a system in which most individuals are covered through insurance programs related to their employment.

[312] National Conference of State Legislatures, 'State Laws Related to Insurance Coverage for Infertility Treatment' (March 2012), at <www.ncsl.org/issues-research/health/insurance-coverage-for-infertility-laws.aspx>. Louisiana law prohibits insurers from excluding coverage for otherwise-covered medical conditions on the basis that the condition leads to infertility. The law does not mandate coverage of any ARTs (La Rev Stat Ann § 22:1036, Public Acts 2001, No 1045, §1).

[313] National Conference of State Legislatures (n 312). The NY statute also excludes GIFT and ZIFT.

[314] For a list of the states requiring some kind of insurance coverage and a description of what is covered in each state, see RESOLVE: The National Infertility Association, 'Insurance Coverage in Your State', at <www.resolve.org/family-building-options/insurance_coverage/state-coverage.html> (listing various types of health insurance laws covering infertility treatments in several states). See also Kindregan and McBrien (n 38); National Conference of State Legislatures (n 312).

voluntary sterilisation), endometriosis, DES exposure or male factors. The statute also limits coverage to treatment involving fertilisation of the patient's eggs with her spouse's sperm.[315] These requirements mean that single women and lesbians are not eligible for coverage, nor are women seeking treatment involving donor eggs.[316] Some state insurance statutes also limit access to coverage through specifying age limits for covered IVF procedures.[317] Thus although eligibility for *treatment* in the US is not restricted by state regulation, the limitation of insurance coverage to specific groups very likely has the effect of restricting eligibility in practice.

Canada's funding picture for infertility treatment, like that in the US, varies by jurisdiction. Although all Canadian jurisdictions cover investigative and diagnostic procedures related to infertility, until very recently only one provided funding for IVF, and only in very limited circumstances.[318] This is remarkable, in that Canada is one of the few jurisdictions with a publicly-funded healthcare system that excludes funding for ART treatment.[319] There has been some change in this picture: in August 2010, the Province of Québec amended its health insurance plan to cover the costs of three cycles of IVF and related procedures,[320] and in October 2010, the Province of Manitoba initiated a tax credit program to help families with some of the costs of fertility treatment.[321] An Expert Panel on Infertility and Adoption has recommended that the Ontario government follow Québec's lead and provide funding for assisted reproduction services.[322]

[315] Ark Stat Ann § 23-85-137, 23-86-118. In order for IVF to be covered, the couple must have been unable to conceive using less expensive treatments. Hawaii law includes these same conditions (Haw Rev Stat § 431-lOA-116.5(a) and 432.1-604), as does Maryland law (Md Code Ann, Ins § 15-810(d) (2010)).

[316] Similar rules are found in other states as well. For example, Texas law mandates insurance coverage only where the gametes used in treatment are the female patient's eggs and her husband's sperm, and where there is a history of infertility (patient and spouse) of 'at least 5 continuous years' or associated with endometriosis, DES exposure, blocked or absent tubes, or oligospermia (Tex Ins Code Ann §1366.005 (2005)). Connecticut law demands coverage where the couple is unable to conceive or sustain a pregnancy over a one-year period; it also specifies the maximum number of covered cycles of various ARTs (Conn Gen Stat §38a-536 (2010)).

[317] Conn Gen Stat §38a-536 (2010) (under 40); NJ Stat Ann §17:48-6xa (2010) (under 45); NY Consolidated Laws, Insurance, § 3221(k)(6); 4303(s) (between 21 and 44); RI Rhode Island General Laws (§ 27-18-30, 27-19-23, 27-20-20 and 27-41-33) (between 25 and 40).

[318] The Province of Ontario provides coverage for up to three cycles of IVF in cases where a woman's fallopian tubes are completely occluded. If a live birth is achieved after IVF treatment, another three cycles may be provided: see, eg, Sharon Ikonomidis and Bernard Dickens, 'Ontario's Decision to Defund In Vitro Fertilization Treatment Except for Women with Bilateral Fallopian Tube Damage' (1995) 21 *Canadian Public Policy* 379; Edward G Hughes and Mita Giacomini, 'Funding in Vitro Fertilization Treatment for Persistent Subfertility: the Pain and the Politics' (2001) 76 *Fertility and Sterility* 431.

[319] Laura Shanner and Jeffery Nisker, 'Bioethics for Clinicians: Assisted Reproductive Technologies' (2001) 164 *Canadian Medical Association Journal* 1589, 1591. See also Beverly Hanck and Katharina Böcker, 'Access to IVF with Reduced Multiple Birth Risks: A Public Health Strategy for Assisted Reproduction in Canada' (Infertility Awareness Association of Canada, 2005), at <www.iaac.ca/print/427>.

[320] An Act Respecting Clinical and Research Activities Relating to Assisted Procreation, RSQ, c A-5.01; Regulation to Amend the Regulation Respecting the Application of the Health Insurance Act, OC 645-2010, 7 July 2010. See also Santé et Services Sociaux Québec's website at <www.msss.gouv.qc.ca/en/sujets/santepub/assisted-procreation.php>; William Buckett, 'Assisted Reproductive Technologies: Moving Toward Universal Access: Québec Government to Provide Public Funding' (Infertility Awareness Association of Canada, 2010), at <www.iaac.ca/print/453>. Although Québec did not cover IVF treatment in the public healthcare system prior to August 2010, since 2002 it has allowed persons undergoing IVF treatment to claim a 30% refundable tax credit (Hanck and Böcker (n 319)).

[321] See, eg, 'News Release: New Fertility Treatment Tax Credit Takes Effect Oct. 1', *Province of Manitoba*, 1 October 2010, at <news.gov.mb.ca/news/index.html?archive=2010-10-01&item=9845>; 'Fertility Treatment Tax Credit', *Province of Manitoba*, at <residents.gov.mb.ca/reference.html?d=details&program_id=5060>.

[322] Ontario, Ministry of Children and Youth Services, Expert Panel on Infertility and Adoption, *Raising Expectations: Recommendations of the Expert Panel on Infertility and Adoption* (Summer 2009) 118–19. See also Nisker (n 10); Jennifer MacMillan, 'Report Calls on Ontario to Foot Fertility Bill', *Globe and Mail*

The funding picture for the rest of the country, at least for the foreseeable future, looks bleak. One province's refusal to cover a particular infertility treatment under its healthcare insurance plan was the subject of an unsuccessful Charter challenge.[323] Nova Scotia's denial of coverage for IVF and ICSI was initially challenged on the basis of sections 7 and 15 of the Charter.[324] Section 7 protects the right not to be deprived of life, liberty or security of the person except in accordance with the principles of fundamental justice. The basis of the section 7 claim was that the right to security of the person includes positive rights to healthcare services. The section 7 claim was given short shrift by the trial judge,[325] which has been the fate of most claims for healthcare funding (or other access to government assistance) made on the basis of section 7.[326]

The plaintiffs also challenged the denial of coverage on the basis that it violated their equality rights under section 15 of the Charter.[327] In order to bring their claim within section 15, the plaintiffs had to establish that infertility is a physical disability. The trial judge held that the government had not discriminated against the plaintiffs as infertile persons in declining to cover infertility treatment services; he therefore found it unnecessary to consider whether infertility amounts to a disability.[328] The Court of Appeal overturned the trial judge's decision, holding that infertility is a physical disability and that the province's failure to fund infertility treatment services created a discriminatory distinction between infertile and fertile persons, as those who are fertile receive full coverage for their reproduction-related healthcare needs. The Court concluded, however, that the exclusion of IVF and ICSI from coverage was saved by the justificatory provision of the Charter (section 1), in that it was related (and proportional) to the pressing objective

(Toronto, 26 August 2009), at <www.theglobeandmail.com/news/national/report-calls-on-ontario-to-foot-fertility-bill/article1264580/> (where a human rights complaint was made against the Ontario government alleging that the government's policy on funding infertility treatment is discriminatory).

[323] *Cameron v Nova Scotia (Attorney General)*, 204 NSR (2d) 1, 177 DLR (4th) 61 (1994) (NSCA), leave to appeal refused [1999] SCCA No 531.

[324] Canadian Charter of Rights and Freedoms, Part I of the Constitution Act, 1982, being Schedule B to the Canada Act 1982 (UK), 1982, c 11.

[325] And was not pursued in the Court of Appeal.

[326] See, eg, Helen Hershkoff, 'Positive Rights and State Constitutions: The Limits of Federal Rationality Review' (1999) 112 *Harvard Law Review* 1131; Diana Majury, 'The *Charter*, Equality Rights, and Women: Equivocation and Celebration' (2002) 40 *Osgoode Hall Law Journal* 297, 330–31. There are exceptions: see, eg, *Eldridge v British Columbia (AG)* [1997] 3 SCR 624, (1997) 151 DLR (4th) 577, where it was held that s 15 of the Charter was violated by British Columbia's failure to pay for sign language interpreters in the context of access to healthcare by deaf persons. See also *New Brunswick (Minister of Health and Community Services) v G (J)* [1999] 3 SCR 46, 216 NBR (2d) 25, where it was held that s 7 of the Charter required the government to provide state-funded counsel to a woman whose children the state sought to remove from the family home. Many scholars have argued in favour of finding positive rights in the Charter; they include Martha Jackman, 'Poor Rights: Using the *Charter* to Support Social Welfare Claims' (1993–94) 19 *Queen's Law Journal* 65; Martha Jackman, 'The Right to Participate in Health Care and Health Resource Allocation Decisions Under Section 7 of the Canadian Charter' (1995–96) 4(2) *Health Law Review* 3; Margot Young, 'Case Comment: Rights, the Homeless, and Social Change: Reflections on Victoria (City) v Adams (BCSC)' (Winter 2009/10) 164 *BC Studies* 103; Barbara Billingsley and Peter Carver, 'Sections 7 and 15(1) of the Charter and Access to the Public Purse: Evolution in the Law?' (2007) 36 *Supreme Court Law Review* 221.

[327] Section 15 of the Charter provides: '(1) Every individual is equal before and under the law and has the right to the equal protection and equal benefit of the law without discrimination and, in particular, without discrimination based on race, national or ethnic origin, colour, religion, sex, age or mental or physical disability. (2) Subsection (1) does not preclude any law, program or activity that has as its object the amelioration of conditions of disadvantaged individuals or groups including those that are disadvantaged because of race, national or ethnic origin, colour, religion, sex, age or mental or physical disability.'

[328] *Cameron v Nova Scotia (Attorney General)*, 172 NSR (2d) 227, 75 ACWS (3d) 219 (1997) (NSSC).

of delivering the best possible healthcare coverage in the context of limited financial resources.[329]

A few years after the decision in *Cameron v Nova Scotia (Attorney General)*, the Supreme Court of Canada heard *Auton (Guardian Ad Litem of) v British Columbia (Attorney General)*, another healthcare services case. In *Auton*, the denial of funding for a specific treatment for autism was challenged on the basis that it violated section 15 of the Charter.[330] The Supreme Court of Canada held that the denial of coverage for a 'non-core' medically necessary service does not amount to discrimination under section 15 of the Charter, as 'the [healthcare] legislative scheme does not promise that any Canadian will receive funding for all medically required treatment'; rather, it leaves non-core services to the discretion of the provinces.[331] Taken together with the Supreme Court's refusal to grant leave to appeal in the *Cameron* case, the decision in *Auton* suggests that any future section 15 claim to funding for infertility treatment will face an uphill battle.

In Australia, the costs of investigative, diagnostic and fertility treatment services are generally provided privately, and are covered under the Medicare rebate system[332] as well as by private insurance plans.[333] Coverage of ART treatment in Australia is very generous, with most of the costs of treatment being covered by Medicare.[334] There is currently no limit on the number of IVF or other ART treatment cycles for which reimbursement may be obtained. Pre-implantation genetic diagnosis is currently not covered by the public scheme, although one Australian IVF clinic has applied to the Government to request that a Medicare billing number be assigned for PGD.[335]

The NHS in the UK provides some funding for infertility treatment services, although the funding is not comprehensive and is in some cases subject to specific eligibility criteria.[336] In spite of efforts aimed at improving access to infertility treatment in the UK, it appears that progress has been slow. In 2004, the UK Government announced plans significantly to improve access to NHS-funded infertility treatment, in the wake of criticism about the inconsistent availability of public funding in various regions of the UK. The Government vowed to tackle what had come to be known as the 'postcode lottery' system, in which access to funding was readily available in some geographical areas and

---

[329] *Cameron v Nova Scotia (Attorney General)* (NSCA) (n 323).

[330] *Auton (Guardian Ad Litem of) v British Columbia (Attorney General)*, 2004 SCC 78, [2004] 3 SCR 657.

[331] *Ibid* para 35.

[332] Australian Government, Department of Health and Ageing, 'Medicare Benefits Schedule Book' (*Medicare Benefits Schedule*, July 2012), at <http://www.health.gov.au/internet/mbsonline/publishing.nsf/Content/700EA EBE8BC5D5FECA257A0F0017617F/$File/201207-MBS.pdf>. See also 'IVF Treatment Costs' (*Melbourne IVF*, 2012), at <www.mivf.com.au/costs/domesti.asp>, for a description of the costs of various infertility treatment procedures.

[333] See, eg, Private Health Insurance Ombudsman, 'Assisted Reproductive Services and Private Health Insurance' (March 2011), at <www.phio.org.au/downloads/file/factsandadvise/factsheet-assistedreproductiveservices.pdf>.

[334] Chambers *et al* (n 307). Additional Medicare rebates are available to those who have reached an annual threshold of out-of-pocket costs, after which Medicare will pay for 80% of the costs of additional services within that same year (Department of Health and Ageing, 'The Extended Medicare Safety Net' (January 2012), at <www.health.gov.au/internet/mbsonline/publishing.nsf/Content/Factsheet-EMSN-1_Jan_2012>; Georgina M Chambers, Maria T Ho and Elizabeth A Sullivan, 'Assisted Reproductive Technology Treatment Costs of a Live Birth: An Age-Stratified Cost–Outcome Study of Treatment in Australia' (2006) 184 *Medical Journal of Australia* 155).

[335] 'Medicare Rebate for Expensive IVF Treatment PGD Sought by Clinics', *Daily Telegraph* (Surrey Hills, 22 July 2011), at <www.dailytelegraph.com.au/news/national/medicare-rebate-for-ivf-treatment-pgd-sought-by-clinics/story-e6freuzr-1226100132291>.

[336] For a detailed discussion, see Jackson (n 6) 197–202.

completely unavailable in others,[337] by implementing an approach based on guidance published by the National Institute for Health and Clinical Excellence (NICE).[338] The NICE guidance called for the provision of three IVF cycles. The new system was to be in place by April 2005, and was to provide one free cycle of IVF to couples who had been trying to conceive for two years where the female partner was between 23 and 39 years of age.[339]

In September 2006, the British Fertility Society (BFS) published the results of a survey of assisted conception treatment providers in England in an attempt to determine the level of uptake of the NICE guidance by health authorities, and to elicit information about the eligibility criteria being applied by Primary Care Trusts (PCTs). The survey found that the vast majority (90 per cent) of responding IVF units were providing only one NHS-funded fresh IVF cycle. Further, half of these cycles were not actually fresh cycles, instead involving the use of embryos that had been cryopreserved following a fresh cycle.[340] Only three of the 37 centres that responded to the survey were providing two fresh cycles of IVF, and none was routinely providing three cycles. The survey results also indicated the application of a wide variety of eligibility criteria by IVF units, with over half of respondents indicating that they used the presence of a 'stable hetero-sexual relationship' as a criterion for selecting patients to receive NHS-funded IVF.[341] In June 2011, a report into NHS IVF provision was commissioned by an all-party Parliamentary group; its findings suggest that while there has been some improvement in the provision of publicly-funded IVF services since the BFS study was published, practice falls far short of full implementation of the NICE guidance. As of March 2011, 73 per cent of PCTs were offering either one or two funded IVF cycles, and only 27 per cent were offering the three cycles recommended by the NICE.[342] The Committee also found that PCTs continue to impose varied eligibility conditions.

Even where women or couples can access NHS-funded IVF treatment, waiting lists can pose a significant barrier. As reported by an NHS Expert Group, waiting lists for

---

[337] 'NHS to Offer One Free IVF Cycle', *BBC News* (25 February 2004), at <news.bbc.co.uk/1/hi/health/3516941.stm>; William L Ledger *et al*, 'The Costs to the NHS of Multiple Births After IVF Treatment in the UK' (2006) 113 *BJOG: An International Journal of Obstetrics and Gynaecology* 21.

[338] National Collaborating Centre for Women's and Children's Health, *Fertility: Assessment and Treatment for People with Fertility Problems CG11* (London, National Institute for Clinical Excellence, 2004). The guidance for IVF services was as follows (*ibid* 16): 'Couples in which the woman is aged 23–39 years at the time of treatment and who have an identified cause for their fertility problems (such as azoospermia or bilateral tubal occlusion) or who have infertility of at least 3 years' duration should be offered up to three stimulated cycles of in vitro fertilisation treatment.' The NICE guidance is currently being updated. The NICE released a draft for consultation in May 2012, recommending (in part) coverage for three full treatment cycles of IVF in women under age 40 who have not conceived after two years of regular unprotected intercourse. The guidance also makes clear that a full treatment cycle includes the transfer of any frozen remaining embryos from a stimulated IVF cycle (National Collaborating Centre for Women's and Children's Health, 'Draft for Stakeholder Consultation – Fertility: assessment and treatment for people with fertility problems (update)' (May 2012) 254, at <www.nice.org.uk/nicemedia/live/12157/59278/59278.pdf>).

[339] *Ibid.* This falls short of the NICE recommendations ('NICE Guidance, Shame About the Implementation' (25 February 2004) 247 *BioNews*, at <http://www.bionews.org.uk/page_11870.asp>).

[340] R Kennedy *et al*, 'Implementation of the NICE Guideline – Recommendations from the British Fertility Society for National Criteria for NHS Funding of Assisted Conception' (2006) 9 *Human Fertility* 181, 182. See also Clare Lewis-Jones, 'IVF: The Continuing Agony of Treatment by Postcode or Bank Balance' (21 April 2006) 355 *BioNews*, at <www.bionews.org.uk/page_37867.asp>.

[341] Kennedy *et al* (n 340) 183.

[342] All Party Parliamentary Group on Infertility, 'Holding Back the British IVF Revolution? A Report into NHS IVF Provision in the UK Today' (June 2011), at <www.garethjohnsonmp.co.uk/uimages/File/appg_IVF_report.pdf>.

NHS-funded treatment range from six months to over six years. As the Expert Group has noted, in light of the diminishing rates of treatment success in older women, 'Waiting lists affect clinical outcomes and cost effectiveness'.[343] Waiting lists for specific fertility services, in particular those involving donated gametes, have contributed significantly to the phenomenon of reproductive tourism. Shenfield's cross-border reproductive care study found that a large majority of patients who travel abroad to access infertility treatment do so in order to avoid legal restrictions on access in their home country, but legal reasons were cited by only 9.4 per cent of those travelling from the UK for fertility treatment.[344] Most UK residents who seek fertility treatment abroad do so because of difficulty (actual or perceived) in accessing treatment in the UK.[345]

i. Should we fund ART treatment?

Several arguments may be made in favour of funding ART treatment. As Philipa Mladovsky and Corinna Sorenson point out,[346] there are a number of factors to consider in determining whether treatment should be publicly funded. One is its cost effectiveness. Another rationale for funding treatment is the claim that infertility is a medical condition that creates a 'medical need'; decisions about funding should be made on that basis, as is the case for other medical treatments. It has also been argued that funding for IVF treatment should be provided on the basis that it is a human right, and that funding is needed to address health inequalities. It has been suggested that IVF treatment can increase the birth rate and reduce population aging, which is important in countries like Canada with a falling birth rate and an aging population.[347] Mladovsky and Sorenseon argue that no one framework should be used on its own to make decisions about funding;[348] as they explain:

> While clinical and economic considerations are likely to remain central to decision-making, this discussion has shown that they cannot be easily detangled from social, political, ethical, and even philosophical dimensions. Many concerns around the cost, efficacy, and safety of ART subtlety [*sic*] blur into broader and more complex questions about what it means in a given society to bear and produce children, or even about life itself. While the rationales for public funding presented here are often divergent, contradictory, overlapping, and inconclusive, taken together they provide guideposts which signal important issues for consideration and highlight where further research, action, and debate are needed.[349]

---

[343] Expert Group on Commissioning NHS Infertility Provision, *Interim Report of the Expert Group on Commissioning NHS Infertility Provision* 8 (Annex D) (Department of Health) 8, at <www.dh.gov.uk/prod_consum_dh/groups/dh_digitalassets/documents/digitalasset/dh_087133.pdf>.

[344] Shenfield *et al* (n 252) 1367.

[345] *Ibid* 1364, noting that 34% of UK residents who sought treatment outside the UK did so for this reason.

[346] Philipa Mladovsky and Corinna Sorenson, 'Public Financing of IVF: A Review of Policy Rationales' (2010) 18 *Health Care Analysis* 113.

[347] See, eg, Stijn Hoorens *et al*, 'Can Assisted Reproductive Technologies Help to Offset Population Ageing? An Assessment of the Demographic and Economic Impact of ART in Denmark and UK' (2007) 22 *Human Reproduction* 2471; Robert PS Jansen and Sandra K Dill, 'When and How to Welcome the Government to the Bedroom' (2009) 190(5) *Medical Journal of Australia* 232; Mark P Connolly, William Ledger and Maarten J Postma, 'Economics of Assisted Reproduction: Access to Fertility Treatments and Valuing Live Births in Economic Terms' (2010) 13 *Human Fertility* 13, 15–18. See also European Parliament Resolution of 21 February 2008 on the demographic future of Europe (2007/2156(INI)), s 26.

[348] Mladovsky and Sorenson (n 346) 124.

[349] *Ibid*.

The effect and significance of funding for ART treatment cannot be overstated. As is clear from the above discussion of treatment costs, the costs of ART treatment are highly variable, being highest by a significant margin in the US. The average gross cost of an IVF cycle as a percentage of disposable income in the US is 50 per cent, compared with approximately 35 per cent in Canada, 18–20 per cent in the UK and 10 per cent in Japan.[350] Research indicates that ART treatment utilisation rates increase where insurance coverage or other funding is available.[351] The European Society of Human Reproduction and Embryology estimates the 'Demand for ART treatment . . . as 1,500 couples per million population'.[352] Australia and Scandinavia come closest to meeting this level of utilisation, with Canada and the US having the lowest levels (only 24 per cent of demand is met in those countries).[353] Australia has one of the highest utilisation rates of ART worldwide,[354] and the reason for the high uptake appears to be closely related to the high level of treatment funding available in that country. The gross costs of an IVF cycle in Australia are markedly reduced by subsidisation – there is 'a 71% reduction in the cost of an ART cycle as a percentage of disposable income, from 19% before government subsidization to 6% after government subsidization'.[355] Recent research demonstrates that access to treatment within the US varies considerably among the states, with higher utilisation rates in states with mandatory insurance coverage.[356]

Given the effect of affordability of treatment on its utilisation, it is clear that eligibility restrictions on insurance coverage play a significant role in determining who can access treatment. But the availability of funding is not the only factor in access to treatment. Ahmad Hammoud and colleagues have studied ART utilisation in the US, and have found that low utilisation is correlated with low availability, lower education levels and less urbanisation, whereas 'higher income and education levels correlated positively with the levels of IVF utilization'.[357] These data correspond with other research showing that even in a state with mandatory insurance coverage (Massachusetts), ART services are principally used by highly-educated, wealthy Caucasians.[358] Tarun Jain and Mark Hornstein speculate that the reasons for the disparities might include 'lack of appropriate information, racial discrimination, lack of referrals from primary care physicians, lack of adequate insurance cover among lower socioeconomic groups and cultural bias against infertility treatment'.[359]

One of the key questions in considering whether treatment should be publicly funded is that of treatment efficacy. If the treatment is not of proven benefit, it ought not to be funded, particularly within a public healthcare system. In Canada, coverage for IVF has

[350] Chambers *et al* (n 307) 2289.
[351] See, eg, Tarun Jain, Bernard L Harlow and Mark D Hornstein, 'Insurance Coverage and Outcomes of In Vitro Fertilization' (2002) 347 *New England Journal of Medicine* 661; J Ryan Martin *et al*, 'Insurance Coverage and In Vitro Fertilization Outcomes: A US Perspective' (2011) 95 *Fertility and Sterility* 964.
[352] Chambers *et al* (n 307) 2285. This is considered to be a conservative estimate.
[353] *Ibid* 2286.
[354] Mark P Connolly, Stijn Hoorens and Georgina M Chambers, 'The Costs and Consequence of Assisted Reproductive Technology: An Economic Perspective' (2010) 16 *Human Reproduction Update* 603, 607.
[355] Chambers *et al* (n 307) 2288–89.
[356] Ahmad O Hammoud *et al*, 'In Vitro Fertilization Availability and Utilization in the United States: A Study of Demographic, Social, and Economic Factors' (2009) 91 *Fertility and Sterility* 1630.
[357] *Ibid* 1634.
[358] Tarun Jain and Mark D Hornstein, 'Disparities in Access to Infertility Services in a State with Mandated Insurance Coverage' (2005) 84 *Fertility and Sterility* 221, 222.
[359] *Ibid* 223. See also Victor Y Fujimoto *et al*, 'Proceedings from the Conference on Reproductive Problems in Women of Color' (2010) 94 *Fertility and Sterility* 7.

been extremely limited since the report of the Royal Commission on New Reproductive Technologies. The Commission took the view that the only evidence-based application of IVF was its use in women with bilaterally occluded fallopian tubes.[360] Since the time of the Royal Commission's report, IVF success rates have increased markedly, and the trend continues.[361] Although many questions remain about the best way to measure treatment efficacy in the case of IVF,[362] the available data suggest that IVF can be an effective treatment for many infertile women and couples, and that funding should not be limited to a narrow subset of infertility patients.

The efficacy of a treatment is not the only factor to consider in deciding whether it should be provided as part of a universal healthcare insurance plan, or whether it should be subject to a coverage mandate (in the US context). Even in the case of highly-effective treatments, it can be very difficult to convince governments to add to the list of health-care services for which they pay,[363] and at present, when world economies are not per-forming at their best, asking a government to fund a costly new treatment will certainly be met with resistance.

In the Canadian system in particular, physicians play a significant role in decision making about Medicare coverage, and it has been argued that one of the reasons that ART treatments are not funded in Canada is the fact that lobbying for coverage has not been a priority for Canadian physicians.[364] Physicians have, however, begun to be more vocal in attempting to secure public funding for IVF. One of the arguments on which physicians often rely is the claim that funding reduces multiple births, particularly if a single-embryo transfer (SET) policy is also put in place for funded treatment cycles.[365] Physicians claim that because of the high costs of IVF, it is difficult to persuade their patients to try SET in the absence of subsidised treatment. They also assert that many patients opt for less expensive but less well-controlled treatments such as fertility drugs alone.[366] It is well known that multiple births are costly to the system, and these costs may be reduced or avoided by implementing a policy of State-funded or subsidised treat-ment linked to SET. Together these mechanisms will help to reduce the multiple birth rate and save the system money in the long run.

---

[360] Royal Commission on New Reproductive Technologies (n 9) 526.

[361] Van Voorhis (n 14) 185. According to CDC data, in 2009, 23% of ART cycles produced a pregnancy (*2009 Assisted Reproductive Technology Success Rates* (n 3) 13); and when fresh donor eggs are used, success rates (defined as a live birth following embryo transfer) are around 50% (*ibid* 62).

[362] In their report, the CDC show six different measures for IVF success rates, all of which show slightly different rates of success (*ibid* 22). See also National Collaborating Centre for Women's and Children's Health (n 338) for a detailed discussion of the complexities involved in assessing IVF success rates.

[363] Colleen M Flood, Mark Stabile and Carolyn Tuohy, 'What Is In and Out of Medicare? Who Decides?' in Colleen M Flood (ed), *Just Medicare: What's In, What's Out, How We Decide* (Toronto, University of Toronto Press, 2006) 15, 31 (noting in particular the lack of enthusiasm for funding new technologies).

[364] Edward Hughes, 'Access to Effective Fertility Care in Canada' (2008) 30 *Journal of Obstetrics and Gynaecology Canada* 389.

[365] When Québec implemented its policy to fund IVF treatment, it also introduced regulations providing for SET, with limited exceptions and where the departure from SET is justified by the physician (Regulation Respecting Clinical Activities Related to Assisted Procreation, c A-5.01, r 1, s 17). See also Annie Janvier, Bridget Spelke and Keith J Barrington, 'The Epidemic of Multiple Gestations and Neonatal Intensive Care Unit Use: The Cost of Irresponsibility' (2011) 159 *Journal of Pediatrics* 409, 412.

[366] Hughes (n 364) 390; Jeff Nisker, 'Distributive Justice and Infertility Treatment in Canada' (2008) 30 *Journal of Obstetrics and Gynaecology Canada* 425; Jocelynn L Cook *et al*, 'Assisted Reproductive Technology-Related Multiple Births: Canada in an International Context' (2011) 33 *Journal of Obstetrics and Gynaecology Canada* 159 (noting that Canada's ART-related multiple pregnancy rate is among the highest seen in industri-alised countries; the twin rate is 28.8% and triplet rate 1.5% of all live births resulting from ART use (*ibid* 161)).

It has been pointed out that to focus on multiple birth rates in the absence of State funding for IVF is perhaps not the best approach, since the profession is in essence asking the government to pay to solve a problem that the profession is responsible for creating. There is no need to fund IVF to encourage SET; instead we could simply mandate SET.[367] This contention gives rise to a number of questions concerning regulation of ARTs. In considering whether ART regulation should be public (ie State-based) or private (based on professional guidelines or individual clinical judgement), I have argued that there is a role for both, and that the best approach to regulation will include a significant role for professional practice guidelines in addition to a public component. A regulatory scheme cannot and should not cover every minute detail related to clinical decision making between patient and provider. Some questions will always be left for professional judgement, and it is essential that any State-based regulatory approach respect the clinical judgement of professionals on such matters, or that public regulation provides sufficient flexibility to enable clinical judgement and physician–patient decision making.

There will of course be situations in which provider judgement leads to serious concerns, as in the case of Nadya Suleman, who gave birth to octuplets in January 2009, after having an IVF procedure in which 12 embryos were transferred to her uterus.[368] Public outcry over the case was intense, particularly after it became clear that Suleman was a single mother who already had six young children and was struggling to support her family. Predictably, one concern raised by many commentators was the lack of regulation of the fertility treatment industry in the US, the claim being that if a regulatory structure had been in place, the so-called 'octomom' case could not have arisen.[369] A great deal of the criticism was directed at Suleman herself for her 'selfish' choices, but also of concern was the notion that IVF would be made available to a woman in her situation – a single mother with several young children and dependent on social assistance.

Aside from the US, all of the jurisdictions under consideration here have put in place (or have attempted to put in place) a far more structured regulatory approach to ART treatment provision. None has adopted strict legal limits on the number of embryos that can be implanted in any given cycle, although in Australia the RTAC Code of Practice speaks to the importance of reducing the rate of ART-related multiple pregnancies.[370] At 11.7 per cent, Australia has the lowest twin rate per live birth following ART treatment by a considerable margin compared to the other three jurisdictions (Canada and the US both have a twin rate of 28.8 per cent, while the UK's twin rate is 23.5 per cent).[371] Australia also provides the most generous funding for IVF of all of these jurisdictions. It certainly seems that a case can be made that funding can affect the multiple birth rate. Together with the concern that a lack of funding creates incentives for patients to request that a higher numbers of embryos be transferred, it is arguable that the most effective way to prevent (or at least reduce the likelihood of) multiple births is to pay for or subsidise IVF treatment.[372]

---

[367] André Picard, 'When the State Funds IVF, the Cost is Too High for Everyone', *Globe and Mail* (Toronto, 11 May 2011), at <www.theglobeandmail.com/life/health-and-fitness/when-the-state-funds-ivf-the-cost-is-too-high-for-everyone/article624953/>.

[368] Madeira (n 206) 341–42; Robertson (n 23).

[369] Robertson (n 23).

[370] NHMRC Guidelines 2007 (n 56)

[371] Cook *et al* (n 366) 161.

[372] Sharon Kirkey, 'Fertility Doctors Back Efforts to Reduce Multiple IVF Births', *Edmonton Journal*, 4 May 2012, at <www.edmontonjournal.com/health/Fertility+doctors+back+efforts+reduce+multiple+births/6568170/story.html>.

Does respect for reproductive autonomy require funded ART treatment? I do not think we can conclude that respect for reproductive autonomy *requires* funding for IVF and related treatments. Reproductive autonomy, while an important interest, does not justify an entitlement to funding for ARTs, given all of the many healthcare needs that place demands on the finite resources of healthcare systems. Even in the context of reproductive health services alone, decisions about funding for ARTs must be weighed against the reproductive-autonomy based justifications for funding other services.

Unquestionably, though, the provision of funding for ART services (or an insurance mandate in the US) can improve one's ability to make meaningful reproductive choices. Given the extremely high cost of such treatment, it is likely that funding will often make the difference in terms of women or couples being able to exercise meaningful choice. Together with all of the other justifications for providing funding, it seems that funding treatment makes practical sense.

A cautionary note is necessary, however, as funding for IVF may be seen as a powerful acknowledgement (or even outright encouragement) that couples should try IVF to exhaust their options before deciding to remain voluntarily childless.[373] Many feminist scholars have raised concerns about the legitimacy of women's options around motherhood in a pronatalist context. While it is important to recognise the potential for such pressures to interfere with reproductive autonomy, in my view, we should not decline to fund ART services on the basis of speculative fears or on the assumption that in a pronatalist society, women's decisions to attempt conception using ARTs cannot be read as authentic exercises of reproductive autonomy.

---

[373] Concerns have been raised about Israeli policy on this front, the concern being that women feel unable to choose not to attempt conception using IVF (Larissa Remennick, 'Childless in the Land of Imperative Motherhood: Stigma and Coping Among Infertile Israeli Women' (2000) 43 *Sex Roles* 821; Daphna Birenbaum-Carmeli and Martha Dirnfeld, 'In Vitro Fertilisation Policy in Israel and Women's Perspectives: The More the Better?' (2008) 16(31) *Reproductive Health Matters* 182; Frida Simonstein, 'IVF Policies with Emphasis on Israeli Practices' (2010) 97 *Health Policy* 202). Israel is something of a special case, however, given the explicit pronatalist stance in that country.

9

Assisted Reproduction: Reproductive Materials and Reproductive Services and Parentage after ART Treatment

ASSISTED REPRODUCTIVE TECHNOLOGIES hold enormous promise for those who wish to procreate but are unable to do so for reasons of biology, sexual orientation or relationship status. They make possible family forms that are thought by some to undermine traditional ideas about the meaning of family and thereby threaten the very fabric of society. In order to mitigate these perceived dangers, or at least to reassure those who are concerned about the future of the family in an ART age, many jurisdictions have established regulatory regimes that restrict access to the technologies, based on either the identity of the treatment-seeker or the uses to which the technologies may be put.

As discussed in the previous chapter, legal regulation of ARTs clearly implicates reproductive autonomy. While many applications of ARTs involve invasive procedures and therefore have a bearing on women's bodily integrity, regulation itself does not directly engage women's interest in bodily integrity. This suggests that ART regulation, in general, falls outside the core of reproductive autonomy, and therefore does not demand the highest level of respect from the State. But as some regulatory decisions around ART use do have the potential to impact women's bodily integrity, regulation requires exceptional care and attention to women's interests.

The previous chapter considered the broad questions of governance and access to treatment; here I reflect on specific applications of ARTs, and on laws around parentage in the ART context. This chapter is concerned with legal issues related to the use of reproductive materials (gametes and embryos) and surrogacy services, as well as with laws dealing with the status of children born using reproductive materials or services provided by a party who will not be a parent of the child. The birth of a child is the aim of ART treatment and is the endpoint when treatment is successful. Given the various parties who might contribute to the conception of a child through providing reproductive materials or services, it is essential to have clear and efficient legal mechanisms for determining who is, and who is not, a parent. The law on parentage in the ART and surrogacy contexts is thus an important aspect of this chapter. In section V., I discuss the phenomenon of reproductive tourism, particularly in the surrogacy context, and through that lens consider the connections between reproductive autonomy and surrogacy and parentage laws.

Each of the topics explored in this chapter could merit its own book, and all have been canvassed at length in the literature. Although a book devoted to regulating reproduction would be incomplete without some consideration of these issues, they will be dealt with relatively briefly. The aim is not to be comprehensive but to highlight some key unresolved or contested issues in ART regulation, and to note their importance and complexity from a reproductive autonomy standpoint. In many of these areas, the reproductive autonomy analysis I adopt leads to answers similar to those arrived at by others who make autonomy-based arguments, particularly in terms of the obvious question about which choices people should be permitted to make. Where my reproductive autonomy argument differs is in relation to the claim that what is needed in order to safeguard reproductive autonomy is State action. This might take the form of (for example) passing legislation to clarify parental status in the ART and surrogacy contexts, or of oversight of surrogacy arrangements. As I argued in chapter eight, oversight or governance of assisted reproduction should be based on a mutually enforcing system involving elements of both professional regulation and State policy. I recognise the potential for State regulation to limit reproductive autonomy, and examples from many of the topics considered throughout this book illustrate that this concern is very real. But a contextualised account of reproductive autonomy reveals that other regulatory structures or approaches can equally limit reproductive autonomy, particularly in respect of those who are relatively less empowered due to existing inequalities. Though there is no way to ensure that regulatory decisions always respect reproductive autonomy, the governance structure I advocate includes government regulation premised upon an explicit mandate to respect the reproductive autonomy interests of the parties using ART services.

I. DONATED GAMETES IN ASSISTED REPRODUCTION

Gametes (sperm and oocytes) are essential elements in assisted reproduction, and their use gives rise to numerous legal and ethical issues. Primarily, the issues centre on the legal status of gametes and the extent to which the gamete donor (whether he or she is the person undergoing treatment or simply a donor) can control the gametes once they are outside of his or her body. Are gametes property? If not property, how are gametes characterised by the law? Another key issue is that of the implications for the non-patient gamete donor from the standpoint of the resulting child. When donor gametes are used, should the law permit the donor to remain anonymous? Does gamete donation carry with it the risk of parental obligations to genetically-related offspring? Or the promise of parental involvement in the child's life?[1]

A. Legal status of gametes

Although some ARTs can accurately be described as 'new', sperm donation and assisted insemination have been practised for well over 100 years.[2] It is noteworthy that even given the lengthy history of the practice, many legal questions remain unresolved. One

---

[1] Parentage in the ART context is considered in section IV. below.
[2] The first reported case of AI using donor gametes is the procedure performed by Dr Pancoast in 1884: see, eg, AT Gregoire and RC Mayer, 'The Impregnators' (1965) 16 *Fertility and Sterility* 130, citing a 1909 letter to the Editor of *The Medical World*. See also K R Daniels, 'To Give or Sell Human Gametes – The Interplay Between Pragmatics, Policy and Ethics' (2000) 26 *Journal of Medical Ethics* 206.

such question is that of the legal status of human gametes. In this section, I briefly consider this question. It should be noted that the cases generally refer to sperm rather than sperm and oocytes; in part this likely reflects the fact that oocytes have not been stored separately (until very recently, it was not possible to cryopreserve oocytes for later use; instead, embryos were created and stored).[3]

Historically the common law has taken the view that there is no property in the body. As Dickens and Cook note, the concept of property is a means of legally protecting 'objects or interests . . . that have value'.[4] The 'no property' rule has been challenged by contemporary medical and scientific developments that demonstrate that body parts (and perhaps by extension, whole bodies) do indeed have value – organs and tissues can be used for transplantation, several body parts (including the genetic information that can be derived from cells and tissues) can have enormous potential research and commercial value, and gametes can be used to create new human life. The value that is placed on human organs, cells and tissues has created challenges for the law governing assisted reproduction, many of which remain unresolved. On one view, gametes should be treated as property that may be disposed of as the 'owner' (or perhaps 'producer') sees fit. Those who oppose this view draw on concerns around commodification of the body and its parts, and assert that a property analysis is neither necessary for adequate protection of one's interests in one's gametes, nor desirable from an ethical standpoint.[5]

In early cases concerning the status of reproductive materials, while recognising the important interests that persons have in their own gametes (or in those of their now deceased spouse[6]), courts shied away from ascribing property interests. In the US, as in all of the other jurisdictions under consideration here, 'the law governing the legal status of sperm remains largely undeveloped'.[7] Although in general property law concepts have not been applied to sperm (in keeping with the rule that body parts are not property), there have been cases in which the interest in sperm has been held to be property-like. In *Hecht v Superior Court*,[8] William Kane had frozen several vials of sperm and bequeathed them to his female partner, Deborah Hecht. After his death, Mr Kane's grown children from his prior marriage (which had ended in divorce) sought to have the sperm destroyed. The California Court of Appeals held that Mr Kane had, 'at the time of his death, . . . an interest, in the nature of ownership, to the extent that he had decisionmaking authority

[3] Debra A Gook, 'History of Oocyte Cryopreservation' (2011) 23 *Reproductive Biomedicine Online* 281.

[4] Bernard M Dickens and Rebecca J Cook, 'The Legal Status of In Vitro Embryos' (2010) 111 *International Journal of Gynaecology and Obstetrics* 91, 91.

[5] See, eg, Margaret Jane Radin, 'Market-Inalienability' (1987) 100 *Harvard Law Review* 1849; Donna Dickenson, *Property in the Body: Feminist Perspectives* (Cambridge, Cambridge University Press, 2007); Sean Cordell *et al*, 'Lost Property? Legal Compensation for Destroyed Sperm: A Reflection and Comparison Drawing on UK and French Perspectives' (2011) 37 *Journal of Medical Ethics* 747.

[6] In *Paraplaix c le Centre d'Etudes et de Conservation de Sperme* (CECOS), JCP 1984 II 20321 Gaz Pal (2e sem) 560, the Court rejected an argument by the widow and parents of Mr Paraplaix that, as his heirs, they now owned his cryopreserved sperm. The Court did however order that the sperm be returned to Mme Paraplaix, on the basis that her deceased husband had intended that she would have access to it after his death. Dickens and Cook point out that the French legislature later reversed the decision (Dickens and Cook (n 4)). In the well-known Diane Blood case, the English Court of Appeal held that the HFEA was legally entitled to refuse Ms Blood's request for access to her deceased husband's sperm, as it had been obtained without his consent (*R (Blood) v Human Fertilisation and Embryology Authority* [1997] EWCA Civ 3092). The Court also held that the sperm could be released to Ms Blood for use outside of the UK.

[7] Charles P Kindregan Jr and Maureen McBrien, *Assisted Reproductive Technology: A Lawyer's Guide to Emerging Law and Science*, 2nd edn (Chicago, IL, American Bar Association, 2011) 83.

[8] *Hecht v Superior Court*, 20 Cal Rptr 2d 274 (Cal App 1993).

as to the use of his sperm for reproduction'[9], and that this interest was sufficiently property-like that the terms of Mr Kane's will as regards the disposition of his cryopreserved sperm could be upheld.

In the Australian case law, there is evidence of similar uncertainty – the general rule that there is no property in one's body or body parts seems to sit uneasily with the way in which sperm is used in assisted reproduction. Although the 'no property' rule has been averted to in the case law, there have been cases in which body parts or tissues have been considered property.[10] For the most part, the cases involve applications by women seeking permission to remove sperm from their deceased husband's body to attempt to conceive a child. In most cases, the applications have been granted. In some Australian states, specific written consent to posthumous use of sperm is required.[11] Some Australian courts have granted orders of possession to the widowed woman to allow her to take the frozen sperm to a jurisdiction where such consent is not required so that she can use the sperm in an attempt to conceive.[12]

Canadian case law around the legal status of gametes is sparse, but to date two Canadian lower courts have held that sperm may be treated as property. In the first case, a decision of the Alberta Court of Queen's Bench, the dispute centred on access and child support in relation to twins born via IVF.[13] The parents had an on-again, off-again sexual relationship. Although they had never been in a committed, long-term relationship, they had been lovers, and had remained friends after their sexual relationship ended. In 1998, AW donated sperm so that CC could attempt IVF. She

---

[9] *Ibid* para 4b.

[10] For a discussion of the authorities, see *Re H, AE* [2012] SASC 146.

[11] Australian Government, National Health and Medical Research Council, *Ethical Guidelines on the Use of Assisted Reproductive Technology in Clinical Practice and Research 2007* (Canberra, Commonwealth of Australia, 2007) ('NHMRC Guidelines') s 6.15 deals with posthumous use of gametes. The section permits such use, in limited circumstances. The primary concern is that the person whose gametes are sought to be used provided 'clearly expressed and witnessed directions consenting to the use of his or her gametes'. In addition, the prospective parent must receive counselling about the implications of this use of gametes, and the use must not 'diminish the fulfilment of the right of any child who may be born to knowledge of his or her biological parents'. Clinics are also instructed to ensure that the parties involved seek guidance from a clinical ethics committee and, where necessary, legal advice. Section 8.4 precludes clinics from storing gametes of a deceased or dying person, or person in a post-coma unresponsive state, in the absence of clearly expressed and witnessed directions consenting to the use of the person's gametes in such circumstances. Posthumous use of gametes is permitted pursuant to the Assisted Reproductive Treatment Act 2008 (Vic) s 46–48. It is prohibited by Directions Supporting the Western Australian Human Reproductive Technology Act 1991 (WA) (Western Australian Government Gazette, '*Human Reproductive Technology Act 1991*: Directions Given by the Commissioner of Health to Set the Standards of Practice Under the *Human Reproductive Technology Act 1991* on the advice of the Western Australia Reproductive Technology Council' (30 November 2004) no 201, 5417, 5435). Szoke discusses some of the cases permitting extraction of sperm from deceased men in Victoria and South Australia (Helen Szoke, 'Regulation of Assisted Reproductive Technology: The State of Play in Australia' in Ian Freckelton and Kerry Petersen (eds), *Controversies in Health Law* (Sydney, Federation Press, 1999) 240, 257).

[12] *Re the estate of the late Mark Edwards* [2011] NSWSC 478. In this case, sperm removed after Mr Edwards' death. The couple had been pursuing IVF treatment. The day before they were to go in and sign consent forms, Mr Edwards died in a workplace accident. A judge's order was sought (and granted) to remove sperm from his body. This was done and his widow then sought possession of the sperm so to export them and use them in a jurisdiction where that would be allowed (it would not be permitted in NSW because s 23(a) of the Assisted Reproduction Technology Act 2007 (NSW) requires written consent to posthumous use of gametes). The order was granted. See also *AB v Attorney-General for the State of Victoria* [2005] VSC 180; *YZ v Infertility Treatment Authority* [2005] VCAT 2655 (these reports are of the same case; the female applicant was allowed to take frozen sperm out of Victoria to seek IVF treatment, which would not have been allowed in Victoria); *Bazley v Wesley Monash IVF Pty Ltd* [2010] QSC 118 (frozen sperm are property).

[13] *C(C) v W(A)* [2005] ABQB 290, 50 Alta LR (4th) 61.

ultimately became pregnant with twins, and AW later successfully sought access to the twins.[14]

In addition to the access dispute, the parties raised the issue of the disposition of four remaining fertilised embryos. The embryos were cryopreserved and stored at an infertility treatment facility in Toronto. When the embryos were initially created, an informed consent form specifying disposition instructions was signed by both parties.[15] The embryos were later moved to a different storage facility and no further agreement as to disposition was made.[16] At the time of the application to vary the original access order, CC also sought the release of the remaining embryos. AW opposed her request and sought to prevent CC from using the embryos to attempt to conceive. Mr Justice Sanderman granted CC's request, stating that the sperm were provided to CC as 'an unqualified gift given in order to conceive children,' and held that both the sperm and the embryos created with them were her property, for her to do with as she wished.[17]

The second Canadian case to consider the legal nature of sperm involved a property dispute over stored sperm purchased by a lesbian couple who had used the sperm to conceive two children.[18] When the couple separated and their property was divided, several remaining straws of cryopreserved donor sperm were inadvertently left out of the property division.[19] One of the women (JCM) later sought to use some of the remaining sperm to conceive a child with her new partner; she offered to pay ANA for the sperm, but ANA instead asked that the remaining sperm be destroyed. The issue for the court was whether the sperm constituted property and, if so, how that property should be dealt with. Relying on Sanderman J's decision in *C(C) v W(A)* (and on the reasoning in *Yearworth v North Bristol NHS Trust*,[20] discussed below), Russell J held that the stored sperm were indeed property; accordingly, she ordered that they be divided equally between the parties.

In 2009, the English Court of Appeal had occasion to consider the question whether men have property interests in their cryopreserved sperm. In *Yearworth*, several men had frozen their sperm in advance of cancer therapy, as the treatment was likely to result in their infertility. The hospital's storage system failed, resulting in the thawing and, therefore, destruction of the men's sperm. The men sued the hospital for breach of its duty to take reasonable care of the sperm;[21] the hospital admitted the breach but denied liability on the basis that the loss of the sperm samples constituted neither 'personal injury' nor 'damage to property'. The Court of Appeal held that the men did have property interests in their stored sperm and that the claims in negligence and bailment could go forward for assessment of damages. The Court stated that 'developments in medical science now require a re-analysis of the common law's treatment of and approach to the issue of ownership of parts or products of a living human body'.[22]

The potential reach of the Court's decision in *Yearworth* is significant. Presumably the Court's reasoning extends to oocytes as well as sperm. If sperm and oocytes are

---

[14] He was also paying child support to CC.
[15] This information was provided to me by one of the parties.
[16] *Ibid.*
[17] *C(C) v W(A)* (n 13) paras 20–21.
[18] *JCM v ANA*, 2012 BCSC 584, 33 BCLR (5th) 140.
[19] *Ibid* para 6.
[20] *Yearworth v North Bristol NHS Trust* [2009] EWCA Civ 37, [2010] 1 QB 1.
[21] Their claims were for mental distress and/or psychiatric injury (*ibid*).
[22] *Ibid* para 45(a).

property (at least for purposes of a claim in negligence and bailment), are they also property for other purposes? If so, what limits can legitimately be placed on transactions involving sperm and oocytes? To what extent does the extension of property to body parts potentially impede a non-commmodification policy agenda?[23] If gametes are property, does the reasoning extend to embryos as well? And if it does, who has property in an embryo?

As Harmon and Laurie have pointed out, the Court did not elucidate a theoretical foundation for its conclusion that Mr Yearworth and his fellow litigants had an ownership interest in their sperm. As a result of this failure, 'we are left to wonder at the foundation and appropriateness of the Court's conclusion that the claimants rightly have a *property* interest in their body products or parts'.[24] The Court's declaration of the existence of a property right is based on the control granted to gamete donors over their gametes by the Human Fertilisation and Embryology Act 1990[25] (HFE Act 1990), and the need for a legal response to the challenges posed by the capability of current medical science and technology. But legitimate questions remain about whether property interests or rights are needed or desirable here.[26] In any case, the reach of the decision in *Yearworth* remains to be seen. In the meantime, several other issues related to the use of gametes in ART treatment require consideration.

B. Consent to use

Whether or not gametes are property, the development of the law has proceeded on the basis that individuals have important interests in deciding how their gametes will be used in the ART context. One important legal response to the challenges posed by ART and its use of gametes is the development of consent laws and policies that apply specifically in the context of assisted reproduction.[27]

The UK, Canada and most of the Australian states with ART-specific legislation have put in place elaborate and detailed consent provisions related to the use of gametes in ART treatment.[28] The consent process seeks to give gamete donors some ability to control the use of their reproductive material, and acknowledges how very important to most participants it is to be able to exert that control. The aim of the consent provisions is to ensure, in part at least, that reproductive autonomy of participants (including gamete donors) is protected.

[23] Shawn HE Harmon and Graeme T Laurie, '*Yearworth v North Bristol NHS Trust*: Property, Principles, Precedents and Paradigms' (2010) 69 *Cambridge Law Journal* 476.
[24] *Ibid* 486.
[25] See HFE Act 1990, Sch 3.
[26] Cordell *et al* (n 5). As Harmon and Laurie note ((n 23) 491), there is an increasing tendency on the part of the courts to recognise the importance of autonomy. They refer to a 'growing judicial affinity for a free-standing right to autnomy' (*ibid*). The reproductive technology context is one in which a right to autonomy could have extremely important implications; it remains to be seen if or how the common law will develop this idea.
[27] There are also equally detailed consent provisions relating to the use of embryos in ART treatment (see section II.B. below).
[28] HFE Act 1990, Sch 3; Human Reproductive Technology Act 1991 (WA), ss 22–24; Assisted Human Reproduction Act, SC 2004, c 2 (AHR Act), s 8; Assisted Human Reproduction (Section 8 Consent) Regulations, SOR/2007-137; Assisted Reproductive Technology Act 2007 (NSW), s 17; Assisted Reproductive Treatment Act 2008 (Vic), ss 20–24. The NHRMC Guidelines include detailed ethical guidance around consent (NHMRC Guidelines 2007 (n 11)).

In general, written informed consent is required before a person's gametes may be used in treatment, whether the gametes are to be used in his or her own (or his or her partner's) treatment, or in the treatment of other persons. Most of the relevant statutes or regulations contain details as to what information must be provided to participants and donors in the consent process, and also include detailed rules about how and when consent to the use of a person's gametes may be withdrawn. Some jurisdictions permit the withdrawal of consent by gamete donors even after the gametes have been combined with those of another person via fertilisation, meaning that withdrawal of consent may take place at any time until the embryo has been transferred to a woman's uterus or used in research.[29] Other jurisdictions permit consent to be varied or withdrawn until the gametes are used, without explicitly defining 'use'. Arguably, 'use' might include being used to create an embryo,[30] meaning that consent can no longer be withdrawn once sperm and oocytes have been combined. The New South Wales legislation explicitly provides that 'consent may be modified or revoked at any time up until: (a) in the case of a donated gamete – the gamete is placed in the body of a woman or an embryo is created using the gamete'.[31] Canada's consent provisions stipulate that where a donor's gametes are to be used to create an embryo for reproductive use by a third party (ie, not the donor or the donor's spouse or partner), the donor may withdraw consent (in writing) at any time until the third party has acknowledged in writing that the 'material has been designated for their reproductive use'.[32]

Consent norms are intimately tied to respect for autonomy, and in healthcare law in general, a great deal of attention has been paid to the need for informed consent and to the appropriate legal response to a failure to respect the right to consent.[33] As genetic and reproductive technologies have developed, issues of consent have been very much a focal point, and consent rules in these areas in particular have become exacting. It is worth considering whether the particularly strict rules around consent are needed and whether they do protect reproductive autonomy effectively. John Harris has argued that the requirement for explicit written consent in respect of donated sperm is 'over-precious' and not reflected in 'custom or practice'.[34] As he explains:

> Men are notorious for leaving their gametes behind in all sorts of places, some of which may well result in the creation of life. They do so almost always without all these requirements for opportunities for counselling, formal consent, and time for reflection . . . We normally accept that they have no say in the outcome one way or another.[35]

---

[29] This is true, eg, of the UK legislation (HFE Act 1990, Sch 3, s 4(2)) and in Victoria, Australia (Assisted Reproductive Treatment Act 2008 (Vic), s 20).

[30] Human Reproductive Technology Act 1991 (WA), s 22(4).

[31] Assisted Reproductive Technology Act 2007 (NSW), s 17(4)(a).

[32] Assisted Human Reproduction (Section 8 Consent) Regulations (n 28), s 5(2)(b). It is not entirely clear precisely when a third party would make this acknowledgement in writing (which is presumably part of the consent process in relation to ART treatment), but it would make sense that this acknowledgement would take place before the gametes are used to create an embryo. Otherwise, the recipients would be vulnerable to a withdrawal of consent even as ART treatment is underway.

[33] See discussion in ch 2, section I.D. See also Neil C Manson and Onora O'Neill, *Rethinking Informed Consent in Bioethics* (Cambridge, Cambridge University Press, 2007); Alasdair Maclean, *Autonomy, Informed Consent and Medical Law: A Relational Challenge* (Cambridge, Cambridge University Press, 2009); Sheila AM McLean, *Autonomy, Consent and the Law* (Abingdon, Routledge-Cavendish, 2010).

[34] John Harris, 'Rights and Reproductive Choice' in John Harris and Søren Holm (eds), *The Future of Human Reproduction: Ethics, Choice, and Regulation* (Oxford, Clarendon Press, 1998) 5, 18.

[35] *Ibid.*

Harris's point cannot be disputed, although it is arguable that some men do indeed care very much about how their gametes are used, and whether or not they have fathered children.[36] But I am not sure how far it takes us in answering the question of where to draw the boundaries around consent in the ART context. Surely men who deliberately participate in a sperm donor program (as distinct from those who 'leave their gametes behind' in less formal circumstances) do want to know how their sperm will be used and are concerned about the implications of such use. Perhaps a more accurate explanation for the perceived need for such strict consent rules has to do with reassuring the public that ARTs are being vigilantly supervised, and reassuring donors that their gametes 'will be used only in accordance with their wishes'.[37]

Certainly, rigorous consent requirements do protect the reproductive autonomy of the gamete donor. But what happens when the donor's reproductive autonomy conflicts with that of another donor or participant in treatment? In *Evans v Amicus Health Care & Others*,[38] the English and European courts considered the issue of withdrawal of consent to the use of an embryo by one of the progenitors. This issue will be discussed in more detail in section II.B. below (in the context of consent to the use of embryos), but it bears brief mention here as well. In *Evans*, the parties were being treated together, in that they each provided gametes for use in IVF. After the embryos had been created but before they had been transferred to Ms Evans' uterus, the male progenitor (Mr Johnston) withdrew his consent to the use of his gametes. Because of the wording of the withdrawal provisions, this meant that Ms Evans could not use the embryos, even though they represented her only chance at conceiving a genetically-related child. Given the implications for someone in Ms Evans' position, it is worth questioning whether the consent rules should be modified to allow for a greater range of options, including the option to waive the ability to withdraw consent in the future.[39] It is also worth asking, as Souzos, Sheldon and Hartshorne do, whether the same rules about withdrawal of consent should apply in cases of anonymous gamete donation as apply to a couple pursuing IVF treatment together with the aim of forming a family.[40]

Respect for reproductive autonomy in this context seems to be a zero-sum game. The reproductive autonomy interests of the parties cannot be reconciled. Honouring the autonomy interests of one party means that the other party's interests cannot be respected. In part this is a reflection of the fact that reproductive autonomy cannot answer all of the complex questions raised by assisted reproduction, but as I shall elaborate below, cases like *Evans* suggest that the issues do need to be canvassed by policy makers more fully than they have been to date. I have argued that reproductive autonomy needs to be viewed through a broad lens, and that we must look beyond consent in thinking about how to respect it. Although it does not demand a particular answer to the question of where the

---

[36] There is case law involving men who are denying parental responsibility (including responsibility for child support) when they have allegedly been deceived by women about the risk of conception, or where women have actively sought to become pregnant by saving sperm from a sexual encounter for later attempts at self-insemination: see, eg, *B(J) v J(C)*, 1994 CanLII 4733 (SKQB). The US case law is discussed in Sally Sheldon, '"Sperm Bandits", Birth Control Fraud and the Battle of the Sexes' (2001) 21 *Legal Studies* 460.

[37] Emily Jackson, *Regulating Reproduction: Law, Technology and Autonomy* (Oxford, Hart Publishing, 2001) 207–08.

[38] *Evans v Amicus Health Care Limited & Others* [2004] EWCA Civ 727, [2005] Fam 1; *Evans v The United Kingdom* (2007) 46 EHRR 34.

[39] Peter D Sozou, Sally Sheldon and Geraldine M Hartshorne, 'Consent agreements for Cryopreserved Embryos: The Case for Choice' (2010) 36 *Journal of Medical Ethics* 230.

[40] *Ibid* 232.

boundaries lie in terms of withdrawing consent to the use of gametes, respect for reproductive autonomy certainly demands thoughtful consideration of these questions.

C. Trade in gametes: payment and egg sharing

In Canada, the purchase and sale of gametes and embryos is prohibited;[41] gametes and embryos may only be donated altruistically. Not only are monetary transactions proscribed, exchanges in kind are also prohibited.[42] It is permissible under the AHR Act to reimburse donors for the expenses actually incurred in donating gametes or embryos, but the relevant section of the Act[43] is not currently in force, as regulations have not been developed. In the meantime, according to the (now defunct) Assisted Human Reproduction Canada (AHRC), until regulations are in place, donors may be reimbursed for their actual expenditures.[44]

Donor gametes are available in Canada to a limited degree. In spite of the ban on paid donation, gametes may be imported from other jurisdictions, even those in which payment to donors is permitted, by clinics that were 'grandfathered' under section 71 of the AHR Act.[45] In light of the fact that Canada currently has only one domestic sperm bank, and that bank has only 45 donors,[46] it seems fairly clear that the majority of donor sperm used in Canada are imported. Most of the sperm are likely imported from the US, meaning that the donor was almost certainly paid for the donation. Egg donation is different from sperm donation in multiple ways. The sperm that are imported into Canada are cryopreserved sperm coming from a sperm bank. There is no direct relationship between donor and recipients. Donated eggs, by contrast, are usually fresh, and the egg donation context more often involves some contact between the donor and recipient. From a legal perspective, this difference could prove significant. It seems that Canadian law permits Canadian women or couples to travel to the US to procure eggs for use in ART treatment, and many Canadian clinics apparently have referral arrangements with donor programs in the US.[47] But as one Canadian fertility lawyer has said, 'the legality of using an out-of-country service to help commit an act (paid egg donation) that is illegal in this country isn't quite so clear'.[48]

---

[41] AHR Act, s 7.

[42] *Ibid* s 7(4) ('In this section, "purchase" or "sell" includes to acquire or dispose of in exchange for property or services.').

[43] *Ibid* s 12.

[44] Assisted Human Reproduction Canada, 'Frequently Asked Questions: Can Sperm or Egg Donors Be Paid For Their Donation?' (2011), at <www.ahrc-pac.gc.ca/v2/faq/monitoringFAQ-surveillanceFAQ-eng.php#a10>.

[45] AHR Act, s 71, which provided: 'Notwithstanding sections 10 to 13, a person who undertakes a controlled activity at least once during the period of one year preceding the coming into force of those sections may subsequently, without a licence, undertake the controlled activity and use any premises required for that purpose until a day fixed by the regulations.' Thus, clinics or practitioners that imported gametes at least once in the year prior to 22 April 2004 were able to continue to do so during the currency of the licensing provisions of the AHR Act. This section was repealed in early 2012 (Jobs, Growth and Long-Term Prosperity Act, SC 2012, c 19, s 738).

[46] ReproMed, in Toronto, is the sole Canadian sperm bank. In January 2013, Repromed's catalogue listed 45 donors (ReproMed, 'Semen Donor Catalogue', at <www.repromed.ca/sperm_donor_catalogue>).

[47] Jessica Werb, 'A Good Egg is Hard to Find' (15 May 2008), at <www.straight.com/article-145554/a-good-egg-hard-find>.

[48] Alison Motluk, 'The Human Egg Trade: How Canada's Fertility Laws Are Failing Donors, Doctors, and Parents', *Walrus Magazine*, April 2010, at <www.walrusmagazine.com/articles/2010.04-health-the-human-egg-trade> (quoting Sherry Levitan).

The Canadian legal regime around ART treatment has a clear agenda of non-commercialisation; indeed, that is one of the guiding principles in the AHR Act.[49] Critics have begun to voice concerns about this approach on two fronts: the lack of availability of donor gametes in Canada, and the apparently flourishing black market in human eggs.[50] The response from those who oppose commercialisation is that the fact that payment for gametes is accepted practice in other jurisdictions does not imply that the practice is ethically sound.[51]

Payment for or commercial trading in human gametes and embryos is also illegal in Australia.[52] Reasonable expenses related to collection, storage and transport of gametes (and storage and transport of embryos once they have become excess ART embryos) may be paid, but 'valuable consideration' may not. Valuable consideration 'includes any inducement, discount or priority in the provision of a service to the person'.[53] Whether a black market in eggs has developed in Australia is less clear, but it does appear that Australian women often seek ART services in other jurisdictions in order to access donor gametes (and also to avoid the effect of the non-anonymity approach that has been adopted in Australia).[54]

The UK's gamete and embryo donation system is also premised on altruism,[55] although donors may be reimbursed for their reasonable expenses. These expenses must be claimed by donors and must relate directly to the donation process.[56] Sperm donors may be paid up to £35 per clinic visit, and egg donors may be compensated to a maximum of £750 per donation cycle.[57] Unlike the situation in either Canada or Australia, however, egg-sharing arrangements are permitted in the UK. The HFE Act 1990 prohibits the giving or receipt of 'money or other benefits . . . unless authorised by directions'.[58] The HFEA has issued directions specifying that 'Gamete donors may receive licensed

---

[49] AHR Act, s 2(f).

[50] See, eg, Motluk (n 48); Megan Ogilvie, 'Hatching Babies: Our Black Market in Human Eggs', *Toronto Star*, 21 November 2009, at <www.thestar.com/life/parent/2009/11/21/hatching_babies_our_black_market_in_human_eggs.html>; Natalie Fraser, 'The Black Market in Sperm and Eggs', *Lawyer's Weekly* (Markham, 30 April 2010) 16, at <www.lawyersweekly.ca/index.php?section=article&articleid=1156>.

[51] Werb (n 47), quoting Patricia Baird.

[52] Prohibition of Human Cloning for Reproduction Act 2002 (Cth), s 21. There is parallel legislation in all Australian jurisdictions except the Northern Territory (Human Reproductive Technology Act 1991 (WA), s 53Q; Human Cloning and Embryo Research Act 2004 (ACT), s 19; Human Cloning for Reproduction and Other Prohibited Practices Act 2003 (NSW), s 16; Human Cloning For Reproduction and Other Prohibited Practices Act 2003 (Tas), s 20; Prohibition of Human Cloning for Reproduction Act 2003 (SA), s 16; Research Involving Human Embryos and Prohibition of Human Cloning for Reproduction Act 2003 (Qld), s 17; Prohibition of Human Cloning for Reproduction Act 2008 (Vic), s 17).

[53] Prohibition of Human Cloning for Reproduction Act 2002 (Cth), s 21(3).

[54] 'Australian Mums Head Overseas to Find Egg Donors', *Sunday Telegraph* (Adelaide, 21 August 2010), at <www.adelaidenow.com.au/news/national/australian-mums-head-overseas-to-find-egg-donors/story-e6frea8c-1225908353524>.

[55] HFE Act 1990, s 12(1). The potential penalty upon conviction for this offence is up to six months' imprisonment, or a fine, or both. In Australia, by contrast, the maximum penalty is imprisonment for 15 years (Prohibition of Human Cloning for Reproduction Act 2002 (Cth), s 21(1)). Canada's AHR Act provides for a maximum penalty of a fine not exceeding $500,000, or a term of imprisonment not exceeding 10 years (AHR Act, s 60).

[56] Human Fertilisation and Embryology Authority, *Code of Practice*, 8th edn (London, HFEA, 2009 (revised April 2012)) para 13.3.

[57] *Ibid* para 13A. Donors may be paid in excess of these amounts if they have incurred actual expenses that exceed the amounts indicated (*ibid* para 13.4). Centres are required to keep records of all expenses claimed and reimbursements paid, including receipts that show excess expenses (*ibid* para 13.7).

[58] HFE Act 1990, s 12(1)(e).

services, such as treatment, . . . in return for supplying gametes for donation'.[59] Egg-sharing arrangements are permitted in relation to donating oocytes both for clinical use and for use in research. This move on the part of the HFEA followed its Sperm, Egg and Embryo Donation (SEED) review in 2005[60] and, not surprisingly, was controversial. Critics raised several concerns, including the potential pressure egg-sharing might place on IVF participants to share eggs, and its potential to undermine the current altruistic systems of donation of other body tissues and human organs. Another significant worry was the incentive such a program might create to over-stimulate participants in the program to secure a higher yield of oocytes from the treatment cycle, with the attendant increased risks of ovarian hyperstimulation syndrome (see further below).[61]

In the US, payment of compensation to donors is typical practice. There are no legal restrictions in place that limit or preclude the ability to pay compensation to gamete donors. Based on data from 2004, Debora Spar estimated the revenue from egg and sperm 'donation' to be over $112 million.[62] It is rare to hear of worries related to compensation for sperm donation within the market framework, but the payment practices surrounding egg donation have given rise to considerable unease.[63] The American Society for Reproductive Medicine (ASRM) has expressed the view that while financial compensation for oocyte donation (either for research purposes or for use in fertility treatment) is ethically justified, 'Total payments . . . in excess of $5,000 require justification and sums above $10,000 are not appropriate'.[64]

In jurisdictions where payment is prohibited, concerns centre on the potential denial of reproductive choice for couples who cannot conceive without donor gametes, and on the creation of an unregulated shadow market, where exploitation of potential donors and recipients is a very real possibility. In the US, by contrast, the focus of concern is on the potential exploitation of women who might donate oocytes, because the high levels of compensation available might lead women to donate eggs when they would not otherwise consider it, or because the promise of significant compensation might lead them to ignore the potential health risks involved in donating oocytes.[65]

---

[59] Human Fertilisation and Embryology Authority, 'Directions Given Under the Human Fertilisation and Embryology Act 1990 as amended: Gamete and Embryo Donation, Ref 0001, version 3' (2009) para 15, at <http://www.hfea.gov.uk/docs/Direction_0001_-_Gamete_and_Embryo_donation.pdf>.

[60] Human Fertilisation and Embryology Authority, 'SEED Report: A Report on the Human Fertilisation and Embryology Authority's Review of Sperm, Egg and Embryo Donation in the United Kingdom' (2005), at <www.hfea.gov.uk/docs/SEEDReport05.pdf>.

[61] *Ibid* 15–17. See also Boon Chin Heng, 'Egg Sharing in Return for Subsidized Fertility Treatment – Ethical Challenges and Pitfalls' (2008) 25 *Journal of Assisted Reproduction and Genetics* 159; Celia Roberts and Karen Throsby, 'Paid to Share: IVF Patients, Eggs and Stem Cell Research' (2008) 66 *Social Science & Medicine* 159.

[62] Debora L Spar, *The Baby Business: How Money, Science, and Politics Drive the Commerce of Conception* (Boston, MA, Harvard Business School Press, 2006) 3.

[63] See, eg, Mark V Sauer, 'Indecent Proposal: $5,000 is not "Reasonable Compensation" for Oocyte Donors' (1999) 71 *Fertility and Sterility* 7; Paul A Bergh, 'Indecent Proposal: $5,000 is not "Reasonable Compensation" for Oocyte Donors – A Reply' (1999) 71 *Fertility and Sterility* 9; Suzanne Holland, 'Contested Commodities at Both Ends of Life: Buying and Selling Gametes, Embryos, and Body Tissues' (2001) 11 *Kennedy Institute of Ethics Journal* 263; Sharon N Covington and William E Gibbons, 'What is Happening to the Price of Eggs?' (2007) 87 *Fertility and Sterility* 1001.

[64] American Society for Reproductive Medicine Ethics Committee, 'Financial Compensation of Oocyte Donors' (2007) 88 *Fertility and Sterility* 305, 305.

[65] A film produced in 2011 by the Center for Bioethics and Culture seeks to highlight this concern in particular. The film, called '*eggsploitation*', follows the stories of several oocyte donors who have suffered ill health that they attribute to their donation experiences. The strong suggestion is that the amounts these women were paid to donate oocytes played a significant role in their decision to do so. The film has also been made into an

Both prohibiting and permitting payment for gametes (or similar exchanges) can give rise to reproductive autonomy-related concerns. A policy that prohibits payment or gamete sharing might lead to a shortage of available gametes for use in ART treatment; this has potential implications for the reproductive autonomy of those who seek to use donated gametes. Where payment is permitted, the argument has been made that the autonomy of gamete donors is or may be compromised by the financial incentive.

The argument against commercial trade in gametes is made almost exclusively in relation to oocyte donation.[66] The claim is premised on the notion that donation is harmful (or at least potentially harmful) to women, given the increased risks of oocyte donation.[67] Oocyte donation typically gives rise to more concern, particularly for feminists, than sperm donation, for a number of reasons. First, the process of oocyte donation is extraordinarily onerous and significantly more risky in comparison to sperm donation. In order to donate eggs, multiple medical procedures are involved, including the use of medications to shut down the woman's natural menstrual cycle, followed by the administration of medications to stimulate the ovaries to produce multiple follicles (compared to the one follicle per cycle normally produced by the ovaries). Extraction of the oocytes requires a minor but invasive surgical procedure, whereby 'Mature oocytes are retrieved under ultrasound guidance by the insertion of a needle through the vagina'.[68] The ASRM Ethics Committee notes that it is 'estimated that oocyte donors spend 56 hours in the medical setting, undergoing interviews, counseling, and medical procedures related to the process'.[69]

Oocyte donation can involve significant risks, including unintended pregnancy (women who are donating oocytes must stop using hormonal contraceptives during the donation cycle) and possibly long-term risks to health and fertility.[70] The most serious risk is ovarian hyperstimulation syndrome (OHSS). Women undergoing ovarian stimulation may experience mild, moderate or severe OHSS. Mild OHSS symptoms include abdominal pain and bloating, while severe OHSS is manifested by significant rapid weight gain (10 pounds in three to five days), severe abdominal pain, shortness of breath, vomiting and diarrhoea.[71] In severe OHSS, women can experience serious complications, including renal insufficiency, ovarian rupture and thrombophlebitis.[72] In extremely rare cases, women have died as a result of these complications.[73]

---

e-book (Jennifer Lahl and Evan C Rosa, *Eggsploitation* (Pleasant Hill, CA, Center for Bioethics and Culture, 2012)).

[66] Although the same non-commodification arguments apply in relation to paid sperm donation (Daniels (n 2)).

[67] Non-commodification arguments are also made in this context, see, eg, Holland (n 63); Cynthia B Cohen, 'Selling Bits and Pieces of Humans to Make Babies: *The Gift of the Magi* Revisited' (1999) 24 *Journal of Medicine and Philosophy* 288; Donna Dickenson, 'Commodification of Human Tissue: Implications for Feminist and Development Ethics' (2002) 2 *Developing World Bioethics* 55.

[68] Robert Steinbrook, 'Egg Donation and Human Embryonic Stem-Cell Research' (2006) 354 *New England Journal of Medicine* 324.

[69] American Society for Reproductive Medicine Ethics Committee (n 64) 308.

[70] *Ibid* 306.

[71] Brooke Ellison and Jaymie Meliker, 'Assessing the Risk of Ovarian Hyperstimulation Syndrome in Egg Donation: Implications for Human Embryonic Stem Cell Research' (2011) 11(9) *American Journal of Bioethics* 22, 23.

[72] *Ibid.*

[73] *Ibid.*

The potential harms of oocyte donation are real, although arguably they have been overstated in the media and some of the literature. The risk of serious complications, including death, as a result of OHSS is extremely low, and it seems to be even lower in cases where the women providing oocytes are otherwise healthy.[74] It is important to emphasise that egg donation itself is not prohibited in Canada, Australia or the UK; only paid 'donation' is ruled out. The underlying assumption must be that the potential harm is a result of the financial aspect of the exchange, rather than the donation process itself. And while it makes intuitive sense that financial incentives (particularly significant financial incentives) might make the risks seem less important to potential donors, to the extent that the risk of exploitation exists, it is also present in the altruistic donation context.[75] There is a lot of speculation, but very little evidence about women's experiences as gamete providers, and almost no evidence to support a claim about exploitation. Indeed, recent research on women who participated in an egg-sharing program suggests that women do not view these transactions as exploitative, neither do they see the value of their oocytes in a manner that rules out the possibility of commercial exchange.[76] Importantly, the study suggests that women want to evaluate the options for themselves, which suggests that reproductive autonomy is not best protected by a blanket prohibition on commercial exchange.[77]

In view of the lack of evidence that gamete donation causes harm to the donors, an argument may be made that reproductive autonomy requires the State to take a position that at least permits the chance of gamete availability. For some individuals, ART treatment (and therefore procreation) will not be successful (or in some cases, even possible) without access to donor gametes. A reproductive autonomy analysis does not imply, however, that those who need donated gametes are entitled to obtain them, or that the State has an obligation to ensure their supply. There is clear potential for conflict here between the autonomy interests of potential donors and recipients, which cannot be resolved by an argument from reproductive autonomy. And though this analysis does demand that the State not rule out the availability of gametes, there is no good evidence that payment is in fact the key to increasing donation rates. The claim has been made that prohibiting paid donation results in limited availability of gametes,[78] and that the State therefore fails to respect reproductive autonomy by prohibiting paid donation. But in the absence of evidence that paid donation is the answer to increasing gamete availability, it is difficult to sustain the argument that restricting donation in this way fails to respect reproductive autonomy. As with many of the ART-related issues, it is essential that research into these issues proceed to help find answers to regulatory and policy dilemmas.

---

[74] *Ibid* 27–28.

[75] Anna Curtis, 'Giving 'Til It Hurts: Egg Donation and the Costs of Altruism' (2010) 22(2) *Feminist Formations* 80.

[76] Erica Haimes, Ken Taylor and Ilke Turkmendag, 'Eggs, Ethics and Exploitation? Investigating Women's Experiences of an Egg Sharing Scheme' (2012) 34 *Sociology of Health & Illness* 1199

[77] *Ibid.*

[78] John A Robertson, 'Commerce and Regulation in the Assisted Reproduction Industry' (2007) 85 *Texas Law Review* 665, 687–88.

D. Gamete donor anonymity

Historically, the practice of donor insemination has been shrouded in secrecy. Not only have the donor and recipients typically not been known to one another, the literature even describes one case where the woman who was inseminated with donor sperm was not aware of the procedure, which took place while she was under anaesthetic.[79]

Early in the history of ART treatment, donor anonymity was typical, based either on legislation that explicitly protected the confidentiality of donor information,[80] or simply through a practice of preserving secrecy.[81] Many parents did not reveal the circumstances of their conception to their donor-conceived children.[82] The secret nature of donor conception was largely related to concerns around the uncertain legal (and ethical) status of the practice, as well as the stigma around male infertility.[83] It was also believed that to reveal to a child that he or she was donor-conceived would be detrimental to family relations.[84] But researchers have claimed that it is better for children to be made aware of the fact that they are donor-conceived,[85] and that secrecy harms rather than helps family relationships.[86] And, over time, as donor-conceived people have begun to express their views, it has become clear that for the most part, those born through the use of donated gametes have a strong preference for being able to learn the identity of their genetic parents, much in the same way as children who have been adopted wish to learn about their genetic families.[87]

Within the last 10 years, the trend has been to shift away from laws that shield donor anonymity, and several jurisdictions that initially permitted secrecy have altered their laws to permit disclosure of donor identity to offspring (and in some cases, to other parties as well).[88] Although none of these laws mandates parental disclosure to donor-conceived

---

[79] The woman herself was never informed about the insemination, although her husband was told later. The story of how Dr William Pancoast inseminated a female patient is reported in many accounts: see, eg, David Plotz, 'The Rise of the Smart Sperm Shopper', *Slate Magazine*, 21 April 2001, at <www.slate.com/id/104633/>; Robin Marantz Henig, *Pandora's Baby: How the First Test Tube Babies Sparked the Reproductive Revolution* (Boston, MA, Houghton Mifflin, 2004) 26–27.

[80] See eg, AHR Act, s 15 (repealed, SC 2012, c 19, s 720); HFE Act 1990, s 31 (this section has been amended by the HFE Act 2008, s 24).

[81] Eric Blyth and Lucy Frith, 'Donor-Conceived People's Access to Genetic and Biographical History: An Analysis of Provisions in Different Jurisdictions Permitting Disclosure of Donor Identity' (2009) 23 *International Journal of Law, Policy and the Family* 174.

[82] And many still do not do so, see, eg, Maggie Kirkman, 'Parents' Contributions to the Narrative Identity of Offspring of Donor-assisted Conception' (2003) 57 *Social Science & Medicine* 2229.

[83] See, eg, Ken R Daniels and Karyn Taylor, 'Secrecy and Openness in Donor Insemination' (1993) 12 *Politics and the Life Sciences* 155; Anna Rumball and Vivienne Adair, 'Telling the Story: Parents' Scripts for Donor Offspring' (1999) 14 *Human Reproduction* 1392; Naomi Cahn, 'Necessary Subjects: The Need for a Mandatory National Donor Gamete Databank' (2009) 12 *DePaul Journal of Health Care Law* 203.

[84] See, eg, SC Klock, 'The Controversy Surrounding Disclosure Among Donor Gamete Recipients' (1997) 14 *Journal of Assisted Reproduction and Genetics* 378; F Shenfield, 'Privacy Versus Disclosure in Gamete Donation: A Clash of Interest, of Duties, or an Exercise in Responsibility?' (1997) 14 *Journal of Assisted Reproduction and Genetics* 371.

[85] Kirkman (n 82) 2240.

[86] See, eg, Daniels and Taylor (n 83); Annette Baran and Reuben Pannor, *Lethal Secrets: The Psychology of Donor Insemination: Problems and Solutions*, 2nd edn (Amistad, Triadoption Publications, 1993).

[87] See, eg, DR Beeson, PK Jennings and W Kramer, 'Offspring Searching for their Sperm Donors: How Family Type Shapes the Process' (2011) 26 *Human Reproduction* 2415.

[88] Blyth and Frith (n 81) 188.

children,[89] several regulators recommend that parents do disclose this information to their children.[90]

Pursuant to the HFE Act 1990, donor identity and other information about donors and those receiving treatment was held by the HFEA in a confidential register.[91] The Act permitted individual applications to the HFEA for disclosure of information – in essence to inform the applicant that 'someone other than the parent of the applicant would or might . . . be a parent of the applicant' (in other words, to inform the applicant that he or she is or might be a child of a gamete donor).[92] The Act did not permit the disclosure of donor identity to either the woman or a couple being treated with donor gametes, or to the child born through the use of donor gametes.[93] In 2002, the issue of donor anonymity reached the English High Court in the context of a claim by two donor-conceived persons: Joanna Rose (then 29 years old) and a six-year-old girl (EM). Their argument was that the HFE Act 1990, by permitting donor anonymity, breached their rights to 'respect for private and family life' as guaranteed by Article 8(1) of the European Convention on Human Rights.[94] In the time between the commencement of the human rights claim and the hearing of the case, the UK Department of Health initiated a consultation on the question of what information ought to be made available to those conceived through the use of donor gametes. The Court therefore decided that many of the issues should be 'stood over pending ministerial decisions on what if any government action was appropriate'.[95] The Court did, however, go on to consider whether the question of access to identifying information about the donor used in their conception engaged the claimants' Article 8 rights. Ultimately, the Court held that Article 8 ECHR was indeed engaged, stating that

> [i]t is . . . entirely understandable that A.I.D. children [*sic*]should wish to know about their origins and in particular to learn what they can about their biological father or, in the case, of egg donation, their biological mother. The extent to which this matters will vary from individual to individual. In some instances, as in the case of Joanna Rose, the information will be of massive importance. I do not find this at all surprising bearing in mind the lessons that have been learned from adoption. A human being is a human being whatever the circumstances of his conception and an A.I.D. child [*sic*] is entitled to establish a picture of his identity as much as anyone else.[96]

---

[89] See, eg, Lucy Frith, 'Gamete Donation and Anonymity: The Ethical and Legal Debate' (2001) 16 *Human Reproduction* 818.

[90] Human Fertilisation and Embryology Authority, 'HFEA Welcomes the Removal of Donor Anonymity' (2004), at <www.hfea.gov.uk/786.html>; Government of Western Australia, Department of Health, *Talking to Children about Donor Conception* (Western Australian Reproductive Technology Council, 2011), at <www.rtc.org.au/publications/docs/Talking_to_Children.pdf>.

[91] HFE Act 1990, s 31.

[92] Donor offspring could also apply to the HFEA for information about whether they might be related to a potential spouse (*ibid* s 31(4).

[93] HFE Act 1990, s 31(3)–(5). Section 31(4) permitted the HFEA to provide only the information required by the regulations, and s 31(5) provided as follows: 'Regulations cannot require the Authority to give any information as to the identity of a person whose gametes have been used or from whom an embryo has been taken if a person to whom a licence applied was provided with the information at a time when the Authority could not have been required to give information of the kind in question.'

[94] European Convention on Human Rights and Fundamental Freedoms (ECHR) 1950, Art 8(1), which provides: 'Everyone has the right to respect for his private and family life, his home and his correspondence.'

[95] *Rose and Another v Secretary of State for Health* [2002] EWHC 1593 (Admin), [2002] 2 FLR 962, para 16.

[96] *Ibid* para 47.

The end result of the Government consultation was the bringing into force of Regulations[97] which made mandatory the disclosure of identifying information about the sperm, egg or embryo donor upon request by a person conceived as a result of egg, sperm or embryo donation.[98] Though welcomed by many, this change has not been uncontroversial, and some have argued that the move to a non-anonymous donation system has led to a crisis in donation rates.[99] Concerns have been voiced about other potential negative effects as well, including the 'pressure to accept donors with sub-optimal characteristics'[100] and the growth of an Internet-based market through which prospective parents may obtain donor semen.[101]

Australia's four states with statutes regulating ART treatment have now all moved to a non-anonymous gamete donation system. Victoria was the first to do so; its 1995 legislation contained provisions permitting donor-conceived persons to access identifying information about their biological parents.[102] Western Australia made a significant change to its law in 2004. Prior to the adoption of the 2004 amendments, offspring could obtain only non-identifying information about their progenitors. Now, donor offspring, upon reaching the age of 16 and undergoing 'approved counselling', will be entitled to access indentifying information.[103] New South Wales adopted an open information

---

[97] Human Fertilisation and Embryology Authority (Disclosure of Donor Information) Regulations 2004 (SI 2004/1511).

[98] *Ibid* reg 2(3). The requirement relates only to information provided to clinics on or after 1 April 2005. These provisions have since been overtaken by further legislative changes (HFE Act 1990, ss 31ZA–31ZE). Donors who provided gametes between 1 August 1991 (the date from which the HFEA has records) and 1 April 2005, and who wish to become identifiable to offspring, may re-register with the clinic at which they donated, or through the HFEA. Those who provided gametes prior to 1 August 1991 can register with UK DonorLink, an organisation which maintains a voluntary contact register.

[99] Ilke Turkmendag, Robert Dingwall and Thérèse Murphy, 'The Removal of Donor Anonymity in the UK: The Silencing of Claims by Would-Be Parents' (2008) 22 *International Journal of Law, Policy and the Family* 283; Olga Craig, 'Where Have All the Donors Gone?', *Telegraph*, 1 May 2006, at <www.telegraph.co.uk/news/uknews/3338979/Where-have-all-the-donors-gone.html>. But see Eric Blyth and Lucy Frith, 'The UK's Gamete Donor Crisis – A Critical Analysis' (2008) 28 *Critical Social Policy* 74 (arguing that the claims that the donor gamete shortage is a result of the removal of donor anonymity cannot be sustained on the basis of the statistics).

[100] Turkmendag, Dingwall and Murphy (n 99) 284.

[101] *Ibid*. See also Craig (n 99).

[102] Infertility Treatment Act 1995 (Vic), s 77. The Act also permitted a donor to apply to receive information about any person born as a result of the use of the donor's gametes (s 76). The new Victorian legislation continues the policy of non-anonymity, although the information is now maintained in a Central Register kept by the Victorian Registrar of Births, Deaths and Marriages (Assisted Reproductive Treatment Act 2008 (Vic), Pt 6). Section 56 governs applications for disclosure of information from the Central Register; s 59 provides that disclosure of identifying information is mandatory upon the application of a donor-conceived person who is an adult, or who is a child whose parents have consented to the application or in respect of whom a counsellor has advised the Registrar that the child is sufficiently mature to understand the consequences of the disclosure. Mandatory disclosure applies only to gametes donated after 31 December 1997, although for gametes donated between 1 July 1988 and 31 December 1997, identifying information may be disclosed with the donor's consent.

[103] Human Reproductive Technology Act 1991 (WA), s 49(2d). The provisions do not apply retroactively, so where the gamete donation took place prior to 1 December 2004, offspring would be permitted to obtain identifying information only if the donor consents to the release of that information, or, more remarkably, where the donation was made prior to 1 December 2004, 'but the Commissioner of Health is satisfied that there is clear evidence that the donor was informed that disclosure of identifying information was likely should there be a future change in the legislation' (Western Australia Reproductive Technology Council, 'Information for Clinics on the Proclamation of the Recent Amendments to the Human Reproductive Technology Act 1991' (29 November 2004), at <www.rtc.org.au/clinics/docs/Information_for_Clinics_on_Proclamation.pdf>).

policy in its statute, which came into force in 2010.[104] Finally, South Australia, though it initially legislated to protect donor anonymity, has also put an end to donor anonymity.[105] As Eric Blyth notes, the change is made indirectly, through the interaction of statutory provisions and national ethics guidelines.[106]

In the US gamete donation practice has traditionally protected the confidentiality of donor information, and while a few states have laws that might permit access to donor records in limited circumstances, no state requires disclosure of donor identity to those who are donor-conceived.[107] Some sperm banks offer 'open donor programs'[108] that permit the possibility of future contact between donor and offspring, but the prevalent practice remains anonymous donation.[109] Regulation of sperm banks and gamete donation generally is almost non-existent, and a thriving marketplace has grown to cater to both research and clinical ART practice.[110]

In Canada, as with much of the ART regulatory picture, it is unclear whether a policy stance protecting donor anonymity is permissible. The AHR Act (as originally passed) prohibited the disclosure of identifying information without the consent of the donor. The section that mandated anonymity absent consent has been repealed, as have all of the sections of the Act concerning information collection and privacy. There are no

---

[104] Assisted Reproductive Technology Act 2007 (NSW), ss 33–40; Assisted Reproductive Technology Regulation 2009 (NSW), Regs 12–16. The provisions permit the parents of a donor-conceived child to receive non-identifying information about the donor. The donor may also obtain non-identifying information (ie sex, year of birth) about any children born through the use of his or her donated gametes. A donor-conceived person aged 18 or older is entitled to obtain identifying information about the donor, including the name and date of birth of the donor.

[105] Donor privacy was protected by the imposition of a penalty of $5,000 or imprisonment for a maximum of six months for unauthorised disclosure of donor identity (Reproductive Technology Act 1988 (SA), s 18(1)).

[106] Eric Blyth, 'Donor Anonymity to Bite the Dust in South Australia' (6 December 2010) 587 *BioNews*, at <www.bionews.org.uk/page_81599.asp>. Briefly, s 15 of the Assisted Reproductive Treatment Act 1988 (SA) permits the Minister for Health to establish a donor conception register. If such a register is kept, it must include the names of the donor, recipient of the donated gametes or embryos and any child born as a result of the donated materials (s 15(2)). Regulation 8(2) of the Assisted Reproductive Treatment Regulations 2010 (SA), imports a requirement of compliance with the NHMRC Guidelines as a condition of registration for ART providers. In turn, the NHMRC Guidelines provide that donor gametes may be used only where 'the donor has consented to the release of identifying information about himself or herself to the persons conceived using his or her gametes' (NHMRC Guidelines 2007 (n 11) s 6.1).

[107] Naomi R Cahn, *Test Tube Families: Why the Fertility Market Needs Legal Regulation* (New York, New York University Press, 2009) 115. Cahn notes that donor anonymity is protected in the contractual arrangements entered into between clinics, donors and recipients. She also notes that there are no reported cases involving children seeking to learn the identity of a donor parent.

[108] See, eg, California Cryobank, 'Open Donor Program', at <www.cryobank.com/How-It-Works/Choosing-Your-Donor/Open-Donor-Program/>.

[109] See American Society for Reproductive Medicine Ethics Committee, 'Interests, Obligations, and Rights of the Donor in Gamete Donation' (2009) 91 *Fertility and Sterility* 22, 24. The Ethics Committee notes that the traditional approach is 'slowly changing' (*ibid* 27).

[110] See, eg, Thomas K Sylvester, 'The Case Against Sperm Donor Anonymity', at <www.donorsiblingregistry.com/sites/default/files/images/docs/legal.pdf>. Sylvester claims (*ibid* 8): 'It wasn't until 2005 that the federal Food and Drug Administration even required sperm banks to test semen for HIV and other communicable diseases. These FDA regulations also require minimal record-keeping to prevent the spread of disease, though in a way that protects donor anonymity. Aside from these limited requirements, sperm banks are free to operate as they choose. There are no legal limits on how often a sperm bank may sell the same man's sperm, raising the specter of incest between half-siblings unaware of their consanguinity. No records are kept on how many children are born as a result of donor insemination (the common estimate of 30,000 DI births a year is based on a twenty-year-old report). Professional associations offer various recommendations and guidelines, but compliance is optional.'

provincial laws on point – even in Québec, where legislation has been passed, donor anonymity is not addressed.[111]

Canada currently has no law in place either to permit or to prohibit access to identifying information about gamete donors. A group of litigants hopes that this may soon change – in 2011, a British Columbia Court ruled[112] that the Province's Adoption Act violates the equality provisions of the Canadian Charter of Rights and Freedoms[113] because it does not give the same rights to information to donor-conceived persons as it grants to those who have been adopted.[114] The relevant legislation, together with its associated regulations, requires the creation and preservation of records relating to the identity and social and medical history of the biological parents of adopted children, and gives adopted persons the right to access the information upon reaching the age of 19. In addition, the provisions allow adopted persons to compare records as to the identity of their biological parents to ensure that they are not related to a potential marriage partner. Because there is no equivalent provision in British Columbia law to allow donor-conceived persons to learn the identity of their biological parent(s), the Court held that British Columbia law discriminates against donor-conceived persons on the basis of the manner in which they were conceived. The Court accordingly declared the impugned provisions 'of no force or effect,' although the declaration of invalidity was suspended for 15 months from the date of the judgment in order to give the Province time to develop an appropriate legislative response without prejudicing the interests of those who benefit from the existing law. The Court also granted a permanent injunction, 'prohibiting the destruction, disposal, redaction or transfer out of B.C. of Gamete Donor Records in British Columbia'.[115] In effect, the ruling prohibited a policy of donor anonymity in British Columbia. The Province successfully appealed the decision, and Pratten has sought leave to appeal to the Supreme Court of Canada.[116]

As noted earlier, most donated gametes used in Canada are imported from the US (in the case of sperm) or involve US oocyte donors. Most of these programs allow anonymous donation, and there are no rules that would prohibit it there. Should the Canadian courts ultimately reach a conclusion such as that of the British Columbia Supreme Court in *Pratten*, the ability of Canadian providers to continue to use sperm from jurisdictions where anonymity is the norm (ie where Canadian law cannot be complied with) will be in question. Legislators would then have to decide whether to include a rule that gametes can be imported only where the circumstances of the donation comply with local law.[117]

---

[111] Québec's legislation does not address the issue of donor anonymity, but it is clear from information found on the Department of Health website that the practice is to use anonymous donors (Santé et Services sociaux Québec, 'Assisted Procreation: Frequently Asked Questions' (2010, at <www.msss.gouv.qc.ca/en/sujets/santepub/faq_procreation.php>).

[112] *Pratten v British Columbia (Attorney General)*, 2011 BCSC 656, [2011] BCJ No 931.

[113] Canadian Charter of Rights and Freedoms, Part I of the Constitution Act, 1982, being Schedule B to the Canada Act 1982 (UK), 1982, c 11.

[114] Adoption Act, RSBC 1996, c 5, ss 6, 8, 9, 32, 48, 56, 58–71; Adoption Regulation, BC Reg 291/96, ss 4, 19–24.

[115] *Pratten v British Columbia* (n 112) para 335(c).

[116] *Pratten v British Columbia (Attorney-General)* 2012 BCCA 480. The Court of Appeal held that the impugned provisions are valid pursuant to s 15(2) of the Charter, as an affirmative action program, and that s 7 of the Charter does not 'guarantee a positive right to "know one's past".' (*Ibid* para 7).

[117] Eric Blyth and Marilyn Cranshaw, 'Countdown Begins for Ending Donor Anonymity in British Columbia: Lessons For Us All?' (6 June 2011) 610 *BioNews*, at <www.bionews.org.uk/page_96105.asp>. Blyth and Cranshaw note that this is the case in the UK, and argue that it is the approach that should be adopted in Canada as well.

What does a reproductive autonomy analysis say about donor anonymity? As in the case of donor payment or compensation, the argument has been made that regimes that mandate disclosure of donor identity fail properly to respect reproductive autonomy because they discourage participation in donor programs and thereby create shortages in the availability of donor gametes.[118] The accuracy of this claim has been disputed,[119] but even if it is the case that gametes are less available as a result of rules that preclude anonymous donation, does a policy of mandatory identity disclosure fail to respect reproductive autonomy?

My argument about the meaning of reproductive autonomy suggests that while reproductive autonomy is an extremely important interest that demands respect from the State, it is somewhat diminished in strength in relation to concerns that do not implicate women's bodily integrity. The ability (or inability) to use donor gametes does not threaten women's bodily integrity and, as such, reproductive autonomy may have to give way to other interests in this context. One such interest might be the interest of the donor-conceived individual to learn about his or her biological origins.

This is in some respects a difficult argument as it prioritises the interests of a not-yet-conceived potential child over those of the potential parents. As Glenn Cohen has argued, the use of the 'best interests of the resulting child' test where there is (as yet) no child whose interests merit protection, is problematic in the reproductive regulation context.[120] Cohen's argument relies on Derek Parfit's identification of the 'non-identity' problem and his discussion of non-person affecting harms.[121] As he explains,

> whenever a proposed intervention will itself determine whether a particular child will come into existence, child-welfare arguments premised on that child's welfare are problematic. So long as a child will *not* be provided a 'life not worth living,' the child cannot be said to be harmed when its counterfactual was not existing, or by having a different child (genetically speaking) substituted for it.[122]

I agree with Cohen that the best interests approach might not be appropriate as a justification for regulation, at least in so far as some ART-related questions are concerned.[123] But in the context of donor anonymity rules, distinct considerations apply. It is indeed the case that those whose interests are protected by requiring disclosure of donor identity do not yet exist when their prospective parents make the decision to use donor gametes. From a practical standpoint, though, there is no way to protect the interests of the people who are conceived with the use of donor gametes other than by protecting or considering these interests in advance. And the empirical evidence suggests that these interests do warrant protection.[124] As there is no other way to protect the interests of

---

[118]   Above (n 99).

[119]   Blyth and Frith (n 99).

[120]   I Glenn Cohen, 'Regulating Reproduction: The Problem with Best Interests' (2011) 96 *Minnesota Law Review* 423; I Glenn Cohen, 'Response: Rethinking Sperm-Donor Anonymity: Of Changed Selves, Nonidentity, and One-Night Stands' (2012) 100 *Georgetown Law Journal* 431.

[121]   Derek Parfit, *Reasons and Persons* (Oxford, Clarendon Press, 1987).

[122]   Cohen, 'Response' (n 120) 435.

[123]   As I explain in ch 8, section V.A.i., I particularly agree that access to ART treatment should not be limited on the basis of welfare considerations where there may never be a child whose welfare is in issue.

[124]   See, eg, Beeson, Jennings and Kramer (n 87); Cahn (n 107); Frith (n 89); Naomi Cahn, 'The New Kinship' (2012) 100 *Georgetown Law Journal* 367. There is also literature suggesting that at least some donors would be interested in and would benefit from the ability to learn about the children that have been conceived using their gametes: see, eg, Jennifer Speirs, 'Semen Donors' Curiosity about Donor Offspring and the Barriers to Their Knowing' (2012) 15 *Human Fertility* 89.

these actual, existing persons, it may be that regulation has to proceed even if it cannot be justified on the basis that failure to regulate causes harm to a specific identifiable individual at the time the regulation affects behaviour.

A full discussion of the 'best interests' argument is beyond the scope of this project, as is full review and analysis of the other potential interests that might fall to be considered in relation to donor anonymity. But it is necessary to note that reproductive autonomy, while important, is not the only consideration in ART regulation, and to point out circumstances in which the interests of others might also play an important role in our decisions about how to regulate. Cohen is quite right that we need carefully to consider the basis upon which we might regulate around donor anonymity, but I do not share his view that we cannot regulate to prohibit donor anonymity.

The use of known donors itself gives rise to another important autonomy-related issue, and that is the possibility that the donor will seek to play a role in the life of the child conceived using his or her gametes. This is of particular concern for lesbian-led families, as courts have been prepared on occasion to grant parental status or access rights to men who have donated sperm to a lesbian couple.[125] While this concern does not necessarily imply that respect for reproductive autonomy demands that women and couples must have the option of using anonymously donated gametes, it does demand that clear parentage rules be put in place. Parentage rules are discussed in more detail in section IV. below.

II. EMBRYOS AND ASSISTED REPRODUCTION

A. Status of the embryo

The scientific or medical definition of an embryo is not contentious – 'embryo' means the products of conception from conception to the fetal stage.[126] But what (if anything) can the scientific definition of an embryo tell us about its moral or legal status?

i. Moral status of the embryo

The status of the embryo has long been a matter of debate and disagreement among ethicists and theologians. It is an intractable problem, not amenable to resolution, and I do not propose to dwell on it here. But the question of the status of the embryo and the importance of its human potentiality has driven much of the debate around permissible uses of embryos in ART practice and in research. So although the discussion of moral status is brief (because it need not do more than set out the competing claims), it is necessary as it highlights themes that underlie so much of what follows.

Few issues have provoked more debate in recent history than the question of the moral status of the embryo. Concerns about this question have been present since the dawn of IVF, and played a significant role in government inquiries into and early regulation of

---

[125] Kindregan and McBrien (n 7) 47–8; Angela Cameron, Vanessa Gruben and Fiona Kelly, 'De-anonymising Sperm Donors in Canada: Some Doubts and Directions' (2010) 26 *Canadian Journal of Family Law* 95.

[126] Which is generally said to begin after eight weeks' gestation (JK Findlay *et al*, 'Human Embryo: A Biological Definition' (2007) 22 *Human Reproduction* 905, 910).

assisted reproduction.[127] Critics of IVF and embryo research have long been concerned that these practices will increasingly lead to a lack of regard for the special status of the embryo.[128] Even many who support (or at least do not oppose) ARTs and embryo research[129] adopt the view that embryos, because of their potential to develop into persons, have a unique moral status and therefore require special consideration.[130]

As Michael Sandel has explained, 'There are three possible ways of conceiving the moral status of the embryo: as a thing, as a person, or as something in between'.[131] Although there is a wide variety of views, Sandel's last category – 'something in between' – best captures the view most take of the human embryo. While few are prepared to argue that a human embryo is a thing, most are also not prepared to equate an embryo with a person.[132] The prevailing view as to embryo status (at least in so far as policy on embryo research and IVF is concerned) may be put fairly simply: although human embryos are distinct from other human tissues (and accordingly deserve more respect than other human tissues), they are not persons and cannot command the respect due to persons.[133] As in the case of the status of the fetus, the idea that embryos require unique treatment in law and policy is based largely on a gradualist perspective of embryonic development, wherein increasing respect is owed to the embryo as its stage of development (and its moral worth) progresses. To be sure, those who believe that the embryo is a person from the moment of conception fervently contest this position, but it does seem to reflect the weight of opinion.[134]

ii. Legal status of the embryo

Like gametes, embryos have long occupied uncertain legal terrain. What, in law, is an embryo? Is it property? A person? Or something in between? If property, to whom does it belong? If a person, how are its rights and interests conceptualised? And how do those

---

[127] Warnock Committee, *Report of the Committee of Inquiry into Human Fertilisation and Embryology* (Cmnd 9314, 1984); Royal Commission on New Reproductive Technologies, *Proceed with Care: Final Report of the Royal Commission on New Reproductive Technologies*, vol 2 (Ottawa, Supply and Services Canada, 1993) 631–38; New York State Task Force on Life and the Law, *Assisted Reproductive Technologies: Analysis and Recommendations for Public Policy* (New York, New York State Task Force on Life and the Law, 1998) 95–117; President's Council on Bioethics, *Reproduction and Responsibility: The Regulation of New Biotechnologies* (Washington, DC, The President's Council on Bioethics, 2004) 123–27.

[128] See, eg, Marian D Damewood, 'Editorial: Ethical Implications of a New Application of Preimplantation Diagnosis' (2001) 285 *Journal of the American Medical Association* 3143; James J McCartney, 'Embryonic Stem Cell Research and Respect for Human Life: Philosophical and Legal Reflections' (2002) 65 *Albany Law Review* 597.

[129] Even that which destroys embryos, such as stem-cell research.

[130] For detailed consideration of the moral status of the embryo, see Carson Strong, 'The Moral Status of Preembryos, Embryos, Fetuses, and Infants' (1997) 22 *Journal of Medicine and Philosophy* 457; Bonnie Steinbock, *Life Before Birth: The Moral and Legal Status of Embryos and Fetuses*, 2nd edn (New York, Oxford University Press, 2011).

[131] Michael J Sandel, 'The Ethical Implications of Human Cloning' (2005) 48 *Perspectives in Biology and Medicine* 241, 245.

[132] But see Jan Deckers, 'Why Current UK Legislation on Embryo Research is Immoral. How the Argument From Lack of Qualities and the Argument from Potentiality Have Been Applied and Why They Should be Rejected' (2005) 19 *Bioethics* 251, 265–70. Deckers argues that embryos have moral status from the beginning of the fertilisation process by virtue of their membership in the human species.

[133] See, eg, Kathryn Ehrich, Clare Williams and Bobbie Farsides, 'The Embryo as Moral Work Object: PGD/IVF Staff Views and Experiences' (2008) 30 *Sociology of Health & Illness* 772, 773–74.

[134] *Ibid.*

rights weigh up against those of its 'progenitors'? If an embryo is neither property nor a person in law, what is it?

As discussed in chapter five, a fetus is not a legal person.[135] Instead, it is generally conceived of, legally speaking, as a part of the woman in whose body it exists. This has implications for our understanding of the legal status of an embryo. If a fetus (which is closer in time and in development to an infant than is an embryo), is not a person then it is difficult to see how an embryo could be. One important distinction in the ART treatment context is that the embryo exists outside of the woman's body, meaning that it can be handled and manipulated without infringing upon a woman's bodily integrity. Thus, calling an in vitro embryo a person does not have identical implications to applying that label to an embryo or fetus in utero. That said, the legal status of the embryo has profound implications in terms of how embryos may be treated, including the uses to which embryos may be put, the need for consent to those uses, whether (and how) embryos can be disposed of.

Several US courts have addressed the question of the legal status of the embryo, albeit not from the perspective of the interests of the embryo itself. In general, the question arises in the context of disputes over the disposition of embryos upon separation of the progenitors. Most American courts have taken the view that the embryo is neither property nor a person,[136] but occupies an intermediate category between the two.[137] This permits the court to deal with the issues from the perspective that the embryo deserves 'special respect' due to its unique potential to become a human person.[138]

Most recently, a number of US state legislatures have sought to grant legal personhood to embryos. These statutes have important implications for reproductive regulation in general, in part because the statutes are often very ambiguous and their full implications are uncertain.[139] To date, none of the so-called 'personhood' laws has been implemented successfully.[140]

B. Consent to use

As in the case of gametes, consent is a cardinal principle in ART practice involving the use of embryos. But when it comes to consent to the use of embryos, the question of

---

[135] See ch 5, section I.

[136] In *Evans v United Kingdom* (n 38), one of the questions before the European Court of Human Rights was whether the embryo has a right to life pursuant to Art 2 ECHR. Referring to its decision in *Vo v France* (2005) 40 EHRR 12, the Court held that in the absence of consensus on the question of when life begins, the issue falls within the 'margin of appreciation' afforded to Member States. As English law does not grant legal status to the embryo, the Court held that the embryo has no right to life pursuant to Art 2 ECHR. See *ibid* paras 54, 56.

[137] See also Margaret Davies and Ngaire Naffine, *Are Persons Property? Legal Debates About Property and Personality* (Dartmouth, Ashgate, 2001).

[138] Charles P Kindregan Jr and Maureen McBrien, 'Embryo Donation: Unresolved Legal Issues in the Transfer of Surplus Cryopreserved Embryos' (2004) 49 *Villanova Law Review* 169, 187–88.

[139] I Glenn Cohen and Jonathan F Will, 'Mississippi's Ambiguous "Personhood" Amendment', *New York Times*, 31 October 2011, at <www.nytimes.com/2011/10/31/opinion/mississippis-ambiguous-personhood-amendment.html?emc=eta1>.

[140] See, eg, Laura Bassett, 'Oklahoma Personhood Measure Struck Down By Supreme Court', *Huffington Post*, 30 April 2012, at <www.huffingtonpost.com/2012/04/30/oklahoma-personhood-fetal-personhood-bill_n_1465657.html?utm_hp_ref=email_share>. Louisiana law grants embryos the status of 'juridical persons' and prohibits their intentional destruction (La Rev Stat Ann §§ 9:121–9:135); the only use that may be made of excess cryopreserved embryos is 'adoption' by a married couple.

whose consent is necessary and sufficient becomes more complex. Where the embryo has been created for the use of a couple seeking ART treatment, the issues are reasonably straightforward as long as the couple's own gametes have been used. But if donated gametes are used, the question of consent becomes less clear.

Different jurisdictions have adopted different approaches to legal rules in this context. In the UK, the HFE Act permits gamete donors to withdraw their consent at any point until the embryo has been used, with 'use' meaning that the embryo has been transferred to a woman's uterus or used in research.[141] Australia's statutory jurisdictions in general provide that consent to the use of an embryo requires consent from both of the gamete providers.[142] The NHMRC Guidelines refer to the need to respect the right of gamete and embryo donors to withdraw or vary their consent at any time,[143] although in the case of gamete donors, the ability to withdraw is limited to the time up to fertilisation,[144] and in the case of embryo donors, until the embryo is transferred to a woman's uterus.[145] In Canada, the Consent Regulations stipulate that in the case of an embryo created for the personal use of an individual who has no spouse or common law partner at the time of embryo creation, the only party who must provide consent to the use of that embryo is the individual.[146] This is the case regardless of the source of the gametes used to create the embryo. Where an embryo is created for the use of a couple (married or in a common law relationship), both members of the couple must provide consent to the use of the embryo (again, regardless of the source of the gametes used in creating the embryo).[147]

The very clearly-delineated consent rules initially outlined in the UK have been largely retained in the 2008 amendments to the HFE Act 1990, although modified slightly in the wake of a high-profile legal battle.[148] Natallie Evans and her fiancé (Howard Johnston) elected to cryopreserve several embryos using their own gametes after learning that Ms Evans had ovarian cancer.[149] Ms Evans' cancer treatment required the removal of her ovaries, meaning that she would no longer be able to produce eggs and therefore would not be able to have genetically-related children in the absence of cryopreserved eggs or embryos. Because cryopreservation of embryos was at the time (and remains) a safer option in success rate terms than cryopreservation of oocytes, and because the clinic could not in any event freeze oocytes, Ms Evans and Mr Johnston were offered the option of creating and freezing embryos.[150] They were both informed that each of them would retain the ability to withdraw their consent to the continued storage and/or use of the embryos at any point until the embryos had actually been transferred to Ms Evans' uterus. When Ms Evans expressed some concern about the fate of the embryos and her only chance at genetic parenthood should the couple decide to split up, Mr Johnston

---

[141] HFE Act 1990, Sch 3, s 4.
[142] Human Reproductive Technology Act 1991 (WA), s 22(e); Assisted Reproductive Technology Act 2007 (NSW), s 19; Assisted Reproductive Treatment Act 2008 (Vic), s 16(2).
[143] NHMRC Guidelines 2007 (n 11) s 9.6.
[144] *Ibid* s 6.14.
[145] *Ibid* s 7.3.
[146] Assisted Human Reproduction (Section 8 Consent) Regulations (n 28), ss 10, 12.
[147] *Ibid.*
[148] The amendments provide that where one gamete donor withdraws consent to continued storage of embryos, the embryos may continue to be stored for a period of 12 months (HFE Act 2008, Sch 3, s 7).
[149] *Evans v Amicus Healthcare Limited & Others* (n 38). The information in this paragraph is drawn from the reasons of the Court of Appeal.
[150] See, eg, Gook (n 3).

assured her that they would remain together. After Ms Evans underwent cancer therapy she was advised to wait for two years before attempting pregnancy with the cryopreserved embryos. Before IVF treatment could be commenced, the relationship broke down and the couple decided to split. Mr Johnston then notified the fertility clinic where the embryos were stored that he wished to withdraw his consent. The clinic, in turn, notified Ms Evans that consent had been withdrawn and that the embryos would have to be destroyed. Ms Evans, wishing to preserve her only chance at genetic parenthood, sought a ruling from the Court allowing her to use the embryos in spite of Mr Johnston's withdrawal of consent. She also challenged the UK legislation on the basis that it infringed her rights under the European Convention on Human Rights.[151]

Ms Evans was unsuccessful before the domestic courts. That the HFE Act 1990 was interpreted as giving Mr Johnston the right to withdraw or vary his consent up until the point at which the embryo had been used was no surprise, given the clear statutory language.[152] After her domestic claim failed, Ms Evans advanced a claim before the European Court of Human Rights, asserting that the consent provisions in the HFE Act 1990 violated the European Convention on Human Rights.[153] Her primary contention was that the Act, in permitting the variation or withdrawal of consent by a gamete donor even after the creation of embryos, precluded her from exercising her Article 8 ECHR rights to respect for her private and family life.[154] Her human rights claim also failed.

All of the judges involved in adjudicating Ms Evans' claim expressed great sympathy for her situation, as have most commentators who have written about the case. There is clearly potential for considerable unfairness in situations like that faced by Ms Evans. Some have suggested that this means the consent provisions should be revised to prevent similar outcomes in the future.[155] Those who argue that the consent provisions are appropriately tailored note that while Ms Evans' case certainly evokes sympathy, it is not possible to justify a legal response that would permit a woman in her position essentially to force a man to become a father against his will.[156]

The sentiment that respect for reproductive autonomy precludes forcing people to become genetic parents is consistent with the US cases that have dealt with embryo disputes;[157] as several commentators have remarked, the most predictable outcome in such cases is one that sees the party wishing to avoid procreation being successful most

---

[151] *Evans v United Kingdom* (n 38).

[152] As Wall J explained: 'In my judgment, this is a simple point, and another issue of fact. The language of the Act is clear, and in the context of this case, "use" can only mean the transfer into either claimant. In my judgment, therefore, none of the frozen embryos in this case has been "used in providing treatment services" within Schedule 3 paragraph 4(2) and there is no impediment to Mr Johnston . . . withdrawing [his] consent on this ground.' (*Evans v Amicus Healthcare Limited & Others* [2003] EWHC 2161 (Fam) para 165)

[153] *Evans v United Kingdom* (n 38).

[154] *Ibid.* Ms Evans also claimed that the consent provisions violated the embryos' right to life, under Art 2 ECHR.

[155] Souzo *et al* (n 39); Heather Draper, 'Gametes, Consent and Points of No Return' (2007) 10 *Human Fertility* 105; Anne Donchin, 'Toward a Gender-Sensitive Assisted Reproduction Policy' (2009) 23 *Bioethics* 28.

[156] For a discussion of the American embryo dispute cases from the standpoint of their comments about forced parenthood, see Ellen Waldman, 'The Parent Trap: Uncovering the Myth of "Coerced Parenthood" in Frozen Embryo Disputes' (2004) 53 *American University Law Review* 1021, 1036–038.

[157] See, eg, *Kass v Kass*, 696 NE 2d 174 (NY 1998); *AZ v BZ*, 725 NE 2d 1051 (Mass 2000); *JB v MB*, 783 A 2d 707 (NJ 2001); *Re the Marriage of Litowitz v Litowitz*, 48 P 3d 261 (Wash 2002). But see *Reber v Reiss*, 42 A 3d 1131 (Pa 2012).

of the time.[158] Disputes over embryo 'ownership' raise complex legal questions (including questions related to the legal status of the embryo, as discussed above). In the US, several cases have arisen wherein the courts have been faced with questions of embryo disposition in the event of a breakdown in the relationship between the progenitors.[159] Although the courts often refer to the need to balance the interests of the progenitors, they most often find in favour of the individual seeking to avoid procreating. In 2012, however, the Pennsylvania Superior Court decided in favour of Ms Reiss, the female member of the couple who sought to use crypreserved embryos to attempt to conceive biologically-related children over the objections of her ex-husband. The court noted the unique facts of the case, including Ms Reiss's age and the very limited possibility of genetic parenthood after her treatment for breast cancer. The court concluded that her 'compelling interests in using the pre-embryos include the fact that these pre-embryos are the option that provides her with what is likely her only chance at genetic parenthood and her most reasonable chance for parenthood at all'.[160]

Case law in Canada and Australia is limited. The one reported Canadian case is *C(C) v W(A)*, in which the Alberta Court of Queen's Bench held that embryos produced by the parties were Ms CC's property, as the donation of the sperm used to create the embryos was an 'unqualified gift'.[161] As the case provides no analysis of the competing arguments around the nature of embryos or the interests implicated in decisions about who owns or controls them, it is difficult to know whether this decision will be followed in future cases. In Australia as well, there is one case on point. In *G and G*, the separating couple disagreed as to disposition of several cryopreserved embryos.[162] At the time the embryos were created, the parties had indicated on the clinic consent form that in the event of separation, the embryos should be discarded. At the time of separation, Mrs G still wished to discard the embryos, but Mr G sought to gain control over the embryos and to donate them to an infertile couple or to use them in a surrogacy arrangement.[163] The Court held that the parties' original agreement to discard the embryos in the event of separation should be implemented, as they 'can no longer achieve the purpose for which they consented to create and use the embryos'.[164]

Embryo disposition cases raise important issues related to reproductive autonomy. Where both parties have an interest in reproductive autonomy, and one party wants to reproduce using the embryos but the other wishes to avoid reproducing now that the relationship has broken down, whose reproductive autonomy prevails? And to what extent should the parties' prior agreement relating to embryo disposition be respected?[165] As in the case of consent to gamete donation, in resolving disputes of this nature, it is not possible to respect the reproductive autonomy of both parties equally. The best we can

---

[158] See, eg, Cahn (n 107) 178–84; Judith F Daar, 'Frozen Embryo Disputes Revisited: A Trilogy of Procreation-Avoidance Approaches' (2001) 29 *Journal of Law, Medicine and Ethics* 197; Deborah H Bell, 'Disputes Over Frozen Embryos' (2011) 81 *Mississippi Law Journal Supra* 105, http://mississippilawjournal.org/wp-content/uploads/2012/04/Supra-81-Prop-26-Symposium-Essay-Bell.pdf.

[159] *AZ v BZ* (n 157); *Re the Marriage of Litowitz v Litowitz* (n 157); *JB v MB* (n 157); *Kass v Kass* (n 157).

[160] *Reber v Reiss* (n 157) 1140.

[161] *C(C) v W(A)* (n 13) para 21.

[162] *G and G* [2007] FCWA 80, para 5.

[163] *Ibid* para 17.

[164] *Ibid* para 61.

[165] See, eg, Carl H Coleman, 'Procreative Liberty and Contemporaneous Choice: An Inalienable Rights Approach to Frozen Embryo Disputes' (1999) 84 *Minnesota Law Review* 55; John A Robertson, 'Precommitment Strategies for Disposition of Frozen Embryos' (2001) 50 *Emory Law Journal* 989.

do is to choose a 'point of no return'[166] after which it is no longer possible for the party who has had a change of heart to prevent the use of the embryos, and to make it clear to both parties at the outset where this boundary lies. This is what most ART legislation seeks to do, and (after the fact) what the courts have done in cases where they have been called upon to decide such disputes.

When we acknowledge that it is not possible to respect the autonomous decisions of both parties equally when a dispute arises, does that end the potential discussion of reproductive autonomy? As noted, different jurisdictions have adopted different points in time as the 'point of no return' for decision making about the use of gametes.[167] This variability makes it clear that there is no one correct approach, but that legislators have made policy choices as to precisely where to draw the line.

The problem with the current approach to resolving disputes over embryos is not so much where the line has been drawn – although some have argued otherwise[168] – but with the lack of consideration given to how best to respect reproductive autonomy in the context of such disputes. In the US, these disputes are generally resolved in the courts, with no policy discussion beyond the arguments of the parties to ground the decisions. Even in jurisdictions where the answer lies in legislation, meaning that some consideration has been given to appropriate policy in crafting the rules, it is arguable that insufficient attention has been paid to reproductive autonomy. None of the ART-related legislation under consideration here explicitly adopts respect for the reproductive autonomy of those using ART services as an objective or guiding principle (although arguably the foundational 'pillar' of consent in the UK legislation seeks to acknowledge autonomy to a degree).

Even though consent is considered crucial to the resolution of disputes around embryos, for the most part regulatory statutes place paramount importance on the welfare of children (and sometimes of society), not on the interests of those who avail themselves of ART treatment. It is legitimate, then, to question whether the point of no return adopted in ART-related statutes has been located appropriately. Take the UK legislation as an example – whether the male progenitor in Ms Evans' case had been her partner or a sperm donor unknown to her, her wish to be a genetic parent could equally have been frustrated by his change of heart. Perhaps in the case of a former partner, it is appropriate to require ongoing consent in order to use the embryos, in that it may be more desirable to limit a woman's ability to be a genetic or biological parent to a child (given that this does not completely preclude her wish to be a parent) than it is to force an unwilling former partner to have a child with a woman he no longer loves and whose values he might no longer share. Given the importance of reproductive decision making to one's very sense of self, it is fair to consider the potential harm done by forcing someone to procreate in such circumstances. It might never be possible to establish empirically which is more harmful, but it is arguable that the harms here may be evenly balanced, and even that the harm of forcing an ongoing parental relationship on the former partner is more pronounced than ruling out a woman's wish to be a genetic parent.

---

[166] Draper (n 155).

[167] See discussion below.

[168] See, eg, Donchin (n 155); Judith F Daar, 'Panel on Disputes Concerning Frozen Embryos' (1999) 8 *Texas Journal of Women and the Law* 285.

But is the same true in the case of a sperm donor who, long after donating sperm, learns that his sperm has been used to create embryos for reproductive use by a woman or couple, and then decides that he no longer wishes to father children through gamete donation?[169] Are the sperm donor's interests in reproductive autonomy equally harmed when weighed against the reproductive autonomy of the woman? In both cases, it is possible that the male progenitor could have missed his opportunity to withdraw consent had the IVF treatment already occurred, but it seems much less likely that the male partner of a woman seeking IVF treatment and questioning the future of the relationship would let matters advance to that point before seeking to exercise his right to withdraw consent. He would at least have the advantage of knowing the stage to which the treatment process had advanced. In the case of a sperm donor, by contrast, once the donation process has ended, there is no way for him to know how far a treatment cycle using his gametes has advanced. His role in the treatment process begins and ends with his donation of sperm. This is not to say that his interest in reproductive autonomy is less important to him than is the reproductive autonomy of someone in Ms Evans' position, or that of the male partner in a situation like that in the *Evans* case. But again, when weighing the interests of a woman in Natallie Evans' circumstances against those of a sperm donor, perhaps we would choose a different point of no return.[170]

The *Evans* case illustrates the way in which law and ethics have come to rely on consent to protect autonomy, and it also shows that consent rules, when conceived in the absence of careful consideration of what autonomy means, cannot do the work we would like to think they do. The sense that consent rules can and do protect reproductive autonomy is clear in the embryo disposition context – instead of asking how to design rules about embryo disposition, we put in place rules requiring consent to embryo disposition. But embryos are created from the gametes of at least two individuals, and consent rules (or rules about withdrawing consent) can really safeguard the reproductive autonomy of only one of them.

I have raised the argument that respecting autonomy in the healthcare context cannot be boiled down to requiring consent to treatment.[171] But at least in the usual consent-to-treatment context, there is only one person whose autonomy interests are implicated. Consent to or refusal of a procedure by one person may have effects on others,[172] but the law gives effect to the autonomy interests of only one person, the one who will have the procedure or treatment. In the assisted reproduction context, there are multiple individuals whose autonomy interests are implicated – the woman undergoing IVF, her male or female partner, the gamete donors (if they are different from the treatment participants). So even if we are right in thinking that requiring consent is enough to protect the autonomy of the surgical or blood transfusion candidate, it is surely readily apparent that consent alone is not sufficient to protect the autonomy interests of all participants in assisted reproduction.

This, then, is one obvious area of legal regulation (and ethical deliberation) that would benefit from a thoughtful, considered approach that takes as its starting point a

---

[169] Souzo *et al* (n 39).

[170] *Ibid*.

[171] See discussion in ch 2, section III.B

[172] In *Re Dubreuil*, 629 So 2d 819 (Fla, 1993), the Florida Supreme Court held that a single mother who wished to refuse a blood transfusion could not be compelled to have the procedure even though her death would leave her children without a mother.

firm understanding of just what we mean by reproductive autonomy. I refer to reproductive autonomy as a starting point, because even assuming that we can agree on what reproductive autonomy means, that does not mark the end of the inquiry. It is not possible to respect equally the reproductive autonomy of two parties who have contributed genetic material to an embryo and who now have opposing views about what should become of that embryo. Even once we have a robust definition of reproductive autonomy to work with, we still have to decide who wins – who can decide what can or cannot be done with the embryo.

Consent to the use of embryos presumes uses that are legally permitted. All jurisdictions where IVF is practised must consider the disposition options that will be available to progenitors of embryos that are not needed or wanted for use in procreation. In general, the options are to cryopreserve embryos indefinitely,[173] to destroy the embryos, to donate them for use in research, or to donate them to another individual or couple for reproductive use.[174] Not all of these options are available in all jurisdictions, and in the most restrictive, none is available. Italian legislation, for example, prohibits the fertilisation of more than three oocytes in any IVF cycle, and mandates that all embryos created in a cycle must be transferred to the woman's uterus (in other words, even cryopreservation of embryos for the same couple's future reproductive use is prohibited).[175] In Japan, donation of embryos to another couple for reproductive use is not permitted.[176] In Canada, while excess IVF embryos may be used for research purposes, guidelines actively discourage requests for fresh (rather than cryopreserved) embryos for use in stem-cell research.[177] Some countries, including the UK and Australia, impose statutory maximum storage periods for cryopreserved embryos.[178]

Where the law precludes particular options in terms of embryo use, there is no possibility of consenting to those uses. But what are the implications of limiting an embryo donor's options for reproductive autonomy? Again, this is an area where policy makers must take explicit account of reproductive autonomy, in conjunction with other policy aims, when crafting law and policy.

---

[173] Although this is not an option in the UK or in Australia, where time limits for embryo storage are in place. The HFE Act 1990 (as amended), s 14(3) specifies a 10-year maximum, as does the Assisted Reproductive Technology Act 2007 (NSW), s 25(3)(c) (where the embryo is created using donor gametes).

[174] Andrea D Gurmankin, Dominic Sisti and Arthur L Caplan, 'Embryo Disposal Practices in IVF Clinics in the United States' (2004) 22(2) *Politics and the Life Sciences* 4.

[175] In 2009, the Italian Constitutional Court held that the legislation is (at least in part) unconstitutional on the basis that protecting embryos must be secondary to the objective of seeking to ensure that the IVF cycle has the best chance of producing a successful pregnancy, and that physician discretion cannot be limited in this way. It is not yet clear what the ultimate result of this legal decision will be, as the Italian Parliament will need to act in order to create new, constitutionally acceptable legislation (PE Levi Setti *et al*, 'Italian Constitutional Court Modifications of a Restrictive Assisted Reproduction Technology Law Significantly Improve Pregnancy Rate' (2010) 26 *Human Reproduction* 376, 376–77).

[176] The prohibition is based on professional guidelines issued by the Japanese Society of Obstetrics and Gynecology (Shizuko Takahashi *et al*, 'The Decision-making Process for the Fate of Frozen Embryos by Japanese Infertile Women: A Qualitative Study' (2012) 13:9 BMC Medical Ethics 1, at <www.biomedcentral.com/1472-6939/13/9>).

[177] Erin Nelson, Roxanne Mykitiuk and Jeff Nisker, 'SOGC Clinical Practice Guideline No 215: Informed Consent to Donate Embryos for Research Purposes' (2008) 30 *Journal of Obstetrics and Gynaecology Canada* 824.

[178] See, eg, NHMRC Guidelines (n 11) s 8.8; Human Reproductive Technology Act 1991 (WA), s 24; Assisted Reproductive Technology Act 2007 (NSW), s 25; Assisted Reproductive Treatment Act 2008 (Vic), s 33; HFE Act 1990 (as amended), s 14(3).

C. Embryo testing and selection

Another contentious aspect of ART regulation as it relates to embryos is the question of how selective prospective parents may be in choosing which embryo(s) to use to attempt pregnancy. In 1990, Alan Handyside and his team reported the first clinical use of pre-implantation diagnosis (PGD). The technique was used to determine the sex of IVF embryos in couples at risk of having offspring with recessive X-linked diseases, so that only unaffected embryos could be transferred to the woman's uterus to establish a pregnancy.[179] The technique very rapidly came into widespread use in the IVF context, and has an ever-increasing number of potential applications as our ability to test for various chromosomal and genetic disorders continues to grow.

Because it raises concerns about the sanctity of life and the special status of the embryo, embryo testing is controversial. The practice of embryo testing and selection implies that embryos that are affected by disability or disease will be discarded; this is seen by some to devalue potential life.[180] Concerns about the potential eugenic implications of PGD are also a feature of the debate,[181] as is the worry that parents will seek to design the characteristics of their children. Such practices have the potential to lead to the further entrenchment of discriminatory attitudes about persons who have certain undesirable attributes that could have been avoided,[182] and the possibility of an emergent genetic 'class divide'.

As the hype surrounding the potential applications of genetic testing has grown, and as PGD techniques have become more refined, the spectre of 'designer babies' has been raised, as commentators became concerned about possible uses for PGD.[183] Parents, we were told, will soon be able to design their children to further morally questionable, if not outright objectionable, desires. Fears of parents being able to choose embryos on the basis of predicted height, IQ, eye colour, disease resistance and other traits were a feature of news reports related to PGD and genetic testing generally.[184] Indeed, some commentators suggested that parents would – sooner rather than later – be able to add desired genetic traits to their embryos so as to customise a child.[185]

---

[179] Alan H Handyside *et al*, 'Pregnancies from Biopsied Human Preimplantation Embryos Sexed by Y-specific DNA Amplification' (1990) 344 *Nature* 768.

[180] Bartha M Knoppers, Sylvie Bordet and Rosario M Isasi, 'Preimplantation Genetic Diagnosis: An Overview of Socio-Ethical and Legal Considerations' (2006) 7 *Annual Review of Genomics and Human Genetics* 201.

[181] Sonia M Suter, 'A Brave New World of Designer Babies?' (2007) 22 *Berkeley Technology Law Journal* 897.

[182] Knoppers *et al* (n 180).

[183] Suzanne Holland, 'Selecting Against Difference: Assisted Reproduction, Disability and Regulation' (2003) 30 *Florida State University Law Review* 401; Bernard M Dickens, 'Preimplantation Genetic Diagnosis and "Savior Siblings"' (2005) 88 *International Journal of Gynaecology and Obstetrics* 91.

[184] See, eg, '"Designer Baby" Ethics Fear', *BBC News*, 4 October 2000, at <news.bbc.co.uk/2/hi/health/955644.stm>; Gautam Naik, 'A Baby, Please. Blond, Freckles – Hold the Colic: Laboratory Techniques That Screen for Diseases in Embryos Are Now Being Offered to Create Designer Children', *Wall Street Journal*, 12 February 2009, at <online.wsj.com/article/SB123439771603075099.html>; Carolyn Abraham, 'Unnatural Selection: Is Evolving Reproductive Technology Ushering in a New Age of Eugenics?', *Globe and Mail* (Toronto, 7 January 2012), at <www.theglobeandmail.com/life/parenting/unnatural-selection-is-evolving-reproductive-technology-ushering-in-a-new-age-of-eugenics/article1357885/?page=all>.

[185] See, eg, Thomas H Murray, *The Worth of a Child* (Berkeley, University of California Press, 1996); Jeremy Rifkin, *The Biotech Century: Harnessing the Gene and Remaking the World* (New York, Jeremy P Tarcher, Putnam, 1998); Michael J Sandel, *The Case Against Perfection: Ethics in the Age of Genetic Engineering* (Cambridge, MA, Harvard University Press, 2009).

The anticipation created by the Human Genome Project as to the significant potential for genetic therapies and genetic enhancement has, to date at least, not translated into clinically useful technologies.[186] While research continues into possible therapeutic applications of genetic technology, gene therapy remains experimental and research trials have given rise to limited success.[187] There is no way, at present, to use genetic technologies to enhance a human being, even at the embryonic stage.[188] But even though the technology does not (yet) exist with which a designer baby could be made, there has been much focus on this concern in the ethical and legal literature, and it has played a role in the regulation of embryo testing.

i. Regulating PGD

Regulation of PGD varies markedly across different jurisdictions. In the UK, it is regulated under the authority of the HFEA.[189] In general, its use is limited to situations in which the embryo is likely to be affected by a 'serious' genetic condition.[190] Before the HFEA can license PGD in respect of a particular condition, it must be satisfied that the condition in question is sufficiently serious to warrant testing. In addition, IVF clinics that are licensed for particular applications of PGD must, when offering such testing, consider the seriousness of the condition to be avoided, taking into account the views of the person or couple being treated.[191] The HFE Act 1990 precludes sex selection for non-medical reasons and the HFE Act 2008 precludes the use of embryo testing to select in favour of disability,[192] but the HFE Act 2008 permits the use of PGD with tissue typing for purposes of conceiving a child who is tissue compatible with an ill sibling.[193]

In Australia, as with ART regulation in general, PGD regulation is not uniform. The NHMRC Guidelines prohibit the use of PGD to test for conditions that do not lead to serious harm.[194] Also prohibited is the use of PGD for non-medical sex selection, or for selecting an embryo with a genetic disease or disability.[195] Selection of an embryo that is tissue compatible with a sibling is permitted, but clinics must seek advice from a clinical ethics committee or state regulatory agency before providing treatment in such cases.[196] In three of the four Australian states with ART legislation, PGD is regulated to some extent within the legislation. In Victoria, providers who do not follow the rules respecting PGD

---

[186] Timothy A Caulfield, 'Underwhelmed: Hyperbole, Regulatory Policy, and the Genetic Revolution' (2000) 45 *McGill Law Journal* 437; James P Evans *et al*, 'Deflating the Genomic Bubble' (2011) 331 *Science* 861.

[187] Pedro R Lowenstein, 'Clinical Trials in Gene Therapy: Ethics of Informed Consent and the Future of Experimental Medicine' (2008) 10 *Current Opinion in Molecular Therapeutics* 428.

[188] M Kiuru and RG Crystal, 'Progress and Prospects: Gene Therapy for Performance and Appearance Enhancement' (2008) 15 *Gene Therapy* 329.

[189] Prior to the 2008 amendments to the HFE Act 1990, the regulation of PGD was fully within the authority of the HFEA, with no legislative direction as to how it should be regulated. The 2008 amendments made a significant change in that they introduced into the HFE Act itself some limitations on justifications for embryo testing (see HFE Act 1990 (as amended), Sch 2, s 1ZA). Embryo testing is generally permitted only in cases where there is a 'significant risk of serious physical or mental disability, a serious illness or any other serious medical condition' (*ibid* s 1ZA(2)).

[190] *Ibid.*

[191] HFEA (n 56) ss 10.5–10.7.

[192] HFE Act 1990 (as amended), s 14(10) (selecting for disability); HFE Act 1990 (as amended), Sch 2, s 1ZB (sex selection).

[193] HFE Act 1990 (as amended), Sch 2, s 1ZA(1)(d).

[194] NHMRC Guidelines 2007 (n 11) s 12.2.

[195] *Ibid.*

[196] *Ibid* s 12.3.

risk criminal prosecution.[197] There, the legislation permits PGD in cases where a provider 'is satisfied, on reasonable grounds,' either that a woman would be unlikely to carry a pregnancy successfully to term, or that she is 'at risk of transmitting a genetic abnormality or genetic disease to a child born as a result of a pregnancy conceived other than by a treatment procedure, including a genetic abnormality or genetic disease for which the woman's partner is the carrier'.[198] In South Australia, a similar eligibility criterion limits the provision of PGD services by registered providers, although the South Australian legislation refers to the risk of transmitting a 'serious' genetic defect, disease or illness.[199] In Western Australia, PGD is permitted for eligible patients[200] where authorised by the Code of Practice or approved by the Reproductive Technology Council.[201] Diagnostic testing can only be authorised where there is a significant risk of transmission of a serious genetic condition.[202] The Reproductive Technology Council must authorise PGD on a case-by-case basis.[203] New South Wales' legislation does not refer to PGD and the NHMRC Guidelines thus govern in that state.[204]

In Canada and the US, PGD regulation is far more limited. Canadian law prohibits sex selection for non-medical reasons,[205] but Canada has no other regulations in place around PGD practice.[206] The practice is virtually unregulated in the US, other than through professional guidelines.[207]

ii. PGD and 'saviour siblings'

Although it is not currently possible to design an embryo that will exhibit particular characteristics, PGD can provide us with a considerable amount of information about an embryo, including its sex and many of its genetic and chromosomal characteristics. It can also tell us which embryos would be both free of an inherited disease and a good tissue match for a sibling with that disease, so that umbilical cord blood and possibly other

[197] Assisted Reproductive Treatment Act 2008 (Vic), s 7.

[198] *Ibid* s 10(2)(iii).

[199] Assisted Reproductive Treatment Act 2008 (SA), s 9(1)(c)(iii). Failure to comply with the conditions of registration, of which this is one, may result in the provider's suspension, or cancellation of his or her registration (*ibid* s 10).

[200] Which include those who are at risk of transmitting a genetic abnormality or disease.

[201] Human Reproductive Technology Act 1991 (WA), s 7(1)(b).

[202] *Ibid* s 14(2b).

[203] Reproductive Technology Council, 'Policy on Approval of Diagnostic Procedures Involving Embryos' (March 2008), at <www.rtc.org.au/clinics/docs/Approval_for_Diagnostic_Testing_of_Embryos_Advice_to_Clinics.pdf>. Pre-implantation genetic screening (PGS) for aneuploidy is authorised by the RTC for patients who meet certain eligibility criteria.

[204] Assisted Reproductive Technology Act 2007 (NSW).

[205] AHR Act, s 5(1)(e).

[206] The SOGC has published practice guidelines on pre-implantation testing (François Audibert, 'SOGC Technical Update No 232: Preimplantation Genetic Testing' (2009) 31 *Journal of Obstetrics and Gynaecology Canada* 761). The Commission de l'éthique de la Science et de la Technologie in Québec has issued a position statement on PGD, although PGD itself is not regulated in the Québec legislation (Commission de l'éthique de la Science et de la Technologie, *Ethics and Assisted Procreation: Guidelines for the Donation of Gametes and Embryos, Surrogacy and Preimplantation Genetic Diagnosis* (Québec, Commission de l'éthique de la science et de la technologie, 2009).

[207] Kathy L Hudson, 'Preimplantation Genetic Diagnosis: Public Policy and Public Attitudes' (2006) 85 *Fertility and Sterility* 1638; Society for Assisted Reproductive Technology Practice Committee and American Society for Reproductive Medicine Practice Committee, 'Preimplantation Genetic Testing: A Practice Committee Opinion' (2008) 90 (Supp 3) *Fertility and Sterility* S136; American Society for Reproductive Medicine Ethics Committee, 'Preconception Gender Selection for Nonmedical Reasons' (2001) 75 *Fertility and Sterility* 861.

tissues could be used in an attempt to cure what would otherwise surely be a fatal illness. This means that parents can use IVF and PGD to choose particular embryos with the aim of providing a 'saviour sibling' for an existing child. The idea of having a child to save or help an existing child is not as new as PGD technology,[208] but the development of PGD has allowed parents to choose a particular child rather than attempt to conceive and hope for the best. This specificity and choice has touched off an ethical firestorm, with parents who have opted to use these technologies being forced to defend a choice that they view simply as doing the best they can for their family.[209]

The first saviour sibling born with the help of IVF and PGD was Adam Nash, whose older sister Molly suffered from Fanconi anemia.[210] After several attempts to conceive a sibling for Molly, Adam was born in August 2000. With his birth came the first headlines raising concerns about the genetic engineering of children, the deliberate destruction of embryos, and renewed questions about the ethics of assisted reproductive and genetic technologies.[211] Since the birth of Adam Nash, several more children have been born who were conceived using PGD and tissue typing to ensure that they would be a healthy, tissue-matched sibling, although this use of ARTs continues to be controversial.[212]

In the UK, the HFEA faced licensing applications for PGD and tissue typing for the first time in 2001, when Mr and Mrs Hashmi, the parents of a boy with ß-thalassaemia, requested permission to use PGD and tissue typing in the hope of conceiving a 'saviour sibling' for their son. The HFEA's decision to grant the licence was unsuccessfully challenged in the English courts;[213] the House of Lords ultimately held that the HFEA had the legislative authority to issue the licence.

At the same time as it granted the Hashmi's application, the HFEA rejected another similar request for PGD and tissue typing from the Whitaker family, whose son suffered from Diamond Blackfan anemia (DBA). This condition is different from Fanconi anemia and from ß-thalassaemia, in that these other conditions are both inherited in an autosomal recessive pattern, while DBA is a rare disease (approximately five to seven

---

[208] The first cord-blood transplant from an HLA-identical sibling took place in 1988 (Eliane Gluckman, 'History of Cord Blood Transplantation' (2009) 44 *Bone Marrow Transplantation* 621). In that case, as pre-implantation genetic diagnosis was not yet available, the fact that the sibling was healthy and HLA-identical was a result of chance, not design. Prior to the development of PGD, parents sometimes tried to conceive a child to provide umbilical cord blood or bone marrow transplants for their ill child, but this was far more of a roll of the dice in terms of knowing whether or not the child would be healthy and whether or not he or she would be a good match for the sibling in need of stem cells.

[209] For more detailed discussion, see Sally Sheldon and Stephen Wilkinson, 'Should Selecting Saviour Siblings be Banned?' (2004) 30 *Journal of Medical Ethics* 533; Colin Gavaghan, *Defending the Genetic Supermarket: The Law and Ethics of Selecting the Next Generation* (Abingdon, Routledge-Cavendish, 2007) (esp 11–39).

[210] Fanconi anemia is an autosomal recessive genetic disorder that leads to severe, progressive bone marrow failure (David I Kutler *et al*, 'A 20-year Perspective on the International Fanconi Anemia Registry (IFAR)' (2003) 101 *Blood* 1249). Affected children usually also manifest abnormalities at birth (such as heart defects, skeletal abnormalities) and are at increased risk of leukemia and other cancers. Many of those with Fanconi anemia die before reaching adulthood.

[211] See, eg, Amanda M Faison, 'The Miracle of Molly', *5280: The Denver Magazine*, August 2005, at <www.5280.com/print/48100>; Dan Vergano, 'Embryo Genetic Screening Controversial – and Successful', *USA Today* (McLean, VA,10 January 2010), at <www.usatoday.com/tech/science/columnist/vergano/2010-01-10-embryo-genetic-screening_N.htm>.

[212] Most recently, this arose in France: see, eg, Antoine Mariotti, Yuka Royer and Joseph Bamat, 'France's First "Saviour Sibling" Stirs Ethical Debate about Biotechnology', *France 24* (Paris, 9 February 2011), at <www.france24.com/en/20110208-france-first-saviour-baby-donor-biotechnology-stem-cell-research-clamart-umut-fryman>.

[213] *Quintavalle, R (on the application of) v Human Fertilisation and Embryology Authority* [2003] EWCA Civ 667, [2004] QB 168, affd [2005] UKHL 28, [2005] 2 WLR 1061.

cases per million births), the cause of which is usually not known.[214] For the HFEA, the fact that DBA was not heritable proved to be a key distinction between the two requests, and while it granted the Hashmi's application, it rejected the Whitaker's. The primary reason given by the HFEA for rejecting the Whitaker's licence application was that the embryos being tested for their HLA properties would not themselves be at risk of DBA. The HFEA concluded that testing an embryo for purposes of tissue typing alone was not in the interests of the embryo, and as such could not meet the legislative requirement to take into account the 'welfare of the child'.

The HFEA came under fire as a result of drawing what many perceived to be an unjustifiable distinction.[215] In 2004, it reviewed its policies on tissue typing and announced that it would now permit tissue typing whether or not the embryo was also to be tested for the presence of a serious disease. The change in policy direction came about after a review of the evidence related to the 'medical, psychological and emotional implications for children and their families,'[216] and the evidence as to the 'safety of the technique'.[217]

When the HFE Act 1990 was amended in 2008, conditions on the permissible applications of embryo testing (including a ban on sex selection for non-medical reasons) were brought within the legislation itself for the first time. All of the restrictions on embryo testing put in place by the legislative amendments are in keeping with the policy positions that had been adopted by the HFEA on these matters, but the policy change is noteworthy in that it removes some aspects of decision making about embryo testing from the HFEA's discretion.[218] Regulation in Victoria, Australia has taken a move in the opposite direction. The former regulator, the Infertility Treatment Authority, had to grant approval to clinics wishing to use PGD for novel purposes. The new regulator (Victorian Assisted Reproduction Treatment Authority, or VARTA) has said that it will no longer be involved in the regulation of PGD techniques; instead, these matters will be handled by IVF clinics.[219]

iii. *PGD and sex selection*

Sex selection is another issue that has generated considerable debate. The earliest use of PGD involved determination of the sex of the embryo in order to avoid the risk of passing on a sex-linked genetic or chromosomal abnormality;[220] thus, the ability to test an embryo to determine whether it is male or female has existed since PGD was first

---

[214] Although in some cases there appears to be a genetic basis for disease (Thiébaut-Noël Willig, Hanna Gazda and Colin A Sieff, 'Diamond-Blackfan Anemia' (2000) 7 *Current Opinion in Hematology* 85).

[215] Sally Sheldon and Stephen Wilkinson, '"Saviour Siblings": Hashmi and Whitaker. An Unjustifiable and Misguided Distinction' (*ProChoice Forum*, 2005), at <www.prochoiceforum.org.uk/irl_rep_tech_2.php>; 'Jamie's Legacy: Look Again at Law on Designer Babies', *Observer*, 22 June 2003, at <www.guardian.co.uk/science/2003/jun/22/genetics.comment>; 'Whitaker Case Sparks Calls for Legal Change' (23 June 2003) 213 *Bionews*, at <www.bionews.org.uk/page_11655.asp>.

[216] Human Fertilisation and Embryology Authority, 'HFEA Agrees to Extend Policy on Tissue Typing', 21 July 2004, at <www.hfea.gov.uk/763.html>.

[217] *Ibid.*

[218] It seems that this change came about in order to respond to concerns about the HFEA and democratic accountability. See discussion in ch 8, section IV.B., respecting concerns about democratic accountability and arm's-length regulators.

[219] Malcolm Smith, 'Changes to PGD Regulation in Victoria, Australia' (15 August 2011) 620 *BioNews*, at <www.bionews.org.uk/page_104140.asp>.

[220] Handyside *et al* (n 179). These diseases include Duchenne Muscular Dystrophy, Lesch-Nyhan Syndrome, adrenoleukodystrophy and Fragile X Syndrome.

developed. Most jurisdictions that have taken steps to regulate PGD have made some provision as to the permissibility of sex selection.[221] While most permit it for medical reasons (specifically, the avoidance of X-linked recessive conditions), a handful of countries ban all uses of sex selection technology.[222]

A number of ethical arguments against sex selection have been made. In addition to the claim that selecting the sex of one's child necessarily entails discrimination on the basis of sex,[223] these arguments also express worries about the skewing of sex ratios at birth, as well as the by-now familiar concern that PGD reduces children to consumer products where parents can simply choose their preferred characteristics so as to design a child.[224]

Sex selection has been an issue of particular concern to feminist scholars and policy makers who raise concerns about the gender bias inherent in seeking to have children of a particular sex. In some regions, the most common gender preference by far is for males, which on its face at least lends support to the gender bias argument.[225] The preference for male embryos (and by extension male children) seems to suggest that the male sex is simply better. This is understandably of concern to those who focus their careers on advocacy of gender equality. However, attempts to limit women's reproductive choices also generate significant feminist unease. While many feminists would be loath to agree that abortion rights could be limited in order to prevent sex-selective abortion,[226] fewer are as concerned about limiting reproductive rights by prohibiting sex selection among embryos. And admittedly, the interference with reproductive decision making is considerably less in the embryo selection context than in the case of a pregnant woman seeking to terminate the pregnancy.

iv. PGD and reproductive autonomy

Pre-implantation genetic diagnosis, whether aimed at avoiding the birth of a disabled child or that of a child of a particular sex, provides options for couples in terms of which types of children they wish to raise. The technology thus has important implications for reproductive autonomy. It has been argued that limits on the permissible uses of PGD

---

[221] Bartha M Knoppers and Rosario M Isasi, 'Regulatory Approaches to Reproductive Genetic Testing' (2004) 19 *Human Reproduction* 2695; Andrea M Whittaker, 'Reproduction Opportunists in the New Global Sex Trade: PGD and Non-Medical Sex Selection' (2011) 23 *Reproductive Biomedicine Online* 609, 609–10.

[222] These countries include Austria, New Zealand, South Korea, Switzerland and Vietnam (Marcy Darnovsky, 'Countries with Laws or Policies on Sex Selection' (*Genetics and Society*, 2009), at <http://genetics andsociety.org/downloads/200904_sex_selection_memo.pdf>).

[223] See, eg, John A Robertson, 'Extending Preimplantation Genetic Diagnosis: Medical and Non-medical Uses' (2003) 29 *Journal of Medical Ethics* 213; Jackie Leach Scully, Sarah Banks and Tom W Shakespeare, 'Chance, Choice and Control: Lay Debate on Social Sex Selection' (2006) 63 *Social Science & Medicine* 21.

[224] Robertson (n 223); Scully *et al* (n 223).

[225] Douglas Almond, Lena Edlund and Kevin Milligan, *O Sister, Where Art Thou? The Role of Son Preference and Sex Choice: Evidence from Immigrants to Canada*, National Bureau of Economic Research Working Paper No 15391 (Cambridge, MA, National Bureau of Economic Research, 2009).

[226] I want to be clear that although most would not wish to preclude abortion for any reason, many feminists have expressed concern about sex-selective abortion: see, eg, Dorothy C Wertz and John C Fletcher, 'Sex Selection Through Prenatal Diagnosis: A Feminist Critique' in Helen Bequaert Holmes and Laura M Purdy (eds), *Feminist Perspectives in Medical Ethics* (Bloomington, Indiana University Press, 1992) 240; Elisabeth Boetzkes, 'Sex Selection and the *Charter*' (1994) 7 *Canadian Journal of Law and Jurisprudence* 173; Drucilla Cornell, *The Imaginary Domain: Abortion, Pornography & Sexual Harassment* (London, Routledge, 1995) 86–88; Jodi Danis, 'Sexism and "the Superfluous Female": Arguments for Regulating Pre-Implantation Sex Selection' (1995) 18 *Harvard Women's Law Journal* 219, 245–52.

are inappropriately restrictive of reproductive autonomy.[227] Indeed, the argument has also been made that not only must we avoid limiting the use of PGD, but that parents are obliged to avail themselves of such technology to ensure they maximally benefit their children.[228] Much has been said in the literature about reproductive autonomy and PGD, including whether reproductive autonomy can justify access to all possible uses of PGD, and whether reproductive autonomy is even a useful analysis in relation to PGD.[229]

A contextualised account of reproductive autonomy such as I argue for here does not necessarily change the discussion to a great degree. While I have argued that the interest in reproductive autonomy is strongest when engaged in relation to women's bodily integrity, and that it is moderated in strength in relation to issues that do not implicate bodily integrity, reproductive autonomy is an important interest that should not be disregarded without good reasons. A nuanced approach to reproductive autonomy should be prepared – in cases that do not engage women's bodily integrity – to weigh other interests and seek a balance among those other interests and reproductive autonomy. The focus of the debate around PGD has been on freedom of choice, both in terms of what it permits or justifies, and whether it is a value worth upholding. Often, concerns about equality are raised in the PGD context, similar to those raised in the context of wrongful birth and wrongful life claims.[230] But it is not clear that restricting the uses of PGD is an appropriate response to equality-based concerns.

Taking reproductive autonomy seriously means that where a choice exists, it must be possible for that choice to be made meaningfully. Equality-based concerns around PGD practice should not direct us to place increasing legal limits on individual choice. Instead, we should seek to ensure that families who face with a decision about whether or not to bear a disabled child have the support they require to make the choice in an autonomous way, as well as the support they need to help them meet their child's needs. In this way, we can foster both reproductive autonomy and equality.

Not only does PGD allow parents to select against disability, it also makes possible selection in favour of embryos affected by disease or disability. Media reports of a lesbian couple who deliberately sought to conceive deaf children (they did so not with PGD but by choosing a known sperm donor who, like them, is congenitally deaf) were met with a great deal of public concern around the potential for parental misuse of embryo selection technologies.[231] The notion that parents might deliberately pursue the birth of a child with a disability is, for many, difficult to understand, as most people see disabling

---

[227] See, eg, Robertson (n 223); John Harris, 'Sex Selection and Regulated Hatred' (2005) 31 *Journal of Medical Ethics* 291.

[228] Julian Savulescu, 'Procreative Beneficence: Why We Should Select the Best Children' (2001) 15 *Bioethics* 413; Julian Savulescu, 'In Defence of Procreative Beneficence' (2007) 33 *Journal of Medical Ethics* 284.

[229] Kathryn Ehrich and colleagues have done some very interesting work on provider views of the ethical considerations involved in PGD and in supporting the ability of their patients to make autonomous decisions, and have suggested that there are limits to the usefulness of prevailing views of autonomy in this context (Kathryn Ehrich *et al*, 'Choosing Embryos: Ethical Complexity and Relational Autonomy in Staff Accounts of PGD' (2007) 29 *Sociology of Health & Illness* 1091). For an excellent discussion of the various concerns raised in relation to PGD, see Susannah Baruch, 'Preimplantation Genetic Diagnosis and Parental Preferences: Beyond Deadly Disease' (2008) 8 *Houston Journal of Health Law & Policy* 245.

[230] See discussion in ch 7. See also Jackie Leach Scully, 'Disability and Genetics in the Era of Genomic Medicine' (2008) 9 *Nature Reviews Genetics* 797; Adrienne Asch and Dorit Barlevy, 'Disability and Genetics: A Disability Critique of Pre-natal Testing and Pre-implantation Genetic Diagnosis (PGD)' (2012) eLS, at <http://onlinelibrary.wiley.com/doi/10.1002/9780470015902.a0005212.pub2/full>.

[231] Merle Spriggs, 'Lesbian Couple Create a Child Who is Deaf Like Them' (2002) 28 *Journal of Medical Ethics* 283.

traits as harmful or at least life-limiting. The HFE Act 2008 in the UK and the NHMRC Guidelines in Australia prohibit the selection of embryos that are affected by an abnormality that leads to a significant risk that the child will be born with 'a serious physical or mental disability, a serious illness, or any other serious medical condition'.[232] But the couple who chose to try to conceive a deaf child do not see their deafness as a disability; rather they consider themselves to be part of a thriving deaf culture and want their children to be able share that culture with them.[233] From the standpoint of respect for reproductive autonomy viewed through a wide lens, it is questionable whether ruling out such uses of PGD technology is appropriate. As Tom Shakespeare has pointed out, such use of IVF and PGD is exceedingly rare, and should be seen (as are most other decisions about ART use) as a matter for individual decision making.[234]

Maneesha Deckha, a Canadian legal scholar, has critiqued the Canadian position on sex selection in particular for failing to acknowledge the parallels between sex selection and disability selection.[235] She argues that the AHR Act's prohibition on sex selection for social reasons, together with the absence of any limit on using PGD to select against disability, instantiates a status quo that takes for granted that parents have good reasons to select against disability while at the same time expressing the view that there are no good reasons for selecting against one of the sexes. In her view, this approach 'sends the additional message that disability selection is not worthy of legal sanction. In this symbolic sense, it has made the situation of people with disabilities "worse off"'.[236]

Deckha makes an interesting point, in that feminists should be concerned with all marginalised groups that face oppression just as they are concerned with women's oppression. But her answer appears to differ considerably from those of many feminists who express concern about both gender and disability selection. Rather than prohibit sex selection and thereby express implicit support for disability selection, Deckha advocates that the prohibition on sex selection be reconsidered as its potentially beneficial effects are outweighed by the problems it may cause, including criminalising women's reproductive decision making.

Embryo testing and selection technologies raise some significant concerns for public policy, including the extent to which it is appropriate to restrict the uses of the technology even though those restrictions might frustrate reproductive autonomy. Respect for reproductive autonomy in the use of PGD and embryo selection creates uncomfortable tensions, as the unrestricted use of such technology may have significant consequences on society. But given the importance of reproductive autonomy, limits on PGD and embryo selection need to be justified, not simply imposed on the basis of speculative concerns. As much as we might wish that no one would want to make use of PGD to select an embryo of a particular sex, it is difficult to see a justification for legal rules that preclude such use, let alone a criminal prohibition backed by fines of up to $500,000 or 10 years' imprisonment,[237] particularly given the lack of any evidentiary foundation of

---

[232] HFE Act 1990 (as amended), s 14(9), (10).

[233] Spriggs (n 231).

[234] Tom Shakespeare, 'Fertilisation Rights and Wrongs' (2009) 65 *Disability, Pregnancy and Parenthood International*, at <www.dppi.org.uk/journal/65/viewpoint.php>.

[235] Maneesha Deckha, '(Not) Reproducing the Cultural, Racial and Embodied Other: A Feminist Response to Canada's Partial Ban on Sex Selection' (2007) 16 *UCLA Women's Law Journal* 1.

[236] *Ibid* 31.

[237] As is the case in the Canadian AHR Act, s 5(1)(e) and s 60.

harm to ground such an approach.[238] So too with the possibility that parents will select in favour of disability. How can we know whether it is harmful to a child to be born deaf into a deaf family, or whether it is more harmful to be born a hearing child in such circumstances? Respect for reproductive autonomy demands a thoughtful and considered approach to these question of limiting access to embryo testing and selection.

III. REGULATING SURROGACY

Surrogacy or surrogate pregnancy is an arrangement wherein one woman carries a pregnancy for a woman who is or a couple who are unable (for medical or social reasons) to do so.[239] Surrogacy may take one of two main forms: gestational surrogacy (where the surrogate is the birth mother but not the genetic mother of the child); and traditional surrogacy, where the surrogate is both birth mother and genetic mother. Gestational surrogacy relies on IVF using either the intended mother's oocyte or that of a third-party donor. Traditional surrogacy may rely on IVF, or may be accomplished via intra-uterine insemination; either way, the surrogate provides the oocyte. The sperm may be provided by the intended father or a third-party donor.

Surrogacy has a lengthy history. As many commentators have noted, the practice is described in The Bible.[240] Since the early days of ARTs, surrogacy has been treated with suspicion by many groups, including feminists and social conservatives, on the basis of its perceived dangers to women and to society as a whole. Like all of the ARTs, surrogacy is potentially disruptive to our traditional ideas about family and the meaning of motherhood, and threatens our sense that we can create meaningful boundaries around these concepts. From a feminist standpoint in particular, the way in which surrogacy appears to make use of women as means to a reproductive end echoes the dystopian vision outlined by Margaret Atwood in her novel *The Handmaid's Tale*.[241]

The *Baby M* case was a defining moment in modern surrogacy.[242] The litigation arose when the surrogate (Mary Beth Whitehead) refused to relinquish the child to the commissioning parents. The arrangement between Ms Whitehead and William and Elizabeth Stern was for traditional surrogacy. Ms Whitehead conceived a child after being inseminated with Mr Stern's sperm. Although a lower court upheld the surrogacy agreement, terminated Ms Whitehead's parental rights and allowed the Sterns to adopt the child, in the end, the New Jersey Supreme Court held that the surrogacy agreement was void. The Supreme Court's decision was based on the view that consent to relinquish one's parental rights could not be given before the child's birth, and on the conclusion that the

---

[238] Timothy Caulfield, 'Clones, Controversy, and Criminal Law: A Comment on the Proposal for Legislation Governing Assisted Human Reproduction' (2001) 39 *Alberta Law Review* 335.

[239] For the purposes of this discussion, the woman who gives birth to the child will be referred to as the 'birth mother' or the 'surrogate mother'. The individuals who seek to enter into a surrogacy arrangement in order to become parents will be referred to either as the 'commissioning parents/mother/father' or the 'intended parents/mother/father'.

[240] Genesis16.

[241] Margaret Atwood, *The Handmaid's Tale* (Toronto, McClelland and Stewart, 1985). Atwood sets her novel in the near future, in the 'Republic of Gilead' (formerly the USA). The Republic is a totalitarian society, formed after the US Government was overthrown by a movement that was expressly concerned about the social and moral decay of the nation.

[242] *In the Matter of Baby M*, 217 NJ Super 313 (Ch Div 1987) rev'd 109 NJ 396 (1988).

payment to Ms Whitehead was illegal.[243] The Court invalidated the adoption and awarded custody to Mr Stern.[244] The matter was remanded to the lower courts to determine visitation rights for Ms Whitehead.

Public scrutiny of the *Baby M* case was intense. A central issue at trial was whether Ms Whitehead was fit to be a parent. A number of prominent feminists responded with a statement declaring their solidarity with Ms Whitehead, claiming that based on the standards by which her ability to mother was being questioned, 'we're all unfit mothers'.[245] A number of these same women joined the Foundation on Economic Trends in filing an *amicus* brief in the *Baby M* appeal,[246] arguing that surrogacy dehumanises and commodifies surrogate mothers.[247]

The uproar over the *Baby M* case does not seem to have dampened surrogacy practice, at least not to a significant degree. It is difficult to assess the incidence of surrogacy or to obtain accurate statistics as to surrogacy trends, for a number of reasons. Many, perhaps most, countries do not track surrogacy incidence.[248] In the US, monitoring of surrogacy itself is not a focal point; ART practice more generally, as well as trends in practice and success rates, are tracked by the Centers for Disease Control (CDC) and the Society for Assisted Reproductive Technologies (SART).[249] In the UK, in spite of a high level of regulatory oversight of assisted reproduction, there is no formalised monitoring of the incidence of surrogacy (although one of the organisations involved in surrogacy has said that it 'celebrated [its] 600th surrogate birth in 2007').[250] In Canada, the practice of surrogacy is perceived to be on somewhat uncertain legal footing, and to the extent that it does take place, it is at present unmonitored by any authority.[251]

[243] 109 NJ 396 (n 242).

[244] *Ibid.*

[245] Iver Peterson, 'Fitness Test For Baby M's Mother Unfair, Feminists Say', *New York Times*, 20 March 1987, (quoting Lois Gould) at <www.nytimes.com/1987/03/20/nyregion/fitness-test-for-baby-m-s-mother-unfair-feminists-say.html>.

[246] Elizabeth Mehren, 'Feminists Fight Court Ruling in Baby M Decision: Steinem, Friedan, Chesler, French Among Supporters', *Los Angeles Times*, 31 July 1987, at <http://articles.latimes.com/1987-07-31/news/vw-147_1_gloria-steinem>.

[247] Joseph F Sullivan, 'Brief by Feminists Opposes Surrogate Parenthood', *New York Times*, 31 July 1987, at <www.nytimes.com/1987/07/31/nyregion/brief-by-feminists-opposes-surrogate-parenthood.html>.

[248] In the UK, it is possible to identify families formed through surrogacy, as the national General Register Offices (there are three GROs: one for Scotland, one for England and Wales, and one for Northern Ireland) maintain Parental Order Registers. Where a child is born via surrogacy, the initial registration of the child's birth shows the surrogate mother and her husband or consenting partner as the child's parents (unless the husband or partner did not consent to the surrogacy arrangement). The commissioning parents may seek a parental order (this is discussed in more detail in section IV.A. below) and the birth is then re-registered, showing the commissioning parents as the child's parents (Eric Blyth, 'Parental Orders and Identity Registration: One Country Three Systems' (2010) 32 *Journal of Social Welfare and Family Law* 345, 348). See also Susan Golombok *et al*, 'Families Created Through Surrogacy: Mother–Child Relationships and Children's Psychological Adjustment at Age 7' (2011) 47 *Developmental Psychology* 1579, 1587 (noting that their study involved families identified with the assistance of the Office of National Statistics).

[249] One author has estimated surrogacy rates in the US, based on data from the CDC and the SART. She suggests that, based on CDC data, 481 births resulted from surrogacy arrangements using IVF (so gestational surrogacy) in 2007, but according to SART data, 1,395 births resulted from surrogacy arrangements in 2008 (Magdalina Gugucheva, *Surrogacy in America* (Cambridge, MA, Center for Responsible Genetics, 2010) 10–12). The author notes that both the CDC and SART estimates are likely underestimates (and in the case of the CDC, a significant underestimate, given that it does not include traditional surrogacy arrangements) (*ibid* 7).

[250] Childlessness Overcome Through Surrogacy (COTS), at <www.surrogacy.org.uk/About_COTS.htm>.

[251] The Canadian law that would have permitted monitoring and data collection by a national agency was only partially implemented when, in late 2010 the provisions creating the agency were declared ultra vires Canada's Federal Parliament (*Reference re Assisted Human Reproduction Act*, 2010 SCC 61, [2010] 3 SCR 457). In the course of outlining its budget priorities for 2012/13, the Federal Government announced that the

But even if countries did attempt to track surrogacy, it would likely be impossible to obtain accurate numbers, because of the possibility of informal surrogacy arrangements.[252] And, given the social disapprobation that some commissioning parents and surrogates fear, it is not surprising that we do not hear a great deal about surrogacy from the participants.[253] Accurate numbers would also be hard to come by in part because many couples seeking surrogacy services do so in jurisdictions other than where they live.

A. Surrogacy law

Canadian law on surrogacy entails both federal and provincial aspects, as it involves criminal law and family law.[254] The law is straightforward, at least in so far as the surrogacy arrangement itself is concerned: surrogacy is legal, but only if done altruistically. The payment of compensation to a surrogate mother is prohibited by the federal AHR Act, as are advertising such payment and the payment of consideration for arranging for a woman to provide surrogacy services.[255] Canadian law does not criminalise the acceptance of payment by the surrogate mother. The AHR Act does not affect the validity of surrogacy agreements, as this is a matter for for provincial law. The law around surrogacy agreements in Canada is unsettled, other than in Québec, where such agreements are null and void.[256] In most other provinces, the law is silent as to the validity and enforceability of surrogacy agreements. However, Alberta law provides that such agreements are not enforceable,[257] and new legislation in British Columbia provides that a surrogacy agreement cannot satisfy the consent requirement for a parentage order.[258]

Although payment for surrogacy services is prohibited, the AHR Act does permit reimbursement of the surrogate mother's expenses in accordance with regulations. To date, no regulations have been developed pursuant to section 12 of the AHR Act,[259] so at present the details of permissible reimbursement remain unclear. There is an open question as to whether, at this point in time, it is at all permissible to reimburse the expenses of a surrogate mother, as the prohibition is in force but the section allowing reimbursement is not.

While Canadian law seems reasonably clear, significant uncertainty exists due to the inaction of federal authorities on the enforcement front. In spite of media reports

agency would be wound down (Government of Canada, 'Chapter 5: Responsible Management to Return to Balanced Budgets' (*Budget 2012*, 2012), at <www.budget.gc.ca/2012/plan/chap5-eng.html#a0>). In June 2012, the provisions of the AHR Act relating to the Agency were repealed in omnibus budget legislation (Jobs, Growth and Long-Term Prosperity Act, SC 2012, c 19).

[252] Elly Teman, 'The Social Construction of Surrogacy Research: An Anthropological Critique of the Psychosocial Scholarship on Surrogate Motherhood' (2008) 67 *Social Science & Medicine* 1104, 1104.

[253] See, eg, *ibid* 1105; Robert J Edelman, 'Surrogacy: The Psychological Issues' (2004) 22 *Journal of Reproductive and Infant Psychology* 123, 127.

[254] As discussed in ch 8, section III.D., the Federal Government holds power over criminal law, and power to make laws related to health is held by provincial/territorial governments. The provinces and territories also have jurisdiction over family law.

[255] AHR Act, s 6.

[256] Civil Code of Québec, RSQ, c C-1991, Art 541.

[257] Family Law Act, SA 2003, c F-4.5, s 8.2(8), The Act also says that the agreement cannot satisfy the consent requirement for purposes of the declaration of parentage.

[258] Family Law Act, SBC 2011, c 25, s 29(6).

[259] AHR Act, s 12.

suggesting that egg donors and surrogate mothers are being paid compensation for eggs and/or for gestational labour, to date the only enforcement measure that has been made public is the execution of a search warrant at the offices of Canadian Fertility Consultants.[260]

In the UK, as in Canada, commercial surrogacy is prohibited.[261] Surrogacy agreements are unenforceable in the UK.[262] Although the law around parentage in surrogacy is far more clear and uniform in the UK than in Canada, depending on the type of surrogacy involved, the rules respecting legal parenthood can vary considerably. Gestational surrogacy, because it involves the creation of an in vitro embryo, is subject to regulation based on relevant provisions of the HFE Act 2008.[263] By contrast, traditional surrogacy is largely unregulated with respect both to requirements related to the surrogacy arrangement itself and to assignment of legal parenthood.[264]

Commercial surrogacy is also prohibited in Australia.[265] Until quite recently, even altruistic surrogacy was proscribed in several jurisdictions. Now in most states it is permitted, although this is a relatively new development; between 2008 and 2010, three Australian states lifted their criminal bans on altruistic surrogacy.[266] As it is difficult to find women willing to enter into surrogacy arrangements without compensation (and as advertising related to surrogacy is generally prohibited), many Australians have sought surrogacy services in other countries. In three Australian states, such surrogacy tourism has now been criminalised. New South Wales,[267] Queensland[268] and the Australian Capital Territory[269] have adopted legislation that prohibits residents from engaging in commercial surrogacy arrangements, even where the contract is made and performed outside of Australia, and even in jurisdictions where commercial surrogacy is allowed. This is accomplished by provisions that state that a geographical nexus exists to the relevant state for purposes of commission of the offence if the person who commits the offence is domiciled or ordinarily resident in the state. Although surrogacy agreements

---

[260] Tom Blackwell, 'Fertility Consultant at Centre of RCMP Raid in the Dark About Reason for Investigation: Lawyer', *National Post* (Don Mills, 1 March 2012), at <http://news.nationalpost.com/2012/03/01/fertility-consultant-at-centre-of-rcmp-raid-in-the-dark-about-reason-for-investigation-lawyer/>.

[261] The Surrogacy Arrangements Act 1985, s 2 prohibits commercial surrogacy arrangements.

[262] *Ibid* s 1A.

[263] HFE Act 2008, ss 33, 35–37, 54.

[264] Kirsty Horsey and Sally Sheldon, 'Still Hazy After All These Years: The Law Regulating Surrogacy' (2012) 20 *Medical Law Review* 67.

[265] See, eg, Surrogacy Contracts Act 1993 (Tas), s 4; Parentage Act 2004 (ACT), s 41; Surrogacy Act 2008 (WA), s 8; Surrogacy Act 2010 (NSW), s 8; Surrogacy Act 2010 (Qld), s 56.

[266] In 2009, the Australian Standing Committee of Attorneys-General (SCAG; now the Standing Council on Law and Justice) sought to create some momentum in favour of harmonising surrogacy laws across Australia (Standing Committee of Attorneys-General, Australian Health Ministers' Conference, Community And Disability Services Ministers' Conference: Joint Working Group, 'A Proposal for a National Model to Harmonise Regulation of Surrogacy' (January 2009), at <www.scag.gov.au/lawlink/SCAG/ll_scag.nsf/pages/scag_pastconsultations>). The stated policy objective of the consultation on surrogacy laws was 'to permit the intended parents to become recognised throughout Australia as the legal parents of the child in place of the birth parent(s)' (*ibid* 2). Another concern in Australia was the high frequency of reproductive tourism within the country. As many states banned both commercial and altruistic surrogacy, the only option for some intended parents was to leave their home state for surrogacy services (Anita Stuhmcke, 'The Criminal Act of Commercial Surrogacy in Australia: A Call for Review' (2011) 18 *Journal of Law and Medicine* 601, 607). Until 2007, eg, NSW was a 'destination' for surrogacy tourism in Australia (Tammy Johnson, 'Queensland's Proposed Surrogacy Legislation: An Opportunity for National Reform' (2010) 17 *Journal of Law and Medicine* 617, 618).

[267] Surrogacy Act 2010 (NSW), s 11.

[268] Surrogacy Act 2010 (Qld), s 54.

[269] Parentage Act 2004 (ACT), s 45.

are not enforceable in Australia, some state legislation enforces the obligation to pay surrogacy costs to the surrogate mother.[270]

Surrogacy laws, like most laws regulating ART services, vary widely among American states.[271] Some states have legislation dealing with surrogacy agreements,[272] and the laws vary in their treatment of surrogacy agreements as to the legality of such agreements, their enforceability and whether compensation is permitted.[273] Other states make surrogacy agreements unenforceable[274] and rely on the common law where legal disputes over custody arise.

B. Surrogacy, regulation and reproductive autonomy

Given the wide variation seen in Canada, the UK, the US and Australia in terms of ART regulation, it is striking to see the degree of consistency among these jurisdictions in relation to surrogacy. The near-uniformity of surrogacy laws (the exception being the variety of approaches taken in the US) suggests general agreement that, among ART practices, surrogacy is a special case requiring extreme caution. As noted earlier, the need to resort to ARTs to form a family has in the past been a source of stigma and unease and has often been kept secret from family, friends and even the resulting children.[275] The unease around the use of ARTs seems most pronounced in the case of surrogacy.

The arguments marshalled against permitting surrogacy include concerns about physical and psychological harm (to both women and children[276]) as well as 'non-harm arguments',[277] such as commodification of reproduction and of children and exploitation of women.[278] While many opponents would be prepared to argue that surrogacy

---

[270] See, eg, Parentage Act 2004 (ACT) (*ibid* s 31); New South Wales (Surrogacy Act 2010 (NSW), s 6) (although the obligation to pay or reimburse surrogacy costs is enforceable); Victoria (Assisted Reproductive Treatment Act 2008 (Vic), s 44(3) ('To the extent that a surrogacy arrangement provides for a matter other than the reimbursement for costs actually incurred by the surrogate mother the arrangement is void and unenforceable')).

[271] For detailed discussions of surrogacy laws in the US, see Kindregan and McBrien (n 7) 151–216; Susan L Crockin and Howard W Jones Jr, *Legal Conceptions: The Evolving Law and Policy of Assisted Reproductive Technologies* (Baltimore, MD, Johns Hopkins University Press, 2010) 209–74.

[272] See, eg, Fla Stat § 742.15 (2010); 750 Ill Comp Stat 47/5 (2010).

[273] See Kindregan and McBrien (n 7) 151–203.

[274] See, eg, DC Code Ann tit 13, § 8–103 (2008); Ind Code Ann § 31–20–1–1(1)–(8) (2009).

[275] See, eg, Robert D Nachtigall, Gay Becker and Mark Wozny, 'The Effects of Gender-Specific Diagnosis on Men's and Women's Response to Infertility' (1992) 57 *Fertility and Sterility* 113; Prasanth Kumar Deka and Swarnali Sarma, 'Psychological Aspects of Infertility' (2010) 3 *British Journal of Medical Practitioners* 32; Ana Galhardo *et al*, 'The Impact of Shame and Self-Judgment on Psychopathology in Infertile Patients' (2011) 26 *Human Reproduction* 2408.

[276] In the main, the harms referred to relate to the physical risks of pregnancy, and the psychological risks relating to potential regret over relinquishing the child: see, eg, Phyllis Chesler, *Sacred Bond: The Legacy of Baby M* (New York, Times Books, 1988); Suze Berkhout, 'Buns in the Oven: Objectification, Surrogacy, and Women's Autonomy' (2008) 34 *Social Theory and Practice* 95; Jennifer Damelio and Kelly Sorensen, 'Enhancing Autonomy in Paid Surrogacy' (2008) 22 *Bioethics* 269; MM Tieu, 'Altruistic Surrogacy: The Necessary Objectification of Surrogate Mothers' (2009) 35 *Journal of Medical Ethics* 171. It has also been suggested that the interests of children born as a result of surrogacy are harmed (Jason KM Hanna, 'Revisiting Child-Based Objections to Commercial Surrogacy' (2010) 24 *Bioethics* 341).

[277] Peter Gaffney, 'Why the "Widespread Agreement" is Wrong: Contesting the Non-harm Arguments for the Prohibition of Full Commercial Surrogacy' (2009) 17 *Journal of Law and Medicine* 280.

[278] See, eg, Elizabeth Anderson, 'Is Women's Labor a Commodity?' (1990) 19 *Philosophy & Public Affairs* 71; R Jo Kornegay, 'Is Commercial Surrogacy Baby-Selling?' (1990) 7 *Journal of Applied Philosophy* 45; Richard J Arneson, 'Commodification and Commercial Surrogacy' (1992) 21 *Philosophy & Public Affairs* 132; Alan

should not be permitted at all, the majority seem to be worried primarily about commercial surrogacy, which treats reproductive labour as something that can be traded in a market-based exchange. These claims have been canvassed (and countered) at length in the literature and need not be recited in detail here.[279] What does bear some attention in a discussion of reproductive autonomy that focuses on the context of women's lives and women's reproductive choices, is what the empirical evidence says about women's experiences of surrogacy.

Do surrogacy arrangements exploit women and children? There is limited evidence about the impact of surrogacy on women or children, but what evidence there is suggests that there is little to be concerned about, at least in the domestic surrogacy context in developed countries such as Canada, Australia, the UK and the US.[280] The research suggests that women who act as surrogates are in general positive about their surrogacy experiences,[281] that they decide to act as surrogates out of altruistic motivations[282] and a desire to help infertile couples, that they are not coerced into surrogacy arrangements[283] and that they are not financially desperate.[284] Based on the available literature, an image of surrogate mothers emerges that situates these women within normal ranges on standardised psychological tests. If they are different in significant ways, women who act as surrogates may be more likely to be 'more independent thinkers . . . less bound by traditional moral values'.[285] Contrary to feminist arguments made in the early days of ARTs, women who act as surrogates are not poor, uneducated women of colour who comprise some sort of reproductive 'underclass' to serve the needs of wealthy white women.[286] They are neither incapable of making advance decisions about their reproductive lives, nor unable to relinquish the infants they bear to the commissioning parents. Busby and Vun note that

[t]he lack of regret and distress experienced by women who choose to be surrogates indicates that they make their decisions with informed consent, an understanding of what the surrogacy

Wertheimer, 'Two Questions about Surrogacy and Exploitation' (1992) 21 *Philosophy & Public Affairs* 211; Stephen Wilkinson, 'The Exploitation Argument against Commercial Surrogacy' (2003) 17 *Bioethics* 169.

[279] See, eg, Chesler (n 276); Berkhout (n 276); Damelio and Sorensen (n 276); Tieu (n 276); Christine Overall, *Ethics and Human Reproduction: A Feminist Analysis* (Boston, MA, Allen & Unwin, 1987) 1, 116–18; Christine Overall, *Human Reproduction: Principles, Practices, Policies* (Toronto, Oxford University Press, 1993); Barbara Katz Rothman, *Recreating Motherhood: Ideology and Technology in a Patriarchal Society* (New York, Norton, 1989).

[280] One article concludes that the 'empirical data offer little support for widely expressed concerns about contractual parenting being emotionally damaging or exploitative for surrogate mothers, children or intended/social parents' (Janice C Ciccarelli and Linda J Beckman, 'Navigating Rough Waters: An Overview of Psychological Aspects of Surrogacy' (2005) 61 *Journal of Social Issues* 21, 29).

[281] See, eg, Teman (n 252); Vasanti Jadva et al, 'Surrogacy: The Experience of Surrogate Mothers' (2003) 18 *Human Reproduction* 2196.

[282] See, eg, Edelman (n 253); Jadva et al (n 281); Eric Blyth, 'I Wanted to be Interesting. I Wanted to be Able to Say "I've Done Something With my Life": Interviews with Surrogate Mothers in Britain' (1994) 12 *Journal of Reproductive and Infant Psychology* 189; Olga van den Akker, 'Genetic and Gestational Surrogate Mothers' Experience of Surrogacy' (2003) 21 *Journal of Reproductive and Infant Psychology* 145.

[283] Ciccarelli and Beckman (n 280). See also Karen Busby and Delaney Vun, 'Revisiting the Handmaid's Tale: Feminist Theory Meets Empirical Research on Surrogate Mothers' (2010) 26 *Canadian Journal of Family Law* 13, 41–52, for a detailed discussion of the literature.

[284] Ciccarelli and Beckman found that 'Surrogate mother's family incomes are most often modest (as opposed to low)' (Ciccarelli and Beckman (n 280) 31).

[285] *Ibid*.

[286] See, eg, Rothman (n 279); Overall, *Ethics and Human Reproduction* (n 279) 1, 116–18; Overall, *Human Reproduction* (n 279).

arrangement requires and a confidence that they can carry through with their initial decision to participate in surrogacy.[287]

Opponents of surrogacy also suggest that such arrangements harm children, but as with the concerns around harm to women, the evidence renders this claim unsustainable. Studies of children born through ART treatment (including surrogacy) and their families have consistently shown that ART-conceived children function normally and enjoy the same levels of psychosocial and cognitive development as do children who are conceived naturally.[288] The studies to date are limited to consideration of fairly young children, meaning that harm to children as a result of surrogacy cannot be ruled out, at least until long-term studies confirm that the findings around family functioning and development are maintained throughout the child's life.

None of this is to suggest that the possibility of exploitation does not exist in the context of surrogacy arrangements. There is no question that both surrogate mothers and commissioning parents can be exploited and harmed. But the evidence suggests that such situations are not the norm (at least not in relatively affluent countries like Canada, Australia, the UK or the US). Arguably, our concern about exploitation should be far more pronounced in developing countries like India, where women are in general less independent and have fewer opportunities for education or for employment that generates an income comparable to what they can earn as surrogate mothers.[289]

To put the point bluntly, respect for reproductive autonomy demands that surrogacy laws be reconsidered and radically altered. Currently, Canada, Australia and the UK permit altruistic surrogacy and criminalise commercial surrogacy. As in the case of egg donation, then, what drives the prohibition is the commercial nature of the arrangement. The underlying assumption must be that the exchange of money for surrogacy services is especially harmful, either because of the power of money to sway women to participate in such arrangements when they otherwise would not, or because of the perceived commodification of reproductive labour and of children. If the concern is that women will be persuaded to act as surrogate mothers against their autonomous wishes, that same concern seems to hold for altruistic surrogacy, in that women who are asked by close friends or relatives might similarly feel pressured.

But in the absence of evidence that commercial surrogacy does unduly influence women's decisions, or that it is harmful or exploitative, it is difficult to argue that parties who wish to engage in surrogacy arrangements should be prohibited from doing so. A contextualised approach to reproductive autonomy instructs that if women wish to act as

---

[287] Busby and Vun (n 283) 73.

[288] Golombok *et al* (n 248); Susan Golombok *et al*, 'Families Created Through Surrogacy Arrangements: Parent–Child Relationships in the 1st Year of Life' (2004) 40 *Developmental Psychology* 400; Susan Golombok *et al*, 'Non-Genetic and Non-Gestational Parenthood: Consequences for Parent–Child Relationships and the Psychological Well-Being of Mothers, Fathers and Children at Age 3' (2006) 21 *Human Reproduction* 1918; Susan Golombok *et al*, 'Surrogacy Families: Parental Functioning, Parent–Child Relationships and Children's Psychological Development at Age 2' (2006) 47 *Journal of Child Psychology and Psychiatry* 213; Katherine H Shelton *et al*, 'Examining Differences in Psychological Adjustment Problems Among Children Conceived by Assisted Reproductive Technologies' (2009) 33 *International Journal of Behavioral Development* 385.

[289] George Palattiyil *et al*, 'Globalization and Cross-Border Reproductive Services: Ethical Implications of Surrogacy in India for Social Work' (2010) 53 *International Social Work* 686, 690–91. See also Usha Rengachary Smerdon, 'Crossing Bodies, Crossing Borders: International Surrogacy Between the United States and India' (2008) 39 *Cumberland Law Review* 15, 53–57; Andrea Whittaker, 'Cross-border Assisted Reproduction Care in Asia: Implications for Access, Equity and Regulations' (2011) 19(37) *Reproductive Health Matters* 107, 111–12.

surrogates and if commissioning parents wish to form their families through the use of surrogacy, then these parties should be permitted to engage in such arrangements. Speculative arguments and concerns – including those based in morality or fears for the future of the family – must not be permitted to take priority over the autonomy-based interests of those who seek to procreate through surrogacy arrangements.

Legal regimes such as those in Canada, the UK and Australia have evolved based on the concerns around harm and exploitation that were raised in the early days of assisted reproduction. These legal approaches seem to conceive of exploitation and harm as the inevitable result of liberal rules around surrogacy (and commercial surrogacy in particular). Canada's ART legislation, which purportedly aims to protect the health, well-being, dignity and rights of the participants in ART treatment,[290] is at present clearly failing the women who participate in these surrogacy (and egg donation) arrangements. The law generates uncertainty which, in turn, creates a greater likelihood of exploitation than would exist with appropriate regulation.[291]

Indeed, given the anecdotal reports suggesting the development of a 'grey market' in Canada for both oocytes and surrogacy services,[292] the law seems to have an effect that is antithetical to its declared principles and objectives. In an effort to protect the interests of women and children from harm, the law has instead created the potential for harm to both by ensuring that surrogacy, when it does take place, occurs in conditions of silence and uncertainty.

Even if I am mistaken about what respect for reproductive autonomy entails, there are other, largely pragmatic considerations that favour permissive regulation. When surrogacy arrangements proceed as the parties hope they will, the end result is the birth of a child. And though the evidence demonstrates that children born as a result of surrogacy arrangements are not harmed by the method of their conception and gestation, legal uncertainty around surrogacy can cause harm to all involved.

Surrogacy, whether commercial or altruistic, should be permitted, but it must be carefully regulated to minimise the potential for harm and to promote the reproductive autonomy interests of both surrogate mothers and intended parents. Regulation should be permissive and allow parties to enter into surrogacy agreements, the terms of which will be respected. The reproductive autonomy analysis that I adopt here requires that such agreements be respected not only to ensure that intended parents who wish to form a family using surrogacy services have a legal means of doing so. It also acknowledges and respects the autonomy interests of the surrogate mother. The suggestion that surrogacy arrangements should be formalised through the mechanism of contract leads to several concerns, in particular the worry that the surrogate mother's ability to make decisions about the pregnancy will be restricted.[293] In order to ensure that the agreements themselves do not impede the reproductive autonomy of any of the parties, surrogacy regulation should include a process whereby surrogacy arrangements are

---

[290] AHR Act, s 2(b).

[291] Busby's study refers to a case where a Canadian woman was acting as a surrogate mother for a European couple (Busby and Vun (n 283) 66). She was being paid, and was required to undergo selective reduction from triplets to twins. She appears to have been told very close to the time of expected delivery that she would have to travel outside of her home province to a province with laws favourable to having commissioning parents' names on the birth certificates. At this stage (after arriving in the other province), she became concerned about the possibility of her own liability for medical costs related to her delivery and sought legal advice.

[292] See, eg, Motluk (n 48).

[293] Damelio and Sorensen (n 276).

evaluated and approved, either judicially or by a regulatory body (such as the Patient Review Panel in Victoria, Australia).[294]

Another aspect of surrogacy that requires close attention from policy makers is the existence of agencies or organisations that facilitate surrogacy arrangements by matching intended parents with potential surrogate mothers. Here, there is significant potential for exploitation and unfairness, as agencies benefit financially from the anxieties of intended parents and from the reproductive labour of surrogate mothers. Given the stakes and vulnerabilities involved in surrogacy arrangements, there is a need for clear information and advice for all parties, and non-professionals may not be able to provide the assistance needed.[295] It is in no one's interests to leave the details of a surrogacy arrangement to chance. But while the help of knowledgeable individuals is essential, care must be taken to ensure that agencies do not take advantage of vulnerable individuals. The monitoring of surrogacy service agencies could be undertaken by the same body that vets surrogacy agreements, as I suggest above.

One argument I have heard many times from feminist colleagues who favour continued restriction of surrogacy (particularly commercial surrogacy) is that although autonomy is an important consideration in reproductive regulation, it is trumped (in this context at least) by equality-based concerns. In other words, surrogacy creates or perpetuates women's inequality, and achieving equality for women is a goal that outweighs the negative effects of the infringement of autonomy occasioned by restrictive regulation. This argument is problematic both for practical reasons and for reasons of principle. From a purely pragmatic standpoint, restrictive regulation of surrogacy is not the way to improve prospects for women's equality. If we are worried that women are choosing to engage in surrogacy because their other options for financial security are so limited or unappealing, our focus should be on finding ways to improve women's opportunities for education and employment, or to support women's decisions to remain at home with their children without facing extreme financial stress. Criminalising surrogacy is not going to move us toward those goals. In any case, reproductive autonomy is an essential ingredient of women's equality, and limiting women's choices (as difficult as they might be for some of us to understand) is not the answer.

As with many of the details of regulation in the ART context, a reproductive autonomy analysis does not resolve all of the questions about the regulation of surrogacy arrangements. The reproductive autonomy analysis in the surrogacy context might be able to tell us whether surrogacy should be legal, whether commercial surrogacy is an option, whether contracts should be enforceable and what freedoms the pregnant woman should have to make decisions about the pregnancy – but where a dispute arises about parentage or custody of the resulting child, this analysis cannot necessarily resolve it. As will be discussed in section IV. below, regulation of surrogacy also requires clear rules about determinations of parentage.

---

[294] Assisted Reproductive Treatment Act 2008 (Vic), ss 39–41.
[295] See *Re G (Surrogacy: Foreign Domicile)* [2007] EWHC 2814 (Fam), [2008] 1 FLR 1047, for a discussion of this concern.

IV. PARENTAGE IN ASSISTED REPRODUCTION

Assisted reproductive technologies create enormous potential for disrupting existing ideas about what it means to be a parent and what constitutes a family. The space that assisted reproduction creates for parental choice is at once the most exciting and (for some) the most dangerous feature of the technologies. One of the most pressing concerns created by assisted reproduction is the potential separation of biological or genetic connection and the work of parenting though the use of donated gametes and the practice of surrogacy. Another is the complexity introduced by the sheer number of possibilities as to who might assert parental rights. As discussed in the previous section, surrogacy in particular has led to significant social concern and legal and ethical debate and discussion.

The potential disengagement of biology from parenting is not limited to the ART context. Adoption also entails the raising of a child to whom one is not biologically related, and even where families are created in a more traditional fashion, the modern family often involves parenting by adults who are connected to the child only through their relationship with one of the child's biological parents. In these situations, law usually plays a role in formalising relationships with children such that there is minimal uncertainty as to the legal status of the adults who play a parental role in the child's life. In the ART context, the law is far less settled.

Law has in some instances been slow to adapt to changing family forms, and in both the legislative and common law realms, it is fair to say that the evolution continues and that the transition has not always been smooth. Judges and policy makers alike have struggled with issues related to assisted reproduction, gay and lesbian parenting, and the prospect of assigning legal parentage to more than two adults, and this has contributed to the slow pace of the evolution of laws addressing the effect of ARTs in the family law realm. Referring to a child support claim in a family formed through assisted reproduction, Gamble and Ghevaert explain that

> [the case] demonstrates that one cannot apply traditional concepts of family law to alternative family structures in which legal, biological and social parentage are not all united in the same parents. Family law usually considers parenting disputes in a pragmatic and discretionary way, led by the best interests of the child. Assisted reproduction law is a very different beast. Its driving force is clarity and certainty, rather than welfare, and parenthood (and by extension financial responsibility is not within the court's gift.[296]

Some jurisdictions have been slower than others to adapt their legal regimes to changing modes of family formation that flow from the availability of ARTs. Legislation is key in this context, in that it sets out explicit rules that lend themselves to far more clarity and consistency than does the common law process, particularly where that process is conditioned – as it often is in the family law context – on a factor as subjective and individually-determined as 'the best interests of the child'. While there are ways to define or determine who is a parent other than through statutory provisions,[297] the significant

---

[296] Natalie Gamble and Louisa Ghevaert, 'Lesbian Mothers in Dispute: T v B' (2010) 40 *Family Law* 1203, 1206.
[297] Social parents may be recognised through the doctrine of *in loco parentis*, where one who has a parental relationship with a child can be treated as a parent in determining issues of child support, custody and access. In Canada, step-parents (or more broadly those standing in the place of a parent vis-à-vis a child) may acquire

advantage provided by statutory rules is the clarity they afford. Where such rules are absent, parties must resort to the judicial process to have their parental status clarified. In turn, judges are placed in the position of applying rules that were not fashioned to deal with families created using ARTs, and inconsistency is often the result.[298] A more fluid common law-based process might work for decision making about support obligations, but it is not amenable to the precision needed on the more fundamental questions that arise in assisted reproduction around parental status. This is a potential problem both for those who donate reproductive materials and for those who use donated gametes or surrogacy services in order to build their families.

Laws relating to parentage in the ART context cover two main situations: the assignment of parentage in cases where donor gametes are used by an individual or a couple to conceive a child, and the assignment of parentage in the context of surrogacy arrangements. In some jurisdictions, the same basic rules cover both circumstances; in other jurisdictions, distinct rules apply. Although early legislative responses to parentage in ART-formed families focused on heterosexual couples seeking to build families using donated sperm or through surrogacy arrangements, more recent legislative responses acknowledge that provision must also be made for additional technologies (such as egg and embryo donation) and for same-sex couples seeking to become parents through these same technologies.[299]

recognition as social parents through the operation of the doctrine, at least in the context of custody, access and support (Alison Harvison Young, 'This Child Does Have 2 (Or More) Fathers . . .: Step-parents and Support Obligations' (2000) 45 *McGill Law Journal* 107; Carol Rogerson, 'The Child-Support Obligation of Step-parents' (2001) 18 *Canadian Journal of Family Law* 9). Similar mechanisms exist in other jurisdictions as well, although the rights and duties acquired depend to some extent on the status of the relationship between the adult and the child's parent. In the US, for example, the courts have begun to recognise the importance of de facto relationships with children (as opposed to insisting on biological relatedness) in establishing parental rights and obligations: see, eg, *Re Custody of HSH-K*, 533 NW 2d 419 (Wis 1995) (holding that a non-biological parent could seek access visits with the child after the adult relationship ended). See also *Elisa B v Superior Court*, 117 P3d 660 (Cal 2005) (where the court held that a woman who 'encouraged her former domestic partner to have a child by intrauterine insemination could be liable for support of the child' (Kindregan and McBrien (n 7) 17)); *Kristine H v Lisa R*, 117 P3d 690 (Cal 2005) (in which the biological mother of the child was 'estopped' from denying her former partner's maternal relationship to the child, as she had consented to her former partner being named as a parent in a pre-birth parenting order).

[298] Angela Campbell, 'Conceiving Parents Through Law' (2007) 21 *International Journal of Law, Policy and the Family* 242, 248.

[299] In the UK, the amendments to the HFE Act extended the parenthood provisions to recognise a lesbian woman's civil partner as the other parent in the ART treatment context (HFE Act 2008, ss 42–43). In Australia, the first legislation to grant parental status to the consenting lesbian partner of a woman undergoing ART treatment was passed in Western Australia (Acts Amendment (Lesbian and Gay Law Reform) Act 2002 (WA), s 26, which created s 6A of the Artificial Conception Act 1985 (WA)). See also Status of Children Act 1974 (Tas), s 10C(1A); Status of Children Act 1974 (Vic), ss 13, 14; Status of Children Act (NT), s 5DA; Status of Children Act 1978 (Qld), s 19C–19E; Status of Children Act 1996 (NSW), s 14(1A); Parentage Act 2004 (ACT), s 11(4). South Australia has recently passed the Family Relationships (Parentage) Amendment Bill 2011 (SA) to amend the Family Relationships Act 1975 (SA), s 10C to extend parental status to a consenting lesbian partner of a woman who conceives using ARTs. Several Canadian provinces also have laws relating to birth registration or parentage in the context of assisted reproduction use by same-sex couples (see the discussion below). Not all of these jurisdictions recognise gay men as parents. In the US, a very small minority of states have addressed parentage in same-sex families with 'consent to inseminate' laws that grant legal parentage to the birth mother's partner or spouse when statutory criteria are met: see, eg, New Mexico Uniform Parentage Act, 2009 NM Laws 215 §§ 7-703, 7-704; Domestic Partnership Judicial Determination of Parentage Act of 2009, DC Code Ann §16 – 909(e)(1) (2010), 56 DC Reg 4269. Oregon has an appellate level decision extending the state's 'consent to inseminate' statute to same-sex couples (*Shineovich v Kemp*, 214 P 3d 29 (Or Ct App 2009).

A. Parentage laws

In the UK, parentage in assisted reproduction (and in gestational surrogacy) is determined on the basis of the status provisions of the HFE Act 2008. These provisions, designed for use in assisted conception but not surrogacy in particular, provide that the birth mother and her consenting spouse or same-sex civil partner are the legal parents of the child, whether or not they are genetically related to the child.[300] If there is no father according to the status rules – where, for example, the surrogate mother is single, or where her spouse or partner does not consent to the assisted conception treatment – the intended father may be considered the legal father of the child.[301]

It is clear that in gestational surrogacy, the intended parents are not the parents of the child at birth. Intended parents can seek what is called a parental order[302] to 'fast-track' adoption of the child. Until the parental order is granted, the intended parents have no parental status and cannot make decisions regarding the child's welfare. This can become extremely significant in cases where the child is born outside of the country as a result of an international surrogacy arrangement, as the law of the child's country of birth may provide otherwise.[303]

To obtain a parental order, intended parents must meet several conditions. The application must be made within a set time frame,[304] and the birth mother and her partner must consent to the order.[305] In addition, at least one of the parents (and there must be two; single parents cannot obtain a parental order[306]) must be genetically connected to the child. Thus where neither parent is able to provide gametes for use in the surrogacy arrangement, a parental order is unavailable. The child must be in the care of and residing with the intended parents when the application is made. Lastly, the court must be satisfied that 'no money or other benefit (other than for expenses reasonably incurred) has been given or received by either of the applicants for or in consideration of' any aspect of the surrogacy arrangement, unless the payment is authorised by the court.[307] The purpose of this last requirement is to discourage intended parents from avoiding the prohibition on commercial surrogacy by participating in commercial surrogacy arrangements outside of the UK. As has been noted by Justice Hedley, however, it will be a rare case in which the child's welfare would not be best served by judicial authorisation of what clearly amounts to a commercial surrogacy arrangement.[308]

---

[300] HFE Act 2008, ss 33, 35–37. In other words, if donor gametes are used, the donor is not the parent; the birth mother and her partner are the parents.

[301] This route to fatherhood exists by virtue of ss 35–37 of the HFE Act 2008. The idea is that the intended father and the surrogate mother received 'treatment together' (Horsey and Sheldon (n 264)). Horsey and Sheldon note that the law may have the effect of encouraging a demand for unmarried women as surrogates.

[302] HFE Act 2008, s 54.

[303] This is discussed in more detail below, section V.

[304] HFE Act 2008, s 54(3). As this condition is mandatory, the UK courts have no discretion to modify the timeline. This could potentially become an impediment where, due to conflicting legal rules, immigration concerns and inaccurate legal advice, the application cannot be made in a timely fashion.

[305] One of the difficulties with the requirement for consent of the birth mother's spouse or partner arises where the couple are estranged. See *Re G* (n 295) paras 30–39.

[306] The intended parents must be married or civil partners (HFE Act 2008, s 54(2)).

[307] *Ibid* s 54(8).

[308] As Hedley J observed: 'I feel bound to observe that I find this process of authorisation most uncomfortable. What the court is required to do is to balance two competing and potentially irreconcilably conflicting concepts. Parliament is clearly entitled to legislate against commercial surrogacy and is clearly entitled to expect that the courts should implement that policy consideration in its decisions. Yet it is also recognised that

Australia is a federal jurisdiction, and as is clear from the discussion in this and the previous chapter, ART regulation is not uniform across the country. However, Australian law-makers have actively sought to harmonise parentage laws to facilitate the ability of intended parents to become the legal parents of their children.[309] In general terms, parentage law in Australia is similar to that in the UK.[310] The surrogate (birth) mother and her partner are parents at birth, regardless of whether they have any genetic connection to the child.[311] In addition, as in the UK, most Australian states have a process whereby intended parents can obtain a court order declaring them to be the child's legal parents.[312] Statutory conditions attach to parentage orders, the specifics of which vary by state. Very generally, the conditions include age and residency requirements for the parties, consent from all of the parties, stipulations that the agreement was made prior to conception and was not a commercial arrangement,[313] and a conclusion by the court that the child's welfare is best served by the order.[314]

In stark contrast to the certainty created by clear parentage rules in both the UK and Australia, few Canadian jurisdictions have explicitly addressed the status of children conceived via the use of ARTs.[315] Even among the provinces that have taken steps to address this issue in legislation, there is no consistency as to where the rules are found, their precise content or how they might be interpreted.[316] And though some provinces have rules that apply to both surrogacy and donor gametes, some are limited to the latter. Manitoba's Vital Statistics Act,[317] for example, says that where a child is born as a result of AI, the birth registration shall be completed showing the birth mother's spouse or common law partner as the father or other parent of the child. Manitoba law thus contemplates same-sex parents, suggesting that a female couple who conceive with the

---

as the full rigour of that policy consideration will bear on one wholly unequipped to comprehend it let alone deal with its consequences (ie the child concerned) that rigour must be mitigated by the application of a consideration of that child's welfare. That approach is both humane and intellectually coherent. The difficulty is that it is almost impossible to imagine a set of circumstances in which by the time the case comes to court, the welfare of any child (particularly a foreign child) would not be gravely compromised (at the very least) by a refusal to make an order.' (*Re X & Y (Foreign Surrogacy)* [2008] EWHC 3030 (Fam), [24])

[309] 'A Proposal for a National Model to Harmonise Regulation of Surrogacy' (n 266).

[310] The UK status provisions include situations involving donated sperm, oocytes or embryos. Most of the Australian legislation refers to sperm and oocyte donors, but not embryo donors.

[311] See, eg, Status of Children Act 1978 (Qld), ss 17–19; Status of Children Act 1996 (NSW), s 14 (dealing with parentage in the case of assisted reproduction); Parentage Act 2004 (ACT), ss 7, 11; Surrogacy Act 2010 (Qld), s 8. But see Jenni Millbank, 'The New Surrogacy Parentage Laws in Australia: Cautious Regulation or '25 Brick Walls'?' (2011) 35 *Melbourne University Law Review* 165 for a detailed discussion and critique of the Australian laws. Millbank argues that the Australian approach is 'unduly complex and inflexible' (*ibid* 206). In her view, a better approach is that found in UK law. As will be discussed below, the Australian laws do appear to be an improvement over the situation in Canada and the US. At least there are laws in place.

[312] See, eg, Status of Children Act 1974 (Vic), s 20; Family Relationships Act 1975 (SA), s 10HB; Parentage Act 2004 (ACT), s 26; Surrogacy Act 2008 (WA), s 19; Surrogacy Act 2010 (NSW), s 12; Surrogacy Act 2010 (Qld), s 21.

[313] Note that Victorian legislation defines what a surrogate mother may be reimbursed for as follows: medical expenses associated with pregnancy and birth, costs of legal advice and counselling, travel expenses incurred in relation to the pregnancy or birth (Assisted Reproductive Treatment Regulations 2009 (Vic), s 10).

[314] See, eg, Status of Children Act 1974 (Vic), ss 20–23; Parentage Act 2004 (ACT), s 26; Surrogacy Act 2010 (NSW), ss 21–38; Surrogacy Act 2010 (Qld), s 22.

[315] The common law thus governs in a number of Canadian jurisdictions: see, eg, *MD v LL*, 2008 CanLII 9374 (ONSC); *WJQM v AMA*, 2011 SKQB 317, 382 Sask R 119.

[316] Some statutes refer to parentage in cases of AI, some refer to donated sperm only, and others refer to donated gametes or genetic material, without reference to whether the material comes from a male or female donor.

[317] Vital Statistics Act, CCSM, c V60, s 3(6).

aid of reproductive technology should both be recognised as the parents of the resulting child. It is not clear, however, whether the law will recognise the persons named as the parents on the birth registration as the legal parents of the child.[318] In Prince Edward Island, the Child Status Act[319] provides that where conception is achieved using ARTs, the spouse or person cohabiting with the child's mother in a conjugal relationship is a parent (unless this person did not consent to assisted conception or was not aware that the mother was seeking to become pregnant via assisted conception). The statute also makes it clear that a gamete donor is not a parent simply by virtue of the gamete donation, and states that a woman who gives birth to a child is deemed to be the child's mother, whether or not she is the genetic mother of the child. Québec's Civil Code also deals with parentage (the Code refers to 'filiation') of children who are born using ARTs.[320] Québec law refers to a 'parental project' involving the use of assisted conception using the genetic material of a person who is not party to the 'parental project'.[321] The Code provides that the party who donates gametes for use in assisted conception by third parties is not a parent of the resulting child.[322] Québec was the first Canadian jurisdiction to recognise that a child could have two female parents by extending the presumption of paternity to a spouse (married or civil union) of either sex.[323]

Alberta's Family Law Act[324] deals explicitly with the complexities of a wider variety of circumstances than most Canadian jurisdictions.[325] The starting point in Alberta's legislation is that the parents of a child are the birth mother and biological father.[326] In the

[318] This was explained by a Manitoba lawyer in a workshop I attended in Winnipeg, Manitoba in February 2012. The workshop, entitled 'New Approaches to Assisted Human Reproduction in Canada', was hosted by the University of Manitoba's Centre for Human Rights Research and the Canadian Journal of Women and the Law/Revue femmes et droit, with additional financial assistance from the Legal Research Institute (at <http://chrr.info/reproductive-and-sexual-rights>).

[319] Child Status Act, RSPEI 1988, c C-6, s 9(5). Similar provisions are found in the Yukon Territory (Children's Act, RSY 2002, c 31, s 13) and in Newfoundland and Labrador (Children's Law Act, RSNL 1990, c C-13, s 12). Newfoundland's Vital Statistics Act, 2009, SNL 2009, c V-6.01, s 5 deals with the naming of the child's parents on the child's birth registration. In the case of AI, the birth mother's spouse or cohabiting partner is to be named as the father or other parent of the child (*ibid* s 5(5)); in the case of surrogacy, s 5(6) provides that the intended parents shall be registered as the parents of the child, where the Registrar General receives a certified copy of an adoption order or a declaratory order respecting parentage pursuant to s 6 or s 7 of the Children's Law Act.

[320] Civil Code of Québec, Arts 538–542.

[321] *Ibid* Art 538.

[322] *Ibid* Art 538.2. It is noteworthy that the Article goes on to provide that 'if the genetic material is provided by way of sexual intercourse, a bond of filiation may be established, in the year following the birth, between the contributor and the child'. As several commentators have noted, the differential treatment of sexual intercourse creates significant potential uncertainty for female couples wishing to embark on a 'parental project' (Campbell (n 298) 254–57; Cameron *et al* (n 125); Robert Leckey, '"Where the Parents are of the Same Sex": Québec's Reforms to Filiation' (2009) 23 *International Journal of Law, Policy and the Family* 62, 68. Case law has borne out this concern: *LC v SG*, [2004] JQ no 7060 (CA)(QL); *LB v Li Ba*, 2006 QCCS 591, affd Droit de la famille – 07527, 2007 QCCA 362.

[323] Civil Code of Québec, Art 538.3. Art 539.1 provides that where both of the child's parents are women, the non-birth mother is assigned the rights and obligations that the law would ordinarily assign to the father.

[324] Family Law Act (AB) (n 257). The discussion of Alberta law that follows is based on the most recent amendments to the Family Law Act. The gender-neutral language in the relevant statutory provisions is in part a response to an equality rights challenge to the former, male-specific language that rendered the provisions inapplicable to the female partner of a birth mother (*Fraess v Alberta (Minister of Justice and Attorney General)* 2005 ABQB 889, 390 AR 280). In a later case, the Alberta courts also found that the legislation violated section 15 of the Charter in failing to extend the assignment of fatherhood to the consenting male partner in the assisted conception context to same-sex couples (*DWH v DJR*, 2011 ABQB 608, 518 AR 165). The provisions had already been amended by the time the Court released its decision.

[325] Family Law Act (AB) (n 257), ss 7, 8.1, 8.2.

[326] *Ibid* s 7(2). In the case of uncertainty or dispute around parentage, an application may be made for a declaration of parentage pursuant to s 9.

assisted conception context, the parents are the birth mother and the man who provides sperm or an embryo for his own reproductive use.[327] Where conception involves the use of donor gametes or donated embryos, the donor is not a parent by reason only of the donation if the gametes or embryo(s) were provided by a donor for the reproductive use of a third party.[328]

In the case of surrogacy arrangements involving assisted reproduction, at birth, the surrogate mother is the mother of the child. Her spouse or conjugal interdependent partner is not the child's legal parent.[329] The Act allows for the making of an application for a declaration of parentage, whereby the birth mother may be declared not to be a parent of the child.[330] If the male commissioning parent is the biological father of the child then his consenting spouse or conjugal interdependent partner is the child's other parent.[331] The Act therefore provides for the possibility of a gay male couple becoming parents of a child through surrogacy.[332] A parallel provision exists for situations where the gametes or embryos are provided by a female commissioning parent.[333] If the court is satisfied that the child was born through assisted reproduction using gametes or an embryo from one of the intended parents, and that the surrogate has consented, the application will be granted.[334] The person declared to be a parent of the child will be deemed to be a parent 'at and from the time of . . . birth'.[335] If the surrogate does not consent to the declaration of parentage then she is the only parent of the child.[336]

As noted earlier, surrogacy agreements are not enforceable and cannot be used as evidence of the surrogate mother's consent for the purposes of a declaration of parentage. Such agreements may, however, be used as evidence of consent by the non-biological parent (ie the parent who did not provide a gamete) to the surrogate's treatment with ARTs; this consent is a condition to the recognition of the non-biological parent as a legal parent.[337] Lastly, the Act states that a declaration of parentage cannot be made if the result of the declaration would be that the child has more than two parents.[338]

British Columbia also has new legislation that deals with issues of parentage in assisted conception and surrogacy.[339] In assisted reproduction, the birth mother and her

---

[327] *Ibid* s 8.1(2). If both partners provide gametes or an embryo, both are parents. Where only one spouse or partner provides gametes or an embryo, that person and the consenting spouse or partner are the parents. Consent to be a parent to a child born via assisted reproduction is presumed where the person is 'married to or in a conjugal relationship of interdependence of some permanence with' the gamete or embryo provider or the birth mother (*ibid* s 8.1(6)).

[328] *Ibid* s 7(4).

[329] *Ibid* s 7(5).

[330] *Ibid* s 8.2. The application is to be brought within 30 days of the child's birth, unless the Court allows the application to be brought later than that (*ibid*, s 8.2(4)).

[331] *Ibid* s 8.1(2).

[332] *Ibid*.

[333] *Ibid* s 8.1(3). Thus, where a woman provides an oocyte or embryo for her own reproductive use and bears the child herself, her partner or spouse is the other parent. If the birth mother is a surrogate and is declared not to be a parent then the embryo or egg provider and partner are the parents.

[334] *Ibid* s 8.2(6). If the surrogate is deceased at the time the application is made, or if she cannot be located after reasonable efforts are made, the consent requirement may be waived (*ibid*, s 8.2(9)).

[335] *Ibid* s 8.2(7).

[336] *Ibid* s 8.1(4)(c).

[337] *Ibid* s 8.1(2)(b)(ii) or s 8.1(3)(b)(ii).

[338] *Ibid* s 8.2(12)(b).

[339] Family Law Act (BC) (n 258). Even before the legislative changes, BC common law allowed intended parents to be registered as the parents of a child born as a result of a surrogacy arrangement (*Rypkema v British Columbia*, 2003 BCSC 1784, 22 BCLR (4th) 233) and allowed for a declaration of parentage to be made in similar cases (*BAN v JH*, 2008 BCSC 808, 86 BCLR (4th) 106).

consenting spouse or partner are the parents, whether or not they are also the genetic parents of the child.[340] In surrogacy arrangements, the intended parents are the parents, provided that the statutory conditions relating to surrogacy arrangements are met.[341] These conditions require that the surrogacy arrangement be formalised in a written agreement that provides that the surrogate mother will not be a parent, that she will surrender the child to the intended parents and that the intended parents will be the parents of the child.[342] As long as no one withdraws from the agreement prior to the child's conception, the surrogate mother provides her consent[343] and the intended parents take the child into their care, the intended parents are the parents of the child.[344] The surrogacy agreement itself cannot satisfy the consent requirement, but it may be used as evidence of the parties' intentions if a dispute arises.[345]

British Columbia's legislation also provides for 'other arrangements' – where a surrogate and the commissioning parents intend to parent together, or where the birth mother, partner and donor all intend to parent together, the parties to the agreement are the parents.[346] There is nothing in the statute that limits the number of parents of a child to two, as found in the Alberta legislation. In the case of a dispute or uncertainty as to parentage, an application may be made for an order declaring parentage.[347] In addition, and perhaps in acknowledgement of the phenomenon of international surrogacy and reproductive tourism, the British Columbia statute also has sections that deal with recognition (within British Columbia) of Canadian and non-Canadian extra-provincial orders.[348]

The US, like Canada and Australia, is a federal system in which family law is state-based.[349] And, as is the case in Canada, American jurisdictions have adopted a variety of approaches to determining parentage in the context of assisted reproduction and surrogacy.[350] Most states have extended the traditionally applicable presumptions of parentage

---

[340] Family Law Act (BC) (n 258) s 27. The section covers donated sperm, oocytes and embryos. Section 28 deals with parentage in the case of conception via assisted reproduction when one of the gamete providers has died prior to the child's conception.

[341] *Ibid* s 29.

[342] *Ibid* s 29(2).

[343] As in Alberta, the consent requirement may be waived if the surrogate is deceased or incapable of providing consent, or where she cannot be located after reasonable efforts are made (*ibid*, s 29(4)).

[344] *Ibid* s 29(3).

[345] *Ibid* s 29(6).

[346] *Ibid* s 30.

[347] *Ibid* s 31.

[348] *Ibid* ss 35 (Canadian orders) and 36 (non-Canadian orders). If a Canadian order is in place, the court must recognise it (unless new evidence is in play that was not available during the out-of-BC proceeding, or unless the court is satisfied that the order was obtained under fraud or duress). If a non-Canadian order is in place, the court must recognise it if at least one of the parents was habitually resident in or had a real and substantial connection with the foreign jurisdiction. As to refusing to recognise the foreign order, the same rules apply, except that the court may also refuse to recognise the foreign order if it is of the view that the order is contrary to public policy. Alberta's legislation does not specify how extra-provincial or foreign orders are to be handled.

[349] Crockin and Jones (n 271) 134.

[350] There is considerable variation, in the states that have taken legislative action, in terms of the aspects of ART procedures that are regulated: see, eg, Cal Fam Code § 7613 (West); Colo Rev Stat § 19-4-106-2 (2000); Wyo Stat Ann § 14-2-902 (2011) (all three of which simply cut off any parental rights of a sperm donor). Other state statutes deal with egg donation: Fla Stat Ann § 742.14 (West 2010) (stating that donors relinquish all rights and obligations with respect to resulting children); ND Cent Code §§ 14-20-01 to -66 (2009); Okla Stat Ann tit 10, §§ 7700-101 to -902 (2009); Tex Fam Code Ann § 160.702 (West 2008); Va Code Ann § 20-158 (2008) (making intended mother the legal mother and relieving egg donor of all rights and obligations). Still others

to the assisted reproduction context through the adoption of legislation along the lines of the 1973 Uniform Parentage Act.[351] These statutes provide that where a married couple use donated sperm to conceive a child, the sperm donor is not a parent of the resulting child.[352] Where a man consents (in writing) to his wife's insemination with donor sperm, as long as the insemination is supervised by a physician and the consent document is registered with the appropriate state department, the man is the legal father of the child borne by his wife.[353] The formalities can be critical, in that a failure to follow the relevant statutory provisions may result in a child having no legal father.[354] Most state laws refer to married couples in contemplating parentage of children born through ART treatment, and in states where marriage is available to same-sex couples, a lesbian non-birth mother may also become a legal parent on the basis of the parentage presumption. A small number of states have passed legislation specifically aimed at clarifying parentage where donated gametes are used.[355] Known as 'consent to inseminate' laws, the statutes grant legal parentage to the non-biological parent where that person intends to parent the child and where the birth mother has consented to the grant of parental status to the non-biological parent.[356]

Some states have adopted more contemporary laws that apply to gamete donation more generally; these laws provide that gamete donors (whether the gametes are oocytes or sperm) who do not intend to parent are not the legal parents of children born through the use of their gametes.[357] To date, only a handful of states have adopted legislation that specifies parentage in the egg donation context specifically,[358] leaving the law unclear in most of the country. Even fewer states have laws that speak to parentage in the situation of embryo donation.[359]

deal with embryo donation: La Rev Stat Ann § 9:130 (West 2000) (Louisiana treats embryo donation like adoption). In Florida and Texas, the statutes provide that embryo donors are not the parents (Fla Stat Ann 742.14 (West 2010); Tex Fam Code Ann § 160.702 (West 2008)). For more detailed discussion of these issues, see Cahn (n 124); Richard F Storrow, 'Parenthood by Pure Intention: Assisted Reproduction and the Functional Approach to Parentage' (2002) 53 *Hastings Law Journal* 597; Helen M Alvare, 'The Case for Regulating Collaborative Reproduction: A Children's Rights Perspective' (2003) 40 *Harvard Journal on Legislation* 1.

[351] The first Uniform Parentage Act (1973) was adopted to address the issue of illegitimacy ('non marital children') and was adopted in some form in 19 states, but 'influenced' the law in all states (Nancy D Polikoff, 'A Mother Should Not Have to Adopt Her Own Child: Parentage Laws for Children of Lesbian Couples in the Twenty-First Century' (2009) 2 *Stanford Journal of Civil Rights and Civil Liberties* 201, 211).

[352] The majority of states have legislation dealing with parentage in the context of assisted reproduction using donor sperm (Crockin and Jones (n 271) 192). Most often, these laws deal with the use of donor sperm by married couples. In the case of single women, there is more variation among states (Cahn (n 107) 90–91). Cahn notes that New Jersey's law provides that the donor is not a parent, whether or not the woman using the donor sperm is married (NJ Stat § 9:17–44b (2007)).

[353] See, eg, Cahn (n 107) 90; Kindregan and McBrien (n 7) 61–62.

[354] *Alexandria S v Pacific Fertility Medical Center, Inc*, 55 Cal App 4th 110 (1997).

[355] Movement Advancement Project, Family Equality Council and Center for American Progress, 'All Children Matter: How Legal and Social Inequalities Hurt LGBT Families' (October 2011) 36–38, at <www.americanprogress.org/wpcontent/uploads/issues/2011/10/pdf/all_children_matter.pdf>.

[356] *Ibid*.

[357] Some of these states have adopted legislation based on some aspects of the 2000 Uniform Parentage Act (Uniform Parentage Act (2000), 9B ULA 299 (2001)). In the case of the male partner of a woman who uses ART procedures, where both intend to become parents (and where conception is accomplished with donor sperm or the male partner's sperm), the male partner is the legal father of the child.

[358] North Dakota has adopted the Uniform Parentage Act; its law states that an oocyte donor is not a parent of the resulting child (ND Cent Code §14–20–60 (2007)), and that a woman may become a child's legal mother by giving birth to the child, or through a court order or legal adoption (ND Cent Code § 14 –20–07(1)(a)–(c)). Oklahoma and Texas have similar legislation (Cahn (n 107) 95).

[359] Cahn (n 107) 96.

There are also some states without any statutory rules in place to determine parentage in assisted reproduction. Where no legislation has been enacted, the common law governs, meaning that questions of legal parentage are handled on a case-by-case basis, creating a significant likelihood of inconsistency. A number of courts that have faced issues of parentage in the ART context have called for legislative action.[360] Naomi Cahn summarises the US law as follows:

> Ultimately, there is no uniformity on parentage or on identity issues when it comes to families formed through ART. Even the model legislation in this area, the Uniform Parentage Act, which provides a gender-neutral approach to donor eggs, sperm, and embryos and which applies to both marital and nonmarital parents, does not address gay and lesbian parenting issues.[361]

Laws relating to determination of parentage in surrogacy arrangements also vary considerably among the states. States take diverse positions on all issues relevant to surrogacy, including whether it is legal, whether surrogacy agreements are enforceable and how parentage should be determined in the surrogacy context. In a small minority of states, pre-birth parentage orders are available to intended parents.[362] Few states have legislation concerning surrogacy, and most have no clear and binding case law.[363] The end result is that similar cases are sometimes decided differently, and 'each state has carved out its own way of dealing with contested surrogacy disputes'.[364]

More than one author has noted that in traditional surrogacy (where the surrogate mother has a genetic connection to the child through providing the oocyte), American courts are fairly consistent in holding that the agreement is not enforceable and that the child's best interests will govern decisions about custody and access.[365] Where, however, a gestational surrogacy arrangement is in place (meaning that the surrogate mother is not genetically connected to the child), the courts generally focus on the parties' intentions or genetic relatedness to award custody to the intended parents.[366] *Johnson v Calvert* is an influential case that exemplifies this approach: genetic ties ultimately prevailed and the intended mother (whose egg was used in the gestational surrogacy arrangement) was named the legal mother, even though California law made it possible to recognise either the genetic or the gestational mother as the legal mother.[367] Although

---

[360] See, eg, *Re adoption of Matthew B*, 284 Cal Rptr 18 (Ct App 1991) 37 ('We urge the Legislature to [act] expeditiously.'); *Belsito v Clark*, 67 Ohio Misc 2d 54 (Ohio Com Pl 1994) 65 ('. . . it would be beneficial to the law of surrogacy for the legislature to act and end this uncertainty.'); *Re Moschetta*, 30 Cal Rptr 2d 893 (Ct App 1994) 903; *Buzzanca v Buzzanca*, 72 Cal Rptr 2d 280 (Ct App 1998) 293 ('Again we must call on the Legislature to sort out the parental rights and responsibilities of those involved in artificial reproduction.').

[361] Cahn (n 107) 112.

[362] Movement Advancement Project *et al* (n 355) 38–9; Kindregan and McBrien (n 7) 361–64.

[363] Kindregan and McBrien (n 7) 157.

[364] *Ibid*.

[365] See, eg, Cahn (n 107) 99; Pamela Laufer-Ukeles, 'Gestation: Work for Hire or the Essence of Motherhood? A Comparative Legal Analysis' (2002) 9 *Duke Journal of Gender Law & Policy* 91, 99. See also Kindregan and McBrien (n 7) 153.

[366] Laufer-Ukeles (n 365) 102.

[367] *Johnson v Calvert*, 851 P 2d 776 (Cal 1993), cert denied, 510 US 874 (1993). The Supreme Court of California took the view that California law allowed for only one legal mother (*ibid* 781): 'Yet for any child California law recognizes only one natural mother, despite advances in reproductive technology rendering a different outcome biologically possible.' The Court 'declined to accept' the ACLU's argument that the child could be found to have two mothers. An even more complex factual situation arose in *JF v DB*, 897 A2d 1261 (Pa Super Ct 2006), where the surrogacy arrangement involved an intended mother, an intended and biological father, an egg donor and a gestational surrogate. All three potential contenders for parent (the egg donor

not often enshrined in legislation in the US, many of the same considerations found in the UK, Australian and Canadian, laws respecting parentage are drawn upon in judicial determinations of legal parentage. These include whether there is a genetic connection between the surrogate and the child, whether the surrogate was paid for her performance of the agreement, the age of the surrogate and the marital status of the intended parents.[368] As with the law on parentage in assisted reproduction generally, the surrogacy parentage cases in the US have little to offer by way of illuminating theoretical or principled approaches to explain how courts are to decide legal parentage in the context of such arrangements. The sole lesson that may be drawn from the cases is that biology is not necessarily determinative.

B. Parentage, law and reproductive autonomy

It is difficult to overstate the importance of parentage laws to reproductive autonomy. The very point of using ART treatment or surrogacy services is to conceive a child and to parent that child. Arguably, of all of the ART-related issues where a reproductive autonomy analysis is relevant, parentage laws are the most important (and the least often considered). Although the laws around how to assign parental obligations in the ART and surrogacy context do not engage women's bodily integrity, they are nevertheless central to reproductive autonomy. While these issues do not neatly fit within the nucleus of the reproductive autonomy model I describe, because they are centrally important to the ability to exercise autonomy interests, they require regulation that demonstrates significant respect for the autonomy interests of those who form their families using technological assistance.

It seems obvious that parentage laws, particularly those in Canada and the US, require significant reform in order to demonstrate respect for reproductive autonomy. Clear legal rules governing the assignment of parental rights and responsibilities in the ART and surrogacy contexts are critical to the ability of prospective parents to create 'legally secure families'.[369] As with most of the other topics considered in this chapter, a reproductive autonomy analysis cannot answer all of the specific questions as to how parentage laws should be designed. But at a minimum, it points to the need for clear parentage laws, spelled out in legislation, that create certainty and security for all of the parties.

Nevertheless, clear laws are only one part of the equation; these laws must also acknowledge the full variety of family forms that are made possible by assisted reproduction. Parentage laws that exclude certain types of families from their reach fail to respect reproductive autonomy in that they limit the ability of some parents to create a legally secure family for their children. Where both members of a couple have actively

---

(Rice), the biological father (Flynn) and the surrogate (Bimber)) asserted parental rights over the triplets who were born via the surrogacy arrangement. Because the parties were in different states, there are judgments from both Pennsylvania and Ohio courts. There is a multiplicity of decisions, all leading to different outcomes. One court assigned legal motherhood to the surrogate, the next found both genetic parents (Flynn and Rice) to be the legal parents, and the last word on parentage and custody comes from the Pennsylvania Superior Court, which awarded sole custody of the triplets to Flynn, as the legal father of the children. For a detailed discussion of the case, see Robert E Rains, 'What the Erie "Surrogate Triplets" Can Teach State Legislatures About the Need to Enact Article 8 of the Uniform Parentage Act (2000)' (2008) 56 *Cleveland State Law Review* 1.

[368] Kindregan and McBrien (n 7) 157.
[369] Crockin and Jones (n 271) 212.

participated in child-rearing but only one is a legal parent, the effects of relationship breakdown (or the death of the legal parent) can be devastating. In lesbian-led families, for example, non-birth mothers who lack legal status as parents are faced with government and school administration practices that misunderstand (and in some cases devalue) their roles in the children's lives[370] and are unable to consent to healthcare for their children.[371] Children, too, struggle with the law's refusal to recognise their family structure as legitimate,[372] and feel the impact of the legal reality in terms that implicate their sense of belonging in their communities. As one child of lesbian mothers explained: 'It would help if the government and the law recognized that I have two moms. It would help more people to understand. It would make my life easier. I want my family to be accepted and included, just like everybody else's family.'[373]

Same-sex parents are in a uniquely difficult position in jurisdictions where parentage laws are ambiguous or insufficiently broad to take account of non-traditional families. Parentage rules that create clear legal relationships from the moment of birth are important to families' abilities to define themselves as such, and to enjoy the security of knowing that the law safeguards their status as a family. The current uncertainty in many jurisdictions around the status of non-birth mothers in lesbian-led families, coupled with the uncertainty as to the potential parental status of sperm donors, leads families to be concerned about their security as a family unit.[374] Where the law on parentage consists solely of a presumption of parentage for a non-biological mother, for example, lesbian-led families are vulnerable to a challenge to the presumption on the part of a sperm donor.[375] In the US, where presumptions of parentage may be contingent on the marital status of the couple, there is a significant risk that the presumption would not hold should the family move to a state which does not recognise same-sex marriage.[376]

When the formal legal status of a prospective or actual parent is in question, not only is family security difficult to attain, the legal obligations of that adult to the child may not align with expectations. In the UK, prior to the 2008 reforms to the HFE Act 1990 that made parentage rules applicable to same-sex couples,[377] the non-birth mother who was not in a civil partnership with the birth mother was not a 'parent' for the purposes of child support.[378] Even now, with the reforms in place, if the couple are not civil partners, the non-birth mother will not be considered a legal parent if conception takes place in an 'informal' way, such as self-insemination with sperm from a known donor or donor insemination outside of the UK, rather than in an HFEA-licensed clinic and after the requisite consent forms are signed.[379]

---

[370] See, eg, Victorian Law Reform Commission, *Assisted Reproductive Technology and Adoption: Final Report* (Victoria, Victorian Law Reform Commission, 2007) 122–31.

[371] *Ibid*. See also Liz Short, '"It Makes The World Of Difference": Benefits for Children of Lesbian Parents of Having Their Parents Legally Recognised *as* Their Parents' (2007) 3 *Gay and Lesbian Issues and Psychology Review* 5, 9.

[372] Campbell (n 298) 265; *MDR v Ontario (Deputy Registrar General)*, (2006) 81 OR (3d) 81, 270 DLR (4th) 90 (ONSC) para 219.

[373] *MDR v Ontario* (n 372) para 219.

[374] Cameron *et al* (n 125) 105–08, 121–30. The authors note the distinct concerns related to the potential abolition of sperm donor anonymity for lesbian-led families and heterosexual families.

[375] *Ibid*.

[376] Cahn (n 107) 107–13.

[377] HFE Act 2008, ss 42–43.

[378] See, eg, Gamble and Ghevaert (n 296) 1206; *T v B (Parental Responsibility: Financial Provision)* [2010] EWHC 144 (Fam).

[379] Gamble and Ghevaert (n 296).

Some might ask why laws around legal parentage are needed, particularly in jurisdictions where partial parental status may be acquired in other ways, such as on the basis of one's parent-like relationship with a child[380] or, if a more formalised status is desired, through adoption. Parents – or those who wish to be legal parents – are seeking more than just knowledge that their social bond is legally acknowledged. As long as all is well within a family, the legal designation as 'parent' may not be needed. But family law rules are generally not put in place for those families in which all is well; they are needed when family relations break down and decisions must be made about the child's place of residence, custody and access, and child support. Reflecting on the significance of formalised legal parentage, Nancy Polikoff explains:

> To a child, in daily life, the absence of an adoption decree makes no difference. . . . The legal status becomes crucial, however, when the child's economic and emotional security are challenged. Then many rights – such as support and custody, public benefits and inheritance – turn not on the child's perception but on the existence of a legally recognized parent–child relationship.[381]

The existence of other routes to parenthood than through clear laws that make explicit provision for ART-formed families is no answer to the reproductive autonomy-based concerns raised here. It is possible in all Canadian jurisdictions, some US states,[382] in the UK[383] and in parts of Australia[384] for gay and lesbian couples to adopt children, and in some jurisdictions this includes second-parent adoption by a non-biological parent of the child.[385] But even where adoption is available as a route to securing legal parentage, it is not an attractive option for many gay and lesbian parents. First, there are questions about whether the adoption would be recognised in other states, or internationally.[386] Secondly, for some, the prospect of adoption 'feels immoral and dishonest'

---

[380]   Above (n 297).

[381]   Polikoff (n 351) 207.

[382]   Adoption by homosexual couples is possible under most state adoption laws and is explicitly permitted in a few states: see, eg, Cahn (n 107) 110; Cynthia R Mabry, 'Joint and Shared Parenting: Valuing All Families and All Children in the Adoption Process with an Expanded Notion of Family' (2009) 17 *American University Journal of Gender, Social Policy & the Law* 659, 661. Until very recently, Florida law expressly prohibited homosexual couples from adopting, but that law has been declared unconstitutional (*Re Gill*, 45 So 3rd 79 (Fla App 2010)).

[383]   Adoption and Children Act 2002 (UK), ss 49, 50(1), 144(4)(b), providing that couples may adopt, and that a couple means 'two people (whether of different sexes or the same sex) living as partners in an enduring family relationship'. The Adoption Act (Northern Ireland) Order 1987 prevents unmarried couples from adopting (*ibid* Arts 14, 15). But see *Northern Ireland Human Rights Commission, Re Judicial Review* [2012] NIQB 77 text following para 83, holding that 'Notwithstanding Articles 14 and 15 of the Adoption (Northern Ireland) Order 1987 it does not prevent couples who are not married, or in a Civil Partnership, from applying to adopt a child pursuant to the terms of that Order. All individuals and couples, regardless of marriage status or sexual orientation are eligible to be considered as an adoptive parent(s); (b) Any guidance published by the Respondent must accord with the declaration at (a) above.'

[384]   Same-sex adoption is permitted in the ACT (Adoption Act 1993 (ACT), s 14), Western Australia (Adoption Act 1994 (WA), ss 38(2), 39(1)(e)), Tasmania (Adoption Act 1988 (Tas), ss 20, 20(2A)(a)(b), where one partner is a parent or relative of the child) and New South Wales (Adoption Act 2000 (NSW), s 28). It is not permitted in Queensland (Adoption Act 2009 (Qld), s 92(1)(h)), or Victoria (Adoption Act 1984 (Vic), s 11(1)).

[385]   Second-parent adoption is available in some US states, and has been held not to be available in others, but its availability is unclear in most of the US: see, eg, Annette R Appell, 'The Endurance of Biological Connection: Heteronormativity, Same-Sex Parenting and the Lessons of Adoption' (2008) 22 *BYU Journal of Public Law* 289, 315–17; Mary Lou Killian, 'The Political is Personal: Relationship Recognition Policies in the United States and their Impact on Services for LGBT People' (2010) 22 *Journal of Gay & Lesbian Social Services* 9, 17–18.

[386]   Cahn (n 107) 109. There are many unresolved questions in this context in the US, including that of whether 'defense-of-marriage' statutes affect states' obligations respecting the recognition of legal parental status in same-sex couples (*ibid* 111–12).

given that the parties both consider themselves to be the parents of the child.[387] There is arguably no distinction between a heterosexual couple who conceive using donor sperm and a lesbian couple who do the same. In most jurisdictions, the infertile man does not have to adopt his child in order to have a legal parent–child relationship, but the non-biological lesbian partner does. This distinction seems particularly problematic where marriage or civil partnership rights have been extended to same-sex couples.

Parentage laws relating to surrogacy and assisted reproduction appear to seek an elusive balance between concern for the welfare of the child and the acknowledgement that there is some utility in giving some (arguably minimal) significance to parental wishes. In the surrogacy context, there is an additional layer of concern related to the potential for exploitation of the women who provide surrogacy services, whether for medical or strictly biological reasons. Even acknowledging the need to consider the welfare of the child and of the surrogate, however, it is difficult to understand the sheer volume of conditions applied in various legislative regimes that allow for declarations of parentage to be made. Why, for example, should it be necessary for intended parents to be at least 25 years old (such as in some Australian states)?[388] How, precisely, does that condition serve to safeguard the welfare of the child or protect against exploitation of the surrogate? And what justifies such restrictions on parents who are not able to have children without the assistance of a surrogate, when no such rules could ever be imposed on those who become parents in a traditional fashion? Likewise, what child welfare-related aims are served by requiring that at least one of the intended parents is a genetic parent of the child?[389] And given that parentage laws only ever have application after there is a child to consider, how can laws that seek to punish parents for engaging in commercial surrogacy be justified?[390]

Perhaps in some instances, these details give legislators some comfort that the practice of surrogacy is strictly regulated and is therefore less susceptible to abuse or exploitation. Or perhaps legislators are so disapproving of resort to surrogacy as a means to create a family that they wish they could refuse to acknowledge the child welfare implications of failing to create clear legal rules around parentage. Instead, they aim to place as many potential obstacles to obtaining a parental order or declaration of parentage as they feel they can get away with.

The failure to enact clear and consistent rules about parentage in assisted reproduction (including surrogacy) is a failure to respect reproductive autonomy. There is no justification for the absence of such laws, or for the existence of rules that protect some, but not all, of the families formed using ARTs.

Regulating parentage of children born using ARTs gives rise to multiple considerations. Reproductive tourism or cross-border reproductive care can intensify the complexity substantially. In the following section, I briefly consider the combined effect of surrogacy regulation and parentage law in the context of international surrogacy arrangements.

---

[387] See, eg, *MDR v Ontario* (n 372) para 218.

[388] See, eg, Surrogacy Act 2008 (WA), s 19; Surrogacy Act 2010 (Qld), s 22(g).

[389] See, eg, HFE Act 2008, s 54(1)(b).

[390] *Ibid* s 54(8); Parentage Act 2004 (ACT), s 45; Surrogacy Act 2010 (NSW), s 11; Surrogacy Act 2010 (Qld), s 54; AHR Act ss 6, 60.

V. REPRODUCTIVE TOURISM, SURROGACY AND REPRODUCTIVE AUTONOMY

Since the adoption of the earliest ART laws, it has been clear that different jurisdictions will adopt distinct regulatory approaches, with some being far more restrictive than others. The inter-jurisdictional variation between countries, and even between regions or states within a single country, has helped to generate and sustain the phenomenon of 'reproductive tourism' or cross-border reproductive care.

While conceivably any aspect of reproductive care may be sought outside of one's home jurisdiction, surrogacy services in particular have been a focus for those seeking to form families, in part because of the significant restrictions many jurisdictions have placed on various aspects of surrogacy arrangements. For example, where commercial surrogacy is prohibited, or where surrogacy agreements are unenforceable, intended parents may look to a jurisdiction where such arrangements are legally permitted or where the contract will be enforced.[391] Even where surrogacy is legal, intended parents may have other motivations to go outside of their home jurisdiction, including access to donor gametes (or access to anonymous donor gametes).[392] Non-legal factors play a role as well, and the cost of surrogacy services is a significant driver of international surrogacy.[393] The relatively low cost of surrogacy services in India, combined with the availability of women willing to provide such services, has created a burgeoning market in that country (the estimated value of the reproductive tourism market in India is almost half a billion dollars).[394]

Based on concerns around the morality and potential harms of surrogacy, some countries have taken a hard legal stance on surrogacy, both prohibiting its practice and refusing to acknowledge the legitimacy of children born via surrogacy arrangements.[395] Even in countries that have not gone so far as to rule out domestic surrogacy, some – including Canada, Australia and arguably the UK – have used law to discourage the practice. These legal restrictions have helped to foster the growth of an international market for surrogacy services, wherein intended parents seek these services abroad and then, once the baby is born, return to their home jurisdiction to live as a family. Parentage laws and citizenship policy are often not amenable to this practice, and can create considerable difficulty for the family after the child is born.

In countries where surrogacy is prohibited and where children born via surrogacy are not recognised as citizens, the result of surrogacy tourism can be stateless children. This

---

[391] Laufer-Ukeles (n 365). The same kinds of concerns are relevant in traditional surrogacy arrangements, where the gametes are contributed by the surrogate mother and the intended father. UK law treats gestational and traditional surrogacy very distinctly, in that only gestational surrogacy is subject to regulation by the HFEA. See Horsey and Sheldon (n 264).

[392] See Françoise Shenfield et al, 'Cross Border Reproductive Care in Six European Countries' (2010) 25 *Human Reproduction* 1361.

[393] It has been estimated that the cost of surrogacy in the US can range from $59,000 to $80,000, whereas in India, the range is $10,000 to $35,000 (all US dollar amounts) (Smerdon (n 289) 32–33; Whittaker (n 289); Casey Humbyrd, 'Fair Trade International Surrogacy' (2009) 9 *Developing World Bioethics* 111). Costs include the fee to be paid to the surrogate, as well as professional expenses (legal advice, counselling), healthcare costs for the surrogate, IVF or AI costs, costs of health and life insurance for the surrogate, agency fees (and other fees related to finding a woman to act as a surrogate for intended parents).

[394] See, eg, Kimberly D Krawiec, 'Altrusim and Intermediation in the Market for Babies' (2009) 66 *Washington and Lee Law Review* 203.

[395] Richard F Storrow, '"The Phantom Children of the Republic": International Surrogacy and the New Illegitimacy' (2012) 20 *American University Journal of Gender, Social Policy & the* Law 561, 595–604.

has led to two notorious cases involving surrogacy services in India. In one, a German couple were unable to leave India for two years with their children, as the children could not obtain travel documents – they were stateless due to the interaction of German and Indian law.[396] The twins were not able to obtain German passports, as German law determines nationality on the basis of the birth mother's nationality. They could not be Indian citizens because Indian law requires that one of the parents must be an Indian citizen at the time of birth. In the second case, known as the *Baby Manji* case,[397] Japanese intended parents used surrogacy services in India. Because Japanese law did not recognise the child as a citizen, Japan refused to issue a passport for her. Indian authorities initially refused to register a birth certificate, as the law requires both mother and father to be listed, and the issuing authorities were unsure whom to list as the child's mother.[398] Without a birth certificate, the child was unable to obtain the documents needed to be able to leave the country. Following several court applications and the handling of further immigration issues, Manji was finally permitted to leave India four months after her birth.[399]

Canadian law permits altruistic surrogacy and, in contrast to Germany and Japan, Canadian immigration authorities will grant citizenship to a child born abroad via surrogacy. In order to be granted automatic Canadian citizenship, the child must be genetically related to at least one parent.[400] In at least two known cases, fertility clinic errors meant that the requisite genetic connection did not exist, and one set of Canadian intended parents returned home without the children they had hoped to raise.[401] The other set of parents remained in India illegally and at great personal and financial cost until the immigration problems could be resolved.[402] In the end, it took six years.

---

[396] The intended parents argued that the birth mother should be considered the legal mother of the twins; they were successful at the High Court of Gujarat, but the decision was overturned on appeal to the Supreme Court of India. See Matt Wade, 'Babies Left in Limbo as India Struggles With Demand for Surrogacy', *Brisbane Times*, 1 May 2010, at <www.brisbanetimes.com.au/world/babies-left-in-limbo-as-india-struggles-with-demand-for-surrogacy-20100430-tzbl.html>; 'German Twins Set to Go Home; SC Stresses on Urgent Need for Surrogacy Laws', *Bar and Bench News* (Bangalore, 27 May 2010), at <http://barandbench.com/brief/2/754/german-twins-set-to-go-home-sc-stresses-on-urgent-need-for-surrogacy-laws>; Dhananjay Mahapatra, 'German or Indian? Surrogate Twins in Legal No-man's Land', *Times of India* (Mumbai, 1 December 2009), at <http://articles.indiaagreement-times.com/2009-12-01/india/28087428_1_surrogate-twins-surrogacy-timesofindia.surrogate-mother>.

[397] *Baby Manji Yamada v Union of India*, Writ Petition (C) No 369 of 2008 (Supreme Court of India). For a detailed description of the case, see Sreeja Jaiswal, 'Commercial Surrogacy in India: An Ethical Assessment of Existing Legal Scenario from the Perspective of Women's Autonomy and Reproductive Rights' (2012) 16 *Gender, Technology and Development* 1.

[398] Jaiswal (n 397) 7. The lack of certainty arose in part because Manji's intended parents separated prior to her birth and the intended mother no longer wished to play a role in raising the child.

[399] And this was only after being granted a unique identity certificate which permitted her to obtain a travel visa for Japan. Japan, for its part, eventually granted a visa to permit Manji to remain in Japan for one year, after which the Japanese authorities would be prepared to allow her father to adopt her in recognition of the relationship that had developed between them.

[400] 'Operational Bulletin 381 – March 8, 2012: Assessing Who is a Parent for Citizenship Purposes Where Assisted Human Reproduction (AHR) and/or Surrogacy Arrangements are Involved' (*Citizenship and Immigration Canada*, 2012), at <www.cic.gc.ca/english/resources/manuals/bulletins/2012/ob381.asp>.

[401] Rick Westhead, 'Troubling Questions Surround Surrogate-born Children in India', *Toronto Star*, 26 April 2010, at <www.thestar.com/life/health_wellness/2010/04/26/troubling_questions_surround_surrogate-born_children_in_india.html>.

[402] See, eg, Raveena Aulakh, 'Baby Quest Traps Couple in India', *Toronto Star*, 21 December 2010, at <www.thestar.com/news/article/910085--baby-quest-traps-couple-in-india>; Raveena Aulakh, 'Couple Fights Federal Surrogacy Policy to Bring Their Boy Back to Canada', *Toronto Star*, 20 August 2011, at <www.thestar.com/news/article/1042222--couple-fights-federal-surrogacy-policy-to-bring-their-boy-back-to-canada>.

Concerns around surrogacy and citizenship have also been in issue in the UK. In one case, UK nationals travelled to Ukraine for surrogacy services.[403] Unlike the law in the UK, Ukrainian law provides that the surrogate mother and her partner or spouse are not the parents of a child born pursuant to a surrogacy agreement. Instead, Ukranian law deprives the birth mother and her partner of all parental rights and obligations, and grants the rights and duties of, and status as, parents to the intended parents.[404] However, according to UK law, the birth mother is the legal mother of the child and her spouse or partner is the father.[405] The intended parents have no status as parents of these children until a parental order is granted. The interaction of the two legal regimes rendered the children stateless and parentless. The intended parents had no legal ability to remain in Ukraine, neither could they take the children home with them, as the children were not UK citizens and the parents had no right to bring them to England.[406]

A number of cases have arisen in the context of international commercial surrogacy wherein the commercial aspect of the arrangement itself is what poses the legal problem. In *Re L (a minor)*,[407] the intended parents were UK nationals who entered into a commercial surrogacy arrangement in the US. The amounts paid to the surrogate exceeded reimbursement of reasonable expenses, meaning that the only way a parental order could be granted would be if the court were to authorise the payments after the fact.[408] In some Australian states, as explained above, domestic and extraterritorial commercial surrogacy are prohibited.[409] In two recent cases, where intended parents sought parental orders in relation to children born as a result of international surrogacy arrangements, the Australian Family Court adverted to the possibility of criminal prosecution of the intended parents.[410] In one of them, the Court ordered that the judgment be provided to the Office of the Director of Public Prosecutions 'for consideration of whether a prosecution should be instituted against the applicants'.[411]

As explained earlier, surrogacy practice is notoriously difficult to track, and it is therefore not possible to be precise about the frequency with which these legal issues arise. However, as a review of the literature makes plain, they do arise and their incidence seems to be increasing.[412] Indeed, as surrogacy lawyer Natalie Gamble notes:

> Indian surrogacy is a hot media topic, with several stories over the past week about couples being stuck in India waiting for British passports for their biological children. As far as we are concerned, this isn't really news – it is the shared experience of every British parent who has had a child through surrogacy in India, and something we deal with on a daily basis.[413]

---

[403] *Re X & Y* (n 308).

[404] *Ibid* para 8.

[405] HFE Act 2008, ss 33, 35–37. The spouse or partner must consent to the receipt of ART treatment by the birth mother in order to be considered the child's parent.

[406] Similar difficulties may arise where the surrogate is a UK citizen and the intended parents are foreign nationals (*Re G* (n 295)).

[407] *Re L (a minor)* [2010] EWHC 3146 (Fam).

[408] The parental order was indeed granted, pursuant to s 54(8) of the HFE Act 1990. See also *Re X & Y* (n 308).

[409] See section III.A. above.

[410] See, eg, *Findlay and Anor & Punyawong* [2011] FamCA 503; *Hubert and Anor & Juntasa* [2011] FamCA 504.

[411] *Findlay and Anor & Punyawong* (n 410) para 3.

[412] See Storrow (n 395) for a thorough review of recent cases in Europe and Asia.

[413] Natalie Gamble, 'The Indian Surrogacy Industry – and Why We Need to Reform UK Surrogacy Law' (6 June 2012) 659 *Bionews*, at <www.bionews.org.uk/page_149168.asp>.

The anecdotal examples described here teach an important lesson: that the well-meaning regulation of surrogacy within one country may have a significantly negative impact on the very interests and persons these laws purport to safeguard. One of the most significant concerns around surrogacy is its potential to lead to commercialisation of reproduction and of children, and exploitation of women and children. Domestic law may attempt (if not always successfully) to regulate in such a way as to discourage or prevent these concerns from materialising. But in a world where reproductive tourism is not only a reality but an increasingly common route taken in the context of family formation, we have to concede the potential harm that law and regulation may cause.

Arguably, in part at least, reproductive tourism is the product of domestic laws that frustrate the exercise of reproductive autonomy. Jurisdictions that restrict surrogacy practice do so in order to safeguard the welfare of the women and children involved, and to demonstrate concern for women's equality. But as a brief review of these cases makes plain, welfare and equality are not protected by restrictive regulation of surrogacy. Couples who seek surrogacy services abroad are made vulnerable by conflicting parentage rules, and the women in developing countries who provide surrogacy services are surely not better protected from an equality and welfare perspective than women in more affluent countries.[414]

Acknowledgement of the concerns raised by international surrogacy – including its disproportionate impact on women, its potential to exploit and to commodify women, children and reproduction, and the health risks to which it gives rise (both to the surrogate herself, and to the tourist destination country in terms of the availability of healthcare services for its citizens)[122] – has led to calls for international regulation of surrogacy. For a number of reasons, it is unlikely that this is realistically achievable.[415] Another possibility is to do what some Australian states have done, and create domestic prohibitions which explicitly provide that they will have extraterritorial application. In my view, this is the wrong approach. Criminalising commercial surrogacy has not prevented its continued practice in domestic contexts, and it will not put an end to international commercial surrogacy, as the Australian examples clearly illustrate. What it will do is drive the practice underground and make exploitation and harm more – not less – likely.[416] As one Australian legal scholar has noted, these decisions arguably create an incentive for parents to be deceptive as to the circumstances of their children's birth and to be reluctant to approach the courts for parental orders in the future.[417] The resulting legal uncertainty around parentage will benefit no one.

As I have said repeatedly throughout this book, reproductive autonomy is an important interest and deserves respect. While it is absolutely not the only value that should guide regulation of reproduction generally, and of ARTs in particular, it is difficult to escape the conclusion that disregard for reproductive autonomy will lead to more harm

---

[414] Humbyrd (n 393); Erica Davis, 'The Rise of Gestational Surrogacy and the Pressing Need for International Regulation' (2012) 21 *Minnesota Journal of International Law* 120.

[415] Davis (n 414); Humbyrd (n 393) 113–14; Kristiana Brugger, 'International Law in the Gestational Surrogacy Debate' (2012) 35 *Fordham International Law Journal* 665, 680. As Brugger notes, 'surrogacy requires regulation in so many areas of law that any comprehensive single instrument will be unlikely to achieve the necessary political support'.

[416] Above (n 410). See also Millbank (n 311).

[417] Millbank (n 311). See also Letitia Rowlands, 'Two Queensland Couples Could Face Criminal Charges For Paying Surrogate Mothers to Carry Their Babies', *Courier-Mail* (Brisbane, July 28, 2011), at <www.the-familylawdirectory.com.au/article/couples-could-face-criminal-charges-under-new-commercial-surrogacy-laws.html>.

than will robust respect for it. The best approach to the growing international problem caused by reproductive tourism may rest largely with domestic regulation. Canada, the UK and Australia (like other countries) have devoted a great deal of time and energy to restrictive domestic regulation of surrogacy. It is time to revisit regulation from a standpoint that takes into account the evidence (or lack thereof) about the need for such restrictive regulation, and that acknowledges the realities of the global market for reproductive services. This demands a shift in attention: we are faced with acknowledging that our focus on protecting women from speculative harms has allowed the development of a situation in which real children and families are harmed. The best way to protect the interests of women involved in surrogacy arrangements – as in the case of all reproductive decision making – is to take the necessary steps to ensure they can make reproductive decisions autonomously.

10

Conclusion

THE TIME IS long past when reproduction was chiefly a matter of chance – when heterosexual intercourse was the only mode of conception, and when the outcome of each pregnancy was a roll of the dice. In the past, reproductive decision making, if it took place at all, was simply a question of whether or not to engage in sexual intercourse. The introduction of reproductive technology – including contraception, medical and surgical abortion, pre-natal and pre-implantation diagnosis, and ARTs – has ushered in a new era in reproductive decision making; an era of complex and complicated choices. And with these choices has come the reality of State involvement in regulating reproduction.

The changing nature of our reproductive lives makes reproductive autonomy and regulation issues of more than just historical and contemporary interest. As technology continues to evolve, decision making will become increasingly complex. Much of the literature concerning the regulation of ARTs concentrates on the morality of the choices being made by prospective parents, and either assumes or contests a broad understanding of reproductive autonomy. Arguments around reproductive autonomy also frequently seem to assume that the essence of reproductive freedom is keeping the State out of one's reproductive business. My concern is not just with the substance of these arguments, but with their focus as well. For the most part, in the context of reproductive autonomy, it seems that we spend a lot of time talking about what choices we should be allowed to make, and not enough time thinking about what it actually means to be autonomous. In both case law and legal literature, there are abundant references to the importance of reproductive autonomy, but no real clarity about what it is.

In the preceding chapters, I have argued that the regulation of reproductive decision making should be based on an ethic of respect for reproductive autonomy. More specifically, I have claimed that reproductive autonomy should be grounded in a contextualised account of autonomy, and that respect for reproductive autonomy should be framed around women's bodily integrity. The notion that the State must respect reproductive autonomy is not new; what is new about my argument is its emphasis on women's reproductive needs and interests. Unlike traditional liberal accounts of reproductive liberty that eschew State involvement in such private matters as procreation, this account of reproductive autonomy demands an active and engaged State; it acknowledges the degree to which women's reproductive autonomy and reproductive health are interwoven, and seeks solutions that will ameliorate both. As a first step toward achievement of this goal, I suggest the adoption of a comprehensive national policy strategy around reproductive autonomy and reproductive health.

The need for an inclusive and thoughtful approach to reproductive regulation stems from the dramatic impact reproduction has on our lives – particularly the lives of women.

Current regulation is fragmentary and *ad hoc* – legal and policy decisions are made in various reproductive contexts as the need arises. This *ad hoc* approach to regulation means that there is no touchstone for legal and policy decision making. As such, it is incapable of appropriately respecting reproductive autonomy.

In chapter nine, I describe a relatively recent Canadian case that illustrates the need for policy development around reproductive autonomy. The case, *C(C) v (W)A*,[1] centered on an access dispute between the parents of two young children. The children were conceived through IVF using Ms CC's oocytes and Mr AW's sperm. At the time the children were conceived, CC and AW were friends. Mr AW donated sperm to Ms CC, but the parties did not intended to parent together. After the children were born, Mr AW sought to play a role in the children's lives. In addition to the access issue, the parties raised the question of the disposition of four remaining frozen embryos. When the embryos were initially created, an informed consent form specifying disposition instructions was signed by both parties.[2] The embryos were created at a facility different from the one at which they were later stored, and no further agreement as to disposition was made.[3] At the time of the application to vary the original access order, Ms CC asked for the release of the remaining embryos. Mr AW opposed this request and sought to prevent her from using the embryos to attempt to conceive. As explained in chapter nine, Justice Sanderman found in favour of Ms CC on the basis that the sperm were provided by Mr AW as an 'unqualified gift', and that the cryopreserved embryos are Ms CC's property and hers to do with as she sees fit.[4]

Justice Sanderman's characterisation of the embryos as property without reference to the ongoing debate around this issue is cause for concern in and of itself.[5] But of even greater concern is his complete failure to acknowledge the larger questions of reproductive autonomy raised by this case. He cites neither authority nor academic commentary related to embryo disposition and reproductive decision making (although there is a wealth of both).[6] It is by no means clear that Mr AW would have been successful in his desire to block Ms CC's future use of the cryopreserved embryos even if issues of reproductive autonomy had been considered, but the fact that these issues received no attention at all is troubling. A national policy strategy relating to reproductive autonomy and reproductive health would not necessarily resolve problems like the one raised in this case, but it could certainly raise the profile of the issues for counsel and the judiciary alike, making it much less likely that these issues will be overlooked.

A comprehensive national strategy around reproductive health is also required in order to tie issues in the regulation of reproductive decision making to questions of reproductive health. In this context, the story of the approval of Gardasil (a vaccine that prevents most cervical cancers) and the implementation of related vaccine mandates in some US states is a ready example. When the vaccine was before regulatory authorities for review and approval, public health experts advocated vaccinating young girls before

---

[1] *C(C) v W(A)* [2005] ABQB 290, 50 Alta LR (4th) 61.
[2] This information was provided to me by one of the parties, who contacted me in 2005 seeking some assistance with a possible appeal of Sanderman J's decision on the embryo dispute.
[3] *C(C) v W(A)* (n 1).
[4] *Ibid* paras 20–21.
[5] See the discussion of this issue in ch 9.
[6] To be fair to Sanderman J, it is not clear whether these issues were raised by counsel.

they become sexually active as the most effective prevention strategy.[7] But the suggestion that girls as young as 11 or 12 should be vaccinated was met with opposition from conservative religious groups, who argued that the use of the vaccine in this age group might send inappropriate messages about sexuality to young girls.[8] Although the approval of the vaccine and the implementation of a vaccine mandate do not call for decisions that are explicitly reproductive, the decision to approve the vaccine and the public health decisions about whom to vaccinate, and when, have clear implications for women's general health, reproductive health and, ultimately, reproductive autonomy.[9] A contextualised account of reproductive autonomy instructs us to be concerned about this potential interference with reproductive health and reproductive autonomy. It also directs us to consider issues of access to this important preventative tool for what is likely to become 'a disease of poor women with little or no access to basic health care'.[10]

My arguments for reproductive autonomy will no doubt face criticism from many feminists who have expressed dismay at the prominence of autonomy in the legal and bioethical literature around reproduction. But in spite of the legitimate worries expressed by feminists, it is essential that we not lose sight of the vital significance – for women – of a strong commitment to reproductive autonomy. Rather than treat the concept itself as suspect due to its traditionally liberal flavour, feminism needs to claim for itself a refigured conception of reproductive autonomy that invokes a rich understanding of autonomy, and that places women's interests at its core. A contextualised approach to reproductive autonomy places reproductive decision making in its full medical, social and political context, and thereby illuminates the disproportionate effects of reproduction (and reproductive decision making) on women's lives. Such an approach also accentuates the need to reflect on the many ways in which oppressive socialisation works against women's development of the capacity for autonomy, and thus illustrates the importance of continuing to advocate for social change. Once such change has come about, we may well decide that we need to reconsider the place of autonomy in reproductive decision making. But until that time, we must seek to empower women and to demonstrate respect for their reproductive decisions.

---

[7] See, eg, Katherine M Stone *et al*, 'Seroprevalence of Human Papillomavirus Type 16 Infection in the United States' (2002) 186 *Journal of Infectious Diseases* 1396, 1400; Gillian D Sanders and Al V Taira, 'Cost Effectiveness of a Potential Vaccine for *Human Papillomavirus*' (2003) 9 *Emerging Infectious Diseases* 37, 42.

[8] See, eg, R Alta Charo, 'Politics, Parents, and Prophylaxis – Mandating HPV Vaccination in the United States' (2007) 356 *New England Journal of Medicine* 1905; Gillian Haber, Robert M Malow and Gregory D Zimet, 'The HPV Vaccine Mandate Controversy' (2007) 20 *Journal of Pediatric and Adolescent Gynecology* 325; Rob Stein, 'Debate Rages on Use of Cervical Cancer Vaccine: While Almost 100% Effective, Some Contend Use Condones Teen Sex', *San Francisco Chronicle*, 31 October 2005, at <www.sfgate.com/cgi-bin/article.cgi?file=/c/a/2005/10/31/MNG2LFGJFT1.DTL>; Cynthia Dailard, 'The Public Health Promise and Potential Pitfalls of the World's First Cervical Cancer Vaccine' (2006) 9(1) *Guttmacher Policy Review* 6.

[9] Cervical cancer treatment usually involves either a hysterectomy or radiation therapy. Hysterectomy quite clearly rules out the possibility of child bearing. Radiation therapy damages the reproductive organs, making future conception unlikely (Steven E Waggoner, 'Cervical Cancer' (2003) 361 *The Lancet* 2217; Lilian T Gien and Allan Covens, 'Fertility-sparing Options for Early Stage Cervical Cancer' (2010) 117 *Gynecologic Oncology* 350). Treatment of pre-cancerous changes in the cervix can also lead to a slight increase in the risk of premature delivery or having a low birth-weight baby (Fiona J Bruinsma *et al*, 'Precancerous Changes in the Cervix and Risk of Subsequent Preterm Birth' (2007) 114 *BJOG: An International Journal of Gynaecology and Obstetrics* 70).

[10] Ben Daitz, 'Vaccine Prevents Cervical Cancer. So, What's the Down Side?', *New York Times*, 23 May 2006, at <www.nytimes.com/2006/05/23/health/23comm.html>. Daitz notes that in the US, cervical cancer ranks eighth in incidence of cancers among women; it ranks second in developing nations.

Bibliography

—— *An Information Paper on Termination of Pregnancy in Australia* (Canberra, National Health and Medical Research Council, 1997)

—— *CMA Policy: Induced Abortion* (Ottawa, Canadian Medical Association, 1988)

—— 'Editorial: Canada's G8 Health Leadership' (2010) 375 *The Lancet* 1580

—— 'Preconception Tort as a Basis for Recovery' (1982) 60 *Washington University Law Quarterly* 275

—— 'Special Issue on Medicalisation' (2002) 324 *British Medical Journal* 859

Abrams, P, 'Reservations about Women: Population Policy and Reproductive Rights' (1996) 29 *Cornell International Law Journal* 1

Abrevaya, J, 'Are There Missing Girls in the United States? Evidence from Birth Data' (2009) 1(2) *American Economic Journal: Applied Economics* 1

Adamson, D, 'Regulation of Assisted Reproductive Technologies in the United States' (2002) 78 *Fertility and Sterility* 932

—— 'Regulation of Assisted Reproductive Technologies in the United States' (2005–06) 39 *Family Law Quarterly* 727

Adjin-Tettey, E, 'Claims of Involuntary Parenthood: Why the Resistance?' in Jason W Neyers, Erika Chamberlain and Stephen GA Pitel (eds), *Emerging Issues in Tort Law* (Oxford, Hart Publishing, 2007) 85

Allan, J, 'You Don't Always Get What You Pay For: No Bill of Rights for Australia' (2010) (24) *New Zealand Universities Law Review* 179

Allen, AL, 'The Proposed Equal Protection Fix for Abortion Law: Reflections on Citizenship, Gender, and the Constitution' (1995) 18 *Harvard Journal of Law & Public Policy* 419

—— 'Coercing Privacy' (1999) 40 *William and Mary Law Review* 723

Almond, D and Edlund, L, 'Son-Biased Sex Ratios in the 2000 United States Census' (2008) 105 *Proceedings of the National Academy of Sciences* 5681

—————— and Milligan, K, *O Sister, Where Art Thou? The Role of Son Preference and Sex Choice: Evidence from Immigrants to Canada* National Bureau of Economic Research Working Paper No 15391 (Cambridge, MA, National Bureau of Economic Research, 2009)

Alstott, AL, 'Private Tragedies? Family Law as Social Insurance' (2010) 4 *Harvard Law and Policy Review* 3

Alvare, HM, 'The Case for Regulating Collaborative Reproduction: A Children's Rights Perspective' (2003) 40 *Harvard Journal on Legislation* 1

Amana, CE, 'Maternal–Fetal Conflict: A Call for Humanism and Consciousness in a Time of Crisis' (1992) 3 *Columbia Journal of Gender and Law* 351

American Academy of Pediatrics, Committee on Bioethics, 'Sterilization of Minors with Developmental Disabilities' (1999) 104 *Pediatrics* 337

American College of Obstetricians and Gynecologists, 'Committee Opinion No 321: Maternal Decision Making, Ethics and the Law' (2005) 106 *Obstetrics & Gynecology* 1127

—— 'ACOG Committee Opinion No 371: Sterilization of Women, Including those with Mental Disabilities' (2007) 110 *Obstetrics & Gynecology* 217

—— 'ACOG Practice Bulletin No 77: Screening for Fetal Chromosomal Abnormalities' (2007) 109 *Obstetrics & Gynecology* 217

—— 'ACOG Practice Bulletin No 88: Invasive Prenatal Testing for Aneuploidy' (2007) 110 *Obstetrics & Gynecology* 1459

American College of Obstetricians and Gynecologists, 'ACOG Committee Opinion No 395: Surgery and Patient Choice' (2008) 111 *Obstetrics & Gynecology* 243

——'ACOG Practice Bulletin No 101: Ultrasonography in Pregnancy' (2009) 113 *Obstetrics & Gynecology* 451

American Society for Reproductive Medicine, *Assisted Reproductive Technologies: A Guide for Patients* (Birmingham, Ala, American Society for Reproductive Medicine, 2011)

——*Infertility: An Overview: A Guide for Patients* (Birmingham, Ala, American Society for Reproductive Medicine, 2012)

American Society for Reproductive Medicine Ethics Committee, 'Preconception Gender Selection for Nonmedical Reasons' (2001) 75 *Fertility and Sterility* 861

——'Financial Compensation of Oocyte Donors' (2007) 88 *Fertility and Sterility* 305

——'Interests, Obligations, and Rights of the Donor in Gamete Donation' (2009) 91 *Fertility and Sterility* 22

——'Child-rearing Ability and the Provision of Infertility Services' (2009) 92 *Fertility and Sterility* 864

——'Human Immunodeficiency Virus and Infertility Treatment' (2010) 94 *Fertility and Sterility* 11

American Society for Reproductive Medicine Practice Committee, 'Guidelines for the Provision of Infertility Services' (2004) 82 (Supp 1) *Fertility and Sterility* 24

American Society for Reproductive Medicine Practice Committee and Society for Assisted Reproductive Technology Practice Committee, '2008 Guidelines for Gamete and Embryo Donation: A Practice Report' (2008) 90 (Supp 3) *Fertility and Sterility* S30

——'Guidelines on Number of Embryos Transferred' (2009) 92 *Fertility and Sterility* 1518

Anderlik, MR, *The Ethics of Managed Care: A Pragmatic Approach* (Indianapolis, Indiana University Press, 2001)

Anderson, E, 'Is Women's Labor a Commodity?' (1990) 19 *Philosophy & Public Affairs* 71

Aneblom, G et al, 'Knowledge, Use and Attitudes Towards Emergency Contraceptive Pills Among Swedish Women Presenting for Induced Abortion' (2002) 109 *BJOG: An International Journal of Obstetrics and Gynaecology* 155

Annas, GJ, 'Forced Cesareans: The Most Unkindest Cut of All' (1982) 12(3) *Hastings Center Report* 16

——'The Supreme Court and Abortion Rights' (2007) 356 *New England Journal of Medicine* 2201

Appell, AR, 'The Endurance of Biological Connection: Heteronormativity, Same-Sex Parenting and the Lessons of Adoption' (2008) 22 *BYU Journal of Public Law* 289

Appleton, SF, 'Reproduction and Regret' (2011) 23 *Yale Journal of Law and Feminism* 255

Arneson, RJ, 'Commodification and Commercial Surrogacy' (1992) 21 *Philosophy & Public Affairs* 132

Asch, A and Parens, E, 'The Disability Rights Critique of Prenatal Genetic Testing: Reflections and Recommendations' in Erik Parens and Adrienne Asch, *Prenatal Testing and Disability Rights* (Washington, DC, Georgetown University Press, 2000) 3

Asch, A, 'Reproductive Technology and Disability' in Sherrill Cohen and Nadine Taub (eds), *Reproductive Laws for the 1990s* (Clifton, NJ, Humana Press, 1989) 69

——'Prenatal Diagnosis and Selective Abortion: A Challenge to Practice and Policy' (1999) 89 *American Journal of Public Health* 1649

——'Disability Equality and Prenatal Testing: Contradictory or Compatible?' (2003) 30 *Florida State University Law Review* 315

Ashe, M, 'Zig-Zag Stitching and the Seamless Web: Thoughts on "Reproduction" and the Law' (1989) 13 *Nova Law Review* 355

Ata, B and Seli, E, 'Economics of Assisted Reproductive Technologies' (2010) 22 *Current Opinion in Obstetrics and Gynecology* 183

Atwood, M, *The Handmaid's Tale* (Toronto, McClelland and Stewart, 1985)

Audibert, F, 'SOGC Technical Update No 232: Preimplantation Genetic Testing' (2009) 31 *Journal of Obstetrics and Gynaecology Canada* 761

Australia, Family Law Council, *Creating Children: A Uniform Approach to the Law and Practice of Reproductive Technology in Australia* (Canberra, Family Law Council, 1985)

Australian Government, Department of Health and Ageing, *Improving Maternity Services in Australia: A Discussion Paper from the Australian Government* (Barton, Commonwealth of Australia, 2008)

Australian Government, National Health and Medical Research Council, *Ethical Guidelines on Assisted Reproductive Technology* (Canberra, Commonwealth of Australia, 1996)

—— *Ethical Guidelines on the Use of Assisted Reproductive Technology in Clinical Practice and Research 2007* (Canberra, Commonwealth of Australia, 2007)

Azzarello, D and Collins, J, 'Canadian Access to Hormonal Contraceptive Drug Choices' (2004) 26 *Journal of Obstetrics and Gynaecology Canada* 489

Baier, A, *Moral Prejudices: Essays on Ethics* (Cambridge, MA, Harvard University Press, 1994)

Backhouse, D and Deckha, M, 'Shifting Rationales: The Waning Influence of Feminism on Canada's Embryo Research Restrictions' (2009) 21 *Canadian Journal of Women and Law* 229

Balkin, JM (ed), *What* Roe v Wade *Should Have Said: The Nation's Top Legal Experts Rewrite America's Most Controversial Decision* (New York, NYU Press, 2005)

Baran, A and Pannor, R, *Lethal Secrets: The Psychology of Donor Insemination: Problems and Solutions*, 2nd edn (Amistad, Triadoption Publications, 1993)

Barker, KK, 'A Ship Upon a Stormy Sea: The Medicalization of Pregnancy' (1998) 47 *Social Science & Medicine* 1067

Barot, S, 'A Problem-and-Solution Mismatch: Son Preference and Sex-Selective Abortion Bans' (2012) 15(2) *Guttmacher Policy Review* 18

Bartlett, KT, 'Gender Law' (1994) 1 *Duke Journal of Gender Law & Policy* 1

Baruch, S, 'Preimplantation Genetic Diagnosis and Parental Preferences: Beyond Deadly Disease' (2008) 8 *Houston Journal of Health Law & Policy* 245

Baruch, S, Kaufman, D and Hudson, KL, 'Genetic Testing of Embryos: Practices and Perspectives of US In Vitro Fertilization Clinics' (2008) 89 *Fertility and Sterility* 1053

Bayer, R and Fairchild, AL, 'Changing the Paradigm for HIV Testing – The End of Exceptionalism' (2006) 355 *New England Journal of Medicine* 647

Baylis, F, 'Dissenting with the Dissent: *Winnipeg Child and Family Services (Northwest Area) v G (DF)*' (1998) 36 *Alberta Law Review* 785

—— 'Human Cloning: Three Mistakes and an Alternative' (2002) 27 *Journal of Medicine and Philosophy* 319

Beal, R, '"Can I Sue Mommy?" An Analysis of a Woman's Tort Liability for Prenatal Injuries to her Child Born Alive' (1984) 21 *San Diego Law Review* 325

Beauchamp, TL and Childress, JF, *Principles of Biomedical Ethics*, 6th edn (New York, Oxford University Press, 2009)

Beauchamp, TL, 'Does Ethical Theory Have a Future in Bioethics?' (2004) 32 *Journal of Law, Medicine and Ethics* 209

Beck, U, *Risk Society: Towards a New Modernity* (London, Sage Publications, 1992)

Becker, G, *The Elusive Embryo: How Women and Men Approach New Reproductive Technologies* (Berkeley, University of California Press, 2000)

Beeson, DR, Jennings, PK and Kramer, W, 'Offspring Searching for their Sperm Donors: How Family Type Shapes the Process' (2011) 26 *Human Reproduction* 1

Bell, DH, 'Disputes Over Frozen Embryos' (2011) 81 *Mississippi Law Journal Supra* 105

Benoit, C *et al*, 'Medical Dominance and Neoliberalisation in Maternal Care Provision: The Evidence from Canada and Australia' (2010) 71 *Social Science & Medicine* 475

Benson, P, 'Feminist Intuitions and the Normative Substance of Autonomy' in James Stacey Taylor (ed), *Personal Autonomy: New Essays on Personal Autonomy and Its Role in Contemporary Moral Philosophy* (Cambridge, Cambridge University Press, 2005) 124

Berer, M, 'Medical Abortion: A Fact Sheet' (2005) 13(26) *Reproductive Health Matters* 20

Berer, M, 'Medical Abortion: Issues of Choice and Acceptability' (2005) 13(26) *Reproductive Health Matters* 25

Berg, BJ, 'Listening to the Voices of the Infertile' in Joan C Callahan (ed), *Reproduction, Ethics, and the Law: Feminist Perspectives* (Bloomington, Indiana University Press, 1995) 80

Bergeron, V, 'The Ethics of Cesarean Section on Maternal Request: A Feminist Critique of the American College of Obstetricians and Gynecologists' Position on Patient-Choice Surgery' (2007) 21 *Bioethics* 478

Bergh, PA, 'Indecent Proposal: $5,000 is not "Reasonable Compensation" for Oocyte Donors – A Reply' (1999) 71 *Fertility and Sterility* 9

Bergum, V, *A Child on Her Mind: The Experience of Becoming a Mother* (Westport, CT, Bergin & Garvey, 1997)

Berkhout, S, 'Buns in the Oven: Objectification, Surrogacy, and Women's Autonomy' (2008) 34 *Social Theory and Practice* 95

—— 'Relational Autonomy on the Cutting Edge' (2012) 12(7) *American Journal of Bioethics* 59

Bhatia, R, 'Ten Years After Cairo: The Resurgence of Coercive Population Control in India' (Spring 2005) 31 *Different Takes* 1

Billingsley, B and Carver, P, 'Sections 7 and 15(1) of the Charter and Access to the Public Purse: Evolution in the Law?' (2007) 36 *Supreme Court Law Review* 221

Bioeffects and Safety Committee on Behalf of the Board of the International Society of Ultrasound in Obstetrics and Gynecology (ISUOG), 'ISUOG Statement on the Non-Medical Use of Ultrasound, 2009' (2009) 33 *Ultrasound in Obstetrics and Gynecology* 617

Birenbaum-Carmeli, D and Dirnfeld, M, 'In Vitro Fertilisation Policy in Israel and Women's Perspectives: The More the Better?' (2008) 16(31) *Reproductive Health Matters* 182

Birk, D, *Human Fertilisation and Embryology: The New Law* (Bristol, Jordan Publishing, 2009)

Black, A *et al*, 'SOGC Clinical Practice Guideline No 143: Canadian Contraception Consensus, Part 1 of 3' (2004) 26 *Journal of Obstetrics and Gynaecology Canada* 143

—— 'SOGC Clinical Practice Guideline No 143: Canadian Contraception Consensus, Part 2 of 3' (2004) 26 *Journal of Gynecology and Obstetrics Canada* 219

——'Contraceptive Use Among Canadian Women of Reproductive Age: Results of a National Survey' (2009) 31 *Journal of Obstetrics and Gynaecology Canada* 627

Black, V and Klimchuk, D, 'Case Comment: *Hollis v Dow Corning*' (1996) 75 *Canadian Bar Review* 355

Blackmer, J, 'Letter: Clarification of the CMA's Position Concerning Induced Abortion' (2007) 176 *Canadian Medical Association Journal* 1310

Blackwell, T, 'Fertility Law Leaves us in Limbo, Doctors Say: Oversight of Burgeoning Industry a "Farce"', *National Post* (Don Mills, 30 April 2010) A1

——'Fertility Spending at Issue: Letter', *National Post* (Don Mills, 2 June 2010) A5

Blyth, E, 'I Wanted to be Interesting. I Wanted to be Able to Say "I've Done Something With my Life"': 'Interviews with Surrogate Mothers in Britain' (1994) 12 *Journal of Reproductive and Infant Psychology* 189

—— 'Parental Orders and Identity Registration: One Country Three Systems' (2010) 32 *Journal of Social Welfare and Family Law* 345

——and Farrand, A, 'Reproductive Tourism – a Price Worth Paying for Reproductive Autonomy?' (2005) 25 *Critical Social Policy* 91

——and Frith, L, 'The UK's Gamete Donor Crisis – A Critical Analysis' (2008) 28 *Critical Social Policy* 74

—— 'Donor-Conceived People's Access to Genetic and Biographical History: An Analysis of Provisions in Different Jurisdictions Permitting Disclosure of Donor Identity' (2009) 23 *International Journal of Law, Policy and the Family* 174

Boetzkes, E, 'Sex Selection and the *Charter*' (1994) 7 *Canadian Journal of Law and Jurisprudence* 173

——'Equality, Autonomy, and Feminist Bioethics' in Anne Donchin and Laura Purdy (eds), *Embodying Bioethics: Recent Feminist Advances* (Lanham, MD, Rowman and Littlefield, 1999) 121

Bonanno, C, Clausing, M and Berkowitz, R, 'VBAC: A Medicolegal Perspective' (2011) 38 *Clinics in Perinatology* 217

Boonstra, H, 'The Impact of Government Programs on Reproductive Health Disparities: Three Case Studies' (2008) 11(3) *Guttmacher Policy Review* 6

Boonstra, H *et al*, 'The "Boom and Bust Phenomenon": The Hopes, Dreams, and Broken Promises of the Contraceptive Revolution' (2000) 61 *Contraception* 9

Boorse, C, 'On the Distinction Between Disease and Illness' (1975) 5 *Philosophy and Public Affairs* 49

Borgmann, CE, 'The Meaning of "Life": Belief and Reason in the Abortion Debate' (2009) 18 *Columbia Journal of Gender and Law* 551

Botkin, JR and Mehlman, MJ, 'Wrongful Birth: Medical, Legal, and Philosophical Issues' (1994) 22 *Journal of Law, Medicine and Ethics* 21

Botti, S, Orfali, K and Iyengar, SS, 'Tragic Choices: Autonomy and Emotional Responses to Medical Decisions' (2009) 36 *Journal of Consumer Research* 337

Boyd, ME, Usher, RH and McLean, FH, 'Fetal Macrosomia: Prediction, Risks, Proposed Management' (1983) 61 *Obstetrics & Gynecology* 715

Boyle, RJ and Savulescu, J, 'Prenatal Testing for "Minor" Genetic Abnormalities is Ethical' (2003) 3(1) *American Journal of Bioethics* 60

Brady, S and Grover, S, *The Sterilisation of Girls and Young Women in Australia: A Legal, Medical and Social Context* (Sydney, Human Rights and Equal Opportunity Commission, 1997)

——, Britton, J and Grover, S, *The Sterilisation of Girls and Young Women in Australia: Issues and Progress* (Sydney, Human Rights and Equal Opportunity Commission, 2001)

Braude, P and the Expert Group on Multiple Births After IVF, *One Child at a Time: Reducing Multiple Births After IVF* (London, Human Fertilisation and Embryology Authority, 2006)

Brazier, M, 'Reproductive Rights: Feminism or Patriarchy?' in John Harris and Søren Holm (eds), *The Future of Human Reproduction: Ethics, Choice, and Regulation* (Oxford, Clarendon Press, 1998) 66

——'Liberty, Responsibility, Maternity' (1999) 52 *Current Legal Problems* 359

Bright, H, 'Access to Emergency Contraception' (2004) 26 *Journal of Obstetrics and Gynaecology Canada* 111

Brock, DW, 'Conscientious Refusal by Physicians and Pharmacists: Who is Obligated to Do What, and Why?' (2008) 29 *Theoretical Medicine and Bioethics* 187

Brodie, J, Gavigan, SAM and Jenson, J, *The Politics of Abortion* (Toronto, Oxford University Press, 1992)

Brody, H, *The Future of Bioethics* (Oxford, Oxford University Press, 2009)

Brodzinsky, AB, 'Surrendering an Infant for Adoption: The Birthmother Experience' in David M Brodzinsky and Marshall D Schechter (eds), *The Psychology of Adoption* (New York, Oxford University Press, 1990) 295

Brown, H and Small, M, 'The Role of the Maternal–Fetal Medicine Subspecialist in Review and Prevention of Maternal Deaths' (2012) 36 *Seminars in Perinatology* 27

Brown, SD, 'The "Fetus as Patient": A Critique' (2008) 8(7) *American Journal of Bioethics* 47

Browne, M, 'Preconception Tort Law in an Era of Assisted Reproduction: Applying a Nexus Test for Duty' (2001) 69 *Fordham Law Review* 2555

Browner, CH and Press, NA, 'The Normalization of Prenatal Diagnostic Screening' in Faye D Ginsburg and Rayna Rapp (eds), *Conceiving the New World Order: The Global Politics of Reproduction* (Berkeley, University of California Press, 1995) 307

——————'The Production of Authoritative Knowledge in American Prenatal Care' (1996) 10(2) *Medical Anthropology Quarterly* 141

Brownsword, R, 'Happy Families, Consenting Couples, and Children with Dignity: Sex Selection and Saviour Siblings' (2005) 17 *Child and Family Law Quarterly* 435

Brugger, K, 'International Law in the Gestational Surrogacy Debate' (2012) 35 *Fordham International Law Journal* 665

Bruinsma, FJ *et al*, 'Precancerous Changes in the Cervix and Risk of Subsequent Preterm Birth (2007) 114 *BJOG: An International Journal of Obstetrics and Gynaecology* 70

Bubela, T and Caulfield, T, 'When Human Dignity is Not Enough: Embryonic Stem Cell Research and Human Cloning in Canada' in Edna F Einsiedel (ed), *Emerging Technologies: From Hindsight and Foresight* (Vancouver, University of British Columbia Press, 2008) 161

Buchanan, A *et al*, *From Chance to Choice: Genetics and Justice* (Cambridge, Cambridge University Press, 2002)

Buckett, WM and Tan, SL, 'Congenital Abnormalities in Children Born After Assisted Reproductive Techniques: How Much is Associated with the Presence of Infertility and How Much with its Treatment?' (2005) 84 *Fertility and Sterility* 1318

Burrow, S, 'On the Cutting Edge: Ethical Responsiveness to Cesarean Rates' (2012) 12(7) *American Journal of Bioethics* 44

Bury, L and Ngo, TD, *'The Condom Broke!' Why do Women in the UK Have Unintended Pregnancies?* (London, Marie Stopes International, 2009)

Busby, K and Vun, D, 'Revisiting the Handmaid's Tale: Feminist Theory Meets Empirical Research on Surrogate Mothers' (2010) 26 *Canadian Journal of Family Law* 13

Butler, J, *Gender Trouble: Feminism and the Subversion of Identity* (New York, Routledge, 1990)

Cahn, N, 'Necessary Subjects: The Need for a Mandatory National Donor Gamete Databank' (2009) 12 *DePaul Journal of Health Care Law* 203

—— *Test Tube Families: Why the Fertility Market Needs Legal Regulation* (New York, New York University Press, 2009)

—— 'The New Kinship' (2012) 100 *Georgetown Law Journal* 367

Calabretto, H, 'Australia: Organized Physician Opposition to Nonprescription Status' in Angel M Foster and Lisa L Wynn (eds), *Emergency Contraception: The Story of a Global Reproductive Health Technology* (New York, Palgrave Macmillan, 2012) 207

Caldwell, JC and Ware, H, 'The Evolution of Family Planning in Australia' (1973) 27 *Population Studies* 7

Calhoun, A, 'The Criminalization of Bad Mothers', *New York Times Magazine*, 25 April 2012, MM30

Callahan, D, 'The WHO Definition of Health' (1973) 1(3) *Hastings Center Report* 77

—— 'Bioethics' in Stephen G Post (ed), *Encyclopedia of Bioethics*, 3rd edn (New York, Macmillan Reference USA, 2004) vol 1, 278

Callahan, JC (ed), *Reproduction, Ethics, and the Law: Feminist Perspectives* (Bloomington, Indiana University Press, 1995)

—— and Roberts, DE, 'A Feminist Social Justice Approach to Reproduction-Assisting Technologies: A Case Study on the Limits of Liberal Theory' (1995–96) 84 *Kentucky Law Journal* 1197

Cameron, A, Gruben, V and Kelly, F, 'De-anonymising Sperm Donors in Canada: Some Doubts and Directions' (2010) 26 *Canadian Journal of Family Law* 95

Campbell, A, 'Conceiving Parents Through Law' (2007) 21 *International Journal of Law, Policy and the Family* 242

Canadian Abortion Rights Action League, *Protecting Abortion Rights in Canada: A Special Report to Celebrate the 15th Anniversary of the Decriminalization of Abortion* (Ottawa, CARAL, 2003)

Canadian Fertility and Andrology Society & Society of Obstetricians and Gynaecologists of Canada, 'Joint Policy Statement: Ethical Issues in Assisted Reproduction' (1999) 21 *Journal of Obstetrics and Gynaecology Canada* 1

Canadian Institute for Health Information, *Reciprocal Billing Report, Canada, 2004–2005, Revised August 2007* (Ottawa, Canadian Institute for Health Information, 2007) F-1

——*Health Care in Canada 2010* (Ottawa, Canadian Institute for Health Information, 2010)

Canadian Institutes of Health Research, Natural Sciences and Engineering Research Council of Canada & Social Sciences and Humanities Research Council of Canada, *Tri-Council Policy Statement: Ethical Conduct for Research Involving Humans* (Ottawa, Interagency Advisory Panel on Research Ethics, December 2010)

Cannold, L, *The Abortion Myth: Feminism, Morality, and the Hard Choices Women Make* (St Leonard's, NSW, Allen & Unwin, 1998)

Cantor, JD, 'Conscientious Objection Gone Awry – Restoring Selfless Professionalism in Medicine' (2009) 360 *New England Journal of Medicine* 1484

Caplan, AL and Patrizio, P, 'Are You Ever Too Old to Have a Baby? The Ethical Challenges of Older Women Using Infertility Services' (2010) 28 *Seminars in Reproductive Medicine* 281

Capron, AM, 'Law and Bioethics' in Stephen G Post (ed), *Encyclopedia of Bioethics*, 3rd edn (New York, Macmillan Reference USA, 2004) vol 1, 1369

Card, R, 'Federal Provider Conscience Regulation: Unconscionable' (2009) 35 *Journal of Medical Ethics* 471

Cargill, Y and Morin, L, 'SOGC Clinical Practice Guideline No 223: Content of a Complete Routine Second Trimester Obstetrical Ultrasound Examination and Report' (2009) 31 *Journal of Obstectrics and Gynaecology* Canada 272

Carroll, DE, 'Parental Liability for Preconception Negligence: Do Parents Owe a Legal Duty to their Potential Children?' (1986) 22 *California Western Law Review* 289

Caulfield, TA, 'Underwhelmed: Hyperbole, Regulatory Policy, and the Genetic Revolution' (2000) 45 *McGill Law Journal* 437

——'Clones, Controversy, and Criminal Law: A Comment on the Proposal for Legislation Governing Assisted Human Reproduction' (2001) 39 *Alberta Law Review* 335

——'Bill C-13: The Assisted Human Reproduction Act: Examining the Arguments Against a Regulatory Approach' (2002) 11 *Health Law Review* 20

——and Bubela, T, 'Why a Criminal Ban? Analyzing the Arguments Against Somatic Cell Nuclear Transfer in the Canadian Parliamentary Debate' (2007) 7(2) *American Journal of Bioethics* 51

——and Nelson, E, '*Winnipeg Child and Family Services (Northwest Area) v DFG*: A Commentary on the Law, Reproductive Autonomy and the Allure of Technopolicy' (1998) 39 *Alberta Law Review* 799

——and Ries, NM, 'Consent, Privacy and Confidentiality in Longitudinal, Population Health Research: The Canadian Legal Context' [2004] *Health Law Journal* Special Supp 1

——and Robertson, G, 'Eugenic Policies in Alberta: From the Systematic to the Systemic?' (1996) 35 *Alberta Law Review* 59

——, Knowles, L and Meslin, EM, 'Law and Policy in the Era of Reproductive Genetics' (2004) 30 *Journal of Medical Ethics* 414

Centers for Disease Control and Prevention, 'Abortion Surveillance – United States, 2008' (2011) 60(15) *Morbidity and Mortality Weekly Report* 6

——American Society for Reproductive Medicine, Society for Assisted Reproductive Technology, *2009 Assisted Reproductive Technology Success Rates: National Summary and Fertility Clinic Reports* (Atlanta, US Department of Health and Human Services, 2011)

Cepko, R, 'Involuntary Sterilization of Mentally Disabled Women' (1993) 8 *Berkley's Women's Law Journal* 122

Chamallas, M, *Introduction to Feminist Legal Theory*, 2nd edn (New York, Aspen Publishers, 2003)

Chambers, GM *et al*, 'The Economic Impact of Assisted Reproductive Technology: A Review of Selected Developed Countries' (2009) 91 *Fertility and Sterility* 2281

——, Ho, MT and Sullivan, EA, 'Assisted Reproductive Technology Treatment Costs of a Live Birth: An Age-stratified Cost–outcome Study of Treatment in Australia' (2006) 184 *Medical Journal of Australia* 155

Charo, RA, 'Children by Choice: Reproductive Technologies and the Boundaries of Personal Autonomy' (2002) 4 *Nature Cell Biology* S23
—— 'Realbioethik' (2005) 35(4) *Hastings Center Report* 13
—— 'The Celestial Fire of Conscience – Refusing to Deliver Medical Care' (2005) 352 *New England Journal of Medicine* 2471
—— 'Politics, Parents, and Prophylaxis – Mandating HPV Vaccination in the United States' (2007) 356 *New England Journal of Medicine* 1905
—— 'Warning: Contraceptive Drugs May Cause Political Headaches' (2012) 366 *New England Journal of Medicine* 1361
Chavkin, W, 'Cocaine and Pregnancy – Time to Look at the Evidence' (2001) 285 *Journal of the American Medical Association* 1626
Chen, YYB and Flood, CM, 'Moving Beyond Hype and Rhetoric: An Evidence-Based Examination of the Implications of Medical Tourism for Health Care Access and Global Equity' (2012) *Journal of Law, Medicine and Ethics* (in press)
Cherry, A, 'Choosing Substantive Justice: A Discussion of "Choice", "Rights", and the New Reproductive Technologies' (1997) 11 *Wisconsin Women's Law Journal* 431
Chervenak, FA and Kurjak, A, *Current Perspectives on the Fetus as a Patient* (New York, Parthenon, 1996)
—— and McCullough, LB, 'Perinatal Ethics: A Practical Method of Analysis of Obligations to Mother and Fetus' (1985) 66 *Obstetrics & Gynecology* 442
—— —— 'An Ethical Critique of Boutique Fetal Imaging: A Case for the Medicalization of Fetal Imaging' (2005) 192 *American Journal of Obstetrics & Gynecology* 31
—— —— 'Conscientious Objection in Medicine: Author Did Not Meet Standards of Argument Based Ethics' (2006) 332 *British Medical Journal* 425
—— *et al*, 'Responding to the Ethical Challenges Posed by the Business Tools of Managed Care in the Practice of Obstetrics and Gynecology' (1996) 175 *American Journal of Obstetrics & Gynecology* 523
Chesler, P, *Sacred Bond: The Legacy of Baby M* (New York, Times Books, 1988)
Chitayat, D, Langlois, S and Wilson, RD, 'Joint SOGC-CCMG Clinical Practice Guideline No 261: Prenatal Screening for Fetal Aneuploidy in Singleton Pregnancies' (2011) 33 *Journal of Obstetrics and Gynaecology Canada* 736
Christman, J, 'Relational Autonomy, Liberal Individualism and the Social Constitution of Selves' (2004) 117 *Philosophical Studies* 143
—— and Anderson, J, 'Introduction' in John Christman and Joel Anderson (eds), *Autonomy and the Challenges to Liberalism: New Essays* (Cambridge, Cambridge University Press, 2005) 1
Chuang, C-C *et al*, 'Age is a Better Predictor of Pregnancy Potential Than Basal Follicle-stimulating Hormone Levels in Women Undergoing In Vitro Fertilization' (2003) 79 *Fertility and Sterility* 63
Cica, N, 'Sterilising the Intellectually Disabled: The Approach of the High Court of Australia in *Department of Health v. J.W.B. and S.M.B*' (1993) 1 *Medical Law Review* 186
Ciccarelli, JC and Beckman, LJ, 'Navigating Rough Waters: An Overview of Psychological Aspects of Surrogacy' (2005) 61 *Journal of Social Issues* 21
Clark, SL, *et al*, 'Maternal Death in the 21st Century: Causes, Prevention, and Relationship to Cesatean Delivery' (2008) 199(1) *American Journal of Obstetrics & Gynecology* 36e1
Cleland, K *et al*, 'Family Planning as a Cost-Saving Preventive Health Service' (2011) 364 *New England Journal of Medicine* e37
Coale, AJ, 'Excess Female Mortality and the Balance of the Sexes in the Population: An Estimate of the Number of "Missing Females"' (1991) 17 *Population and Development Review* 517
Code, L, 'Second Persons' in Lorraine Code, *What Can She Know: Feminist Theory and the Construction of Knowledge* (Ithaca, NY, Cornell University Press, 1991)
Cohen, CB, 'Selling Bits and Pieces of Humans to Make Babies: *The Gift of the Magi* Revisited' (1999) 24 *Journal of Medicine and Philosophy* 288

Cohen, IG, 'Beyond Best Interests' (2012) 96 *Minnesota Law Review* 1187

——'How To Regulate Medical Tourism (And Why It Matters For Bioethics)' (2012) 12 *Developing World Bioethics* 9

——'Response: Rethinking Sperm-Donor Anonymity: Of Changed Selves, Nonidentity, and One-Night Stands' (2012) 100 *Georgetown Law* Journal 431

——and Sayeed, S, 'Fetal Pain, Abortion, Viability, and the Constitution' (2011) 39 *Journal of Law, Medicine and Ethics* 235

Cohen, J, 'Assisted Hatching of Human Embryos' (1991) 8 J*ournal of In Vitro Fertilization and Embryo Transfer* 179

Cohen, SA, 'The Broad Benefits of Investing in Sexual and Reproductive Health' (2004) 7(1) *Guttmacher Report on Public Policy* 5

——'Abortion and Women of Color: The Bigger Picture' (2008) 11(3) *Guttmacher Policy Review* 2

——'Family Planning and Safe Motherhood: Dollars and Sense' (2010) 13(2) *Guttmacher Policy Review* 12

——'US Overseas Family Planning Program, Perennial Victim of Abortion Politics, Is Once Again Under Siege' (2011) 14(4) *Guttmacher Policy Review* 7

Coleman-Cowager, VH *et al*, 'Current Practice of Cesarean Delivery on Maternal Request Following the 2006 State-of-the-Science Conference' (2010) 55 *Journal of Reproductive Medicine* 25

Coleman, CH, 'Procreative Liberty and Contemporaneous Choice: An Inalienable Rights Approach to Frozen Embryo Disputes' (1999) 84 *Minnesota Law Review* 55

Collier, R, 'Surge in Down Syndrome Prenatal Testing Anticipated' (2012) 184 *Canadian Medical Association Journal* E449

Commission de l'éthique de la science et de la technologie, *Ethics and Assisted Procreation: Guidelines for the Donation of Gametes and Embryos, Surrogacy and Preimplantation Genetic Diagnosis* (Quebec, Commission de l'éthique de la science et de la technologie, 2009)

Committee to Consider the Social, Ethical and Legal Issues Arising from In-vitro Fertilization, *Consolidated Reports of the Victorian Inquiry into IVF and Related Issues, 1982 –1984* (Melbourne, Committee to Consider the Social, Ethical and Legal Issues Arising from In-vitro Fertilisation, 1990)

Connolly, MP, Hoorens, S and Chambers, GM, 'The Costs and Consequence of Assisted Reproductive Technology: An Economic Perspective' (2010) 16 *Human Reproduction Update* 603

Connolly, MP, Ledger, W and Postma, MJ, 'Economics of Assisted Reproduction: Access to Fertility Treatments and Valuing Live Births in Economic Terms' (2010) 13 *Human Fertility* 13

Conrad, P, 'Medicalization and Social Control' (1992) 18 *Annual Review of Sociology* 209

Cook, H, 'Unseemly And Unwomanly Behaviour: Comparing Women's Control of Their Fertility in Australia and England from 1890–1970' (2000) 17 *Journal of Population Research* 125

Cook, JL *et al*, 'Assisted Reproductive Technology-Related Multiple Births: Canada in an International Context' (2011) 33 *Journal of Obstetrics and Gynaecology Canada* 159

Cook, RJ, 'Reservations to the Convention on the Elimination of All Forms of Discrimination Against Women' (1990) 30 *Virginia Journal of International Law* 643

——'International Human Rights and Women's Reproductive Health' (1993) 24(2) *Studies in Family Planning* 73

——and Dickens, BM, 'Voluntary and Involuntary Sterilization: Denials and Abuses of Rights' (2000) 68 *International Journal of Gynaecology and Obstetrics* 61

——— 'Access to Emergency Contraception' (2003) 25 *Journal of Obstetrics and Gynaecology Canada* 914

——— 'In Response' (2004) 26 *Journal of Obstetrics and Gynaecology Canada* 112

——— 'Reply' (2004) 26 *Journal of Obstetrics and Gynaecology Canada* 706

——— and Fathalla, MF, *Reproductive Health and Human Rights: Integrating Medicine, Ethics, and Law* (Oxford, Oxford University Press, 2003)

Cook, RJ and Fathalla, MF, 'Advancing Reproductive Rights Beyond Cairo and Beijing' (1996) 22 *International Family Planning Perspectives* 115

Cordell, S *et al*, 'Lost Property? Legal Compensation for Destroyed Sperm: A Reflection and Comparison Drawing on UK and French Perspectives' (2011) 37 *Journal of Medical Ethics* 747

Corea, G, *The Mother Machine: Reproductive Technologies from Assisted Insemination to Artificial Wombs* (New York, Harper & Row, 1985)

Cornell, D, 'Bodily Integrity and the Right to Abortion' in Austin Sarat and Thomas R Kearns (eds), *Identities, Politics, and Rights* (Ann Arbor, University of Michigan Press, 1995) 21

—— *The Imaginary Domain: Abortion, Pornography & Sexual Harassment* (London, Routledge, 1995)

Council on Ethical and Judicial Affairs, American Medical Association, 'Ethical Issues in Managed Care' (1995) 273 *Journal of the American Medical Association* 330

Covington, SN and Gibbons, WE, 'What is Happening to the Price of Eggs?' (2007) 87 *Fertility and Sterility* 1001

Crockin, SL and Jones Jr, HW, *Legal Conceptions: The Evolving Law and Policy of Assisted Reproductive Technologies* (Baltimore, MD, Johns Hopkins University Press, 2010)

Crosignani, PG *et al*, 'Multiple Gestation Pregnancy' (2000) 15 *Human Reproduction* 1856

Curtis, A, 'Giving 'Til It Hurts: Egg Donation and the Costs of Altruism' (2010) 22(2) *Feminist Formations* 80

Daar, JF, 'Regulating Reproductive Technologies: Panacea or Paper Tiger' (1997) 34 *Houston Law Review* 609

—— 'Assisted Reproductive Technologies and the Pregnancy Process: Developing an Equality Model to Protect Reproductive Liberties' (1999) 25 *American Journal of Law & Medicine* 455

—— 'Panel on Disputes Concerning Frozen Embryos' (1999) 8 *Texas Journal of Women and the Law* 285

—— 'Frozen Embryo Disputes Revisited: A Trilogy of Procreation-Avoidance Approaches' (2001) 29 *Journal of Law, Medicine and Ethics* 197

Dada, OA *et al*, 'A Randomized, Double Blind, Noninferiority Study to Compare Two Regimens of Levonorgestrel for Emergency Contraception in Nigeria' (2010) 82 *Contraception* 373

Dailard, C, 'The Public Health Promise and Potential Pitfalls of the World's First Cervical Cancer Vaccine' (2006) 9(1) *Guttmacher Policy Review* 6

Damelio, J and Sorensen, K, 'Enhancing Autonomy in Paid Surrogacy' (2008) 22 *Bioethics* 269

Damewood, MD, 'Editorial: Ethical Implications of a New Application of Preimplantation Diagnosis' (2001) 285 *Journal of the American Medical Association* 3143

Daniels, K, 'To Give or Sell Human Gametes – The Interplay Between Pragmatics, Policy and Ethics' (2000) 26 *Journal of Medical Ethics* 206

—— and Taylor, K, 'Secrecy and Openness in Donor Insemination' (1993) 12 *Politics and the Life Sciences* 155

Danis, J, 'Sexism and "the Superfluous Female": Arguments for Regulating Pre-Implantation Sex Selection' (1995) 18 *Harvard Women's Law Journal* 219

Darroch, JE, Sedgh, G and Ball, H, *Contraceptive Technologies: Responding to Women's Needs* (New York, Guttmacher Institute, 2011)

Davidson, AR and Kalmuss, D, 'Topics For Our Times: Norplant Coercion – An Overstated Threat' (1997) 87 *American Journal of Public Health* 550

Davies, M and Naffine, N, *Are Persons Property? Legal Debates About Property and Personality* (Dartmouth, Ashgate, 2001).

Davis, E, 'The Rise of Gestational Surrogacy and the Pressing Need for International Regulation' (2012) 21 *Minnesota Journal of International Law* 120

Davis, VJ, 'SOGC Clinical Practice Guideline No 184: Induced Abortion Guidelines' (2006) 28 *Journal of Obstetrics and Gynaecology Canada* 1014

Dawson, A, 'The Human Fertilisation and Embryology Authority: Evidence Based Policy Formation in a Contested Context' (2004) 12 *Health Care Analysis* 1

de Costa, CM *et al*, 'Early Medical Abortion in Cairns, Queensland: July 2006–April 2007' (2007) 187 *Medical Journal of Australia* 171

——, Russell, DB and Carrette, M, 'Correspondence: Abortion in Australia: Still to Emerge from the 19th Century' (2010) 375 *The Lancet* 804

de Crespigny, LJ and Savulescu, J, 'Pregnant Women with Fetal Abnormalities: The Forgotten People in the Abortion Debate' (2008) 188 *Medical Journal of Australia* 100

De Rycke, M, Liebaers, I and Van Steirteghem, A, 'Epigenetic Risks Related to Assisted Reproductive Technologies: Risk Analysis and Epigenetic Inheritance' (2002) 17 *Human Reproduction* 2487

Deans, Z, 'Conscientious Objections in Pharmacy Practice in Great Britain' (2013) 27 *Bioethics* 48

Deckers, J, 'Why Current UK Legislation on Embryo Research is Immoral. How the Argument From Lack of Qualities and the Argument from Potentiality Have Been Applied and Why They Should be Rejected' (2005) 19 *Bioethics* 251

Deckha, M, '(Not) Reproducing the Cultural, Racial and Embodied Other: A Feminist Response to Canada's Partial Ban on Sex Selection' (2007) 16 *UCLA Women's Law Journal* 1

DeCoste, FC, '*Winnipeg Child and Family Services (Northwest Area) v DFG*: The Impossibility of Fetal Rights and the Obligations of Judicial Governance' (1998) 36 *Alberta Law Review* 725

Deka, PK and Swarnali, S, 'Psychological Aspects of Infertility' (2010) 3 *British Journal of Medical Practioners* 32

Dekkers, W, Hoffer, C and Wils, J-P, 'Bodily Integrity and Male and Female Circumcision' (2005) 8 *Medicine, Health Care and Philosophy* 179

DeNavas-Walt, C, Proctor, BD and Smith, JC, US Census Bureau, *Current Population Reports, P60-239, Income, Poverty, and Health Insurance Coverage in the United States: 2010* (Washington, DC, US Government Printing Office, 2011)

Department for Constitutional Affairs, *Mental Capacity Act 2005 Code of Practice* (London, The Stationery Office, 2007)

Department of Health, *Choosing Health: Making Healthy Choices Easier*, Cm 6374 (London, The Stationery Office, 2004)

——*Review of the Human Fertilisation and Embryology Act: Proposals for revised legislation (including establishment of the Regulatory Authority for Tissue and Embryos)* Cm 6989 (London, The Stationery Office, 2006)

——*Findings of the Baseline Review of Contraceptive Services* (London, The Stationery Office, 2007)

——*Government Response to the Report from the Joint Committee on the Human Tissue and Embryos (Draft) Bill*, Cm 7209 (London, The Stationery Office, 2007)

——*Human Tissue and Embryos (Draft) Bill*, Cm 7087 (London, The Stationery Office, 2007)

Department of Justice, *Report of the Committee on the Operation of the Abortion Law* (Ottawa, Minister of Supply and Services, 1977)

Department of Reproductive Health and Research, World Health Organization, *Unsafe Abortion: Global and Regional Estimates of the Incidence of Unsafe Abortion and Associated Mortality in 2008*, 6th edn (Geneva, World Health Organization, 2011)

Dickens, BM, *Abortion and the Law* (Bristol, MacGibbon & Kee, 1966)

——'Informed Consent' in Jocelyn Downie, Timothy Caulfield and Colleen M Flood (eds), *Canadian Health Law and Policy*, 2nd edn (Markham, Butterworths, 2002) 148

——'Preimplantation Genetic Diagnosis and "Savior Siblings"' (2005) 88 *International Journal of Gynaecology and Obstetrics* 91

——'Conscientious Objection and Professionalism' (2009) 4 *Expert Review of Obstetrics & Gynecology* 97

——'Legal Protection and Limits of Conscientious Objection: When Conscientious Objection is Unethical' (2009) 28 *Medicine and Law* 337

Dickens, BM, and Cook, RJ, 'The Scope and Limits of Conscientious Objection' (2000) 71 *International Journal of Gynaecology & Obstetrics* 71

——— 'The Legal Status of In Vitro Embryos' (2010) 111 *International Journal of Gynaecology and Obstetrics* 91

Dickenson, D, 'Commodification of Human Tissue: Implications for Feminist and Development Ethics' (2002) 2 *Developing World Bioethics* 55

——— *Property in the Body: Feminist Perspectives* (Cambridge, Cambridge University Press, 2007)

Dickinson, JE, 'Late Pregnancy Termination within a Legislated Medical Environment' (2004) 44 *Australia and New Zealand Journal of Obstetrics and Gynaecology* 337

Ding, QJ and Hesketh, T, 'Family Size, Fertility Preferences, and Sex Ratio in China in the Era of the One Child Family Policy: Results from National Family Planning and Reproductive Health Survey' (2006) 333 *British Medical Journal* 371

Dodds, S, 'Choice and Control in Feminist Bioethics' in Catriona Mackenzie and Natalie Stoljar (eds), *Relational Autonomy: Feminist Perspectives on Autonomy, Agency, and the Social Self* (Oxford, Oxford University Press, 2000) 213

Donchin, A, 'Reworking Autonomy: Toward a Feminist Perspective' (1995) 4 *Cambridge Quarterly Healthcare Ethics* 44

——— 'Autonomy, Interdependence, and Assisted Suicide: Respecting Boundaries/Crossing Lines' (2000) 14 *Bioethics* 187

——— 'Understanding Autonomy Relationally: Toward a Reconfiguration of Bioethical Principles' (2001) 26 *Journal of Medicine and Philosophy* 365

——— 'Toward a Gender-Sensitive Assisted Reproduction Policy' (2009) 23 *Bioethics* 28

——— 'Reproductive Tourism and the Quest for Global Justice' (2010) 24 *Bioethics* 323

Donnelly, M, 'Best Interests, Patient Participation and the Mental Capacity Act 2005' (2009) 17 *Medical Law Review* 1

Downie, J and Sherwin, S, 'A Feminist Exploration of Issues Around Assisted Death' (1996) 15 *St Louis University Public Law Review* 303

Draper, H, 'Gametes, Consent and Points of No Return' (2007) 10 *Human Fertility* 105

Dresser, R, 'Long-term Contraceptives in the Criminal Justice System' in Ellen Moskowitz and Bruce Jennings (eds), *Coerced Contraception? Moral and Policy Challenges of Long-Acting Birth Control* (Washington, DC, Georgetown University Press, 1996) 134

——— 'Regulating Assisted Reproduction' (2000) 30(6) *Hastings Center Report* 26

Driscol, DA and Gross, S, 'Prenatal Screening for Anueploidy' (2009) 360 *New England Journal of Medicine* 2556

Dubuc, S and Coleman, D, 'An Increase in the Sex Ratio of Births to India-born Mothers in England and Wales: Evidence for Sex-Selective Abortion' (2007) 33(2) *Population and Development Review* 383

Duden, B, *Disembodying Women: Perspectives on Pregnancy and the Unborn* (Lee Hoinacki tr) (Cambridge, MA, Harvard University Press, 1993)

Dudley, S and Mueller, S, *Fact Sheet: What is Medical Abortion?* (Washington, DC, National Abortion Federation, 2008)

Dunphy, BC *et al*, 'Female Age, the Length of Involuntary Infertility Prior to Investigation and Fertility Outcome' (1989) 4 *Human Reproduction* 527

Dworkin, G, *The Theory and Practice of Autonomy* (Cambridge, Cambridge University Press, 1988)

Dworkin, R, *Life's Dominion: An Argument About Abortion, Euthanasia, and Individual Freedom* (New York, Alfred A Knopf, 1993)

Dyer, C, 'New Life for the HFEA?' (2011) 342 *British Medical Journal* 258

Edelman, RJ, 'Surrogacy: The Psychological Issues' (2004) 22 *Journal of Reproductive and Infant Psychology* 123

Eggertson, L, 'News: Abortion Services in Canada: A Patchwork Quilt with Many Holes' (2001) 164 *Canadian Medical Association Journal* 847

——'Ontario Pharmacists Drop Plan B Screening Form' (2006) 174 *Canadian Medical Association Journal* 149

——'Plan B Comes Out From Behind the Counter' (2008) 178 *Canadian Medical Association Journal* 1645

——'New Reproductive Technology Board Belies Expert Selection Process' (2007) 176 *Canadian Medical Association Journal* 611

——and Sibbald, B, 'Privacy Issues Raised Over Plan B: Women Asked for Names, Addresses, Sexual History' (2005) 173 *Canadian Medical Association Journal* 1435

Ehrenreich, N, 'The Colonization of the Womb' (1993) 43 *Duke Law Journal* 492

Ehrich, K *et al*, 'Choosing Embryos: Ethical Complexity and Relational Autonomy in Staff Accounts of PGD' (2007) 29 *Sociology of Health & Illness* 1091

——, Williams, C and Farsides, B, 'The Embryo as Moral Work Object: PGD/IVF Staff Views and Experiences' (2008) 30 *Sociology of Health & Illness* 772

El Feki, S, 'The Birth of Reproductive Health: A Difficult Delivery' (2004) 1(1) *Public Library of Science Medicine* 010

Ellertson, C, 'History and Efficacy of Emergency Contraception: Beyond Coca-Cola' (1996) 28 *Family Planning Perspectives* 44

——*et al*, 'Extending the Time Limit for Starting the Yuzpe Regimen of Emergency Contraception to 120 Hours' (2003) 101 *Obstetrics & Gynecology* 1168

Ellison, B and Meliker, J, 'Assessing the Risk of Ovarian Hyperstimulation Syndrome in Egg Donation: Implications for Human Embryonic Stem Cell Research' (2011) 11(9) *American Journal of Bioethics* 22

Elster, NR, 'Book Review of *Test Tube Families: Why the Fertility Market Needs Legal Regulation*' (2009) 119 *Journal of Clinical Investigation* 3501

Emanuel, EJ and Dubler, NN, 'Preserving the Physician–Patient Relationship in the Era of Managed Care' (1995) 273 *Journal of the American Medical Association* 323

Epps, T, 'Regulation of Health Care Professionals' in Jocelyn Downie, Timothy Caulfield and Colleen M Flood (eds), *Canadian Health Law and* Policy, 4th edn (Markham, LexisNexis Canada, 2011) 75

Erdman, JN and Cook, RJ, 'Protecting Fairness in Women's Health: The Case of Emergency Contraception' in Colleen M Flood (ed), *Just Medicare: What's In, What's Out, How We Decide* (Toronto, University of Toronto Press, 2006) 137

——, Grenon, A and Harrison-Wilson, L, 'Medication Abortion in Canada: A Right-to-Health Perspective' (2008) 98 *American Journal of Public Health* 1764

Espey, E, Cosgrove, E and Ogburn, T, 'Family Planning American Style: Why It's So Hard to Control Birth in the US' (2007) 34 *Obstetrics & Gynecology Clinics of North America* 1

Evans, JP *et al*, 'Deflating the Genomic Bubble' (2011) 331 *Science* 861

Faden, RR and Beauchamp, TL, *A History and Theory of Informed Consent* (Oxford, Oxford University Press, 1986)

Falconer, AD *et al*, 'Scaling Up Human Resources for Women's Health' (2009) 119 (Supp 1) *BJOG: An International Journal of Obstetrics and Gynaecology* 11

Fan, HC *et al*, 'Non-invasive Prenatal Measurement of the Fetal Genome' (2012) 487 *Nature* 320

Farquharson, RG, Jauniaux, E and Exalto, N, 'Updated and Revised Nomenclature for Description of Early Pregnancy Events' (2005) 20 *Human Reproduction* 3008

Fasouliotis, SJ and Schenker, JG, 'Maternal–Fetal Conflict' (2000) 89 *European Journal of Obstetrics & Gynecology, and Reproductive Biology* 101

Faunce, T and Jefferys, S, 'Abandoning the Common Law: Medical Negligence, Genetic Tests and Wrongful Life in the Australian High Court' (2007) 14 *Journal of Law and Medicine* 469

Feldman, GB and Frieman, JA, 'Prophylactic Cesarean Section at Term?' (1985) 312 *New England Journal of Medicine* 1264

Fentiman, LC, 'Pursuing the Perfect Mother: Why America's Criminalization of Maternal Substance Abuse is Not the Answer – A Comparative Legal Analysis' (2009) 15 *Michigan Journal of Gender and Law* 389

Fertility Society of Australia, Reproductive Technology Accreditation Committee, *Code of Practice for Assisted Reproductive Technology Units* (Melbourne, Fertility Society of Australia, 2010)

Fessler, A, *The Girls Who Went Away: The Hidden History of Women Who Surrendered Children for Adoption in the Decades Before* Roe v Wade (New York, Penguin Press, 2006)

Filippi, V *et al*, 'Maternal Health in Poor Countries: The Broader Context and a Call for Action' (2006) 368 *The Lancet* 1535

Findlay, JK *et al*, 'Human Embryo: A Biological Definition' (2007) 22 *Human Reproduction* 905

Fineman, M and Karpin, I (eds), *Mothers in Law: Feminist Theory and the Legal Regulation of Motherhood* (New York, Columbia University Press, 1995)

Fineman, MA, *The Autonomy Myth: A Theory of Dependency* (New York, The New Press, 2004)

Finer, LB *et al*, 'Timing of Steps and Reasons for Delays in Obtaining Abortions in the United States' (2006) 74 *Contraception* 334

——*et al*, 'Reasons US Women Have Abortions: Quantitative and Qualitative Perspectives' (2005) 37 *Perspectives on Sexual and Reproductive Health* 110

—— and Zolna, MR, 'Unintended Pregnancy in the United States: Incidence and Disparities, 2006' (2011) 84 *Contraception* 478

Fitzgerald, FT, 'The Tyranny of Health' (1994) 331 *New England Journal of Medicine* 196

Flavin, J and Paltrow, LM, 'Punishing Pregnant Drug-Using Women: Defying Law, Medicine, and Common Sense' (2010) 29 *Journal of Addictive Diseases* 231

Flenady, V *et al*, 'Major Risk Factors for Stillbirth in High-Income Countries: A Systematic Review and Meta-analysis' (2011) 377 *The Lancet* 1331

——, 'Stillbirths: The Way Forward in High-Income Countries' (2011) 377 *The Lancet* 1703

Fletcher, JC and Evans, MI, 'Maternal Bonding in Early Fetal Ultrasound Examinations' (1983) 308 *New England Journal of Medicine* 392

Flood, CM and Thomas, B, 'Canadian Medical Malpractice Law in 2011: Missing the Mark on Patient Safety' (2011) 86 *Chicago-Kent Law Review* 1053

——, Stabile, M and Tuohy, C, 'What Is In and Out of Medicare? Who Decides?' in Colleen M Flood (ed), *Just Medicare: What's In, What's Out, How We Decide* (Toronto, University of Toronto Press, 2006) 15

Fodden, SR, *Family Law* (Toronto, Irwin Law, 1999)

Ford, J, 'The Sterilisation of Young Women with an Intellectual Disability: A Comparison Between the Family Court of Australia and the Guardianship Board of New South Wales' (1996) 10 *Australian Journal of Family Law* 236

Fortin, JES, 'Is the "Wrongful Life" Action Really Dead?' (1987) 9 *Journal of Social Welfare Law* 306

Fossum, GT, Davajan, V and Kletzky, OA, 'Early Detection of Pregnancy with Transvaginal Ultrasound' (1988) 49 *Fertility and Sterility* 788

Fovargue, S and Miola, J, 'The Legal Status of the Fetus' (2010) 5 *Clinical Ethics* 122

Fox, M, 'A Woman's Right to Choose? A Feminist Critique' in John Harris and Søren Holm (eds), *The Future of Human Reproduction: Ethics, Choice, and Regulation* (Oxford, Clarendon Press, 1998) 77

—— 'The Human Fertilisation and Embryology Act 2008: Tinkering at the Margins' (2009) 17 *Feminist Legal Studies* 333

Franklin, S, *Embodied Progress: A Cultural Account of Assisted Conception* (London, Routledge, 1997)

Fredman, S, *Women and the Law* (Oxford, Clarendon Press, 1997)

Free, C, Lee, RM and Ogden, J, 'Young Women's Accounts of Factors Influencing Their Use and Non-use of Emergency Contraception: In-depth Interview Study' (2002) 325 *British Medical Journal* 1393

Friedman, M, 'Feminism and Modern Friendship: Dislocating the Community' in Cass R Sunstein (ed), *Feminism and Political Theory* (Chicago, Ill, University of Chicago Press, 1990) 143

—— 'Autonomy and Social Relationships: Rethinking the Feminist Critique' in Diana Tietjens Meyers (ed), *Feminists Rethink the Self* (Boulder, CO, Westview Press, 1997) 40

—— *Autonomy, Gender, Politics* (Oxford, Oxford University Press, 2003)

—— 'Autonomy and Male Dominance' in John Christman and Joel Anderson (eds), *Autonomy and the Challenges to Liberalism: New Essays* (Cambridge, Cambridge University Press, 2005) 150

Frith, L, 'Gamete Donation and Anonymity: The Ethical and Legal Debate' (2001) 16 *Human Reproduction* 818

Fujimoto, VY *et al*, 'Proceedings from the Conference on Reproductive Problems in Women of Color' (2010) 94 *Fertility and Sterility* 7

Furedi, A, 'Britain: Contradictory Messages about Sexual Responsibility' in Angel M Foster and Lisa L Wynn (eds), *Emergency Contraception: The Story of a Global Reproductive Health Technology* (New York, Palgrave Macmillan, 2012) 123

Furrow, BR *et al*, *Health Law: Cases, Materials and Problems*, 3rd edn (St Paul, West Group, 1997)

Gaffney, P, 'Why the "Widespread Agreement" is Wrong: Contesting the Non-harm Arguments for the Prohibition of Full Commercial Surrogacy' (2009) 17 *Journal of Law and Medicine* 280

Galhardo, A *et al*, 'The Impact of Shame and Self-Judgment on Psychopathology in Infertile Patients' (2011) 26 *Human Reproduction* 2408

Gallagher, J, 'Fetus as Patient' in Sherrill Cohen and Nadine Taub (eds), *Reproductive Laws for the 1990s* (Clifton, NJ, Humana Press, 1989) 185

—— 'Collective Bad Faith: "Protecting" the Fetus' in Joan C Callahan (ed), *Reproduction, Ethics, and the Law: Feminist Perspectives* (Bloomington, Indiana University Press, 1995) 343

Gamble, N, 'Considering the Need for a Father: The Role of Clinicians in Safeguarding Family Values in UK Fertility Treatment' (2009) 19(1) *Reproductive Biomedicine Online* 15

—— and Ghevaert, L, 'Lesbian Mothers in Dispute: T v B' (2010) 40 *Family Law* 1203

Gan, C *et al*, 'The Influence of Medical Abortion Compared with Surgical Abortion on Subsequent Pregnancy Outcome' (2008) 101 *International Journal of Gynaecology & Obstetrics* 231

Ganatra, B, 'Maintaining Access to Safe Abortion and Reducing Sex Ratio Imbalances in Asia' (2008) 16(31 Supp) *Reproductive Health Matters* 90

Garrow, DJ, 'Significant Risks: Gonzales v Carhart and the Future of Abortion Law' (2007) 1 *The Supreme Court Review* 1

Gavaghan, C, *Defending the Genetic Supermarket: The Law and Ethics of Selecting the Next Generation* (Abingdon, Routledge-Cavendish, 2007)

Gee, RE *et al*, 'Behind-the-counter Status and Availability of Emergency Contraception' (2008) 199 *American Journal of Obstetrics & Gynecology* 478.e1

Gemzell-Danielsson, K, 'Mechanism of Action of Emergency Contraception' (2010) 82 *Contraception* 404

Germain, A, 'Playing Politics with Women's Lives' (2004) 305 *Science* 17

Gianelli, DM, 'Shock-Tactic Ads Target Late-Term Abortion Procedure', 5 July 1993, *American Medical News*, 3

Giddens, A, 'Risk and Responsibility' (1999) 62 MLR 1

Gien, LT and Covens, A, 'Fertility-sparing Options for Early Stage Cervical Cancer' (2010) 117 *Gynecologic Oncology* 350

Gilligan, C, *In a Different Voice: Psychological Theory and Women's Development* (Cambridge, MA, Harvard University Press, 1982)

Gillon, R, 'On Sterilising Severely Mentally Handicapped People' (1987) 13 *Journal of Medical Ethics* 59

Gillon, R, 'Ethics Needs Principle – Four Can Encompass the Rest – And Respect For Autonomy Should be "First Among Equals"' (2003) 29 *Journal of Mediacl Ethics* 307

Glasier, A and Baird, D, 'The Effects of Self-Administering Emergency Contraception' (1998) 339 *New England Journal of Medicine* 1

——*et al*, 'Advanced Provision of Emergency Contraception Does Not Reduce Abortion Rates' (2004) 69 *Contraception* 361

Gleeson, K, 'The Other Abortion Myth – The Failure of the Common Law' (2009) *Journal of Bioethical Inquiry* 69

Gluckman, E, 'History of Cord Blood Transplantation' (2009) 44 *Bone Marrow Transplantation* 621

Gnoth, C *et al*, 'Definition and Prevalence of Subfertility and Infertility' (2005) 20 *Human Reproduction* 1144

Gold, RB, 'Insurance Coverage and Abortion Incidence: Information and Misinformation' (2010) 13(4) *Guttmacher Policy Review* 7

——*et al*, *Next Steps for America's Family Planning Program: Leveraging the Potential of Medicaid and Title X in an Evolving Health Care System* (New York, Guttmacher Institute, 2009)

——and Nash, E, 'Troubling Trend: More States Hostile to Abortion Rights as Middle Ground Shrinks' (2012) 15(1) *Guttmacher Policy Review* 14

Goldberg, S, 'Cloning Matters: How *Lawrence v Texas* Protects Therapeutic Research' (2004) 4 *Yale Journal of Health Policy, Law, and Ethics* 305

Golder, B, 'From *McFarlane* to *Melchior* and Beyond: Love, Sex, Money and Commodification in the Anglo-Australian Law of Torts' (2004) 12 *Torts Law Journal* 1

Goldhar, J, 'The Sterilization of Women with an Intellectual Disability – A Lawyer Looks at the Medical Aspects' (1990–91) 10 *University of Tasmania Law Review* 157

Golditch, IM and Kirkman, K, 'The Large Fetus: Management and Outcome' (1978) 52 *Obstetrics & Gynecology* 26

Golombok, S *et al*, 'Families Created Through Surrogacy Arrangements: Parent–Child Relationships in the 1st Year of Life' (2004) 40 *Developmental Psychology* 400

————'Surrogacy Families: Parental Functioning, Parent-Child Relationships and Children's Psychological Development at Age 2' (2006) *Journal of Child Psychology and Psychiatry* 213

————'Non-Genetic and Non-Gestational Parenthood: Consequences for Parent-Child Relationships and the Psychological Well-Being of Mothers, Fathers and Children at Age 3' (2006) 21 *Human Reproduction* 1918

————'Families Created Through Surrogacy: Mother-Child Relationships and Children's Psychological Adjustment at Age 7' (2011) 47 *Developmental Psychology* 1579

Goodwin, M, 'A View from the Cradle: Tort Law and the Private Regulation of Assisted Reproduction' (2010) 59 *Emory Law Journal* 1039

Gook, DA, 'History of Oocyte Cryopreservation' (2011) 23 *Reproductive Biomedicine Online* 281

Gottweiss, H, 'The Endless hESC Controversy in the United States: History, Context, and Prospects' (2010) 7 *Cell Stem Cell* 555

Government of Canada, 'Regulations Amending the Food and Drug Regulations (1272 – Levonorgestrel)' (2004) 138 *Canada Gazette* 1633

Grady, A, 'Legal Protection for Conscientious Objection by Health Professionals' (2006) 8 *Virtual Mentor* 327

Gray, E and McDonald, P, 'Using a Reproductive Life Course Approach to Understand Contraceptive Method Use in Australia' (2010) 42 *Journal of Biosocial Science* 43

Grayson, N, Hargreaves, J and Sullivan, EA, *Use of Routinely Collected National Data Sets for Reporting on Induced Abortion in Australia AIHW Cat No PER 30* (Sydney, Australian Institute of Health and Welfare, National Perinatal Statistics Unit, 2005)

Greenberg, JA, 'Reconceptualizing Preconception Torts' (1997) 64 *Tennessee Law Review* 315

Gregoire, AT and Mayer, RC, 'The Impregnators' (1965) 16 *Fertility and Sterility* 130

Grey, A, 'Harriton v Stephens: Life, Logic and Legal Fictions' (2006) 28 *Sydney Law Review* 545

Grimes, DA, 'Switching Emergency Contraception to Over-the-Counter Status' (2002) 347 *New England Journal of Medicine* 846

——et al 'Unsafe Abortion: The Preventable Pandemic' (2006) 368 *The Lancet* 1908

——and Peipert, JF, 'Electronic Fetal Monitoring as a Public Health Screening Program: The Arithmetic of Failure' (2010) 116 *Obstetrics & Gynecology* 1397

Gugucheva, M, *Surrogacy in America* (Cambridge, MA, Center for Responsible Genetics, 2010)

Guilmoto, CZ, 'The Sex Ratio Transition in Asia' (2009) 35 *Population and Development Review* 519

Gurmankin, AD, Sisti, D and Caplan, AL, 'Embryo Disposal Practices in IVF Clinics in the United States' (2004) 22(2) *Politics and the Life Sciences* 4

Gwatkin, DR, 'Political Will and Family Planning: The Implications of India's Emergency Experience' (1979) 5 *Population and Development Review* 29

Haber, G, Malow, RM and Zimet, GD, 'The HPV Vaccine Mandate Controversy' (2007) 20 *Journal of Pediatric and Adolescent Gynecology* 325

Habiba, M et al, 'Late Termination of Pregnancy: A Comparison of Obstetricians' Experience in Eight European Countries' (2009) 116 *BJOG: An International Journal of Obstetrics and Gynaecology* 1340

Hadley, J, *Abortion: Between Freedom and Necessity* (Philadelphia, Pa, Temple University Press, 1996)

Haimes, E, Taylor K and Turkmendag, I, 'Eggs, Ethics and Exploitation? Investigating Women's Experiences of an Egg Sharing Scheme' (2012) 34 *Sociology of Health & Illness* 1199

Halpern, SA, 'Medical Authority and the Culture of Rights' (2004) 29 *Journal of Health Politics, Policy and Law* 835

Halsey, J, 'The Shortcomings of Contemporary Political Rhetoric' (2012) 8(2) *Pitt Political Review* 9.

Hammoud, AO et al, 'In Vitro Fertilization Availability and Utilization in the United States: A Study of Demographic, Social, and Economic Factors' (2009) 91 *Fertility and Sterility* 1630

Hampton, T, 'Abstinence-Only Programs Under Fire' (2008) 299 *Journal of the American Medical Association* 2013

Handyside, AH et al, 'Pregnancies from Biopsied Human Preimplantation Embryos Sexed by Y-specific DNA Amplification' (1990) 344 *Nature* 768

Hanigsberg, JE and Ruddick, S (eds), *Mother Troubles: Rethinking Contemporary Maternal Dilemmas* (Boston, MA, Beacon Press, 1999)

Hanna, JKM, 'Revisiting Child-based Objections to Commercial Surrogacy' (2010) 24 *Bioethics* 341

Harmon, SHE and Laurie, GT, '*Yearworth v North Bristol NHS Trust*: Property, Principles, Precedents and Paradigms' (2010) 69 *Cambridge Law Journal* 476

Harris, J, 'Rights and Reproductive Choice' in John Harris and Søren Holm (eds), *The Future of Human Reproduction: Ethics, Choice, and Regulation* (Oxford, Clarendon Press, 1998) 5

——'Is There a Coherent Social Conception of Disability?' (2000) 26 *Journal of Medical Ethics* 95

——'Sex Selection and Regulated Hatred' (2005) 31 *Journal of Medical Ethics* 291

Harris, LH, 'Rethinking Maternal–Fetal Conflict: Gender and Equality in Perinatal Ethics' (2000) 96 *Obstetrics & Gynecology* 786

——'Second Trimester Abortion Provision: Breaking the Silence and Changing the Discourse' (2008) 16(31 Supp) *Reproductive Health Matters* 74

——et al, 'Obstetrician-Gynecologists' Objections to and Willingness to Help Patients Obtain an Abortion' (2011) 118 *Obstetrics & Gynecology* 905

Harvison Young, A, 'This Child Does Have 2 (Or More) Fathers ... : Step-parents and Support Obligations' (2000) 45 *McGill Law Journal* 107

——and Wasunna, A, 'Wrestling with the Limits of Law: Regulating New Reproductive Technologies' (1998) 6 *Health Law Journal* 239

Haynes, J and Miller, J (eds), *Inconceivable Conceptions: Psychological Aspects of Infertility and Reproductive Technology* (Hove, Brunner-Routledge, 2003)

Health Canada, Health Products and Food Branch, *Guidance Document For Industry and Practitioners – Special Access Programme for Drugs* (Ottawa, Health Canada, 2008)

Henderson, H, 'Case Reignites Debate on Forced Sterilization', *Toronto Star*, 8 June 2002, M15

Henderson, JT *et al*, 'Safety of Mifepristone Abortions in Clinical Use' (2005) 72 *Contraception* 175

Heng, BC, 'Egg Sharing in Return for Subsidized Fertility Treatment – Ethical Challenges and Pitfalls' (2008) 25 *Journal of Assisted Reproduction and Genetics* 159

Henig, RM, *Pandora's Baby: How the First Test Tube Babies Sparked the Reproductive Revolution* (Boston, MA, Houghton Mifflin, 2004)

Hensel, WF, 'The Disabling Impact of Wrongful Birth and Wrongful Life Actions' (2005) 40 *Harvard Civil Rights – Civil Liberties Law Review* 141

Herrin, BW, 'Tort Law – *Etkind v Suarez*: When Do the Joys of Being a Parent Become a Burden?' (1999) 23 *American Journal of Trial Advocacy* 481

Hershkoff, H, 'Positive Rights and State Constitutions: The Limits of Federal Rationality Review' (1999) 112 *Harvard Law Review* 1131

Hesketh, T, Lu, L and Xing, ZW, 'The Effect of China's One-Child Family Policy After 25 Years' (2005) 353 *New England Journal of Medicine* 1171

Hewlett, SA and Luce, CB, 'Off-Ramps and On-Ramps: Keeping Talented Women on the Road to Success' (2005) 83(3) *Harvard Business Review* 43

Hickman, SE *et al*, 'The POLST (Physician Orders for Life-Sustaining Treatment) Paradigm to Improve End-of-Life Care: Potential State Legal Barriers to Implementation' (2008) 36 *Journal of Law, Medicine and Ethics* 119

Hitt, J, 'Pro-Life Nation', *New York Times Magazine*, 9 April 2006, 40

Hobbs, MK *et al*, 'Pharmacy Access to the Emergency Contraceptive Pill: A National Survey of a Random Sample of Australian Women' (2011) 83 *Contraception* 151

Hochschild, A, *The Second Shift* (New York, London Books, 1989)

Hogan, MC *et al*, 'Maternal Mortality for 181 Countries, 1980–2008: A Systematic Analysis of Progress Toward Millennium Development Goal 5' (2010) 375 *The Lancet* 160

Holland, S, 'Contested Commodities at Both Ends of Life: Buying and Selling Gametes, Embryos, and Body Tissues' (2001) 11 *Kennedy Institute of Ethics Journal* 263

—— 'Selecting Against Difference: Assisted Reproduction, Disability and Regulation' (2003) 30 *Florida State University Law Review* 401

Hollister, GD, 'Parent–Child Immunity: A Doctrine in Search of Justification' (1982) 50 *Fordham Law Review* 489

Holsinger, MC, 'The Partial Birth Abortion Ban Act of 2003: The Congressional Reaction to *Stenberg v Carhart*' (2002/2003) 6 *New York University Journal of Legislation and Public Policy* 603

Hoorens, S *et al*, 'Can Assisted Reproductive Technologies Help to Offset Population Ageing? An Assessment of the Demographic and Economic Impact of ART in Denmark and UK' (2007) 22 *Human Reproduction* 2471

Horne, T and Abells, S, *Public Remedies, Not Private Payments: Quality Health Care in Alberta* (Edmonton, AB, Parkland Institute, 2004)

Horsey, K and Sheldon, S, 'Still Hazy After All These Years: The Law Regulating Surrogacy' (2012) 20 *Medical Law Review* 67

House of Commons Standing Committee on Health, *Assisted Human Reproduction: Building Families* (Ottawa, Public Works and Government Services Canada, 2001)

Howard, R and Hendy, S, 'The Sterilisation of Women with Learning Disabilities – Some Points for Consideration' (2004) 50 *British Journal of Developmental Disabilities* 133

Howlett, MJ, Avard, D and Knoppers, BM, 'Physicians and Genetic Malpractice' (2002) 21 *Medicine and Law* 661

Hoyano, LCH, 'Misconceptions about Wrongful Conceptions' (2002) 65 MLR 883

Hudson, KL, 'Preimplantation Genetic Diagnosis: Public Policy and Public Attitudes' (2006) 85 *Fertility and Sterility* 1638

Hughes, E, 'Access to Effective Fertility Care in Canada' (2008) 30 *Journal of Obstetrics and Gynaecology Canada* 389

——and Giacomini, M, 'Funding in Vitro Fertilization Treatment for Persistent Subfertility: the Pain and the Politics' (2001) 76 *Fertility and Sterility* 431

Human Fertilisation and Embryology Authority, *Code of Practice* (London, HFEA, 1991)

——*Code of Practice*, 7th edn (London, HFEA, 2007)

——*Code of Practice*, 8th edn (London, HFEA, 2009 (revised April 2012))

——*Fertility Facts and Figures 2008* (London, HFEA, 2010)

Humbyrd, C, 'Fair Trade International Surrogacy' (2009) 9 *Developing World Bioethics* 111

Humphries, D, *Crack Mothers: Pregnancy, Drugs, and the Media* (Columbus, GA, Ohio State University Press, 1999)

Ikemoto, LC, 'The Code of Perfect Pregnancy: At the Intersection of the Ideology of Motherhood, the Practice of Defaulting to Science, and the Interventionist Mindset of Law' (1992) 53 *Ohio State Law Journal* 1205

——, 'Reproductive Tourism: Equality Concerns in the Global Market for Fertility Services' (2009) 27 *Law and Inequality* 277

Ikonomidis, S and Dickens, B, 'Ontario's Decision to Defund In Vitro Fertilization Treatment Except for Women with Bilateral Fallopian Tube Damage' (1995) 21 *Canadian Public Policy* 379

Ingham, R *et al*, 'Reasons for Second Trimester Abortions in England and Wales' (2008) 16(31 Supp) *Reproductive Health Matters* 18

Institute of Medicine, *Clinical Preventive Services for Women: Closing the Gaps* (Washington, DC, National Academies Press, 2011)

Intromasso, C, 'Reproductive Self-Determination in the Third Circuit: The Statutory Proscription of Wrongful Birth and Wrongful Life Claims as an Unconstitutional Violation of *Planned Parenthood v Casey*'s Undue Burden Standard' (2003) 24 *Women's Rights Law Reporter* 101

Iyengar, S, *The Art of Choosing* (New York, Twelve, 2010)

Jackman, M, 'Poor Rights: Using the *Charter* to Support Social Welfare Claims' (1993–94) 19 *Queen's Law Journal* 65

——'The Right to Participate in Health Care and Health Resource Allocation Decisions Under Section 7 of the Canadian Charter' (1995–96) 4(2) *Health Law Review* 3

Jackson, A, 'Wrongful Life and Wrongful Birth: The English Conception' (1996) 17 *Journal of Legal Medicine* 349

Jackson, E, 'Abortion, Autonomy and Prenatal Diagnosis' (2000) 9 *Social & Legal Studies* 467

——*Regulating Reproduction: Law, Technology and Autonomy* (Oxford, Hart Publishing, 2001)

——'Conception and the Irrelevance of the Welfare Principle' (2002) 65 MLR 176

Jacobs, M, 'Sterilization Issue in Court's Hands', *Edmonton Sun*, 2 June 2002, 27

Jadva, V *et al*, 'Surrogacy: The Experience of Surrogate Mothers' (2003) 18 *Human Reproduction* 2196

Jain, T and Hornstein, MD, 'Disparities in Access to Infertility Services in a State with Mandated Insurance Coverage' (2005) 84 *Fertility and Sterility* 221

——, Harlow, BL and Hornstein, MD, 'Insurance Coverage and Outcomes of In Vitro Fertilization' (2002) 347 *New England Journal of Medicine* 661

Jaiswal, S, 'Commercial Surrogacy in India: An Ethical Assessment of Existing Legal Scenario from the Perspective of Women's Autonomy and Reproductive Rights' (2012) 16 *Gender, Technology and Development* 1

Jamieson, A, 'Parents Wrestling with Sterilization Issues Deserve Compassion', *Vancouver Sun*, 5 June 2002, A15

Jansen, RPS and Dill, S, 'When and How to Welcome the Government to the Bedroom' (2009) 190(5) *Medical Journal of Australia* 232

Janvier, A, Spelke, B and Barrington, KJ, 'The Epidemic of Multiple Gestations and Neonatal Intensive Care Unit Use: The Cost of Irresponsibility' (2011) 159 *Journal of Pediatrics* 409

Jelen, TG and Wilcox, C, 'Causes and Consequences of Public Attitudes Toward Abortion: A Review and Research Agenda' (2003) 56 *Political Research Quarterly* 489

Jerdee, AL, 'Breaking Through the Silence: Minnesota's Pregnancy Presumption and the Right to Refuse Medical Treatment' (2000) 84 *Minnesota Law Review* 971

Jha, P *et al*, 'Trends in Selective Abortion of Girls in India: Analysis of Nationally Representative Birth Histories from 1990 to 2005 and Census Data from 1991 to 2011' (2011) 377 *The Lancet* 1921

Joffe, C and Parker, WJ, 'Editorial: Race, Reproductive Politics and Reproductive Health Care in the Contemporary United States' (2012) 86 *Contraception* 1

Johanson, R, Newburn, M and Macfarlane, A, 'Has the Medicalisation of Childbirth Gone Too Far?' (2002) 324 *British Medical Journal* 892

Johnson, T, 'Queensland's Proposed Surrogacy Legislation: An Opportunity for National Reform' (2010) 17 *Journal of Law and Medicine* 617

Jones, BS and Weitz, TA, 'Legal Barriers to Second-Trimester Abortion Provision and Public Health Consequences' (2009) *American Journal of Public Health* 623

Jones, M, 'A Miracle and Yet', *New York Times Magazine*, 15 July 2001, 39

Jones, M, and Salter, B, 'Proceeding Carefully: Assisted Human Reproduction Policy in Canada' (2010) 19 *Public Understanding of Science* 420

Jones, MB, *Birthmothers: Women Who Have Relinquished Babies for Adoption Tell Their Stories* (Chicago, Ill, Chicago Review Press, 1993)

Jones, RK and Finer, LB, 'Who Has Second-trimester Abortions in the United States?' (2012) 85 *Contraception* 544

——and Kooistra, K, 'Abortion Incidence and Access to Services In the United States, 2008' (2011) 43 *Perspectives on Sexual and Reproductive Health* 41

Jones, WG, 'Sterilization Can Be Decision of a Loving Mother', *Halifax Daily News*, 8 October 2002, 28

Joshi, H and Davies, H, *Childcare and Mothers' Lifetime Earnings: Some European Contrasts* (London, Centre for Economic Policy Research, 1992)

Jütte, R, *Contraception: A History* (Cambridge, Polity Press, 2008)

Kaiser, HA, 'Mental Disability Law' in Jocelyn Downie, Timothy Caulfield and Colleen M Flood (eds), *Canadian Health Law and Policy*, 2nd edn (Markham, Butterworths, 2002) 298

Kale, R, 'Editorial: "It's a Girl!" – Could be a Death Sentence' (2012) 184 *Canadian Medical Association Journal* 387

Kalish, RB, McCullough, LB and Chervenak, FA, 'Decision-making About Caesarean Delivery' (2006) 367 *The Lancet* 883

Kaplan, D, 'Prenatal Screening and Diagnosis: The Impact on Persons with Disabilities' in Karen H Rothenberg and Elizabeth J Thomson (eds), *Women and Prenatal Testing: Facing the Challenges of Genetic Technology* (Columbus, Ohio State University Press, 1994) 49

Katz, P *et al*, 'Costs of Infertility Treatment: Results from an 18-month Prospective Cohort Study' (2011) 95 *Fertility and Sterility* 915

Kavanaugh, ML, Williams, SL and Schwarz, EB, 'Emergency Contraception Use and Counseling After Changes in United States Prescription Status' (2011) 95 *Fertility and Sterility* 2578

Kennedy, I and Grubb, A, *Medical Law*, 3rd edn (London, Butterworths, 2000)

Kennedy, R *et al*, 'Implementation of the NICE Guideline – Recommendations from the British Fertility Society for National Criteria for NHS Funding of Assisted Conception' (2006) *Human Fertility* 181

Keown, J, *Abortion, Doctors and the Law: Some Aspects of the Legal Regulation of Abortion in England from 1803 to 1982* (Cambridge, Cambridge University Press, 1988)

Khalaf, Y *et al*, 'Selective Single Blastocyst Transfer Reduces the Multiple Pregnancy Rate and Increases Pregnancy Rates: A Pre- and Postintervention Study' (2008) 115 *BJOG: An International Journal of Obstetrics and Gynaecology* 385

Khan, T and McCoy, MA, 'Access to Contraception' (2005) 6 *Georgetown Journal of Gender and the Law* 785

Killian, ML, 'The Political is Personal: Relationship Recognition Policies in the United States and their Impact on Services for LGBT People' (2010) 22 *Journal of Gay & Lesbian Social Services* 9

Kim, D-S, 'Missing Girls in South Korea: Trends, Levels and Regional Variations' (2004) 59 *Population* (English Edition) 865

Kimmelman, D, 'Poverty and Norplant: Can Contraception Reduce the Underclass?', *Philadelphia Inquirer*, 12 December 1990, A18

Kindregan Jr, CP and McBrien, M, 'Embryo Donation: Unresolved Legal Issues in the Transfer of Surplus Cryopreserved Embryos' (2004) 49 *Villanova Law Review* 169

——— *Assisted Reproductive Technology: A Lawyer's Guide to Emerging Law and Science*, 2nd edn (Chicago, Ill, American Bar Association, 2011)

King, J, 'Duty to the Unborn: A Response to Smolensky' (2008) 60 *Hastings Law Journal* 377

Kirkman, M, 'Parents' Contributions to the Narrative Identity of Offspring of Donor-assisted Conception' (2003) 57 *Social Science & Medicine* 2229

—— *et al*, 'Reasons Women Give for Abortion: A Review of the Literature' (2009) 12 *Archives of Women's Mental Health* 365

Kitzman, JO *et al*, 'Noninvasive Whole-genome Sequencing of a Human Fetus' (2012) 4(137) *Science Translational Medicine* 137ra76

Kiuru, M and Crystal, RG, 'Progress and Prospects: Gene Therapy for Performance and Appearance Enhancement' (2008) 15 *Gene Therapy* 329

Klar, LN, *Tort Law*, 5th edn (Toronto, Thompson Carswell, 2012)

Klees, BS, Wolfe, CJ and Curtis, CA, *Brief Summaries of Medicare & Medicaid: Title XVIII and XIX of the Social Security Act* (Washington, DC, Centers for Medicare and Medicaid Services, Department of Health and Human Services, 2010)

Klein, R, 'From Test-Tube Women to Bodies Without Women' (2008) 31 *Women's Studies International Forum* 157

Klock, SC, 'The Controversy Surrounding Disclosure Among Donor Gamete Recipients' (1997) 14 *Journal of Assisted Reproduction and Genetics* 378

Knoppers, BM, 'Reflections: The Challenge of Biotechnology and Public Policy' (2000) 45 *McGill Law Journal* 559

——, Bordet, S and Isasi, RM, 'Preimplantation Genetic Diagnosis: An Overview of Socio-Ethical and Legal Considerations' (2006) 7 *Annual Review of Genomics and Human Genetics* 201

—— and Isasi, RM, 'Regulatory Approaches to Reproductive Genetic Testing' (2004) 19 *Human Reproduction* 2695

Kolder, VEB, Gallagher, J and Parsons, MT, 'Court-Ordered Obstetrical Interventions' (1987) 316 *New England Journal of Medicine* 1192

Kornegay, RJ, 'Is Commercial Surrogacy Baby-Selling?' (1990) 7 *Journal of Applied Philosophy* 45

Koyama, A and Williams, R, 'Abortion in Medical School Curricula' (2005) 8 *McGill Journal of Medicine* 157

Krawiec, KD, 'Altruism and Intermediation in the Market for Babies' (2009) 66 *Washington and Lee Law Review* 203

Kukla, R, 'Conscientious Autonomy: Displacing Decisions in Health Care' (2005) 35(2) *Hastings Center Report* 34

—— *Mass Hysteria: Medicine, Culture, and Mother's Bodies* (Lanham, MD, Rowman and Littlefield, 2005)

Kukla, R, *et al*, 'Finding Autonomy in Birth' (2009) 23 *Bioethics* 1

Kutler, DI *et al*, 'A 20-year Perspective on the International Fanconi Anemia Registry (IFAR)' (2003) 101 *Blood* 124

Lader, D and the Office for National Statistics, *Opinions Survey Report No 41: Contraception and Sexual Health, 2008/09* (Newport, Office for National Statistics, 2009)

Lahey, W, 'Medicare and the Law: Contours of an Evolving Relationship' in Jocelyn Downie, Timothy Caulfield and Colleen M Flood (eds), *Canadian Health Law and Policy*, 4th edn (Markham, LexisNexis Canada, 2011) 1

Lahl, J and Rosa, EC, *Eggsploitation* (Pleasant Hill, CA, Center for Bioethics and Culture, 2012)

Lake, C, 'The Kid and the Cash: Categorising Damage in Wrongful Birth and Wrongful Pregnancy' (2009) 17 *Torts Law Journal* 55

Lalor, J, Begley, CM and Galavan, E, 'Recasting Hope: A Process of Adaptation Following Fetal Anomaly Diagnosis' (2009) 68 *Social Science & Medicine* 462

Lambert, RD, 'Safety Issues in Assisted Reproduction Technology: The Children of Assisted Reproduction Confront the Responsible Conduct of Assisted Reproductive Technologies' (2002) 17 *Human Reproduction* 3011

Langille, DB, Allen, M and Whelan, AM, 'Emergency Contraception: Knowledge and Attitudes of Nova Scotian Family Physicians' (2012) 58 *Canadian Family Physician* 548

Laufer-Ukeles, P, 'Gestation: Work for Hire or the Essence of Motherhood? A Comparative Legal Analysis' (2002) 9 *Duke Journal of Gender Law & Policy* 91

——'Reproductive Choices and Informed Consent: Fetal Interests, Women's Identity, and Relational Autonomy' (2011) 37 *American Journal of Law & Medicine* 567

Law Reform Commission of Canada, *Medically Assisted Procreation (Working Paper 65)* (Ottawa, Minister of Supply and Services Canada, 1992)

Lawrence, RE and Curlin, FA, 'Physicians' Beliefs about Conscience in Medicine: A National Survey' (2009) 84 *Academic Medicine* 1276

Leckey, R, '"Where the Parents are of the Same Sex": Quebec's Reforms to Filiation' (2009) 23 *International Journal of Law, Policy and the Family* 62

Ledger, WL, 'Regulation of Reproduction in the UK' (2005) 8 *Human Fertility* 65

——*et al*, 'The Costs to the NHS of Multiple Births After IVF Treatment in the UK' (2006) 113 *BJOG: An International Journal of Obstetrics and Gynaecology* 21

Lester, B and Veer, S, 'A Measure of Justice for Regina McKnight' *The State* (Columbia, 1 July 2008)

Levine, EM, 'The Constitutionality of Court-Ordered Cesarean Surgery: A Threshold Question' (1994) 4 *Albany Law Journal of Science and Technology* 229

Lewis, G, 'Saving Mothers' Lives: The Continuing Benefits for Maternal Health from the United Kingdom (UK) Confidential Enquiries into Maternal Deaths' (2012) 36 *Seminars in Perinatology* 19

Linden, AM and Feldthusen, B, *Canadian Tort Law*, 9th edn (Markham, LexisNexis Canada, 2011)

Lisonkova, S *et al*, 'Temporal Trends in Maternal Mortality in Canada I: Estimates Based on Vital Statistics Data (2011) 33 *Journal of Obstetrics and Gynaecology Canada* 1011

————'Temporal Trends in Maternal Mortality in Canada II: Estimates Based on Hospitalization Data' (2011) 33 *Journal of Obstetrics and Gynaecology Canada* 1020

Litman, MM, 'Fiduciary Law and For-Profit and Not-For-Profit Health Care' in Timothy A Caulfield and Barbara von Tigerstrom (eds), *Health Care Reform and the Law in Canada: Meeting the Challenge* (Edmonton, University of Alberta Press, 2002) 85

Little, MO, 'Abortion and the Margins of Personhood' (2007/08) 39 *Rutgers Law Journal* 331

Llewellyn, JJ and Downie, J, 'Introduction' in Jocelyn Downie and Jennifer J Llewellyn (eds), *Being Relational: Reflections on Relational Theory and Health Law* (Vancouver, UBC Press, 2012) 1

Lowe, P *et al*, '"Making it all Normal": The Role of the Internet in Problematic Pregnancy' (2009) 19 *Qualitative Health Research* 1476

Lowenstein, PR, 'Clinical Trials in Gene Therapy: Ethics of Informed Consent and the Future of Experimental Medicine' (2008) 10 *Current Opinion in Molecular Therapeutics* 428

Lucke, J et al, 'Unintended Pregnancies: Reducing Rates by Improving Access to Contraception' (2011) 40 *Australian Family Physician* 849

Lumley, J, 'Through a Glass Darkly: Ultrasound and Prenatal Bonding' (1990) 17 *Birth* 214

Lupton, D, 'Risk and the Ontology of Pregnant Embodiment' in Deborah Lupton (ed), *Risk and Sociocultural Theory: New Directions and Perspectives* (Cambridge, Cambridge University Press, 1999)

Lyerly, AD et al, 'Risk and the Pregnant Body' (2009) 39(6) *Hastings Center Report* 34

——, Little, MO and Faden, RR, 'A Critique of the "Fetus as Patient"' (2008) 8(7) *American Journal of Bioethics* 42

Mabry, CR, 'Joint and Shared Parenting: Valuing All Families and All Children in the Adoption Process with an Expanded Notion of Family' (2009) 17 *American University Journal of Gender, Social Policy & the Law* 659

Macaluso, M et al, 'A Public Health Focus on Infertility Prevention, Detection, and Management' (2010) 93 *Fertility and Sterility* 16e1

MacDonald, C, 'Relational Professional Autonomy' (2002) 11 *Cambridge Quarterly of Healthcare Ethics* 282

MacIntyre, A, *After Virtue: A Study in Moral Theory*, 2nd edn (Notre Dame, IN, Notre Dame University Press, 1980)

Mackenzie, C, 'Abortion and Embodiment' (1992) 70 *Australasian Journal of Philosophy* 136

—— 'Relational Autonomy, Normative Authority and Perfectionism' (2008) 39 *Journal of Social Philosophy* 512

—— and Stoljar, N, 'Introduction: Autonomy Refigured' in Catriona Mackenzie and Natalie Stoljar (eds), *Relational Autonomy: Feminist Perspectives on Autonomy, Agency, and the Social Self* (Oxford, Oxford University Press, 2000) 3

MacKinnon, CA, *Feminism Unmodified: Discourses on Life and Law* (Cambridge, MA, Harvard University Press, 1987)

—— *Toward a Feminist Theory of the State* (Cambridge, MA, Harvard University Press, 1989)

—— 'Reflections on Sex Equality Under Law' (1991) 100 *Yale Law Journal* 1281

MacLean, A, 'Advance Directives and the Rocky Waters of Anticipatory Decision-Making' (2008) 16 *Medical Law Review* 1

—— *Autonomy, Informed Consent and Medical Law: A Relational Challenge* (Cambridge, Cambridge University Press, 2009)

Macones, GA et al, 'The 2008 National Institute of Child Health and Human Development Workshop Report on Electronic Fetal Monitoring: Update on Definitions, Interpretation, and Research Guidelines' (2008) 37 *Journal of Obstetric, Gynecologic and Neonatal Nursing* 510

Madeira, JL, 'Woman Scorned?: Resurrecting Infertile Women's Decision-Making Autonomy' (2012) 71 *Maryland Law Review* 339

Magnusson, BM et al, 'Contraceptive Insurance Mandates and Consistent Contraceptive Use Among Privately Insured Women' (2012) 50 *Medical Care* 562

Mahowald, MB, 'As If There Were Fetuses Without Women: A Remedial Essay' in Joan C Callahan (ed), *Reproduction, Ethics and the Law: Feminist Perspectives* (Bloomington, Indiana University Press, 1995)

Major, B et al, 'Psychological Responses of Women After First-Trimester Abortion' (2000) 57 *Archives of General Psychiatry* 777

———— 'Abortion and Mental Health: Evaluating the Evidence' (2009) 64 *American Psychologist* 863

Majury, D, 'The *Charter*, Equality Rights, and Women: Equivocation and Celebration' (2002) 40 *Osgoode Hall Law Journal* 297

Malat, J, 'Racial Differences in Norplant Use in the United States' (2000) 50 *Social Science & Medicine* 1297

Manson, NC and O'Neill, O, *Rethinking Informed Consent in Bioethics* (Cambridge, Cambridge University Press, 2007)

Marks, JF, 'OKC Meth Mom Wins Early Release', *NewsOK, Oklahoma City*, 20 November 2008

Martin, JR *et al*, 'Insurance Coverage and In Vitro Fertilization Outcomes: A US Perspective' (2011) 95 *Fertility and Sterility* 964

Martin, L, 'Reproductive Rights and New Technologies: Lessons from Law Reform' (1986) 58 *The Australian Quarterly* 375

Mason, JK, *The Troubled Pregnancy: Legal Wrongs and Rights in Reproduction* (Cambridge, Cambridge University Press, 2007)

——and Laurie, GT, *Mason and McCall Smith's Law and Medical Ethics*, 8th edn (Oxford, Oxford University Press, 2011)

Mastenbroek, S *et al*, 'In Vitro Fertilization with Preimplantation Genetic Screening' (2007) 357 *New England Journal of Medicine* 9

Mathieu, DR, *Preventing Prenatal Harm: Should the State Intervene?*, 2nd edn (Washington, DC, Georgetown University Press, 1996)

McCandless, J and Sheldon, S, 'The Human Fertilisation and Embryology Act (2008) and the Tenacity of the Sexual Family Form' (2010) 73 MLR 175

McCarthy, M, *Sexuality and Women with Learning Disabilities* (London, Jessica Kingsley, 1999)

——'Contraception and Women with Intellectual Disabilities' (2009) 22 *Journal of Applied Research in Intellectual Disabilities* 363

McCartney, JJ, 'Embryonic Stem Cell Research and Respect for Human Life: Philosophical and Legal Reflections' (2002) 65 *Albany Law Review* 597

McClain, LC, 'Reconstructive Tasks for a Liberal Feminist Conception of Privacy' (1999) 40 *William and Mary Law Review* 759

McCullough, LB and Chervenak, FA, 'A Critical Analysis of the Concept and Discourse of "Unborn Child"' (2008) 8(7) *American Journal of Bioethics* 34

——————*Ethics in Obstetrics and Gynecology* (New York, Oxford University Press, 1994)

McDonald, K, Amir, LH and Davey, M-A, 'Maternal Bodies and Medicines: A Commentary on Risk and Decision-Making of Pregnant and Breastfeeding Women and Health Professionals' (2011) 11 (Supp 5) *BioMed Central Public Health* S5

McGee, G, 'Bioethics for the President and Bioethics for the People' (2002) 2(2) *American Journal of Bioethics* 1

McGuire, A and Hughes, D, *The Economics of Family Planning Services: A Report Prepared for the Contraceptive Alliance* (London, Contraceptive Alliance, 1995)

McLaren, A, *A History of Contraception: From Antiquity to the Present Day* (Oxford, Basil Blackwell Inc, 1990)

——*Our Own Master Race: Eugenics in Canada, 1885–1945* (Toronto, McClelland and Stewart, 1990)

——and McLaren, AT, *The Bedroom and the State: The Changing Practices and Politics of Contraception and Abortion in Canada, 1880–1997*, 2nd edn (Toronto, Oxford University Press, 1997)

McLean, SAM, *Autonomy, Consent and the Law* (Abingdon, Routledge-Cavendish, 2010)

McLeod, C, 'Women's Autonomy and the "G" Case' (May 1998) 3 *Canadian Bioethics Society Newsletter* 6

——*Self-Trust and Reproductive Autonomy* (Cambridge, MA, MIT Press, 2002)

——and Baylis, F, 'Feminists on the Inalienability of Human Embryos' (2006) 21(2) *Hypatia* 1

——and Sherwin, S, 'Relational Autonomy, Self-Trust and Health Care for Patients who are Oppressed' in Catriona Mackenzie and Natalie Stoljar (eds), *Relational Autonomy: Feminist Perspectives on Autonomy, Agency, and the Social Self* (Oxford, Oxford University Press, 2000) 259

Medoff, MH, 'State Abortion Politics and TRAP Abortion Laws' (2012) 33 *Journal of Women, Politics & Policy* 239

Mello, MM and Rosenthal, MB, 'Wellness Programs and Lifestyle Discrimination – The Legal Limits' (2008) 359 *New England Journal of Medicine* 192

Menard, G, Pineau, M and Laplante, S, 'Abstract: A Cost-minimization Analysis Comparing Mirena® with Oral Contraceptives' (2001) 4 *Value in Health* 165

Meyers, DT, 'Personal Autonomy and the Paradox of Feminine Socialization' (1987) 84 *Journal of Philosophy* 619

—— *Self, Society, and Personal Choice* (New York, Columbia University Press, 1989)

—— 'Feminism and Women's Autonomy: The Challenge of Female Genital Cutting' (2000) 31 *Metaphilosophy* 469

—— 'Intersectional Identity and the Authentic Self? Opposites Attract!' in Catriona Mackenzie and Natalie Stoljar (eds), *Relational Autonomy: Feminist Perspectives on Autonomy, Agency, and the Social Self* (Oxford, Oxford University Press, 2000) 151

Mill, JS, *On Liberty*, 2nd edn (Cambridge, MA, Ticknor and Fields, 1863)

Millbank, J, 'The New Surrogacy Parentage Laws in Australia: Cautious Regulation or '25 Brick Walls'?' (2011) 35 *Melbourne University Law Review* 165

Millns, S, 'Exploring the Boundaries of Reproductive Autonomy' (2003) 9 *Res Publica* 87

Min, JK, Claman, P and Hughes, E, 'Joint SOGC-CFAS Guideline No 182: Guidelines for the Number of Embryos to Transfer Following In Vitro Fertilization' (2006) 28 *Journal of Obstetrics and Gynaecology Canada* 799

Minkler, M, 'Personal Responsibility For Health? A Review of the Arguments and the Evidence at Century's End' (1999) 26 *Health Education and Behavior* 121

Minkoff, H, 'The Ethics of Cesarean Section by Choice' (2006) 30 *Seminars in Perinatology* 309

—— and Chervenak, FA, 'Elective Primary Cesarean Delivery' (2003) 348 *New England Journal of Medicine* 946

—— and Lyerly, AD, 'Samantha Burton and the Rights of Pregnant Women Twenty Years after *In re A.C.*' (2010) 40(6) *Hastings Center Report* 13

Mitchinson, W, 'Agency, Diversity, and Constraints: Women and Their Physicians, Canada, 1850–1950' in Susan Sherwin *et al* (eds), *The Politics of Women's Health: Exploring Agency and Autonomy* (Philadelphia, Pa, Temple University Press, 1998) 122

Mladovsky, P and Sorenson, C, 'Public Financing of IVF: a Review of Policy Rationales' (2010) 18 *Health Care Analysis* 113

Montgomery, J, 'Rhetoric and "Welfare"' (1989) 9 *OJLS* 395

Morgan, D, 'Ethics, Economics and the Exotic: The Early Career of the HFEA' (2004) 12 *Health Care Analysis* 7

Morgan, KP, 'Contested Bodies, Contested Knowledges: Women, Health, and the Politics of Medicalization' in Susan Sherwin *et al* (eds), *The Politics of Women's Health: Exploring Agency and Autonomy* (Philadelphia, Pa, Temple University Press, 1998) 83

Morris, K, Savell, K and Ryan, CJ, 'Psychiatrists and Termination of Pregnancy: Clinical, Legal and Ethical Aspects' (2012) 46 *Australian and New Zealand Journal of Psychiatry* 18

Mosher, WD and Jones, J, 'Use of Contraception in the United States: 1982–2008' (2010) Series 23, No 29 *Vital and Health Statistics* 1

Mullan, Z and Horton, R, 'Comment: Bringing Stillbirths out of the Shadows' (2011) 377 *The Lancet* 1291

Mullin, A, *Reconceiving Pregnancy and Childcare: Ethics, Experience, and Reproductive Labor* (New York, Cambridge University Press, 2005)

Munk-Olsen, T *et al*, 'Induced First-Trimester Abortion and Risk of Mental Disorder' (2011) 364 *New England Journal of Medicine* 332

Murphy, S, 'Access to Emergency Contraception' (2004) 26 *Journal of Obstetrics and Gynaecology Canada* 705

Murphy-Lawless, J, *Reading Birth and Death: A History of Obstetric Thinking* (Bloomington, Indiana University Press, 1998)

Murray, TH, *The Worth of a Child* (Berkeley, University of California Press, 1996)

Murtaugh, MT, 'Wrongful Birth: The Courts' Dilemma in Determining a Remedy for a "Blessed Event"' (2007) 27 *Pace Law Review* 241

Mykitiuk, R, 'Beyond Conception: Legal Determinations of Filiation in the Context of Assisted Reproductive Technologies' (2001) 39 *Osgoode Hall Law Journal* 771

—— and Turnham, S, 'Legal Dimensions of Adolescent Sexuality' (2004) 26 *Journal of Obstetrics and Gynaecology Canada* 991

—— and Wallrap, A, 'Regulating Reproductive Technologies in Canada' in Jocelyn Downie, Timothy Caulfield and Colleen M Flood (eds), *Canadian Health Law and Policy*, 2nd edn C Markham, Butterworths, 2002) 399

Nachtigall, RD, Becker, G and Wozny, M, 'The Effects of Gender-Specific Diagnosis on Men's and Women's Response to Infertility' (1992) 57 *Fertility and Sterility* 113

Nass, SJ and Strauss, JF (eds), *New Frontiers in Contraceptive Research: A Blueprint for Action* (Washington, DC, The National Academies Press, 2004)

National Collaborating Centre for Women's and Children's Health, *Fertility: Assessment and Treatment for People with Fertility Problems* CG11 (London, National Institute for Clinical Excellence, 2004)

National Collaborating Centre for Women's and Children's Health for the National Institute for Health and Clinical Excellence, *Caesarean Section Clinical Guideline* (London, Royal College of Obstetricians and Gynaecologists Press, 2011)

National Health and Medical Research Council, *Ethical Guidelines on the Use of Assisted Reproductive Technology in Clinical Practice and Research 2007* (Canberra, Commonwealth of Australia, 2007)

National Health Law and Family Law Sections, Canadian Bar Association, 'Submission on Draft Legislation on Assisted Human Reproduction' (2001) 10 *Health Law Review*

Nedelsky, J, 'Reconceiving Autonomy: Sources, Thoughts and Possibilities' (1989) 1 *Yale Journal of Law and Feminism* 7

—— 'Law, Boundaries, and the Bounded Self' (1990) 30 *Representations* 162

—— 'Reconceiving Rights as Relationship' (1993) 1 *Review of Constitutional Studies* 1

—— *Law's Relations: A Relational Theory of Self, Autonomy, and Law* (New York, Oxford University Press, 2011)

Nelson, AR, 'Medicine: Business or Profession, Art or Science?' (1998) 178 *American Journal of Obstetrics and Gynecology* 755

Nelson, E, 'The Fundamentals of Consent' in Jocelyn Downie, Timothy Caulfield and Colleen M Flood (eds), *Canadian Health Law and Policy*, 2nd edn (Markham, Butterworths, 2002) 122

—— 'Reconceiving Pregnancy: Expressive Choice and Legal Reasoning' (2004) 49 *McGill Law Journal* 593

—— 'Comparative Perspectives on the Regulation of Assisted Reproductive Technologies in the United Kingdom and Canada' (2006) 43 *Alberta Law Review* 1023

—— 'Informed Consent: Reasonableness, Risk and Disclosure' in Jocelyn Downie and Elaine Gibson (eds), *Health Law at the Supreme Court of Canada* (Toronto, Irwin Law, 2007) 145

—— and Caulfield, T, 'You Can't Get There From Here: A Case Comment on *Arndt v Smith*' (1998) 32 *University of British Columbia Law Review* 353

——, Mykitiuk, R and Nisker, J, 'SOGC Clinical Practice Guideline No 215: Informed Consent to Donate Embryos for Research Purposes' (2008) 30 *Journal of Obstetrics and Gynaecology Canada* 824

New South Wales Law Reform Commission, *Report 49 (1986): Artificial Conception: Human Artificial Insemination* (Sydney, The Commission, 1986)

——*Discussion Paper 15 (1987): Artificial Conception: In Vitro Fertilisation* (Sydney, The Commission, 1988)

——*Report 60 (1988): Artificial Conception: Surrogate Motherhood* (Sydney, The Commission, 1988)

New York State Task Force on Life and the Law, *Assisted Reproductive Technologies: Analysis and Recommendations for Public Policy* (New York, New York State Task Force on Life and the Law, 1998)

Newkirk, KL, 'State-compelled Fetal Surgery: The Viability Test is Not Viable' (1998) 4 *William and Mary Journal of Women and the Law* 467

Newman, D, 'An Examination of Saskatchewan Law on the Sterilization of Persons with Mental Disabilities' (1999) 62 *Saskatchewan Law Review* 329

Ngai, SW *et al*, 'A Randomized Trial to Compare 24h Versus 12h Double Dose Regimen of Levonorgestrel for Emergency Contraception' (2005) 20 *Human Reproduction* 307

Nisker, J, 'Distributive Justice and Infertility Treatment in Canada' (2008) 30 *Journal of Obstetrics and Gynaecology Canada* 425

——'Socially Based Discrimination Against Clinically Appropriate Care' (2009) 181 *Canadian Medical Association Journal* 764

Norman, WV, 'Induced Abortion in Canada 1974–2005: Trends Over the First Generation with Legal Access' (2012) 85 *Contraception* 185

Nussbaum, MC, *Sex and Social Justice* (Oxford, Oxford University Press, 1999) 55

O'Neill, N, 'Sterilisation of Children with Intellectual Disabilities' (1996) 2 *Australian Journal of Human Rights* 262

O'Neill, O, *Autonomy and Trust in Bioethics* (Cambridge, Cambridge University Press, 2002)

O'Rourke, K, *Background Paper: Time for a National Sexual and Reproductive Health Strategy for Australia* (Public Health Association of Australia, Sexual Health and Family Planning Association of Australia and Australian Reproductive Health Alliance, 2008)

Oberman, M, 'Commentary: The Control of Pregnancy and the Criminalization of Femaleness' (1992) 7 *Berkeley Women's Law Journal* 1

——'Sex, Drugs, Pregnancy, and the Law: Rethinking the Problems of Pregnant Women Who Use Drugs' (1992) 43 *Hastings Law Journal* 505

——'Mothers and Doctors' Orders: Unmasking the Doctor's Fiduciary Role in Maternal–Fetal Conflicts' (1999–2000) 94 *Northwestern University Law Review* 451

Ontario Law Reform Commission, *Report on Human Artificial Reproduction and Related Matters* (Toronto, The Commission, 1985)

Ontario, Ministry of Children and Youth Services, Expert Panel on Infertility and Adoption, *Raising Expectations: Recommendations of the Expert Panel on Infertility and Adoption* (Summer 2009)

Oshana, MAL, 'Personal Autonomy and Society' (1998) 29 *Journal of Social Philosophy* 81

Overall, C, *Ethics and Human Reproduction: A Feminist Analysis* (Boston, MA, Allen & Unwin, 1987)

——*Human Reproduction: Principles, Practices, Policies* (Toronto, Oxford University Press, 1993)

Palattiyil, G *et al*, 'Globalization and Cross-Border Reproductive Services: Ethical Implications of Surrogacy in India for Social Work' (2010) 53 *International Social Work* 686

Palermo, G *et al*, 'Pregnancies After Intracytoplasmic Injection of a Single Spermatozoa into an Oocyte' (1992) 340 *The Lancet* 17

Paltrow, LM, 'Punishment and Prejudice: Judging Drug-Using Pregnant Women' in Julia E Hanigsberg and Sara Ruddick (eds), *Mother Troubles: Rethinking Contemporary Maternal Dilemmas* (Boston, MA, Beacon Press, 1999) 59

——, Cohen, DS and Carey, CA, *Year 2000 Overview: Governmental Responses to Pregnant Women Who Use Alcohol or Other Drugs* (Philadelphia, Pa, Women's Law Project, 2000)

Parens, E and Asch, A, 'The Disability Rights Critique of Prenatal Genetic Testing: Reflections and Recommendations' in Erik Parens and Adrienne Asch (eds), *Prenatal Testing and Disability Rights* (Washington, DC, Georgetown University Press, 2000) 3
—————*Prenatal Testing and Disability Rights* (Washington, DC, Georgetown University Press, 2000)
——and Knowles, LP, 'Reprogenetics and Public Policy: Reflections and Recommendations' (July 2003) Special Supplement *Hastings Center Report* S1
Parfit, D, *Reasons and Persons* (Oxford, Clarendon Press, 1987)
Parliament of Victoria, Legislative Council Legislation Committee, *Report on the Consideration in Detail of the Assisted Reproductive Treatment Bill 2008* (Melbourne, Government Printer, 2008)
Paul, ME *et al*, 'Early Surgical Abortion: Efficacy and Safety' (2002) 187 *American Journal of Obstetrics & Gynecology* 407
Pennings, G, 'Legal Harmonization and Reproductive Tourism in Europe' (2004) 19 *Human Reproduction* 2689
——*et al*, 'Cross Border Reproductive Care in Belgium' (2009) 24 *Human Reproduction* 3108
Performance Assessment Tool for Quality Improvement in Hospitals (PATH), World Health Organization, United Nations Population Fund, *Essential Medicines for Reproductive Health: Guiding Principles for their Inclusion on National Medicines List* (Seattle, Wash, PATH, 2006)
Perry, JEC, 'Return of the Burden of the "Blessing"' (1999) 149 *New Law Journal* 1887
Petchesky, RP, 'Fetal Images: The Power of Visual Culture in the Politics of Reproduction' (1987) 13 *Feminist Studies* 263
——*Abortion and Woman's Choice: The State, Sexuality, and Reproductive Freedom* (Boston, Northeastern University Press, 1990)
Petersen, K, 'Criminal Abortion Laws: An Impediment to Reproductive Health?' in Ian Freckelton and Kerry Petersen (eds), *Controversies in Health Law* (Sydney, The Federation Press, 1999) 28
——'The Regulation of Assisted Reproductive Technology: A Comparative Study of Permissive and Prescriptive Laws and Policies' (2002) 9 *Journal of Law and Medicine* 483
——'Early Medical Abortion: Legal and Medical Developments in Australia' (2010) 193 *Medical Journal of Australia* 26
——'Abortion Laws and Medical Developments: A Medico-Legal Anomaly in Queensland' (2011) 18 *Journal of Law and Medicine* 594
Petrie, KJ and Wessely, S, 'Modern Worries, New Technology, and Medicine' (2002) 324 *British Medical Journal* 690
——*et al*, 'Thoroughly Modern Worries: The Relationship of Worries about Modernity to Reported Symptoms, Health and Medical Care Utilization' (2001) 51 *Journal of Psychosomatic Research* 395
Phelan, JP, 'The Maternal Abdominal Wall: A Fortress Against Fetal Health Care?' (1991) 65 *Southern California Law Review* 461
Phillips, A, 'Feminism and Liberalism Revisited: Has Martha Nussbaum Got It Right?' (2001) 8 *Constellations: An International Journal of Critical and Democratic Theory* 249
Picard, EI and Robertson, GB, *Legal Liability of Doctors and Hospitals in Canada*, 4th edn (Toronto, Thomson Carswell, 2007)
Plomer, A, 'A Foetal Right to Life? The Case of *Vo v France*' (2005) 5 *Human Rights Law Review* 311
Polikoff, ND, 'A Mother Should Not Have to Adopt Her Own Child: Parentage Laws for Children of Lesbian Couples in the Twenty-First Century' (2009) 2 *Stanford Journal of Civil Rights and Civil Liberties* 201
Pollitt, K, 'Pregnant and Dangerous' (26 April 2004) 278(16) *The Nation* 9
Pope, TM, 'Legal Briefing: Conscience Clauses and Conscientious Refusal' (2010) 21 *Journal of Clinical Ethics* 163

Population Council, *Norplant, Levonorgestrel Implants: A Summary of Scientific Data* (New York, The Population Council, 1990)

Powers, M, 'Some Reflections on Disability and Bioethics' (2001) 1(3) *American Journal of Bioethics* 51

President's Council on Bioethics, *Reproduction and Responsibility: The Regulation of New Biotechnologies* (Washington, DC, The President's Council on Bioethics, 2004)

Press, N, 'Assessing the Expressive Character of Prenatal Testing: The Choices Made or the Choices Made Available?' in Erik Parens and Adrienne Asch (eds), *Prenatal Testing and Disability Rights* (Washington, Georgetown University Press, 2000) 214

——and Browner, CH, 'Why Women Say Yes to Prenatal Diagnosis' (1997) 45 *Social Science & Medicine* 979

Priaulx, N, 'Joy to the World! A (Healthy) Child is Born! Reconceptualizing 'Harm' in Wrongful Conception' (2004) 13 *Social & Legal Studies* 5

——'Damages for the "Unwanted" Child: Time for a Rethink?' (2005) 73 *Medico-Legal Journal* 152

Public Health Agency of Canada, *What Mothers Say: The Canadian Maternity Experiences Survey* (Ottawa, Public Health Agency of Canada, 2009)

Purdy, L, 'A Feminist View of Health' in Susan M Wolf (ed), *Feminism & Bioethics: Beyond Reproduction* (New York, Oxford University Press, 1996) 163

Radin, MJ, 'Market-Inalienability' (1987) 100 *Harvard Law Review* 1849

Rains, RE, 'What the Erie "Surrogate Triplets" Can Teach State Legislatures About the Need to Enact Article 8 of the Uniform Parentage Act (2000)' (2008) 56 *Cleveland State Law Review* 1

Ranney, ML, Gee, EM and Merchant, RC, 'Nonprescription Availability of Emergency Contraception in the United States: Current Status, Controversies, and Impact on Emergency Medicine Practice' (2006) 47 *Annals of Emergency Medicine* 461

Rao, M, *From Population Control to Reproductive Health: Malthusian Arithmetic* (New Dehli, SAGE, 2004)

Rapp, R, *Testing Women, Testing the Fetus: The Social Impact of Amniocentesis in America* (New York, Routledge, 2000)

Raymond, JG, *Women as Wombs: Reproductive Technology and the Battle Over Women's Freedom* (San Francisco, CA, Harper Collins, 1993)

——'RU486: Progress or Peril?', in Joan C Callahan (ed), *Reproduction, Ethics, and the Law: Feminist Perspectives* (Bloomington, Indiana University Press, 1995) 284

Raz, J, *The Morality of Freedom* (Oxford, Clarendon Press, 1986)

Reid, B *et al*, 'A Meta-Synthesis of Pregnant Women's Decision-Making Processes with Regard to Antenatal Screening for Down Syndrome' (2009) 69 *Social Science & Medicine* 1561

Reilly, E, 'The "Jurisprudence of Doubt": How the Premises of the Supreme Court's Abortion Jurisprudence Undermine Procreative Liberty' (1998) 14 *Journal of Law and Politics* 757

Reinarman, C and Levine, HG (eds), *Crack in America: Demon Drugs and Social Justice* (Berkeley, University of California Press, 1997)

Remennick, L, 'Childless in the Land of Imperative Motherhood: Stigma and Coping Among Infertile Israeli Women' (2000) 43 *Sex Roles* 821

Reproductive Health Technologies Project and the Alan Guttmacher Institute, *The Unfinished Revolution in Contraception: Convenience, Consumer Access and Choice* (Washington, DC, Alan Guttmacher Institute, 2004)

Reuter, S, 'The Emergency Intrauterine Device: An Endangered Species' (2003) 29(2) *Journal of Family Planning and Reproductive Health Care* 5

Rhoden, N, 'The Judge in the Delivery Room: The Emergence of Court-Ordered Cesareans' (1986) 74 *California Law Review* 1951

Riddle, JM, *Eve's Herbs: A History of Contraception and Abortion in the West* (Cambridge, MA, Harvard University Press, 1997)

Rifkin, J, *The Biotech Century: Harnessing the Gene and Remaking the World* (New York, Jeremy P Tarcher, Putnam, 1998)

Roberts, C and Throsby, K, 'Paid to Share: IVF Patients, Eggs and Stem Cell Research' (2008) 66 *Social Science & Medicine* 159

Roberts, D, *Killing the Black Body: Race, Reproduction, and the Meaning of Liberty* (New York, Vintage, 1997)

——'Punishing Drug Addicts Who Have Babies: Women of Color, Equality, and the Right of Privacy' (1991) 104 *Harvard Law Review* 1419

——'Racism and Patriarchy in the Meaning of Motherhood' (1993) 1 *American University Journal of Gender & the Law* 1

Roberston, GB, *Mental Disability and the Law*, 2nd edn (Toronto, Carswell, 1984)

Robertson, JA, 'Procreative Liberty and the Control of Conception, Pregnancy and Childbirth' (1983) 69 *Virginia Law Review* 405

——'Procreative Liberty and Human Genetics' (1990) 39 *Emory Law Journal* 697

——*Children of Choice: Freedom and the New Reproductive Technologies* (Princeton, NJ, Princeton University Press, 1994)

——'Precommitment Strategies for Disposition of Frozen Embryos' (2001) 50 *Emory Law Journal* 989

——'Extending Preimplantation Genetic Diagnosis: Medical and Non-medical Uses' (2003) 29 *Journal of Medical Ethics* 213

——'Procreative Liberty in the Era of Genomics' (2003) 29 *American Journal of Law & Medicine* 439

——'Procreative Liberty and Harm to Offspring in Assisted Reproduction' (2004) 30 *American Journal of Medicine* 7

——'Commerce and Regulation in the Assisted Reproduction Industry' (2007) 85 *Texas Law Review* 665

——'Assisting Reproduction, Choosing Genes, and the Scope of Reproductive Freedom' (2008) 76 *The George Washington Law Review* 1490

——'The Octuplet Case – Why More Regulation is Not Likely' (2009) 39(3) *Hastings Center Report* 26

——'Embryo Stem Cell Research: Ten Years of Controversy' (2010) 38 *Journal of Law, Medicine & Ethics* 191

Robinson, JC, 'The End of Managed Care' (2001) 285 *Journal of the American Medical Association* 2622

Rodgers, G, 'Yin and Yang: The Eugenic Policies of the United States and China: Is the Analysis that Black and White?' (1999) 22 *Houston Journal of International Law* 129

Rodgers, S, 'The Legal Regulation of Women's Reproductive Capacity in Canada' in Jocelyn Downie, Timothy Caulfield and Colleen M Flood (eds), *Canadian Health Law and Policy*, 2nd edn (Markham, Butterworths, 2002) 331

——'A Mother's Loss Is the Price of Parenthood: The Failure of Tort Law to Recognize Birth as Compensable Reproductive Injury' in Sanda Rodgers, Rakhi Ruparelia and Louise Bélanger-Hardy (eds), *Critical Torts* (Markham, LexisNexis Canada, 2009) 161

——and Downie, J, 'Guest Editorial: Abortion: Ensuring Access' (2006) 175 *Canadian Medical Association Journal* 9

Rodrigues, I, Grou, F and Joly, J, 'Effectiveness of Emergency Contraception Pills Between 72 and 120 Hours After Unprotected Sexual Intercourse' (2001) 184 *American Journal of Obstetrics & Gynecology* 531

Rogerson, C, 'The Child-Support Obligation of Step-parents' (2001) 18 *Canadian Journal of Family Law* 9)

Rooney, MJ and Rooney, CM, 'Parental Tort Immunity: Spare the Liability, Spoil the Parent' (1990–91) 25 *New England Law Review* 1161

Rosenthal, D *et al*, *Understanding Women's Experiences of Unplanned Pregnancy and Abortion: Final Report* (Melbourne, The Key Centre for Women's Health in Society, Melbourne School of Population Health, University of Melbourne, 2009)

Roth, R, *Making Women Pay: The Hidden Costs of Fetal Rights* (Ithaca, NY, Cornell University Press, 2000)

Rothman, BK, *The Tentative Pregnancy: Prenatal Diagnosis and the Future of Motherhood* (New York, Viking, 1986)

—— *Recreating Motherhood: Ideology and Technology in a Patriarchal Society* (New York, Norton, 1989)

Rothman, DJ, 'The Origins and Consequences of Patient Autonomy: A 25-Year Retrospective' (2001) 9 *Health Care Analysis* 255

Rothschild, C, 'Abstinence Goes Global: The US, the Right Wing, and Human Rights' in Gilbert Herdt and Cymene Howe, *21st Century Sexualities: Contemporary Issues in Health, Education, and Rights* (New York, Routledge, 2007) 178

Rothstein, MA, 'The Growth of Health Law and Bioethics' (2004) 14 *Health Matrix* 213

Rowland, R, *Living Laboratories: Women and Reproductive Technologies* (Bloomington, Indiana University Press, 1992) 248

Royal College of Obstetricians and Gynaecologists, 'Ethics Committee Guideline No 1: Law and Ethics in Relation to Court-Authorised Obstetric Intervention' (London, Royal College of Obstetricians and Gynaecologists, September 2006)

—— *The Care of Women Requesting Induced Abortion: Evidence Based Clinical Guideline Number 7* (London, Royal College of Obstetricians and Gynaecologists, November 2011)

Royal College of Obstetricians and Gynaecologists Clinical Effectiveness Support Unit, *National Audit of Induced Abortion 2000: Report of England and Wales* (London Royal College of Obstetricians and Gynaecologists, September 2001)

Royal Commission on New Reproductive Technologies, *Proceed with Care: Final Report of the Royal Commission on New Reproductive Technologies*, vols 1 and 2 (Ottawa, Supply and Services Canada, 1993)

Rumball, A and Adair, V, 'Telling the Story: Parents' Scripts for Donor Offspring' (1999) 14 *Human Reproduction* 1392

Rybak, EA, 'Hippocratic Idea, Faustian Bargain and Damocles' Sword: Erosion of Patient Autonomy in Obstetrics' (2009) 29 *Journal of Perinatology* 721

Sabatino, CP, 'The Evolution of Health Care Advance Planning Law and Policy' (2010) 88 *Milbank Quarterly* 211

Sack, RA, 'The Large Infant: A Study of Maternal, Obstetric, Fetal, and Newborn Characteristics; Including a Long-Term Pediatric Follow-Up' (1969) 104 *American Journal of Obstetrics and Gynecology* 195

Sadasivam, B, 'The Rights Framework in Reproductive Health Advocacy – A Reappraisal' (1997) 8 *Hastings Women's Law Journal* 313

Sage, WM, 'Over Under or Through: Physicians, Law and Health Care Reform' (2009) 53 *Saint Louis University Law Journal* 1033

Sandel, M, *Liberalism and the Limits of Justice* (Cambridge, Cambridge University Press, 1982)

—— 'The Ethical Implications of Human Cloning' (2005) 48 *Perspectives in Biology and Medicine* 241

—— *The Case Against Perfection: Ethics in the Age of Genetic Engineering* (Cambridge, MA, Harvard University Press, 2009)

Sandelowski, M, 'Fault Lines: Infertility and Imperiled Sisterhood' (1990) 16 *Feminist Studies* 33

Sanders, GD and Taira, AV, 'Cost Effectiveness of a Potential Vaccine for Human Papillomavirus' (2003) 9 *Emerging Infectious Diseases* 37

Sandor, D, 'Sterilisation and Special Medical Procedures on Children and Young People: Blunt Instrument? Bad Medicine?' in Ian R Freckelton and Kerry Anne Petersen, *Controversies in Health Law* (Sydney, Law Federation Press, 2000) 2

Santello, DM, 'Maternal Tort Liability for Prenatal Injuries' (1988) 22 *Suffolk University Law Review* 747

Sauer, MV, 'Indecent Proposal: $5,000 is not "Reasonable Compensation" for Oocyte Donors' (1999) 71 *Fertility and Sterility* 7

——'Italian Law 40/2004: A View from the "Wild West"' (2006) 12 *Reproductive Biomedicine Online* 8

Savell, K, 'Sex and the Sacred: Sterilization and Bodily Integrity in English and Canadian Law' (2004) 49 *McGill Law Journal* 1093

Savulescu, J, 'Sex Selection: The Case For' (1999) 171 *Medical Journal of Australia* 373

—— 'Procreative Beneficence: Why We Should Select the Best Children' (2001) 15 *Bioethics* 413

—— 'Deaf Lesbians, "Designer Disability" and the Future of Medicine' (2002) 325 *British Medical Journal* 771

—— 'Editorial: Is There a "Right Not to be Born"? Reproductive Decision Making, Options and the Right to Information' (2002) 28 *Journal of Medical Ethics* 65

—— 'Conscientious Objection in Medicine' (2006) 332 *British Medical Journal* 294

—— 'In Defence of Procreative Beneficence' (2007) 33 *Journal of Medical Ethics* 284

Saxton, M, 'Born and Unborn: The Implications of Reproductive Technologies for People with Disabilities' in Rita Arditti, Renate Duelli Klein and Shelley Minden (eds), *Test-Tube Women: What Future for Motherhood?* (London, Pandora Press, 1984) 298

—— 'Disability Rights and Selective Abortion' in Rickie Solinger (ed), *Abortion Wars: A Half Century of Struggle, 1950 to 2000* (Berkeley, University of California Press, 1998) 374

—— 'Why Members of the Disability Community Oppose Prenatal Diagnosis and Selective Abortion' in Adrienne Asch and Erik Parens (eds), *Prenatal Testing and Disability Rights* (Washington, DC, Georgetown University Press, 2000) 147

Schaff, E, 'Mifepristone: Ten Years Later' (2010) 81 *Contraception* 1

Schmidt, H, Voigt, K and Wikler, D, 'Carrots, Sticks, and Health Care Reform – Problems with Wellness Incentives' (2010) 362 *New England Journal of Medicine* e3

Schneider, C, *The Practice of Autonomy: Patients, Doctors, and Medical Decisions* (New York, Oxford University Press, 1998)

Schuchman, M, 'Stalled US Plan for Plan B' (2005) 173 *Canadian Medical Association Journal* 1437

Schwartz, B, *The Paradox of Choice: Why More is Less* (New York, Harper Perennial, 2004)

Science and Technology Committee, *Human Reproductive Technologies and the Law* (HC 2004–05, 7-I)

——*Human Reproductive Technologies and the Law* (HC 2004–05, 7-II, Oral and Written Evidence)

Scott, R, *Rights, Duties and the Body: Law and Ethics of the Maternal-Fetal Conflict* (Oxford, Hart Publishing, 2002)

—— 'Prenatal Testing, Reproductive Autonomy, and Disability Interests' (2005) 14 *Cambridge Quarterly of Healthcare Ethics* 65

Scully, JL, 'Disability and Genetics in the Era of Genomic Medicine' (2008) 9 *Nature Reviews Genetics* 797

——, Banks, S and Shakespeare, TW, 'Chance, Choice and Control: Lay Debate on Social Sex Selection' (2006) 63 *Social Science & Medicine* 21

Sedgh, G et al, 'Induced Abortion: Incidence and Trends Worldwide from 1995 to 2008' (2012) 379 *The Lancet* 625

Segal, JA, Timpone, RJ and Howard, RM, 'Buyer Beware? Presidential Success Through Supreme Court Appointments' (2000) 53 *Political Research Quarterly* 557

Séguin, L et al, 'Effects of Low Income on Infant Health' (2003) 168 *Canadian Medical Association Journal* 1533

Select Committee of the Legislative Council, *Report of the Select Committee of the Legislative Council on Artificial Insemination by Donor, In-Vitro Fertilisation and Embryo Transfer Procedures and Related Matters in South Australia* (Adelaide, Government Printer, 1987)

Sen, A, 'Women's Survival as a Development Problem' (1989) 43 *Bulletin of the American Academy of Arts and Sciences* 14

Sermon, K, Van Steirteghem, A and Liebaers, I, 'Preimplantation Genetic Diagnosis' (2004) 363 *The Lancet* 1633

Sethna, C and Doull, M, 'Far From Home? A Pilot Study Tracking Women's Journeys to a Canadian Abortion Clinic' (2007) 27 *Journal of Obstetrics and Gynaecology Canada* 640

Setti, PEL *et al*, 'Italian Constitutional Court Modifications of a Restrictive Assisted Reproduction Technology Law Significantly Improve Pregnancy Rate' (2010) 26 *Human Reproduction* 376

Seymour, J, *Childbirth and the Law* (Oxford, Oxford University Press, 2000)

Shaffer, ER, Sarfaty, M and Ash, AS, 'Contraceptive Insurance Mandates' (2012) 50 *Medical Care* 559

Shah, KR, 'Increasing Cesarean Rates: The Balance of Technology, Autonomy, and Beneficence' (2012) 12(7) *American Journal of Bioethics* 58

Shakespeare, T, 'Choices and Rights: Eugenics, Genetics and Disability Equality' (1998) 13 *Disability and Society* 665

Shanner, L, 'Pregnancy Intervention and Models of Maternal-Fetal Relationship: Philosophical Reflections on the *Winnipeg C.F.S.* Dissent' (1998) 36 *Alberta Law Review* 751

——and Nisker, J, 'Bioethics for Clinicians: Assisted Reproductive Technologies' (2001) 164 *Canadian Medical Association Journal* 1589

Shapira, A, '"Wrongful Life' Lawsuits for Faulty Genetic Counselling: Should the Impaired Newborn be Entitled to Sue?' (1998) 24 *Journal of Medical Ethics* 369

Shaw, J, *Reality Check: A Close Look at Accessing Abortion Services in Canadian Hospitals* (Ottawa, Canadians for Choice, 2006)

Shaw, MW, 'The Potential Plaintiff: Preconception and Prenatal Torts' in Aubrey Milunsky and George J Annas (eds), *Genetics and the Law II*, 2nd edn (New York, Plenum Press, 1980)

Sheldon, S, '"Who is the Mother to Make the Judgment?" The Constructions of Woman in English Abortion Law' (1993) 1 *Feminist Legal Studies* 3

——*Beyond Control: Medical Power and Abortion Law* (London, Pluto Press, 1997)

——'"Sperm Bandits", Birth Control Fraud and the Battle of the Sexes' (2001) 21 *Legal Studies* 460

——'A Missed Opportunity to Reform an Outdated Law' (2009) 4 *Clinical Ethics* 3

——'Only Skin Deep? The Harm of Being Born a Different Colour to One's Parents' (2011) 19 *Medical Law Review* 657

——'*Evans v Amicus Health Care; Hadley v Midland Fertility Services* – Revealing Cracks in the "Twin Pillars"?' (2012) 16 *Child and Family Law Quarterly* 437

——and Wilkinson, S, 'Should Selecting Saviour Siblings be Banned?' (2004) 30 *Journal of Medical Ethics* 533

Shelton, KH *et al*, 'Examining Differences in Psychological Adjustment Problems Among Children Conceived by Assisted Reproductive Technologies' (2009) 33 *International Journal of Behavioral Development* 385

Shenfield, F, 'Privacy Versus Disclosure in Gamete Donation: A Clash of Interest, of Duties, or an Exercise in Responsibility?' (1997) 14 *Journal of Assisted Reproduction and Genetics* 371

——*et al*, 'Cross Border Reproductive Care in Six European Countries' (2010) 25 *Human Reproduction* 1361

Sherwin, S, *No Longer Patient: Feminist Ethics and Health Care* (Philadelphia, Pa, Temple University Press, 1992)

——'A Relational Approach to Autonomy in Health Care' in Susan Sherwin *et al* (eds), *The Politics of Women's Health: Exploring Agency and Autonomy* (Philadelphia, Pa, Temple University Press, 1998) 19

——'Normalizing Reproductive Technologies and the Implications for Autonomy' in Rosemary Tong, Gwen Anderson and Aida Santos (eds), *Globalizing Feminist Bioethics: Crosscultural Perspectives* (Boulder, CO, Westview Press, 2001) 96

Sherwin, S, 'Looking Backwards, Looking Forward: Hopes for *Bioethics'* Next Twenty-Five Years' (2011) 25 *Bioethics* 75

Shmueli, B, 'Love and the Law, Children Against Mothers and Fathers: Or, What's Love Got To Do With It?' (2010) 17 *Duke Journal of Gender Law & Policy* 131

Short, L, '"It Makes The World Of Difference": Benefits For Children Of Lesbian Parents Of Having Their Parents Legally Recognised *As* Their Parents' (2007) 3 *Gay and Lesbian Issues and Psychology Review* 5

Sibbald, B, 'Nonprescription Status for Emergency Contraception' (2005) 172 *Canadian Medical Association Journal* 861

Siegel, R, 'Reasoning from the Body: An Historical Perspective on Abortion Regulation and Questions of Equal Protection' (1992) 44 *Stanford Law Review* 261

—— 'Abortion as a Sex Equality Right: Its Basis in Feminist Theory' in Martha Albertson Fineman and Isabel Karpin (eds), *Mothers in Law: Feminist Theory and the Legal Regulation of Motherhood* (New York, Columbia University Press, 1995) 43

Silver, RM *et al*, 'Work-up of Stillbirth: A Review of the Evidence' (2007) 196 *American Journal of Obstetrics & Gynecology* 433

Simonstein, F, 'IVF Policies with Emphasis on Israeli Practices' (2010) 97 *Health Policy* 202

Singer, S, '*Rees v Darlington Memorial Hospital NHS Trust* [2004] 1 AC 309' (2004) 26 *Journal of Social Welfare and Family Law* 403

Singh, S *et al*, *Adding it Up: The Costs and Benefits of Investing in Family Planning and Maternal and Newborn Health* (New York, Guttmacher Institute and the United Nations Population and Development Fund, 2009)

——, Sedgh, G and Hussain, R, 'Unintended Pregnancy: Worldwide Levels, Trends, and Outcomes' (2010) 41 *Studies in Family Planning* 241

Smerdon, UR, 'Crossing Bodies, Crossing Borders: International Surrogacy Between the United States and India' (2008) 39 *Cumberland Law Review* 15

Smith, J, 'Burden of Care v Burden of Proof', *National Post* (Don Mills, 1 June 2002) A23

Smith, M, 'Reviewing Regulation of Assisted Reproductive Technology in New South Wales: The Assisted Reproductive Technology Act 2007 (NSW)' (2008) 16 *Journal of Law and Medicine* 120

Smith, VP, 'Doctors', Freedom of Conscience' (2006) 332 *British Medical Journal* 425

Smolensky, KR, 'Creating Children with Disabilities: Parental Tort Liability for Preimplantation Genetic Interventions' (2008) 60 *Hastings Law Journal* 299

Snow, D and Knopff, R, 'Assisted Reproduction Policy in Federal States: What Canada Should Learn from Australia' (2012) 5(12) *School of Public Policy Research Papers* 1

Society for Assisted Reproductive Technology Practice Committee and American Society for Reproductive Medicine Practice Committee, 'Preimplantation Genetic Testing: A Practice Committee Opinion' (2008) 90 (Supp 3) *Fertility and Sterility* S136

Society of Obstetricians and Gynaecologists of Canada, 'SOGC Policy Statement No 237: Mifepristone' (2009) 31 *Journal of Obstetrics and Gynaecology Canada* 1180

——Association of Women's Health, Obstetric and Neonatal Nurses of Canada, Canadian Association of Midwives, College of Family Physicians of Canada and the Society of Rural Physicians of Canada, 'SOGC Clinical Practice Guideline No 221: Joint Policy Statement on Normal Childbirth' (2008) 30 *Journal of Obstetrics and Gynaecology Canada* 1163

Sonfield, A, 'Contraception: An Integral Component of Preventive Health Care for Women' (2010) 13(2) *Guttmacher Policy Review* 2

——and Gold, RB, 'Editorial: Holding on to Health Care Reform and What We Have Gained for Reproductive Health' (2011) 83 *Contraception* 285

Sozou, PD, Sheldon, S and Hartshorne, GM, 'Consent agreements for Cryopreserved Embryos: The Case for Choice' (2010) 36 *Journal of Medical Ethics* 230

Spar, DL, *The Baby Business: How Money, Science, and Politics Drive the Commerce of Conception* (Boston, MA, Harvard Business School Press, 2006)

Speirs, J, 'Semen Donors' Curiosity about Donor Offspring and the Barriers to Their Knowing' (2012) 15 *Human Fertility* 89

Spriggs, M, 'Lesbian Couple Create a Child Who is Deaf Like Them' (2002) 28 *Journal of Medical Ethics* 283

Spurgeon, D, 'Abortion Doctor Suffers Second Attack in Six Years' (2000) 321 *British Medical Journal* 197

Srinivas, KR and Kanakamala, K, 'Introducing Norplant: Politics of Coercion' (1992) 29 *Economic and Political Weekly* 1531

Stansfield, AJ, Holland, AJ and Clare, ICH, 'The Sterilisation of People with Intellectual Disabilities in England and Wales During the Period 1988 to 1999' (2007) 51 *Journal of Intellectual Disability Research* 569

Starr, P, *The Social Transformation of American Medicine* (New York, Basic Books, 1982)

Statistics Canada and Canadian Institute for Health Information, *Health Care in Canada* (Ottawa, Canadian Institute for Health Information, 2005)

Stein, R, 'A Boy for You, a Girl for Me: Technology Allows Choice: Embryo Screening Stirs Ethics Debate', *Washington Post*, 14 December 2004, A01

Steinbock, B, 'Symposium: Opening Remarks' (1999) 62 *Albany Law Review* 805

—— *Life Before Birth: The Moral and Legal Status of Embryos and Fetuses*, 2nd edn (New York, Oxford University Press, 2011)

Steinbrook, R, 'Egg Donation and Human Embryonic Stem-Cell Research' (2006) 354 *New England Journal of Medicine* 324

—— 'Imposing Personal Responsibility for Health' (2006) 355 *New England Journal of Medicine* 753

Steptoe, PC and Edwards, RG, 'Birth After the Reimplantation of a Human Embryo' (1978) 2 *The Lancet* 366

Stevenson, GS, Ryan, T and Anderson, S, 'Principles, Patient Welfare and the Adults with Incapacity (Scotland) Act 2000' (2009) 32 *International Journal of Law and Psychiatry* 120

Steverson, JW, 'Prenatal Drug Exposure: The Impetus for Overreaction by the Legal Community or a Serious Problem Needing a Serious Solution?' (2008) 28(4) *Children's Legal Rights Journal* 41

Stone, KM *et al*, 'Seroprevalence of Human Papillomavirus Type 16 Infection in the United States' (2002) 186 *Journal of Infectious Diseases* 1396

Stormer, N, 'Seeing the Fetus: The Role of Technology and Image in the Maternal–Fetal Relationship' (2003) 289 *Journal of the American Medical Association* 1700

Storrow, RF, 'Parenthood by Pure Intention: Assisted Reproduction and the Functional Approach to Parentage' (2002) 53 *Hastings Law Journal* 597

—— '"The Phantom Children of the Republic": International Surrogacy and the New Illegitimacy' (2012) 20 *American University Journal of Gender, Social Policy & the* Law 561

Strasser, M, 'Wrongful Life, Wrongful Birth, Wrongful Death and the Right to Refuse Treatment: Can Reasonable Jurisdictions Recognize All But One?' (1999) 64 *Missouri Law Review* 29

Stretton, D, 'The Birth Torts: Damages for Wrongful Birth and Wrongful Life' (2005) 10 *Deakin Law Review* 319

Strickland, SLM, 'Conscientious Objection in Medical Students: A Questionnaire Survey' (2012) 38 *Journal of Medical Ethics* 22

Strong, C, 'The Moral Status of Preembryos, Embryos, Fetuses, and Infants' (1997) 22 *Journal of Medicine and Philosophy* 457

Stuhmcke, A, 'The Criminal Act of Commercial Surrogacy in Australia: A Call for Review' (2011) 18 *Journal of Law and Medicine* 601

Suter, SM, 'A Brave New World of Designer Babies?' (2007) 22 *Berkeley Technology Law Journal* 897

Szoke, H, 'Regulation of Assisted Reproductive Technology: The State of Play in Australia' in Ian Freckelton and Kerry Petersen (eds), *Controversies in Health Law* (Sydney, Federation Press, 1999)

Task Force on Postovulatory Methods of Fertility Regulation, 'Randomised Controlled Trial of Levonorgestrel Versus the Yuzpe Regimen of Combined Oral Contraceptives for Emergency Contraception' (1998) 352 *The Lancet* 428

Taylor, JS, 'Autonomy and Informed Consent: A Much Misunderstood Relationship' (2004) 38 *The Journal of Value Inquiry* 384

Taylor, KA, 'Compelling Pregnancy at Death's Door' (1997) 7 *Columbia Journal of Gender and Law* 85

Teliska, H, 'Obstacles to Access: How Pharmacist Refusal Clauses Undermine the Basic Health Care Needs of Rural and Low-Income Women' (2005) 20 *Berkeley Journal of Gender, Law and Justice* 229

Teman, E, 'The Social Construction of Surrogacy Research: An Anthropological Critique of the Psychosocial Scholarship on Surrogate Motherhood' (2008) 67 *Social Science & Medicine* 1104

Tew, M, *Safer Childbirth? A Critical History of Maternity Care*, 3rd edn (London, Free Association Books, 1998)

Thomson, M, 'Legislating for the Monstrous: Access to Reproductive Services and the Monstrous Feminine' (1997) 6 *Social & Legal Studies* 401

—— *Reproducing Narrative: Gender, Reproduction and Law* (Aldershot, Ashgate, 1998)

Thorpe, LJ, 'The Caesarean Section Debate' (1997) 27 *Family Law* 663

Thorpe, R *et al*, 'New Assisted Reproductive Technology Laws in Victoria: A Genuine Overhaul or Just Cut and Paste?' (2011) 18 *Journal of Law and Medicine* 835

Tietze, C and Lewit, S, 'Abortion' (1969) 220 *Scientific American* 21

Tieu, MM, 'Altruistic Surrogacy: The Necessary Objectification of Surrogate Mothers' (2009) 35 *Journal of Medical Ethics* 171

Trussell, J and Jordan, B, 'Editorial: Mechanism of Action of Emergency Contraceptive Pills' (2006) 74 *Contraception* 87

Turkmendag, I, Dingwall, R and Murphy, T, 'The Removal of Donor Anonymity in the UK: The Silencing of Claims by Would-Be Parents' (2008) 22 *International Journal of Law, Policy and the Family* 283

Turnbull, L, *Double Jeopardy: Motherwork and the Law* (Toronto, Sumach Press, 2001)

Twerski, AD and Cohen, NB, 'Informed Decision-Making and the Law of Torts: The Myth of Justiciable Causation' (1988) *University of Illinois Law Review* 607

United Nations, Department of Economic and Social Affairs, Population Division, 'World Contraceptive Use 2010' (POP/DB/CP/Rev2010)

United Nations Millennium Project, Task Force on Child Health and Maternal Health, *Who's Got the Power? Transforming Health Systems for Women and Children* (London, Earthscan, 2005)

University of Aberdeen, Faculty of Family Planning and Reproductive Health Care Clinical Effectiveness Unit, 'FFPRHC Guidance: Emergency Contraception' (2003) 29(2) *Journal of Family Planning and Reproductive Health Care* 9

van den Akker, O, 'Genetic and Gestational Surrogate Mothers' Experience of Surrogacy' (2003) 21 *Journal of Reproductive and Infant Psychology* 145

van Doorslaer, E, Masseria, C and Koolman, X, 'Inequalities in Access to Medical Care by Income in Developed Countries' (2006) 174 *Canadian Medical Association Journal* 177

Van Voorhis, BJ, 'Outcomes from Assisted Reproductive Technology' (2006) 107 *Obstetrics & Gynecology* 183

Verlinsky, Y *et al*, 'Preimplantation Diagnosis for Fanconi Anemia Combined with HLA Matching' (2001) 285 *Journal of the American Medical Association* 3130

Victora, CG and Barros, FC, 'Beware: Unnecessary Caesarean Sections may be Hazardous' (2006) 367 *The Lancet* 1796

Victorian Law Reform Commission, *Law of Abortion: Final Report, No 15* (Melbourne, Victorian Law Reform Commission, 2008)

Villar, J *et al*, 'Caesarean Delivery Rates and Pregnancy Outcomes: The 2005 WHO Global Survey on Maternal and Perinatal Health in Latin America' (2006) 367 *The Lancet* 1819

Vogel, L, 'Sex Selective Abortions: No Simple Solution' (2012) 184 *Canadian Medical Association Journal* 286

von Hertzen, H *et al*, 'Low Dose Mifepristone and Two Regimens of Levonorgestrel for Emergency Contraception: A WHO Multicentre Randomised Trial' (2002) 360 *The Lancet* 1803

Waggoner, SE, 'Cervical Cancer' (2003) 361 *The Lancet* 2217

Waldman, E, 'The Parent Trap: Uncovering the Myth of "Coerced Parenthood" in Frozen Embryo Disputes' (2004) 53 *American University Law Review* 1021

Waldron, J, 'Moral Autonomy and Personal Autonomy' in John Christman and Joel Anderson (eds), *Autonomy and the Challenges to Liberalism: New Essays* (Cambridge, Cambridge University Press, 2005) 307

Walker, K, 'The Bishops, The Doctor, His Patient and the Attorney-General: The Conclusion of the McBain Litigation' (2002) 30 *Federal Law Review* 507

Walker, RL, 'Medical Ethics Needs a New View of Autonomy' (2009) 33 *Journal of Medicine and Philosophy* 594

Wang, YA *et al*, *Assisted Reproductive Technology in Australia and New Zealand 2009* (Canberra, Australian Institute of Health and Welfare, 2011)

Warnock Committee, *Report of the Committee of Inquiry into Human Fertilisation and Embryology* (Cmnd 9314, 1984)

Warnock, M, *Making Babies: Is There a Right to Have Children?* (Oxford, Oxford University Press, 2002)

Watson, P, 'Legal and Ethical Issues in Wrongful Life Actions' (2002) 26 *Melbourne University Law Review* 736

Webster, PC, 'Nutrition and Integrated Health Care to Highlight Canadian Plan to Fight Child and Maternal Mortality, Minister Says' (2010) 182 *Canadian Medical Association Journal* E397

Weil, E, 'A Wrongful Birth?', *New York Times Magazine*, 12 March 2006, 52

Weiss, D, 'Court Delivers Controversy' *The Times Leader* (Wilkes-Barre, 16 January 2004) 1A

Weitz, TA, 'What Physicians Need to Know About the Legal Status of Abortion in the United States' (2009) 52 *Clinical Obstetrics and Gynecology* 130

Wellington, K, 'Maternal Liability for Prenatal Injury: The Preferable Approach for Australian Law?' (2010) 18 *Tort Law Review* 89

Wertheimer, A, 'Two Questions about Surrogacy and Exploitation' (1992) 21 *Philosophy & Public Affairs* 211

Wertz, DC and Fletcher, JC, 'Sex Selection Through Prenatal Diagnosis: A Feminist Critique' in Helen Bequaert Holmes and Laura M Purdy (eds), *Feminist Perspectives in Medical Ethics* (Bloomington, Indiana University Press, 1992) 240

Wertz, RW and Wertz, DC, *Lying-In: A History of Childbirth in America* (New York, Schocken Books, 1979)

West, RL, 'The Difference in Women's Hedonic Lives: A Phenomenological Critique of Feminist Legal Theory' (1987) 3 *Wisconsin Women's Law Journal* 81

—— 'Jurisprudence and Gender' (1988) 55 *University of Chicago Law Review* 1

Whitfield, A, 'Common Law Duties to Unborn Children' (1993) 1 *Medical Law Review* 28

Whittaker, A, 'Cross-border Assisted Reproduction Care in Asia: Implications for Access, Equity and Regulations' (2011) 19(37) *Reproductive Health Matters* 107

—— 'Reproduction Opportunists in the New Global Sex Trade: PGD and Non-Medical Sex Selection' (2011) 23 *Reproductive Biomedicine Online* 609

Wiebe, E *et al*, 'Comparison of Abortions Induced by Methotrexate or Mifepristone Followed by Misoprostol' (2002) 99 *Obstetrics & Gynecology* 813

Wiesenfeld, HC *et al*, 'Subclinical Pelvic Inflammatory Disease and Infertility' (2012) 120 *Obstetrics & Gynecology* 37

Wilkinson, S, 'The Exploitation Argument against Commercial Surrogacy' (2003) 17 *Bioethics* 169

Williams, JC, 'Deconstructing Gender' (1989) 87 *Michigan Law Review* 797

—— 'Gender Wars: Selfless Women in the Republic of Choice' (1991) 66 *New York University Law Review* 1559

Willig, T-N, Gazda, H and Sieff, CA, 'Diamond-Blackfan Anemia' (2000) 7 *Current Opinion in Hematology* 85

Winikoff, B and Davis, AR, 'Comment: Abortion is for Women' (2007) 369 *The Lancet* 1904

Wolf, D, 'An Opinion on Regulating the Assisted Reproductive Technologies' (2003) 20 *Journal of Assisted Reproduction and Genetics* 290

Wolfe, J, 'APA Condemns Prosecution of Pregnant Drug Abusers' (2012) 47(9) *Psychiatric News* 12a

Wolpe, PR, 'The Triumph of Autonomy in American Bioethics: A Sociological Perspective' in Raymond De Vries and Janardan Subedi (eds), *Bioethics and Society: Constructing the Ethical Enterprise* (New York, Prentice Hall, 1998)

Wong, S *et al*, 'SOGC Clinical Practice Guideline No 256: Substance Use in Pregnancy' (2011) 33 *Journal of Obstetrics and Gynaecology Canada* 367

Wood, AJJ, Drazen, JM and Greene, MF, 'A Sad Day for Science at the FDA' (2005) 353 *New England Journal of Medicine* 1197

Woodhandler, S and Himmelstein, DU, 'Extreme Risk: The New Corporate Proposition for Physicians' (1995) 333 *New England Journal of Medicine* 1706

Wool, C, 'Systematic Review of the Literature: Parental Outcomes After Diagnosis of Fetal Anomaly' (2011) 11 *Advances in Neonatal Care* 182

World Health Organization, *The World Health Report 2005 – Make Every Mother and Child Count* (Geneva, World Health Organization, 2005)

—— *WHO Model List of Essential Medicines*, 16th edn (Geneva, World Health Organization, 2010)

—— *Trends in Maternal Mortality 1990–2010: WHO, UNICEF, UNFPA and The World Bank Estimates* (Geneva, World Health Organization, 2012)

Wynn, LL, 'United States: Activism, Sexual Archetypes, and the Politicization of Science' in Angel M Foster and Lisa L Wynn (eds), *Emergency Contraception: The Story of a Global Reproductive Health Technology* (New York, Palgrave Macmillan, 2012) 39

—— and Foster, AM, 'The Birth of a Global Reproductive Health Technology: An Introduction to the Journey of Emergency Contraception' in Angel M Foster and Lisa L Wynn (eds), *Emergency Contraception: The Story of a Global Reproductive Health Technology* (New York, Palgrave Macmillan, 2012) 3

You, JJ *et al*, 'Proliferation of Prenatal Ultrasonography' (2010) 182 *Canadian Medical Association Journal* 143

Young, M, 'Case Comment: Rights, the Homeless, and Social Change: Reflections on Victoria (City) v Adams (BCSC)' (Winter 2009/10) 164 *BC Studies* 103

Yusuf, F and Briggs, D, 'Legalized Abortion in South Australia: The First 7 Years' Experience' (1979) 11 *Journal of Biosocial Science* 179

—— and Siedlecky, S, 'Patterns of Contraceptive Use in Australia: Analysis of the 2001 National Health Survey' (2007) 39 *Journal of Biosocial Science* 735

Yuzpe, AA and Lancee, WJ, 'Ethinylestradiol and dl-Norgestrel as a Postcoital Contraceptive' (1977) 28 *Fertility and Sterility* 932

—— *et al*, 'Post Coital Contraception – A Pilot Study' (1973) 13 *Journal of Reproductive Medicine* 53

Zegers-Hochschild, F *et al*, 'International Committee for Monitoring Assisted Reproductive Technology (ICMART) and the World Health Organization (WHO) Revised Glossary of ART Terminology, 2009' (2009) 92 *Fertility & Sterility* 1520

Zinn, C, 'Health Minister is Stripped of his Right to Veto Use of Abortion Pill' (2006) 332 *British Medical Journal* 441

Zite, N and Borrero, S, 'Female Sterilisation in the United States' (2011) 16 *European Journal of Contraception & Reproductive Health Care* 336

Zweben, JE and Payte, JT, 'Methadone Maintenance in the Treatment of Opioid Dependence: A Current Perspective' (1990) 152 *Western Journal of Medicine* 588

Index